# HEIMSKRINGLA
## OR THE LIVES OF THE
## NORSE KINGS

by Snorre Sturlason

*Edited with notes by*
ERLING MONSEN
*And translated into English*
*with the assistance of*
A. H. SMITH

DOVER PUBLICATIONS, INC., New York

Published in Canada by General Publishing Company, Ltd., 30 Lesmill Road, Don Mills, Toronto, Ontario.

This Dover edition, first published in 1990, is an unabridged republication of the work originally published by W. Heffer & Sons, Ltd., Cambridge, England, in 1932 (the copy used for reproduction had "Heffer" on the spine but no imprint whatsoever on the title page). The location of some of the plates has been changed. Two errata indicated on an inserted slip in the original have been corrected directly in the text of the present edition.

Manufactured in the United States of America
Dover Publications, Inc., 31 East 2nd Street, Mineola, N.Y. 11501

*Library of Congress Cataloging-in-Publication Data*

Snorri Sturluson, 1179?–1241.
    [Heimskringla. English]
    Heimskringla, or The lives of the Norse kings / by Snorre Sturlason ; edited with notes by Erling Monsen and translated into English with the assistance of A. H. Smith.
       p.    cm.
    Translated from the Old Norse.
    Reprint. Originally published: Cambridge : W. Heffer, 1932.
    ISBN 0-486-26366-5
    1. Scandinavia—History.    I. Monsen, Erling.    II. Smith, A. H. (Albert Hugh), 1903–1967.    III. Title.    IV. Title: Lives of the Norse kings.
PT7277.E5L3    1990
839'.61—dc20
                                    89-25924
                                    CIP

# CONTENTS

# CONTENTS

# PLATES

# MAPS

FACSIMILE OF A PAGE IN THE FLATEYJARBÓK
Reproduced by kind permission of Levin and Munksgaard, Copenhagen

# INTRODUCTION

## TO THE TRANSLATION OF SNORRE'S
### *HISTORY OF THE NORSE KINGS*

### I. SNORRE'S LIFE

SNORRE STURLASON belonged to a powerful family of Icelandic chiefs, and could reckon several distinguished men amongst his earlier ancestors. It was Snorre's paternal grandfather, Tord Gilson, who first rose to the rank of leadership. But Tord's mother was the maternal granddaughter of Haldor Snorrason of Hjardarholt (cf. 'History of Harald Hardrade', chapter 9) and Tord himself had married a great-great-granddaughter of the same Haldor. Tord's son Sturla Tordson of Hvamm (A.D. 1115–83) was the father of the *Sturlungs* by his marriage. His wife, Gudny, on her father's side was descended from the Myra-men, the famous family of scalds to which Egil Skallagrimson and Einar Skulason belonged; through her paternal grandmother, Gudny was also a descendant of the famous lawyer and scald, Markus Skeggjason. Sturla was described as wise and shrewd, vindictive and ambitious. In his later years he quarrelled with Paul Salveson of Reykjaholt, a powerful priest and leader, but Sturla was worsted, for John Loftson of Odda (mentioned in 'History of Magnus the Blind', chapter 9, and in 'History of Magnus Erlingson', chapter 21), the strongest and most renowned man in the island, took up Paul's case and secured him justice. To reconcile Sturla to his defeat, John offered to bring up his three-year-old son, Snorre—an honour which Sturla found flattering and which knit the bonds of friendship between the family of Odda and the Sturlungs.

When Sturla died in 1183 he divided his wealth amongst his three sons; the two elder, Tord and Sigvat, at once took over their share, whilst Snorre, then only five years old, who throughout his boyhood lived with his foster-father, had his mother as guardian of his share. John Loftson's homestead at Odda (in the Southland) was a centre of culture. His paternal grandfather, Sæmund the Wise, had been famed as a learned priest with a remarkable knowledge of the earlier history of Iceland and Norway. He had kept a private school for the training of priests which was continued by his son

Loft, likewise a priest. Loft's son John had also had an ecclesiastical training and was consecrated a deacon. At Odda, Snorre no doubt had an ecclesiastical education; he had learned to read and write, and knew probably a good deal of Latin, and he soon occupied himself with the historical writings which were to be found in the homestead. Poetic composition was also to be found in John Loftson's circle. Thus even in his early days Snorre received impulses towards the activity he displayed later as an author and historian. Here, too, he studied the law, such as secular chiefs needed when they had to act as judges at the quarter sessions and as members of the law-giving and adjudicating gatherings at the *Althing*. He also learned to understand the chiefs of Iceland and became intimate with their characters and individual qualities.

After John's death in 1197, Snorre, who was now 19 years old, still stayed on at Odda with John's eldest son Sæmund, who even allowed Snorre to appear on his behalf in a legal action. Snorre was then comparatively poor, for his mother had wasted his heritage. In 1199, however, he made a marriage with Herdis, the rich daughter of Bersi of Borg.

The fortune that Snorre had acquired by his marriage he knew how to use wisely; like his father and brothers he was a very enterprising and energetic landowner; like them he was eager for wealth and power. It is clear that at an early date he had gained possession of many big and goodly estates in the west and south of Iceland; to him belonged Hvamm, Stafaholt, Bessastadir and many others. At Reykjaholt, Snorre established himself as the virtual owner, although the estate was only left to his management; he built houses and enlarged them, raised a protective wall as well as a timber-hall, and the old bathing-place, which had already been in use in the tenth century, was most probably renovated by Snorre, as it is still called Snorralaug (Snorre's bath).

To the east of the garth lies Skrifla (pron. Skribla), one of the hot springs frequent in Iceland. From the spring there runs a partly covered-in water-race of masonry (about 110 yards long). The water-race opens out below the garth into a circular open bath, about 4 yards in diameter, built of flat rectangular blocks of stone, 1 yard deep. The temperature of the water is 97° centigrade, but it drops to 65° on its way to the bath. In order to get a temperature suitable for a hot bath it is only necessary to put a stone at the outlet of the water-race, whereby the water is diverted into a side-channel; if the stone is put there in the evening the water in the bath will be cooled to a proper temperature the morning after. This bath still exists in Iceland.

Snorre at an early age was noticed as a clever scald and a man well versed in the law. His earliest known poem was a *drapa* about King Inge's half-brother, Hacon the Jarl. This poem (which is now lost) Snorre wrote down and sent written copies to Norway. Hacon the Jarl received it with great pleasure, and bade him also compose a poem about his Swedish wife, Kristin, which Snorre did. Snorre had already been summoned by the Archbishop of Trondheim in 1211 and he now thought seriously of going to Norway in the summer of 1214, but in the spring it was reported in Iceland that the jarl had died in January of the same year, and he therefore put off the journey. He was now so well known as a lawyer that in 1215 he was chosen as Speaker (i.e. *lögsögumann*) of the *Althing*.

In 1218 Snorre carried out his former plan of going to Norway. The object of the journey was twofold: to gain honour and standing as a poet with the Norse rulers and to get to know the land, the history of whose kings had long occupied him. He went to Bergen in the autumn and from there he went along the coast to the Vik where he met King Hacon and Skuli the Jarl, just as the final peace was concluded between the Birchlegs and the Baglers, and the latter had submitted to the king. The winter he spent with the jarl in Tönsberg and he probably then composed a poem for him. In the spring Snorre went to Gautland to visit Hacon the Jarl's widow, who had married Eskil the Lawman. Kristin greeted Snorre well and thanked him for the poem he had written about her. In the autumn of 1219 Snorre returned to Norway and during the winter he was with Skuli the Jarl, who was then in Trondheim with King Hacon.[1] This winter Snorre was engaged at the king's court, not as one of the bodyguard, but as a gentleman-in-waiting (chamberlain), the highest rank in the court. On this occasion Snorre had sworn allegiance to the Norse king; but as the king's power did not extend to Iceland, he pledged his oath to the king only for the time he was in Norway and afterwards to grant the king only such services in Iceland as would not curtail his personal independence.

In the autumn of 1220 Snorre returned to Iceland and landed in the Southland. The report about his stay at the king's court, his new title and his task as peacemaker aroused distrust. But happily for Snorre an internal dissension broke out in the Southland and this impaired Sæmund Johnson's power.

1 Hacon Haconson (d. 1263).

So far he had kept his promise to the Norse king and the jarl, and in 1221 he also sent his son John to Norway, where the latter was taken into the court of Skuli the Jarl. But Snorre had done little or nothing to bring about the submission of his countrymen to the Norse king, and there is no doubt that he was constrained by circumstances to let himself be bound to such a promise. It also looks as though Skuli the Jarl after the division of the kingdom between the king and himself had released Snorre from his oath, for in 1224 the jarl let Snorre's son go home to Iceland.

In the autumn of 1222 Sæmund Johnson died. That summer Snorre had again agreed to be chosen as Speaker at the Althing. Snorre also sought to establish his powerful position by a clever family and marriage policy which was not unknown amongst the great men of Iceland and Norway. After Sæmund's death Snorre thought of marrying Sæmund's wealthy daughter Solveig, but his nephew, Sturla Sigvatson, forestalled him and married her in the spring of 1223. This resulted in enmity amongst the Sturlungs. The discord continued for several years, but it did not come to a straight fight between Snorre and Sturla. Thus when Snorre's son-in-law, Torvald of Vatsfjord, was slain in 1228 by Sturla's supporters, and Torvald's sons by an earlier marriage tried to kill Sturla, it was believed that Snorre had known of the plan. Not even when Sturla avenged himself by attacking and slaying Torvald's son Tord (1232) was there a break between Sturla and Snorre; on the contrary, they were easily reconciled. Snorre had a clear advantage by Tord's death, for Snorre's infant grandson Einar (born 1227) was now the heir to Vatsfjord, and Snorre took charge of his inheritance, so that he had also temporary power at any rate in the West-fjords in the north-western part of the land.

Snorre soon saw that the time had come when he must vindicate his position by force of arms. He gathered troops, and put Bodvar Tordson his nephew with an armed following to winter in Reykjaholt; and he sent word to his son Urökja who also provided himself with men and was ready to fight for his father. But when it came to the point, his courage deserted Snorre, who was neither warlike nor used to fighting; he made an offer of terms to Sturla and Sigvat and bade Urökja send his men home. But Sigvat and Sturla would no longer hear of peace; they came down to Borgarfjord with an army of 1000 men, and Snorre left everything and fled from Borgarfjord south to Bessastadir. Sigvat and Sturla seized all Snorre's possessions in Borgarfjord, whilst Snorre now felt no longer secure in Bessastadir and pushed on to the Eastland, where he spent the summer as the guest of one of the local chiefs. Urökja upheld his father's party by carrying on a kind of sea warfare in the West-fjords, but he had soon no power to continue the fight. A peace meeting was now arranged and in the meantime Urökja was able to return to Stafaholt. From there Sturla treacherously enticed him to Reykjaholt, where he was taken prisoner and forced to promise to go to Norway. This he did. Meantime, Snorre summoned up his courage to continue the fight, and he got help from his powerful cousin, Torleiv Tordson, but it was too late. With eight hundred men they went north to Borgarfjord, but when Torleiv would not follow out Snorre's plan of battle, Snorre left him, and Torleiv had to fight the battle out alone. In the battle Torleiv was defeated and had to submit to Sturla, who ordered him and many of his supporters to go to Norway. Snorre also thought it best to go to Norway. He found an excuse for this in a summons which the king, Skuli the Jarl and the Archbishop had sent out to Iceland in the spring of 1237 calling the Icelandic chiefs to Norway; the king and the jarl wished to bring about peace between the chiefs, and the Archbishop wanted to clear up the confused ecclesiastical conditions. Like a broken man, almost in flight, Snorre had this time to leave Iceland, in contrast to his departure nineteen years before, when he went to Norway to win honour and repute.

In Norway Snorre found things much changed. Many of his former friends such as Dagfinn Bonde were dead; his powerful patron Skuli was no longer lord of the land but a vassal under his former ward, King Hacon, who had by degrees made himself a strong ruler. The king had planned amongst other things to subdue Iceland to Norway's rule and as his tool he had chosen Sturla, not Snorre, whom he found too weak. Snorre must also have felt himself to be in disfavour with the king, and when soon after his arrival he saw the opposition smouldering between Skuli and the king he had no other choice but to fall in with Skuli. During the winter (1237-8) the Icelanders were in Trondheim, and Snorre was the guest of Skuli's son Peter, and the following summer he was with the duke with whom he lived and who showed him much friendship. The following autumn news came from Iceland that Sturla Sigvatson, who after Snorre's departure had started an open fight with Gissur Torvaldson about the lordship, had forced the latter into a pact with Kolbein the Young in Skagafjord, which had resulted in a decisive battle between them at Örlygstadir (Aug. 1238) where the old Sigvat Sturlason fell and Sturla was slain by Gissur's own hand. Snorre, it is said, was deeply moved by the death of his near kinsman and he expressed his sorrow in a verse which he sent to Sturla's brother Tord in Bergen. On the other hand, now that Sturla was dead, his hopes of regaining his power and wealth revived, and he at once decided to go back to Iceland together with his son Urökja and his cousin Torleiv. But as King Hacon had now lost his spokesman in Iceland he would not allow Snorre to work against him, and in early spring in 1239 he sent word to Trondheim that Snorre and the other Icelanders were not to leave the land before it was agreed what their business should be. At the same time the king also called the duke to a meeting in Bergen. The duke did not openly refuse to present himself, but despite the king's orders he gave Snorre leave to go and moreover got him a place on a ship which belonged half to himself and half to the Northlander Gudleik of Skartastadir, who was called 'Snorre's friend'. It appeared too that Skuli had blessed Snorre's plans of revolt and had promised to make him jarl of Iceland if he won the fight. On hearing that the Icelanders were all making ready to go, the king again sent a letter to Trondheim, which expressly forbade the Icelanders to leave that summer; they received it when they were lying off Nidarholm ready to sail, but when the letter was shown to Snorre, he took no notice of it and left.

Snorre and his friends arrived safely in Iceland and Snorre was greeted on his arrival by Halveig, his second wife; they went together to Reykjaholt where Snorre again took up residence. Torleiv and Urökja went to Stafaholt. Snorre now appeared as Sturla's avenger and at the same time he and Torleiv demanded the punishment of those who had fought against them at Bær. It was not long before Snorre took up his former powerful position in Borgarfjord and the surrounding parishes. Peace was this time broken by King Hacon who was greatly enraged at Snorre's disloyalty, and after Duke Skuli's death the king decided upon revenge. He chose Gissur Torvaldson as his agent and in 1240 he sent Arne Ureida, Snorre's former son-in-law, and the Norseman Eyvind Bratt to Iceland with a letter to Gissur which bade him send Snorre over to Norway whether he liked it or no—or else slay him, for he had gone out to Iceland against the king's orders. Gissur accepted the king's task but kept it secret, and, as for Snorre, he only arranged a meeting for the next summer (1241) at the Althing, where they were to come to terms about the fines for the slaying of Sturla and

Sigvat. Both came to the meeting, Snorre with but one hundred and twenty men; he clearly suspected nothing. But suddenly Gissur's ally, Kolbein the Young, appeared at the thing with an army of six hundred men. Snorre had to flee quickly into the church at Thingvold, but he drew up his men outside and they presented such a warlike array that Kolbein dared not come to grips with them and drew back. Gissur was then forced to come to terms with Snorre and everything seemed to end in a friendly way. But a short time afterwards Halveig, Snorre's wife, died, and Snorre, who grieved much over her death, had now to proceed to the disagreeable task of sharing her estate with his step-sons. The latter made claims to half the joint estate, whilst Snorre protested that the manors of Reykjaholt and Bessastadir with others were not included in the estate. It was then agreed that to start with they would share the movable property and the books, whilst the sharing of the rest should be delayed. The step-sons Klæing and Orm now sought the help of their uncle Gissur, and the latter gladly accepted this pretext for throwing himself upon Snorre. He held a meeting up in the fells (towards the Northland) with Kolbein the Young and arranged an attack; he then summoned his supporters and submitted the king's letter, saying he by no means wished to oppose the king's order to take Snorre prisoner. Klæing joined Gissur, but Orm his younger brother, who had been brought up by Snorre, would take no part in the attack and turned home. Snorre had received warning in a letter, written in secret characters, and from this he saw that he must protect himself. Whilst Kolbein was coming in from the north against Snorre's supporters in the Westland, Gissur came unexpectedly to Reykjaholt with seventy men; they passed unopposed into the garth and broke into the house where Snorre slept; Snorre, however, escaped down into the cellar. They found him, and by Gissur's orders five men went down into the cellar. There was no talk of peace and Gissur's servant, Simon Knut, straightway bade one of the men, Arne Beisk by name, to strike Snorre. Accustomed as he was to commanding, Snorre tried to overawe his murderer by saying, "Thou shalt not strike!" But Simon repeated his order and the fatal blow fell. At his death, in September 1241, Snorre was sixty-three years old.

King Hacon declared afterwards that it had not been his intention to punish Snorre by death, if he had submitted.

We have no notion of Snorre's outward appearance, for the Sturlunga Saga gives no information thereof. As to his character,

P. A. Munch says of him that he was avaricious, ambitious and aspiring, but nowhere is it said that he was cruel and bloodthirsty as were most of the chieftains of his time; his victories were not marked, as were those of others, by the maiming or killing of the vanquished, and eager as he may have been for power, it is clear that he was greatly trusted. The sons of Sæmund Johnson chose him to divide their inheritance, and it is specially mentioned in his favour that he was always on a friendly footing with such a man as Rafn Sveinbjörnson. Indeed, his unshaken attachment to the irrational though well-meaning Bishop Gudmund shows that his piety could be stronger than his statesmanship. And lastly his patriotism stands out more plainly and more strongly than did that of most of his countrymen.

## II. SNORRE'S WRITINGS

It has already been mentioned that Snorre Sturlason had from his youth been engaged in literary work and had appeared as a poet before the contemporary Norse rulers. But literary work was essentially historical composition—poems in honour and in memory of rulers—and from olden times poets were historians, and history became the most important subject for Snorre's study. We have seen that books formed such a conspicuous part of his possessions that his library was mentioned in the division of his wealth amongst his step-sons. He had begun to collect books at an early age and it is certainly a well-founded conjecture to suppose that he had already inherited books from John Loftson, his step-father, and that he had likewise got many more by his marriage with Halveig, John's grand-daughter. It is quite clear that he had by him almost everything that Icelandic literature had produced up to his own time; this is shown by his ability to cite so many verses of older and younger poets and by the fact that he could make so good a selection from what he had read. Besides this he was certainly conversant with foreign chronicles written in Latin. He first appears as an author rather late in life, for his first chief work, the *Edda*, was completed about 1220, and his second, the *History of the Norse Kings*, was written probably ten or fifteen years later.

The *Edda*[1] is a primer for young poets, showing how poetic

---

[1] The word means 'the poetic art'. Snorre's *Edda* is often called the *Younger Edda* and is, of course, quite distinct from the *Elder Edda*.

diction and forms are to be applied. It is in three parts, and was perhaps written at different periods, though they form a unity. The first part is called *Gylfaginning* (that is, the beguiling of Gylfi). The second part is called *Skaldskapar-mal* (i.e. poetic diction).

The third part is called *Hattatal* (that is, list of verse-forms) and contains a poem of one hundred and twenty verses, composed by Snorre for Skuli the Jarl and King Hacon. *Hattatal* is accompanied by a learned prose exposition of the rules and different applications of the verse-forms.

Snorre's *Edda* is a unique work, without any predecessors or parallel.

As the author of the *History of the Norse Kings*, Snorre has had many imitators, but he rises above them all and his work is the most complete of its kind. Icelandic historical writings are considered to have began with the priest Ari Torgilson the Wise (1067–1148) who soon after 1120 wrote the older history of his country in his *Islendinga-bok*, where he also gives a short sketch of the history of the mother-country, Norway. This book was lost long ago, but it is known in an abbreviated form. Ari was a conscientious and accurate scholar who strove to discriminate between truth and fiction.

In Norway also short Latin chronicles were written about the kings of Norway, partly from Icelandic sources. Tjodrek, a monk in Nidarholm (Trondheim) covers the period from Harald Hairfair to the death of Sigurd the Crusader, and *Historia Norvegiæ*, written by a Bergen priest, perhaps went farther, but only the part down to St Olav's time has survived.

Snorre knew and valued the work of Tjodolv of Kvin, a poet contemporary with Halvdan the Black and Harald Hairfair, who had told of the whole succession of Halvdan's forefathers right back to the old gods.

Snorre, when he comes to the period of Harald Hairfair, was guided by the writings of Ari the Wise. From Ari the Wise he also probably borrowed his chronology.

With the help of Tjodolv of Kvin and Ari the Wise, Snorre tested the work of his predecessors and selected from them for his purpose. Besides this, he had probably gathered much material on his two journeys to Norway and Sweden.

The historical saga was principally concerned with biography. Snorre's work is a collection of biographies with description of character as an outstanding feature. The special quality of his work is the skilful composition by which all irrelevant matter is kept out and each detail belongs to a whole. His collection of biographies of the Norse kings has therefore become a family history, where each single member stands out with his own distinctive stamp of character.

When reading these narratives the same question must occur to everybody: How can those parts of the accounts which were handed down from man to man (and not taken from written accounts or foreign chronicles) have been so well remembered, and how is it possible that they can have been truthfully related? What wonderful memories these men must have had! To this we have no hesitation in answering that there can be little doubt that their memories were highly developed, much more so than in modern days when we employ endless historical books, newspapers, dictionaries, etc., for constantly refreshing our knowledge of the past. It may almost be said that we do not need a memory for history nowadays! But it was essential to the scalds and historians of the Viking Age. Snorre touches upon the subject of memory in his preface, also upon the truthfulness of the narratives. He says: "No one would dare tell the king himself such deeds of his as all listeners and the king himself knew to be lies and loose talk; that would be mockery, but not praise".

Not only must these men have had trained memories, inherited through generations, but they were trustworthy and had a keen sense of honour.

## III. THE MANUSCRIPTS

The copies of Snorre's *History of the Norse Kings* were known both in Iceland and Norway. The oldest known copy on parchment was called *Kringla*. It includes *Skaldatal*. The latter gives an account of all the court scalds known in historical times, mentioning the Norse kings and princes for whom they composed. The list of scalds ends with Olav Hvitaskald (d. 1259) and Sturla Tordson (d. 1284), Snorre's nephews. It is not unlikely that Sturla Tordson had taken the book with him to Norway, when he went there in 1263; at any rate it is certain that *Kringla* came to Norway at an early date and was kept in or near Bergen till the end of the sixteenth century. Later on the book was sent from Bergen to the University Library in Copenhagen; but it had then lost its first page, and the second page (which was now the first) began with the words *Kringla heimsins* (the world's circle); after this the book has been called *Heimskringla*. At the end of the seventeenth century two well-executed copies were made of *Heimskringla*, one in 1682 by Jon Eggertson, an Icelander in Swedish service who took his copy to Stockholm; the second by the Icelander Asgeir Jonsson. It was done just in time, for in 1728 the book was burned together with most of the University Library's treasures in the great fire of Copenhagen. One leaf of it was saved, however, as Jon Eggertson had taken it with him to Stockholm, where it was handed over to the Royal Library.

## IV. PREVIOUS TRANSLATIONS

The first complete translation of the *History of the Norse Kings* into Norwegian and Danish was made by a Norwegian clergyman, Peder Claussön, who became Archdeacon of the Cathedral at Stavanger (b. 1545; d. 1614). He had frequented a high ecclesiastical school at Stavanger and came into possession of some written copies of the sagas. In 1599 he commenced translating Snorre at the request of Axel Gyldenstjerne, the Governor-General of Norway.

By order of the Swedish king, Charles XI, Johan Pering-skiold translated *Heimskringla* into Swedish and Latin. His book was printed in Stockholm in 1697. The O.N. text is also given. Peringskiold was probably the first to call Snorre's book *Heimskringla*, a name it has retained ever since.

In Copenhagen a Norwegian historian, Gerhard Schöning, made another translation of *Heimskringla* into Danish by order of the Danish and Norwegian Crown Prince Frederick (later Frederick VI). Schöning's book was printed in 1777, and gives the O.N. text as well as a Latin translation.

Peringskiold's and Schöning's books contain practically the same number of chapters, but the spelling of the O.N. text is somewhat different. The well-known Norwegian historian, P. A. Munch, printed in 1859 his translation of *Heimskringla*, and forty years later Gustav Storm made another translation of the book by order of the Norwegian Government. Munch has left out the scalds' poems, which he considered would lose their beauty if they were translated. Storm followed a different course. He has admirably translated the scalds' poems into modern Norwegian, but decided to leave out a number of interesting chapters—most of these belonging to the second half of his book. He also left out three chapters in the 'History of Olav Trygvason', and one chapter in the 'History of Magnus the Good'. Both Munch and Storm leave out eight chapters concerning the Norsemen's voyages to America (Vinland), although they are printed in Peringskiold's and Schöning's editions. These chapters describe in detail the voyages to Vinland by Leif Ericson and others, whilst Eric the Red's discovery of Greenland and Leif Ericson's discovery of Vinland are recorded elsewhere in the book without any particulars. That others besides Leif Ericson should have attempted to go to America is highly probable, considering the short distance between Greenland and the North American coast. It was an age when the spirit of adventure among the Norsemen stood at its zenith, and to discover new lands and form new colonies had a powerful attraction for these enterprising men. The two versions of Eric the Red's Saga were in existence when Snorre Sturlason wrote his book and it may safely be assumed that he knew all the details of the voyages and that chapters 97 to 104 formed part of *Heimskringla* in accordance with Johan Peringskiold and Gerhard Schöning's editions. As these accounts, however, are written in a somewhat different style from the rest of the book, they may have been inserted in a later handwritten copy by Snorre or his clerical scribes after the first dictation was finished. This would explain the altered style and character, also why they do not quite seem to fit in where they are placed. It has often been contended that the eight chapters are interpolations by Peringskiold, but no convincing argument in support of this has ever been put forward. At the end of chapter 104, p. 202, occurs the following remark: "Nobody has given a clearer account than Karlsefni of the happenings on these voyages, of which something has here been told". This is an observation typical of Snorre, but most of the other contents do not resemble Snorre and may have been to a large extent taken from Eric the Red's Saga. It is, of course, true that Snorre or his clerical scribes could have made a slight addition to chapter 96 by stating that the following chapters give all the details of the Vinland voyages. This would have brought chapter 96 into line with what follows (excepting for Biarne Herjulfson's meeting with Eric the Jarl). But if the narratives were inserted after Snorre had finished his first dictation, the first written text was probably on purpose left unaltered.

The first translation of the *History of the Norse Kings* into English was made by Samuel Laing, whose book was printed in London in 1844 in three volumes. It is an admirable work, most conscientiously executed. In his notes and explanations Laing mentions that he has obtained great assistance from Jacob Aal, who made a Norwegian translation, printed in 1838. Laing was born at Kirkwall (Orkneys) in 1780. He had an enthusiastic admiration for the old vikings, and spared no pains in testifying to the great influence which the Nordic races have had upon the British people, an influence which was yet to be further cemented by the Normans who sprang from the same race. Laing might justly be called the "father of the Nordic cult in the British Isles". Carlyle and Longfellow were so impressed by the Norse sagas that Carlyle wrote his well-known book *The Early Kings of Norway*, and included St Olav in his *Heroes and Hero-Worship*; and Longfellow wrote some of his best poems on the subject. Another edition of Laing's book was issued in 1889 by Rasmus B. Anderson, at one time United States Minister to Denmark. A third edition of Laing has recently been issued by Dent, in 'Everyman's Library'.

Another English translation of *Heimskringla* was made by William Morris and Eiríkr Magnússon, printed in London in four volumes in 1893. This is a magnificent literary work. The text is translated into English direct from O.N. and a number of old-fashioned English words are used, so as to bring out Snorre Sturlason's forceful and vivid style. The historical part is not much in evidence until one reaches the fourth volume, but in this volume a very complete index with explanations is given. The names of historical persons, however, have often been translated directly into English in such a way as to make them almost unrecognisable. But apart from this defect it is a book that should appeal to all British lovers of the sagas. That William Morris was another true enthusiast of the Nordic cult can be seen from the following words which he writes in connection with the mythical *Volsunga Saga*: "This is the great story of the north, which should be to all our race what the tale of Troy was to the Greeks: to all our race first, and afterwards when the change of the world has made our race nothing more than a name of what has been—a story too—then should it be to those that come after us no less than the tale of Troy has been to us".

The subject of the *Volsunga Saga* had also an irresistible attraction for Richard Wagner, the greatest musical genius the world has ever seen. The old German poem *Nibelungenlied* or *Nibelunge Nôt* is to a great extent based on the *Volsunga Saga*. In fact, it is difficult to understand the former thoroughly without reference to the latter. But it is doubtful whether the legend in the German versions has ever been given such a dramatic and heroic rendering as in the original Norse form.

## V. CHARACTER AND CUSTOMS OF THE NORDIC RACES

In 1889 Paul du Chaillu, the explorer, published in London in two volumes *The Viking Age, or the Early History, Manners and Customs of the Ancestors of the English-speaking Nations.* This book deals with archæology as well as mythology and history and goes far to prove that the old Nordic people were, judging by the standard of the time, a highly cultured race. Numerous illustrations of archæological finds are given, and du Chaillu writes with conviction of what he calls "the archæological wealth of the north".

We still cling to the mistaken idea that these people were barbarians and pirates, but is it not time that we in our enlightened age should commence to revise our opinions about them? They were, according to modern ideas, pirates, but it must not be forgotten that piracy was considered a serious business in those days, and was practised by every country whose inhabitants had acquired the sea sense. The vikings held for several centuries the mastery of the sea and there was nobody to dispute this right. It enabled them to colonise other countries, and we should be living in a different world at present if this process had not taken its course. We still talk of the cruel Danes and the cruel Norsemen, but were they really so cruel? Certainly not when they are again compared with the standard of the time in which they lived. They punished with cruelty; but so did every other nation in Europe, and this was continued by other nations for many centuries after the Viking Age. Even in our civilised age cruelties have sometimes been committed for political and other offences which would appal and dismay the most hard-hearted viking. Snorre's *Heimskringla* gives many instances in which the vikings showed great clemency towards their enemies, and we hear of no mass murders. They were attached to their kinsmen and faithful to their friends. It may be surprising to read that they gave way to grief at the funerals of their kings and leaders—in fact Snorre tells us that they even shed tears. It has been handed down to us that they often exclaimed during raids: "Kill not the bairns". How can they therefore have been such brutes as they are depicted to us? No other people in the north of Europe had the vikings' understanding of literature or their love for poetry (scaldcraft); and the respect in which they held their womenfolk evinces probably more than anything else their high intellectual discipline. They harried other countries and fought against the inhabitants because it was a question of killing others or of being killed themselves. This was not cruelty, but probably cleaner warfare than that which is waged in modern times! They invaded the north of Germany, the Baltic Provinces and Russia as well as Holland, Belgium and the north of France; but it was the British Isles which had the greatest attraction for them. These islands were more vulnerable on account of the long coast line, and the sea was always a safe road for retreat. The German historians have for years been in the habit of telling us that the Nordic people are part of the Germanic race and that they originated in the plains of Germany, but the Nordic people had little in common with the Celtic and Slavonic races in Germany, excepting the relationship which Snorre Sturlason alleges to exist between them (cf. 'Ynglinga Saga,' p. 3). It is, however, generally acknowledged that over-population in the barren countries of the north was the cause of many Scandinavians settling in North Germany, after the invasions by the Goths and Huns had spent their force. This mixture of races has made the Germans the most intellectual people in Europe. After the passing of the Viking Age the German people in their turn commenced exercising a great influence upon the customs and manners of the Scandinavian peoples, and many Germans settled in the north. Before that time the Nordic people had for centuries developed their race in the hard and frosty climate of the northern countries, among their mountains, fjords and extensive coast lines, and it was in these surroundings that the people acquired their strong physique, their sea sense and independence of character. It was also here that the Nordic mythology became firmly established.

## VI. THE ORIGIN OF THE NORDIC RACES; THE NORSE KINGS

Snorre Sturlason tells us in the 'Ynglinga Saga' where the chief branch of the Nordic people originated. It contains legends and myths, a fact which Snorre does not deny; but when everything is considered, this saga still stands forth, giving us much food for thought and guidance for further research work. When we come to the sagas of the kings Snorre Sturlason is on more sure ground and it is evident from the narrative that he is anxious to tell us the history of the kings and the people, as he had it related to him by wise and truthful men, and as he had read about it in old books and foreign chronicles. The word 'history', being of Latin origin, was not in use among the Icelandic writers, who principally wrote in O.N. They used the O.N. word *saga* (sing.), *sögur* (plur.), both for historical, mythical and fictitious writings. As *Heimskringla* is essentially historical we have in this translation used the word 'history' instead of 'saga', as being more consistent with present ideas about historical writings.

The narratives of the Norse kings from Halvdan the Black (839–60) until Magnus Erlingson (1161–77) contain all the principal events that happened during each king's reign and give a vivid description of battles both on land and sea. Snorre also gives a certain amount of information about settlements in foreign countries, but it is obvious that he was in possession of only scant knowledge of the numerous raiding and colonising expeditions undertaken by the Norsemen. Doubtless of many he knew nothing, whilst others he did not consider worth while mentioning. The most important colonising expedition of which he tells us is Rolf the Ganger's conquest of the north of France, which ever since has retained its name of 'Normandy', after the invaders. The French called him Rollon or Rou as in Robert Wace's *Roman de Rou*. Snorre tells us that he came from Norway, and with his usual thoroughness he gives a full account of Rolf's family. In this is included his half-brother Einar (Turf-Einar) who became Earl of Orkney, and from whom many subsequent Earls of Orkney have descended. This is all dealt with in the 'History of Harald Hairfair'. The well-known English chronicler William of Malmesbury, who lived about 1090–1143 (or a hundred years before Snorre), corroborates Snorre's information about Rolf's origin, and agrees with Snorre's statement that Rolf was banished from Norway by command of the king. About Rolf and the origin of his followers there is further evidence in the chronicles written by Roger de Hoveden, another well-known English chronicler, who lived about the same time as Snorre. Hoveden writes the following passage of William the Conqueror: "For he [i.e. William] stated that his ancestors and those of nearly all the Barons of Normandy had been Norwegians and had formerly come from Norway".

*La Cronique d'Alberic* (in the 9th volume of the *Histoires de France*) speaks thus about Rolf's origin: "Rollone duce qui de nobili, sed per vetustatem obsoletá prosapiá Noricorum editus, regis præcepto patria pulsus, multos quos æs alienum vel conscientia scelerum agitabat, magnis speciebus sollicitans, ditatos secum abduxit".

Le Moine de Fontanelle also writes that Rolf was expelled from Norway.

It may further be mentioned that the eminent English historian John Richard Green in *A Short History of the English People*, and the well-known French historian G. B. Depping (1784–1853) in *Histoire des Expéditions Maritimes des Normands*, after verifying the various English and French chroniclers, consider it proved beyond doubt that Rolf was a Norseman. Most of the English and French chroniclers give the Norsemen and Danes who settled in Britain and France the collective name of Danes. Hence the confusion that has often arisen as to the origin of Rolf and his followers.

The Norsemen have left their unmistakable mark on the population of Normandy. This is to-day probably more pronounced than it was a thousand years ago. Now the Nordic element is prevalent in the cottages, whereas at that time the Norse rulers were obviously in the minority. Numerous personal and place names are of Norse origin. G. B. Depping, in the work mentioned above, states that in most place names ending with 'ville' the first part of the name is of Norse origin. The reason is simple to find in the fact that Rolf the Ganger divided the land among his men, who gave their names to the farms or holdings, adding the Latin name 'villa' instead of 'ham', 'by', or 'tun'. Depping mentions names from Seine-Inférieure such as Froberville, Beuzeville, Gauzeville, Rouville, Rolleville, Triguerville, Houppeville, Tancarville, Norville, Normanville, Varengeville, Guizorville. Rolf gave lands to Arngaut, Biorn, Folkvard, Geirmund, Harald and Grani, and their homesteads were called Angoville, Borneville, Foucarville, Grimondville, Heronville, and Granville. The ending *bec* meaning in O.N. 'little river', is found in place names such as Bolbec, le Bec, Caudebec,

Foulbec, Holbec, Robec, etc. The old name for Harfleur was Herosfluet or Harflue. For Barfleur, Robert Wace wrote Barbeflue and Barbeflot. Here is the O.S. ending *fljot*, i.e. 'river' (the same as *fleet* in English). The old name for Painbeuf was Penteboe (from O.N. *bö*, *bær*) and in Seine-Inférieure two places are called Grandes Dalles and Petites Dalles respectively. Other names ending with *dale* are Oudale near Beaucamp, Crodale, Danestal (Calvados), Dieppedale, Croixdal and Bruquedalle (Seine-Inférieure). The name *gard* (or *garth*) is also found in the villages of Normandy. For instance Auppegard and Epegard (Depart. de l'Eure). The Cape La Hogue or Hogue is the Scand. *haug* (howe). The name *ness* is found in names such as Blancnez, Grisnez and Nez de Carteret. Le Houlme near Rouen is the Nordic *holme*, and Havre and Dieppe are probably also of Scand. origin. Cherbourg, called at times Chierisburch, is obviously Skerriesbourgh or O.S. Skerjaborg (on account of its skerries outside the harbour). In Guernsey, Jersey and Chausey we have the O.S. *ey* meaning 'island'. It may be asked, how is it that the old French chroniclers have shown such disregard for the influence which the Nordic people exercised upon the north of France and wrote as little as possible about them? Only when they rose to be the rulers of the land and built and endowed churches did the chroniclers write about them and praise their actions. The reason can only be found in the altered conditions of religious life in France and other countries from the time when the vikings first made their appearance. A new religion had come into being and the Roman Church was bent upon suppressing the knowledge of these pirates and of depreciating the influence which the heathens exercised. A similar policy was adopted in England, and this indifference shown them by the early teachers of history has been handed down to us to this day.

The history of Rolf the Ganger has led us into a somewhat lengthy digression on place names and Nordic influence in the north of France, and now we return to the Norse kings. We shall first mention Halvdan the Black (839–860). He was the father of Harald Hairfair (860–933) who united the whole of Norway into one kingdom by conquering all the lesser kings. Rolf was outlawed by Harald and it was this circumstance that made him settle in Normandy.

After Harald Hairfair comes the fascinating history of his son Hacon the Good, also called Hacon Athelstan's foster-son, as he was brought up by King Athelstan from boyhood. This famous English king and his grandfather King Alfred should rank side by side as the two greatest rulers in England before the Conquest. Hacon left England for Norway on the death of his father in 933. The English chroniclers do not mention Athelstan's foster-sons; but besides fostering Hacon the Good, as Snorre tells us, we hear from French sources that he also fostered Louis d'Outremer, who afterwards became King Louis IV of France, and Alan de Bretagne. Hacon was the first to introduce Christianity into Norway; but the people would not give up their old and trusted gods, and Hacon was forced to allow them to keep to their old faith. After Hacon the Good, his half-brothers succeeded to the kingship; but they were tyrannical and therefore unpopular, and finally Hacon the Jarl—the strong warrior jarl who lived in the county of Trondheim—virtually became the ruler of the country, though without the kingly title, as he was not of royal stock. Then we come to Olav Trygvason, the glorious sea-king who had lived for years in foreign countries and at last arrived home to claim his heritage. There is no more picturesque king in the sagas than Olav Trygvason. He was the embodiment of sportsmanship, bravery and strength combined at times with recklessness; and the vivid account of his last battle at Svold—the finest description given by Snorre of any sea battle—goes far to depict the proud and ambitious spirit of this great king.

The next great king is Olav Haraldson (St Olav) and Snorre's history of him excels all the other sagas. It is evident that Snorre was in possession of numerous details of this king, who must have appealed to him both as a brave warrior and as a prudent and sagacious ruler. As the champion of Christianity—which he finally established in Norway—he obtained more renown than any other king and after his death was made a saint. He fought many battles both in foreign countries and in Norway, and, as often happens with geniuses living before their time, he received full recognition only after his death. He fell at the battle of Stiklestad (near Trondheim) in 1030. Many tales of miracles were told about him, and Snorre relates some of them, but without comment. It is now nine hundred years since St Olav fell, and commemoration services were held last year all over Norway and also in the churches dedicated to him which still exist in England.

St Olav's son was Magnus the Good. He made a treaty with King Hardicanute by which he had the right to succeed to the thrones of Denmark and England should Hardicanute die before him. On the death of Hardicanute, Magnus went to Denmark and was elected king by the Danes. Later he sent messengers to Edward the Confessor claiming the English Crown. Magnus finally decided "to let Edward have his realm in peace, and to hold fast to the kingdoms which God has let me win".

After Magnus, his uncle Harald Hardrade became King of Norway. Among all the hero kings of Norway he must be placed in the front rank. He had for many years been the leader of the Værings (the Greek emperor's warriors at Constantinople) and fought all the enemies of the Greek emperors in the Mediterranean. Coming home to Norway via Russia he married the daughter of the Russian monarch, and became a most powerful king. In the end his ambitious nature had the better of him and he consented at the request of Earl Tosti (the brother of Harold Godwinson, the last of the O.E. kings) to bring an army to England and try to conquer the country for himself and Earl Tosti. This was not such an impossible enterprise as we may think, because on the death of Edward the Confessor England was left without a legitimate ruler, and the Norsemen spoke practically the same language as the English. They were not foreigners in the same sense as the Normans, who spoke Norman French and were not liked by the common people. Harald defeated the English army outside York and became so elated by his victory that he and his men took few precautions and went to battle against Harold Godwinson without wearing the usual armour. The chroniclers relate that it was the fiercest battle ever fought in England, and in the end the Norsemen were defeated and Earl Tosti and Harald Hardrade were slain. It may be said that they paved the way for William the Conqueror, who landed at Pevensey four days afterwards, but we have no reason to believe that William worked in conjunction with Harald Hardrade. Norway had now seen enough of fighting, and Harald Hardrade's son Olav Kyrre (or the Peaceful) decided to live on friendly terms with his neighbours, but matters took a different course when his son Magnus Barefoot (or Bareleg, because he wore a kilt) came to the throne. He was inspired by his grandfather's ambition and fighting spirit, and Norway again suffered by the calling up of levies for war. Henry the First (the son of the Conqueror) was now the powerful monarch of England, and Magnus thought it most fitting to avenge his grandfather's death by attacking England from the west and by way of Ireland. Ordericus Vitalis gives lengthy descriptions of Magnus Barefoot's expeditions to England and Ireland, some of which are mentioned in the footnotes. Magnus was slain by treachery in Ireland in 1103.

Another picturesque king, Sigurd the Crusader, now came to the throne of Norway. He was Earl of Orkney for a few years and went back to Norway on the death of his father, Magnus Barefoot. He is best known for his voyage to Jerusalem and Constantinople, of which Snorre Sturlason gives full details. After his death in 1130 the various pretenders to the throne fight between themselves and civil warfare becomes the order of the day. One king succeeds the other and each king is kept busy in maintaining his position and right to the throne. The last king in this book is Magnus Erlingson, who ruled until 1184, but Snorre's history of him finishes in 1177. He had no legal right to the throne, because he descended from the royal stock only through his mother. The Viking Age was now gradually fading away; in fact it began to die with Sigurd the Crusader in 1130. But Norse history (written by Snorre's successors) tells us of two more prominent kings who held the realm of Norway—King Sverre and Hacon Haconson. The latter has become notorious because he led the last army that landed in Britain from abroad. He quarrelled with the Scottish King Alexander and fought him at the battle of Largs in 1263. The battle was indecisive and Hacon left for Kirkwall, where he died the same winter. Three years afterwards his son Magnus made peace with the Scots and sold the Hebrides and Isle of Man to the Scottish king for 4000 marks, which were never paid. The Norsemen had now lost two important strategical points, but it was not till 1468 that they parted with their last two possessions in the British Isles, viz. the Orkney and Shetland Isles. These islands were in that year pledged by King Christian the First to the Scottish Crown as security for his daughter's dowry, which was not redeemed. For strategical as well as commercial purposes the islands had long since lost their importance to Norway, and it may be considered a blessing in disguise that they were ceded in this way and that they did not cause any further fighting and bloodshed.

## VII. THE JUTES, ANGLES AND SAXONS

If the Norse, and to a lesser degree the Swedish, elements played an important rôle in the Midlands and Scotland, in Ireland and in the Northern and Western Isles, the Danes concentrated their energy in the south. According to the English chroniclers the first Nordic people to land in England were the Jutes from Jutland. They were invited by Vortigern to help him against the Picts and Scots after the

Romans, almost to the last man, had left the country in 410 in order to rescue Rome. Under their leaders Hengest and Horsa the Jutes landed at Ebbsfleet in 449 and were given the Isle of Thanet by the ancient Britons. Finally they possessed themselves of the whole of Kent. The chroniclers tell us further of other races that soon afterwards invaded England, viz. the Angles and the Saxons. As a district immediately to the north-east of Sleswick is still called Angeln or Angel-land, the tradition is that the Angles came from this part of Denmark, and it is generally assumed that the Saxon tribes lived round the River Elbe (the mouth of which was partly Danish) and the River Weser. The Saxon tribes must have been closely allied to the Danes or to that part of the Danish nation which occupied the land between Sleswick and Hamburg. Living round the coasts of Denmark and North-west Germany the invaders were familiar with the sea and any excess of population had to look abroad for its livelihood. It was over two hundred years after these races had settled down in England, before any other recorded invasions took place. They were mostly Norsemen and Danes, but Swedes, Frisians and Flemings also came across. The chroniclers tell us of 'the army' which made its appearance year after year during the ninth century, and King Alfred's treaty of Wedmore in 878, concluded with all the Scandinavians settled in England, did not stop new forces from landing. John Richard Green in his *Short History of the English People* deals at length with the English invasions and characterises the Nordic race as follows: "No other race has ever shown a greater power of absorbing all the nobler characteristics of the people with whom they came in contact, or of infusing their own energy into them". Dr John Beddoe in his book, *The Races of Britain*, writes as follows in connection with Normandy: "The Scandinavian conquerors were partly Norwegian and partly Danish, the former specially numerous about the Seine, where Rollo's companions chiefly settled, the latter in the Cotentin, where Harald Bluetooth's army found land to their liking. Physically, they must have been among the purest specimens among that restless, roving, adventurous type of men, blond or rufous, with straight profile and elliptical head, which evermore crops up among the people of the west of Europe whenever deeds of adventurous daring have to be done".

## VIII. ENGLAND'S DANISH KINGS

We have briefly in this introduction named some of the most important Norse kings mentioned in the *Heimskringla*, and now we come to two Danish kings who were destined to play a great rôle in the history of the British Isles, viz. Swein Forkbeard and Canute the Great, of whom Snorre has a good deal to say.

Swein Forkbeard appears, according to the chroniclers, to have arrived in England in the first instance in 994 in company with Olav Trygvason (who soon afterwards became King of Norway), but Snorre is silent about this joint expedition and writes all the time about Olav's enmity to Swein, which ended with the battle of Svold related in the 'History of Olav Trygvason'. Swein harried in England for several years and went back to Denmark at intervals. In 1003 he brought his army across again and this time apparently in order to avenge the massacre of the Danes on St Brice's Day the previous year, when his sister Gunhild was among the victims. From now onwards he fights continually to wrest the English Crown from King Ethelred. The battle of London Bridge was fought in 1013, when Ethelred, assisted by King Olav (the later St Olav) and Thorkel the High, temporarily forced him to retire to Wallingford and later to Bath. Swein finally succeeded in his designs and Ethelred left for Normandy, to return to England a few months later on the death of Swein in 1014. But Swein's son Canute was immediately elected king by the Danes in England and more fighting followed. Ethelred died of illness in 1016 and after his death King Canute gradually got the upper hand and was elected King of England by some of his English adherents in the autumn of 1016 and during the following year the whole of England submitted to his rule. King Canute was a wise and able ruler and soon became a popular king among the common people as well as among the nobles. He was not looked upon as a foreigner in the same sense as were the Normans, for being a Dane he spoke a very similar language to that of the Old English and all the Scandinavians already settled in England. He undertook a voyage to Rome in 1031, which secured him great renown. The story told about King Canute attempting to stem the tide is a curious misrepresentation of facts. It was due to his courtiers' flattery that he agreed to place his chair on the sea shore, and when the tide mounted, as he knew it would, he gave them a well-deserved rebuke. He wanted to show them how absurd they were in their flattery. Canute died in 1035 at Shaftesbury and was buried at

Winchester, where his tomb is still shown. His sons Harold Harefoot and Hardicanute were not of the same stamp as their father and their reigns were of short duration. In 1043 England reverted to her own royal stock and Ethelred's son, Edward the Confessor, came to the throne.


## IX. CONCLUSION

A short résumé of events related by Snorre Sturlason has been given above, in order to make the reader acquainted with an outline of the contents of Snorre's book. The English invasions have also been briefly dealt with, although they are not mentioned by Snorre.

It was the study of various English chronicles that caused this translation of *Heimskringla* to be undertaken. By collating the chroniclers with Snorre it has often been possible to solve problems which have hitherto been obscure, and although we do not profess to have solved them in their entirety we believe that we have shown the right way for further research work in this uncertain and difficult part of English and Scandinavian history. There are times when Snorre relates events connected with English history which are not mentioned by the English chroniclers. Often it may be that these events have not been considered important enough; but in any case the chroniclers' silence is no proof that Snorre gives information which is not historical. Only when Snorre's narrative is strictly opposed to that of the chroniclers have we assumed that the latter were in possession of information which gives us the correct version. Sometimes the chain of events can be linked together, one book supplementing the other. These comparisons have been pointed out in the numerous footnotes, each chronicler being mentioned as Snorre's narrative proceeds, but because certain events do not apparently at once agree with the chroniclers, it is of no use to get impatient as did, for instance, E. A. Freeman when he read the saga narratives about the battles of St Olav and Thorkel the High in England. He could not make head or tail of them and exclaimed: "The northern tradition here, like most of the accounts of the sagas, is utterly unintelligible". We have endeavoured in our footnotes on pp. 227, 228 to bring the saga account on these events into line with the chroniclers, from whom we hear that more fighting actually took place than Snorre tells us about. Freeman also criticises the saga narratives of the battle at Stamford Bridge. His remarks here are even less justified. Snorre's account of the battle is plain and simple enough, and the only fault that English readers may find with it is that Snorre puts Earl Tosti in a more favourable light than his brother Harold Godwinson, and it is a great question whether Snorre after all is far wrong in this. William had never anything good to say about Harold. This was partly due to prejudice; but William was broadminded enough at times to overlook and excuse the faults and misdeeds of his enemies.

Instead of leaving out the scalds' poems an endeavour has been made to translate them into English, and although it may be looked upon as a most difficult, if not a hopeless task, it seemed preferable to translate them in order to give the reader some idea of their contents; but to appreciate them fully they must be read in Old Norse. The *Norröna* tongue, however, is a very difficult language on account of its complicated grammar. It might have been assumed that the Old Scandinavians had a language as easy and plain as the simple (though turbulent) lives they led, and as clear and lucid as their fjords and lakes, but it was not so. It is far more complicated than modern English or the present Scandinavian languages. For instance the proper and common nouns are divided into four conjugations and the prepositions govern either the genitive, dative or accusative case of the noun. It has been thought more in keeping with these old-world narratives to employ old-fashioned English words and expressions as far as possible and to retain the Norse spelling of some of the place names and personal names, particularly those among the latter which are no longer in use. Names like Aki, Ani, Ari, Bui, Karlsefni, Loki, Skuli, Yngvi, etc., are put in the text as they are spelt in O.N. in the nominative form. When 'son' is added to the name the genitive form should be applied and the names then become Akason, Anason, Arason, Buason, Skulason, Yngvason, etc. It would be too much of a good thing to carry the conjugations any further, and 'Aki's daughter', 'Bui's brother', and 'Skuli's sister' have been written, although the correct form would be 'daughter of Aka', 'brother of Bua' and the 'sister of Skula'. The personal names still in use are written according to present practice, viz. Atle, Arne, Bruce, Eric, Inge, Ivor, John, William, etc., but we do not claim to have been consistent in this method, and no hard and fast rule has been followed. In surnames ending with *son* the form with only one *s* has been used, such as Björnson, Haraldson, Sigurdson, etc., in accordance with the generally adopted modern practice. In O.N. they are invariably written as Björnsson, Haraldsson and Sigurdsson. In the footnotes a few repetitions have been made in order to assist the reader's memory.

Some of the illustrations are reproductions of drawings by the late Halvdan Egedius, who was an artist of rare talent. Unfortunately he died while engaged on a Norwegian edition of Snorre, at the early age of twenty-one. His mother, Mrs Egedius, has allowed me to reproduce his drawings. Others have been produced by kind permission of the famous Norwegian painter, Erik Werenskiold, whose brilliant style and conception of the saga events and personalities have been much valued in Norway. The drawings of another Norwegian painter, the late Chr. Krohg, have also been reproduced in this book by kind permission of Mrs Oda Krohg. His drawings are masterpieces of their kind.

I also owe a debt of gratitude to the well-known Norwegian publishers, Messrs J. M. Stenersen's Forlag of Oslo, for allowing me to reproduce the illustrations contained in their magnificent Norwegian edition of Snorre Sturlason, printed in 1899.

Many thanks are due to Dr A. H. Smith of University College, London, and formerly of Upsala University, for having undertaken the spade work of making the first draft of the translation into English. As a Yorkshireman he has used many old-fashioned words and expressions familiar to him, and he has also furnished me with several historical data of great value. I am also indebted to my Icelandic friend Dr Jon Stefansson of King's College, London, for helping me not only with the O.N. language, but also with the spelling of the O.N. personal and place names. Last, but by no means least, my gratitude goes forth to my wife, who has been a constant helpmate to me with the compiling both of the book and the index.

Last year, 1930, was the great year for the Althing celebrations in Iceland, and England and the three Nordic countries as well as the United States sent representatives to do homage to the Icelandic nation, that virile little country which can boast of its own Parliament for a thousand years. It was the Norsemen who settled in Iceland in 874 and it was the Norsemen who as early as 930 laid the foundations for representative government in the island. It is of course true that it was not exactly a democratic assembly in the beginning. The members elected themselves and consisted of landed proprietors and leaders of men. Those who had intelligence, power and wealth took the responsibility of ruling the country, and everybody looked upon this as only just and right.

Snorre Sturlason was twice Speaker of the Althing and held as such a dominating position in the island.

The Nordic peoples owe a tremendous debt to Iceland for its wonderful literature and historical writings, with which her ancient, noble sons have enriched the world in general and the northern countries in particular, a debt that can never be paid.

And to those who are critical and sceptical about Snorre's great work we can only say with the French philosopher:

> La vérité peut attendre.
> Elle restera toujours aussi jeune,
> Et sera sûre d'être un jour reconnue.

E. M.

1931

SNORRE STURLASON

(1178–1241)

Born and died in Iceland

# SNORRE STURLASON'S PREFACE

IN THIS BOOK I have had written the old narratives about the chiefs who have had realms in the Northlands and who spoke the Danish tongue,[1] even as I have heard wise men, learned in history, tell, besides some of their family descents even as I have been taught them; some of this is found in the family successions in which kings and other men of great kin have traced their kinship; some is written according to old songs or lays, which men have had for their amusement. And although we know not the truth of these, we know, however, of occasions when wise old men have reckoned such things as true. Tjodolv of Kvin was a scald to Harald Hairfair; and about King Ragnvald the Glorious he made the song which is called Ynglinga-tal. Ragnvald was the son of Olav Geirstader-Alf, the brother of Halvdan the Black. In the poem he mentions thirty of his forefathers and there he speaks of the death and burial-place of each. Fjölnir is the name of the son of Yngvi-Frey, to whom the Swedes made offerings for a long time after, and from whom the Ynglings take their name. Eyvind Scaldaspiller also gives an account of Jarl Hacon the Mighty's forefathers in the poem which is called Haleygia-tal and which was composed about Hacon. There is first mentioned Sæming, the son of Yngvi-Frey; there too is it told of each man's death and burial-howe. From Tjodolv's poem are the lives of the Ynglings first written and thereto are added matters from the lore of wise men.

The first Age is called the Age of Burning, for then they burned the dead and raised stones in memory of them, but after Frey had been buried in a howe at Upsala, many chiefs made howes no less than standing-stones to the memory of their kinsmen. But after Dan the Proud, the Danish king, had had a howe made for himself and bade them bear him thither after death in his kingly garb and armour, with horse and saddle trappings and with other goods, many men of his family did the same and this was the beginning of the Mound Age in Denmark; but the Burning Age continued long after amongst the Swedes and Norsemen.

---

1 *Danish tongue* (*Dönsk tunga*) was the name often used in olden times for the languages spoken in the Scandinavian countries; but the word *Norröna* (meaning 'Nordic') was also in use.

When Harald Hairfair was king in Norway, Iceland was settled. With Harald there were scalds, and even now their songs are known, as well as the songs about all the kings who were in Norway after this; and we find the best evidence in the poems which were offered to the kings themselves or to their sons; we take everything for true which is found in their poems about their journeys or battles. It is the way of scalds, of course, to give most praise to him for whom they composed, but no one would dare tell the king himself such deeds of his as all listeners and the king himself knew to be lies and loose talk; that would be mockery, but not praise.

The priest Ari the Wise, son of Torgils Gellison, was the first man to write here in Iceland in the Norröna speech about older times ancient and modern. In the beginning of his book he wrote mostly about how Iceland was settled and its laws founded, and how long each of the law-speakers had pronounced the law; he reckoned the years first to the time when Christianity came to Iceland and thereafter right down to his own days. Thereto he added many happenings in the lives of the kings in Norway and Denmark and likewise in England, besides the great events which had befallen in this land. And it seems to me that all his accounts are very trustworthy; he was very understanding and he was so old that he had been born the year after Harald Sigurdson's death.[1] He wrote, as he himself tells us, about the lives of the kings of Norway according to the reports of Odd Kollson, grandson of Hall of Sida; Odd got his knowledge from Torgeir Afradskoll who was a wise man and so old that he lived at Nidarnes when Jarl Hacon the Mighty was slain; in the same place King Olav Trygvason had the market town built which is there now. When seven years old, Ari the Priest came to Haukadale[2] to Hall Torarinson and was with him for fourteen years. Hall was a very wise man and of good memory; he remembered that Tangbrand the Priest baptised him when he was three years old; that was the year before Christianity was made law. Ari was twelve years old when Bishop Isleif died. Hall had travelled between the countries and was in partnership with King St Olav and got much gain therefrom; he therefore knew much about his reign. And when Bishop Isleif died almost eighty years had passed since the fall of King Olav Trygvason. Hall died nine years after Bishop Isleif and he was then ninety-four years old. He was thirty years old when he settled in Haukadale, and he lived there sixty-four years; so writes Ari. Teit, son of Bishop Isleif, was brought up with Hall

1 In 1066.        2 *Haukadale* is in South-west Iceland.

in Haukadale and lived there afterwards; he taught Ari the Priest and gave him much information about former times, which Ari afterwards wrote down. Ari also got much knowledge from Thurid, daughter of Snorre Godi; she was very wise and she could remember her father, who was nearly thirty-five years old when Christianity came to Iceland and died the year after the fall of St Olav. It is not strange that Ari knew the truth of old events both here and abroad, for he had got his knowledge from old and wise men, and he himself was eager to learn and had a good memory. But the poems, I think, are most trustworthy if they are rightly interpreted and are read with understanding.

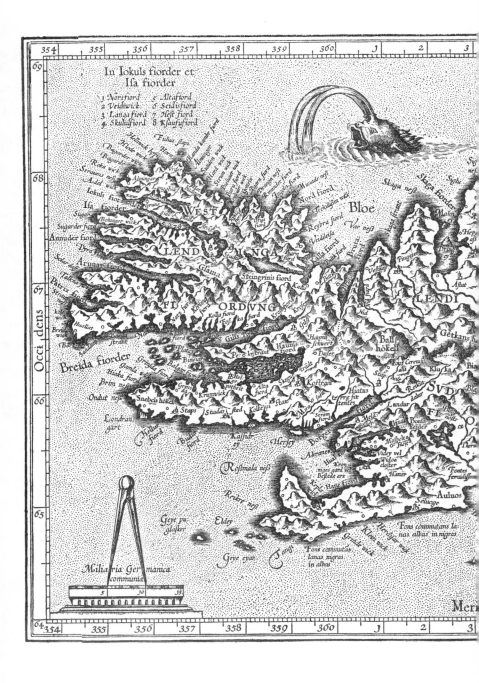

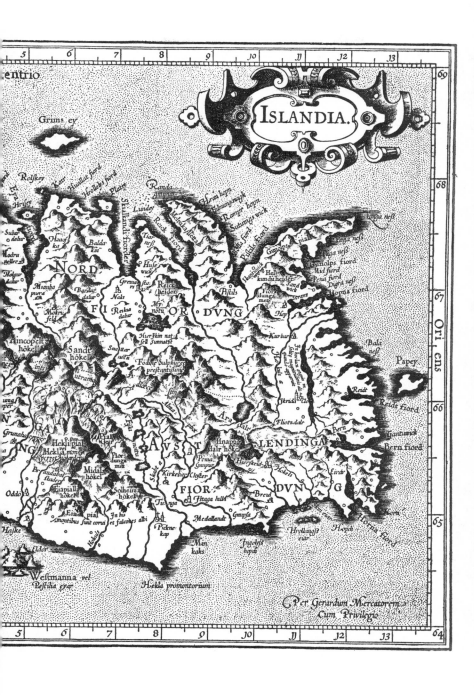

ISLANDIA.

Per Gerardum Mercatorem
Cum Privilegio

# ABBREVIATIONS

M.S. = Modern Scandinavian.
O.E. = Old English.
O.S. = Old Scandinavian.
O.N. = Old Norse or Old Norwegian.

Both O.S. and O.N. are used. They signify the old Norröna tongue spoken in the northern countries.

# I

# YNGLINGA SAGA

1. The earth's round face, whereon mankind dwells, is much cleft because great gulfs run up into the land from the ocean. It is known that a sea stretches from Norvasund[1] to Jorsalaland,[2] and from the sea there goes towards the north-east a bight which is called the Black Sea. It is there that one finds the division between the three parts of the earth: to the east it is called Asia, but the land to the west is sometimes called Europa, sometimes Enea.[3] But to the north of the Black Sea there stretches the great but icy Sweden; Sweden the Great[4] some men reckon as large as the great Serkland,[5] others equate it with the great Blaland.[6] The northern part of Sweden the Great lies unpeopled through frost and cold, just as the southern part of Blaland is wasted by the heat of the sun. In Sweden there are many great lordships, many kinds of people, and many tongues; there are giants and there are dwarfs and there are black men, and there are many kinds of strange creatures, there are great savage beasts and dragons. To the south of the fells which lie outside all the inhabited land there runs through Sweden the Great a river which in proper speech is called the Tanais;[7] it was formerly called the Tanakvisl or Vanakvisl; it flows out into the Black Sea. In the olden days the land between the Vanaforks was called Vanaland or Vanaheim.[8] This river divides the

---

1 Straits of Gibraltar.   2 The land of Jorsalir, i.e. Jerusalem.   3 *Enea*, because in the Middle Ages it was thought that many European peoples (the Romans, and others) derived their origin from Eneas and the Trojans. 4 Russia.   5 *The great Serkland* is North Africa. The name Serkland is also used for the country of the Saracens in Asia as well as for Spain.   6 *Blaland* = where the negroes live in Africa. The negroes are called in O.S. *blamenn* = the blue men.   7 River Don in Russia.   8 *Vanaheim*, the home of the Vanes. The O.E. word *ham* in Nottingham, Birmingham, etc., was pronounced *hām* and is cognate with the O.S. *heim*. In Whittinghame *hame* is pronounced like the Scand. *heim*. Nottingham's original name was Snotingaham—according to Asser: 'place of caves'. In O.S. *snöttungr* means 'robbers'. The words are possibly connected. The name 'Hamburg' (in Danish 'Hamborg') is no doubt also of Scand. origin, as is probably the name of the village of Ham, adjoining the town. Flensborg (in Sleswick), Middelburg (in Holland), Cherbourg (in France) are all names of Scand. origin. The Danish frontier up to 1848 extended as far south as Altona (adjoining Hamburg) and it is generally recognised that the Scandinavians before coming to Britain and France made raids and settled on the coasts of North Germany, Holland and Belgium as well as on the coasts of Finland, Russia and the Baltic Provinces. Rörik of Jutland is considered the founder of the Romanoff dynasty in Russia by some historical writers.

world into parts; that to the east is known as Asia, and that to the west as Europe.

2. The land in Asia to the east of the Tanakvisl was called Asaland or Asaheim and the chief town in the land was called *Asagarth* (or *Asagard*). In the town there was the chief who was known as Odin and it was a great place for sacrificing. It was the custom for twelve

chief priests of the temple to direct the sacrifices and to judge between men; they were called *diar* or *drottnar*; and them should all people serve and obey. Odin was a mighty warrior who had wandered far and won for himself many kingdoms; he was so victorious that he won every battle, and through that it came about that his men believed he must needs be winner in every fight. It was his wont when he sent his men to battle or on any other journey to lay his hands on their heads and give them his blessing; they then believed that all would go well with them. And so it was with his men: when they were hard beset on sea or land, they called on his name and always thought they got help from it; in him had they all their trust. He often went so far away that he was many years on the journey.

3. Odin had two brothers; one was called Ve, the other Vili. These two ruled the kingdom when he was away. It once happened when Odin was gone far away and had been a long time from home that his people thought he would not come back. Then his brothers took it upon themselves to divide his goods in succession to him, but they both took to wife his spouse Frigga. But a little later Odin came home and once more took his wife to himself.

4. Odin[1] went with his army against the Vanes, but they withstood him well and defended their land. Each of them was in turn winner; both sides harried one another's land, and did each other great scathe. And when they both became weary of it, they arranged a meeting to make peace and gave each other hostages. The Vanes gave them their highest men, Niord the Wealthy and his son Frey, and the people of Asaland in return gave the man called Hænir, whom they

---

[1] From Odin (in O.E. Woden) Wednesday derives its name; from Tyr or Tys (genitive), Tuesday; from Thor, Thursday; from Freya, Friday.

thought well fitted to be a leader, being a big and handsome man. With him they sent Mimir, the wisest of men, and the Vanes in return gave the wisest of their men called Kvasir, and when Hænir came to Vanaheim he was chosen as leader and Mimir gave him every advice. But when Hænir was at the thing or at gatherings, where any difficult matter came before him, then he always answered the same (unless Mimir was present), "Now get the counsel of others", said he. Then the Vanes had a suspicion that the Asaland people had played them false in the exchange of men. They therefore took Mimir and beheaded him and sent his head to the Asaland people. Odin took the head, smeared it with such herbs that it could not rot, quoth spells over it and worked such charms that it talked with him and told him many hidden things. Odin sent Niord and Frey to the temple priests and they now became priests. Niord's daughter was Freya. She was a priestess and she first taught the Asaland people wizardry, which was in use with the Vanes. Whilst Niord was with the Vanes he had espoused his own sister (for that was lawful with them), and their children were Frey and Freya. But in Asaland it was forbidden to wed such near kin.

5. A great ridge of mountains goes from north-east to south-west dividing Sweden the Great from other kingdoms. To the south of the fells it is not far to the land of the Turks where Odin had great possessions. At that time the Roman Emperors were going far and wide over the world and in battle beat down all people; because of the unrest many lords fled from their lands. When Odin looked into the future and worked magic, he knew that his offspring would dwell and till in the northern parts of the earth. He, therefore, set his brothers Ve and Vili over Asagarth and he himself went away and with him went all the priests and many of his folk. First he went to Gardarik[1] and from there he went south to Saxland.[2] He had many sons; he won kingdoms far over Saxland and set his sons as rulers over them. From there he fared north to the sea and found himself a dwelling on an island which is now called Odensö in Fyn. Then he sent Gefion north-east over the sound to look for land; she then came to Gylfi,[3] who gave her a ploughland. Next she went to a giant's home and there begot four sons with a giant. She shaped them in the likeness of oxen, yoked them to a plough and broke up the land unto the sea westwards opposite Odensö; it was called Selund,[4] and there she dwelt after-

---

1 Russia.  2 Germany.  3 King Gylfi of Sweden, of whom Snorre Sturlason has written in his *Edda*.  4 *Selund* is the old name for Zealand in Denmark.

wards. Skjold,[1] Odin's son, took her to wife and they lived in Leidra.[2] There where she ploughed is now a lake or sea called Löginn; the fjords in Löginn answer to the nesses in Selund. Thus said Bragi the Old:

| | |
|---|---|
| Gefion drew with gladness | The oxen bore eight eyes |
| From the gold-rich Gylfi | And four heads. |
| Denmark's new increase | There they went forth, |
| (So that it reeked from the beasts). | Far over Vinö's bay. |

And then when Odin got to hear that there was good land to the east in Gylfi's country he went there and Gylfi came to terms with him because he deemed he had no power to withstand the Asaland people. Many dealings had Odin and Gylfi between themselves in cunning and charms, but the Asa people always won. Odin set his dwelling near Lögrinn[3] where it is now called Gamla-Sigtun,[4] and where he built a large temple for blood offerings according to the customs of his people. He conquered all the land round it, and called his place Sigtun. He gave the temple priests dwelling-places; Niord lived in Noatun, Frey near Upsala, Heimdal by the Himenfell, Thor in Trudvang, Balder in Breidablik; to all of them he gave good lands.[5]

6. It is said with truth that when Asa-Odin and the *diar* (priests) came to the northern lands, they brought in and taught others the sports and crafts which were plied there for a long time afterwards. Odin was the cleverest of all, and from him they learned all because he knew most of them first. And why he was so honoured shall be told of him for this reason: when he sat with his friends he was so fair and noble in looks that all were joyful; but when he was with his army then he seemed terrifying to his foes. It was said that he understood such tricks of cunning that he could change himself and appear in any

---

1 *Skjold,* according to various chroniclers, was the founder of the old Danish Skjoldung line of kings and is identified with Scyld Sceafing of the Old English poem *Beowulf.* 2 *Leidra* was later called Leire near Roskilde in Zealand, where all the Danish kings are buried even in our time. 3 Lake Mälar in Sweden. 4 *Gamla* or Old Sigtun (= Old Sigtown) was situated on the east side of the Upsala fjord, near the present Sigtuna. 5 *Noatun, Himenfell, Trudvang* and *Breidablik* are places in Sweden, which cannot now be identified; these names are held to be mythical. Snorre Sturlason mentions Himenheid (cf. chapter 35) where King Anund was killed through a landslip; and in Tjodolv's verses on this incident the scene of Anund's death is called 'Himenfell'.

form he would, and it was said that he talked so glibly and shrewdly that all who heard him must needs take his tale to be wholly true; he said everything in rime in a manner which is now called scaldcraft. He and his temple priests were called song smiths because the scaldic art in the northern land had its beginning from them. In battle Odin could make his foes blind or deaf or terrified and their weapons were as nothing more than sticks; but his own men went about without armour and were mad like hounds or wolves, and bit their shields and were strong as bears or bulls; they slew men, but neither fire nor steel would deal with them. This was called a berserk's-gang.

7. Odin often changed himself; at those times his body lay as though he were asleep or dead, and he then became a bird or a beast, a fish or a dragon, and went in an instant to far-off lands on his own or other men's errands. He could do this also: with sacrificial words he slaked fire, stilled the sea or turned winds in what way he would. He had a ship which was known as *Skidbladnir*; on it he went over mighty seas, but it could also be rolled up together like a table-cloth. Odin had with him Mimir's head and it told him many tidings of other worlds; and sometimes he awoke dead men from the earth and sat himself down under men who had been hanged; and so he was called Lord of the Ghosts or the Hanged Men. He owned two ravens, which he had taught to talk; they flew far over the land and told many tidings. Through all this he became very wise. All these crafts he taught with runes and songs which were called *galdrar* (enchantments) and so the Asa people were called *galdra* smiths. Odin knew and practised that craft which brought most power and which was called *seid* (witchcraft), and he therefore knew much of man's fate and of the future, likewise how to bring people death, ill-luck or illness, or he took power and wit from them and gave it to others. But in promoting this sorcery, lack of manliness followed so much that men seemed not without shame in dealing in it; the priestesses were therefore taught this craft. Odin also knew where any treasure pit was hidden and knew such songs that the earth and hills and rocks and howes opened themselves for him, and he bound with spells those who might be dwelling therein, so that he could go in and take all that he wished. By these crafts he became very renowned; his foes feared him, but his friends took pride in him and trusted in his craft and in him. But most of the crafts he taught the priests; they came nearest to him in all wisdom and wizardry. And many others learned much thereof; from them sorcery has therefore spread widely and long endured. Men sacrificed to Odin and his twelve chiefs and called them their

gods and long afterwards believed in them. From Odin's name was the name Audun formed, and by it men called their sons, and from the name Thor are formed Tor-e and Tor-aren or it is joined with other names as in Steintor or Havtor, or varied in other ways.

8. Odin set in his land the laws which had formerly been upheld by the Asa folks; thus, he bade that they burn all the dead and bear their possessions on to the firebale with them. He said that every man should come to Valhall with such riches as he had with him on the firebale and that each should use what he himself had buried in the earth. They should bear the ashes out on the sea or bury them down in the earth;[1] for a renowned man they should build a howe as a mark of remembrance, and for all men in whom there was some manliness they should raise standing-stones, and this custom held good for a long time after. Near winter's day[2] they should sacrifice for a good season, in the middle of winter for a good crop, and near summer's day[3] it was the sacrifice for victory. Over all Sweden they gave Odin scot[4] (or taxes) for every nose, and he would protect their land from war and do sacrifices for them for a good season. Niord took a wife called Skadi; she would not live with him and afterwards gave herself to Odin. They got many sons and one of them was called Sæming: about him Eyvind Scaldaspiller has made this:

Hail, lord!
The chief was begotten
By the kin of the god
With the giantess,
In those days of old
When the prince's friend

Was Skadi's mate
In the Manheims,
And the fell-sliding
Ski-goddess
Begot with Odin
Many sons.

From Sæming, Jarl Hacon the Mighty reckons his race, man for man. This Sweden they called the Manheims, but Sweden the Great they called the Godheims, about which they tell many tidings.

9. Odin died in his bed in Sweden, and when he was near death he had himself marked with a spear point and dedicated to himself all men who died through weapons; he said that he should now fare to the Godheims and there welcome his friends. The Swedes now believed that he had gone to the old Asagarth and would live there for ever. Then began anew the belief in Odin and prayers to him arose afresh. The Swedes often seemed to see him clearly before great battles began; to some he gave victory, but others he bid come to him;

1 All the relics found in the *Kungshögar* at Gamla-Upsala show distinct traces of thorough cremation.    2 *Winter's day* was the middle of October.    3 *Summer's day* was the middle of April.    4 'Scotfree' probably originates from the Scand. *skatfri* (tax free)

both fates seemed good to them. Odin was burned after his death and the fire was very glorious. It was their belief that the higher the reek went up aloft, the higher place in Heaven would he receive whose body was burned, and the more goods that were burned with him, the richer he became. Niord of Noatun then took the rule over the Swedes and upheld the sacrifices; then the Swedes called him their *Drott* (or Sovereign) and he then took scot from them. In his days there was peace, and the seasons were so good that the Swedes believed that Niord had power over the crops and the well-being of mankind. In his days most of the *diar* (or priests) died and all were burned, and afterwards they sacrificed to them. Niord died in his bed; he also had himself marked for Odin before his death. The Swedes burned him and wept much by his grave.

10. So Frey took the rule after Niord; he was called *Drott* (or Sovereign) of the Swedes and took scot from them; he had many friends and brought good seasons like his father. Frey built near Upsala a great temple, and set there his chief seat, and endowed it with all his income from land and chattels. That was the beginning of the Upsala Crown property[1] which has lasted ever since. In his days began the peace of Frode;[2] then there was also a good season over all the land. The Swedes gave Frey credit for it, and he therefore was much more worshipped than the other gods, as the land folk in his days became richer on account of peace and good seasons than ever before. Gerd, the daughter of Gymir, was the name of Frey's wife, and their son was called Fjölnir. Frey was known by a second name Yngvi; that name was used long after in his race as a name of great worth, and his kinsmen were afterwards called Ynglings. Frey then fell sick, and as he neared death, his men took counsel, and let few men come to him; and they built a great howe with a door and three holes in it. And when Frey was dead they bore him in loneliness to the howe, and told the Swedes that he was still alive; they watched him then for three years, and all scot they hid down in the howe, in one hole the gold, in another the silver, and in the third copper pennies. The good seasons and peace continued. Freya held to the sacrifices still, for she alone of the gods still lived. She then became so very

---

1 *Upsala Crown property* or *Upsala Öde* (O.S.), lit. the Upsala Wealth, was the Crown property belonging to the Swedish kings in various parts of Sweden.    2 Snorre Sturlason here refers to what he has related in his *Edda*: Frode took over the kingdom (in Denmark) after his father Fridleiv at a time when the Emperor Augustus made peace all over the world and Christ was born. As Frode was the mightiest king in the northern countries the peace was attributed to him and named after him.

renowned, that they called all their noble women by her name, even as they are now called *fruer*; so every woman is called Freya (*Frue*), who rules over her own property, but she is called house-freya (*husfrue*), who has a household.

Freya was shifty of mind. Her husband was called Od and their daughters were called Noss and Gersimi;[1] they were very beautiful and from them are named the most costly things. When all the Swedes marked that Frey was dead, but that good seasons and peace still continued, they believed that it would be so, so long as Frey was in Sweden; therefore, they would not burn him, but called him god of the earth, and ever after sacrificed to him, most of all for good seasons and peace.

11. Fjölnir, Yngvi-Frey's son, next ruled over the Swedes and the Wealth of Upsala;[2] he was mighty and brought good seasons and peace. At that time Peace Frode dwelt in Leidra.[3] Between him and Fjölnir there was friendship, and they invited each other to meet. Then Fjölnir went to Frode at Selund; a great feast was ready there, and many were bid to it from far over the land. Frode had great dwelling-houses, therein was made a great vat, many ells high and fastened together with stocks of timber. It stood in a room on the ground floor, and higher up was a loft with an opened floor, so that from it men poured down the drink and mixed the vat full of mead. The drink was very strong. In the evening Fjölnir was led to his bedroom in the next loft and his followers with him. In the night he walked out into the passage to seek himself a certain place. He was then heavy with sleep and dead drunk. Then he went back to his sleeping-place. Then he walked along the passage to the door of another loft and went through it; there he slipped with his foot, and so fell into the mead vat, and was drowned. Thus says Tjodolv of Kvin:

| | |
|---|---|
| There went forth | And the generous prince |
| In Frode's dwelling | In the mead-vat's |
| The behest of Death, | Windless wave |
| Which was borne to Fjölnir, | Found his death. |

Svegdir took the kingdom after his father. He made a vow to look for the Godheims and Odin the Old. He went with twelve men far about the world; he came right out into the land of the Turks and Sweden the Great and found there many kinsmen. On the journey

---

[1] Snorre Sturlason relates in *Edda*: "Freya and Od's daughter was Noss; she was so fair and beautiful that from her name is everything called 'noss' which is beautiful and costly". The O.S. word is spelt *hnoss*. [2] Upsala Crown property. [3] Near Roskilde (in Denmark).

he was five winters,[1] and so he came back and then stayed at home for a while. Out in Vanaheim he had taken a wife called Vana; their son was named Vanlandi.

12. Svegdir again went out to look for the Godheims. In the east of Sweden there is a great town called Stein;[2] there is a stone as big as a great house. One evening after sunset he went from the drinking to the sleeping-bower; and, as he came to the stone, he saw a dwarf sitting under it. Svegdir and his men were very drunk, and ran towards the stone. The dwarf stood in the door, and called to Svegdir, and bade him go in, if he wished to meet Odin. Svegdir leaped into the stone, and it straightway locked itself, and Svegdir never came back. Thus says Tjodolv:

| | |
|---|---|
| But Durin's[3] kinsman, | Dusla's offspring[4] |
| Who shunned the daylight, | Leaped after the dwarf, |
| The warden of the hall, | And Sokkmimi's[3] |
| Duped Svegdir, | Bright abode, |
| When into the stone | The hall of the giants, |
| The great-hearted | Carried away the king. |

13. Svegdir's son hight Vanlandi, and he took the kingdom after him and ruled over the Wealth of Upsala. He was a great warrior and went far over the land. He had stayed one winter in Finland with Snæ the Old, and there married his daughter Driva. In the spring he went away, whilst Driva stayed behind, and he promised to come back after three winters, but he came not for ten winters. Then Driva had Huld the witch woman called to her, and sent Visbur, hers and Vanlandi's son, to Sweden. Driva paid Huld the witch woman to draw Vanlandi to Finland with sorcery or else to kill him. When the spell was being furthered, Vanlandi was in Upsala, and he had a longing to go to Finland, but his friends and advisers forbade him, and said that it certainly was Finnish witchcraft[5] which caused his wanderlust. Then he became sleepy and said that the Mare[6] was treading on him. His men sprang up and would help him, but when they came to his head she trod on his feet, so that they were nigh broken; then they resorted to the feet, but then she smothered the head, so that he died there. The Swedes took his body and burned it

---

1 I.e. years.   2 Probably a town in Estland, see chapter 32.   3 *Durin* and *Sokkmimi* are names of dwarfs.   4 *Dusla's offspring*: meaning uncertain.   5 The Old Scandinavians believed that the Finns, both in Finland and in Finmark (north of Norway) were full of witchcraft.   6 *Mare* (O.S. *mara*) is thought to be an old woman who disturbs people in their sleep by sitting on them. In O.S. *martröð*; in English, *nightmare*; and in French, *couchmar*.

near a river which was called Skuta; there was his standing-stone set up. Thus says Tjodolv:

| | |
|---|---|
| But on the way | Sorceress |
| To Vili's brother[1] | On the warrior lord. |
| Evil wights | And there was burned |
| Bore Vanlandi; | On the Skuta bank |
| Then there trod | That generous man |
| The troll-wise | Whom the Mare killed. |

14. Visbur took his inheritance after his father Vanlandi; he took to wife a daughter of Aud the Wealthy and gave her as a wedding gift three great estates and a gold necklace; they had two sons, Gisl and Andur. Afterwards Visbur left her, and took another wife, but she went to her father with her sons. After that Visbur had a son who was called Domaldi; Domaldi's stepmother had witchcraft worked to bring him ill-luck. When Visbur's sons were twelve and thirteen years old they went to their father and craved their mother's wedding gift, but he would not give it up. Then they foretold that the golden necklace should be the bane of the best man in his race, and thereupon they went off home. Then again they had witchcraft worked, to the end that they should know how to kill their father. The witch Huld told them that even so she would work the spell, and also that slaughter of their kin should always be with the race of the Ynglings; they agreed to it. Thereafter they gathered folk together and unexpectedly came upon Visbur in the night and burned him inside his house. Thus says Tjodolv:

| | |
|---|---|
| And Visbur's | Loosed |
| Body | The heated wood |
| The sea's fiery brother | And the flames |
| Swallowed up, | That howled |
| When the seat wardens | Against the king |
| Against their father | In his own house. |

15. Domaldi took the inheritance after his father Visbur and ruled over the land. In his days there was famine and need in Sweden. The Swedes then held a great sacrifice near Upsala. For the first harvest they sacrificed oxen, but the crop was not bettered by it; for the next harvest they sacrificed men, but the crop was the same or even worse. And for the third harvest many Swedes came to Upsala at the time when the sacrifice should be held. The chiefs then took counsel, and held to a man that Domaldi their king must be the cause of the bad seasons and also that they should have to sacrifice him in order to have

---

1 *Vili's brother* is Odin.

a good season, that they should bear their weapons against him and kill him and dye the altars with his blood. And so they did. Thus says Tjodolv:

It was long ago
That the earth was dyed
With the blood of the king,
Spilled by the sword-bearers;
And the land warriors
With happiness

Bore against Domaldi
Their blood-reddened weapons,
When the Swedish folk,
Weary of want,
Had sacrificed
The foe of the Jutes.

16. Domaldi's son was called Domar, and he next held the kingdom. He ruled for a long time, and there were good seasons and peace in his days. About him nothing else is told, but that he died in his bed in Upsala, was borne to the Fyrisvold,[1] and burned there on the river bank where his standing-stone is. Thus says Tjodolv:

And often I
From wise men
Have learned
Of the grave of the Ynglings,
Where Domar
By the roaring

Fiery bane of Halv[2]
Was borne away.
Now do I know
That the pain-stricken
Offspring of Fjölnir
Was burned near Fyris.

17. His son was called Dygvi, who next ruled over the land, and about him nothing more is said than that he died in his bed. Thus says Tjodolv:

I do not doubt
That Dygvi's grave
The goddess in Glitnir
Had for game,
For the wolf
And the dragon's sister

Must choose
A kingly man;
And Loki's daughter[3]
Has taken to herself
The noble prince
Of Yngvi's race.

Dygvi's mother was Drott, daughter of King Danp, the son of Rig who was first called 'king' in the Danish tongue. His kinsmen ever after bore the name of 'king' as the name of highest worth. Dygvi was the first in his race to be called 'king', but before that they were called *drottnar*, their wives *drottningar* and the ruler's men *drott*. But every man in the race was always called Yngvi or Ynguni and all of them

1 The *Fyris* is the river which flows through Upsala.  2 *Halv's bane* was fire, as King Halv was burned in his house.  3 *Hel* was daughter of Loki and sister of the wolf (Fenri) and the dragon (Midgardsworm). Hel ruled in one of the nine underworlds, where all those were sent that died from sickness and old age.

together were called Ynglings. Queen Drott was sister to King Dan the Proud, from whom Denmark afterwards took its name.

18. Dag was the name of King Dygvi's son, who had the kingdom after his father; he was so wise a man that he understood the song of the birds. He had a sparrow which told him many tidings; it often flew to other lands. It happened once that the sparrow flew to Reidgotland,[1] to a town which was called Vörva; it swooped down to a bonder's field and fed there. The bonder came up, took up a stone, and slew the sparrow dead. King Dag became uneasy in his mind because the sparrow did not come home, went to the sacrifice of atonement to ask about it and received the answer that his sparrow was killed in Vörva. He afterwards ordered out a great army and went to Gotland; but when he came to Vörva he went up with his army and harried there; the folk fled far and wide from him. When it was near evening Dag led his army back to the ships after he had killed or taken many men. But when they crossed the river near a place called Skjotansvad or Vapnavad, a workman leaped forth from the wood to the river bank and cast a hayfork into the host of men, and it fell on the king's head. He straightway fell from his steed and died. At that time a prince who went harrying was called a *gram*, and his chief men were called *gramir*. Thus says Tjodolv:

Hel, the goddess of death

I have heard that Dag,
The deed lusty man,
On a journey of death
Had to fare.
When he, the wise
Spear-thrower,
Came to Vörva
To avenge the sparrow.

On the East Way
The king's men
Bore from the fight
That word
That the fork which pitched
Sleipnir's[2] fodder
Gave death
To the warrior lord.

19. Dag's son was called Agni, who became king after him, a great chief, mighty and renowned and a hardy man withal. One summer when King Agni fared with his army to Finland he went

---

1 I.e. probably Jutland. Sometimes *Reidgotland* is also used for part of North Germany.
2 *Sleipnir*, i.e. horse. This was the name of Odin's horse.

ashore and harried it. The Finns gathered together a great host and drew to battle; Frosti was the name of their chief. There was a great battle, and King Agni had the victory; Frosti fell there and a great band with him. King Agni went with his army about Finland, laid it under him and took much booty; he seized and took with him Frosti's daughter Skjalv and her brother Loga. Then he came home to the west, stayed near Stoksund,[1] and set his tents on the south fields; a wood was there then. King Agni had then the gold necklace which Visbur had owned. He went to take Skjalv to wife; she begged the king to make a funeral feast for her father. He then bade his chief men come to him and make a great feast. He became very famous through that war. Then there was a great drinking feast held. But when King Agni was drunk, Skjalv bade him heed the necklace which he had on his neck. He took the necklace and bound it fast round his neck before he went to sleep. The camp stood near the wood and over the tent was a high tree which would shield it from the sun's heat. When King Agni was asleep, Skjalv took a thick cord, and fastened it under the necklace. Her men then knocked down the tent-pole, but cast a loop of the cord into the fork of the tree, and after that drew it up, so that the king was hanging down near the tree fork; that was his bane. Skjalv and her men leaped out on a ship and rowed away. King Agni was burned there and the place west of Stoksund on the east side of the Taur[2] was afterwards called Agna-fet.[3] Thus says Tjodolv:

| | |
|---|---|
| I call it wondrous | With the necklace |
| If Agni's men | The god's kinsman, |
| Should praise | Who by the Taur |
| Skjalv's counsel, | Should tame |
| When Loga's sister | The cold steed |
| Heaved aloft | Of Signy's bridegroom.[4] |

20. Agni's sons were called Alrek and Eric, and they were kings after him. They were mighty and able men, great warriors and skilled in all sports. It was their wont to ride horses and tame them to canter and jump; they could do it best of all men. They competed with each other to see which rode best or had the best horses. It happened once that the two brothers rode away from the other men on their best steeds and rode over certain level lands, but came not back. Men went to look for them and found them both dead with wounded heads,

1 *Stoksund* is the present Norrström between Lake Mälar and the sea, on the north side of Old Stockholm. 2 *Taur*, Old Swedish *Tör*, is the peninsula between Lake Mälar and the sea. 3 *Agna-fet* is situated on the south side of Old Stockholm. 4 *Signy's* (Signe's) *bridegroom* was Hagbard, who was hung by Sigar. His horse = the gallows.

but they had no weapons except horses' bridles, so that men thought
that with them they had slain each other. Thus says Tjodolv:

| | |
|---|---|
| Alrek fell | Dag's kinsmen |
| There where Eric | Slew each other. |
| At his brother's hand | It was unheard of |
| Got his death, | That horses' gear |
| And where with the headgear | By Frey's offspring |
| Of the horse | Was borne into fight. |

21. Alrek's sons were Yngvi and Alf who next took the kingdom
of Sweden. Yngvi was a great warrior and very victorious, handsome
and the greatest in sports, strong and bold in battle, open-handed and
very cheerful; by all this he drew many friends to him, and was much
talked about. King Alf, his brother, sat at home and was never on a
raid; he had the by-name Elfsi, and he was a silent, domineering and
friendless man; his mother was called Dageid, daughter of King Dag
the Mighty, from whom the Daglings have descended. Alf had a
wife of the name Bera, fair and bold and very lively. Yngvi Alrekson
came home to Upsala one harvest time from a viking raid and was
then very famous. He often sat for a long time in the evening drinking but King Alf often went early to bed. Queen Bera often sat up
in the evening and she and Yngvi often talked together. Alf many
times told her about it and bade her go to bed earlier, and said that
he would not lie awake for her. She answered that that woman was
lucky who could have Yngvi rather than Alf for a husband; often
when she said this he became very wroth about it. One evening Alf
went into the hall, whilst Yngvi and Bera sat on the high-seat and
were talking together; Yngvi had a sword lying across his knees. The
men were very drunk and gave no heed when the king came in. King
Alf went to the high-seat, drew his sword from under his cape, and
stuck it into Yngvi, his brother. Yngvi leaped up, swung his sword
and struck Alf a death blow; both of them fell dead on the floor. Alf
and Yngvi were buried in a howe on the Fyrisvold.[1] Thus says
Tjodolv:

| | |
|---|---|
| And the warden | It was hardly true |
| Of the holy stall, | That Bera urged |
| Slain by Alf, | The men so bold |
| Met his death, | On to battle, |
| When the kinsman of Dag | When the brothers were |
| Drew his sword | Each other's death |
| Through envy | With no cause |
| Against Yngvi. | For their zeal. |

1 Cf. p. 11, n. 1.

22. Alf's son was called Hugleik, who took the kingdom of the Swedes after the brothers, because Yngvi's sons were minors. King Hugleik was no warrior and sat at home at his ease; he was very rich but niggardly with his goods. He welcomed to his court all kinds of minstrels, harpers, jig players and fiddlers; he had also with him wizards and all kinds of sorcerers. Haki and Hagbard were the names of two famous brothers; they were sea kings and had a great host; sometimes they both went together, sometimes each went by himself. Each of them had many champions in their army. King Haki went with his army to Sweden against King Hugleik, but Hugleik gathered the folk to meet him. Then there came two brothers to his help, Svipdag and Geigad, both famous men and mighty champions. King Haki had with him twelve champions and amongst them was Starkad the Old; King Haki was also a great champion. They met on the Fyrisvold; there was a great battle and many of Hugleik's men fell at once. Then the champions Svipdag and Geigad went forth but Haki's champions were six against each of them, and they took the two prisoner. King Haki then went to a camp, attacked King Hugleik there and slew him there with his two sons. Thereafter the Swedes fled, and King Haki laid the lands under him and made himself King of the Swedes. He stayed in the land three years, and in the time of peace his champions went forth on viking raids and thus gathered booty for themselves.

23. The sons of Yngvi Alrekson were called Jörund and Eric; all this time they had lain out on their warships and were great warriors. One summer, they harried in Denmark and met King Gudlaug, King of the Haleygers.[1] They had a battle with him and the end of it was that Gudlaug's ship was cleared but he himself was seized; they moved him to land on Strömönes and hanged him there. His men there threw up a howe for him. Thus says Eyvind Scaldaspiller:

But Gudlaug
Tamed the grim
Steed of Sigar[2]
When the victory was won
By the eastern kings,
And the sons of Yngvi
Hanged on the gallows
The generous prince.

And bearing the body
There stands on the ness
The gallows tree,
Where the sea parts the land,
There by the king's grave
(Marked by a stone)
Where it was called
Strömönes.

Jörund and Eric became very famous by that deed and were now deemed much more powerful than before. They heard from afar that

1 *Haleygers*, inhabitants of Halogaland in North Norway.    2 *Steed of Sigar* = the gallows.

King Haki of Sweden had sent his champions from him; then they made for Sweden and afterwards gathered an army. But when the Swedes learned that the Ynglings had come there they sent a great army to them. Then they proceeded up Lögrinn and made for Upsala against King Haki, but he met them on the Fyrisvold with a much smaller army. Then there was a great battle; the king himself set forth so hardily that he felled all those who came near him; and in the end slew King Eric and hewed down the standard of the brothers. Then King Jörund fled with all his host to the ships. King Haki got in the battle so many wounds that he saw the days of his life would not be long. Then he had a ship brought up that he owned, and had it laden with dead men and weapons, had it floated out to the sea, had the rudder shipped and the sail hoisted, and had fire put to pitch wood and a firebale made on the ship. The wind blew from the land; King Haki was then dead or nearly dead when he was laid on the firebale. The burning ship then sailed out on the sea and that was much talked about for a long time after.

24. King Yngvi's son Jörund now became king in Upsala; he ruled the land, but was often away in the summer harrying. One summer he went with his army to Denmark, harried round about in Jutland and in the autumn went into the Limfjord, where he harried; he lay with his ships in Oddasund.[1] Then came there with a great army Gylaug, King of the Haleygers, son of Gudlaug who is mentioned above. He went to battle with Jörund; but when the men of the country became aware of it, they gathered from all quarters with big and little ships. Then was Jörund overthrown and his ship cleared. He himself leaped overboard, but was seized and taken on to the land. Then King Gylaug had a gallows raised, led Jörund thereon and had him hanged. So ended his days. Thus says Tjodolv:

| | |
|---|---|
| Jörund at last | Had to bear |
| Found his death | The bane of Gudlaug, |
| And was bereft of life | And the lord of Herser |
| In the Limfjord, | Was hard grasped |
| When the high-breasted | About the neck |
| Gallows | By Hagbard's halter. |

25. Jörund's son was called Aun or Ani, who became king over the Swedes; he was a wise man and a great sacrificer but no warrior, for he stayed at home in his land. At that time when these kings who have just been named were in Upsala, Dan the Proud was the first king in Denmark—he was now very old. After him came his son Frode

---

1 *Oddasund*, now Oddesund, on the western part of the Limfjord (in Denmark).

the Proud or Peaceful, and after him his sons Halvdan and Fridleiv; they were great warriors. Halvdan was the eldest of them and the foremost in all things; he went with his army to Sweden against King Aun; they had several battles and Halvdan always had the victory, so that King Aun at length fled to West Gautland.[1] He had been king in Upsala for twenty-five winters[2] and was in Gautland for another twenty-five winters whilst King Halvdan was in Upsala. King Halvdan died of sickness in Upsala and was there buried in a howe. After that

Aun will sacrifice his last son

King Aun came back to Upsala when he was sixty years old, and he then offered a great sacrifice in order to have long life; he gave to Odin his son who was then sacrificed to him. King Aun had this answer from Odin, that he should still live for sixty years. Aun was king in Upsala for another twenty-five years until Ali the Bold, son of Fridleiv, came with his army to Sweden against King Aun; they fought several battles and Ali always won. Then King Aun fled a second time from his kingdom and went to West Gautland. Ali was king in Upsala for twenty-five years until Starkad the Old slew him. After Ali's death, King Aun went back to Upsala and ruled the kingdom again for twenty-five years. He then made a great sacrifice and offered his second son; Odin then told him he should go on living as long as he

1  In the western part of Sweden.　　2  *Winters* = years.

gave him a son every ten years and further gave a name to each of the districts of his land according to the number of those sons he offered up to Odin. When he had offered up seven of his sons he lived for ten years till he could not walk and had to be borne on a stool. Then he sacrificed his eighth son and lived for ten more years, but now he had to lie in his bed. Then he offered up his ninth son and lived for another ten years, but now he drank from his horn like a baby. Aun had now one son left, and would sacrifice him; he wanted to give Odin Upsala and the lordships which lie thereto and he had it called Tiundaland.[1] But the Swedes forbade him and the offering was put off. Thereupon King Aun died and was buried in a howe near Upsala. It was afterwards called Ana-sott when a man died of old age without any sickness. Thus says Tjodolv:

At last Aun
In Upsala
Began to feel
Ana-sott.
A long life
He should live.
Yet once more,
Like a young child,

When from the point
Of the ox's horn
The slayer of his sons
Drank lying down;
For the eastern king
Had no might
To hold up
The mead horn.

26. The son of Aun the Old was called Egil, who was king in Sweden after his father; he was no fighter but sat at home at his ease. His thrall was named Tunni and he had been scot-gatherer to Aun the Old. But when Aun was dead, Tunni took great treasure and buried it in the earth. When Egil became king he put Tunni amongst the other thralls; Tunni took this badly and ran away and with him went many thralls. They now unearthed the treasure he had hidden and he gave it to his folk, and they took him as their leader. Afterwards many evil men went to him; they lay out in the woods and at times they rushed into dwellings and robbed or killed the folk there. When King Egil heard of this he went with his men to look for them. But when in the evening he had taken his lodging for the night Tunni suddenly came upon them with his army and slew many of the king's men. When King Egil marked this uproar he wanted to stop it and set up his standard, but many of his army had fled from him. Tunni and his men fought him boldly, and then King Egil had naught to do but flee. Tunni followed them as they fled right into the woods, but he afterwards came back to the building, harried and robbed, but no one withstood him. All the goods which Tunni took in that district

1 *Tiundaland* can, according to Snorre Sturlason's version, be described as the tenth land or the tenth lordship's land.

he gave to his men; thereby he drew many friends and got great help from the people.

King Egil gathered his troops together and went to fight against Tunni; in the battle Tunni had the victory, and King Egil fled and lost many of his men. King Egil and Tunni fought eight battles and Tunni had the victory in them all. Thereupon King Egil fled from the land to Denmark, to Frode the Bold in Zealand. He promised King Frode scot from Sweden if he would give him help; Frode then gave him an army and his own warriors. King Egil then went to Sweden and when Tunni heard of it he went with his army to meet him. Then there was a great battle; Tunni fell and King Egil took back his kingdom; the Danes went home. King Egil sent King Frode a great and goodly gift each year, but paid no scot to the Danes; friendship, however, still held between Egil and Frode. After Tunni's death, King Egil ruled for three years. It then befell in Sweden that an ox which was to be used for the offering had grown old and was overmuch fattened so that it became dangerous, and when they wanted to take it, it dashed to the wood, became mad and was for a long time a scathesome beast in that wood. King Egil was a great hunter, and he often rode in the daytime to the wood to hunt wild animals. It once happened when he had ridden hunting with his men that he followed an animal for a long time and had ridden after it into the wood away from all his men. Then he came upon the ox, so that he rode towards it to slay it, but the ox turned on him. The king struck at it but his spear sheered off and the ox stuck its horns into the flank of the horse which straightway fell down flat and the king with him. The king then leaped up again and would draw his sword, but the ox stuck its horns into his breast so that they went deep in. Then the king's men came up and slew the ox, but the king lived only a short while and was buried in a howe near Upsala. Thus says Tjodolv:

Before Tunni's might
The highly praised
Offspring of Tyr
Fled from the land.
But the straying[1] ox
Locked its horn,
Much stained with blood,
In Egil's breast.

That ox in the east
Oft and long
Its lofty head
Had borne.
And the sword-like horn
Stood deep in the heart
Of the Skilvings'[2]
Fair offspring.

1 In the O.S. text the word *flæming* is used. In O.S. *fara undan i flæmingi* means to move to and fro in order to escape a blow: 'to dodge'. The race name Fleming is probably connected with O.S. *flæming*.   2 *Skilving* was the name of the old stock of the Swedish kings—the 'Scylfings' of *Beowulf*.

27. Egil's son was called Ottar, who took his country and kingdom after him. He was not friendly towards Frode, who then sent men to King Ottar to demand the scot which Egil had vowed him. Ottar answered that the Swedes had never paid scot to the Danes nor would he do so; the messengers went back. Frode was a mighty warrior, and one summer he went with his army to Sweden, attacked it and harried there, killed many folk and took others prisoner; he got much booty, burned dwellings far and wide and did great scathe. Next summer he went to harry on the Östervei[1] and then King Ottar learned that King Frode was not at home. He then went aboard his warships, fared out to Denmark, harried there and was not withstood. He heard that there was a great army gathered in Zealand, and thereupon he sailed south to Jutland; he lay in the Limfjord, harried on the Vendel[2] and burned and laid waste the land. Vatt and Fasti were the names of Frode's jarls whom he had set to rule the land in Denmark whilst he was away. When they heard that the king of the Swedes was harrying in Denmark, they gathered an army, leaped on to their ships and sailed south to the Limfjord. There they came very suddenly upon King Ottar and straightway came to battle. The Swedes met them well, and men fell on both sides; but as some of the Danes fell, others came up, man for man, and they hurried there from the districts round about, and others likewise that were at hand came too, with all their ships. The end of the fight was, that King Ottar fell there with most of his men. The Danes took his body, moved it ashore and laid it on a howe, letting beasts and birds tear at it. They took a tree crow, sent it to Sweden, and said that their King Ottar was worth no more. Ottar they afterwards called the Vendel crow. Thus says Tjodolv:

| | |
|---|---|
| The able Ottar | I know that deed |
| Fell beneath | Of Vatt and Fasti |
| The eagle's cliff | Is told in tales |
| Before the Danish weapons. | Amongst the Swedes, |
| The body | How Frode's jarls |
| Of the far-farer | On the island |
| The ravens tore asunder | Had slain |
| On Vendel. | The stalwart king. |

1 Östervei means Eastway, i.e. the Baltic and the lands east of Sweden.    2 Vendel is the land lying north-west of the Limfjord but there is also a place called Vendel about twenty miles north of Upsala, having a great mound similar to the Kungshögar at Upsala, both in structure and in the various charred remains. Its date must be about the same as that of the Kungshögar. This mound might also be connected with King Ottar, and what lends point to this is the fact that in the seventeenth century it was called Utter's Högen or Otter's Högen.

28. Ottar's son was called Adils,[1] who took the kingdom after him; he was king for a long time and was very wealthy. Some summers he also went on viking raids. Once he came with his army to Saxland[2] which was ruled by a king called Geirtjov, whose queen was known as Alov the Mighty; their children were never spoken of. The king at that time was not at home. King Adils and his men leaped up

Queen Alov tells Yrsa about her family

to the king's house and robbed there, and some of them drove the cattle down to be killed on the shore; the herd was minded by thralls, both men and women, and all these they took away with them. Among them there was a markedly beautiful maid, who called herself Yrsa. King Adils now went home with his booty. Yrsa was not set amongst

1 In the Old English poem of *Beowulf*, we are told that Othere (Ottar) the King of Sweden had a brother Onela (Ali) who succeeded him. Othere's sons, Eadgils (Adils) and Eadmund, rebel and are sent from Sweden; they go to the Geatas (Gauts), and these people, being enemies of Onela, are now attacked by him and lose their king, who is succeeded by Beowulf himself. The latter then supports Eadgils (Adils) in his return attack on Onela (Ali) and in the battle which ensued (as mentioned in chapter 29) Onela is slain and his nephew Eadgils (Adils) takes the throne. These events took place about the beginning of the sixth century.    2 *Saxland* is Germany; in this case no doubt the north coast round Mecklenburg.

the thrall women, for they soon found that she was wise and fair-spoken and was cunning in all things; everybody liked her and most of all the king. It came about that the king made a bridal feast with her, and Yrsa then became queen in Sweden and seemed to be an able woman.

29. King Helgi,[1] Halvdan's son, was then ruling in Leidra; he came to Sweden with so great an army that King Adils saw naught for it but to flee thence. King Helgi went with his army up into the land and harried, taking much booty; he took Queen Yrsa, brought her with him to Leidra and took her in wedlock; their son was called Rolf Krake. When Rolf was three winters old, Queen Alov came to Denmark and then told Yrsa that King Helgi, her husband, was also her father, and that Alov was her mother. Then Yrsa went back to Adils in Sweden and was queen there as long as she lived. King Helgi fell in battle, and Rolf Krake, who was then eight years old, became king in Leidra. King Adils had a long struggle with a king who was called Ali the Uplander, who was from Norway. They held battle on the Väner-ice,[2] where Ali fell and Adils had the victory; that battle is told of at length in the Skjoldungasaga,[3] where it is also told how Rolf Krake came to Adils in Upsala and then sowed the gold on the Fyrisvold. King Adils was very happy in owning good steeds, for he had the best of horses at that time. One of them was called Slöngvir; another which he had taken from the fallen Ali was called Ravn, and from him he bred another horse, Ravn, which he sent to Haloga-land[4] to King Godgest. King Godgest rode it, but he could not hold on to it, so that he fell off and came to his death; that happened in Amd in Halogaland. King Adils was at sacrifice to the goddesses and rode on his horse around the temple; the horse stumbled under him and fell; so the king also rolled over, and his head fell against a stone, so that his skull burst and his brains lay on the stone. That was his death; he died in Upsala and there now is his howe.[5] The Swedes called him a mighty king. Thus says Tjodolv:

1 *King Helgi* is the Halga of *Beowulf* and father of Hrothulf (Rolf Krake) who later became King of Denmark.    2 Lake Väner (in Sweden).    3 *Skjoldungasaga* = the Saga of the Skjoldungs, an account of the Danish kings. An extract of this saga relating to Rolf Krake is mentioned in Snorre Sturlason's *Edda*. The saga is not now extant, but a Latin abstract of it is preserved.    4 *Halogaland* = North Norway, the land of the Haleygers.    5 North of Upsala there are three great mounds known as the *Kungs-högar* = The kings' howes. These were explored between 1847 and 1874 and from the nature of the finds (mostly charred) and the structures (a heap of stones covered with earth) they are said to belong to the early part of the sixth century. Bearing in mind the chronology of the events taking place about this time (cf. chapter 29) we find only three kings mentioned as being buried in a howe at Upsala; these were Aun, Egil his son, and Adils his great-grandson. For the absence of Aun's grandson Ottar cf. p. 20, n. 2.

I have also heard
That evil sprites
Should waste
Adils's life,
And the proud
Offspring of Frey
Must fall
From his steed's back,

And mingled
Should be the brains
Of that high king
With the hard gravel;
The deed-lusty
Foe of Ali
Should die
In Upsala.

30. Adils's son was called Eystein, who next ruled over Sweden. In his days, Rolf Krake died in Leidra. At that time kings, both Danes and Norsemen, were harrying in Sweden. There were many sea kings, who had great armies but had no land. They alone seemed to have the right to be called sea kings who never slept under the sooty beams nor drunk in the ingle nook.

31. Salve, son of Hogni in Njardöy,[1] was the name of a sea king who was at that time harrying in the Baltic; he had great possessions in Jutland. He steered his ship to Sweden when King Eystein was visiting a district called Lovund. There King Salve came suddenly in the night, surrounded the house, and burned the king in it with all his men. Then Salve went to Sigtun[2] and claimed for himself the name of king and demanded homage, but the Swedes gathered an army and wanted to protect their land; then there was a great battle, said to have lasted eleven days. King Salve had the victory and was then king over Sweden for a long time, till the Swedes broke trust with him and slew him. Thus says Tjodolv:

I know that the end
Of Eystein's life
Was closed
On Lovund,
And Swedes said
The king
Was burned
By Jutish men.

And, tearing him away,
The sooty fire of wood
Seized the king
In his own house,
When the timbered
Dwelling place
Full of folk
Was burned with the prince.

32. King Eystein's son[3] was called Yngvar, who thereafter became king in Sweden. He was a great warrior and was often out in his warships, for Sweden had been much harried both by Danes and

---

1 Now Næröy by the Namdale or Naumadale in Norway.  2 On *Sigtun* see p. 4, n. 4.
3 *Eystein* is generally written as *Öistein* in modern Scandinavian. 'Austin' and 'Austen' are probably corruptions of the O.S. name. Others consider that these two names derive their origin from the Latin *Augustinus*.

by men from the Baltic. He made peace with the Danes and took to harrying in the Baltic. One summer, he brought out his army, went to Estland, and harried there during the summer in a spot called Stein.[1] Then came down the Estland men with a mighty army and they held battle; the army of the Estland men was so strong that the Swedes could not withstand it. King Yngvar fell and his folk fled; he was buried in a howe by the sea in Adalsysla.[2] After that defeat the Swedes went home. Thus says Tjodolv:

And it came about
That Yngvar was
By the folk of Sysla
Slain dead,
And the hoary chief,
Near the rocky heart of the sea,

Was killed
By the Estland men's army.
And now the Baltic waves
Sang songs, for the sport
Of the sea god,
Over the Swedish prince.

33. Yngvar's son was called Anund, who next took the kingdom in Sweden; in his days there was great peace in the land and he became wealthy. King Anund went with his army to Estland to avenge his father; he went ashore, harried far over the land and took much booty; in the harvest he went back home to Sweden. In his days, too, there were good seasons in Sweden and he became the best liked of all kings. Sweden was a much-wooded land, and the wastes were so wide that it took many days to ride over them. King Anund went to great trouble and cost in ridding the land of woods and making clearings; he also had roads built over the wastes. The land was cleared far into the woods and great lordships were formed there. In that way the land was peopled, for there were plenty of people to cultivate it. King Anund had roads made over all Sweden, over marsh, wood and fell, and for that he was called Braut-Anund.[3] He made himself estates in every part of Sweden and went visiting throughout his land.

34. Braut-Anund had a son who was called Ingjald. At that time the king in Fjadrundaland[4] was Yngvar, who had by his wife two sons whose names were Alf and Agnar. They were almost the same

---

1 This town is mentioned in chapter 12.   2 *Adalsysla* is the O.N. name for the mainland opposite the island of Ösel, the latter being called *Eysysla* (island district). *Adalsysla* signified the main *syssel* and the whole of Estland was called a *sysla* (or *syssel*) which can be translated by 'district', or 'shire'.   3 I.e. Road-Anund, *Braut* from O.S. *brjota*, i.e. to break up.   4 In the 'History of St Olav' (see chapter 77), Snorre calls Fjadrundaland also by the name of Vestmanland. The present Vestmanland is probably smaller in size than the old Fjadrundaland.

age as Ingjald. There were now district kings in Sweden and Braut-Anund ruled over Tiundaland,[1] in which Upsala stands and where all the things of the Swedes are held. There a great offering was held and to it there came many kings; it was about midwinter.[2] And one winter when many folks were gathered in Upsala, King Yngvar was there with his sons, who were six winters old. Alf, King Yngvar's son, and Ingjald, King Anund's son, started some boyish game, and each commanded his own army, but when they played with each other, Ingjald was not so strong as Alf and it seemed so unfair to him that he wept loudly. Then came his foster-brother Gautvid, and led him away to Svipdag the Blind, his foster-father, and told him that things were ill with Ingjald; he was not so strong or skilful in the game as Alf, King Yngvar's son. Then Svipdag answered that it was a great shame. The next day Svipdag had the heart taken from a wolf, stuck it on a spindle, and afterwards gave it to Ingjald the king's son to eat; after that Ingjald became the grimmest and most hasty-tempered of all men. When he was grown up, Anund wooed for him Gauthild, the daughter of King Algaut, the son of Gautrek the

:INGIALD: GAVTVID: SVIPDAG BLINDE:

Generous, the son of Gaut, from whom Gautland[3] took its name. King Algaut seemed to think that his daughter would wed well if she wed the son of King Anund and if he were like his father. The maid was sent to Sweden (East Sweden) and Ingjald held a bridal feast with her.

35. One harvest, King Anund went through his towns with his men, and came to a place called Himenheid;[4] there are some narrow dales with high fells on each side. There was at that time much rain, and snow had fallen on the fells; a great landslide shot down rock and

---

1 See p. 18, n. 1.  2 Midwinter night was the 12th of January, when the old Scandinavians held their Yuletide (cf. 'History of Hacon the Good', chapter 13). 3 *Gautland* is the present Götland which is divided into Vestergötland and Östergötland (West Gautland and East Gautland).  4 Cf. p. 4, n. 5.

clay; King Anund and his men were under it, and in that way the king got his death and many men with him. Thus says Tjodolv:

Anund was stopped
By the falling rock—
The sorrow of
Jonakr's sons—
Under the Himenfell;
And the king,
The Estland men's tamer,

Was badly struck
By the fall of stones;
And his army,
His valiant warriors,
All of them
Were covered over
By the landslide.

36. King Anund's son Ingjald became king in Upsala, and at the time when there were many district kings, the Upsala kings had been uppermost in Sweden from the time that Odin was chieftain there. The kings who sat in Upsala were alone kings over all Sweden till Agni's death, when the kingdom was first shared between brothers, as is written above (chapter 20), and afterwards the rule and kingdom were further split up amongst the royal family, as each of the members separated; some kings cleared the great woodland and peopled it, and so eked out their realms. And when Ingjald took the rule and kingdom, there were many district kings, as is written above (chapter 34). King Ingjald then had a great feast made ready, which he wished to give in memory of his father, King Anund; he had a hall prepared as big and noble as the Upsala[1] itself and he called it the seven kings' hall, and therein were raised seven high-seats. King Ingjald then sent men over all Sweden to bid kings and jarls and other outstanding men come to him. To that funeral feast came King Algaut, his kinsman, and King Yngvar of Fjadrundaland with his two sons, Agnar and Alf, King Sporsnjall of Närike, King Sigverk of Attundaland; but King Granmar of Sudermannaland[2] did not come. There the six kings were given seats in the new hall, and one of the high-seats which King Ingjald had had prepared, was then wasted. All the number who had come there then took their seats in the new hall. King Ingjald had given his courtiers and all his folk places in the Upsala. It was their wont at that time, when they made a funeral feast for kings or jarls, that he who made the feast and was entitled to come into the inheritance should sit on the step before the high-seat until the cup which was called the *Bragi* cup[3] was borne in. Then should he stand up with the

---

1 His hall at Upsala. *Upsala* means 'Upper hall'. 2 Now Södermanland. 3 In O.S. *bragafull* was a cup which an heir should empty at an heirship feast on succeeding to his father's property. *Bragi* was the god of eloquence. In Mallet's *Northern Antiquities*, *bragr*, which in O.S. signifies 'poetry', has in English become 'brag' and a poet a 'braggart'. It is further mentioned that the name is probably connected with 'brain'; in French *brein* and Low German *bregen*, and that O.S. *brugga*, in English *brew*, in French *brasser*, and in German *brauen* are likewise connected with 'Bragi's bumper' or O.S. *bragafull*.

*Bragi* cup, make a vow and thereupon drink the cup dry; after that he would be led to the high-seat which his father had had, and he then had a right to all the inheritance. Now it happened that when the *Bragi* cup came in, King Ingjald stood up and took a great horn; he made a vow that he would double the size of his kingdom towards every corner of the earth or else he would die; after that he drank the horn dry. And when in the evening the folk were drunk, King Ingjald told Svipdag's sons, Gautvid and Hulvid, to arm themselves and their men in the evening, as they had proposed. And these men went

Svipdag's sons and their men proceed to the new hall

out to the new hall, bore fire there, and next set it aflame and burned therein the six kings and all their men; those that tried to come out were straightway slain. After that, King Ingjald put under himself all the kingdoms which those kings had had and he took tribute from them.

37. King Granmar heard these tidings and seemed to think that the same fate was meant for him unless he took care of himself. King Hjörvard, who was called Ylving, the same summer came with his army to Sweden and lay by in the fjord which is called Myrkvafjord;[1] when King Granmar heard that, he sent men to him to ask him and his men to be his guests. Hjörvard accepted the invitation, for he had

1 *Myrkvafjord*, now Mörköfjärd, by Södertelje in Södermanland.

not harried in King Granmar's kingdom, and when he came to the feast there was great rejoicing. In the evening when they drank their cups, it was the custom of kings who stayed in his land or sat at his feasts (which they had caused to be made ready), that they should sit drinking two by two, a man and a woman together by themselves as far as possible, but they who were over should sit together by themselves. But it was the law of the vikings that when they were in a guest house they should all sit drinking together. King Hjörvard's high-seat was raised opposite King Granmar's high-seat, and all his men sat on this bench. Then King Granmar told his daughter Hildegunn to make herself ready and bear ale to the vikings; she was a very beautiful woman. Then she took a silver bowl, filled it and went before King Hjörvard and said, "Hail, all Ylvings, in memory of Rolf Krake". She drank half of it and then handed it to King Hjörvard. He now took the bowl and her hand with it and said that she should go and sit with him; she answered that it was not the wont of vikings to sit out in pairs with women.[1] Hjörvard answered that there was more to look forward to, if he made a change in giving up the vikings' custom and drinking with her. So Hildegunn sat with him, and they both drank together and talked much during the evening. The next day, when the Kings Granmar and Hjörvard met, Hjörvard wooed Hildegunn. King Granmar bore the news to his wife Hild and to his chief men and said they would get great help from King Hjörvard. Now this was greatly approved of and all thought it advisable, and so it ended in Hildegunn being betrothed to King Hjörvard, who then held a bridal feast with her. King Hjörvard now remained with King Granmar, for Granmar had no son to rule the kingdom after him.

38. The same harvest time King Ingjald gathered an army and wished to go against Granmar and his kinsman; he had men from all those kingdoms which he had put under him. And when the kinsmen learned of it they gathered the folk in their kingdom and to their

---

1 The viking custom of the women retiring after meals and leaving the men behind still prevails in England and Scotland. The custom of 'kissing under the mistletoe' is connected with Balder, the Apollo of Scandinavian mythology. Balder was killed by a mistletoe arrow given to the blind Höder by Loki, the god of mischief. Balder was restored to life and the mistletoe was placed under the care of Frigga, Odin's wife, so as never again to be an instrument of evil until it touches the earth, the empire of Loki. Hence it was always suspended from ceilings, and when persons of opposite sex pass under it, they give each other the kiss of peace and love in the full assurance that the epiphyte is no longer an instrument of mischief. In O.S. mistletoe was called *mistilteinn*. See further Brewer's *Dictionary of Phrase and Fable* (new and revised edition), pp. 722, 712. Others consider that the custom originates from the druids, although the English word 'mistletoe' is closely connected with the Scand. word *mistilteinn*.

help there came King Hogni and his son Hildir who ruled over East Gautland.[1] Hogni was the father of Hild whom King Granmar had taken to wife. King Ingjald went ashore with his army and had far more men. They fought together and the battle went hard, and when they had fought for a short while, the chiefs fled who ruled over Fjadrundaland, West Gautland, Närike and Attundaland together with the army which had come from these lands, and they all made for their ships. Thereupon King Ingjald met with dire need, got many

King Hogni and his men go warring in Sweden

wounds and thereafter escaped to his ship, but his foster-father Svipdag the Blind with both his sons, Gautvid and Hulvid, fell there. After that King Ingjald went back to Upsala and was ill pleased with his expedition; he seemed to think that the army, which he had had from those parts of his kingdom that he had won by force, had been faithless to him. Afterwards there was little peace between King Ingjald and King Granmar. When this had gone on for a long time, the friends of both of them tried to bring about a reconciliation; the kings Ingjald and Granmar and his kinsman Hjörvard arranged a talk between themselves, met, and made their peace and agreed that it should last as long as the three kings lived; they made it binding by oaths, and protestations of good faith. The next spring King Granmar went to Upsala to the blood offering which was usually held

1 See p. 25, n. 3.

about summer's day in order that the peace should last. Then it was prophesied at the offering that he could not live long.[1] Thereafter he went home to his kingdom.

39. The next harvest King Granmar and his kinsman Hjörvard went to meet guests on an island called Sili[2] at their own estates, and whilst they were at the feast King Ingjald came during the night with all his army, surrounded the dwelling and burned them inside with all their folk. He then laid under himself all the kingdom which these kings had had and set chiefs over it. King Hogni and his son Hildir often rode up into Sweden and slew the men that Ingjald had set over the kingdom which their kinsman Granmar had owned. Then was there a great strife for a long time between King Hogni and King Ingjald. Hogni, however, kept his kingdom against King Ingjald right to the day of his death. King Ingjald had by his wife two children; the first was called Asa, the second, Olav the Tree-feller. Gauthild, King Ingjald's wife, sent the boy to her foster-father Bovi in West Gautland, and he was there brought up with Bovi's son Saxi, who was called *Fletta*.[3] It is a folk tale that King Ingjald slew twelve kings and broke his trust with them all, and he got the name of Ingjald the

Ill-minded; he was king over most of Sweden. His daughter Asa he gave in wedlock to King Gudröd in Scania;[4] she was like her father in temper and she made him slay his brother Halvdan, who was father to Ivor the Widefathom. She also brought about the death of her husband Gudröd.

40. Ivor the Widefathom came to Scania after the death of Gudröd, his father's brother, and straightway gathered a large army and went up to Sweden. Asa the Ill-minded had already gone to her father. King Ingjald was at a feast in Räning[5] when he learned that King Ivor's army had come in the neighbourhood. Ingjald seemed to have no strength to fight with Ivor, and the state of affairs appeared so clear to him that if he prepared for flight, his foes would

1 This was done by cutting splints or shavings from a holy tree and the gods' wishes were read from the position in which they fell.   2 Now Sela-ön in Lake Mälar, north-east of Strängnäs.   3 *Fletta* means 'plaited hair'.   4 *Scania*, the most southern part of Sweden.   5 *Räning* is an estate at Tosterön in Lake Mälar, west of Sela-ön (in Södermanland).

be gathering against him from all quarters. Then he and Asa decided
on the well-known plan of making all their folk dead drunk and afterwards setting fire to the hall; the hall was burned and all who were
in it together with King Ingjald. Thus says Tjodolv:

| | |
|---|---|
| And Ingjald's life spark | And the fate |
| The smoke-raising pile | (That he himself |
| Did waste | Dauntlessly |
| On Räning, | Should end |
| When the house thief | His own life) |
| With fire | Seemed to all |
| Destroyed | The people in Sweden |
| The god's prince, | Most likely. |

41. Ivor the Widefathom laid under himself all Sweden; he also
won for himself all Denmark, a great part of Saxland,[1] all the Östrik,[2]
and a fifth part of England. From his race have come those Danish
and Swedish kings who there have had the sole rule. After Ingjald
the Ill-minded the Upsala kingdom went from the race of the Ynglings, who have been spoken of, man for man.

42. When King Ingjald's son Olav learned of his father's death,
he went away with such men as would follow him, for all the Swedish
peasantry stood up with one accord to drive out King Ingjald's race
and all his friends. Olav first went up to Närike, but when the Swedes
there heard about him he could not stay. He then went west along
the forest road to the river which falls from the north into Väner[3] and
is called the Elv;[4] there they remained and set about clearing and
burning the wood and building a settlement. A great lordship soon
rose there and they called it Värmland; there was good living there.
But when they heard in Sweden about Olav, how he was clearing the
woods, they called him Tree-feller and his position seemed to them
disgraceful. Olav took a wife who was called Solveig, or Solva, the
daughter of Halvdan Gold-tooth from the west in Solör.[5] Halvdan
was the son of Salve, the son of Salvar, the son of Salve the Old, who
first cleared Solör. Olav Tree-feller's mother was called Gauthild,
and her mother was Alov, the daughter of Olav the Sharp-sighted,
king in Närike. Olav and Solva had two sons, Ingjald and Halvdan;
Halvdan was brought up in Solör with his mother's brother Salve,
and he was called Halvdan Whiteleg.

43. A great number of folk fled from Sweden because of King

1 North Germany.   2 I.e. the Baltic Provinces.   3 Lake Väner.   4 *Elv*
means 'river'—in this case Klar-Elven (in Värmland) or Götaelven (which runs into
the sea by Gothenburg).   5 In South-east Norway.

Ivor. They learned that Olav Tree-feller had good living in Värmland and so they drove thither to him in such big numbers that the land could not support them and there was much poverty and hunger there; they gave their king the blame for it, just as the Swedes were wont to give the king the blame both for good and bad years. Olav did not give many blood offerings and the Swedes liked that ill and thought that bad seasons came through it. They gathered an army, went against King Olav, surrounded the house and burned him in it; they gave him to Odin and made blood offerings in order to have a good season. That happened near Lake Väner. Thus says Tjodolv:

| | |
|---|---|
| And in the bay | Sweated the clothes |
| By the lake's side | Of the Svia king.[1] |
| The fire consumed | From Upsala |
| Olav's body. | The prince |
| And the glowing | Of loved kin |
| Son of Fornjot | Withdrew long ago. |

The wisest men of Sweden found out that hard times were due to the folk being more numerous than the land could support, and the king was not to blame for it. They now took counsel to go with all the army to the west over Eidaskog[2] and they suddenly came forth into Solör. They slew King Salve and took Halvdan Whiteleg prisoner, but they made him their chief and gave him the name of king. He then laid Solör under himself; afterwards he went with the army out into Raumarik,[3] harried there and with his army he took the land.

44. Halvdan Whiteleg was a mighty king; he married Asa, the daughter of Eystein the Hardrede,[4] king of the Uplanders and ruler over Hedemark. Halvdan had by her two sons, Eystein and Gudröd. He obtained possession of much of Hedemark, Tote and Hadeland and much of Vestfold.[5] He grew to be an old man and died in his bed in Tote, and was afterwards borne out to Vestfold and buried in a howe at a place called Skæreid in Skiringsal.[6] Thus says Tjodolv:

| | |
|---|---|
| Everyone heard | In Tote took |
| That over Halvdan | The folk-king. |
| The bonders | And Skæreid |
| Shed tears, | In Skiringsal |
| When the slaying maid,[7] | Enclosed the bones |
| The hand of death, | Of the armoured prince. |

1 *Svia king* = Swedish king; *Sviar*, the old name for the Swedes.    2 *Eidaskog* = Eidskogen, the frontier forest between Värmland and Solör.    3 *Raumarik* in the county of Akershus (South-east Norway).    4 Hard to rede or counsel.    5 *Vestfold* is the present Vestfold Fylke (or shire) (Norway).    6 *Skiringsal* is probably the present district of Tjölling between Larvik and Sandefjord.    7 *The slaying maid* was *Hel*, the daughter of Loki.

45. Halvdan's brother Ingjald was king in Värmland, and after his death King Halvdan laid Värmland under himself, took tribute and set jarls over it for as long as he lived.

46. Halvdan Whiteleg's son Eystein, who after him became king in Raumarik and Vestfold, married Hild, the daughter of Eric Agnarson who was king in Vestfold. Agnar, Eric's father, was the son of King Sigtryg in Vendel. King Eric had no son, and he died whilst Halvdan Whiteleg was still living. Eystein and his father Halvdan then took to themselves all Vestfold, and Eystein ruled there as long as he lived. At that time there was a king in Varna[1] called Skjold; he was very troll-wise. King Eystein went with some warships over to Varna and harried there; he took such clothes as he found, various other things and bonders' tools and made a raid on their cattle on the shore; after that they went away. When King Skjold came to the strand, King Eystein was away and had gone across the fjord, and Skjold saw the sails of his ships. He took his cape, waved it and blew into it. When they sailed past Jarlsöy,[2] King Eystein sat at the helm; another ship sailed near him; there was some swell and the sail boom of the second ship swept the king overboard; that was his bane. His men took his body and it was carried into Borro;[3] a howe was cast up for him out by the sea near Vadla. Thus says Tjodolv:

| | |
|---|---|
| The sail boom caused | Out by the sea |
| Eystein to fare | The Chief of the Warriors. |
| To Hel, the daughter | There near the Gautish king |
| Of Byleist's brother Loki. | Comes the icy cold |
| And there now rests | Vadla stream[4] |
| Under the rocky howe | Up to the calm creek. |

47. King Eystein's son was called Halvdan, who took the kingdom after him; he was called the Generous and the Food-stinter, for it is said that to keep his men he gave them as many gold pennies as other kings gave silver pennies but he starved them in food. He was a great warrior, he was often for a long time on viking raids, and he won goods for himself. He married Liv, the daughter of King Dag of Vestmare.[5] His chief town was Holtar[6] in Vestfold; there he died

---

1 *Varna* in the district of Rygge in Smalenene (Norway) where the present estate Værne Kloster is situated. About the year 1200 it became a hospital for old warriors.   2 Now Jersöy, at the entrance of Tönsberg.   3 *Borro* = Borre district, near Horten (Norway). 4 *Vadla stream* probably refers to a current in a sound between the mainland and an island. 5 *Vestmare* is probably the coast land west of Vestfold. A place with similar ending called Grenmar is situated in the Langesundsfjord. This ending may be connected with the ending in names such as Thirlmere, Grasmere, etc. The Lake District is well known to abound in Old Norse names.   6 *Holtar*, now Holtan in Borre district.

in his bed and he was buried in a howe in Borro. Thus says
Tjodolv:

| | |
|---|---|
| And at the thing | Had to suffer |
| Loki's maiden, Hel, | The Norns' doom. |
| Bade the third king | And the victorious |
| Leave his life. | Chieftain |
| Then Halvdan | Was shrouded |
| Who dwelt at Holtar | In Borro. |

48. Halvdan's son was called Gudröd, who took the kingdom after
him; he was called Gudröd the Magnificent, and some called him the
Hunting king. He had a wife who was called Alfhild, the daughter
of King Alvaren of Alvheim, and with her he received half of Vingulmark;[1] their son was Olav, who was called Geirstader-Alf. Alvheim
was then the name of the land between Raumelv and Gautelv.[2] And
when Alfhild died, King Gudröd sent his men to the west to Agder[3]
to the king who was ruling there, called Harald Redbeard; they were
to ask the king for Asa his daughter, but Harald refused it. The men
thus sent came back and brought the king the answer. Some time
after this, King Gudröd launched his ships and went out with a
great army to Agder; he came there very suddenly, made a landing
and in the night came about King Harald's houses. And when Harald
was aware that an army had come against him, he went out with such
men as he had. There was battle and a great clash of men. There fell
King Harald and his son Gyrd, and King Gudröd took great booty. He
took home with him King Harald's daughter, Asa, and held a bridal
feast with her; they had one son who was called Halvdan. But in the
harvest, when Halvdan was a year old, King Gudröd fared on a round
of feasts; he lay with his ship in Stivlesund,[4] and there was much
drinking and the king became very drunk. In the evening, when it
was dark, the king went from his ship; and when he came to the
end of the gangway a man leaped out and stuck a spear into him,
and that was his bane. The man was straightway slain, and the next
morning when it was light he was recognised as Queen Asa's shoe
lad. She did not deny that it was done by her counsel. Thus says
Tjodolv:

| | |
|---|---|
| Gudröd the Generous | When a death plan |
| Was encircled | Of revenge |
| By guile | Against the drunken prince |
| For a long time, | Found outlet, |

---

1 *Vingulmark*, the land round Oslo and Smalenene.    2 *Raumelv* = Glommen;
*Gautelv* = Göta River.    3 *Agder* = the present counties of Nedeness and Lister and
Mandal.    4 Unidentified.

| And to win money | And the prince |
|---|---|
| That sneaky carl | Was stabbed |
| Of Asa | On the shore |
| Won against the king, | Of Stivlesund. |

49. Olav took the kingdom after his father; he was a mighty man and a great warrior, and he was very good-looking and had grown big. He had only Vestfold, for King Alvgeir had subdued all Vingulmark, over which Alvgeir set his son King Gandalv. Gandalv and his father went often into Raumarik and got for themselves the greatest part of that kingdom and its people. Hogni was the name of the son of Eystein the Mighty, the Upland king; at that time he put under himself all Hedemark and Tote and Hadeland. Then Värmland was also lost to Gudröd's sons and the Värmer began to pay tribute to the Swedish kings. Olav was in his twentieth year when Gudröd died, and then Halvdan, his brother, took the kingdom with him, and they shared it between themselves; Olav took the western half and Halvdan the eastern. Olav had his seat at Geirstader.[1] He died from a foot disease and was buried in a howe at Geirstader. Thus says Tjodolv:

| And now in Norway | Till a foot ache |
|---|---|
| A Branch | In the Fold[2] |
| Of the god's race | Overcame |
| Had grown: | The bonders' friend. |
| Olav once | At Geirstader |
| Strongly ruled | The generous king |
| Far and wide | Now lies, |
| Over Vestmare, | Buried in a howe. |

50. King Olav's son was named Ragnvald, who was king in Vestfold after his father; he was called 'the Glorious'. About him has Tjodolv of Kvin edited the Ynglinga-tal; there he says:

| I know best | That Ragnvald |
|---|---|
| Under the blue heaven | The rudder-steerer |
| The most famous name | Is now called |
| Which a king owned, | 'The Glorious'. |

1 Now Gjerstad in Tjölling district (between Larvik and Sandefjord in Norway).
2 *Fold* = Oslofjord.

# II

# THE HISTORY OF HALVDAN THE BLACK

1. Halvdan was one winter[1] old when his father was slain. His mother Asa straightway went west with him to Agder and there she set herself in the kingdom which her father had had. There Halvdan grew up and became very big and strong and black-haired; he was called Halvdan the Black. When he was nineteen winters old he took the kingdom of Agder and straightway went to Vestfold and shared that kingdom with his brother Olav. The same harvest he went with his army to Vingulmark against King Gandalv, and they had many battles; each of them won in turn, and at last they agreed to these terms: that Halvdan should have all Vingulmark which his father Gudröd had formerly had. Thereafter he went up to Raumarik and subdued it. King Sigtryg, the son of King Eystein, learned this; he had his seat in Hedemark, and had already subdued Raumarik. King Sigtryg, therefore, went with his army against King Halvdan, and there was a great battle in which Halvdan had the victory. When they took flight, King Sigtryg was wounded by an arrow in the left hand and he died there. After that Halvdan laid all Raumarik under him. Eystein was the name of a younger son of King Eystein; he was the brother of King Sigtryg, and he then became king in Hedemark. And when Halvdan was gone out to Vestfold, King Eystein went out with his army to Raumarik and subdued the land far and wide.

2. Halvdan the Black learned that there was unrest in Raumarik, and he therefore drew his army together and went against King Eystein; they held battle and Halvdan had the victory, whilst Eystein fled to Hedemark. King Halvdan went with his army after him up to Hedemark, and there they held another battle; Halvdan won and Eystein fled to Gudbrand, a district chief in Dale[2] in the north. There he gathered to him the people and afterwards, during the winter, he went out to Hedemark. He met Halvdan the Black on a great island which lies in Mjöse,[3] and there they held battle; Halvdan had the victory and many people fell on both sides, and amongst them was Guthorm, the son of Gudbrand the Chief, who was the youth of great-

1 A year.    2 The well-known Gudbrandsdale in Norway.    3 *Mjöse*, a great lake in East Norway.

est hope in the Uplands. Then King Eystein fled back to the north to Dale, and after that he sent his kinsman, Halvard the Rogue, to King Halvdan to seek terms, and for the sake of friendship Halvdan gave King Eystein half of Hedemark. Halvdan now subdued Tote and the district called Land, and he also took Hadeland; he was now a mighty king.

3. Halvdan the Black now took a wife who was called Ragnhild; she was the daughter of Harald Goldbeard who was king in Sogn.[1]

Halvdan the Black arms himself

They had a son to whom King Harald gave his own name, and he was brought up in Sogn with his mother's father King Harald. When Harald became infirm and he had no son, he gave his kingdom to his daughter's son Harald and had him made king; a little later Harald died. The same winter his daughter Ragnhild died, and the next spring Harald, the young king in Sogn, died in his bed, when he was ten winters old. As soon as Halvdan the Black learned of his death, he set out with many men and went to Sogn, where he was well received. He claimed the kingdom and inheritance after his son, and as he was not opposed, he laid the kingdom under him. Then Jarl

1 *Sogn* in West Norway round the well-known Sognefjord.

Atle the Small, who was a friend of King Harald, came to him from Gaular,[1] and the king set him to be jarl over the Sygnafylke,[2] to carry out the law of the land and collect the tribute. From there King Halvdan went to the Uplands.

4. In the autumn, King Halvdan went out to Vingulmark, and it happened one night when Halvdan was at a feast that the man who had kept watch on the horses came to him in the middle of the night and told him that an army had come near the place. The king straightway stood up and bade his men arm themselves; he went quickly out and drew up his army. Thereupon came Gandalv's sons, Hysing and Helsing, with a great force. There was a mighty battle, and as Halvdan was outnumbered by his enemies, he fled to the wood and lost many men; there fell Ölvir the Wise, Halvdan's foster-father. After that the folk gathered to King Halvdan; he went out to seek Gandalv's sons, and they met on Eid[3] near Öieren and fought there; Hysing and Helsing fell, but their brother Haki fled. After that King Halvdan subdued Vingulmark and Haki fled to Alvheim.

5. Sigurd the Hart was the name of a king in Ringerik; he was greater and stronger than any other, and he was also the most handsome of men. His father was Helgi the Sharp-tongued and his mother was Aslaug, the daughter of Sigurd Serpent's-eye, the son of Ragnar Lodbrok. So it is said that Sigurd the Hart was only twelve years old when he killed in single battle Hildebrand the Berserk and eleven men with him; many mighty deeds he did and there is a long saga written about him. He had two children: his daughter was called Ragnhild, and she was the grandest of women and at that time twenty years old when her brother Guthorm was half grown. And this must be told of Sigurd's death, how he rode out alone into the wastes, as was his wont, how he hunted great and dangerous beasts, in which sport he was most eager, and how, when he had ridden a long way, he came out into a clearing near Hadeland and there came against him Haki, the Berserk, with thirty men with whom he fought, and how Sigurd the Hart fell and twelve men on Haki's side, and how Haki himself lost a hand and had three other wounds. Thereafter Haki rode to Sigurd's dwelling, and there took his daughter Ragnhild and her brother Guthorm; he carried them away with him together with many goods and treasures and bore them home to Hadeland, where he had great estates. Then he had a feast made ready and wished to

---

1 *Gaular* is situated in Holmedale inside the Dalsfjord in Söndfjord.   2 *Sygnafylke* = the Sogn folk district or shire.   3 *Eid* is the present Askim and part of Trögstad, south of Lake Öieren.

hold a bridal feast with Ragnhild, but some time passed before he could do so, because his wounds healed slowly. Haki Hadeberserk kept to his bed during harvest time and part of the winter. About Yuletide when King Halvdan was in Hedemark, he learned all these tidings, and early one morning when he was clad, he called to him Harek the Wolf and told him to go over to Hadeland and bring back to him Sigurd the Hart's daughter Ragnhild. Harek went out with a hundred men, and he arranged the journey so well, that they crossed the water early in the morning to Haki's dwelling. There they set watch on the doors of the room where the folk slept. After that they went to the dwelling in which Haki lay, broke in, and took away Ragnhild and her brother Guthorm and all the goods that were there; they burned the house and all who were in it. Then they fitted an awning over a splendid wagon and set Ragnhild and Guthorm in it, and after that they went to the ice. Haki got up and for a short time went after them, but when he came to the ice he turned down the hilt of his sword and laid himself on the point, so that the sword went through him. There he got his death and he was buried in a howe on the bank of the lake. King Halvdan saw them crossing the water on the ice, for he was very sharp-sighted; he saw a covered wagon and then he knew that they had done the errand as he had wished. He had his table made ready, he sent folk far and wide in the district, and he called many men to him. That day there was a great feast and at that feast Halvdan wedded Ragnhild, and she became a mighty queen. Ragnhild's mother was Torny, the daughter of King Klak-Harald of Jutland and sister of Tyri, Queen of Denmark, who had married Gorm the Old, the ruler of Denmark.

6. Queen Ragnhild dreamed mighty dreams, and she was very wise. In one of her dreams she seemed to be standing in her garden and to take a thorn from her gown, and as she held it, it grew so much that it became a big tree. One end went down into the

Queen Ragnhild's dream

earth and straightway became deeply rooted, and the other end of the tree quickly grew high aloft; thereupon the tree seemed to her so big that she could only see over it with difficulty; it was very thick. The nethermost part of the tree was red like blood, up the trunk it was light green, and out in the branches it was snow-white; there were great twigs on the tree, some longer above, others longer below. The branches of the tree were so big that they seemed to her to spread themselves over all Norway and even farther.

7. King Halvdan never dreamed; it seemed strange to him, and he told it to a man called Torleiv the Wise and sought his counsel as to what he should do about it. Torleiv told him what he did when he wished to know anything; he went to sleep in a pigsty, and then it always happened that he dreamed. The king did this, and he had this dream: he seemed to have grown a good head of hair and it was full of locks, some growing as low as the ground, some to the middle of his legs, some to his knee, some to his thighs, some to his hip and some to his neck, and others no more than little wisps springing from the crown of his head like knots, and his locks were of all colours, though one stood out from all the rest in beauty, fairness and greatness. He told this dream to Torleiv, who interpreted it in this way: a great race would descend from him, and it would rule the land with great glory, but not all would be of like greatness, and from his race one man would come, who would be greater and more glorious than the others; it was held for true, that this lock of hair meant King St Olav. King Halvdan was a wise and just man; he made laws and kept them himself and made others keep them, so that pride could not override the law; he himself also made a *sak-tal*,[1] fixing penalties for every man according to his birth and rank. Queen Ragnhild bore a son; he was sprinkled with water and called Harald. He very soon became big and bold and he grew up and quickly became skilled in all sports and he was of good understanding. His mother loved him much, but his father loved him less.

1 *Sak-tal* means 'a code of law recording penalties, mulcts and compensations'. The penalty, compensation, or *mannbot* for every injury, due to the party injured, or to his family and next of kin if the injury was the death or premeditated murder of the party, appears to have been fixed for every rank and condition, from the murder of the king down to the maiming or beating of a man's cattle or his slave. A man for whom no compensation was due was a dishonoured person, or an outlaw. It appears to have been optional with the injured party, or his kin if he had been killed, to take the mulct or compensation, or to refuse it, and wait an opportunity of taking vengeance for the injury on the party who inflicted it, or on his kin. A part of each mulct or compensation was due to the king; and these fines or penalties appear to have constituted a great proportion of the king's revenues, and to have been settled at the things held in every district for administering the law with the lagman (lawman).

8. King Halvdan kept Yule in Hadeland. There on Christmas Eve a strange thing happened; when the men were gone to the table, and a great gathering was present, all the food and ale vanished from the table. The king remained behind full of wrath, but all the others went home. And in order to find out who had caused it, the king had a Finn taken who was troll-wise, and he required him to tell the truth; he tortured him, but even then he got nothing out of him. The Finn

Halvdan the Black falls through the ice in Rökensvik

asked Halvdan's son Harald for help, and Harald begged mercy for him, but still did not get it; so Harald helped him to get away against the king's will and he himself followed. They came to where a chief was holding a great feast and they were received, as they thought, with gladness. And when they had been there till spring, the chief one day said to Harald, "Thy father reckoned it a great shame that I took some food from him this winter, but I shall requite thee with good tidings. Thy father is now dead, and thou shalt go home. Thou shalt have all the kingdom he has had, and therewith shalt thou win all Norway".

9. Halvdan the Black drove on a sledge from the feast in Hadeland and his way so lay that he went over the lake of Rand.[1] It was in the spring and it was thawing. They drove over Rökensvik;[2] during

1 *Rand* = the present Randsfjord.    2 On the east side of the Randsfjord.

the winter there had been a cattle branding and when the dung had fallen on the ice it had eaten itself in during the thaw. And when the king drove over it, the ice burst under him, so that he was drowned and many men with him. He was then forty winters old. Of all the kings he had been the most fortunate one in having good seasons; and all loved him so highly that, when they learned he was dead and his body was being taken to Ringerik (where they would give him a grave), the great men of Raumarik and Vestfold and Hedemark went there and they all demanded his body for themselves to lay it in a howe in their own district, for they expected good seasons if they had the body. Finally it was agreed that they should divide the body into four parts, and the head was laid in a howe at Stein[1] in Ringerik, whilst each of the others took home his part and laid it in a howe, and all these howes were called Halvdan's-howes.

1 The present farm of Stein at Hole in Ringerik.

## CHRONOLOGY

### HALVDAN THE BLACK. 820–860

820. Birth of Halvdan the Black.
821. Death of Ragnvald the Glorious.
836. Torgils or Turgesius subdued the Irish by his conquest of Dublin. According to the Irish chronicler Giraldus Cambrensis, he and his followers were Norsemen.
839. Halvdan the Black becomes king.
845. Turgesius killed by treachery in Ireland.
850. Birth of Harald Hairfair.
860. Death of Halvdan the Black; Harald Hairfair becomes king.

# III

# THE HISTORY OF HARALD HAIRFAIR

1. Harald took the kingdom after his father when he was ten winters old; he was bigger and stronger and more handsome than other men, very clever and energetic. Guthorm, his mother's brother, was the head of the king's guard[1] and adviser in all affairs of state; he was a 'duke' of the army. After Halvdan the Black's death many chiefs went against the kingdom he had left behind. First there was King Gandalv and next the brothers Hogni and Frode, sons of King Eystein of Hedemark, together with Hogni Karason, who went far over Ringerik. Haki Gandalvson went out against Vestfold with 300 men, and they went along the upper ways through certain long valleys and intended to come suddenly on King Harald, but King Gandalv stopped at home with his army and would from there cross the fjord to Vestfold. And when Duke Guthorm learned this, he gathered an army and went with King Harald; he first turned to meet Haki up in the country and they met in a valley; there a great battle took place and King Harald had the victory; there King Haki fell with a great part of his army; this place was afterwards called Haka-dale.[2] After that King Harald and Duke Guthorm turned back, but King Gandalv had then arrived in Vestfold; both troops now went towards each other, and when they met there was a hard fight; King Gandalv fled and lost the greatest part of his army, and so came back to his kingdom. When King Eystein's sons in Hedemark learned these tidings, they soon expected strife. They sent behests to Hogni Karason and Gudbrand Herse[3] and arranged a meeting in Ringsaker[4] in Hedemark.

2. After these battles, King Harald and Duke Guthorm went with all the army they had gathered against the Uplanders and fared mostly through forest ways. They learned where the Upland kings had agreed to meet and came there at midnight, and as the watchmen were not aware of them, they came to the room which Hogni Karason was in, and to that in which Gudbrand slept. They set fire to both.

1 The *hird* or *king's guard* was a company of men-at-arms, kept in pay and holding guard by night, even on horseback (as seen in the 'History of Halvdan the Black', chapter 4) and appears to have been an establishment coeval with kingly power itself.  2 *Hakadale* is situated in Nittedale, the lower part of Raumarik.  3 *Herse* means 'district chief'.  4 *Ringsaker* is in the northern part of Hedemark (on the east side of Lake Mjöse).

Eystein's sons, Hogni and Frode, came out with their men and fought for a short while, but they both fell. After the fall of these four chiefs, King Harald, by the skill and power of his kinsman Guthorm, now possessed himself of Ringerik, Hedemark, Gudbrandsdale and Hadeland, Tote and Raumarik, and all the northern part of Vingulmark. After that King Harald and Duke Guthorm had unrest and fighting with King Gandalv, and it ended with King Gandalv's fall in the last battle; King Harald won the kingdom south, right to the Raumelv.

Gyda gives Harald Hairfair's men her answer

3. King Harald sent his men after a maiden, who was called Gyda, daughter of King Eric of Hordaland; she was being fostered by a wealthy *bonder*[1] in Valders; he wished to take her as his mistress, for she was a very handsome and high-spirited maiden. When the messengers came there, they put forth their message for the maiden. She answered, that she would not waste her maidenhood in such manner as to take for a husband a king who had not a bigger kingdom to rule than some shires; "and to me it seems strange", she said, "that there is no king who will possess himself of Norway, so that he alone has rule over it, as King Gorm has in Denmark or Eric in Upsala". To the messengers it seemed that she answered over-boldly. They asked her about the meaning of that answer; they said, that Harald was so

1 A farmer who owns his own land.

mighty a king that he was fully good enough for her; but although she answered to their message otherwise than they would have, they now saw no chance of taking her away with them, unless she wished it, and they made themselves ready to go home. When they were ready to leave, men led them out. Then Gyda spoke to the messengers and bade them bear her words to King Harald, that she would only become his wife when he had first for her sake laid under himself all

King Gryting is brought as prisoner to King Harald

Norway and ruled over the kingdom as freely as King Eric in Sweden or King Gorm in Denmark, "for then for the first time", she said, "it seems to me that he can be called a folk king".

4. The messengers now went back to King Harald and told him the maiden's words. They called her very bold and witless and found it probable that the king would send many men for her and dishonour her. King Harald answered that this maiden had not talked ill or acted so as to call for revenge, but that she should have great thanks for her words. "She has reminded me of those things", he said, "which it now seems strange I have not thought of before"; and thereto he added, "and I make this vow, and the god who made me and

rules all things shall be my witness, that never shall my hair be cut or combed till I have possessed myself of all Norway in *scot*,[1] dues and rule—or else die." For these words Duke Guthorm thanked him and said that it was a kingly work to fulfil his vow.

5. After that King Harald and his kinsman gathered a great army and first went to the Uplands, then north through the Dales and so north over the Dovre-fell, and when he came down to the peopled countryside,[2] he had all the men slain and the houses burned. But when the folk became aware of it, everyone who could, fled, some down to Orkedale, some to Guldale, some to the woods, but others sought for peace and all got it who came to the king; they became his men. They were not withstood till they came to Orkedale, where men had gathered against them. There they had the first battle against a king who was called Gryting. King Harald had the victory and Gryting was taken; many of his folk fell, but he himself went before King Harald and swore him his troth. After that all the folk in Orkedale submitted to King Harald, and became his men.

6. King Harald set the law wherever he won land, that he was possessed fully of all the land by *odal*[3] right and he made all bonders, great and small, pay him a land tax. Over each shire he set a jarl who should administer the law and justice in the land and gather the fines and land dues, and every jarl should have a third of the tribute for living and costs. Every jarl should have under him four or more district chiefs, and each of them should have an income from the land of twenty marks. Each jarl should muster for the king's army sixty warriors and each district chief (*herse*) twenty men. But so much had King Harald increased the tribute and land taxes, that his jarls had greater incomes than the kings had had aforetime, and when that was learned in Trondheim, many great men sought King Harald and became his men.

1 *Scot* or *Scat* was a tax paid to the king in money or kind from all lands, and was adjudged by the thing to each king on his accession. In Orkney, where the land has been feudalised since the annexation by Scotland in 1468, the *odal* tax remains as an item in the feu duties payable to the Crown.    2 This district is probably Opdal.  3 *Odal* lands are freehold lands held in many cases by the Norwegian bonders and their descendants for generations. The same family has always the first option on the land, in case of decease of an owner with no direct heir. Harald Hairfair made himself owner of all the land and the bonders that occupied it had to pay him land dues. William the Conqueror adopted a similar procedure, when he won England. But Harald Hairfair's land dues were abolished about sixty years later, during the reign of his son Hacon the Good. Hacon offered to make all the bonders 'free born', doing away with the land dues and giving them the land in *odal* tenure. The *odal* law is still in force in Norway and is zealously guarded by the bonders.

7. It is said that Jarl Hacon Grjotgardson came to King Harald west from Yrjar[1] and had many men to help King Harald. After that, King Harald went into Guldale, fought a battle there, killed two kings and possessed himself of their kingdoms; they were the Guldale and the Strind districts. Then King Harald went into Stjordale and there he fought a third battle, won the victory and took that district. After that the up-country men by Trondheim gathered together, and four kings came with their armies; one ruled over Værdale, another over Skaun,[2] a third over the Sparbyggja folk and a fourth over Inderöy; he had the Öyna district. These four kings went with their army against King Harald, and he held battle with them and had the victory; some of the kings fell and the rest fled. King Harald in all fought eight or more battles round Trondheim, and after the fall of the eight kings he owned all the Trondheim districts.

8. North in Naumadale two brothers were kings, Herlaug and Rollaug. They had been three summers making a howe, which was built of stone, chalk and stocks of timber, and when the howe was finished the brothers learned the tidings that King Harald was coming against them with an army. Then King Herlaug had much food and drink carried to the howe, and thereafter he went into the howe with eleven men, and then he had the howe closed. King Rollaug went up on the howe on which the kings were wont to sit, had the king's high-seat placed there and sat himself down in it. Thereupon he had pillows laid on the steps where the jarls were wont to sit and tumbled himself down from the high-seat to the jarl's seat and gave himself the name of jarl. After that King Rollaug went to King Harald, gave him all his kingdom and offered to become his man and told him of all his doings. Then King Harald took a sword and fastened it to his belt, hung a shield about his neck, made him jarl and led him to the high-seat. After that he gave him the Naumadale-shire and made him jarl over it.

9. King Harald then went back to Trondheim and stayed there during the winter; ever after he reckoned it his home and there he raised a great estate which is called Lade.[3] That winter he took to wife Asa, daughter of Jarl Hacon Grjotgardson, and Hacon then had much say in the king's affairs. The next spring the king built ships for himself. He had laid down during the winter a dragon-head ship with splendid fittings. In it he set his bodyguard and

---

1 *Yrjar*, on the north-west side of the Trondheimsfjord.   2 Now Skogn.   3 *Lade* is a great property situated about two miles north-east of Trondheim.

berserks; the stem men were the best chosen, for they had the king's standard. The part which went from the stem back to the bailing place was called *rausn*; there the berserks took their place. They alone became guardsmen to King Harald, who were foremost in strength or boldness, or most skilled, and they alone came on his own ship, for he now had good opportunity of choosing himself guardsmen from every shire. He had a great army and many longships and many mighty men followed him. It was told by Hornklove in Glymdrapa that King Harald had fought a battle in the woods of Opdale with the Orkedale men, before he went on this sea expedition.

10. King Harald brought this army out from Trondheim and turned south towards Möre. Huntjov was the name of the king who ruled over Möre-shire;[1] his son was called Salve Klove—they were great warriors. And the king who ruled over Raumsdale was called Nökkvi; he was Salve's mother's father. These chiefs drew together a great army when they heard about King Harald. They went against him and were met near Solskel;[2] there the strife began, and King Harald had the victory. Thus says Hornklove:

| | |
|---|---|
| The ship by the wind was driven | And those heated princes |
| Thither from the north, so that | Were greeted without words, |
| The king aboard went to fight | But with whizzing darts in battle; |
| With the Dagling twins,[3] | The clashing song of shields was heard. |

Both kings fell, but Salve got clear by flight. Then King Harald laid these two shires under him, stayed there a long time during the summer and arranged for their rule; in the autumn he got himself ready to turn back to Trondheim. Ragnvald, Jarl of Möre, son of Eystein Glumra, then became King Harald's man. King Harald set him as chief over these two shires, Nordmöre and Raumsdale, and gave him the support of both leaders and bonders and also ships to keep the land from unrest. Ragnvald was called the Mighty, or the Shrewd, and it is said that both by-names were true. The winter after, King Harald was in Trondheim.

11. The next spring King Harald gathered a great army in Trondheim, and said that he would sail to Söndmöre with it.[4] Salve Klove had lain out in a warship during the winter and harried in Nordmöre and slew there many of King Harald's men and committed robbery; at times during the winter he had been in Söndmöre with

---

1 *Möre* is situated on the coast south of Trondheim.    2 *Solskel* is a small island northeast of Christiansund, inside the island of Smölen.    3 *Dagling* means 'prince'.
4 *Söndmöre* is South Möre.

his kinsman, King Arnvid. But when they learned of King Harald, they gathered an army and got many folk, for many of them wanted to revenge themselves on King Harald. Salve Klove went south to the Fjords[1] to King Audbjörn who ruled there and asked him for help to go with his army to support him and King Arnvid. He said this: "We can all see that the first care we have is to rise all together against King Harald; then shall we have strength enough and then fate must decide the victory; otherwise we can only become his thralls, and that is no condition for those men who have names no less famous than Harald. My father thought it better to fall in his own kingdom than

The battle of Solskel

to become King Harald's under-man". Salve was so persuasive in his talk that Audbjörn vowed to go, and he drew his army together and went north to King Arnvid; they then had a very big force. They then learned that King Harald had come southwards. They met near Solskel. It was then the custom when they fought on ships to lash the ships together and fight on the stems. It was so done now; King Harald brought his ship against King Arnvid's ship, and the strife became very hard; many men fell on both sides, and soon King Harald became so heated and wroth that he went forth into the *rausn* of his ship and fought so boldly that all the men in the stem of Arnvid's

1 *South to the Fjords* means to Nordfjord and Söndfjord.

ship fell back to the mast and others were killed; King Harald then boarded the ship, but King Arnvid's men sought flight and he himself was slain in his own ship. There King Audbjörn also fell, but Salve fled. Thus says Hornklove:

| The hero king roused a flight of spears | ˙Whilst the men fell lifeless |
| (The arrows would be whistling past) | Before the king in the prow. |
| In Skogul's[1] war; the wounds | He won the victory and |
| Were rushing red with blood | The swords sang against shields. |

In King Harald's army there fell his Jarls Asgaut and Asbiorn[2] and his kinsmen Grjotgard and Herlaug, the sons of Hacon Ladejarl. After that Salve was for a long time a great viking and often did much scathe in King Harald's kingdom.

12. King Harald put under himself Söndmöre, and Audbjörn's brother Vemund ruled over the Firda-folk.[3] That was late in the autumn and it was agreed that King Harald should not go south of Stad.[4] Then King Harald made Ragnvald jarl over both Möre-shires and Raumsdale and he had many folk about him. King Harald then went to Trondheim and the same winter Ragnvald the Jarl went the inner way over Eidet[5] and thereupon south to the Fjords. He had news of King Vemund and in the

Odin and his ravens

night he came to Nautsdale, where King Vemund was in guest-quarters. Ragnvald the Jarl surrounded the house and burned the king therein with ninety men. After that Kari came from Berdla[6] to Ragnvald the Jarl with a fully equipped longship and they both went north to Möre, and Ragnvald took the ships which King Vemund had owned and all the chattels he could seize. Berdla-Kari went north to King Harald and became his man; he was a mighty berserk. The following spring King Harald went south along the land and laid under himself the Firda-folk. Afterwards King Harald sailed east along the land and came forth to the Vik,[7] but he left behind Hacon

1 *Skogul* is one of Odin's warrior maidens (Valkyries). 2 The name *Asbiorn* has in English become 'Osborn'. The Danes called it Esbern and the Normans Osbern. Cf. p. 730, n. 4. 3 *Firda-folk*, the districts of the Fjords (see p. 49, n. 1). 4 *Stad* is situated on the west coast, on the border of Söndmöre and the Fjord district. 5 *Eidet*, inside Stad, either the present-day Mandseidet or Birkedalseidet. 6 *Berdla*, now Berle in Nordfjord. 7 Oslofjord.

Grjotgardson and gave him the rule over the Firda-folk. When the king had gone east, Hacon the Jarl sent bidding to Jarl Atle the Small, that he should go away from Sogn and be jarl in Gaular as he had formerly been; Hacon said that King Harald had given him the Sygnafylke.[1] Atle the Jarl then sent word back, that he would hold fast to the Sygnafylke and also Gaular, until he had found King Harald. The jarls quarrelled over it till they both gathered armies; they met in Stafanesvag,[2] in Fjalir, and there they had great strife. Hacon the Jarl fell there, whilst Atle the Jarl was mortally wounded; they went with him to Atleöy[3] and there he died. Thus says Eyvind Scaldaspiller:

| | |
|---|---|
| There was Hacon | And there, where sunk |
| The warrior, | The friendly troop |
| Slain, when he | Of Grjotgard's son |
| Went to battle, | On Stafanesvag, |
| And in the spear play | Was spilled |
| Frey's heir | The blood of men |
| Ended his life | In the strife god's |
| In Fjalir. | Mighty clashings. |

13. King Harald came with his army east into the Vik and lay in by Tunsberg, which was then a trading town; he had then stayed four years in Trondheim and had not in that time come to the Vik. He learned there the tidings that the Swedish king, Eric Emundson, had laid under himself Värmland, taken tribute from all the wood districts, and seized West Gautland as far north as Svinasund, so that the king of the Swedes called the western land[4] along the sea his kingdom and took tribute therefrom. He had set over it a jarl, called Rani the Gaut; he had all the rule between Svinasund and the Göta River and he was a mighty jarl. King Harald was told about the Swedish king's words, that he would not stop till he had as great a kingdom in the Vik as Sigurd Ring or his son Ragnar Lodbrok had formerly had; and that extended to Raumarik and Vestfold as far as to Grenmar, as well as Vingulmark and all the land to the south. In all these districts many chiefs and many others had rendered themselves obedient to the Swedish king. That pleased King Harald very ill, so he straightway called a thing of the bonders near Fold[5] and bore complaint against them for treason. Some bonders got witnesses to show that they were guiltless, others paid fines and others let themselves be punished. All

---

1 Cf. 'History of Halvdan the Black', p. 38, n. 2.    2 *Stafanesvag*, now Stangfjord, on the south side of the Fördefjord.    3 On the south side of the Fördefjord.    4 The land between Svinesund and the Göta River.    5 *Fold* is the Oslofjord.

the summer he went through the whole district in this way. In the harvest he went up to Raumarik and there he acted in the same way. Then in the beginning of the winter he learned that Eric, the king of Sweden, was riding with his guard in Värmland on a round of feasts.

14. King Harald went to the east over Eidaskog[1] and came forth into Värmland, where he went about to feasts. Aki was the name of a man who was the mightiest bonder in Värmland and who was very rich and at that time old; he sent men to King Harald and bade him to a feast and the king agreed to come on the appointed day. Aki also bade King Eric to the feast and agreed with him for the same meeting day. Aki had a great feast-hall which was then old; so he had another new hall built, just as big and handsomely adorned. This hall he had furnished with new hangings, but the old with old hangings. And when the kings were come to the feast, King Eric and his men were given their places in the old hall, and King Harald and his men in the new; so also were all the table utensils divided; Eric's men had old vessels and horns, though still golden and well finished, and King Harald's men all had new vessels and horns, well adorned with gold. All of them were smooth and polished, and the drink in both places was very good. Aki had formerly been Halvdan the Black's man. And when the day came on which the feast ended, the kings made themselves ready to go away, and the horses stood ready. Then went Aki before King Harald and with him brought his son, twelve years old, called Ubbe. Aki said, "My lord, if that goodwill which I have shown you in my feast seems to you worthy of friendship, then grant it to my son; him I give to you as your serving-man". The king thanked him with many fair words for his welcome and vowed to give him in return his full friendship; thereupon Aki brought forth great gifts which he gave the king. Afterwards Aki went to the Swedish king; Eric was then clad and ready to ride away, and he was rather displeased. Aki then took some things of great worth and gave them to him. The king answered little and mounted his horse. Aki followed him on the way and spoke with him. A wood was near them and the way went through it, and when Aki came to the wood the king asked him: "Wherefore didst thou arrange the welcome between me and King Harald in such a way that he had the best of everything? Thou knowest thou art my man". "I think", said Aki, "that you, my lord, and your men have lacked nothing in your welcome at this feast, and when it was an old hall where you drank, that happened because you are now an old man, and King Harald is now

1 *Eidaskog* is the frontier wood between Värmland and Solör.

in the bloom of youth, and therefore I gave him the new hall. And when you reminded me that I should be your man, then I know no less than that you are my man." Then the king drew his sword and smote him to death. He afterwards rode away. When King Harald was about to mount his steed, he bade them call Aki the bonder to him, and when they were seeking him, some leaped thither where King Eric had ridden; there they found Aki dead, and afterwards they went back and told it to the king. And when he learned this, he ordered his men to avenge Aki the bonder. Then King Harald rode on the way that King Eric had taken, till they got sight of each other. Then both troops rode as fast as they were best able, till King Eric came to the wood which divides Gautland and Värmland. King Harald then turned back to Värmland. He put all the land under him, and he slew King Eric's men where he came across them. In the winter King Harald went back to Raumarik.

15. In the winter King Harald went out to Tunsberg to his ships; he made them ready and steered to the east across the fjord and then subdued all Vingulmark. He was out on his ship all the winter and harried in Ranrik.[1] Thus says Torbjörn Hornklove:

Away from home
Shall he drink at Yule,
If he alone will rule,
And as the valiant king of all
He will play the game of Frey,[2]

This youth weary of the fireplace,
And of sitting indoors,
Weary of heated rooms,
And of down-lined gloves.

16. The Gauts gathered against him throughout the land. In the

spring, when the ice was loosening, the Gauts set piles across the Göta River, so that King Harald could not bring his ships up into the land.

1 *Ranrik* is the land between Göta River and Svinesund. See chapter 13.    2 On *Frey*, cf. 'Ynglinga Saga', chapter 10.

But King Harald brought his ships up the river and moored them to the piles, harried on both banks and burned the district. Thus says Hornklove:

| | |
|---|---|
| The battle-bird's friend laid | And this large-minded king |
| The land and people under him. | Used to the horror of war |
| South of the sea (for this hero | Moored to the piles |
| Was hard in battle). | By the shore his dragon ship. |

Afterwards the Gauts rode thither with a great army and fought with King Harald; there was a great slaughter of men, and King Harald had the victory. Thus says Hornklove:

| | |
|---|---|
| The axes were often raised, | Then had the foe of the Gauts |
| The long spear whistled, | The victory, whilst the weapons' |
| And the mighty death-dealing sword | High song could be heard |
| Of the king's men could bite; | About the warriors' necks. |

17. King Harald went far over Gautland with his troops, held many battles there on both sides of the Göta River and most often had the victory, though in one of these battles Rani the Gautlander fell. After that King Harald subdued all the land north of the Göta River and west of Väner and all Värmland. And when he turned away from there, he left behind, as ruler, Guthorm the Duke and many men with him, and he then went to the Uplands and stayed there for a time; next he went north over the Dovre-fell to Trondheim and was again there for a long time. Then he got his first children; by Asa he had these sons: Guthorm, who was the eldest, Halvdan the Black and Halvdan the White, who were twins, and Sigfröd who was the fourth. They were all fostered in Trondheim with great honour.

18. The tidings were learned from the south of the land that Horders and Rygers, Agders and Telers[1] had gathered together and had called out ships, weapons and warriors. The leaders were Eric, king in Hordaland, Sulki, king in Rogaland, with his brother, Soti the Jarl; Kjotvi the Rich, king in Agder, and his son, Tore Haklang; from Telemark there were two brothers, Roald Rygg and Hadd the Hard. But as soon as King Harald first knew these tidings, he drew together his army, set the ships on the water, then got ready his army and made for the south along the land; he had many men from every shire. And when he had come as far south as Stad,[2] King Eric heard of it. He had also gathered an army which he knew was biding for

---

1 The men from Hordaland and Rogaland (West Norway), Agder (South Norway) and Telemark (in East Norway).    2 *Stad*, see p. 50, n. 4.

him, and then he went to the south to meet those which he knew were coming from the east to his help. The whole army then met to the north of Jæderen[1] and put into Hafursfjord.[2] There King Harald lay all ready with his forces. Now was there straightway a great strife both hard and long. The end of it was that King Harald had the victory, and there were killed King Eric, King Sulki and his brother, Soti the Jarl. Tore Haklang had drawn his ship against King Harald's, and Tore was a mighty berserk; there was a hard fight before Tore Haklang was slain, and then was all his ship cleared. King Kjotvi fled to an island where there was a great fort; and after that all

The battle of Hafursfjord

their men fled, some on ships, some leaping up on land, and thence by the upper ways south through Jæderen. Thus says Horn-klove:

Hast thou heard, where yonder,
In Hafursfjord, there fought
This king of mighty race
Against Kjotvi the Rich?

Ships came from east-way,
All eager for battle,
With grim gaping heads
And rich carved prows.

1 *Jæderen* is the flat land between Stavanger and Egersund (West Norway). 2 *Hafurs-fjord* is a small fjord close to Stavanger (situated west of the town).

They carried a host of warriors,
With white shields
And spears from the Westlands[1]
And Welsh[2] wrought swords.
The berserks were roaring
(For this was their battle),
The wolf-coated warriors howling,
And the irons clattering.

They egged on the valiant
King of the Eastmen,[3]
Who taught them to flee,
Who was bider at Utstein;[4]
He stopped the ships
When the strife he expected,
Blows struck on shields
Ere Haklang was fallen.

Weary of warding
His land from the thick-haired[5]
Was bull-necked King Kjotvi.
He let the holme shield him.
Those who were wounded
Sank under the boards
Upthrowing their buttocks,
Their heads in the bottom.

The cool-headed men
Let the shivering shields
Flash on their backs
When stones were striking them.
Eastward they fled
Home over Jadar;[6]
They thought of the mead horns.

1 *Westlands*, i.e. Great Britain and Ireland. This should indicate that Norsemen from Ireland or Great Britain took part in the battle. Chas. Haliday in *The Scandinavian Kingdom of Dublin* asserts that King Cearbhall (Carroll) of Ossory (Ireland) was accompanied by Onund Trefotr (who lost his leg in the battle of Hafursfjord and substituted for it a wooden one) from the Hebrides to Ireland soon after the battle had been fought. King Cearbhall's presence in the Hebrides is not easy to explain unless he took part in the battle of Hafursfjord, perhaps in company with his father-in-law, Eyvind Austman. King Cearbhall reigned 872–885.   2 The O.N. word in the text is *Valscra*, which means 'French' from the O.N. word *Valland* = North of France. But the inhabitants of Brittany and Cornwall were called 'Galli-Bretons' or 'West Welsh', so the word *Valscra* may also refer to Cornwall or Wales. The Scandinavians called Wales 'Bretland'.   3 *King of the Eastmen*, Harald Hairfair's name among the British and Irish.   4 King Harald had an estate at Utstein (cf. p. 71, n. 5).   5 *The thick-haired* is Harald Hairfair.   6 *Jadar*, i.e. Jæderen; see p. 55, n. 1.

19. After that battle King Harald was not any more withstood in Norway, for then all his worst foes had fallen and others had fled from the land and they were a great number, and at that time great waste lands were peopled. Then were Jämtland and Helsingeland inhabited, but they had both been partially settled before by Norsemen. Amid all the unrest, when Harald was seeking to subdue all the land of Norway, the Faroes and Iceland, lands out beyond the sea, were found and settled. At that time also there was a great faring to Shetland and many great men fled as outlaws from Norway and they went

King Harald's messengers
come to see Gyda

on viking raids to the west; in the winter they were in the Orkneys and the Hebrides, but in the summer they harried in Norway and did great scathe there in the land. But many also were the great men who handed themselves up to King Harald and became his men and settled in the land with him.

20. King Harald was now the only ruler in all Norway, and then he remembered what the large-minded maid had told him; he sent men to her, had her brought to him and married her. These were their children; Alov was the eldest, and then came Rörik, then Sigtryg, Frode and Torgils.

21. King Harald had many wives and many children. He next took the woman called Ragnhild, the daughter of King Eric of Jutland. She was called Ragnhild the Mighty, and their son was Eric Blood-axe. Besides her he had Svanhild the daughter of Eystein the Jarl, and their children were Olav Geirstader-Alf, Björn and Ragnar Rykkel. Lastly King Harald had Ashild, the daughter of Ring Dagson from Ringerik, and their children were Dag and Ring, Gudröd Skirja and Ingegerd. They say that when King Harald took Ragnhild the Mighty, he had divorced himself from nine women. About that Hornklove says:

The maids of Holme-Rygers,[1]     The maids of Halgi's race,[2]
Of Hordaland,                      The mighty king gave up
And Hedemark.                      When he took the Danish woman.

[1] *Holme-Rygers* = inhabitants of the islands in Rogaland (round Stavanger).    [2] *Halgi's race* = Haleygers from Halogaland (North Norway).

King Harald's children were brought up, each with his mother's family. Guthorm the Duke had sprinkled water over King Harald's eldest son and given him his own name; he sat the boy on his knee[1] and fostered him and brought him east to the Vik where he was with Guthorm the Duke. When the king was away, the Duke Guthorm had the whole rule of the Vik and the Uplands.

22. King Harald learned that the vikings who in the winter were in the Westlands[2] were harrying in the Midlands.[3] He went out to war each summer and ransacked the islands and the outlying rocks, but when his army came near the vikings they all fled, most of them out to sea. And when the king was weary of this, it happened one summer that he sailed west with his army across the sea. First he came to Shetland and there slew all the vikings who had not fled thence. Next he sailed south to the Orkneys and cleansed them all of vikings. Thereafter he went right to the Hebrides[4] and harried there; he slew many vikings who before had warriors under them and he held there many battles and most often had the victory. So too he harried in Scotland and had battle there; but when he came west to the Isle of Man, where they had learned what damage had been done in the land, he found that all the folk had fled thence into Scotland, that the land held no people and that they had also carried off all the goods they could. Thus, when King Harald and his men went up on the land, they got no booty. Thus says Hornklove:

| | |
|---|---|
| The cool, generous chief | Whilst it chanced that all |
| Led many warriors | The Scottish army in horror |
| To the town by the sea, | Had to flee from the land |
| And he won the victory on the sands, | Before the valiant prince. |

In one of these battles there fell Ivor, the son of Ragnvald the Jarl of Möre, and to requite his death King Harald when he sailed homewards gave the Jarl Ragnvald the Orkneys and Shetland, but Ragnvald straightway gave both lands to his brother Sigurd, and he stayed behind in the west when the king sailed eastwards, but before he did so, he gave Sigurd the name of jarl. To join him there came Torstein the Red, the son of Olav the White,[5] and Aud the Pensive. They harried in Scotland and possessed themselves of Caithness[6] and

1 This was a general custom in adopting a child.    2 Great Britain and Ireland.
3 *Midlands* meant West Norway, the later *Gulathing*.    4 The *Hebrides* were called by the Norsemen, *Suðreyar*. This word is still retained in the title of the Bishop of *Sodor* and Man.    5 *Olav the White* was king in Dublin until 870 or 871 when he was slain in battle. According to Irish sources he had a son called Eystein and also a son Torstein the Red.    6 *Caithness* was called *Katanes* by the Norsemen.

Sutherland[1] right to the River Oykell.[2] Sigurd the Jarl slew the Scottish jarl, Melbridge Tooth, and bound his head to his saddle strap, but the calf of his leg was wounded by a tooth which stood out from his head; it festered, and he got his death from it; he was buried in a howe by the River Oykell. Then his son Guthorm ruled over the land for a winter and died childless. After that the vikings, Danes and Norsemen settled firmly in these lands.

23. King Harald was feasting in Möre with Ragnvald the Jarl, and he had then subdued the whole of the country. There King Harald took a bath and had his hair combed; and then Ragnvald the Jarl cut off the hair, which had been uncut and uncombed for ten years. Hitherto he had been called Harald Thick-hair, but now Ragnvald the Jarl gave him a by-name and called him Harald Hairfair[3] and all said who saw him that it was the truest name, for he had both thick and beautiful hair.

24. Ragnvald[4] the Jarl was King Harald's dearest friend and the king valued him highly. Ragnvald had for his wife Hild the daughter of Rolf Nevja, and their sons were Rolf and Tore. He also had bastard sons, one called Hallad, the next Einar and the third Rollaug. They were full grown when their legitimate brothers were still children. Rolf was a great viking; he was grown so big that no steed could bear him and he therefore walked everywhere; he was called Rolf the Ganger. He harried much in the eastern countries. One summer when he had come to the Vik from a viking raid in the east he made a

Hild pleads with King Harald for her son Rolf the Ganger

shore raid. King Harald was then in the Vik, and when he learned of this he became very wroth, for he had strongly forbidden robbery in the land. At the thing, therefore, King Harald declared Rolf to be an outlaw in Norway. But when Rolf's mother heard that, she

---

1 *Sutherland* in O.N. is *Suðrland* (the land to the south). 2 The banks or braes of the *Oykell*, the Norsemen called *Ekkjalsbakki*. The Norse domination in Scotland comprised all land north of *Ekkjalsbakki*. 3 *Hairfair* is the most suitable translation for O.N. *Harfagr*, which does not mean fair hair but beautiful and thick hair. 4 *Ragnvald* has in Scotland and England become 'Ronald'.

went to the king and asked frith for Rolf. But the king was so wroth that her asking availed her naught. Then quoth Hild:

| | |
|---|---|
| The name of Nevja is torn; | Evil it is by such a wolf, |
| Now driven in flight from the land | Noble prince, to be bitten; |
| Is the warrior's bold kinsman. | He will not spare the flock |
| Why be so hard, my lord? | If he is driven to the woods. |

Rolf the Ganger afterwards crossed the sea to the Hebrides and from there went south-west to France; he harried there and possessed himself of a great jarldom; he settled many Norsemen there, and it was afterwards called Normandy.[1] From Rolf are descended the jarls in Normandy. Rolf the Ganger's son was William, the father of

[1] *Normandy* takes its name from O.N. *Norðmann* = Norseman. In M.S. a Norwegian is called *Nordmand*. As regards the date of Rolf the Ganger's arrival in Normandy and the length of his reign, the various English and French chroniclers differ to a great extent. The *Anglo-Saxon Chronicle* states that in 876 Rolf overran Normandy with his army and ruled for fifty years; later that he was succeeded by his son William in 928. Roger de Hoveden mentions that Rolf, the first duke of the Normans, entered Normandy in 876, but omits his death. Roger of Wendover states that in 897 Rolf came to England and proceeded to France. In 912 he records his baptism, and later that King Athelstan made a close friendship with him in 928. Wendover is very descriptive about the various happenings to Rolf in England and in France and gives a long genealogy, which, however, is of little value. He places his death in 935. Matthew of Westminster follows Wendover's narrative in all details. William of Malmesbury writes about Rolf's conquest of Normandy in 876. He states that Rolf was born of noble lineage among the Norsemen, though obsolete from its extreme antiquity, and was banished by the king's command from his own country. This corresponds, as will be noticed, with Snorre Sturlason. He omits his death. Florence of Worcester writes that Rolf and his band landed in Normandy on the fifteenth calends of December (17th Nov.) 876, but put his death in 917. Simeon of Durham mentions his arrival in Normandy on the fifteenth calends of December 876, but gives his death in the year 906. When we come to the Norman and French chronicles, these are also greatly at variance. *La Chronique de Cornerus* fixes Rolf's arrival in 880. *La Chronique d'Alberic* in 882 and Gabriel du Moulin in 872. Dudon de St Quentin agrees upon the year 876, as do most of the English chroniclers. The French historian Depping considers 876 to be the right year for Rolf's first arrival in the Seine; but states that he left Rouen in 878 and returned to England in order to aid King Alfred, who offered him half his kingdom in recompense. Rolf, remembering Alfred's previous help with ships and men, readily went to Alfred's assistance, subdued the rebels and re-established Alfred on his throne. The only English chronicler who records any such aid being given to Alfred is John Wallingford. Rolf refused Alfred's offer of half his kingdom, preferring his old life of sea raiding, and went harrying up the Rhine, in Holland and in Flanders. His return to the Seine must have been about 885. From now onwards his various wars commence against the French king, ending with the treaty of Saint-Clair-sur-Epte in 912, when Rolf was baptised. In 928 he abdicated in favour of his son William Longsword. His death is generally believed to have taken place in 931. Gabriel du Moulin states that he was buried in Notre Dame (i.e. the cathedral) in Rouen and cites the Latin epitaph in the church. He further asserts that part of Rolf's body was moved about 1060 to Fécamp, and adds that some say the whole body was moved to this town, citing the Latin epitaph placed on the tomb at Fécamp. This story is not mentioned by other

Richard, the father of another Richard, the father of Robert Long-sword,[1] the father of William the Bastard, King of England, from whom are descended all the later kings of England. Queen Ragnhild the Mighty lived three years after she came to Norway; after her death Eric, the son of King Harald and her, went to be brought up in the Fjords[2] by Tore Herse, the son of Roald, and he was fostered there.

25. King Harald went one winter a-feasting in the Uplands and had a Yule feast made ready for himself in Toftar.[3] On the eve of Yule, Svasi came without the door whilst the king was at the table and he sent a messenger to the king to go out to him. But the king was wroth at that behest and the same man who brought in the behest bore out the king's anger, but notwithstanding, Svasi bade him carry the same message a second time; he said he was the Finn whom the king had allowed to set his hut on the other side of the stream there. The king then went out and agreed to go home with him and crossed the stream, egged on by some of his men but discouraged by others. There Snæfrid, Svasi's daughter, stood up, the most beautiful of women, and she offered the king a cup full of mead; he drank it all and also took her hand, and straightway it was as though fire passed through his body, and at once he would lie with her that same night. But Svasi said that it should not be so except by force, unless the king betrothed Snæfrid and wed her according to the law. The king took Snæfrid and wed her, and he loved her so witlessly that he neglected his kingdom and all that was seemly for his kingly honour. They got four sons, Sigurd the Giant, Halvdan Highleg, Gudröd Gleam and Ragnvald Rettlebone. Afterwards Snæfrid died, but the colour of her skin never faded and she was as rosy as before when she lived. The king always sat over her and thought that she would come to life again, and thus it went on for three winters that he sorrowed over her death and all the people of his land sorrowed over his de-

---

Norman chroniclers. The present tombs of Rolf and his son William in the cathedral in Rouen are not the original ones, and were installed in the thirteenth century, the old church having been destroyed in the year 1200. The English chroniclers call Rolf *Rolla* or *Rollo*, whilst the French call him *Rollon*, sometimes *Rou* and *Robert*, by which latter name he was baptised.    1 Rolf's son William was called Longsword. It is not known that the Conqueror's father Robert the Magnificent was also called Longsword; but the Norman dukes had many appellations. Richard I was called *Aux Longues Jambes* or *Sans Peur*, Richard II *Le Bon* and Robert the Magnificent was also called *Le Libéral* and *Le Diable*. The English King John was called by the Normans *Jean le Méchant* and *Jean Sans Terre*, before he became King of England. It is noteworthy that the Normans continued the O.S. traditions of calling their rulers by some descriptive name. 2 Cf. p. 49, n. 1.    3 *Toftar*, now Tofte in Gudbrandsdale.

lusion. And to stop this delusion Torleiv the Wise came to his help; he did it with prudence, in that he spoke to him first with soft words, saying, "It is not strange, O king, that thou shouldst remember so bright and noble a woman and honour her with down and goodly web[1] as she bade thee. But thy honour and hers is still less than it seems, in that she has lain for a long while in the same clothes, and it is fitter that she should be raised and the clothes changed under her". But as soon as she was raised from the bed, so there rose from the body a rotten and loathsome smell and all kinds of evil stink; speedily a funeral bale was then made and she was burned. But before that all the body waxed blue and out crawled worms and adders, frogs and paddocks and all manner of foul reptiles. So she sank into ashes, and the king came to his wits and cast his folly from his heart and afterwards ruled the kingdom and was strengthened and gladdened by his men, and they by him and the kingdom by both.

26. After King Harald had proved the treachery of the Finnish woman, he became so wroth that he drove from him all the sons he had had by her and would not see them. But Gudröd Gleam went to Tjodolv, his foster-father, and bade him go with him to the king, for Tjodolv was the king's dear friend; the king was then in the Uplands. So they went, and when they came to the king late in the evening, they took a distant seat and hid themselves. The king walked on the floor and looked on the benches. He held a feast and the mead was mixed. Mumbling he said this:

| | |
|---|---|
| Very eager for mead | Who have come hither, |
| Are my white-haired warriors | What makes ye come so many? |

Then answered Tjodolv:

| | |
|---|---|
| We had many blows | For the wise prince. |
| In the sword play | We were not then too many. |

Tjodolv took his hat off and the king knew him and greeted him well. Then Tjodolv bade the king not to cast off his sons, "for fain would they have had a better-born mother, if thou hadst given them one". The king agreed with him and bade him keep Gudröd at home with him as he had been before, and Sigurd and Halvdan he sent to Ringerik and Ragnvald to Hadeland. They did as the king bade, and all became bold men and well endowed in all sports. King Harald now settled quietly in the land, and there was peace and the seasons were good.

27. Ragnvald, Jarl of Möre, learned of his brother Sigurd's death,

---

1 O.N. *gudvefr* was a costly woven material for bedcovers, etc.

and that the vikings had settled in the land. Then sent he his son Hallad to the west; Hallad took the name of jarl and he had many men with him in the west. And when he came to the Orkneys, he settled himself firmly in the land; but both in autumn, in winter, and in spring, did vikings go about the islands, landed on the nesses and made shore raids. Then did Hallad grow weary of sitting in the isles; he cast aside his jarldom and assumed the rights of a *hold*,[1] and after that he went east to Norway. But when Ragnvald the Jarl learned of it, he was ill pleased with Hallad's journey and said that his sons would be unlike their forefathers. Then answered Einar: "I have little honour with thee, I have little love to part from. I will go west to the isles, if thou wilt give me some backing. I will promise thee something about which thou wilt be very glad; I will not come back to Norway". Ragnvald said it would please him well that he should not come back, "for I little think that thy kin will get honour from thee, for all thy mother's kin were thrall-born". Ragnvald gave Einar a longship and fitted it out for him. About harvest time Einar sailed west across the sea and when he came to the Orkneys he met the vikings, Tore Treebeard and Kalv Scurvy with two ships. Einar straightway came to battle with them and had the victory and they both fell. Then was this sung:

> When he gave Treebeard to the trolls
> Turf-Einar slew Scurvy.

He was called Turf-Einar,[2] because he was the first to cut peat and use it for burning, for there was no wood in the Orkneys. After that Einar was jarl over the isles and became a mighty man; he was ugly and one-eyed, but still he was very sharp-sighted.

28. The Duke Guthorm was most often in Tunsberg, and when the king was not by he had the rule over all the Vik, and he was also warding the land. It was much exposed to viking raids and there was no peace with Gautland as long as King Eric Emundson lived. He died when King Harald Hairfair had been king over Norway for ten winters.

1 A *hold*, in O.N. *höldr*, had less privileges than a jarl. He was a *holder* of inherited land, not purchased but received by hereditary rights. The *Chronicle* of Henry of Huntingdon mentions in 905 about Ysop the *Hold* and Osketel the *Hold*. In 906 mention is made of the *Holds* Othulf, Benesing, Anlaf (Olav) the Black, Thurferth and Osferth, the collector of revenue, also Agmund the *Hold* and Guthferth the *Hold*. Huntingdon refers to these men as belonging to 'the Army' and having been slain by the English at a battle in Mercia. As *hold* is assumed to have been a Norse title, it may be inferred that 'the Army' often contained many Norse elements and not only Danes and Swedes. The Danish historian I. Steenstrup considers *hold* to be a Norse title. Cf. further p. 108, n. 1. 2 In O.S. *peat* is called *torf*; in M.S. the same word is still used.

29. After Eric, his son Björn was king in Sweden for fifty winters; he was father of Eric the Victorious and of Olav, the father of Styrbjörn. Guthorm the Duke died in his bed in Tunsberg and then King Harald gave the rule of all that kingdom to his son Guthorm and set him as chief over it.

30. When King Harald was forty years old, many of his sons were fully grown and they all ripened early to manhood. And it came about they little liked the fact that the king gave them no kingdoms, but set jarls in every shire; they thought jarls were not so high-born as themselves. One spring Halvdan Highleg and Gudröd Gleam went off with a great band of men; they came suddenly upon Ragnvald, Jarl of Möre,[1] drew a ring round his house and burned him in it with sixty men. Thereupon Halvdan took three longships which he fitted out and he afterwards sailed west on the sea, but Gudröd settled himself firmly where Ragnvald the Jarl had formerly had his seat. When King Harald learned that, he straightway went against Gudröd with a great army and Gudröd saw no other lot for himself but to put himself in King Harald's power; the king sent him east to Agder. King Harald then set Tore, the son of Ragnvald the Jarl, over Möre and married him to his own daughter Alov, who was called Arbot. Jarl Tore the Silent had then such rule as his father Ragnvald had had.

31. Halvdan Highleg came very suddenly west to the Orkneys and straightway Einar the Jarl fled from the isles, but the same harvest he came back and then suddenly attacked Halvdan. They met, but the battle was short, for Halvdan fled; that was about night time. Einar and his men lay without *tjald*[2] during the night and in the morning when it dawned they followed the fleeing men about the islands and every man was slain where he was found. Then said Einar the Jarl: "I wot not, if I can see out on Ronaldsey[3] a man or a bird; sometimes it lifts itself up, sometimes it lays itself down". Afterwards they went there and found Halvdan Highleg whom they took prisoner. On the evening before he went to battle Einar the Jarl said this verse:

The spear doth not fly
From Rolf nor Rollaug[4]
Against the hostile band.
I shall avenge my father.

And to-night whilst we
Bold expect battle, there sits
The silent Jarl Tore
In Möre with his ale-pot.

1 *Ragnvald, Jarl of Möre*, the father of Rolf the Ganger, who conquered Normandy. Cf. chapter 24.    2 *Tjald* was the tent or awning that was used at night on the ships. 3 *Ronaldsey* was called in O.N. *Rinansey*.    4 *Rolf* the Ganger and *Rollaug*, Einar's half-brothers.

Then Einar the Jarl went to Halvdan; he carved an eagle on Halvdan's back in this way: he stuck his sword into the body by the backbone, cut all the ribs away down to the loins and there drew out the lungs.[1] That was Halvdan's death. Then quoth Einar:

The Norns decided right,
And for my quarter share
I have avenged Ragnvald's death.
The prince is now fallen.

Bold swains, they cast
Stones on Highleg,
(For in the battle we won),
I sent him hard tribute.

Afterwards, Einar set himself firmly in the Orkneys which he had had before. But when these tidings were learned in Norway, his brothers were very wroth and said it should be avenged and many others confirmed it. And when Einar the Jarl heard it, he said:

On good grounds do many
Of the grasping high-born sons
From other parts
Seek my life,

But they know not yet
(Till they have killed me)
Who is fated to stoop
Under my eagle's claws.

32. King Harald called his men out, drew together a great army and then went west to the Orkneys; and when Einar the Jarl learned that the king was come west, he crossed to Caithness. Then he quoth a song:

The fair swain is made peaceless
For the slaughter of sheep,
But among the sea-beat islands
For a king's son's slaying, I fall.

I hear that the vengeance
Of the hard king threatens me;
I have struck a blow on Harald's shield
And I shall not sorrow.

Then men with messages went between the king and the jarl. It came about that a meeting was arranged; they met and the jarl gave himself up entirely to the king's judgment. King Harald deemed that Einar the Jarl and all the Orkneys should pay him sixty gold marks. That seemed too much to the bonders; then did the jarl offer to pay all himself, but he would acquire all the land by *odal* right. They agreed to this, mostly because the poor had small lands and the rich thought they would redeem their *odal* lands as soon as they wished. The jarl paid all the fine to the king, and in the harvest the king went back east. It lasted for a long time that the jarls had all the *odal* lands in the Orkneys, until Sigurd Lodverson gave back to the bonders the *odal* rights.

33. Guthorm, King Harald's son, had rule of the land in the Vik and he went with warships outside the islands and fjords; and when he lay in the mouth of the Göta River, Salve Klove came there and fought with him; Guthorm fell. Halvdan the Black and Halvdan the

---

[1] This kind of death was called *rista örn* = to carve an eagle.

White were on a viking raid and were harrying in the eastern countries. They had a great battle in Estland, where Halvdan the White fell. Eric was fostered by the chief Tore Roaldson in the Fjords; King Harald loved him best of all his sons and honoured him most. When Eric was twelve years old, King Harald gave him five longships and then Eric went raiding, first in the eastern countries, then south through Denmark and round about Friesland and Saxland; he remained on this journey four years. After this he went west across the sea and harried in Scotland and Wales, Ireland and France, and was there another four years. Afterwards he went north to Finmark and right to Bjarmaland,[1] had a great fight and won the victory. When he came back to Finmark, his men found a woman in a turf hut, the like of whom for beauty they had never seen; she was called Gunhild and she said that her father dwelt in Halogaland and was called Assur Toti; "I have been here", she said, "to learn witchcraft from the two Finns who are the cleverest men in Finmark. Now have they gone a-hunting and both of them wish to wed me. They are so wise that they can follow tracks like hounds, both in thaws and on hard snow; they are so good on skis that nothing, man or beast, can escape them and they hit everything they shoot at. So too have they made an end of everyone who has come near here; and if they are wroth, the very earth turns before their eyes; and if any living creature comes before their glance, then it straightway falls down dead. Now for anything in the world do not come in their way, but I will hide you here in the hut; we shall then see if we can manage to kill them". They agreed that she should hide them. She took a linen sack and they thought there were ashes in it. She put her hand in it and scattered it about the hut, both within and without. A little while after, the Finns came home; they asked if anything had come there, but she answered that nothing had come. That seemed strange to the Finns, for they had followed the spoor right to the hut, but they found nothing. Then they made themselves a fire and made ready the food. When they were satisfied, Gunhild went to her bed. For three nights before, when Gunhild slept, it happened that each of them watched the other through jealousy. Then she said, "Come hither now and each of you lie on either side of me". They were glad of it and did so. She then put her arms round their necks. They straightway fell asleep, but she woke them and again they straightway fell asleep and this time so fast that she could scarcely wake them; and

1 *Bjarmaland* is the old name for the country round the White Sea, especially the western part and the mouth of the River Dvina.

again they slept and then she could in no way waken them. She then rose but they still slept on. She took two big sealskin bags, drew them over their heads and bound them firmly below their hands. Then she gave the king's men the hint; they leaped forth and bore their weapons against the Finns; they slew them and dragged them out of the hut. The next night there was so great a thunderstorm that they could not go away, but the next morning they went to the ship, took Gunhild with them and bore her to Eric. Eric then went south with her to Halogaland. He called Assur Toti to him and said that he would have his daughter. Assur agreed to it and Eric then wedded Gunhild and had her with him in the south of the land.

34. King Harald was fifty years old when some of his sons were full grown and others dead. Many of them were very unruly in the land and were not friends amongst themselves; they drove the king's jarls out of their lands or slew them. King Harald then called a great thing in the east of the land and called the Uplanders to it. Then he gave his sons the name of king and laid down the law that each of his descendants should take the kingdoms after his father, but those who were come of his stock on the mother's side should take jarldoms. He divided the land between them, and Vingulmark, Raumarik, Vestfold and Telemark he gave to Olav, Björn, Sigtryg, Frode and Torgils; and Hedemark and Gudbrandsdale he gave to Dag, Ring and Ragnar; to Snæfrid's sons he gave Ringerik, Hadeland, Tote and all that belongs thereto. He had already given Guthorm the rule over Ranrik from the Göta River to Svinasund; he had set him to rule in the east as far as to Landsend,[1] as is already written. King Harald himself was most often in the Midlands;[2] Rörik and Gudröd were usually in attendance on the king and they had great incomes from land in Hordaland and Sogn. Eric was with his father King Harald; he loved him best of all his sons and honoured him most; to him he gave Halogaland, Nordmöre and Raumsdale. In the north, the rule in Trondheim he gave to Halvdan the White, Halvdan the Black and Sigröd. He gave his sons half the income with himself from each of these shires and it was agreed that they should sit in high-seats, one step higher than the jarls, but one step lower than himself. Each of his sons hoped for that seat after Harald's death. Harald himself wished Eric to have it and the Tronds[3] wished Halvdan the Black to have it, but the men of the Vik and the Uplanders each thought him best who ruled over

---

1 *Landsend* or O.S. *Landsendi* was the old frontier between Sweden and Norway by the Göta River (Gothenburg).    2 Cf. p. 58, n. 3.    3 *Tronds* are the inhabitants of Trondelag (the Trondlaw) round the Trondheim country.

them. But according as they thought they had little rule, they went fighting, and as mentioned already Guthorm fell in battle with Salve Klove in the Göta River. After that Olav took the kingdom which Guthorm had had. Halvdan the White fell in Estland, Halvdan Highleg in the Orkneys. To Torgils and Frode King Harald gave warships and they went on a viking raid to the west and harried in Scotland, Wales and Ireland. They were the first Norsemen to conquer Dublin. So it is said that Frode was given poison and that Torgils was king of Dublin for a long time, till he was betrayed by the Irish and slain there.[1]

35. Eric Blood-axe intended to become king over all his brothers and King Harald also wished it; he and his father were nearly always together. Ragnvald Rettlebone had Hadeland; there he learned magic and became a wizard. King Harald did not like wizards. In Hordaland there was a wizard called Vitgeir. The king sent him a behest to leave off his wizardry. He answered and sang:

> It is little strange  
> If we do wizardry,  
> Who are the sons of carls  
> And of low-born mothers,  
>
> When Ragnvald Rettlebone,  
> Harald's noble son,  
> Can be a wizard  
> In Hadeland.

When King Harald heard that said, Eric Blood-axe went by his counsel to the Uplands and came to Hadeland. There he burned his brother Ragnvald and eighty wizards with him and that work was much praised. Gudröd Gleam was during the winter as guest with his foster-father, Tjodolv of Kvin;[2] he had a well-fitted vessel and

---

1 The Irish annals are not clear on this question. Chas. Haliday, in his history *The Scandinavian Kingdom of Dublin*, after considering the various sources (which he names), comes to the conclusion that Thorgils (i.e. the servant of Thor and better known as Turgesius) is no other than Ragnar Lodbrok, but his arguments are not convincing. Dr Todd, in his book *Wars of the Gædhill with the Gaill*, fixes the reign of Turgesius from 832 to 845. On the other hand Thomas Wright in his revised edition of Giraldus Cambrensis considers that Cambrensis is wrong in his date when he mentions that Turgesius came to Ireland in 838 and that he was Torgils, the son of Harald Hairfair. Wright has been influenced by Snorre Sturlason in this respect, whose statement that Torgils (Harald Hairfair's son) was the first Norse king in Dublin is obviously wrong, because there is ample evidence to prove that besides Turgesius, the Norseman Olav the White (cf. p. 58, n. 5) established his dynasty there in 852 and was son of Ingvald, a king of the Uplands (in Norway), a Norse descendant of the above-mentioned Ragnar Lodbrok. Olav's widow, Queen Aud (cf. chapter 22), left Ireland on Olav's death in 870 or 871 and was destined to play a great rôle in the history and settlement of Iceland. Torgils (Harald Hairfair's son) could not have come to Ireland much before 910. Turgesius's ancestry is not known, but Giraldus Cambrensis calls him and his followers Norsemen.
2 *Tjodolv of Kvin* was the great scald whose poems are often quoted. Snorre Sturlason derived much information from them.

wished to go north to Rogaland. A great storm came on and Gudröd
was anxious to proceed and would not wait. Then said Tjodolv:

| | |
|---|---|
| Go not from here, till the fairway | Wait here, thou travelled prince, |
| Of the ship is improved, | Till the wind doth stop. |
| Gudröd! The sea now turns | Stay, till the fair wind comes, |
| The mighty rocks against the shore. | The breakers are now round Jadar.[1] |

But Gudröd still left in spite of what Tjodolv said. When they came
outside Jæderen, the ship sank and they were all drowned.

36. King Harald's son Björn was then ruling over Vestfold and
was almost always in Tunsberg[2] and was seldom out fighting. To

The Farman's Howe

Tunsberg came many merchant ships, both from the Vik and from
the northern districts, from Denmark and Saxland in the south. King
Björn also had merchant ships going to other lands and acquired
thereby costly wares and other goods for which he seemed to have
need. His brothers called him the farman[3] or the chapman.[4] Björn
was a wise man, calm and full of promise to become a leader; he made

1 *Jadar*, i.e. Jæderen; cf. p. 55, n. 1.    2 Now Tönsberg (East Norway).    3 In O.S.
*farmann* means skipper who sails on trading journeys, whilst *farmr* means load or burden.
Odin was also called *farma-guð*: the god who carried the heavy burdens.    4 *Chapman*
in O.S. is *kaupmann*, in modern Norwegian and Danish *kjöbmand*. The O.S. verb is
*kaupa*, modern Norw. *kjöpe*, to buy. *Chap* is from O.E. *ceap*, ultimately connected with
O.S. *kaupa*. 'Cheapside' and 'Eastcheap' in London originate from these words. In
the State Papers published for the reigns of Henry VIII and Queen Elizabeth,
Copenhagen is called *Copmanhaven* or *Copmannehaven*. This corresponds with the
O.S. form *Kaupmannahöfn*, viz. Merchants' Haven.

a good and fitting marriage and had one son who was called Gudröd. Eric Blood-axe came from the eastern countries with his warships and many men; he asked his brother Björn for the tribute and the money which King Harald had from Vestfold, but it was a custom that Björn should himself take the tribute to the king, or send men with it. He would still have it so and would not part with the tribute. But Eric had need of food and drink and shelter. The brothers quarrelled fiercely about it, but Eric did not get his wish and went away from the town. Björn also left the town in the evening and went up to Seim.[1] Eric waited about and in the night he went up to Seim after Björn; he came there as they sat over the drink. Eric surrounded the house and Björn and his followers went out and fought. There Björn fell and many men with him. Eric took much booty and went north into the land. That was ill-liked by the men of the Vik and Eric became hated there. Word went about that Olav would avenge Björn, if he got the chance. King Björn lies in the Farman's Howe[2] in Seim.

37. In the next winter King Eric went north to Möre and was feasted at Sölva[3] within Agdenes. When Halvdan the Black learned that, he went there with an army and drew a ring of men round the house. Eric was sleeping in an outer house and with four men came out into the wood, whilst Halvdan's men burned up the main houses and all who were inside. Eric came to King Harald with these tidings. The king was violently wroth, gathered an army and went against the Tronds. And when Halvdan the Black heard that, he bade his army and ships out, gathered a great following and put out to Stad within Torsbjerg. King Harald then lay with his army out by Reinsletta;[4] men went between them. An excellent man called Guthorm Sindri was then in the following of Halvdan the Black, but before that he had been with King Harald and was a good friend of both. He was also a great poet and had composed a poem about the father and another about the son. They had offered to pay him for it, but he had declined it and had asked if they would grant him a boon and they had agreed. He now went to King Harald and bore the word of peace between them and then asked each of them to fulfil his boon, namely, that they should be reconciled, and the kings did him so great an honour that they were reconciled through his boon. Many other

1 *Seim*, later called Sem, the present Jarlsberg.    2 *Farman's Howe* is situated about one mile south of Jarlsberg towards the Tönsbergfjord. This howe has lately been examined but no grave was found, so either the nature of the soil has demolished everything, or it had already been opened, and destroyed, which has happened with other viking graves.    3 *Sölva*, now Selven, inside Agdenes on the south side of the Trondheimsfjord.    4 *Reinsletta* on the north side of the Trondheimsfjord, and *Stad* on the south side.

noble men backed up his words. So it was agreed that Halvdan should have all the kingdom that he had had before, but that he should leave his brother Eric in peace. About this affair, Jorunn, the maiden poet, has composed some lines in the Sendebit; she quoths:

Halvdan (I know) had heard Hard mood and it seemed
Of Harald Hairfair's That his future was black.

38. Hacon Grjotgardson, Jarl of Lade, had all the rule in Trondheim when King Harald was elsewhere in the land, and Hacon had the greatest influence in the Trondlaw[1] over the king. After his death, his son Sigurd took over his country and became jarl in Trondheim; he had his seat in Lade. With him were brought up King Harald's sons, Halvdan the Black and Sigröd, and they had before been with his father Hacon. Harald's sons and Sigurd were almost of the same age. Sigurd the Jarl married Bergliot, the daughter of Jarl Tore the Silent; her mother was Alov (Arbot), Harald Hairfair's daughter. Sigurd the Jarl was a very wise man. When King Harald was growing old he often settled down at the great estates he had in Alrekstader[2] or Seim,[3] Fitjar[4] or Utstein[5] and Agvaldsnes[6] in Karmt. When the king was nearly seventy years old, he had a son by a woman called Thora Mosterstang, who came from a family at Moster[7] and had good relations; she reckoned herself related to Horda-Kari. She was a beautiful and fine woman and was called the servant-maid of the king, for at that time many were obliged to become the king's servants, both men and women, although they were of good lineage. It was the custom with children of great men, that they should be careful in the choice of men to sprinkle water over them or to give them names, and as the time arrived when Thora was expecting to give birth to the child, she wished to go to King Harald, for he was then north in Seim, whilst she was at Moster. She then went north in Sigurd the Jarl's ship. During the night they stayed ashore and there Thora brought forth a child at Hella[8] near to the quay wall; it was a boy.[9] Sigurd the Jarl sprinkled water over the boy and called him Hacon after his own father Hacon the Jarl of Lade. The boy soon became handsome and well grown and very much like

1 Cf. p. 67, n. 3. 2 *Alrekstader*, now Arstad by the Lungegard's Lake at Bergen. 3 *Seim* in Alversund district on the peninsula north of Osterfjord, in North Hordaland. 4 *Fitjar*, now Fitja on the north-west of Stord, in South Hordaland. 5 *Utstein*, now Utstein's Kloster on the island of Utstein in Ryfylke, by Stavanger. 6 *Agvaldsnes*, now Avaldsnes on the north-east side of the island of Karmöy by Haugesund, between Stavanger and Bergen. 7 *Moster*, now Mosteröy, an island in South Hordaland. 8 Now Helleren by Vatleströmmen (Vatlestream) south-west of Bergen. Also called Hakonshella. 9 The later Hacon the Good.

his father. King Harald let the boy remain with his mother and they stayed on the king's estates whilst the boy was little.

39. Athelstan was the name of the king in England who had lately taken the kingdom; he was called the Victorious and the Faithful. He sent men to Norway to King Harald with that kind of greeting that the messenger went before the king and handed him a sword with a hilt and grip of gold and a scabbard all chased with gold and costly stones. The messenger handed the hilt of the sword to the king and said, "Here is the sword which King Athelstan said thou shouldst take". The king took the grip and forthwith the messenger said, "Now dost thou take the sword as our king would wish and now shalt thou be his man since thou dost take his sword". King Harald now thought that it was done as an insult, for he would be nobody's man, but he yet remembered that, as was his wont when at any time heat or wrath came over him, he would first hold himself in check and let such anger go from him and act without wrath. Now again he did so and related the matter to his friends and they all found that it was best to let the messengers go home unscathed.

40. The summer after King Harald sent a ship west to England and set Hauk Habrok as its helmsman, for he was a mighty champion and a good friend of the king. With him the king sent his son Hacon. Hauk then sailed west to England to King Athelstan and found him in London, when there was a feast and a splendid banquet. Hauk told his men in what order they should go in, when they came to the hall; he said, "He shall go last out, who went first in", and after that all should stand in equal distance in front of the table and each should have his sword on his left side with his cape fastened over, so that the sword could not be seen. Afterwards they went into the hall; they were thirty men. Hauk went before the king and greeted him and the king bade him welcome. Then did Hauk take the boy Hacon and set him on King Athelstan's knee. The king looked at the boy and asked Hauk why he had done this. Hauk answered, "King Harald bade thee foster for him the child of his servant-maid". The king was very wroth and snatched his sword which lay beside him and drew as though he would kill the boy. "Thou hast him seated on thy knee",[1] said Hauk, "now canst thou murder him if thou wilt, but thereby wilt thou not slay all the sons of King Harald." After that Hauk and all his men departed and went their way to the ship, and put to sea

1 To set a child on one's knee was used in old Scandinavia as a symbol of adoption. (Cf. also p. 58, n. 1.) In England the expression, "Come, let me nurse you", meaning to take a child on one's knee, may be connected with the O.S. custom.

when it was ready and came back to Norway to King Harald; he liked this well for it is reckoned by men that he who fosters another's child is less important. In these dealings between the kings it was found that each of them would be greater than the other, but still no harm was done to the honour of either of them; each of them was sovereign lord in his own kingdom till the day of his death.[1]

Hauk Habrok with King Athelstan

41. King Athelstan had Hacon christened and taught him the right faith and good habits and all kind of learning and manners. He loved him much, more than he did all his own kin, and so did everyone who knew the boy. He was afterwards called Athelstan's foster-son. He was the greatest in sports, bigger and stronger and more handsome than any other. He was wise, of fair speech and a good Christian. King Athelstan gave Hacon a sword of which the hilt and grip were of gold but the blade was even better; with it Hacon cleaved a millstone to the eye and it was afterwards called the Kvernbit (or

[1] William of Malmesbury is the only chronicler who mentions Harald Hairfair's friend-ship with King Athelstan. He states: "Harald, King of Norway, sent him a ship with a golden beak and a purple sail, furnished within with a compacted fence of gilded shields. The names of the persons sent with it were Helgrim and Offrid, who being re-ceived with princely magnificence in the city of York, were amply compensated by rich presents for the labour of their journey". Malmesbury writes this under the year 926.

millstone-biter). It was the best sword that ever came to Norway. Hacon had it till his death day.

42. King Harald was now eighty years old; he then became so heavy of foot that he did not care to travel through the land or manage the kingly affairs. He then led his son Eric into the high-seat and gave him the rule of the whole land. But when King Harald's other sons heard this, Halvdan the Black set himself in the high-seat and took all Trondheim into his power; in that act all the Tronds to a man were with him. After the death of Björn the Chapman his brother Olav took his kingdom in Vestfold and fostered Björn's son Gudröd. Olav's son was called Trygvi and he and Gudröd were foster-brothers and almost of the same age, both were promising and doughty men; Trygvi was bigger and stronger than any other man. When the Vik men learned that the Hordalanders had taken Eric as sovereign king, they took Olav as king of the Vik and he held the kingdom. Eric liked that very ill. Two years later Halvdan the Black died a sudden death at a feast in Trondheim and it was said that Gunhild King's Mother[1] had bought over a witch wife to give him *bane* drink.[2] After that the Tronds took Sigröd as their king.

43. King Harald lived three years after he had given Eric sole rule over the kingdom; he was then in Rogaland or Hordaland on one of the great estates he owned. Eric and Gunhild had a son over whom King Harald sprinkled water and to whom he gave his name; he said that he should be king after his father Eric. King Harald married most of his daughters to jarls in the land and from them sprang many great branches of his race. King Harald died in his bed in Rogaland and was buried in a howe at Haugar.[3] Near Haugesund stands a church[4] and in the north-west corner of the churchyard is Harald Hairfair's howe; on the west of the church lies King Harald's grave-stone, which had been laid over his grave in the mound; it is thirteen and a half feet long and nearly two ells broad. King Harald's grave was in the middle of the howe; a stone was set by his head and another by his feet, and a flat stone was across them both; and below on either side it was filled up with stones. These stones, which were then in the howe and have just been mentioned, are now standing in the church-yard. So say men of knowledge that Harald Hairfair had been

1 Here is meant Gunhild, the spouse of King Eric. She was sometimes called Gunhild King's Mother. 2 Poison. 3 Near Haugesund (West Norway) between Stavanger and Bergen. 4 The church on the king's estate Haugar (later called Gar) was pulled down in the sixteenth century, but its site was where Harald's monument was erected in 1872. The big gravestone has been included in the monument. The church was probably built by St Olav.

the finest and strongest and biggest of all men, generous with his goods and friendly towards his men; he was a mighty warrior in his early days and this was foreshadowed by the big tree which his mother saw in a dream before his birth and of which the lower part was red as blood. That the trunk was fair and green above they took to betoken the flourishing of his kingdom, and when the tree was white above they knew that he would become old and white-haired. The twigs and branches of the tree betokened his offspring, who spread themselves all over the land, and from his kin have come ever after the kings of Norway.

44. The next winter after King Harald's death, King Eric took all the income which the king had in the Midlands,[1] whilst Olav did the same in the Vik and their brother Sigröd had all in Trondlaw. Eric was right ill-content at this, and word went about that he would seek his brothers with force if he could get the sole rule over the land as his father had given it to him. And when Olav and Sigröd learned of it, messengers fared between them; upon this they arranged a meeting and in the spring Sigröd went east to the Vik. He and his brother Olav now met in Tunsberg and stayed there for a time. The same spring Eric fitted out a great army and ships and sailed east to the Vik. He had so fair a wind that he sailed day and night and no knowledge of his journey went before him. When he came to Tunsberg, Olav and Sigröd went east from the town with their army to a hill[2] and gathered their troops. Eric had a much greater army; he had the victory and both Olav and Sigröd fell there; the grave mounds of both of them are on the hill where they lay fallen. Eric now went about the Vik, laid it under him and stayed there long during the summer. Trygvi and Gudröd fled to the Uplands. Eric was a big, good-looking man, strong and powerful, a great and victorious warrior, hot-tempered, cruel, unfriendly and of few words. Gunhild, his wife, was the fairest of women, wise and skilful in magic, glad of speech, crafty and very cruel. These were the children of Eric and Gunhild: Gamle (the eldest), Guthorm, Harald, Ragnfröd, Ragnhild, Erling, Gudröd, Sigurd Sleva. All Eric's children were good-looking and manly.

1 In O.N. *Mitt-land*, meaning West Norway.    2 This hill is the present Möllebakken (the Mill-hill) in the east part of Tönsberg. Here are still two great howes, which are no doubt those of the two kings.

HARALD HAIRFAIR. KING OF NORWAY FROM 860,
ABDICATED 930 AND DIED 933

872. The battle of Hafursfjord.
874. First settlement of Iceland.
876. Rolf the Ganger's first arrival in the Seine.
878. Harald's expedition to the west.
      Ragnvald, Jarl of Möre, obtains Orkneys.
      Sigurd becomes jarl of Orkneys.
      Rolf the Ganger left Normandy for England to aid King
      Alfred.
c. 885. Birth of Eric Blood-axe.
919. Birth of Hacon the Good.
928. Rolf the Ganger abdicates in favour of his son William.
930. Eric Blood-axe becomes King of Norway on Harald Hair-
      fair's abdication.
931. Death of Rolf the Ganger, the illustrious founder of
      Normandy.
933. Death of Harald Hairfair.

# IV

# THE HISTORY OF HACON THE GOOD

1. Hacon, Athelstan's foster-son, was in England when he learned of the death of his father, King Harald, and he straightway made ready to go home. King Athelstan gave him men and good ships and fitted him out nobly for the journey; in the harvest he came to Nor-

King Hacon speaks at the thing to the Tronds

way. He then learned of the fall of his brothers and also that King Eric was then in the Vik. Hacon then sailed north to Trondheim[1] and went to Sigurd the Jarl who was then the wisest man in Norway; he was greeted well and they made a covenant. Hacon promised Sigurd great power, if he became king. Then they had a great thing of the people summoned and at that thing Sigurd the Jarl spoke for Hacon and offered him to the bonders as king. After that Hacon himself stood up and spoke. Then they talked two and two together

1 The present town of Trondheim was built by King Olav Trygvason. Often when Trondheim is mentioned, Snorre Sturlason means the surrounding county. Olav Trygvason called the town *Nidaros*.

and said that here Harald Hairfair was come back and was young for a second time. Hacon began his speech by asking the bonders to give him the name of king and also to grant him support and help to maintain his kingdom; in return he offered to make all the bonders *odal*-born to their lands, and the lands whereon they lived he offered to give back to them free of tax. That speech caused so great a stir that the whole body of bonders shouted and cried out that they would take him as their king. And thus it came that the Tronds took Hacon as king over all the land. He was then fifteen winters old; he then engaged a bodyguard and went over all the land. These tidings were learned in the Uplands, that the Tronds had taken as their king one who was like Harald Hairfair in all things, except that Harald had thrall-bound and cowed all the people in the land, whereas Hacon wished every man well and had offered to give back to the bonders their *odal* lands which Harald had taken from them. At these tidings all were glad; one man told another till the news flew like fire in dry grass right east to Landsend.[1] Many bonders went from the Uplands to meet King Hacon, some sent messengers, some words and tokens[2] and all made it known that they would be his men. The king took them all thankfully.

2. In the beginning of the winter King Hacon went to the Uplands and called things; all the folk who could come gathered to him and he was taken as king by all the things; he then went east to the Vik. There Trygvi and Gudröd, the sons of his brother, came to him and many others who reckoned up all the sorrows they had borne from his brother Eric. Eric's unfriendliness also grew, the more all men wished to win Hacon's friendship and the more everyone had courage to speak as they thought. King Hacon gave to Trygvi and Gudröd the name of king and the land which King Harald had given to their fathers; to Trygvi he gave Ranrik[3] and Vingulmark[4] and to Gudröd he gave Vestfold, and because they were young and but children, he set great and wise men to rule the land with them; he gave them the land with the provision, which had formerly held, that they should have half the taxes and tribute with him. When spring came, King Hacon went north overland through the Uplands to Trondheim.

1 The frontier between Sweden and Norway by the Göta River was called *Landsendi* in O.S., as mentioned in 'History of Harald Hairfair', p. 67, n. 1.   2 Tokens were called in O.S. *Jartegnir*. They were certain signs or objects, which passed between two men, in token of the good faith of the messengers who carried them.   3 Cf. 'History of Harald Hairfair', p. 53, n. 1.   4 *Vingulmark*, the land round Oslo and Smalenene (on the east and south sides).

3. King Hacon drew a great army together in Trondheim in the spring and procured ships; the men of the Vik also had drawn out a great army and would meet Hacon. Eric also called an army out from the Midlands, but he got few men, for many chiefs fell away from him and went to Hacon; and when he could see no way of standing against Hacon's army, he sailed west across the sea with the men who would follow him. He went first to the Orkneys and there he got many men; afterwards he sailed south towards England and harried in Scotland wherever he came near land. He

Queen Gunhild is baptised by an English bishop

also harried right to the north of England. Athelstan, the King of England, sent word to Eric, bidding him to take of him a kingdom in England; he said that his father King Harald was a good friend of King Athelstan, so that he would let it avail also for his son. Men then went between the kings and made an agreement that King Eric should hold Northumbria for King Athelstan[1] and there protect the

1 The English chroniclers are brief and vague in their description of the many short-lived Kings of Northumberland and the evidence relating to the advent of Eric Blood-axe is also hazy and contradictory. The *Anglo-Saxon Chronicle* states that the English king Edred ravaged Northumberland in 948 and expelled Eric, and that in the year 952 King Anlaf (Olav) was expelled and Eric, Harald's son, received as king, to be deposed again in 954. Roger de Hoveden states that Eric was taken as king in 947 and expelled in 948. Simeon of Durham and Florence of Worcester mention the years 949 and 950. Nothing is said about what happened to Eric afterwards. The only chroniclers who give a clearer although still incomplete record of Eric Blood-axe are Roger of Wendover and Matthew of Westminster. They state, among other things, that in 947 the Northumbrians broke their faith with King Edred and took Eric for their king and that Eric was deposed again in 948. It is further mentioned that Eric by the treachery of Earl Osulf was slain by a nobleman called Macon (Maccus), a son of King Anlaf (Olav)—at a lonely spot called Steinmore in 950, together with his son Henry and his brother Reginald. Steinmore is situated near Kirkby Stephen in Westmoreland. But all the chroniclers are silent about Eric having been made King of Northumberland by Athelstan. Their silence on this particular subject is, however, not conclusive evidence that Eric first became king in 947; in fact there are good reasons for thinking that Snorre Sturlason is right, when he mentions that Athelstan made Eric king in order to assist him against the vikings, but his first reign must have been of short duration, otherwise it would probably not have been ignored. As mentioned above, the *Anglo-Saxon Chronicle* states that Eric was expelled in 948, came back in 952 and ruled until 954, so here we have support for our contention that Eric had two reigns in Northumberland; but the dates are obviously wrong and contrary to all the other chroniclers. In comparing this discordant evidence we may well assume that Athelstan made Eric king a year or two before his death (940), and that he had to leave when

land against Danes and other vikings. Eric was to let himself be baptised with his wife and children and all the men who had followed him thither. Eric accepted these conditions and he was then baptised and took the true faith. Northumbria is reckoned a fifth part of England. He had his seat in York,[1] where it is said the sons of Lodbrok[2] had formerly had their seat. Northumberland was mostly peopled by Norsemen. After the sons of Lodbrok had won the land, Danes and Norsemen often harried there when they had lost their power in the land. Many names there are in the Norröna tongue,[3] such as Grimsby[4] and Hauksfljot[5] and many others.

4. King Eric had many folk about him and he had a great number of Norsemen who had gone from the east with him, also many of his friends afterwards came from Norway. He had little land, therefore in the summer he was usually raiding, and he harried in Scotland and in the Hebrides, Ireland and Wales, and thereby got himself wealth. King Athelstan died in his bed; he had been king for fourteen winters, eight weeks and three days.[6] Afterwards his brother Edmund became King of England; he liked not the Norsemen and King Eric

Edmund, his enemy, came to the throne. When Edmund died, he sought to recover his lost kingdom and now we come to the year 947 mentioned by the chroniclers, when Eric was taken as king, and the Northumbrians decided to break their faith with Edred. They would hardly have done this unless Eric had not been well known to them from previous times. It is further inconceivable that Eric would ever have become King of Northumberland without the support of the English king, and Athelstan was the only king who would have given him this support, as both Edmund and Edred were hostile to him. The *Encyclopædia Britannica* (9th ed. Edinburgh, 1886), vol. xxi, p. 479, states: "Athelstan died two years after Brunanburgh, but before his death granted Northumberland to Eric Blood-axe son of Harald Haarfagr, who was almost immediately expelled by Irish Danes. Athelstan even after so great a victory could not annex Northumberland, much less Scotland, to his dominions". The battle of Brunanburgh was fought in 938 and the poem composed about it and cited in the *Anglo-Saxon Chronicle* is Anglo-Norse in substance and diction. (See further Kershaw's *Anglo-Saxon and Norse Poems*, Cambridge University Press, 1922.)   1 York was called *Jorvik* by the old Scandinavians.   2 *Sons of Lodbrok*: Ingvar (or Ivor), Ubbe and Halvdan were the leaders of 'the Army', which landed in England in 865 and conquered York in 866. Halvdan became King of Northumberland in 875.   3 *Norröna tongue* means the language spoken by the Scandinavian peoples in olden times.   4 *Grimsby*, now in Lincolnshire, was at that time in Lindsey. Snorre Sturlason writes about it in connection with Northumbria, and this county bordered on the River Humber in the tenth century. 5 *Hauksfljot* is probably the same as *Humrafljot*, i.e. River Humber. The tradition is that the river takes its name from Humber, a chief of the Huns, defeated by Locrin, King of England, and drowned in the River Abus, ever since called the Humber. O.S. *fljot* is connected with *fleet*, which occurs in many place names in England. 6 The *Anglo-Saxon Chronicle* states: "King Athelstan reigned fourteen years and ten weeks".

had no friendship with him. Word went about that King Edmund would set another chief over Northumbria. And when King Eric learned that, he went on a viking raid to the west and he had with him from the Orkneys, Arnkel and Erlend, the sons of Turf-Einar. He then went to the Hebrides and there were many vikings and fighting kings who went into his following. He then sailed with all his army to Ireland and he took with him as many men as he could get. He afterwards went to Wales and harried there. After that he sailed south along England, where he harried in many places, all the folk fleeing before him wherever he went. And as Eric was a bold warrior and had a great army, he believed so much in his strength that he went up into the land and harried and pursued the folk. Olav was the name of the king whom King Edmund had set to rule the land there; he drew together a mighty army and went against King Eric. There was now a great battle. Many of the English fell, but where one fell, there came three in his stead from over the land. Later in the day the loss of men turned to the Norsemen's side and many of them fell; by the end of the day King Eric had fallen and with him five kings; these were Guthorm and his two sons, Ivor and Harek, besides Sigurd and Ragnvald and the sons of Turf-Einar, Arnkel and Erlend. There was great slaughter amongst the Norsemen and those who came away went to Northumberland and told these tidings to Gunhild and her sons.

5. When Gunhild and her sons were aware that King Eric had fallen and that he had been harrying in the King of England's land, they knew that they could expect no peace there. They straightway made ready to go from Northumberland and took with them all the ships that King Eric had had; they took also all the folk who would follow them and much loose property, which they had drawn together in England from tribute or from raiding. They sailed north with their army to the Orkneys and stayed there for a time. At that time Tor-finn Hausakljuv, the son of Turf-Einar,[1] was jarl there. Eric's sons then took to themselves the Orkneys and Shetlands and had scot from them; they stayed there during the winter, but in the summer they went on viking raids to the west and harried in Scotland and Ireland.

1 *Turf-Einar* (cf. 'History of Harald Hairfair, p. 63) was half-brother of Rolf the Ganger, who conquered Normandy. Einar's son, Torfinn Hausakljuv, Earl of Orkney, married Grelauga (in O.N. *Grelad*), daughter of Duncan, Earl of Duncansbay, and Torfinn's grandson was Sigurd the Stout. (Cf. 'History of Harald Hardrade', p. 536, n. 1.)

About this Glum Geirason says:

The far-faring chieftain,
The young rider of sea steeds,
Had gone from hence
A long journey to Scania.
The shrewd war lord
In Scotland sent troops to Odin;
A wound-bitten band they were.

To the sport of the Valkyries' ravens
They did harm to the Irish dwellings.
When the folk escaped in flight
The victory-seeking land chief
In the south dyed the edge of his sword
Red with the blood of the folk
And the fallen men.

6. King Hacon, Athelstan's foster-son, put under him all Norway, when his brother Eric fled away. The first winter he went west in the land, then north to Trondheim and settled there. But when peace seemed not likely, if King Eric came east across the sea with his army,

Queen Gunhild receives the news of Eric's death

he settled with his army in the middle of the land, in the Firda district and Sogn, in Hordaland and Rogaland. Hacon set Sigurd the Jarl of Lade over all Trondlaw, such as he and his father Hacon had formerly held of King Harald Hairfair. When King Hacon learned of the death of Eric, his brother, and that Eric's sons could not get help in England, it seemed to him that he could have little fear of them and so he went east with his army to the Vik. At that time the Danes were harrying much in the Vik and did great scathe there, and when they learned that King Hacon was come thither with a great army they all fled thence, some south to Halland, but others who were nearer to King Hacon sailed out to sea, and thereupon went south to Jutland.[1] When King Hacon heard that, he sailed after them with all his army and when he came to Jutland and the folk there were aware of it, they drew their army together to protect their land and sought battle with King Hacon. There was a great fight and King Hacon fought so boldly that he was in front of his banner and had neither helm nor coat of mail.[2] King Hacon had the victory and drove the fleeing men far up into the land. Thus says Guthorm Sindri in Hacon's drapa:

The king crossed on the blue way
Of the boat with the sea spray
From the oars. The noble prince
Slew the Jutes in battle.

Odin's sated birds
Afterwards clawed the fliers;
The ravens sought their food,
And glutted their lust.

1  *Jutland* was in O.S. called *Jotland*, whilst in M.S. it is called *Jylland*.
2  *Coat of mail* was called in O.S. *brynja*; in M.S. *brynje* (or *brynie*).

7. King Hacon with his army then went north (east) to Zealand to seek the vikings. He rowed forth with two boats into Öresund[1] and there met eleven viking ships and straightway fell to battle with them; the end of it was that he won the victory and cleared all the viking ships. Thus says Guthorm Sindri:

> The glad warrior chief,
> With only two warships,
> Went south to Zealand's
> Green sea-shore,
>
> When all eleven ships
> Of the Danes were cleared
> By the wroth sword-swinger,
> Afterwards far-renowned.

8. After that King Hacon harried far about in Zealand and plundered and slew some of the folk and took others prisoner; from some he took great fines and was not any more withstood. Thus says Guthorm Sindri:

> The sea king then neared Zealand
> To lay it under himself
>
> To gain Vendish booty
> Far along Scania side.

Afterwards King Hacon went east along the coast of Scania and harried everywhere; he took money and tribute from the land and slew all vikings where he found them, both Danes and Vends. He went as far east as Gautland[2] and harried there and took much money from the land. Thus says Guthorm Sindri:

> The shield-bearer took toll
> From the Gauts far and wide;
>
> The generous gold-giver
> Had profit from his journey.

In the harvest King Hacon went back with his army and he had gained a great many goods. He settled for the winter in the Vik to protect it, if Danes and Gauts should make an inroad there.

9. That autumn King Trygvi Olavson came from a western viking raid; he had before this been harrying round about Ireland and Scotland. The next spring King Hacon went north in the land and set King Trygvi, his brother's son, over the Vik to protect it from unrest and to obtain as many taxes as he could of the land in Denmark from which King Hacon had taken scot the previous summer. Thus says Guthorm Sindri:

> As king in the East
> (In the oaklands),
> The battle-tried king set
> The skilful young Trygvi,
>
> Who, bold warrior,
> Was lately come home
> From Ireland with his ships,
> His swans' way's skis.[3]

10. King Harald Gormson was then ruling in Denmark and he little liked King Hacon harrying in his land. Word went about that

---

1 The Sound.    2 *Gautland* in Sweden.    3 The *swans' way* = the sea. The
*skis* = the ships.

the Danish king would avenge himself, but no action was taken in a hurry. And when Gunhild's sons learned that there was trouble between Denmark and Norway, they and Gunhild made ready to go east. They married Eric's daughter Ragnhild to Arnfinn, the son of Torfinn Hausakljuv; then Torfinn the Jarl again took the rule in the Orkneys as Eric's sons had gone away. Gamle Ericson was a little older than the others, but even so he was not full grown. And when Gunhild came to Denmark with her sons, she went to King Harald and was greeted well. King Harald gave them incomes from land in his kingdom big enough to keep themselves and their men; he took Harald Ericson as his foster-son and set him on his knee; he was brought up in the Danish king's household. Some of Eric's sons went raiding as soon as they were old enough and so gathered wealth; they harried about the eastern countries. They were soon handsome men and they had grown in skill and prowess more quickly than in years. About it Glum Geirason says in Grafeld's drapa.

The prince, generous to many scalds,
Went to battle
In the eastern lands,
He always won the fight;

The lord of the sword-play oft let
His hefty weapon sing,
And the grim chief sent many
Great warriors to their death.

Eric's sons also turned north with their army to the Vik and harried there; King Trygvi would lead out his army and go to meet them. They had many fights and each had the victory in turn. Sometimes Eric's sons would harry in the Vik, sometimes Trygvi would harry in Halland and Zealand.

11. When Hacon was King in Norway, there was good peace amongst bonders and chapmen, so that neither did scathe to the other or the other's goods; and there were good seasons both on land and sea. King Hacon was the blithest of all men, the sweetest spoken and the kindest; he was a very wise man and gave much time to law giving. By the counsel of

King Hacon sprinkles water on the jarl's son

Torleiv the Wise, he set up the Gulathing's law; by the counsel of Sigurd the Jarl and others of the wisest of the Tronds, he set up the Frostathing's law; the Heidsævi law[1] had Halvdan the Black set up, as is written

---

1 Cf. 'History of Halvdan the Black', p. 40, n. 1. Although Snorre Sturlason does not specially mention the name *Heidsævi* law in this chapter, it is evident that this law thing was founded by Halvdan the Black and had its seat at Eidsvold, on the south bank of Lake Mjöse.

already. King Hacon had a Yule feast in Trondheim, which Sigurd the Jarl had made ready for him at Lade. The first night of Yule, the jarl's wife Bergliot gave birth to a boy. The day after, King Hacon sprinkled water on the boy and gave him his name. The boy grew up and afterwards became a mighty and great man. Sigurd the Jarl was King Hacon's dearest friend.

12. Eystein, the King of the Uplanders, who was by some called the Mighty, but by others the Evil, harried in Trondheim and subdued the Öyna folk and the Sparbyggja folk and set his son over them, but the Tronds slew him. Once more King Eystein raided Trondheim and harried far and wide and again put the land under him. He then asked the Tronds to choose whether they would have as their king a thrall of his called Tore the Hairy or his dog Saur; they chose the dog, for they believed that they would then rule mostly themselves. Then they bewitched the dog with the wit of three men, so that it barked two words but spoke every third word. They had made for it a collar and leash of silver and gold, and when it was muddy the king's guardsmen bore it on their shoulders; a high-seat was raised for it and it sat on the howe like a king and dwelled on Inderöy and had its seat in the place called Saurshowe.[1] It is said that this was its death; wolves came on its flocks and herds and the guardsmen egged it on to protect its sheep; it went from the howe thither where the wolves were and they straightway tore it asunder. Many other strange things King Eystein did against the Tronds, and because of the raids and unrest many chiefs and many folk fled from their *odal* lands. Ketel Jämte, the son of Jarl Anund of Sparabu,[2] went east over the Kjöl[3] with a great troop of men and they had cattle with them. They cleared woods and made there great lordships and it was afterwards called Jämtland. Ketel's grandson was Tore Helsing and because of a case of manslaughter he went east from Jämtland over the woods which are there and settled; many folks went with him and it was called Helsingeland; it reached east right to the sea. The Swedes had inhabited the east of Helsingeland along by the sea, but when King Harald Hairfair had cleared the kingdom for himself, there had fled from the land a great number of men, Tronds and men of Naumadale, and new districts were made east in Jämtland, and some went right into Helsingeland. The Helsings had trade in

---

1 *Saurshowe*, now Saxhaug.    2 *Sparabu*, now Sparbuen in the Sparbyggja district.
3 *Kjöl* (Keel) is the frontier between Norway and Sweden. Some of the frontier is formed by mountains or mountainous land, going from north to south, hence its name 'Keel' (of a ship).

Sweden and were subservient to Sweden in everything. But the men of Jämtland were almost in the middle between Norway and Sweden and no notice was taken of them, before Hacon made peace and sent trading people to Jämtland and made friends of the great men there. They often went west to him, vowed him homage and paid tribute and became his men; they heard nothing but good of him and they would rather be in his kingdom than in that of the Swedes, for they were of Norse stock; he set up laws and land rights for them. The same did also all those Helsings who had come of kin north of the Kjöl.

13. King Hacon was a good Christian when he came to Norway and because all the land was heathen and there was much blood offering and many powerful men, and because he seemed to have great need of the help and good will of many of them, he took the advice to fare privily with Christianity. He kept Sundays and fasted on Fridays and he made it a law that they should keep Yule at the same time as Christian men, that every man should then hold a guest feast with ale made of one measure of malt and keep it holy as long as the ale lasted or else pay a fine; formerly the first night of Yule was hogmanay night,[1] that is midwinter night,[2] and Yule was held for three nights. He thought when he had settled firmly in the land, and had fully subdued it, that he could then send forth the message of Christianity. First he drew to Christianity those men who were dearest to him and through his friendship many were baptised, though some still kept to the blood offerings. He stayed for long periods in Trondheim, for there lay the land's greatest strength. And when King Hacon seemed to have the support of some of the great men in upholding Christianity, he sent to England for a bishop and other priests; and when they came to Norway, King Hacon made it clear that he would have Christianity over all the land; but the men of Möre and Raumsdale referred the matter to the Tronds. King Hacon then had some churches consecrated and set priests in them, and when he came to Trondheim he called a thing of the bonders and bade them take up Christianity. They answered that they would defer the matter for decision at the thing at Frosta[3] and wished men to come thither from all the folks who were in Trondlaw and said that then they would answer the difficult matter.

1 *Hogmanay night* is used in Scotland for the last day of the year. In O.S. it is called *höggu nott*, and is supposed to take its name from hogging or hewing down cattle before the festival.    2 *Midwinter night*, the commencement of the heathen Yule, was the 12th of January.    3 *The thing at Frosta* was held on the Frosta peninsula in the Trondheimsfjord.

14. Sigurd, the Jarl of Lade, was a great sacrificer and so had been Hacon his father. Sigurd the Jarl upheld all the blood offerings for Trondlaw on the king's behalf. It was an old custom, when they made an offering, for all the bonders to come to the temple and bring their eatables which they would need as long as the offering lasted. At that offering all men should have ale. There they also slew all kinds of cattle and horses, and all the blood which flowed from them was called *laut*, the bowls in which the blood stood were called *laut-bowls* and *laut-teinar*, which were made like a sprinkler; with all this they should stain the stalls red and likewise the temple walls inside and out and likewise sprinkle it on all the men; the flesh was cooked as meat for the guest feast. There should be fires in the midst of the temple floor and thereover should hang kettles; they should carry bowls to the fire and he who was making the offering and was chief should bless the bowl and all the flesh, but he should first bless Odin's bowl (which should be drunk for the king's victory and power) and afterwards the bowls of Niord and Frey for good seasons and peace. It was usual to drink last Bragi's bowl; they also drank bowls for their howe-laid kinsmen and that was called *minni*.[1] Sigurd the Jarl was very generous; he did work which was much spoken of, in that he made a great feast at Lade and alone bore all the cost of it. About this Kormak[2] Agmundson says in Sigurd's drapa:

No man bore cup
Or basket with him
To the jarl's feast.
(The gods betrayed Tjassi)

Who would not with joy
Go to the blood offering
Which the generous prince gave.
(The king fought for gold.)

15. King Hacon came to the Frosta thing and thither was come a great number of bonders. When the thing sat, King Hacon spoke; he said first that it was his behest and offer to the bonders and labourers, great and small, and young men and old, rich and poor, women and men, that they should become Christians and believe in one God, Christ, the son of Mary, and give up all blood offerings and

---

1 In M.S. *minde*, in O.S. *minni*, meaning 'to mind' or 'remember'. 2 *Kormak* is an Irish name met with in the sagas. In Ireland and Scotland it has become McCormack or McCormick. The Norse name Per or Pehr has in Scotland become McPherson or Pearson (the son of Per). Ole or Ola is a similar Christian name, which in Scotland has become Macauley or Macoley (the son of Ole). The ending *son* in many names in Britain denotes Scandinavian origin, although in some cases it has no doubt been adopted by families which did not trace their descent from the northern countries. The Normans adopted the Scandinavian custom of adding *son* to some of their names by using the Norman-French *Fitz* (i.e. *fils*) and placed it in front of the name. Hence words like Fitzherbert, Fitzmaurice, etc. Later this custom was principally used by families which traced their descent from royalty.

heathen gods, keep holy the seventh day and not work, and fast every seventh day. And as soon as the king had said that before the people, there was straightway a mighty uproar; the bonders growled that the king would take their work from them, and said that in that way they could not till the land; the labourers and thralls thought that they could not work, if they should get no food. They also said that it was the hereditary vice of King Hacon and his father and their kinsmen to be niggardly with food, although they were generous with gold. Asbiorn from Medalhus[1] in Guldale stood up and answered his speech thus: "We bonders thought, King Hacon", said he, "when thou hadst the first thing here in Trondheim and we took thee as king and got back from thee our *odal* lands, that we had taken heaven in our very hands. But now we know not if we indeed have got our freedom, or if thou wilt thrall-bind us anew in this strange wise, that we must forgo the faith which our fathers and all our forefathers had before us, first in the burning age and now in the howe age;[2] they were much greater than we and all the same this faith has availed us well. We have shown thee so great a love that we let thee have thy way in making all the laws and the land rights. Now it is our will and the bonders' also, to keep the laws which thou madest for us here at the Frosta thing and into which we entered; we will all follow thee and hold thee for king as long as there is alive one of the bonders here at the thing, if thou, O king, wilt forbear with us and bid us only such things as we can give thee and which are not unmeet for us to do. But if thou wilt take up this matter with so great zeal and use force and might over us, then have we bonders made up our mind to part from thee and take us another king who can help us freely to hold the faith that we wish. Now shalt thou, O king, choose between these two ways by the time the thing is ended". At these words the bonders cried out and said that so would they have it.

Asbiorn of Medalhus answers the king

16. When everything was still, Sigurd the Jarl answered and said that "it is King Hacon's wish to agree with you bonders and never to be parted from your friendship". The bonders said they wished

---

1 *Medalhus*, now Melhus in Guldale near Trondheim.    2 About *burning age* and *howe age*, cf. Snorre Sturlason's Preface, p. xxxvi.

the king to sacrifice for them for good seasons and peace, as his father had done. The uproar then ceased and the thing ended. Sigurd the Jarl afterwards spoke with the king and said that he must not altogether fail to do what the bonders wished and that there was nothing else for it. "It is, O king, as thou thyself canst hear, the will and anxious demand of the leaders and therewith all the folk. We shall, O king, soon enough find some good counsel", and that was now arranged between the king and the jarl.

17. In the autumn towards Winter Day there was a blood offering at Lade and thither the king went. Formerly, when he was present where there was an offering, he had always been wont to hold a meal with a few men in a little house; but the bonders now complained that he sat not in his high-seat, when this would please his people most; the jarl then said that he should not now do so and then it happened that the king did sit in his high-seat. And when the first bowl was poured out, Sigurd the Jarl spoke and blessed it in the name of Odin and drank to the king from the horn. The king took it and made the sign of the Cross over it. Then said Kar of Gryting,[1] "Wherefore does the king so? Will he even now not sacrifice?" Sigurd the Jarl answered, "The king does as all do, who trust in their skill and strength; he blesses his bowl in the name of Thor, and makes the sign of the hammer over it before he drinks". All was quiet in the evening, but the day after, when they went to the table, the bonders thronged round the king and said that he must now eat horse flesh. That would the king in no wise do. They bade him drink the soup, but he would not. Then they bade him eat the fat; he would not do that either; and then they nearly turned against him. Sigurd the Jarl said that he would make it up with them and bade them keep back their anger; he bade the king gape over the kettle handle where the steam of the soup had blown and made it greasy. The king went and put a linen cloth on the handle and gaped over it, and thereafter went to the high-seat; but none of them was satisfied.

18. The following winter, Yule feast was prepared for the king in Mæren.[2] When it was near Yule the eight chiefs, who mostly controlled the offerings in the whole of Trondlaw, held a meeting amongst themselves. From the outskirts of Trondheim there were four, Kar of Gryting, Asbiorn of Medalhus, Torberg of Varnes[3] and Orm of

---

1 Kar is very like Kerr and Carr. The names are pronounced in the same way in Norse. *Gryting* was the old name for the present vicarage (with farm adjoining) in the Orkedale. 2 *Mæren* was situated in Sparebuen district. 3 *Varnes*, now Værnes in Nedre Stjordalen (or Nether Stjordale).

Ljoxa;[1] and among the Inner Tronds were Blotolv of Ölvi's haug,[2] Narfi of Stav[3] in Værdale, Trond Haki of Egge[4] and Tore Skegg of Husebö[5] at Inderöy. These eight men agreed that the four of the Outer Tronds should destroy Christianity and the four of the Inner Tronds should require the king to come to the offering. The

Sigurd the Jarl prevails upon the king to give in to the bonders

Outer Tronds went with four ships south to Möre, slew there three priests and burned three churches; they then went home. And when King Hacon and Sigurd the Jarl came into Mæren with their army, the bonders were come there in great numbers. The first day of the guest feast the bonders thronged about the king and bade him make the offering and otherwise threatened him with force. Sigurd the Jarl went between them and it came about that King Hacon ate some bits of horse liver and then drank all the 'remembrance' (*minni*) bowls which the bonders poured out for him, without making the sign of the Cross. And when the guest feast was at an end, the king and the jarl went out to Lade. The king was very unhappy and wished straightway to go away from Trondheim with all his army, and said that another time he would come to Trondheim with a mightier force and then would reply to the Tronds for that enmity which they had shown him. Sigurd the Jarl bade the king not give the Tronds cause for that, and said that it would not be good for the king to threaten or harry the people in the land and least of all where the land's greatest strength was, in Trondheim. The king was so wroth that no man could come to speak with him; he went away from Trondheim south to Möre and stayed there during the winter and the spring, but when summer came he drew folk to him. Word went about that he was going with this army against the Tronds.

19. King Hacon went on board his ships and had there many men. Tidings then came to him south from the land, that Eric's sons had come south from Denmark to the Vik and news further followed that they had driven King Trygvi Olavson from his ships, east by Sotanes;[6] then they had harried far and wide in the Vik and

---

1 *Ljoxa*, now Lexviken on the west side of the Trondheimsfjord.   2 *Ölvi's haug*, now Alstahaug in Skogn district.   3 *Stav*, a big farm in the Værdale (which no longer exists). 4 *Egge*, in Egge district.   5 *Husebö*, now Hustad at Inderöy.   6 *Sotanes* is a peninsula in Ranrik west of the Abyfjord.

many men had gone over to them. When the king learned these tidings, he thought he had need of help from the people; he then sent word to Sigurd the Jarl and the other chiefs from whom he expected help, to come to him. Sigurd the Jarl came and brought with him a great army; in it were all the Tronds who most of all in the winter had forced the king to make the offering; they were all reconciled to the king at the request of Sigurd the Jarl. King Hacon then went south along the land and when he came near by Stad, he learned that Eric's sons had come to North Agder. Both armies then went to meet each other; they met near Karmt.¹ Both armies went up from their ships and fought on Agvaldsnes;² both were strong in men and there was now a great battle. King Hacon went forth boldly and against him came King Guthorm Ericson with his following and they exchanged blows with one another. There fell King Guthorm, his standard was hewn down and many men fell about him. After that the army of the sons of Eric was put to flight and they fled to their ships and rowed away; they had lost many folk. About it Guthorm Sindri says:

> The ring waster let his swords     There went one king from the strife
> Swing over the warriors' head.     Slain by the weapons of another.

King Hacon went to his ships and sailed east after Gunhild's sons (Eric's sons); both armies went as fast as they could till they came to East Agder. Then the sons of Eric sailed out to sea and went south to Jutland. About that Guthorm Sindri says:

> The kin-host began     The shield-bearer steered
> To feel the sword-bearer's     His ships out to sea,
> Great might (I am often     And all Eric's sons
> Mindful of that gladly).     Had to flee thence.

Afterwards King Hacon went back north to Norway and Eric's sons then stayed a long time in Denmark.

20. After that battle King Hacon enacted a law over all the land along the coast and as far inland as the salmon leaps and made all the districts into *Skipreider*, and further divided the *Skipreider* amongst the various shires.³ It was then arranged how many and how big should be the ships that each shire supplied, to be ready from each

---

1 *Karmt* is the island Karmöy, situated close to Haugesund (West Norway).    2 Cf. 'History of Harald Hairfair', p. 71, n. 6.    3 Each *Skipreide* had to supply the king with a certain number of ships and men in case of war. The Cinque Ports in England was a somewhat similar institution, for which the first existing charter dates back to the beginning of Edward I's reign. This charter refers to previous charters made by the Conqueror and Edward the Confessor.

shire when the full levy was called out, and full levy was demanded
whenever foreign armies were in the land. It was also part of the
men's duty to make beacons on the high fells near enough to be
seen one by another, and so say men that the calling up of the army
went from the southernmost beacon to the most northerly thing in
Halogaland within seven nights.

21. Eric's sons were often raiding in the eastern countries and
sometimes they harried in Norway, as already related, but when
King Hacon was ruling the land, there were good seasons and peace
in the land and he was the most beloved of kings.

22. When King Hacon had been King of Norway for twenty
years, Eric's sons came from the south from Denmark and they had
a great army. There were many who had followed them on their raids,
and still greater was the army of Danes which Harald Gormson had
given them. They had a fair wind and sailed out from Vendel and
came into Agder; they steered north along the land and sailed night
and day, but the beacons were not lighted because it was the custom
to start the beacons along the land from the east, but the eastern men
were not aware of the raid. Besides if the beacons were wrongfully
lighted the king had made great penalties for those men who were by
law found guilty of it, because warships and vikings often went by
the outer isles and harried. The landsmen would then often believe
that Eric's sons had arrived and then the bale fires would be lighted
and the call to arms fly through the whole land. But Eric's sons
would go back to Denmark if they did not have with them the Danish
army but only their own folk; at other times it might be other kind
of vikings. King Hacon was very wroth over this, when it only ended
in troubles and expense and no gain; the bonders also complained of
it on their side when this happened, and this was the reason why no
news came out about Eric's sons' raid, till they got as far north as
Ulvasund.[1] There they lay for seven nights; then tidings were sent
along the upper way over Eidet[2] north to Möre, but King Hacon was
then in South Möre on an island called Frædi,[3] on his estate Birkestrand,[4] and he had no folk with him except his household and the
bonders who had been his guests.

23. Spies came to King Hacon and brought him news that Eric's

---

1 *Ulvasund,* the sound between Vagsöy and the mainland near Moldöy, the northern
part of Nordfjord.    2 *Eidet,* i.e. Mandseidet in Statland.    3 The island of *Frædi,*
now Fredöy, is situated in North Möre (Nordmöre), but it might have belonged to South
Möre (Sondmöre) at that time.    4 *Birkestrand* is on the east side of Fredöy, some
distance north-east of Frey's Church (Frei Kirke) and Frey's Howe (Freihaugen).

sons were lying to the south of Stad with a great army. He then called to him those men present who were wisest and sought their counsel whether he should fight with Eric's sons, although they had a great multitude against them, or whether they should fare northwards and gather a greater army. Egil Wool-Sark[1] was the name of a bonder who was there at the time. He was very old but had been greater and stronger than all others and a great warrior; he had long borne King Harald Hairfair's standard. Egil answered the king's speech: "I have been in some of the battles of King Harald, your father; he sometimes fought with a greater army, sometimes with a smaller, but he always had the victory; I have never heard him seek counsel that his friends should teach him how to flee. We would rather not teach you that counsel, king, for we are thought to have a brave chief and you shall have powerful help from us". Many others also supported that speech. The king also said that he had most desire to fight with such as he could gather. That was agreed upon. The king then bade them shear up arrows which he sent in all directions and he drew together as many men as he could get. Then said Egil Wool-Sark: "For a while during the long peace, I feared that I should die of old age in my straw bed, but I would rather fall in battle following my chief; it may now be that it will so happen".[2]

24. Eric's sons sailed north round Stad as soon as they had a fair wind. When they came there they learned where King Hacon was and went against him. King Hacon had nine ships; he lay with his vessels north under Frædarberg[3] in Féeyarsund, but Eric's sons lay to the south of the same cape and they had more than twenty ships. King Hacon sent them word bidding them go on land and said that he had hedged in with hazel boughs a place of battle on Rastarkalf,[4] where there is a flat field at the foot of a long and rather low ridge. Eric's sons then left their ships, proceeded north through the pass over Frædarberg and forth into Rastarkalf. Egil then spoke to King Hacon and asked for ten men and ten standards. The king granted this, and Egil went up under the ridge[5] and King Hacon went down on the level land with his men, set up his standard, drew up his men and said: "We shall have a long line so that they cannot surround us if they have more men than we". They did so and there was a great and sharp battle. Egil then had his ten standards set up and dispersed the men who bore them in such a way that they should go as near the

1 The O.N. for *Woolsark* was *Ullserc* or *Ullserk*.　　2 To die on a bed of sickness was considered dishonourable.　　3 *Frædarberg*, now Freihaugen on Fredöy.　　4 *Rastarkalf* is the field north of Freihaugen.　　5 This ridge is called Skrubhaugen.

bank as possible and leave a great space open between each of them. They did so and they went forth near the bank as if they were coming behind the army of Eric's sons. Those who stood uppermost in the line of Eric's sons' troops saw that many standards were waving and fluttering over the bank; they thought that many men followed who would come upon them from behind, between them and their ships. There was a great uproar and everyone told the other what was astir. Thereupon was there flight among their army, and when the kings saw it they also fled. King Hacon pursued them hardily, followed the fleeing men and slew many.

25. When Gamle Ericson came up on to the pass above the hill, he turned round and then saw that there were no more people following them than they had fought with and that it was a trick. Then King Gamle had a war blast blown, set up his standard and drew up his line. All his Norse followers answered the call but the Danes fled to their ships, and when King Hacon and his men came up to them there was again the keenest of fights; this time King Hacon had more men. The end was that Eric's sons fled. They made for the south over the pass and some of their folk took the way to the south towards the hill, and King Hacon followed them. To the east of the pass and on the west of the hill there is a flat piece of ground, but steep rocks lie on the west side. Then Gamle's men went thence on to the hill, but King Hacon came upon them so boldly that he slew some, whilst others leaped down from the rocks and all were killed; the king left not till every man was slain.

26. Gamle Ericson also fled from the pass down to the flat ground to the south of the hill. Then King Gamle again turned about and continued to battle; men came back to him and his brothers also came with a great following. Egil Wool-Sark was the foremost of Hacon's men and pressed forward; he exchanged blows with King Gamle. King Gamle got great wounds, but Egil fell and many men with him. Then King Hacon came up with the troop which had followed him and there was another fight. King Hacon pressed forward hardily and struck blows on both sides of him and slew one after another. Thus says Guthorm Sindri:

| | |
|---|---|
| The coward army fled | The warrior who had struck |
| Before the brisk warrior, | So dauntless a blow |
| The strong-minded king | Guarded himself without shields |
| Went fighting before the standard. | In the Valkyries' meeting. |

Eric's sons saw their men falling on all sides and then they turned in flight to their ships, but those, who had fled to the ships before, had run the ships out and some of them lay up on the beach. Then Eric's sons and all the men who were with them leaped out into the sea. Gamle Ericson fell there, but his other brothers reached the ships and then sailed away with the men who had escaped and afterwards went south to Denmark.

27. King Hacon took the ships which lay on the beach and which Eric's sons had owned and he had them drawn up on land. There in a ship King Hacon had Egil Wool-Sark laid and those of his men who had fallen with him; he had earth and stones borne to it. King Hacon also had other ships set up and the dead laid in them, and these howes are still seen to the south of Frædarberg. When Glum Geirason in his verse vaunted the death of King Hacon, Eyvind Scalda-spiller composed this verse:

> Once the victorious prince
> Dyed his sword in Gamle's blood
> (When anger swelled
> In the beach fighters' breasts),
>
> And he drove out to sea
> All Eric's heirs.
> Deeply now the warriors
> Mourn over the king.

Standing-stones on Egil
Wool-Sark's grave

High standing-stones were raised on Egil Wool-Sark's howe.

28. When King Hacon, the foster-son of Athelstan, had been king in Norway for twenty-six winters after his brother Eric had left the land, he happened to be in Hordaland and held a feast at Fitjar in Stord;[1] he had there his household and many bonders as his guests. And when the king sat at breakfast the watchmen who were without saw that many ships were sailing from the south and were not far from the island. Then they said one to another that the king should be told that they thought an army was coming against them; but it seemed not easy for some to give the king the war cry, for he had set penalties for any who did so. Yet it seemed wrong that the king should not know it. Then one of them went into the room and bade Eyvind Finnson come straightway out with him; he said that it was very necessary. Eyvind at once went, and came out to where the ships could be seen; then he saw that a great army was

1 The island of Stord in Hordaland (south of Bergen).

sailing there, and went straight back to the room before the king
and said:         Quickly does the hour fleet,
                  But long sit men at meat.

The king looked at him and said: "What is astir?" Eyvind said:

| | |
|---|---|
| The Avengers of Blood-axe | Hard it is to utter the war cry; |
| Are calling us to the keen clash | Though I readily wish thy honour, |
| Of swords; we are given | O king! Now shall we go |
| No chance of sitting. | Straight to take up the weapons. |

The king said: "Thou art so good a man, Eyvind, that thou wilt not
say the war cry unless it is true". He then had the table taken down,
and went out and saw the ships; he then saw that they were warships
and spoke to his men about the plan they should take, whether they
should fight with such folk as they had or whether they should go to
their ships and sail thence to the north. "It is easy for us to see", he
said, "that we shall now have to fight against a much greater army
than we have yet done, though we have often seemed to have great
difference in numbers, when we have had to fight with Gunhild's
sons." They gave no hasty answer to this. Then said Eyvind:

| | |
|---|---|
| Warrior king! It is not fitting | Now it is, that Harald leads |
| For the sea warrior | The broad boats from the south |
| To steer the ship farther north | On the sea king's swelling ways; |
| (But we will not dally). | We will quickly take up our shields. |

The king answered, "Manfully is that speech and near to my own
mind; but yet will I hear what other men think about this". And
when the men understood how the king would have it, many answered and said that they would rather fall in manly fight than flee
from the Danes without trying; they also said that they had often had
the victory even though they had had fewer men. The king thanked
them well for their words and bade them arm themselves and so they
did. The king threw on his brynie (armour) and took his sword
Kvernbit (i.e. the millstone-biter),[1] set on his head a golden helmet,
had a spear in his hand and a shield by his side. Thereupon he drew
up his guard in line and the bonders with it and set up his standards.

29. Harald Ericson was at that time the chief of his brothers after
Gamle's death. They had gathered in the south a great army from
Denmark. In their following there were with them their mother's
brothers, Eyvind Skröia and Alf Askman. These men were strong
and able and the greatest of man-killers. The sons of Eric steered
their ships to the island, went up on land and arrayed their men.

1 Cf. 'History of Harald Hairfair', p. 73.

So it is said that the proportion of their men could not have been less than six to one, so great was the man strength of Eric's sons.

30. King Hacon then had drawn up his line and it is said that the king threw off his brynie before the battle began. Thus says Eyvind Scaldaspiller in Hakonarmal:

> There they found Björn's brother, etc. (See p. 99.)
> He egged on the Haleygers, etc. (See p. 99.)
> The warriors' lord flung off his war clothes, etc. (See p. 99.)

King Hacon chose men for his guard much according to strength and courage, just as his father Harald had done. Toralv the Strong, the son of Skolm, was there and walking by the king's side; he had helm, shield and spear and a sword which was called *Fetbreid*; it was said that he and the king were equally strong, and about it Tord Sjarekson says in the poem he made about Toralv:

> There where those battle-hardened       In Stord at Fitjar;
> Warriors fought boldly,                  And this warrior dared to go
> The army went gladly to sword-play   Nearest to the Norsemen's king.

And when the armies came together, there was a hot and bloody battle; when they had shot their spears, the men drew their swords and then King Hacon and Toralv with him went forth by the standard and struck out on all sides. Thus says Eyvind Scaldaspiller:

> Then the sword rested, etc. (See p. 100.)
> Shields and hard skulls, etc. (See p. 100.)

King Hacon was easier to recognise than other men; his helmet lit up as the sun shone on it and many bore their weapons against him. Then Eyvind Finnson took a hat and set it over the king's helmet.

31. Eyvind Skröia then shouted loudly: "Doth the Norsemen's king now hide himself or has he fled, for where is now the golden helmet?" Then Eyvind and his brother Alf went forth and struck out on all sides and bore themselves as though they were frantic or mad. King Hacon shouted loudly to Eyvind, "Hold forth as thou art, if thou wilt find the Norsemen's king!"[1] Thus says Eyvind Scaldaspiller:

> The warrior who was grim        If thou, in thy lust for victory,
> Towards gold but true to his own,   Wilt seek the battle's leader,
> Bade Skröia not to turn            So hold thou forth
> Away from fighting,                Against the Norsemen's king.

There was little time to wait till Eyvind came thither, lifted his sword and struck at the king. Toralv shot his shield against it and Eyvind

---

[1] The O.N. text reads: *ef þu vilt finna Nordmanna konung.*

staggered therewith; the king then took the sword Kvernbit in both hands and struck Eyvind over the helm and so cleft the helm and the head right down to the shoulders. Thereupon Toralv slew Alf Askman. Thus says Eyvind Scaldaspiller:

I know that the sword
Held in both hands of the king
Did little good
To the warship's steersman.

The warrior king, who harried
The Danes, cleft the viking's head
Right down to the shoulders
With the gold-hilted sword.

After the fall of both brothers, King Hacon went forth so hardily that all fell back before him. Terror came into the army of Eric's sons and at last flight. King Hacon was foremost of his own army and followed fast the fleeing men and struck both sharp and hard. Then flew a kind of arrow (called a *flein*)[1] which struck King Hacon's arm in the muscle below the shoulder; and it is said by many men that Gunhild's shoe boy (who was called Kisping) leaped forth in the crowd shouting, "Make room for the king's bane-man", and shot the arrow at King Hacon, but others say that no one knows who shot it and it can well be so, for arrows and spears and all kinds of shooting weapons were flying as thickly as the snow drifts. Many men of Eric's sons fell both on the battlefield and on the road to the ships or on the beach and many leaped into the sea. All Eric's sons and many others reached the ships and rowed away forthwith with Hacon's men after them. Thus says Tord Sjarekson:

Thus shall peace be ended:
The slayer of robbers, foremost of his
      people,
Protected his land widely
(He could not approach old age).
The battle begun, when Gunhild's heirs
Landed from the south
(The generous prince put them to flight,
But the warrior fell in the fight).

Weariness was seen, when the
      wounded
Bonders sank down on the seats
Where they were rowing.
So one after another fell.
Well is it said of manliness
That the mighty warrior who gave
Drinks of blood to Hugin[2]
Went nighest to Hacon in the fight.

32. King Hacon went out on his ship and let them bind his wound, but the blood ran so strongly that no man could stop it and when it drew near evening he lost strength. He then said that he would go north to Alrekstader[3] to his house there; and when they came north to Hakonshella,[4] they lay in there. The king was then nearing death

---

1 *Flein* is an arrow with two hooks at the point.    2 *Hugin* and *Munin* (i.e. mind and memory) were the two ravens that sat on Odin's shoulders, and told him news from the four quarters of the world. See further Brewer's *Dictionary of Phrase and Fable*, new and revised edition, p. 634.    3 Cf. 'History of Harald Hairfair', p. 71, n. 2.
4 Cf. 'History of Harald Hairfair', p. 71, n. 8.

and he called his friends to him and told them the settlement of the kingdom that he wished. He had only one daughter, Thora, and no son.[1] He bade them send word to Eric's sons, that they should be the kings of the land; and he bade them show goodness towards his friends and kinsmen. "And even if I shall be granted life," he said, "yet will I go from the land unto Christian men and atone for what I have done in sin against God, and if I die here in heathendom, so give me a grave as seems best to you".[2] A little after this King Hacon died there at the place where he was borne. They sorrowed so much over him that both friends and foes wept over his death and said that never again would such a good king come to Norway. His friends bore his body north to Seim,[3] in North Hordaland, and there they threw up a great howe and laid the king in it, fully armed with the best of his array, but with no other goods. They spoke by his grave, as was customary among heathen men, and showed him to Valhall. Eyvind Scaldaspiller made a poem about King Hacon's death and how he was received in Valhall. It is called Hakonarmal, and the beginning of it reads thus:

Gauta-Tyr sent the Valkyries
Gondul and Skogul[4]
To choose[5] amongst the kings
Which of Yngvi's race
Should go to Odin
And be in Valhall.

There they found Björn's brother
Arrayed in his brynie,
The king most costly
Coming 'neath the standard.[6]
Bows were drawn;
Spears trembled;
The battle began.

He egged on the Haleygers[7]
And all the Holmerygers;[8]
The bane of the jarls
Hastened to battle.
Good was the prince's
Following of Norsemen;
The slayer of Danes
With his helm shining.

The warriors' lord
Flung off his war clothes,
Slipped off his brynie,
Before he began.

---

1 The law of Norway prevents a woman from occupying the throne.  2 The O.N. text reads: *Enn ef ec dey her i heidni, þa veiti mer her gröpt þann er ydr syniz.*  3 Cf. 'History of Harald Hairfair', p. 71, n. 3.  4 The name of two Valkyries, Odin's swift fighting-maids. In O.N. they were called *Göndol* and *Scögol*.  5 In O.N. *kiosa*, i.e. to choose or elect. The Parliament of the Manxmen, the House of Keys, derives its name from O.N. *kiosa*.  6 The text in O.N. reads *Kominn und gunnfana*, i.e. 'Coming (or had come) under Gonfanon'. *Gonfanon* was the name of the standard which the Normans—true to their Norse traditions—used at the battle of Hastings in 1066. See further the celebrated Norman historical work *Roman de Rou* by Robert Wace (in edition printed at Rouen in 1827 on pp. 170 and 195). Robert Wace lived 1112–84.  7 The men from Halogaland (North Norway).  8 *Holmerygers*, i.e. the inhabitants of the islands (holmes) in Rogaland (in the Stavanger district).

The gladdest of fighters
He played with his liegemen;
Under his gold helm
He would guard the land.

Then the sword rested
In Sikling's hand[1]
In Valfather's[2] clothes,
As through the water
The sword points crashed,
Shields were turned,
Swords whistled
On the wounded skulls.

Shields and hard skulls
Were both cleft
By the hardy blows
Of the Norsemen's lord,
In the island battle,
Where the kings dyed
The bright ramparts of shields
In the blood of warriors.

Wound brands burned
In bloody sores,
Long axes stooped
To take life.
High swelled the wound seas
On the ness of swords;
The arrows flew
On the shore of Stordöy.[3]

The spear waves raged
In Skogul's cloud storm
Under the red shield's heaven,
The blood waves roared in Odin's gale;
Many a warrior sank
Under the sword stream.

There sat the Daglings[4]
With swords drawn,
Their shields were split,
And brynies stricken.
That army was not glad of heart;
It was on the way to Valhall.

Gondul said
As she took a spear shaft,
"The Asers'[5] following grows,
When Hacon the High
Goes with so great an army
To the bourgh of the gods".

The king heard
What the battle maids said,
Those quick horsewomen,
They were ready to strike,
As they sat helmeted,
With shields by their side.

(Hacon said)
"Why, Skogul, hast thou
So fated the battle?
We were still worthy to win!"
(Skogul said)
"We willed it,
That thou held the wold
And thy foes are fled!"

Said the rich Skogul,
"Gondul and I shall ride
To the gods' green home
To tell Odin
That quickly the prince
Comes himself to see him".

"Hermod and Bragi",
Said the war father Odin,
"Go forth to meet Hacon,
For that warrior king
Is called hither to the hall."

The king said this—
He came from the fight,
And there he stood bloody and
    pale:
"Fierce in mind
Odin me seems,
Ill is his look".

1 *Sikling* = sea king.    2 *Valfather*, i.e. Odin.    3 *Stordöy*, the island of Stord.
4 *Dagling* = prince.    5 *Aser* or *Æser* = the gods in Valhall.

"*Einherjar*",[1] quoth Bragi,
"Be ye welcome.
Take ale[2] with the Asers,
O ruler of jarls,
Thou hast here
Eight of thy brothers".

"Our weapons",
Said the wise king,
"Shall we ourselves guard;
Cared for by us shall be
Both helmet and brynie.
Good it is to have them whole."

Now it is known
That the king had guarded
Well the temples,
So Hacon the Good
Was welcomed with gladness
By the kind gods.

That warrior king is born
On a lucky day
Who has such lofty mind.
His time here
Shall always be
Full of praise and glory.

Unbound
Against all the world
The wolf Fenri[3] will go,
Till in his destroying tracks
Kings of equal worth
Are found.

Wealth dies,
Kinsmen die,
The land is laid waste.
Since Hacon fared
To the heathen gods
Many are thralls and slaves.[4]

## CHRONOLOGY

### HACON THE GOOD. KING OF NORWAY 934–961

934. Hacon, Athelstan's foster-son, comes from England and is made King by the Trondheim people.
935. Eric Blood-axe goes raiding.
939. Eric Blood-axe becomes King of Northumberland.
940. Death of King Athelstan.
      Eric is expelled.
945. Hacon the Good fights in Denmark and Sweden.
947. Eric is again elected King of Northumberland.
950. Death of Eric Blood-axe at Steinmore in England.
955. Battle of Rastarkalf.
961. Death of Hacon the Good after the battle on the island of Stord.

1 *Einherjar* was the name of the warriors who came to Odin in Valhall.    2 In the O.N. text *öl* is used for ale. In *Alvismal* (the Elder Edda) it is stated in verse 35 that "*öl* among men is called *bior* among the gods".    3 The wolf *Fenri* was Loki's offspring begotten with a giantess. Cf. 'Ynglinga Saga', p. 11, n. 3.    4 This is supposed to allude to Hacon's successor, who was tyrannical and disliked.

# V

## THE HISTORY OF ERIC'S SONS
### (961–963)

1. Eric's sons now took over the kingdom of Norway, after King Hacon had fallen. Harald was the most honoured amongst them, and of those who were then alive he was the eldest. Their mother Gunhild had much of the ruling with them and she was called the King-Mother. At that time there were the following chiefs in the land: Trygvi Olavson had the land in the east, Gudröd Björnson had Vestfold, Sigurd Ladejarl had Trondheim and Gunhild's sons had the Midlands. The first winter, words and messengers went between Gunhild's sons and the kings Trygvi and Gudröd, and it was arranged that the latter should have just as big a share of the kingdom from Gunhild's sons as they had formerly held of King Hacon. There was a man called Glum Geirason, who was King Harald's scald and a bold man. He made this verse about King Hacon's fall:

| | |
|---|---|
| Well has Harald avenged | When the ravens |
| Gamle, and Hacon's swains | Drank Hacon's blood. |
| Found death; but fame | The sword from across the sea |
| Did the war leader win | Was, as I heard, all dyed with blood. |

That verse was very much liked, and when Eyvind Finnson heard it, he uttered a verse which is written above:

Once the victorious prince, etc. (See 'History of Hacon the Good', p. 95.)

That verse was also often given forth. But when King Harald heard it he threatened him with his death for it, until the friends of both of them reconciled them on the understanding that Eyvind should be his scald, just as he had been King Hacon's. There was near kinship between them, in that Eyvind's mother was Gunhild the daughter of Halvdan the Jarl, and her mother was Ingebjörg, daughter of Harald Hairfair. Then did Eyvind make a verse about King Harald:

| | |
|---|---|
| Little they said, lord | Nor when thou didst swing |
| Of Hordaland, thou lost heart | The bloody, biting, sword in thy hand, |
| When the wound hail burst the brynies, | Nor when thou, Harald, |
| | Didst stem the wolves' hunger. |
| And the bows all bent together, | |

Gunhild's sons stayed mostly in the Midlands, for it seemed safer to them not to be with either the Tronds or the men of the Vik, who had been King Hacon's best friends; furthermore, there were many great men in both places. Then men went bearing offers of peace between Gunhild's sons and Sigurd the Jarl, for never before had they had scot (tribute) from Trondheim. At last it came to this: the kings and the jarl made a treaty and bound it with oaths. Sigurd the Jarl was to have from them as big a land in Trondheim as he had formerly had from King Hacon; and so they were well-nigh reconciled. All Gunhild's sons were called miserly and it was said that they had hidden treasure in the earth. About that Eyvind Scaldaspiller made the following:

| | |
|---|---|
| In the whole of King Hacon's days | Always in Hacon's time |
| We had in our lands | There shone in the scald's hands |
| Such seed as was sown on the Fyrisvold,[1] | Gold like that |
| O thou sword-fighter! | In Fulla's headband. |
| But now has the foe of the folk | Now is the gleaming gold hidden |
| Hidden in Thor's own mother earth | In the giant-killing Thor's |
| Such meal as King Frode's women thralls | Mother earth—but the |
| Ground in their mill.[2] | Hard men's will is unmoved. |

When King Harald learned the truth of this verse, he sent for Eyvind, bidding him come to him; and when Eyvind came, the king accused him and said he was no friend of his; "and it will be ill with thee to show me falseness", he said, "for thou hast already been made my man". Then Eyvind quoth a verse:

| | |
|---|---|
| One chief have I had, | I was true to the generous prince, |
| Till I knew thee; | For I never yet bore two shields. |
| But age overpowers me, | O king, thy flock can I follow, |
| So I expect not a third. | For age will soon fell me. |

King Harald then gave his judgment. Eyvind had a big and good gold ring called Moldi; it had formerly been taken out of the earth. Now the king said he would have that ring and there was no other choice. Then quoth Eyvind:

| | |
|---|---|
| Ruler of ships! I suppose at length | If only thou hadst this gold ring |
| I should win thy goodness | Which my father had so long. |

Eyvind thereafter went home and it is not said whether he ever met King Harald after that.

2. Gunhild's sons had taken up Christianity in England, as is written already ('History of Hacon the Good', chapter 3). But when they came to rule in Norway they could do nothing to make the men

---

1 *The seed on the Fyrisvold* = gold, because Rolf Krake used to sow gold on the Fyrisvold. Cf. 'Ynglinga Saga', chapter 29.    2 The women thralls of King Frode ground gold in their mill.

of the land Christians; but wherever they came they broke down temples and destroyed the sacrifice and from that they got many foes. It happened in their days that the seasons became bad in the land, for the kings were many and each of them had his own separate guards. Their costs were high and moreover they were greedy for goods. They did not keep the laws which King Hacon had made, except those which pleased them. They were all very good-looking men, strong and big and skilful in all sports. Thus says Glum Geirason in the poem he made about Harald Gunhildson:

> The open-handed prince,　　　　Knew twelve different games,
> Who went forth to battle,　　　All of them kingly ones.

Often all the brothers went together, but sometimes each went for himself. They were grim and crafty men, great warriors and very victorious.

3. Gunhild the King-Mother and her sons often met together in counsel and talked and planned about the ruling of the land; and one

Gunhild the King-Mother upbraids her sons and urges them to fight

time Gunhild asked her sons: "What are you doing to let things go so badly north in Trondheim? You bear the name of kings, just as your forefathers before you have done; but you have few men and little land and you are too many to share the land. In the east Trygvi and Gudröd have the Vik and they have some claim upon it by their birth; but Sigurd the Jarl rules all over the Trondlaw and I know not what obligation you have to let only a jarl rule over so great a land; unless you also have some say. It seems strange to me that you go every summer on viking raids to other lands, but you let a jarl in the land take your father's legacy from you. It would seem a small matter for King Harald, thy father's father whom thou art called after, to take from a jarl his land and life—he who won all Norway for himself and ruled over it afterwards till his death". Harald answered, "It is not", he said, "like cutting up a kid or a calf, to slay Sigurd the Jarl. Sigurd the Jarl is of high birth and has many kinsmen and he is friendly and wise; I think that if he learns with truth to expect enmity from us, then all the Tronds will be there where he is. We shall then have no errand thither, except an ill one. It seems to me as if it would not be safe for any of us brothers to stay amongst the Tronds". Then said Gunhild: "We shall then take another way with our plan, that will give us less trouble. Harald and Erling shall stay in the autumn in North Möre and I will also go with you: we shall all try together what we can do". Now did they act in this wise.

4. Sigurd the Jarl's brother was called Grjotgard and he was much younger and much less honoured, nor had he the name of jarl, although he had followers and during the summer went on viking raids and got himself goods. King Harald sent men into Trondheim to Sigurd the Jarl with friendly gifts and friendly words. They said that King Harald would have such friendship with him as Sigurd the Jarl had formerly had with King Hacon. It also followed with the sending of such words that the jarl should come to King Harald and they would then knit their friendship fully. Sigurd the Jarl received well the messengers and the king's friendship; he said that because of much business he could not go to the king, but he sent him friendly gifts and words both good and blithe in thanks for his friendship. The messengers went away; they went to Grjotgard and bore the same message to him—King Harald's friendship and invitation and goodly gifts therewith. And when the messengers went home, Grjotgard promised to come. On the appointed day Grjotgard came to King Harald and Gunhild. They received him gladly and he was held in so great favour that he was taken into counsels of importance and many secret talks. It came about that the plan which the king and queen had arranged about Sigurd should now be taken up. They mentioned to Grjotgard how the jarl had made him a small man, but if he would be with them in that plan, then the king promised that Grjotgard should be his jarl and have all the land which Sigurd the Jarl had formerly had. The outcome of it

was that they were wholly agreed that Grjotgard should spy for the best time to fall upon Sigurd the Jarl and then send word to King Harald. After that Grjotgard went home and had goodly gifts from the king.

5. In the autumn, Sigurd the Jarl went into Stjordale and was there on a round of feasts. From there he went out to Aglo[1] and began feasting. The jarl had always many men about him whilst he trusted ill the kings, but as soon as the words of friendship had gone between him and King Harald, he did not have any great following. Grjotgard then sent word to King Harald that never again would it be so easy to go against the jarl. And straightway in the same night the Kings Harald and Erling went up into Trondheim. They had four ships and many men and they sailed during the starlit night. Grjotgard came to meet them and late that night they came to Aglo, where Sigurd the Jarl was at the feast. They put fire to the house and burned the dwellings with the jarl and his folk all inside. Early in the morning they went out into the fjord and from there they sailed south to Möre, where they stayed a long time.

1 *Aglo* is the later Skatval Sogn in Nether (or Nedre) Stjordale.

# VI

# THE HISTORY OF HACON THE JARL

HIS LEADERSHIP COMMENCED ABOUT 963

1. Sigurd the Jarl's son Hacon was at that time in Trondheim when he learned these tidings, and straightway gathered a great army from all over Trondheim; every ship which was fit for fighting was drawn down into the sea. And when the army came together they took Hacon, the son of Sigurd the Jarl, as their jarl and as leader of the army. He took the fleet out into Trondheimsfjord. And when Gunhild's sons learned that, they fared south to Raumsdale and South Möre. Both forces kept watch on each other. Sigurd the Jarl was slain two years after King Hacon's fall. Thus says Eyvind Scaldaspiller in Haleygia-tal:

And Sigurd,
Who gave
To Odin's ravens
The red blood

To drink,
Fell in death
At Aglo
Before Eric's sons.

And the prince
Undaunted
In the heat
Must give up

His life
When the land's lords
Faithlessly betray
Tyr's own kinsman.

Hacon the Jarl with the help of his kinsmen held Trondheim for three years, so that Gunhild's sons could get no scot (tribute) there. He had some battles with Gunhild's sons and they slew many men on either side. About that Einar Skalaglam says in Vellekla, which he made about Hacon the Jarl:

The oath-fast warrior
Drew out his broad fleet;
The warrior, who was glad
In Gondul's storms, stayed not long.

And the heated warriors
Heaved up the shield
When he would stop
The kings' lust for strife.

No one was able to say
That the men—the ravens' meat—

Would in that downpour of arrows
Be wanting in courage.

The warrior shook from his shield
The arrows which came like hail
From the bows.
He grimly saved the life of the wolves.

Many mighty battles
Befell, before the jarl
Inherited the eastern lands,
After the will of the gods.

Furthermore, Einar tells how Hacon the Jarl avenged his father:

For the revenge, which the lord
Of the swelling sea-horse had for his
 father,
I bring forth praise:
He learned to swing the sword.

The rain of weapons poured
Down far on the hersers' life.

The storm of swords greatly increased
Odin's strong following.

And against the life of the holds[1]
The leader of the ocean steeds
Let wax the death-cold
Gale of swords.

After that the friends of both went between them and made peace,
for the bonders were weary of this
fighting and unrest in the land. And
with the counsel of mighty men it
came about that terms were made
between them by which Hacon the
Jarl was to have the land his father
Sigurd the Jarl had had, and the
kings were to have the land that
King Hacon had had before them.
It was bound with oaths. There

A great friendship sprang up between
Gunhild and Hacon the Jarl

was a great friendship between Hacon the Jarl and Gunhild, but
sometimes they laid sly traps for each other. So it went on for
another three years and Hacon then stayed peacefully in his land.

2. King Harald stayed most often in Hordaland and Rogaland
and likewise did many of his brothers, who often stayed in Hardanger.
One summer it was, that there came from Iceland an ocean-going
ship owned by men of Iceland. It was laden with skins and they
steered the ship into Hardanger, for they had heard that there was a
great gathering of folk. But when the men came to deal with them
no one would buy the skins. Then the steersman went to King Harald
(for he had known him before) and he told Harald about his trouble.
The king said that he would come to them, and so he did. King
Harald was a kindly and a very hearty man. Thither he came in a
full-manned boat. He looked on their wares and said to the steersman, "Wilt thou give me one of the grey skins?" "Willingly", said
the steersman, "and more than that." The king then took a skin and
put it about him, and after that he went down to the boat. And before
they rowed away each of his men had bought himself a skin. A few
days later there were so many men who all wished to buy skins that

1 About *holds* cf. 'History of Harald Hairfair', p. 63, n. 1. In the O.E. *Nord-leoda
laga* (VII, ch. 2, § 1), the *wergild* for a *hold* is 3000 scill. Mercian money; for a
*thegn* 1500 and for a *ceorl* 200.

not half of those who would could buy them. After that the king was called Harald Greyskin.

3. Hacon the Jarl went one winter to the Uplands to a feast, and there he slept with a woman of low birth. As the time passed the woman went with child and when it was born it was a boy; he was sprinkled with water and called Eric. The mother took the boy to Hacon the Jarl and said that he was the father. The jarl let the boy be brought up with a man called Torleiv the Wise, who dwelt up in Medaldale.[1] He was a mighty and a rich man and a good friend of the jarl. Eric soon gave great promise, he was very good-looking and early became big and strong. The jarl liked him little. Hacon himself was also very fair to look upon, not tall but strong and a great man in all sports, wise and a great warrior.

4. One harvest, Hacon the Jarl went to the Uplands and there when he came out into Hedemark, King Trygvi Olavson and King Gudröd Björnson came against him: there also came Gudbrand of the Dale. These men had counselled together and sat a long time in talk and it became known that each would be the other's friend. After that they parted and each went home to his own land. Gunhild and her sons learned that and they had misgivings that these men had been planning against the kings: they often spoke about it between themselves. And when springtime came, King Harald and his brother King Gudröd made known that in the summer they were going on a viking raid over the sea to the west or else to the eastern countries, as they were wont. Thereupon they drew their folk to them, set their ships on the water and fitted them out. And when they drank their ale of departure, there was a great drinking and over their drink many things were said. It came about that they began comparing men and something was then said about the kings themselves. One man said that King Harald was in all things the foremost of his brothers and upon that Gudröd grew very wroth and said that in no thing did he stand behind Harald and he was ready to prove it. Both then became so wroth that they bade each other fight and both ran for their weapons. But they who were wiser and less drunk, stopped them and leaped between them. They both went to their ships, but it was not now to be expected that they would fare together. Gudröd sailed east along the land, but Harald made out to sea and said he would sail to the west. When, however, he came out by the isles he made for the outer fairway to the east along the land. King Gudröd sailed east on the inner fairway to the Vik and then east across Folden.[2] He then sent a message to King Trygvi to come and

1 *Medaldale*, now Meldale in Orkedale.    2 *Folden* = Oslofjord.

meet him and they would go together in the summer and harry in the eastern countries. King Trygvi took the tidings well and readily. He heard that Gudröd had few men and Trygvi went to meet him with only one boat. They met on the east of Sotanes[1] near Veggir.[2] But when they came to talk, Gudröd's men leaped forth and slew King Trygvi and twelve men with him. He lies there where it is now called Trygvi-rör.[3]

5. King Harald sailed mostly on the outer lode; he steered into the Vik and came during the night to Tunsberg. He then learned that King Gudröd Björnson was in guest-quarters up in the land a short way from there. King Harald and his men went up, came there during the night and drew a ring round the house. King Gudröd and his men went out and there was a short fight in which Gudröd fell and many men with him. King Harald then went away to meet his brother, King Gudröd, and the two now laid the whole of the Vik under them.

6. King Gudröd Björnson had got himself a good and fitting wife and they had a son called Harald, who was sent to be brought up in Grenland,[4] by Roe the White, a chief of the land. Roe's son was Rani the Wide-faring and he and Harald were almost of the same age and were foster-brothers. After the fall of his father Gudröd, Harald, who was called "the Grenlander", fled first to the Uplands and with him there was his foster-brother Rani and a few men. There he stayed a while with his kinsmen. Now Eric's sons often sought out those men who were at strife with them and mostly those from whom they expected the strongest opposition. Harald's kinsmen and friends counselled him to go away from the land and then Harald the Grenlander went east into Sweden and sought to get on board ships, so that he could follow those men who went raiding to get themselves goods. Harald was a very doughty man. There was in Sweden a man called Tosti, one of the mightiest and greatest amongst those who did not have any title. He was a great warrior and spent much time in raiding; he was called Skogul-Tosti. Harald the Grenlander came into his following; he was with Tosti on a viking raid during the summer and he was well thought of by every man. The winter after, Harald stayed with Tosti. Tosti's daughter was called Sigrid: she was young and beautiful and very bold-minded. She was married

1 *Sotanes* (in Ranrik) between the Abyfjord and the Sotafjord (now belonging to Sweden). Cf. also 'History of Hacon the Good', chapter 19.    2 *Veggir*, now Wägga, east of Grafvarna Church, the southern part of Sotanes.    3 At *Tryggön*, on the west side of the Sotanes peninsula.    4 *Grenland* is the present Lower Telemark and Bamle district in Bratsberg.

THE HISTORY OF HACON THE JARL

afterwards to the Swedish King Eric the Victorious and their son was Olav the Swede, who was afterwards King of Sweden. Eric died in his bed at Upsala, ten winters after the fall of Styrbjörn.

7. Gunhild's sons drew a great army out from the Vik and so went north along the coast: they had men and ships from every district. They made it known that with this host they were making for Trondheim against Hacon the Jarl. These tidings were learned by the jarl, who then gathered an army together and fitted out ships. When he heard about Gunhild's sons and how great their army was, he steered with his army to Möre in the south. He harried wherever he came and slew many men; and then he sent back the Tronds' army and a troop of bonders, but he himself went warring over both Mörer and Raumsdale and kept men right in the south near Stad to spy on the army of Gunhild's sons. And when he learned that they were come to the Fjords and were waiting for a south wind to sail north round Stad, Hacon himself sailed south by Stad in the outer fairway, so that his sails could not be seen from the land. He then proceeded outside the skerries to the east along the coast and came to Denmark, sailed from there to the eastern countries and harried there in the summer. Gunhild's sons brought their army north to Trondheim, stayed there a very long time and took all scot and dues. When the summer was advancing, Sigurd Sleva and Gudröd stayed there but Harald and his other brothers went east to the Vik and with them the war host which had followed them during the summer.

8. In the autumn, Hacon the Jarl went to Helsingeland and there drew up his ships. He then went by land through Helsingeland and Jämtland, and west over the Kjöl,[1] so that he came down into Trondheim. Straightway the folk came to him and he got himself ships and steered out along the fjord. Hacon the Jarl went out to Lade and settled there during the winter, but Gunhild's sons settled in Möre. Both made raids on each other and slew many men on either side. Hacon the Jarl held fast to his lands in Trondheim and was most often there during the winter. Sometimes in the summer he went east to Helsingeland, took there his ships and went to the eastern countries harrying; sometimes, however, he sat in Trondheim and sent out his army so that Gunhild's sons could not stay north of Stad.

9. Harald Greyskin went north one summer with his army to Bjarmaland,[2] harried there and had a great fight with the Bjarmers on

1 *Kjöl*. Cf. 'History of Hacon the Good', p. 85, n. 3.     2 Cf. 'History of Harald Hairfair', p. 66, n. 1.

the banks of the Vina;[1] there King Harald had the victory and slew many; he harried far and wide in the land and got himself no end of goods. About it Glum Geirason says:

| | |
|---|---|
| In the east, the princes' foe | Well did the prince greet the spear storm |
| Swung his burning sword | When he fared on Vina's bank. |
| In the homesteads of the north, | About the young king's courage |
| Where I saw the Bjarmers run. | Word went far and wide. |

King Sigurd Sleva came to the estate of Klypp the Herse, who was the son of Tord, Horda-Kari's son; he was a mighty man and of great kin. Klypp, however, was not at home, but his wife Alov greeted the king well and there was a good feast and much drinking. Alov, the

Klypp the Herse kills King
Sigurd Sleva

wife of Klypp the Herse, was the daughter of Asbiorn and sister of Jarnskeggji from Yrjar in the north. Asbiorn's brother was Reidar, the father of Styrkar, the father of Eindridi, the father of Einar Tambarskelver. During the night the king went to Alov's bed and lay with her against her will; after that the king went away. The following autumn King Harald and his brother Sigurd went up to Voss and arranged a meeting with the bonders. At the thing the bonders went against them with weapons and would have slain them, but they betook themselves off and went away. King Harald went to Hardanger and King Sigurd to Alrekstader. And when Klypp the Herse heard this, he and his kinsmen gathered together and went against the king. The leader was Vemund Volva-break. When they came to the dwelling they bore their weapons against the king. Klypp the Herse stuck his sword right through the king and that was the death of him. But Erling the Old straightway slew Klypp on the spot.

10. King Harald Greyskin and his brother King Gudröd drew together a great army from the lands in the east, and with that army they went north to Trondheim. When Hacon heard it he gathered his folk to him, sailed south to Möre and harried there. At that time his father's brother Grjotgard was there and he was to keep the land for Gunhild's sons. He called the army out just as the kings had sent bidding. Hacon the Jarl went to meet him in battle and there Grjotgard fell with two jarls and many other men.

1 The *Vina,* i.e. the River Dvina.

About it Einar Skalaglam says:

The hardy prince had fallen
On his foes with the helm storm
And Odin's vine[1]
Started waxing.

Then three brave men,
Sons of jarls, lost their lives
In the gale of swords; and gave
Honour to the folk's friend.[2]

After that Hacon the Jarl sailed out to sea and went by the outer fairway south along the land. He came forth in the south to Denmark
and went to Harald Gormson, the Danish king. There he was welcomed and stayed with him over the winter. There was with the
Danish king another man called Harald: he was the son of Knut
Gormson and he was King Harald's brother's son; he had lately come
from a viking raid, had harried for a long time and had got himself a
good deal of riches, so that he was called Gold-Harald. He seemed
to have a certain right to become king in Denmark.

11. King Harald Greyskin and his brothers brought their army
north to Trondheim and were not withstood, so that they took scot
and dues and all the king's income and made the bonders pay great
sums of money, because the kings had for a long time got little scot
from Trondheim since Hacon the Jarl had settled there with great
strength and had no peace with the kings. In the harvest King Harald
went south in the land with the greater part of the army which had its
home there, and King Erling stayed behind with his men. Even then
he made great demands on the bonders and made their lot hard, and
the bonders growled and bore the scathe badly. So in the winter, the
bonders gathered themselves together; they had a great troop of men
and then went against King Erling where he was feasting and held
fight with him. There King Erling fell and a great number of men
with him. When Gunhild's sons were ruling over Norway there was
great want in the land and the longer they ruled the more it grew.
The bonders blamed the kings for it, so much the more as the kings
were greedy for goods and were hard on the bonders. So bad it became that the land folk well-nigh lacked everywhere corn and fish.
In Halogaland there was such great hunger and need that almost no
corn was grown there and the snow lay over all the land in the middle
of summer. Thus quoth Eyvind Scaldaspiller when he went out one
day and the snow was driving hard:

In the middle of summer
It snows on Odin's wife, the earth;

And so like the Finns we fodder
The cattle with birch brooms.[3]

---

1 *Odin's vine*, i.e. the scaldic art, poetry.   2 The king.   3 In O.N. *birkibrum* means
the buds on the birch trees.

Eyvind made a poem about all the men of Iceland and they rewarded him in such a way that every bonder gave him a scot-penny amounting to three pennies of weighed silver and which were white when broken. But when the silver came to the Althing,[1] they agreed to get a smith to refine the silver; then with the silver the smith made a cape brooch, and when the smithing was paid for, the brooch was worth fifty marks. They sent it to Eyvind, but he had the brooch cut up and with it he bought cattle for himself. About the springtime there came a shoal of herrings to certain outlying fishing places nearby. Eyvind took his huscarls and tenants in a rowing boat and rowed there where the herrings were. He said:

| | |
|---|---|
| Let us spur to the south | To learn (O noble woman!) |
| The sea steed with oars | To buy for my friends |
| After the long-tailed herring, | The roots of the sea, |
| The fish in the long net, | Which the billow swine uprooteth.[2] |

Then had his money all gone with which he had bought goods, so that he bought herrings with his arrows. He said:

| | |
|---|---|
| We bartered for the fjord-fishing | Now must I sell mostly |
| The fair cape brooch | My own arrows |
| Which the Icelanders | In order to gather |
| Sent us from afar. | The sea's good gifts. |

1 *Althing* is the famous legislative assembly in Iceland dating from 930.    2 *Billow swine*, i.e. fishing net. In some recent Norwegian translations of Snorre Sturlason the words in the O.N. text: *unn svin*=billow swine, are considered a kenning for a ship; but the scalds had more poetical expressions than this for the old viking ships!

THIS PART FINISHES 968

# VII

# THE HISTORY OF OLAV TRYGVASON

1. Astrid was the name of a woman whom King Trygvi Olavson had married. She was the daughter of Eric Bjodaskalli, a mighty man who lived in Oprostader.[1] And after Trygvi's fall she fled secretly with what loose property she could take with her. She was followed by her foster-father who was called Torolv Louse-beard and he never left her, but her other trusted men went to spy out what was told of her foes or where they were. Astrid was with child by King Trygvi, so she had herself taken out on a lake and hid herself on an island there and had a few folks with her. There she brought forth a child and it was a boy.[2] When he was sprinkled with water he was called Olav after his grandfather. There Astrid stayed secretly during the summer, but when the nights became dark and the days began to be shorter and the weather colder, she went away and took Torolv and a few others with her. They travelled secretly through peopled parts and only during the night, and they came not amongst people. They came one evening to Astrid's father, Eric, at Oprostader. They fared privily and Astrid sent a messenger to the house to tell it to Eric. He then bade his people take them to a little building and there spread a table for them with the best of cheer. And when Astrid had stayed there a short time, her followers went home, but she remained behind and kept with her two servant-maids, her son Olav, Torolv Louse-beard and his son Torgils who was six winters old; they remained there during the winter.

2. After the death of Trygvi Olavson Harald Greyskin and his brother Gudröd went to those estates which Trygvi had owned. But Astrid was then away and they learned nothing of her. The rumour came to them that she was probably with child by Trygvi. In the autumn they went north in the land, as is written above ('History of Hacon the Jarl', chapter 7), and when they found their mother Gunhild they told her the news of all that had happened on their journey. She asked carefully about Astrid and they told her the rumour that they had heard about her. But because Gunhild's sons had been

---

1 There is an important place of this name at Jæderen (near Stavanger), but judging from Snorre Sturlason's narrative Astrid's father must have lived at a farm of similar name in the east of Norway. The three sons of Eric Bjodaskalli had estates in East Norway, cf. p. 158.  2 The later Olav Trygvason.

fighting with Hacon the Jarl the same autumn and in the following winter as is written above ('History of Hacon the Jarl', chapter 8), Astrid and her son were not sought out that winter.

3. The next spring Gunhild sent spies to the Uplands right down to the Vik to find out how things stood with Astrid. And when the messengers came back they told Gunhild that Astrid was probably with her father Eric. They also said that it was likely that she was there rearing King Trygvi's and her son. Then Gunhild straightway called up messengers and fitted them out well with weapons and clothes. They were thirty men and their leader was a mighty man

Gunhild bids Hacon to bring her Olav Trygvason

and a friend of Gunhild, called Hacon. She bade them go to Oprostader to Eric and take from there King Trygvi's son and bring him to her. Thereupon the messengers went their way. And when they were a short way from Oprostader, Eric's friends became aware of their journey and one evening they brought Eric a report about it. Straightway in the night Eric bade Astrid make herself ready to go away, gave her good guides and sent her east to Sweden to his friend Hacon the Old, a mighty man. They went away when there was still much of the night left. The next day about evening they came to a lordship called Skaun,[1] saw there a great house and went and asked for a night's lodging for themselves. They kept their names secret and wore simple clothes. The bonder there was called Björn Eiterkveisa, a rich but evil man. He drove them away, but the same evening they came to a farm a short way from there, called Vizkar.[1] Torstein[2] was the name of the man there and he harboured them well and gave them help for the night; there they slept in good beds.

4. Early in the morning Hacon came with Gunhild's men to Oprostader and asked for Astrid and her son. Eric said she was not there and so Hacon and his men searched all over the buildings. They stayed far into the day and obtained some news of Astrid's journey.

---

1 Neither *Skaun* nor *Vizkar* can definitely be traced, but there are two districts in East Norway of the name of Skaun.   2 *Torstein* is a name often met with in the Sagas. In Normandy it has become *Toustain*, but Robert Wace in *Roman de Rou* calls William's standard-bearer at Hastings *Tostein*. In England and Scotland the name has become Turstin, Thurstan and Thurston. In O.N. *þorstein*, i.e. Thorstein.

They rode the same way and late in the evening they came to Björn Eiterkveisa in Skaun and went in there. Hacon then asked Björn if he could tell him anything about Astrid. Björn said that some people had come there during the day and had asked for a night's lodging; "but I drove them away and I expect they are lodged somewhere in the neighbourhood". In the evening Torstein's workman went from the wood and came to Björn's house, for it was on his way. He became aware that they had guests there and knew what their errand was; he told this to Torstein the bonder. Whilst there was still a third part of the night left Torstein woke his guests up, bade them go away and spoke harshly to them. And when they were gone a short way from the house Torstein told them that Gunhild's messengers were with Björn and were seeking them. They asked him for help and he gave them a guide and some food. The guide showed them the way into the wood where there was a lake and an island overgrown with sedge. They could wade to the island and hide there. Early next day Hacon rode from Björn's house out into the district and wherever he came he asked after Astrid. When he came to Torstein, he asked if they were come there. He said some folk were come there but that they had gone at dawn east into the wood. Hacon bade Torstein go with them, for he knew the ways and the hiding places. Torstein went with them; and when he came to the wood, he brought them right away from where Astrid was. They went looking for them all the day but found them not. They afterwards went back and told Gunhild how things had gone. Astrid and her folk went their way and came forth into Sweden to Hacon the Old. There Astrid and her son Olav stayed for a long time and were well cared for.

5. Gunhild the King-Mother learned that Astrid and her son Olav were in Sweden. She then again sent Hacon and a good following with him east to Eric King of Sweden with good gifts and words of friendship. The messengers were welcomed and had good cheer there. Then Hacon bore his errand to the king and said that Gunhild sent this word, that the king should grant him help so that he could take Olav Trygvason with him to Norway: "Gunhild will foster him". The king gave him men and they rode to Hacon the Old. There with many friendly words Hacon asked for Olav to go with him. Hacon the Old answered in a friendly way and said that Olav's mother should decide his journey, but Astrid would in no way let the boy go. The messengers went away and told the answer to King Eric. They then made ready to go home and again asked the king to give them help to take the boy away, whether Hacon the Old would

or not. The king once more gave them a troop of men. The messengers now came to Hacon the Old and craved that the boy should go with them, but when he was not willing to do that they uttered mighty words, threatened with violence and grew wroth. Then there leaped forth a thrall called Bursti and would smite Hacon, so that they had to retire in a hurry, lest the thrall had beaten them. Afterwards they went back home to Norway and told Gunhild about their journey and also that they had seen Olav Trygvason.

6. Astrid's brother was called Sigurd, the son of Eric Bjodaskalli; he had long been away from the land and been east in Gardarik[1] with King Valdemar.[2] Sigurd there had great honour. Astrid wished to go there to her brother Sigurd, and Hacon the Old gave her a good following and fitted her out well; she went with some merchants. She had been two years with Hacon the Old, and Olav was then three winters old. When they were sailing east on the sea, vikings came against them; they were men from Estland. They took both men and goods; some they slew and others they shared amongst themselves as thralls. There was Olav parted from his mother and an Estland man called Klerkon took him and Torolv and Torgils. Klerkon thought that as Torolv was too old for a thrall he would be no use, so he slew him. But he took the boys with him and sold them to a man called Klerk for a good buck; a third man bought Olav and gave for him a good gown or cape; this man was called Reas, his wife was called Rekon and their son Rekoni. Olav was there a long time and was well looked after and the bonder thought much of him. Olav was six winters in Estland in those circumstances.

7. Sigurd Ericson came to Estland on an errand from King Valdemar of Holmgard[2] and was to gather the king's tribute in that land. Sigurd went forth mightily with many men and much wealth. In the market place he saw a fair boy, whom he knew to be a foreigner, and he asked him his name and birth. He called himself Olav and his father Trygvi Olavson and his mother Astrid the daughter of Eric Bjodaskalli; then Sigurd knew that the boy was his sister's son. Sigurd asked how he was come there and Olav told him all that had befallen him. Sigurd bade him follow him to the bonder Reas; and when he came to Reas, he bought the boys Olav and Torgils and took them with him to Holmgard and kept it secret that Olav was of royal descent.

8. Olav Trygvason stood one day in the market place and there

1 *Gardarik*, i.e. Russia. In O.S. *Garðariki*.   2 Vladimir the Great of Russia (980–1015) became Grand Duke of Novgorod (Holmgard) in 970.

were many folk present. And there he recognised Klerkon who had slain his foster-father Torolv Louse-beard. Olav had in his hand a little axe and he drove it into the head of Klerkon so that it struck down to the brain. He ran straightway home to the house and told it to his kinsman Sigurd. Sigurd at once took him to the queen's house and told her the news. She was called Allogia and Sigurd bade her help the boy. She looked at the boy, said that no man should kill so fine a boy and called to her fully weaponed men. In Holmgard a law was in force, that any man would forfeit his life if he had killed an un-judged man. According to their custom and law all the people rushed together and sought out where the boy had gone. It was said that he was in the queen's house and there amidst an armed troop; this was told to the king. He then went down to his men and wished them not to fight. The king decided the fine and the queen paid it. Olav was afterwards with the queen and she was very fond of him. It was the law in Gardarik that king-born men should not be there without the wish of the king. Then Sigurd told the queen of what kin Olav was and the reason why he had come there—that because of strife he could not be in his own land—and he asked her to speak with the king about it and she did so. She asked the king to help this king's son, so hard a lot had he had, and thus by her asking it came about that the king granted her boon and he took Olav into his protection and kept him in such honour as was meet for a king's son. Olav was nine winters old when he came to Gardarik and he stayed another nine winters with King Valdemar. Olav was very good-looking, big and strong, and in all kinds of sport surpassed all the Norsemen who are spoken of.

9. Hacon Sigurdson the Jarl was with the Danish King Harald Gormson during the winter, after he had fled from Norway before Gunhild's sons. He had so much to brood over during the winter that he lay in his bed. He often lay awake and ate and drank only just enough to keep his strength up. Then secretly he sent his men north to Trondheim to his friends and made a plan with them to kill King Erling if it was possible. He said he would turn back to his land when summer came. That winter the Tronds slew Erling, as is written above.[1] Between Hacon and Gold-Harald there was great friendship. Harald made his thoughts known to Hacon; he said he would settle in the land and no longer would he be on board his war-ship; he asked Hacon what he thought of King Harald sharing the kingdom with him, if he claimed it. "I think", said Hacon, "that the Danish king will not deny thee any right; but thou wilt get to

[1] 'History of Hacon the Jarl', chapter 11.

know more than I can tell thee, if thou speakest about it to the king; I think thou wilt not get the kingdom if thou dost not crave it." A short time after this meeting, Gold-Harald spoke to King Harald at a time when there were present many great men and friends of both. Then Gold-Harald craved of King Harald to share with him half the kingdom, such as his birth and kin gave him right to in Denmark. On that request Harald became very wroth and said that no man had craved King Gorm, his father, to be half-king in Denmark, or his father Harda-Knut, nor Sigurd Serpent's Eye, nor Ragnar Lodbrok. He waxed so wroth that no man could talk with him.

Hacon the Jarl is bedridden and worries about the future

10. Gold-Harald liked his position still less now than before; he had now no more kingdom than before, but only the king's wrath. He then came to his friend Hacon, complained to him of his distress and asked him for good counsel if he had any, so that he could get the kingdom. He said he had almost thought of getting it by might and weapons. Hacon bade him not say that to anyone so that it would not be reported. "It may cost thee thy life," he said; "think for thyself what power thou canst have to do it; for such great deeds thou art asked to be bold and firm, to spare nothing good or bad, so that thou mayest be successful in what thou hast undertaken. But it is ignoble to take up great enterprises and afterwards lay them down with dishonour." Gold-Harald answered, "So shall I take up this plan; that not once shall I spare my hands from slaying even the king if I can get so far, as he now denies me that kingdom which I ought to have by right". They now ended their meeting. Thereafter King Harald went to Hacon and they began to talk together. The king told the jarl what claim Gold-Harald had raised against him about the kingdom, and what answer he gave him; he said that he would in no way lessen his kingdom: "but if Gold-Harald will hold fast to this claim, then I do not mind having him killed, for I trust him little, if he will not give it up". The jarl answered, "I think that Harald has set it forth too eagerly for him to let it drop again. I think that if he raises strife here in the land he will get good help and mostly for his

father's many friendships; but it would be the most ill luck for thee to slay thy kinsman, for by that death all men would call him blameless. I would rather not give thee that counsel, to make thyself a lesser king than Gorm thy father was: he also increased his kingdom much and lessened it in no way". Then said the king, "What then is thy counsel, Hacon? Shall I neither share my kingdom nor yet shake this unrest from my neck?" "We shall meet in a few days", said Hacon the Jarl, "and I shall first think over this difficult matter and then give answer." The king and all his men then went away.

11. Hacon the Jarl had now again much earnest thought and meditation and he would have few men in the house with him. A few days later, Harald came to the jarl and they talked together. The king asked if the jarl had now considered in his mind on the matter they had talked over the other day. "I have lain awake", said the jarl, "both day and night, and I find it best for thee to have and to hold all the kingdom which thy father had and which thou tookest after him, and to get thy kinsman Harald another kingdom from which he can get honour." "What kingdom is there", said the king, "that I can

Death of King Erling

give to Harald, if I do not share the kingdom of Denmark?" The jarl said, "There is Norway. The kings who are there are hated by the land folk and every man wishes them as much ill as possible". The king said, "Norway is a great land and there is a hardy folk and it is difficult to attack with a foreign army. Thus it was with us, when Hacon defended the land, that we lost many men but won no victory. Besides, Harald Ericson is my foster-son and has sat on my knee". Then said the jarl: "Long have I known that thou hast helped Gunhild's sons, but they have not repaid thee with aught but ill. But we shall get Norway in a much easier way than by fighting with the whole Danish army to take it. Send a behest to thy foster-son Harald and bid him take of thee the land and fiefs which they formerly had here in Denmark. Call him to thee, for then may Gold-Harald in a short time win a kingdom in Norway from King Harald Greyskin". The king answered that it would be called an ill deed to betray his own foster-son. "The Danes", said the jarl, "will well say that it is better to slay a Norse Viking than his own Danish brother's son." They now talked about it for a long time, until they were agreed about it.

12. Gold-Harald came again to speak with Hacon, and the jarl told him that he had now so furthered the matter that there was good hope that a kingdom would soon be ready for him in Norway. "Shall we two then", he said, "hold fast by our fellowship? I shall then be able to help thee a great deal in Norway. Get thou that kingdom; King Harald is moreover very old, and hath a bastard son, whom he likes but little." The jarl spoke about it to Gold-Harald till he said he was well content with it. The three of them, the king and the jarl and Gold-Harald, often talked together about it. After that, the Danish king sent his men north to Norway to Harald Greyskin. Their expedition was well fitted out and they were well greeted when they found King Harald. They told the tidings that Hacon the Jarl was in Denmark, lying at death's door and nigh out of his wits, and they told other tidings that the Danish King Harald bade his foster-son Harald Greyskin to him to take such fiefs of him as he and his brothers had formerly had in Denmark, and bade him come to him in Jutland. Harald Greyskin bore this message to Gunhild and his other friends. They were not of one mind about it, for some seemed to think that such a journey as was arranged was not trustworthy; but there were many more who wished him to go, for there was so much hunger in Norway that the kings could hardly feed their own men. It was after this time that the fjord where the kings sat most often got its name Hardanger.[1] But in Denmark the season was fairly good and they thought they would get all they required if King Harald had fief and rule there. It was settled before the messengers went away that King Harald would come in the summer to the Danish King and take from him the conditions that he offered.

13. In the summer King Harald Greyskin went to Denmark with three longships: Arenbjörn the Herse from the Fjords steered one of them. King Harald sailed out from the Vik to Limfjord and then lay in by Hals.[2] He was told that the Danish king would come forthwith. But when Gold-Harald got to hear of it, he sailed there with nine ships, which he had before fitted out for a viking raid. Hacon the Jarl had also fitted out his army and would likewise go on a viking raid, and he had twelve ships, all great. And when Gold-Harald was

1 In O.N. *angr* means 'sorrow', 'grief', or 'affliction'. Connected with place-names such as Leikanger, Stavanger, Tananger, etc. it means harbour or haven and also narrow place.    2 *Hals* is by the entrance of the *Limfjord* in Denmark on the north-east side.

gone away, Hacon the Jarl said to the king: "Now I know not whether we shall not have to row to the meeting[1] and still pay the fines. Now will Gold-Harald slay Harald Greyskin and afterwards take the kingdom of Norway. Dost thou think he will be true to thee when thou givest him so great might? Last winter he said before me that he would slay thee if only he could get the chance. Now will I win Norway under thee and slay Gold-Harald, if thou wilt promise that I may

Harald Greyskin fares to Denmark

easily be reconciled with thee for this deed; I will be thy jarl and by my oath will I bind myself to win Norway with thy help and afterwards to hold the land under thy rule and to pay thee scot; then shalt thou be a greater king than thy father, if thou dost rule over two peoples". The king and the jarl became of one mind about it, and then did Hacon go with his men to seek Gold-Harald.

14. Gold-Harald came to Hals in Limfjord and straightway bade Harald Greyskin fight, but though Harald Greyskin had fewer men, yet he straightway went up on land, made himself ready to fight and drew up his men. And before the battle began, Harald Greyskin strongly egged on his men and bade them draw their swords. He himself leaped forth straightway at the head of his folk and struck on both sides. Thus says Glum Geirason in Greyskin's drapa:

Bold words spake
The sword-fighter who dared
Dye the battlefield
With the blood of his foes.

Harald bade his warriors
Now swing the swords
In fight. Noble to men
Did the king's words seem.

There fell King Harald Greyskin. Thus says Glum Geirason:

The shield-bearer, who was true
To his ships, must in death
Lie on the broad
Shore of the Limfjord.

The generous chief
Fell on the sand near Hals.
The smooth-spoken kinsman
Of the prince wrought this murder.

There most of King Harald's men fell with him; there fell Arenbjörn the Herse. Fifteen years had gone since the fall of Hacon, Athelstan's foster-son, and thirteen from the fall of Sigurd the Jarl of Lade. So it is said by the priest Ari Torgilson that Hacon the Jarl ruled over his father's lands in Trondheim for thirteen years before Harald Greyskin fell, but in the last six years that Harald Greyskin was alive, says

1 A fine was imposed upon those who did not turn up to an army meeting.

Ari, Gunhild's sons and Hacon were always fighting against each other and were in turn obliged to leave the land.

15. Hacon the Jarl and Gold-Harald met a little while after Harald Greyskin fell. Hacon the Jarl went to battle and there he had the victory. Harald was taken and Hacon had him fastened on the gallows. Hacon the Jarl afterwards went to the Danish king and easily was he reconciled with him for the slaughter of the king's kinsman Gold-Harald. After that King Harald called out the army from all his kingdom and sailed forth with 600 ships. There were with him Hacon the Jarl and Harald the Grenlander, son of King Gudröd, and many other great men who had fled from their *odal* lands because of Gunhild's sons. The Danish king steered north with his army to the Vik and there all the people submitted to him. And when he came to Tunsberg a great host of men came to him, and all that army which came to him in Norway he gave into the hands of Hacon the Jarl and he gave him the rule of Rogaland and Hordaland, Sogn, the Fjords,[1] South Möre, Raumsdale and North Möre. These seven shires did King Harald give to Hacon the Jarl to keep with such rule as Harald Hairfair had entrusted to his sons, except that Hacon should himself own all the king's estates and land dues there, as in Trondheim; he was also to have such of the king's income as he needed if there were war in the land. King Harald gave to Harald the Grenlander, Vingulmark, Vestfold and Agder as far as Lidandisnes[2] with the name of king, and he let him there have the land on such terms as his kinsmen had had before and such as Harald Hairfair gave to his sons. Harald the Grenlander was then eighteen years old and he afterwards became a well-known man. Harald the Danish king then went home with all the Danish army.

16. Hacon the Jarl went north along the coast with his men. And when Gunhild and her sons heard these tidings, they gathered an army but had trouble in getting folk. They took again the same plan as before, to sail west over the sea with such as would follow them. They went first to the Orkneys and stayed there for a while. Lodver, Arnvid, Ljot and Skuli, the sons of Torfinn Hausakljuv (Skullsplitter) were now jarls there. Hacon the Jarl put all the land under him and stayed that winter in Trondheim. About it Einar Skalaglam says in Vellekla:

> The noble jarl, who beareth        Hath taken to himself seven shires;
> The silken band on his brow,       Lucky it was for the land.

---

1 The land round Northfjord and Southfjord.    2 The present Lindesnes, the most southerly point of Norway; in English, 'the Naze'.

When Hacon the Jarl went north along the coast in the summer and the people gave themselves up to him, he bade them keep up the temples and blood offering all over the land and so it was done. So is it said in Vellekla:

The wise folk leader
Now let the once harried
Temple lands of Thor and the gods
Be free for all men's use.
The shield-bearer brought
Home with honour his ship
All across the sea.
(Him the gods lead!)

And friendly to men, the gods
Turn their minds
To the offering; the mighty
Shield-bearer thereby wins fame.
Now grows the earth as of yore;
Again the generous prince
Leads the glad men
To build the gods' houses.

Now lies under the jarl
All land north of the Vik.
The lordships of Hacon,
The fighter, go far and wide.

Gunhild in the Orkneys

The first winter that Hacon ruled the land, the herring came up all round the land; and in the autumn before, corn grew everywhere it had been sown. And in the spring they got themselves seed corn, so that most of the bonders sowed their land and it soon promised to be a good year.

17. King Ragnfröd, Gunhild's son, and Gudröd, another son of Gunhild, were now the only sons of Eric and Gunhild who were still alive. Thus says Glum Geirason in Greyskin's poem:

Half my hope of wealth
Fell, when the battle
Took the chieftain's life.
Harald's death me scathed.

But I know that both
His brothers have vowed me
Good gifts, and all the guardsmen
Look to them for luck.

Ragnfröd made himself ready to sail in the spring when he had been in the Orkneys one winter. He then sailed east to Norway and had a fine army and big ships. When he came to Norway, he learned that Hacon the Jarl was in Trondheim. Ragnfröd sailed north round Stad and harried round about in South Möre, and some folk gave themselves up to him, as it often happens, when war troops visit a land, that those whom they meet ask for help and accept it wherever it can be most easily obtained. Hacon the Jarl learned the tidings that there was unrest in the south in Möre. The jarl then gathered his ships and bade the war arrows be sheared, fitted himself out hastily and sailed out along the fjord. It was easy for him to obtain followers; he and Ragnfröd met in the north of South Möre. The jarl straightway came to battle; he had more men but smaller ships. The battle was hard and it went unluckily for Hacon; they fought on the stems as at that time was usual. There was a strong current in the sound and all the ships drifted together on to the land. The jarl steered his ships to a place where it seemed to him best to land. And when the ships grounded, the jarl and all his men left them and drew them up so that their foes should not drag them out. After that the jarl drew up his men on the beach and egged on Ragnfröd to come up. Ragnfröd's men lay farther out and for a time they shot at one another; but Ragnfröd would not go ashore and thereupon they parted. Ragnfröd brought his army south round Stad, for he feared that a land army would gather for Hacon the Jarl. But the jarl did not seek battle, for he thought the difference in size between their ships seemed too great. In the autumn he went north to Trondheim and was there during the winter, but King Ragnfröd held all land to the south of Stad: the Fjords, Sogn, Hordaland and Rogaland. He had a great force during the winter and when it came to springtime he bade his men muster and got many men. He then went himself over all these districts to gather men and ships and everything else he needed.

18. When it was spring, Hacon the Jarl called men out from the land right to the north. He had many men from Halogaland and Naumadale, so that right from Byrda[1] to Stad he had men from all the seaboards, and an army came to him from all over Trondlaw, also from Raumsdale. So it was said that he had an army from four shires; seven jarls followed him and together they had a great gathering of men. So it was said in Vellekla:

Minded should be that the war-lusty
Folk-saver of the Mörers
Let fare from the north
An army to Sogn;
From four folk lands
The warriors brought arms.
He saw help therein
For all the land folk;
And to the shield meeting
There hastened to the ships
Seven land rulers
With their war-chief.
When the sea warriors clashed together
All Norway was shaken.
Before the nesses there floated
The masses of dead men's bodies.

1 *Byrda* is Böröy in the Roan (Björnör) district near the frontier between Naumadale and North Möre.

Hacon the Jarl sailed to the south with all this army round by Stad. Then he learned that King Ragnfröd had gone with his army into Sogn; so he brought his men there and met with Ragnfröd. The jarl steered his ships to the land and chose a field of battle for King Ragnfröd. Thus is it said in Vellekla:

| | |
|---|---|
| The Vender-slayer met | The warrior lord bade them steer |
| The warrior lord in another fight, | The bows towards the land, |
| And then a wide-known | And brought his ships |
| Fall of men befell. | To the shire's foremost shore. |

There a great strife took place. Hacon the Jarl had a much greater army and got the victory. The fight was on Thinganes,[1] where Sogn and Hordaland meet. King Ragnfröd fled to his ships but 300(360) men of his army fell. Thus it is said in Vellekla:

| | |
|---|---|
| The fight was hard until, | Over the heads |
| 'Neath the carrion crow's claws, | Of the ocean-dwellers |
| Three hundred men | The victorious prince could go |
| Were wanted by the war-chief. | From there, and gladly he did so. |

After that battle King Ragnfröd fled from Norway and Hacon the Jarl kept peace in the land and let the great army which had followed him in the summer go back north; but he stayed there during the autumn and winter.

19. Hacon the Jarl took as his wife a woman called Thora, the daughter of Skagi Skoftason, a mighty man. Thora was very pretty. Their sons were Swein and Heming and their daughter was Bergliot, who afterwards was wed to Einar Tambarskelver. Hacon the Jarl was very fond of women and had many children. One daughter was called Ragnhild and he married her to Skofti Skagason, Thora's brother. The jarl loved Thora so much that Thora's kinsmen were dearer to him than other men; but Skofti, his son-in-law, had still most to say of all his kinsmen. The jarl gave him big land rents in Möre. And whenever they went fighting, Skofti would lay his ship near the jarl's and no other was allowed to lay his ship between theirs.

20. It was one summer that Hacon the Jarl went out to sea, and Torleiv the Wise was steering his ship for him. Eric was also there and he was then ten or eleven winters old. And when they came to a harbour in the evening, Eric would hear of nothing else than that they should lay at anchor nearest the jarl's ship. And when they came

---

1 *Thinganes*, now Dingenes, at the mouth of the Sognfjord (on the south side) was a thing stead. A *thing* was often held at a place which was easily accessible by water.

south to Möre, the jarl's son-in-law, Skofti, came with a well-fitted longship. And as they rowed towards the fleet Skofti shouted that Torleiv should make room in the haven for him and move his anchorage. Eric answered sharply and bade Skofti find another anchorage. Hacon the Jarl heard it, that his son Eric now seemed so mighty that he would not give way to Skofti. The jarl called out at once that they should move from their anchorage or it would go much worse with them; he said they would get blows. When Torleiv heard that, he

Hacon the Jarl brings up his ships for the night

called on his men and bade them loosen the ship from its moorings; and so it was done. Skofti lay his ship in the anchorage such as he was wont to have nearest the jarl's ship. Skofti used to tell the jarl all the news when they were both together and the jarl told Skofti tidings if he heard them first: so he was called Tidings-Skofti. The next winter Eric was with his foster-father Torleiv and early in the spring Eric got himself a following of men. Torleiv gave him a fifteen-seated ship with all gear, tents and food. Then Eric steered out along the fjord and so south round Möre. Tidings-Skofti was going between his coastal estates with a full-manned fifteen-seated ship and Eric straightway lay by to meet him in battle. There Skofti fell and Eric gave quarter to the men who were still alive. Thus says Eyolf Deed-scald in Banda drapa:

On the sea king's ski the young man
Sailed late in the day,
With such great strength
Against the stark herse of the far-shore.

Then before him who swung
The bloody sword Skofti fell.
The provider of meat for the wolves
Oft gave the ravens food.

After this Eric sailed along the land to the south and came forth into Denmark. He then went to King Harald Gormson and was with him during the winter. And the next spring the Danish king sent Eric north to Norway and gave him the name of jarl, and therewith he gave him Vingulmark and Raumarik to rule in such manner as under-kings had formerly done. Thus says Eyolf Deedscald:

The folk ruler,
Few winters old,
Stayed south and drank
In the ale-boats;

Before the gold-rich
Princes would give
The young, helmeted
Leader, land to rule.

Eric the Jarl was afterwards a great chief.

21. Olav Trygvason was all this time in Gardarik[1] and had there the greatest honour from King Valdemar and friendship from the queen. King Valdemar made him chief of that army which he sent out to guard his land. Olav fought some battles and showed himself to be a doughty leader. He had himself a great company of warriors at his own cost with the means the king gave him. Olav was generous to his men and became therefore well befriended by them. But, as often befalls when foreign men are raised to power or to so great honour that they go before the natives, it happened that many were envious that he was dear to the king and no less to the queen. Many spoke about it before the king and said that he should take heed of himself lest he make Olav too mighty; "for such a man is dangerous to thee, if he lends himself to do harm to thee or thy kingdom, when he is as doughty and beloved as this man is; nor do we know what he and the queen are for ever talking about". Now it was a common custom with mighty kings that the queen should have half the body-guard and keep it at her own cost, and for that to have scot and dues such as were needed. So was it also with King Valdemar: the queen had a bodyguard not smaller than the king's and much did they vie to win gallant men: each would have them for themselves. Now it happened that the king put faith in such tales as came to him and he became somewhat short-spoken and unfriendly towards Olav. And when Olav noted it he told it to the queen and added that he wished

___
1 In O.S. *Garðariki*, i.e. Russia.

to go to the Northlands. He said that his kinsmen had had rule there before and it seemed to him most likely that he would get on farthest there. The queen bade him farewell and said that he would be thought a valiant man wherever he might be. Olav then manned his ship, went aboard and so sailed out into the Baltic. And when he sailed to the west, he came to Borgundarholm,[1] made a landing and harried. The men of the island came down and held battle with him, but Olav had the victory and got much booty.

22. Olav lay near Borgundarholm; they had there rough weather

Olav and his men fare to Queen Geira

and storm in the sea, so that they could not stay there, and they sailed south by Vendland and there got a good haven; they went about peacefully and stayed there a time. The king in Vendland was called Burislav;[2] his daughters were Geira, Gunhild and Astrid. The king's daughter Geira had lands and rule where Olav came to land. The man who had most to say with Queen Geira was called Dixon. And when they learned that unknown men were come into the land who bore themselves in a seemly manner and behaved peacefully, then went Dixon to them with words from Queen Geira. She asked the men who were come there to stay during the winter, for there was

1 Now Bornholm (in the Baltic).    2 *Burislav,* i.e. Boleslav I of Poland (992–1025). Boleslav's father Miesco died in 992, but he must have abdicated before his death in favour of his son.

little left of the summer, the weather was hard and there were great storms. And when Dixon came thither, he straightway became aware that it was a fine man, both of kin and aspect, who led them. Dixon told them that the queen bade them go to her with offers of friendship. Olav took the behest and went during the winter to Queen Geira. They both seemed to like each other, so that Olav wooed Queen Geira and so it happened that Olav wed Geira that winter. He shared the rule of that kingdom with her. About it Halfred Vandradascald says in the poem he made about King Olav:

On Holmen,[1] the war lord,          Had the hard swords dyed with blood:
And east in Gardar,[2]               Why shall it be hidden?

23. Hacon the Jarl ruled over Norway and paid no scot on the grounds that the Danish king granted him all the scot which the king had from Norway, for the labour and costs that the jarl had in guarding the land against Gunhild's sons.

24. The Emperor Otta was then ruling over Saxland.[3] He sent bidding to the Danish king Harald that he and the folk he ruled should become Christian and take the true faith;[4] otherwise, said the Emperor, he would fare against him with his army. The Danish king made his army ready and guarded well the Dane-work[5] and manned his warships. Thereupon he sent bidding to Hacon the Jarl in Norway that he should come to him early in the spring with all the army he could gather. In the spring, Hacon the Jarl called out an army from all over his kingdom and he got a great strength of men. With this army he sailed to Denmark and went to meet the Danish king, who greeted him well. With the Danish king there were many other chiefs who gave him their help: he had then a very mighty host.

25. Olav Trygvason had been in Vendland during the winter, as is written above (chapter 22), and in that winter he went to the lordships in Vendland which had been under Queen Geira, but which had withdrawn all loyalty and tribute to her. There Olav harried and slew many men, burned some, took much booty and put those kingdoms under him; he then went back to his fortified castle. Early in the spring Olav made his ships ready and then sailed out on the sea. He sailed near Scania and made a landing there. The landsmen

1 *Holmen*, i.e. Bornholm.    2 *Gardar* (*Gardarik*), i.e. Russia.    3 *The Emperor Otta* is Otto II (973–983).    4 According to other sources the Emperor Otto's war was undertaken to punish the Danish king and make him obedient to the Emperor's wishes. 5 *Dane-work* is in O.S. *Danavirki*, the frontier fortifications in South Denmark. In the same way Southwark (in London, on the south bank of the Thames) was called in O.S. *Suðvirki*, where the Danes fortified themselves against Ethelred. Cf. 'History of St Olav', chapter 12.

gathered together and fought against him, but Olav got the victory and great booty. After this he sailed east to Gotland,[1] where he took a merchant ship which the Jämters[2] owned. They defended themselves well, but in the end Olav cleared the ship, slew many men and took all their goods. A third battle he had in Gotland where he had the victory and got much booty. Thus says Halfred Vandradascald:

| | |
|---|---|
| After this the temple's foeman | The hersers' sword-bold lord |
| Slew the Jämtlandmen | Struck out on the Gots. |
| And the Vends in battle | I have heard that this gold-giver |
| (Used to this he was early); | Fain took booty in Scania. |

26. The Emperor Otta drew together a great army; he had men from Saxland, Frankland and Friesland, and from Vendland King Burislav followed him with a great army and in that following with Burislav was Olav Trygvason, his son-in-law.[3] The Emperor had a great host of riders and a much greater army of foot warriors; also, he had a great army from Holtseteland.[4] Harald the Danish king sent Hacon the Jarl with the army of Norsemen that followed him south to the Dane-work to guard the land. So is it said in Vellekla:

| | |
|---|---|
| It also befell that sea steeds | And in the wintertide |
| Rushed down from the north, | Would the generous king |
| Under their cool riders, | Of the murky woodlands try |
| To Denmark in the south. | This warrior who came from the north, |
| And the Horders' lord, | When this hardy fighter |
| Whose head was decked with helm, | Had bidding from |
| This ruler of Dovre, sought | The great king, to guard |
| To meet the Danish princes. | Dane-work against the foe. |

The Emperor Otta came up with his army from the south to the Dane-work and Hacon the Jarl guarded the bourgh walls with his men. The Dane-work lies thus: two fjords go into the land one on either side of it, and between the heads of the fjords the Danes had made a great wall of stones and peat and trees and had dug a broad and deep ditch on the outside and raised towers near each gate. Then was there a great battle. About this it is said in Vellekla:

| | |
|---|---|
| It was not gladly | When the warriors from the south |
| That they went against their armies, | Went with forces of Frisians, |
| For the shield-bearers | Of Franks and of Vends, |
| Wrought great scathe, | And the sea fighter egged on to battle. |

Hacon the Jarl set up troops over all the bourgh gates, but the greatest part of his army he drew up along the walls and defended them wherever the foe came up. Many of the Emperor's army fell there

---

1 The island of Gotland (in the Baltic).    2 *Jämters* means 'men from Jämtland' (in Sweden).    3 This report that Boleslav and Olav Trygvason joined the Emperor Otto is not mentioned in the German History.    4 I.e. Holsten.

and they won no part of the fortress. The Emperor then turned away and no longer resumed the fight. So is it said in Vellekla:

| | |
|---|---|
| The spear shafts were smashed | The sea steed's steerer |
| When in the fighting they bore | Drove the *Saxers* in flight, |
| Shields against each other, | The grim war lord |
| And the opposers yielded not. | Guarded the walls against the foe. |

After that battle Hacon the Jarl went back to his ships and then made up his mind to sail home to Norway, but he had no fair wind, so he lay outside in Limfjord.

27. The Emperor Otta now turned with his army to Sle.[1] He there drew to himself a fleet of ships and took his men over the fjord

Hacon the Jarl shot upon land all the priests and learned men

to Jutland.[2] And when the Danish king Harald learned that, he went to meet him with his army; there was a great fight and at last the Emperor won the victory. The Danish king fled thence to Limfjord and went out to Morsö.[3] Men went between him and the Emperor, and peace and a meeting were arranged. The Emperor Otta and the Danish king met in Morsö. Then a holy bishop, Poppa, made known the true faith to King Harald; the bishop bore glowing iron in his hand and showed King Harald his hand unburned. After that, King Harald let himself and all the Danish army be baptised. Before this, whilst he was in Morsö, King Harald had sent bidding to Hacon the

1 Sleswick.   2 South Jutland (Sönder Jylland).   3 *Morsö* is a large island in the Limfjord.

Jarl to come to his help, and the jarl came just when the king had let himself become Christian, and then the king sent bidding to the jarl to come to him. And when they met, the king made the jarl take up Christianity. And then Hacon the Jarl and all the men who followed him were baptised. The king gave him priests and other learned men and said that the jarl should have all the folk in Norway converted to Christianity. Thus they parted and Hacon the Jarl went out to sea and waited there for a south wind. And when the wind came which he thought would bear him out to sea he shot up on to the land all the priests and learned men, and then he sailed out on the sea. The wind changed round to south-west and west, and the jarl sailed east through Öresund and he harried the land on either side; he then sailed east along Scania and harried here and there wherever he came to land. And when he came east along the Gautaskerries[1] he came to land and made there a great blood offering. Then came flying thither two ravens and they screeched loudly. The jarl seemed to know that Odin had taken the offering well and that now he would have good luck in battle. The jarl burned all his ships, went up on land with the whole of his army and went everywhere with the shield of war. Against him came Ottar the Jarl who ruled over Gautland; they had a great battle and there did Hacon get the victory, whilst Ottar the Jarl and a great number of his men fell. Hacon the Jarl now went over East and West Gautland everywhere with the shield of war, till he came to Norway. He then went overland right north to Trondheim. About this it is said in Vellekla:

The foe of the fleeing
Went to offer on the meadow
And got answer that day
All would go well in fight.
Then the battle guider
Saw the stark ravens.
The chief of the temple would
Take the life of the Gauts.

A sword thing now the jarl held
Where (before him) no man
With shield on his arm
Had been able to harry.

No man from the sea
Had on so long a way borne
The golden shield: through
All Gautland he went.

The warrior filled the field
With heaps of dead men.
The Asers' kin took the victory:
Odin took the fallen.
Can men doubt that the crushing
Of kings is by the gods ruled?
Strong powers, I know,
Strengthen Hacon's rule.

28. The Emperor Otta went back to his kingdom in Saxland and he and the Danish king parted in friendship. So it is said that the Emperor

---

1  The *Gautaskerries* (or Götaskjär in modern Scandinavian) are situated outside East Gautland and Kalmar (East Sweden).

Otta became godfather to King Harald's son Swein[1] and gave him his own name, and he was christened and ever afterwards called Otta Swein. Harald the Danish king kept to Christianity right to the day of his death. King Burislav went back to Vendland and with him his son-in-law, Olav Trygvason. About the battle Halfred Vandrada-scald says in Olav's drapa:

<table>
<tr><td>The warship's steerer<br>In Denmark to the south,</td><td>Off Hedeby,[2] struck<br>The warriors asunder.</td></tr>
</table>

29. Olav Trygvason was three years in Vendland till his wife Geira took a sickness which brought on her death. That seemed to Olav so great a sorrow that he liked not Vendland after that. He then

Olav sorrows over Queen Geira's death

manned his warships and went back to fighting, harrying first in Friesland, then in Saxland as far as Flanders. Thus says Halfred Vandradascald:

<table>
<tr><td>Trygvi's son did strike<br>Soon against the Saxers,<br>So that their mangled bodies<br>Lay as food for the wolves.<br>The well-loved prince<br>Far and wide gave the wolves</td><td>The brown blood of many<br>Frisians to drink.<br>The mighty sea king struck<br>In the south as far as Valkere.[3]<br>The prince gave to the ravens<br>The Flemings' flesh to eat.</td></tr>
</table>

30. After this Olav Trygvason sailed to England and harried far and wide in the land. He sailed right north to Northumbria and harried there; from there he went north to Scotland and harried there

---

1 *Swein*, later Swein Forkbeard, father of King Canute of England.    2 *Hedeby* was the old town of Sleswick, situated opposite the present town (on the north side of the river).
3 *Valkere*, i.e. the island Walcheren (in Holland).

far and wide. Thence he sailed to the Hebrides and had some battles there. After that he sailed south to the Isle of Man and fought there. He also harried far and wide in Ireland, whence he sailed to Wales[1] and harried much in the land and so too in Cumberland. From there he sailed (south)-west to Valland[2] and harried there, and from there he sailed from the (south)-west and intended going to England. But he came to the Scilly Isles in the west of England. Thus says Halfred Vandradascald:

| | |
|---|---|
| The young king unsparingly | The bearer of the elm bow |
| Harried the English. | Brought death to the army |
| The maker of the spear rain avenged | Of the Isles and of the Irish, |
| The murder of the Northumbrians. | For yearning for fame was the prince. |
| The battle-glad wolf feeder | The king knocked the dwellers |
| Wasted the Scots widely | Of Bretland and struck down |
| With the sword. The dealer of gold | The Cumberlanders, and greed |
| Made the sword play in Man. | Did leave the vultures. |

Olav was four years on this journey from the time when he went from Vendland until he came to the Scilly Isles.

31. When Olav was in the Scilly Isles he learned that there was on the island a soothsayer who foretold forthcoming tidings, and many believed that things often went according to his words. Olav

Olav is carried to his ship

had a list to prove this man's sooth-saying; so he sent the most handsome and biggest of his men, clad as finely as possible, and bade him say that he was the king, for Olav was known all over the land in that he was more handsome, bolder and bigger than all other men. But after he went from Russia he used no other name than to say he was called Ali and that he was a Russian. And when the messenger came to the soothsayer and told him he was the king, he got this answer: "Thou art not the king: but this is my counsel that thou be true to thy king". He said no more to the man. The messenger went back to the king and told Olav, who now had a much greater list to find this man, when he had such an answer from him. He now had no

1 *Wales,* in O.N. *Bretland.*    2 I.e. north of France.

doubt that he was a true soothsayer. Olav then went to him and asked what he foretold about Olav's future, if he would have kingdoms or other luck. The hermit answered with holy soothsaying: "Thou shalt be a glorious king and bring forth glorious work. Thou shalt bring many men to the truth and to become Christian. Thereby shalt thou help thyself and many others, and that thou shalt not have doubt about my answer, thou canst have this evidence: near to thy ships wilt thou meet treachery and foes and wilt come to battle; thou wilt lose some of thy men and thou thyself wilt be wounded. From that wound thou shalt near be dead and be borne on the shields to thy ship; but from that wound thou wilt be well in seven nights and shortly after wilt thou be baptised". After that, Olav went down to his ships and there he met foes, who would slay him and his men. But the meeting ended as the hermit had told him, so that Olav was borne wounded out to his ship and likewise was he well after seven nights. Then it seemed clear to Olav that this man had told him the truth and that he was a true soothsayer, from whom he had this foretelling. Olav then went again to find the man, spoke much with him and asked carefully whence he had this wisdom by which he foretold the future. The hermit said that the God of Christian men let him know all he wished, and then he told Olav of many great works of God and after all these words Olav agreed to be baptised, and so it came about that Olav and all his following were baptised. He stayed there very long and learned the right faith and took with him from there priests and other learned men.

32. From the Scilly Isles, Olav sailed in the autumn to England; he lay there in a haven, and now went about peacefully, for England was a Christian country and he was also a Christian. Then it happened that messages were sent all over the land summoning a thing. And when the thing was met, there came a queen called Gyda, the sister of Anlaf Cuaran,[1] who was King of Dublin in Ireland. She had been married to a mighty jarl in England; he was now dead, but she ruled the land after him. But there was in her county a man called Alvini, a great warrior and a fighter of duels. He had wooed her, but she answered that she would herself choose whom she wanted from the

1 *Anlaf Cuaran* (in O.S. *Olaf Kvaran*) is often mentioned in English history during the reigns of Athelstan, Edmund and Edred. Gyda, his sister, or probably half-sister, must have been considerably younger than Anlaf in order to marry Olav Trygvason. Chas. Haliday in his history *The Scandinavian Kingdom of Dublin* also mentions Gyda as Anlaf Cuaran's sister, and states that Anlaf lived to an old age and is supposed to have died in 992. Snorre Sturlason often makes no distinction between children borne by different mothers and merely calls them brothers and sisters.

men of her county, and for that reason was the thing gathered so that Gyda should choose herself a husband. There did Alvini come, decked out in the best clothes, and many others there were well clad. Olav was come there and wore his bad-weather clothes covered by a shaggy cape; he stood with his men farther off than the others. Gyda went and looked over every man who seemed to her to be manly. And when she came where Olav stood she looked up into his face and

asked what man he was. He called himself Ali: "I am a foreigner", he said. Gyda asked, "Wilt thou have me? So will I choose thee". "I will not say nay to that", he said, and asked about her name, parents and descent. "I am a king's daughter", she said, "from Ireland. I was wed here in this land to the jarl who ruled this county. Now after he died have I ruled it. Many men have wooed me, but there is no one to whom I will be wed. I am called Gyda." She was young

Queen Gyda chooses a husband

and beautiful, and she and Olav now talked about the matter and were of one mind about it. Olav now betrothed himself to Gyda. Alvini liked it little; but there was a custom in England that when two men rivalled each other about anything, so should there be a duel.[1] Alvini challenged Olav on this matter. They agreed on a place of battle and that there should be twelve on either side. And when they met, Olav told his men to do as he did: he had a great axe. And when Alvini would strike him with his sword he swept the sword from his hand and with a second blow he struck Alvini so that he fell. After that Olav bound Alvini fast. So it fared with all Alvini's men: they were beaten and bound and so brought home to Olav's dwelling. He then bade Alvini leave the land and never come back; Olav took all that he owned. Olav then wed Gyda and stayed in England, though sometimes in Ireland. Once when Olav was in Ireland and was on a great raid, they went in ships and had need of making a shore raid: men went up on the land and drove down a great number of cattle. Then came a bonder and he bade Olav give him the cows he owned. Olav bade him take his cows if he could find them, "but hinder not

1 The Norsemen called a duel *holmganga,* because they fought their duels on a holme (or small island).

our journey". The bonder had there a great collie dog, to which he showed the herd, which consisted of many hundreds of cattle; but the hound ran round in the whole of the herd and drove out just as many as the bonder said he had and they were all marked in the same way. They knew then that the dog had chosen rightly and he seemed remarkably clever. Then Olav asked the bonder if he would give him the hound. "Readily", said the bonder. In return Olav straightway gave him a gold ring and vowed his friendship. The hound was called Vigi and it was the best of all hounds. Olav had it for a long time after that.

33. The Danish king Harald Gormson learned that Hacon the Jarl had cast away Christianity and had harried far and wide in the Danish king's land. Then Harald, the Danish king, called out the army and went to Norway. And when he came to the land where Hacon the Jarl had the rule, he harried there and wasted all the land, and he then came with his army to the islands called Solunder.[1] Only five farms were left unburned in Læradale in Sogn, and all the folk fled to the fells and woods with all that they could get. And then the Danish king would sail with his army to Iceland to avenge himself, because all the Icelanders had made shameful verses about him. It had been made a law in Iceland that for every man in the land a scurvy verse should be made about the Danish king. The fact of the matter was that a ship owned by Iceland men had stranded in Denmark and the Danes took all the goods and called it wreckage, and he who had planned it was the king's farm bailiff, called Birger. Shabby verses were made about them both; this is one of them:

| | |
|---|---|
| The murderous Harald | But the powerless Birger |
| Rode on the sea steed from the south | A wreck of the land sprites |
| In the shape of Faxi the stallion, | (As all must see) |
| The Vend-slayer was nothing but wax. | Practised like a mare. |

King Harald bade a troll-wise man go to Iceland in the shape of some animal and see what he could tell him; he went in the shape of a whale. And when he came to the land he went west along the north side. He saw that all the fells and howes were full of land sprites, some big, others small. And when he came outside Vapnafjord, he went into the fjord and wished to go ashore. Then came a great dragon down from the dale followed by many serpents, toads and adders, and they blew poison at him. Then he went away west along the land till he was outside Eyjafjord. He went into the fjord, but there came against him a bird so big that its wings neared the fells

---

1 *Solunder*, now Solund, outside the Sognfjord.

on both sides of it; with it there were a big number of other birds, both great and small. He went away from there towards the west round the land and then south to Breidafjord,[1] and there he went into the fjord. Towards him came a great ox that waded out in the sea and began to bellow horribly; a great many land sprites followed him. Away he went from there to the south round by Reykjanes[2] and would go up to Vikarskeid.[3] But against him there came a great hill giant who had an iron staff in his hand and bore his head higher than the fells, and many other giants there were a-following him. From there he went east all the way along the land: "There was nothing", he said, "but sand and deserts and great burned clearings without, but so great is the sea between the lands that no man can sail there with longships". At that time Brodd Helgi was in Vapnafjord, Eyolf Valgerdson in Eyjafjord, Tord Gelli in Breidafjord and Torodd the Good in Olfus. After that the Danish king turned south with his army alongside the land and went south to Denmark. But Hacon the Jarl had all the farms rebuilt and afterwards paid no scot to the Danish king.

34. King Harald's son Swein—he who was afterwards called Forkbeard[4]—craved a kingdom of his father, King Harald. But just as before, King Harald would not share Denmark and would give him no kingdom. Thereupon Swein gathered warships and said he would go on a viking raid. But when the whole of his army was come together and Palna Toki of the Jomsvikings[5] was come to his help, Swein steered to Zealand and into Isefjord. There lay his father, King Harald, with his ships, and they were manned to go to battle. Swein came to battle with him and there was a great fight. But then folk turned to King Harald so that Swein was overpowered and fled. There King Harald got such wounds that he died. After that Swein was taken as king in Denmark. Sigvaldi was at that time the jarl in Jomsborg[5] in Vendland; he was the son of King Strut-Harald who had ruled over Scania, and Sigvaldi's brothers were Heming and Thorkel the High.[6] There were also with the Jomsvikings as chieftains Bui Digre of Borgundarholm[7] and his brother Sigurd; there

---

1 *Breidafjord* is the great bay on the western coast of Iceland.   2 *Reykjanes* is the most south-westerly point in Iceland.   3 *Vikarskeid*, now Skeid, a flat beach outside the River Olfus on the southern shore.   4 *Swein Forkbeard*, the father of King Canute; cf. chapter 28.   5 *The Jomsvikings* came from *Jomsborg*, a fortified town on the east side of Wollin, the big island at the mouth of the River Oder. Jomsborg does not exist in our days. 6 *Thorkel the High* later came to England in company with St Olav, joined forces with King Ethelred and defended London against the Danes; cf. 'History of St Olav', chapter 12.   7 I.e. Bornholm (in the Baltic) belonging to Denmark; cf. chapters 21 and 22.

were also Vagn, son of Aki and Torgunna, the son of the sister of
Bui and Sigurd. Sigvaldi the Jarl had taken King Swein prisoner
and brought him to Jomsborg in Vendland and forced him to make
peace with Burislav, king of the Vends, and to let Sigvaldi secure the
peace between them (for Sigvaldi the Jarl had then wed Astrid, King
Burislav's daughter); otherwise, said the jarl, he would give King
Swein into the Vends' hands. And the king knew that they would
torture him to death, and he therefore agreed to let the jarl make the
peace. The jarl deemed that King Swein should take King Burislav's
daughter Gunhild, and King Burislav should wed Tyri Harald's
daughter, King Swein's sister; each should have his kingdom and
there should be peace between the lands. After that King Swein went
home to Denmark with his wife Gunhild: their sons were Harald and
Canute the Mighty. At that time the Danes often threatened to go
with an army to Norway against Hacon the Jarl.

35. King Swein made a great feast and called to him all the chiefs
who were in his kingdom; he would take the inheritance[1] after his
father Harald. A little before this there had also died Strut-Harald
in Scania, and Veseti in Borgundarholm, the father of Bui Digre.
The king sent bidding to the Jomsvikings that Sigvaldi the Jarl and
Bui and their brothers should come there and take the inheritance
after their fathers at that feast just as the king did. The Jomsvikings went to the feast with all the boldest of their folk; they had
forty ships from Vendland and twenty from Scania; and a great many
men came there together. The first day of the feast, before King Swein
stepped into his father's high-seat, he drank his cup of remembrance
and made a vow that ere three years were gone he would go to
England with his army and slay King Ethelred or drive him from the
land.[2] That cup of remembrance should all drink who were at that
feast. Then was poured out for the chiefs of the Jomsborg vikings
the strongest drink there was and in the biggest horns. And when
that cup was drunk up all men should drink a cup of remembrance for
Christ, and always to the Jomsvikings was borne the fullest horn and
the strongest drink. The third was the cup of St Michael and all drank
it. After that Sigvaldi the Jarl drank his father's cup and made a vow
that ere three years were gone he would come to Norway and slay
Hacon the Jarl or drive him from the land. Then Thorkel the High,
his brother, vowed to follow Sigvaldi to Norway and not fly from
battle so long as Sigvaldi was fighting. Bui Digre then vowed that

1 It was a custom for the successor to hold a feast and drink the heirship ale.    2 Cf.
'History of St Olav', chapter 12.

he would go with them to Norway and not fly before Hacon the Jarl from battle. Then his brother Sigurd vowed that he would go to Norway and not fly so long as the greatest part of the Jomsvikings were fighting. Vagn Akason vowed that he would go with them to Norway and not come back before he had slain Thorkel Leira and

Sigvaldi the Jarl makes a vow at the cup of remembrance to his father

lain in bed with his daughter Ingebjörg. Many other chiefs made vows about other things. That day the men drank the inheritance ale, but next morning when the Jomsvikings had slept it off, they thought they had said big words and now held a meeting and counselled how they should carry out their promises. They agreed to arm themselves as quickly as possible and make ready their ships and men. And the rumour of it spread far and wide in the lands.

36. Eric the Jarl, son of Hacon, learned these tidings when he was in Raumarik. He straightway drew folk to him and went to the Uplands and then over the fells to Trondheim to his father, Hacon the Jarl. About that Tord Kolbeinson says in Eric's drapa:

And truly there came far
From the south great tales
Of war and steel-clad fighters,
And the bonders feared strife.

The ships' ruler learned
That the Danish longships
Were dragged from the strand
And down to the sea.

37. Hacon the Jarl and Eric the Jarl bade the war arrows be sent over all Trondlaw and sent bidding to both North and South Möre and to Raumsdale as far north as Naumadale and Halogaland,

and then called up a full levy of men and ships. So is it said in Eric's drapa:

| | |
|---|---|
| The scald's praises grow! | When the mighty warrior |
| The shield-bearer let many | Would guard with the shield |
| Longships, cutters and boats | His father's land: a great fleet |
| Be borne to the sea, | Then lay off the land. |

Hacon the Jarl went straight south to Möre to spy and gather men, and Eric drew the army together and took it towards the south.

38. The Jomsvikings sailed with their army to Limfjord and therefrom they sailed out to sea; they had sixty ships. They came to Agder and then sailed straightway north to Rogaland and thereupon began to harry as soon as they came into Hacon the Jarl's land; they continued sailing northwards, everywhere with the shield of war. There was a man called Geirmund who went with a speedy boat and some men. He came forth into Möre and found Hacon the Jarl, went straight before the table and told the jarl the tidings that

Geirmund bears witness to Hacon the Jarl by showing him his struck-off hand

in the south of the land there was an army come from Denmark. The jarl asked if he knew it to be true. Geirmund thrust up one arm of which the hand was struck off and said that there was clear witness that an army was in the land. Then the jarl asked carefully about this army, and Geirmund said that the Jomsvikings were there and that they had slain many men and robbed far and wide. "And yet do they go", said he, "both swiftly and eagerly. I think that it will not be long before they come forth hither". The jarl rowed then through all the fjords, in along one side and out along the other; he went day and night and had spies on the upper way over Eidet,[1] both south in the Fjords[2] and likewise in the north,

1 *Eidet*, i.e. Mandseidet in Statland. Cf. 'History of Hacon the Good', chapter 22.
2 *The Fjords*, i.e. Nordfjord and Söndfjord.

where Eric went with his army. About that is it said in Eric's drapa:

| | |
|---|---|
| The doughty battle jarl, | Many oars trembled, |
| Who had longships on the sea, | But there was no fear of death |
| Brought against Sigvaldi | Amongst the seamen, who pulled |
| His high-built stems. | The oar blades. |

Eric the Jarl went south with his army as quickly as he could.

39. Sigvaldi the Jarl sailed north with his army round Stad and came first to the Heröys.[1] And although the vikings found the land folk, they never told the truth of what the jarl was doing. The vikings harried wherever they came. They lay in by the Isle of Hod,[2] went ashore there and harried, and they brought to the ships both men and cattle, and all weapon-bearing carls they slew. And when they went down to the ships an old bonder came up to them and Bui's men were near. The bonder said: "Ye go not forth like warriors, driving to the strand both cows and calves; it would be a greater capture for you to take the bear, now ye are come so near the bear's den". "What sayeth the carl?" they shouted: "canst thou tell us aught of Hacon the Jarl?" The bonder answered: "Yesterday he went into Hjorundarfjord:[3] he had a ship or two, not more than three, and he had then heard nothing about you". Bui and his men began at once to leap to their ships and left all their booty behind. Bui said: "Let us now make good use of the news we have had, so that we be nighest unto victory". And when they came up to the ships, they straightway rowed away. Sigvaldi the Jarl shouted to them and asked for tidings, and they said that Hacon the Jarl was there in the fjord. Then the jarl weighed anchor and they rowed round the north of the Isle of Hod and so in and about the island.

40. Hacon the Jarl and his son Eric lay in Halkelsvik[4] where all their army was gathered. They had one and a half hundred ships.[5] They had then learned that the Jomsvikings had lain in by Hod. The jarl then rowed north to seek them, and when they came to where it is called Hjorungavag,[6] they met. Both drew up their armies for battle. Sigvaldi the Jarl's standard was in the middle of his army and right against it Hacon the Jarl arrayed his ships. Sigvaldi the Jarl had twenty ships and Hacon sixty. In Hacon the Jarl's troop there were the chiefs Thore the Hart from Halogaland and Styrkar from Gimsar. On the one wing of Sigvaldi's army were Bui Digre and his

---

1 Islands west of Hareidland. 2 Now Hareidland. 3 Now Hjörundfjord, east of Hareidland. 4 *Halkelsvik* is situated within Voldenfjord, south of Hareidland. 5 I.e. 160. 6 *Hjorungavag*, now Liavag, inside the Hjöringsnes, the north-east point of Hareidland.

brother Sigurd with twenty ships, and against them lay Jarl Eric Haconson with sixty ships and with him the chiefs Gudbrand the White from the Uplands and Thorkel Leira from the Vik. On the other wing of the Jomsborg army stood forth Vagn Akason with twenty ships, and against them Swein Haconson with Skeggi of Ophaug from Yrjar and Ragnvald from Ærvik in Stad with sixty ships. So is it said in Eric's drapa:

The fleet sailed on by the
    land
And the ocean-going boats
Hasted to the battle-meet
Against the Danish ships;
The jarl at Möre
Cleared many ships
Of the Vikings' following;
They drifted about, full of
    warm bodies.

Eyvind Scaldaspiller also says this in Haleygiatal:

That early morn
Was least of all
A meeting of joy
For the foes
Of Yngvi-Frey,
When 'gainst the Danes
The land rulers
Brought longships,
And when the sword elf
Steered from the south
The sea steeds
Against their host.

After this they brought the fleets together and now was there the grimmest of battles and many fell on both sides, but more by far on Hacon's, for the Jomsvikings fought both skilfully, boldly and sharply and they shot right through the shields; so many weapons were borne against Hacon the Jarl that his coat of mail was altogether cut up and so useless that he cast it from him. About that Tind Halkelson says:

The kirtle, which the bejewelled
Woman had made for the jarl,
Could not be borne
As the sword's whine grew louder,
And the mailed prince
Had to cast off

The sea king's sark
(For the sea steeds were cleared).
Then from the jarl was blown
Sorle's ring-woven shirt
Yonder on the sand.
He still bears the mark of it.

41. The Jomsvikings had bigger and higher-built ships, but on both sides they went forth boldly. Vagn Akason lay so hard against Swein Haconson's ship that Swein was turning thence and began to flee. Then Eric the Jarl came up and went into the line against Vagn. Vagn turned back and the ships now lay as they had lain at first. Eric turned back to his own army, where his men were falling back; and Bui, who had cut his fastenings, was setting off after the fleeing men. Eric then laid himself alongside Bui's ship and there was a sharp battle of axe blows and two or three of Eric's ships came up against Bui's one. Then a storm arose and hail fell so great that one hailstone weighed an öre. Sigvaldi then cut his fastenings and turned his ship as if to flee. Vagn Akason shouted to him and bade him not flee, but Sigvaldi would not listen to what he said. Vagn then shot a spear after him and it struck him who sat by the tiller. Sigvaldi the Jarl rowed away with thirty-five ships and left behind twenty-five. Hacon the Jarl then drew up his ship on the other side of Bui's; Bui's men then got little time between the blows. Vigfus, Vigaglum's son, took up a pointed anvil which lay on the boards and which a man had just used to solder the hilt of his sword. Vigfus was a very strong man and he cast the anvil with both hands and drove it into the head of Aslak Holmskalli, so that the point went down to his brain. No weapon had bitten upon Aslak earlier and he had struck out on both sides; he was Bui's foster-son and stem man. Another man was Howard the Hewer[1] and he was the strongest of men and very bold.

---

1 In O.N. *Hávard* (pronounced Hovard), in M.S. *Haavard*. This name is often met with in Scandinavia, and has probably come to England with the vikings or the Normans. The Scandinavian letter *aa* or *å* is pronounced as the English *o*. Hence most Scandinavian names with an *å* become *o* in English. Both *Howard* and *Haward* are family names in England.

During this battle Eric's men went up on Bui's ship and went aft on the quarterdeck against Bui. Then did Thorstein Midlang strike Bui across the nose and cleft the nose-guard; that was a great wound. Bui struck Thorstein right in the middle of his side so that he cut him in two. Bui then caught up two chests full of gold and called out: "Overboard, all Bui's men". Bui leaped overboard with the chests and many of his men followed him, but many others fell on the ship, for it was no use to ask for quarter. Then was the whole of Bui's ship cleared from stem to stern and afterwards all the others, one

The storm during the battle of Hjorungavag

after the other. After this Eric the Jarl lay to by Vagn's ship and was boldly withstood, but at last the ship was cleared and Vagn himself and thirty others were taken prisoner. They were bound and brought ashore. Then went Thorkel Leira to them and said: "That vow didst thou make, Vagn, to slay me, but it seems to me more likely that I shall slay thee". Vagn and his men sat together on a tree trunk. Thorkel had a great axe and he struck him who sat on the outside of the tree trunk. Vagn and his men were bound in such a way that a rope was knotted about their feet, but their hands were free. Then said one of them: "I have in my hand a clasp and I will stick it in the earth if I know aught when my head is off". His head was struck off and the clasp fell down from his hand. There, too, sat a handsome man with fine hair; he swept the hair over his head and held forth his neck and said: "Let no blood come on my hair". A man then took the hair in his hand and held it fast and Thorkel swung the axe to strike. The viking pulled his head away sharply and he who held the hair went forward and the axe fell down on both his hands and cut

"Wilt thou have peace, Sigurd?" said Eric the Jarl

them off, so that the axe stopped in the earth. Then Eric the Jarl came up and asked: "Who is this handsome man?" "Sigurd they call me", he said, "and I am held to be a son of Bui; not yet are all the Jomsvikings dead." Eric said, "Indeed thou must be a true son of Bui! Wilt thou have peace?" "That depends on who offers it", said Sigurd. "He offers it who has might thereto; Eric the Jarl!" "Then I will", he said; he was then loosened from the rope. Then said Thorkel Leira: "If thou wilt let all these men have peace, jarl, yet never shall Vagn Akason come from it with his life", and so he rushed forward with the lifted axe. But the viking Skardi threw himself on the rope and he fell before Thorkel's feet. Thorkel fell full length over him; Vagn grabbed the axe, swung it up and struck Thorkel his death blow with it. Then said the jarl, "Vagn, wilt thou have peace?" "I will", he said, "if we all have it." "Loosen them from the rope", said the jarl, and so was it done. Eighteen men were slain and twelve got peace.

42. Hacon the Jarl and many of his men sat on a tree trunk and a bowstring twanged on Bui's ship; the arrow fell on Gissur of Valders, a lord of the land, who sat nearest the jarl, and was proudly clad. Some went on board the ship and found Howard the Hewer standing on his knees by the ship's bulwark, for his legs were smitten from him: he had the bow in his hand. And when they came out on the ship, Howard asked, "Who fell from the tree trunk?" They said that he was called Gissur. "Then was my luck less than I would." "The bad luck was great enough", they said, "and thou shalt do no more", and they slew him. The slain were then ransacked and the booty borne away to be dealt out. Twenty-five ships of the Jomsvikings were cleared. Thus says Tind:

He, who bade the raven flocks  
To feed (the swords struck his legs),  
Long they fought  
Against the Vender's friend,  

Till he, who ruined  
The shields, had cleared  
Five and twenty ships:  
Perilous was the fight.

After that the armies parted. Hacon the Jarl went to Trondheim and liked it ill that Eric had given Vagn Akason quarter. It is a tale among men that Hacon the Jarl had in that battle sacrificed his son Erling to get victory, and that after the hailstorm came, the Jomsvikings lost many men. Eric the Jarl then went to the Uplands and then east into his own lands, and Vagn Akason went with him. Eric married Vagn to Ingebjörg, the daughter of Thorkel Leira, gave him a goodly longship with all gear and manned it. They parted the best of friends. Vagn then went home south to Denmark and afterwards became a well-known man; many mighty men are come from him.

43. Harald the Grenlander was king in Vestfold as is written above (chapter 15); he married Asta, the daughter of Gudbrand Kula. One summer when Harald the Grenlander was on a raid in the eastern countries to win himself goods, he came to Sweden. Olav the Swede was king there at that time and he was the son of Eric the Victorious and Sigrid, the daughter of Skogul-Tosti. Sigrid was now widowed and she had many great estates in Sweden. And when she heard that her foster-brother Harald the Grenlander was come into the land not far from there, she sent men to him and bade him to a feast; he was at once ready and went there with a great following of men. It was a great feast; the king and the queen sat in the high-seats and both drank together in the evening, and the drink was well

poured out for his men. In the evening when the king went to bed, his bed was covered with a rich spread and hung with costly clothes; in the house there were few men. And when the king was undressed and had gone to bed, the queen came to him and herself poured out drink for him; she urged him much to drink and she was very blithe. The king was very drunk and so was she. Then he went to sleep, and the queen also went to her bedroom. Sigrid was a very wise woman and foresaw many things. The next morning the drinking began again. But it happened, as often it does when people get drunk, that the next day most of them were more careful with the drink; but the queen was merry and she and Harald talked together. She said she held that the possessions and estates she had in Sweden were worth no less than his kingdom and possessions in Norway. By that speech the king became sad and found little joy in anything. He would go away and was sick at heart, but the queen was glad and saw him off with great gifts. In the autumn Harald went back to Norway; he was at home in the winter and was by no means happy. The next summer he went east with his army and sailed to Sweden; he sent word to Sigrid that he wished to meet her. She rode down to him and they talked together. Straightway he came out with the words, would Sigrid wed him? She answered that it was silly of him, for he was already so well married that it was a good marriage for him. Harald said that Asta was a good and clever woman, "but she is not of such good lineage as I". Sigrid answered, "It may be that thou art of greater kin than she; yet I should think that with her rests the good fortune of both of you". They exchanged few words before Sigrid rode away. King Harald was then very heavy in his mind. He made himself ready to ride up into the land and again meet Queen Sigrid. Many of his men counselled him against it, but none the less he went with a great following of men and came to the estates which the queen owned. The same evening another king came thither; he was called Vissavald[1] and came from the east from Gardarik; he came to woo the queen. The kings and all their folk took their seats in a great and ancient hall: so old, too, were all the fittings of the hall. Over-much drink there was in the evening and drink so strong that all were drunk and both the chief guard and the night watch were asleep. Then in the night Queen Sigrid bade her men fall on them with fire and weapons. There were burned both the hall and the men who were in it, and they who dragged themselves out were slain. Sigrid said that in this way would she make these small kings loathe coming from

1 The Russian name 'Vsevolod'.

other lands to woo her: she was afterwards called Sigrid the Strong-minded.

44. The battle of the Jomsvikings in Hjorungavag had been fought during the winter before. When Harald went up into the land, Rani had been left behind with the ships and was at the head of the men who stayed behind. And when they learned that Harald had lost his life, they forthwith went back to Norway and told these tidings. Rani went to Asta and told her all about that journey and likewise on what errand Harald had gone to Queen Sigrid. Asta

Asta hears of the unfaithfulness of her husband, Harald the Grenlander

straightway went to the Uplands to her father when she learned these tidings and he received her well. But both were very wroth over what had happened in Sweden and because Harald had thought to leave her. In the summer, Asta, Gudbrand's daughter, bore a son; the boy was called Olav[1] when he was sprinkled with water. Rani it was who sprinkled him with water. The boy was at first brought up with Gudbrand and his mother Asta.

45. Hacon the Jarl ruled over all Norway along the sea coast and he had sixteen folk districts[2] to mind. But after Harald Hairfair had made a law that there should be a jarl in every folk district, this

1 The later St Olav.    2 *Folk districts*, or shires.

custom was long kept up. Hacon the Jarl had sixteen jarls under him. Thus is it said in Vellekla:

Where else is it known
That one land ruler reigns
Over the fortune of sixteen jarls?
The army should be mindful of that.

To all corners of heaven[1]
The fame is now raised
Of the mighty leader's
Heroic actions.

Whilst Hacon the Jarl was ruling over Norway, there were good seasons in the land and good peace between the bonders within. The jarl was befriended by the bonders for the greater part of his life. But as time went on, it often happened with the jarl that he was improper in his dealings with women; the report went far and wide that the jarl had the daughters of mighty men taken and brought home to him; he lay with them a week or two and then sent them home. Hereby he was shown great unfriendliness by the women's kinsmen and the bonders began to grumble just as the Tronds are wont to do over anything which goes against them.

46. Hacon the Jarl heard something to the effect that there was a man across the sea in the west who called himself Ali and who was held as king; and the jarl gathered from the talking of some men that he might be a man of Norse royal blood. He was told that Ali called himself a Gardarik-man by birth, and the jarl had learned that Trygvi Olavson had had a son who had gone east into Gardarik and that he was there brought up with King Valdemar, and that he was called Olav. The jarl himself had also asked much about this man and gathered that he had come into the Westlands. There was a man called Thore Klakka, a good friend of Hacon the Jarl; he spent much time on viking raids, but often he went on trading journeys and knew the lands far and wide. Hacon the Jarl sent this man west across the sea, bade him go on a trading journey to Dublin, as at that time many were used to do, and find out what man this Ali was. And if he learned for a truth that it was Olav Trygvason or some other of the Norse kings' blood, Thore should lay traps of guile against him if he could.

47. Thereupon Thore went west to Ireland to Dublin and asked about Ali, who was there with his brother-in-law Anlaf Cuaran. After this Thore managed to get Olav in talk: Thore was very wise of speech and when they had talked together for a long time, Ali began to ask about Norway, first about the Upland-kings and which of them were now alive or what kingdom they had; he also asked about Hacon the Jarl, how much liked he was in the land. Thore answered: "The jarl is so mighty a man that no one dare say any

1 *Heaven* was called in O.S. *hifinn* or *himinn*.

other than that which he wishes, but the fact of the matter is that there is no other man in authority; but to tell you the truth, I know the mind of many great men and so too of the people, who would be most happy and ready if some king of Harald Hairfair's race came to the kingdom; but now we know no likelihood of that and mostly on the ground that to struggle against Hacon the Jarl has been proved to bring ill-reward". And when they had often talked about this, Olav confessed to Thore his name and race and asked his counsel, whether he thought that the bonders would take Olav as king if he went to Norway. Thore egged him on to that journey eagerly and praised him and his doughtiness over-much. Olav then began to wish to go to the kingdom of his fathers. Thereafter he sailed from the west with five ships, first to the Hebrides. Thore was on the journey with him. He then sailed to the Orkneys and at that time Jarl Sigurd Lodverson lay in Asmundvag[1] in Ronaldsey with a longship and intended going over to Caithness. Olav then sailed with his army from the west to the isles and lay in the harbour there, for Pentland Firth was not navigable. And when the king found out that the jarl lay there, he called him to talk with him. And when the jarl came to the king, they had not talked long before the king said that the jarl and all his folk should become Christian, otherwise he should die forthwith; the king said he would go with fire and sword over the isles and waste the land if the folk would not take up Christianity. But such was the position of the jarl that he chose to take baptism; he was then baptised and so too were all the folk who were there with him. After this the jarl swore oaths to the king and became his man, gave him his son (who was called Whelp or Hound) as a hostage; him did Olav take with him to Norway. Olav now sailed east on the sea and reached the coast by Moster.[2] There he first came to land in Norway and had mass sung there in a land tent; in that same spot a church was afterwards built. Thore Klakka told the king that it was advisable that he should not make known who he was and not let the least news of him go forth, and that he should fare as quickly as he could to the jarl and come upon him suddenly. King Olav did so: he went north night and day just as the wind served and let the land folk know nothing about the journey he was taking there. And when he came north to Agdenes,[3] he learned that Hacon the

1 *Asmundvag*, now Osmondwall, is a harbour in the island of Hoy, opposite South Ronaldsey; it is still used for waiting for a favourable tide to cross the Pentland Firth. The tide at times is very strong and unfavourable for crossing to Scotland in sailing vessels. 2 In South Hordaland, inside Bömmelöy. 3 *Agdenes*, at the entrance of the Trondheimsfjord.

Jarl was within the fjord and also that he was not at one with the bonders. And when Thore heard this news, it was rather otherwise than he had expected, for after the battle with the Jomsvikings all men in Norway had become friendly to Hacon the Jarl on account of the victory he had won and because he had freed the whole land from unrest. But now, by ill-luck, a great leader had come into the land and the bonders were at enmity with the jarl.

48. Hacon the Jarl was at a feast in Medalhus[1] in Guldale, but his ships lay outside by Vigg.[2] There was a man called Orm Lyrgja, a mighty bonder, who dwelt on Bynes.[3] He had a wife called Gudrun, daughter of Bergtor of Lundar.[4] She was known as the Sun of Lundar; she was a very beautiful woman. The jarl sent his thralls to Orm on the errand of bringing Orm's wife Gudrun to him. The thralls went forth on their errand and Orm bade them first go to their supper; and before the thralls were done with the food, there came to Orm from the houses many men whom he had sent for. Orm said then that Gudrun should by no means go with the thralls. And Gudrun bade the thralls tell the jarl that she would not come to him unless he sent Thora of Rimol[5] for her: Thora was a mighty lady and one of the jarl's mistresses. The thralls said that they would come there again so that the bonder and his wife would quickly repent of it, and they used great threats before they went away. And Orm bade the arrow of war be sent over all the four roads of the district and let word follow with the behest that all should go with weapons against Hacon the Jarl and slay him. He also sent bidding to Haldor of Skerdingstedja[6] and forthwith Haldor sent out the arrow of war. A little before this the jarl had taken the wife of a man called Brynjulv and that deed had done much harm and an army had then nearly been raised. After the call all the folk ran forth and went to Medalhus. But the jarl had news of it and got away with his men to a deep dale, now called Jarlsdale, and they hid themselves there. The next day the jarl kept a lookout for the army of bonders, who had placed men on all the roads and thought most that the jarl had gone to his ships, but his son Erlend, a hopeful young man, looked after the ships. And when night fell, the jarl sent his folk away and bade them go by the wood paths out into Orkedale: "No man will do you harm, if I am not somewhere in the neighbourhood; send word to Erlend that

1 Cf. 'History of Hacon the Good', p. 88, n. 1.    2 *Vigg*, now Viggen by the Orkedale's fjord.    3 In Guldale.    4 *Lundar*, now Lunde in Guldale.    5 *Rimol*, now Romol on the west side of the Gulelven (the Gul River) opposite Medalhus. 6 *Skerdingstedja*, now Skerdingstad, south of Medalhus (Melhus).

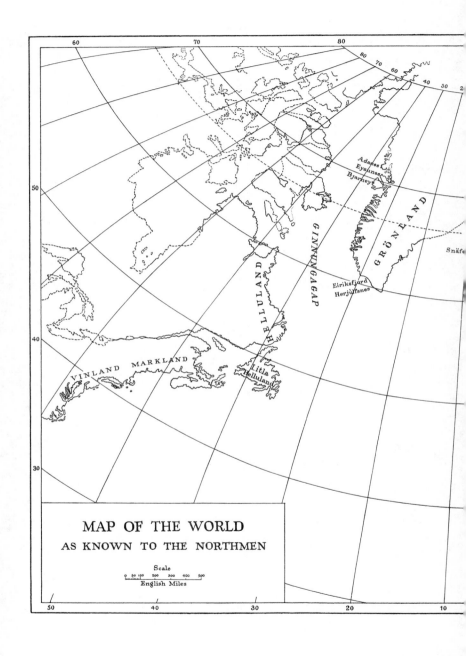

MAP OF THE WORLD
AS KNOWN TO THE NORTHMEN

Scale
0  50 100   200    300   400   500
English Miles

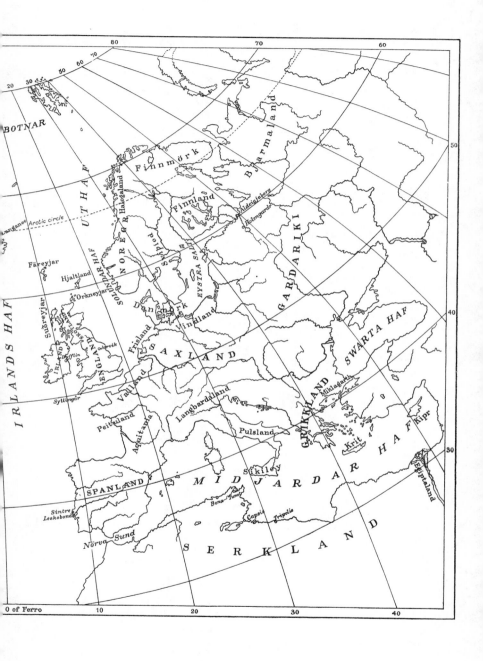

BOTNAR

IRLANDS HAF

Færeyjar

Hjaltland

Orkneyjar

Snöreyjar

UTHAF

Finnmörk

Finnland

Bjarmaland

Aldeigjuborg

Holmgardr

GARDARIKI

SOLUNDAR HAF

NOREGR

Halogaland

Danmörk

Vindland

SAXLAND

ENGLAND

Frisland

SWARTA HAF

Valland

Peituland

Aquitania

Langbardaland

GRIKKLAND

Miklagardr

SPANLAND

Sintre

Leskobondi

Norva Sund

MIDJARDAR HAF

Sikiley

Bona

Capsa

Tripolis

Krit

Kipr

Egiptaland

SERKLAND

0 of Ferro

Arctic circle

EYSTRA SALT

he shall go out of the fjord, so that we can meet at Möre. I can manage to hide myself yet from the bonders". Thereafter the jarl left and with him his thrall, who was called Kark. Ice lay on the Gulelven and into it the jarl drove his horse and left his cape behind, and they went into the cave which was afterwards called Jarlsheller. There they slept, and when Kark awoke he told his dream, that a black fell man came near the cave and he was afraid that he would come in; but the man told him that "Ulli" was dead. The jarl said that Erlend must have been slain. Again Tormod Kark slept for a second time and shouted in his sleep; and when he awoke he told his dream, that he saw the same man going down and he bade him tell the jarl that now were all the sounds blocked. Kark told the jarl his dream: he thought that such a dream must betoken a short life for him. He stood up and they went to the houses at Rimol. The jarl then sent Kark to Thora and bade her come secretly to him; she did so and she greeted him well. The jarl bade her hide him for a few nights until the bonders broke up their gathering. "Here will they seek you", she said, "in my houses, both without and within, for many will know that I am eager to help you all I can; but there is a place in my farmstead where I know they would not look for such a man; it is the swine-sty." They went to it and the jarl said, "Here shall we now fit ourselves up: we must first take heed of our lives". Then the thrall dug there a great hole and bore the earth away; then he laid boards over it. Thora told the jarl the tidings that Olav Trygvason was come into the fjord and had slain his son Erlend. The jarl now went into the hole that had been dug, and Kark went with him. Thora spread boards over it, swept earth and muck over all, and drove the swine over it. That swine-sty lay under a great rock.

49. Olav Trygvason sailed into the fjord with five longships and Hacon the Jarl's son Erlend rowed out against him with three ships. And when the ships neared each other, Erlend and his men gathered that there was unrest and they turned towards the land. When Olav had seen the longships going out along the fjord and rowing towards him, he thought that Hacon the Jarl must be there and bade his men row after them as fast as they could. And when Erlend's men had almost come to land, they rowed aground and straightway leapt overboard and made for the land. Then Olav's ships came up. Olav saw where a very handsome man was swimming, so he grabbed the tiller and cast it after the man and the blow fell on the head of Erlend, the jarl's son, so that his skull burst right down to the brain: there Erlend lost his life. Olav's men slew many men, but some got away by flight

and some they took prisoner and gave them quarter and then had tidings from them. Olav was told that the bonders had driven Hacon the Jarl away, he had fled from them and all his troops were dispersed. After that the bonders came to Olav; both sides were glad to meet and they straightway agreed to combine. The bonders took him as their king and together they agreed to search for Hacon the Jarl. They went up to Guldale and it seemed to them most likely that the jarl would be at Rimol, if he were at any of the farms, for Thora was the dearest friend he had in the dale. They now went there and looked for the jarl within and without but found him not. Olav then held a husthing out in the farmstead and he himself stood up on a great rock which was near the swine-sty. Then Olav spoke and his words were in this wise, that he would reward both with goods and honour that man who brought scathe to Hacon the Jarl. The jarl and Kark heard this speech: they had a light with them. The jarl said: "Why art thou so wan and sometimes as black as the earth? Is it not that thou wilt betray me?" "Nay", said Kark. "We two were born on one night", said the jarl; "it will be but a short while between our deaths." Towards evening Olav went away and when it was night the jarl was awake, but Kark slept and bore himself ill. The jarl woke him and asked what he dreamed. He said, "I was then in Lade, and Olav Trygvason put a gold necklet about my neck". The jarl answered, "Then will Olav Trygvason lay a blood-red ring about thy neck if thou dost meet him. Watch now for it; but of me thou wilt have goods as before, if thou betray me not". After that they both kept awake, as if each were keeping watch on the other: but towards day the jarl slept and bore himself ill, and so much so that he shot his heels and the back of his head under him as if he would stand up, and he shrieked loudly and horribly. Kark became afraid and horror-struck and he grabbed a great knife from his belt, stuck it in the jarl's throat and cut it out. That was the death of Hacon the Jarl. After this, Kark cut off the jarl's head and sprang out and came the next day to Lade and brought the jarl's head to King Olav. He told him then all the happenings of the journey of Hacon the Jarl and himself, as it is already written. King Olav had him taken away and had his head struck off.

50. King Olav and a great many bonders with him went out to Nidarholm;[1] he had with him the heads of Hacon the Jarl and Kark. The island was at that time used for the slaying of thieves and felons,

[1] *Nidarholm*, now Munkholmen by the mouth of the Nidelven (River Nid), Trondheim.

and a gallows stood there. He had the heads of Hacon the Jarl and Kark brought to it. The whole army gathered there and shouted and cast stones at them and said that there could the one outcast fare with the other. Afterwards the folk went up to Guldale, took out the body, dragged it away and burned it. The strength of the enmity, which the Tronds now showed towards Hacon the Jarl, became so great that no one dared name him in any other way than as "the evil jarl"; this by-name was used long after. But it is still true to say about Hacon the Jarl that he had many abilities to make him a leader, first great lineage and then wisdom and insight to use his power, boldness in battle and thereto the good luck of winning victories and slaying his foes. Thus says Torleiv Raudfeldarson:

Hacon! We have not
A more noble jarl
'Neath the path of the moon.
In strife did he win honour,
Nine heirs to Odin
Didst thou send—their bodies
The ravens ate. For that
Canst thou now be lord of much.

The most generous of men was Hacon the Jarl, but for such a chief he had the greatest ill-luck on his death day. But now matters were brought to a head; the time was come when blood offerings and the blood priests were foredoomed, and in their place came the holy faith and the right worship.

51. At a general thing in Trondheim, Olav Trygvason was taken as king over all the land that Harald Hairfair had had. The people in great numbers got up and would hear no other than that Olav Trygvason should be their king. Olav then went over the whole land and put it under him: all men in Norway turned in obedience to him; even the chiefs in the Uplands and the Vik, who had before held their lands from the Danish king, now became Olav's men and held their land of him. Thus he went over the land during the first winter and in the following summer. Eric Haconson the Jarl and his brother Swein and their other kinsmen and friends fled from the land, made east to Sweden to King Olav the Swede and had good welcome there. Thus says Tord Kolbeinson:

Thou robber-foe! Fate
Can quickly alter much!
Short was the time ere treachery
Of men sent Hacon to his death.
But to that land, which the stalwart
Warrior had won in fight,
There now did come the son
Of Trygvi, who had fared from the
    west.

More in his mind had Eric
Against that king
Than now we will say,
For such must be expected of
    him.
Wrathfully the jarl sought
Counsel with the Swedish king,
But the Tronds became stubborn,
No man could hinder it.

52. Lodin was the name of a man from the Vik, rich and of great lineage: he was often on trading journeys, but sometimes he went a-raiding. One summer Lodin went trading in the eastern countries and he owned the whole ship and had a great cargo. He sailed to Estland and during the summer was busy with trade. Whilst the market was open many kinds of wares were brought thither; there were also many thralls for sale. Lodin saw a woman who had been sold as a thrall, and when he looked on the woman he knew that she was Astrid, Eric's daughter,[1] whom King Trygvi had had. She was now unlike what she had been, when he saw her before, for she was now wan and thin and ill-clad. He went to her and asked how things were with her and she said: "It is heavy to tell about that; I have been sold as a thrall and am brought hither to be sold". After that they knew each other and Astrid had good knowledge of him. She asked him if he would buy

Lodin's meeting with Astrid in Estland

her and take her home with him to her kin. "I will give thee choice about that", he said; "I will take thee to Norway, if thou wilt wed me." And as Astrid was now in great need, and as she knew that Lodin was of great lineage and a bold and rich man, she promised him that, in order to be freed. Lodin then bought Astrid, took her home with him to Norway and wed her with the goodwill of her kinsmen. Their children were Thorkel Nevja, Ingerid and Ingegerd. Her daughters by King Trygvi were Ingebjörg and Astrid. Now the sons of Eric Bjodaskalli were Sigurd Karlshead, Jostein and Thorkel Dydrill, who were all noble and wealthy men, and had their estates in the east of the land. And two brothers, called Torgeir and Hyrning, who dwelt east in the Vik, wed the daughters of Lodin and Astrid.

53. When the Danish king Harald Gormson had taken the Christian faith, he sent bidding over all his kingdom that all men should be baptised and should turn to the true faith. He himself followed on

1 *Astrid, Eric's daughter*, the mother of Olav Trygvason; cf. chapter 6, where Olav was parted from her.

the heels of that behest and moreover used might and punishment, when nothing else availed. He sent two jarls, called Urguthrjot and Brimilskjar,[1] with many men to Norway; they were to order Norway to become Christian; this was also done in the Vik where King Harald's might prevailed and many men of that land were baptised. But after Harald's death, his son Swein Forkbeard went soon on a raid both to Saxland and Friesland and at last to England. But in Norway those who had taken up Christianity fell back to the blood offering just as they had also done before in the north of the land. But when Olav Trygvason became king of Norway, he stayed a long time during the summer in the Vik. There came to him many of his kinsmen, some that were allied to him, and many who had been his father's good friends. He welcomed them with great love. Olav then called to him his mother's brothers, his step-father Lodin and his brothers-in-law Torgeir and Hyrning. And with the greatest warmth he put before them a matter which they should take up with him and afterwards help on with all their skill, namely, that he intended to have Christianity throughout the whole of his kingdom. He said he would set out to convert all Norway to Christianity or otherwise die. "I shall make you all great and mighty men, for I trust you most on the grounds of kinship and friendship." All these men agreed to do as he bade and, together with those who would follow their advice, to help him in everything he wished. King Olav straightway opened the matter with the common folk, that he would ask all men in his kingdom to become Christian. Those who had already promised to do so, agreed first to that behest, and they were the mightiest present: all the others followed them. Thereupon all the men in the east in the Vik were baptised. Now the king went north in the Vik and bade all men take up Christianity, and those who spoke against it he dealt with hard; some he slew, some he maimed and some he drove away from the land. So it came about far and wide over all the kingdom which his father King Trygvi had formerly ruled and likewise over that which his kinsman Harald the Grenlander had had, that all the folk took up Christianity as Olav bade. And in that summer and the following winter the folk in the whole of the Vik were all converted to Christianity.

54. Early in the spring, King Olav went out of the Vik and had

---

1 In a recent Norwegian translation of Snorre Sturlason there appears to be some misunderstanding about these two names. It is contended that they do not exist in Snorre's text. As Peringskiold, Schöning and P. A. Munch mention the names in their translations, they must have been found in the text which they used.

many men with him: he went north (west) to Agder and at every place where he held a thing with the bonders, he bade men be baptised and all men took up Christianity, for none of the bonders dared oppose the king and wherever he went the folk were baptised. In Hordaland there were many bold men who were come of the stock of Horda-Kari. He had four sons. One was Torleiv the Wise, the second Agmund, the father of Torolv Skjalg, the father of Erling of Sola;[1] the third was Tord, the father of Klypp the Herse who slew Sigurd Sleva, the son of Gunhild,[2] and the fourth was Almod, the father of Askel who was the father of Aslak Fitjaskalli.[3] This family was the greatest and noblest in Hordaland. And when these kinsmen learned of the hard tidings, that the king was going from the east through the land with a great army and was breaking the old laws, and that all who spoke against him were marked out for torments and mishandling, then the kinsmen arranged to hold a meeting amongst themselves to take common counsel, for they knew well that the king would soon come there. And they were of one mind about going with a great strength of men to the Gulathing and arranging there to meet King Olav Trygvason.

55. Olav called the thing as soon as he came to Rogaland; and when the behest came to the bonders, they gathered together in great force and were fully weaponed. When they came together they held talk and made plans, and then they chose three men who were the fairest spoken in their gathering to answer King Olav at the thing and speak against him and to make it known that they would not undergo lawlessness, even if the king himself bade it. And when the bonders came to the thing and the thing was set, King Olav stood up and first spoke blithely to the bonders. Yet it seemed from his speech that he wished them to take up Christianity; first with fair words he bade them do it, but at length he vowed that they who spoke against him and would not fall in with his behest should have from him wrath and torment and hard dealing everywhere. And when the king ended his speech, there stood up among the bonders one who was the best-spoken and was first chosen to answer King Olav. And when he wished to speak, there came upon him such a cough and choking in the chest that he could not bring forth one word and he sat himself down. Then stood up the second bonder and he would

1 *Erling of Sola* was known as Erling Skjalgson. He lived on a great estate still known as Sola on the north coast of Jæderen, near Stavanger.    2 Cf. 'History of Hacon the Jarl', chapter 9.    3 *Aslak Fitjaskalli* came from Fitjar. Cf. 'History of Harald Hairfair', p. 71, n. 4.

not let his answer fall flat even though things went badly with the first. But when he began to speak he stammered so much that he could not bring forth a word and all who heard it began to laugh: the bonder then sat down. Then the third man stood up to speak against King Olav, but when he began to speak he was so hoarse and thick of his speech that no one could hear what he said, and he had to sit down. Then was there no one of the bonders to speak against the king. And when the bonders had no one to answer the king, no one rose up to withstand him. And it came about that all agreed to

The most eloquent bonder rose to speak

what the king bade, and all the folk at the thing were baptised, before the king parted from them.

56. King Olav proceeded with his folk to the Gulathing, for the bonders had sent word that there they would answer this matter of his. And when both parties of men came to the thing, the king wished first to have a talk with the chiefs. When they were all gathered, he put forth his errand and bade them be baptised according to his behest. Then said Almod the Old: "We kinsmen have spoken about this matter between ourselves and we all shall be of one counsel. If thou, O king, thinkest to drive us kinsmen to such things, to break our laws and break us under thee by force, then shall we withstand thee with all our might and may fate then decide the victory. But if thou,

O king, wilt give us kinsmen some useful gifts, then wilt thou do a right thing and we shall all turn to thee in full obedience". The king said: "What will ye crave of me, that our peace be of the best?" Then said Almod: "First, that thou wilt wed thy sister Astrid to our kinsman Erling Skjalgson, whom we reckon the most hopeful of all the young men in Norway". The king said that it seemed likely that it would be a good wedding, as Erling was of good lineage and of goodly looks, but still, he said, Astrid herself must answer that matter. Thereupon the king spoke with his sister about it. "Little good I get", she said, "of being a king's daughter and a king's sister, if I have to be wed to a man without the name of prince: I would rather bide a few more winters for another wedding", and therewith for the time being they ended their talking.

57. Olav had a hawk taken, which Astrid owned, and had all the feathers plucked out of it and sent it back to her. Then said Astrid "Wroth now is my brother!" After this she stood up and went to the king who greeted her in a friendly way. Astrid said that she wished the king would arrange about her wedding just as he desired. "I thought", said the king, "that I should get might enough in the land here to make whomsoever I will a jarl." The king then called Almod and Erling and all their kinsmen to a meeting; a marriage was talked about, and the end of it was that Astrid was betrothed to Erling. Then the king called the thing and bade the bonders take up Christianity. Almod and Erling were the foremost men in promoting this matter of the king and with them were all their kinsmen. No one had spoken against it and so all the folk were baptised and converted to Christianity.

58. Erling Skjalgson held his wedding in the summer and a great many folk were present: King Olav was also there and he offered to give Erling a jarldom.[1] But Erling said: "Hersers[2] have my kinsmen always been and I will have no higher rank than they. Yet this will I take from thee, O king, if thou wilt let me be the greatest of that name in this land". The king promised him that and at their parting

1 The O.N. text has *jarldom*. This name appears closely connected with the English 'earldom'; but opinions are divided whether 'earl' is of English or Scandinavian origin. Thomas Forester in his translation of Henry of Huntingdon considers that the dignity of Earl (the Norse Jarl) was not introduced into England till 906. This is obviously wrong because earls are mentioned before this time both by Florence of Worcester and William of Malmesbury, although principally in connection with the Scandinavian earls that came over with 'the Army', and Bede's *Ecclesiastical History* mentions that Earl Puch and Earl Addi were living in Yorkshire as early as 686. The Norwegian Professor Alexander Bugge considered that 'earl' was an O.E. title and did not originate from O.S. 'jarl'.
2 *Herse*, district chief, plur. *herser*. In O.S. *hersir*, plur. *hersar*.

he gave his brother-in-law Erling the land north from Sognsjö, and as far east as Lidandisnes,[1] to rule in such a manner as Harald Hairfair had given land to his sons, as is written already.

59. The same harvest King Olav called a thing of four shires north in Stad at Dragseid,[2] and to it the Sognings, the Fjordings, the South Mörings and Raumdalers[3] were to come. King Olav went there with a great following of men, whom he had brought with him from the east of the land and with them also some who had come to him in Rogaland and Hordaland. And when King Olav came to the thing, he bade them take Christianity as he had done in other places. And since the king had there a very great strength of men, they were afraid of this; and at last the king gave them two choices, either that they should take up Christianity and let themselves be baptised, or otherwise that they should hold battle with him. And when the bonders saw no hope in fighting with the king, the former choice was taken, so that all the folk were baptised. King Olav went with his army to North Möre and baptised that folk. After this he sailed into Lade and had the temple broken down and took all the goods and ornaments from the temple and from the god. And from the temple door he took a great gold ring which Hacon the Jarl had caused to be made: then King Olav had the temple burned down. And when the bonders became aware of that, they sent out the war arrow to all the folks, called out the army and intended going against the king. King Olav sailed out with his army along the fjord and stood by on the north side of the land and thought he would go north to Halogaland to baptise that district. But when he came to Björnör,[4] he learned from Halogaland that they had an army out and were minded to guard their land against the king. The chiefs of that army were Harek from Tjotta,[5] Thore the Hart from Vagar[6] and Eyvind Rough-chin. When Olav heard this he turned back on the way and sailed south along the land. And as he came south round Stad, he went more slowly, but still he came right east to the Vik by the beginning of the winter.

60. Queen Sigrid of Sweden, who was called the Strong-minded, was living on her estates, and during the winter men went between

---

1 *Sognsjö* was the border between Sogn and Hordaland, so that Erling was made ruler of Hordaland, Rogaland and the west part of Agder as far south as Lindesnes (the Naze). 2 *Dragseid* is the outer part of Statland, between Drage (south) and Leikvang (north). 3 The men from Sogn and Northfjord and South Fjord and the men from South Möre and Raumsdale. 4 *Björnör* was the most northerly district in North Möre (now called Roan district). 5 *Tjotta*, south of Alstahaug in Halogaland. 6 *Vagar*, now Vaagen at Vagöy in Lofoten (North Norway).

King Olav and Queen Sigrid, and for King Olav they begged Queen Sigrid's hand. She took the offer kindly and the matter was agreed upon. King Olav then sent Queen Sigrid a big gold ring he had taken from the door of the temple at Lade and it seemed to be a very costly gift. And about this matter there was to be a meeting at the landmark by the Elv.[1] And when this ring, which King Olav had sent Queen

Baptism of St Olav

Sigrid, was much praised by all men, there were with the queen two of her smiths, who were brothers. But when they took the ring, felt its weight in their hands and talked alone between themselves, the queen had them called and asked them why they were mocking over the ring. They denied it. But she said that they must needs let her know what they had found out about the ring. They said that there was falseness about it. After this she had the ring broken asunder and there was brass inside it. Then the queen was wroth and said that Olav would even betray in more things than this. That same winter Olav went up to Ringerik and converted everybody to Christianity there. Shortly after the death of Harald the Grenlander, Asta, Gudbrand's daughter, had married a man called Sigurd Syr,[2] who was King of Ringerik. He was the son of Halvdan, who was the son of Sigurd the Giant, the son of Harald Hairfair. At that time, Olav, her son by Harald the Grenlander, was with Asta. In his childhood, Olav had been brought up with his step-father Sigurd Syr. And when King Olav Trygvason came to Ringerik to bid them become Christian, Sigurd Syr let himself be baptised along with Asta his wife and her son Olav,[3] to whom Olav Trygvason was godfather at the baptism and who was

1 *Elv*, i.e. the Göta River by Gothenburg.    2 *Syr* in O.N. means a 'pig'. He was called by this name because he "rooted in the earth like a pig", i.e. occupied himself with looking after his estates.    3 The later St Olav. Other sources relate that St Olav was baptised in Normandy, and although Snorre Sturlason states that he was baptised when he was three years old, it is not unlikely that another baptism took place in Normandy by the high Norman ecclesiastics, who might not have been satisfied with his first baptism. It must be remembered that it took many years before the new religion was regularly taught in churches and before it was firmly established in Norway. When

then three winters old. King Olav then went back to the Vik and was there during the winter; and that was the third year he had been king over Norway.

61. Early in the spring, King Olav went east to Konungahella[1] to meet Queen Sigrid. And when they met they spoke about the matter which had been discussed during the winter, that they should be married, and things were progressing well. Then King Olav said that Sigrid should be baptised and take the true faith. She answered, "I will not go from the faith I have had before, and my kinsmen before me. I will not say anything against thee if thou believe in the god that pleases thee". King Olav was very wroth and answered hastily,

Sigrid said, "This may well be thy death!"

"Why should I wed thee, thou heathen bitch?" and he struck her in the face with the glove he was holding in his hand. After that he stood up and she likewise and Sigrid said, "This may well be thy death!" They parted, and the king went north to the Vik and the queen east into Sweden.

62. King Olav went to Tunsberg and there again he had a thing, at which he bade all the men who were openly or secretly dealing with wizardry and troll craft to go away from the land. The king made them ransack for such men in the districts which were in the neighbourhood, and he bade them all come before him. And when they came, there was amongst them a man called Eyvind Kelda, who was the grandson of Ragnvald Rettlebone,[2] the son of Harald Hairfair. Eyvind was a wizard and very troll-wise. King Olav had all these men gathered in a room and had it all well laid out; he made a great feast for them and gave them strong drink; and when they were

Olav Trygvason died in the year 1000, the bonders reverted to their old heathen faith and St Olav in his childhood and youth had probably no opportunity of being brought up in the new religion. 1 Now Kungälf on the north side of the mouth of the Göta River. 2 Cf. 'History of Harald Hairfair', chapter 35. Ragnvald Rettlebone was also occupied with wizardry.

drunk Olav had the place set on fire and burned it and all the folk who were therein, except Eyvind Kelda, who got away through the smoke hole. And when he had got far away, he met on the road the men who were going to the king and bade them tell the king that Eyvind Kelda had escaped the fire and he would never again come into King Olav's power, and he would always continue in the same way as he had always done, with all his magic arts. And when these men came to King Olav, they told him such things as Eyvind had bid them. The king was full of wrath that Eyvind was not dead.

The wizards and troll-wise folk on Scrat-Skerry

63. When spring came, King Olav went out along the Vik and held feasts on his big estates, and he sent bidding over all the Vik that he would have an army out in the summer and would go north in the land. After that he went north-west to Agder, and when Lent was nearly over, he sailed north to Rogaland and came on Easter Eve to Agvaldsnes in Karmt.[1] There an Easter feast was made ready for him and he had nigh on 300 men. The same night Eyvind Kelda came to the island and he had a longship fully manned with wizards and other troll-wise folk. Eyvind and his following went up from the ship and practised their craft. Eyvind made by magic so great a darkness through fog that the king and his men could not see them. But when they came near to the houses at Agvaldsnes, it had become daylight and things went otherwise than Eyvind had wished: the darkness

1 Now Karmöy, near Haugesund.

which he had made by magic came over him and his folk so that they could no more see with their eyes than with their necks, and they went round and round in rings. And the king's watchmen saw where they were going but knew not what folk they were. The king was told, and he and all his men rose and clothed themselves. And when the king saw where Eyvind and all his folk were going, he bade his men arm themselves and go and see what folk they were. When the king's men there recognised Eyvind, they took him and all the others prisoner and brought them before the king. Then Eyvind told all that had befallen on his journey. The king had them all taken out and brought to a skerry which was under water at high tide and he had them bound there. Eyvind and the others thus lost their lives. The skerry was afterwards called Scrat-Skerry.[1]

64. Thus is it said[2] that when King Olav was at the feast at Agvaldsnes there came one evening an old man of wise words, who had a broad hat and was one-eyed;[3] the man could tell of all lands. He happened to talk with the king, who found much fun in his talk; the king asked him about many things and the guest gave answer to all the questions; the king sat with him for a long time in the evening. Then the king asked if he knew who Agvald had been, after whom the ness and the estate were called. The guest said that Agvald was a king and a great warrior and he sacrificed mostly to a cow, which he had with him wherever he went; it seemed good for his health always to drink her milk; "King Agvald fought with a king called Varin and in that battle King Agvald fell. He was buried in a howe here a short way from this house and the howe stones were set up which are still standing. And at a spot close by the cow was also buried in a howe". Such things and many others he told about the kings and about other old tidings. And when they had sat far into the night, the bishop minded the king that it was time to go to sleep and the king did so. And when he was undressed and had laid himself on his bed, the guest sat on the footboard and again talked long with the king. The bishop then spoke to the king and said that it was now time to go to sleep. The king did so and the guest went out. A little later the king woke up and asked after the guest and bade him be called to him. But the guest was nowhere to be found. So next morning the king called to him his cook and his butler and asked them if some unknown man had come to them. They said that when they were getting the

---

1 The O.N. word is *Skratta-sker* = wizard or troll skerry.   2 The addition "thus is it said" shows how careful Snorre Sturlason is when relating things, the truthfulness of which he does not warrant or believe himself.   3 Odin was one-eyed.

meat ready a man came and said that they were cooking the flesh badly for the king's table and thereupon he gave them two thick, fat flitches of meat and they cooked them with the other flesh. Then the king said that all that meat should be wasted and that this guest was no human being, but it must have been Odin in whom the heathen had so long believed; and he said that Odin should have no chance of betraying them.

65. King Olav that summer drew a great army together from the east of the land and sailed north with it to Trondheim and first lay in by Nidaros.[1] He sent bidding all round the fjord that he would hold a thing and called a thing of eight shires at Frosta;[2] but the bonders turned this bidding to the thing into an arrow of war[3] meeting, and all the men from over Trondheim gathered together. And when the king came to the thing, the body of bonders were come there fully weaponed. When the thing met, the king spoke to the folk and bade them take up Christianity. And when he had spoken for a little time the bonders shouted and bade him be quiet, saying that otherwise they would go against him and drive him away. "Thus we did", they said, "with Hacon the foster-son of Athelstan, when he came to us with such behest and we think no more of thee than of him." And when King Olav saw the heated temper of the bonders and likewise that they had so great an army that he could not withstand them, he changed his speech and turned in assent with the bonders: he said, "I wish that we shall be friends again, as we have formerly agreed between ourselves. I will go there where ye have your greatest offering and see your worship. Then shall we all take counsel about what worship we shall have and we shall all be as one about it". And when the king spoke mildly to the bonders, they were softened in their minds and all their talk was reasonable and peaceful, and it was at last agreed that there should be a midsummer offering at Mæren, and thither were all the chiefs and mighty bonders to come, as was their wont, and thither also was King Olav to come.

66. There was a man named Skeggi, a mighty bonder who was also known as Iron-Skeggi, and he dwelt at Ophaug in Yrjar.[4] Skeggi was the first man at the thing to speak against King Olav and he was the bonders' foremost speaker against Christianity. In

---

1 *Nidaros* was at the mouth of the River Nid (Nidelven).    2 Cf. 'History of Hacon the Good', p. 86, n. 3.    3 If a thing was summoned and all the men were asked to bring their weapons, the arrows sent round had a piece of rope or string fastened on them. 4 Cf. 'History of Harald Hairfair', p. 47, n. 1.

this way, the thing was dissolved; the bonders went home and the king went over to Lade.

67. King Olav lay with his ships in the River Nid and he had thirty ships and many bold men; the king himself was often in Lade with his own guard. And when the time drew nigh for the offering to be made at Mæren,[1] King Olav held a great feast in Lade; and he had sent bidding into Strind and up into Guldale, calling to him the chiefs and other great bonders. But when the feast was ready, and the bidden guests were come, there was great feasting the first evening: the drink was good and they became very drunk. And the night after all the men slept peacefully. Next day, when the king was clad, he had Mass sung, and when it was over he had a husthing called by bugle; all his men went up from the ships to the thing. And when it was met, the king stood up and spoke thus: "We held a thing in Frosta and I bade the bonders let themselves be baptised; but they bade me turn myself to sacrificing with them, just as King Hacon the foster-son of Athelstan had done. Then we came to an agreement between ourselves to meet at Mæren and there make a great offering. But if I turn to the offering with you, then I will have you make the greatest sacrifice that can be made, and sacrifice men. Nor will I choose thralls or evil men, but as gifts to the gods we must choose the best men and to that end I name Orm Lygra of Medalhus, Styrkar of Gimsar, Kar of Gryting, Asbiorn Torbergson of Varnes, Orm of Ljoxa and Haldor of Skerdingstedja", and there besides he named five others who were of the noblest; he said that he would offer them for good seasons and peace, and bade his men fall on them straightway. And when the bonders saw that they had no strength of men to meet the king, then they begged for peace and put all their rule in the king's hands. Then it was agreed that all the bonders who were come there should be baptised, and they swore oaths to the king to keep the true faith and put aside all sacrificing. The king then kept all these men at his feast, until they gave their sons or brothers or other near kinsmen as hostages to the king.

68. King Olav went with all his army into Trondheim, and when he came to Mæren, all those chiefs of the Tronds were there who had most withstood Christianity, and they had with them all the great bonders who had formerly held the offerings in that place. There was a great number present, in the same way as there had formerly been at the Frosta thing. The king had the thing called and both troops went to it fully weaponed. And when the thing was met, the king

---

[1] Cf. 'History of Hacon the Good', p. 89, n. 2.

spoke and bade the men become Christian. Iron-Skeggi answered the king's speech on the bonders' behalf and said that the bonders wished the king as before not to break down their laws. "We wish thee, O king", he said, "to sacrifice as other kings have done here before thee." To this speech the bonders gave a great applause and said they wished everything to be just as Skeggi had said. The king said he would go into the temple and see their worship when they sacrificed. That pleased the bonders well, and so both troops went to the temple.

69. King Olav now went into the temple with a few of his men and a few of the bonders, and when he came thither where the gods

were, he saw Thor sitting there, the most honoured of all the gods and adorned with gold and silver. King Olav then heaved up a gold-chased spike-axe that he had in his hand and struck at Thor so that he fell from his place. The king's men leaped up and thrust down all the gods from their places; and whilst the king was in the temple Iron-Skeggi was slain outside the temple door; the king's men did it. When the king came out to his men, he bade the bonders choose between two things: one was that they should all take up Christianity, and the other was that they should hold battle with him. But after the fall of Skeggi there was no leader in the bonders' army to raise the standard against King Olav, so what they chose was to go to the king and do as he bade. King Olav had all the folk who were there baptised, and took hostages of the bonders that they should hold to Christianity. After that, King Olav let his men go round all the folk districts in Trondheim; no man spoke against Christianity and all the folk in Trondlaw were baptised.

King Olav went into the temple

70. King Olav went out with his army to Nidaros and he had houses built on the banks of the Nid and arranged that there should be a market place. He gave men tofts for them to build themselves houses, and he had a king's house built above Skipakroken.[1] Thither in the autumn he caused to be moved all the goods which

1 A little bay on the west side of the River Nid, at the end of the present Strandgate in Trondheim.

would be needed for settling there for the winter and he had a great number of folk.

71. King Olav arranged to meet Iron-Skeggi's kinsmen and offered them compensation. And there were many noble men to answer. Iron-Skeggi had a daughter who was called Gudrun and it was at last agreed that King Olav should wed her. When the bridal night came, King Olav and Gudrun both got into one bed. And the first night they lay together she drew out a knife as soon as the king was asleep and wished to stick it in him. But the king was aware of it; he took the knife from her, got up from the bed and went to his men, saying what had happened. Gudrun and all the men who had followed her then took their belongings and went away; Gudrun never came back to the same bed as King Olav.

72. The same autumn King Olav had a great longship built on the shores of the Nid; it was a cutter and on it the king had many shipwrights working. And when the ship was ready at the beginning of the winter she had thirty rowing seats and a high stem and stern but not big otherwise. The king called the ship the *Crane*.

After Iron-Skeggi's death, his body was moved out to Yrjar and it lies now in Skeggi-howe on Austratt.[1]

73. When King Olav Trygvason had been king in Norway for two years there was with him a Saxon[2] priest called Tangbrand. He was a powerful but murderous man, but a good scholar and a bold man. But on the grounds that he was a wild man, the king would not have him with him; so he gave him an errand to go and preach Christianity in Iceland. He received a merchant ship and of his journey it is said that he came to Iceland in the Eastfjords in South Alptafjord, and the winter after he was with Hall of Sida.[3] Tangbrand preached Christianity in Iceland and after his words Hall let himself and all his folk and many other chiefs be baptised. But there were many more who spoke against it. Thorvald the Wily[4] and Veterlidi the Scald made scurvy rimes about Tangbrand, but he slew them both. Tangbrand stayed two years in Iceland and he was the death of three men before he went away.

74. There was a man called Sigurd and another called Hauk.

---

1 This howe was in existence at the beginning of the nineteenth century, south of the farm Östraat (Austratt).    2 The O.N. text reads: *Saxneskr*, meaning 'Saxon English'.    3 *Sida* is near Skapta in the western Skaptarfells district. Hall lived near Tvatta in the south part of Alptafjord; but Snorre Sturlason calls him Hall of Sida, which was probably his first home.    4 In O.N. he was called Torvaldr Veili, the word *veili* meaning 'false, unfaithful, suspicious or dishonourable'. The word is connected with *wily*, only it has a somewhat different meaning in English. It is not known in modern Scandinavian.

They were from Halogaland and were often on trade journeys. One summer they had been west to England, and when they came back to Norway they sailed along the land and in North Möre they met King Olav's men. When the king was told that certain heathen men were come from Halogaland, he had the steersmen called before him. He asked them if they would let themselves be baptised, but to that they answered 'nay'. After this the king spoke to them in many ways, but it was of no use; he then vowed them death or maiming, but they did not yield for that. So he had them clapped in irons and had them with him for some time thus held in chains. The king often talked to them, but it availed naught. One night they got away, but no one learned anything of them or how they had got away. But in the autumn they came north to Harek of Tjotta; he greeted them well and they were well kept by him during the winter.

75. One fine day in spring, Harek was at home on his farm; he

King Olav requests Harek of Tjotta to be baptised

had few men with him and time fell heavy on him. Sigurd asked him if they should row out a little and amuse themselves. That pleased Harek well. They went down to the shore and drew forth a six-oared boat; Sigurd took from the boat-house such sails and tackle as belonged to the ship, for they were often wont to have a sail with them when they went out to amuse themselves. Harek went out in the boat and fixed the rudder. Sigurd and his brother went fully weaponed, just as they were wont to do at home with the bonder. They were both strong men. Before they had gone out in the ship, they threw in some butter and a bread basket, and between them they carried a great barrel of beer out to the ship. Then they rowed from the land; and when they were away from the island, the brothers hoisted the sail and Harek steered and they quickly went from the island. The brothers then moved over to where Harek was sitting and Sigurd said to the bonder: "Now shalt thou choose between certain things: one is that thou lettest us brothers be master of this journey and its course; the second is that thou lettest us bind thee; and the third is that we slay thee". Harek saw how things were arranged for him. He could not be a match for more than one of the brothers, even if they were likewise armed. He therefore chose what seemed to him most reasonable, to let them manage the journey. He swore them oaths thereon, and gave them his troth. After that Sigurd went to the rudder and steered south along the land. The brothers took good care not to meet other folk and they had a very good wind. They did not stop in the journey ere they came south to Trondheim and went into Nidaros and there found King Olav. After that, King Olav had Harek called to talk with him and he bade him be baptised, but Harek spoke against it. The king and Harek talked about it for many a day, sometimes in the company of men, sometimes alone; but they were not agreed. And at last the king said to Harek: "Now shalt thou go home and I will do thee no ill this first time. One reason is that there is close kinship between us, and another is that thou mayest say that I got thee by treachery. But know it for a truth that I think to come north in the summer and I shall seek ye Haleygers.[1] Ye shall then learn if I can punish those who withstand Christianity". Harek thought himself lucky to get away from there as quickly as possible. King Olav gave him a good boat, which was rowed by ten or twelve men on either side, and he had the ship fitted out with the best of things that were needed. He let him take with him thirty men, bold and well armed.

76. Harek of Tjotta went away from the town as quickly as he could, but Hauk and Sigurd stayed with the king and let themselves be baptised. Harek went his way till he came to Tjotta. He sent a messenger to his friend Eyvind Rough-chin and bade him tell Eyvind that Harek had found King Olav, and that he had not let himself be cowed into taking up Christianity. Harek also bade the messenger tell Eyvind that Olav thought of going against them with an army in the summer and that they must show wariness, and he bade Eyvind come to him as soon as possible. And when these tidings were borne to Eyvind he said that no king should get the upper hand over them. So Eyvind went as quickly as possible with a light skiff and a few men in it. And when he came to Tjotta, Harek greeted him well; and Harek and he straightway fell to talking on the other side of the farm. And when they had talked together for a short time, there came Olav's men who had followed Harek north; they took Eyvind prisoner, put him in the ship with them and went away

1 I.e. men from Halogaland (North Norway).

to the south with him. They did not stop their journey until they came to Trondheim, and found King Olav in Nidaros. Eyvind was then brought to a talk with King Olav, who bade him be baptised like other men. To that Eyvind answered 'nay'. The king then bade him with many blithe words take up Christianity and told him many good grounds for it, and the bishop did likewise. But Eyvind did not agree. The king then offered him gifts and great land rents, but Eyvind turned everything from him. So the king vowed him injury or death, but Eyvind did not give way. After that the king had a bowl brought in, full of glowing cinders, and set it on Eyvind's stomach,[1] and very soon the stomach[1] burst asunder. Then said Eyvind: "Take the bowl from me: I will speak some words ere I die"; and so it was done. Then the king asked him, "Eyvind, wilt thou now believe in Christ?" "Nay," he said, "I cannot receive baptism; I am a spirit quickened in man's body by the wizardry of the Finns, for my father and mother had no child before that was done." After this Eyvind died and he had been the most troll-wise of men.

77. The next spring Olav had his ships and men fitted out. The king himself had the *Crane,* and a great and very fine army. And when he was ready he sailed with it out of the fjord, then north by Byrda and so north into Halogaland. And wherever he came to land he held things and bade all the folk there take baptism and the true faith. No one had the strength to speak against him and all the land became Christian wherever he went. King Olav was at Tjotta as the guest of Harek, who with all his men was baptised. Harek gave the king gifts at parting, became his man and got from the king both the land rents and the title of district chief.

78. Raud the Strong was the name of a bonder who lived in Godöy in the fjord called Salpti.[2] He was a very rich man and had many huscarls; he was a mighty man and there followed him a great number of Finns whenever he had need of them. Raud was an ardent sacrificer and very troll-wise. He was a good friend to the man afore-named (chapter 59), Thore the Hart, and they were both mighty chiefs. And when they learned that King Olav was going about in Halogaland with an army, they gathered an army, ordered out ships and got many men. Raud's ship had a great dragon with golden heads; she had thirty rowing seats and was spacious for her size. Thore the Hart also had a great ship. They sailed with their army to the south against King Olav, and when they met they went to

---

1 The O.S. name for stomach is *magi* or *kvidr*; but the modern Scandinavian word is *mave,* similar to the Old English *maw.*    2 *Salpti,* i.e. Salten (North Norway).

battle against the king. It was a hard fight and there was soon a great number slain, but the loss of life turned on the army of the Haleygers, their ships were cleared and at last fright and terror came over them. Raud then rowed with his dragon ship out to sea and hoisted his sail. He always had the wind where he wished to sail and it came by wizardry. To speak shortly of Raud's journey, it may be said that he sailed home to Godöy. Thore the Hart fled inland and there they leaped from their ships. But King Olav followed them, and his men also leaped from their ships, followed the others and slew them. The king was again foremost as always when such things were done. He saw where Thore the Hart was running, and Thore was fleet footed. The king ran after him, followed by his hound Vigi.[1] Then said the king, "Vigi, take the Hart!" Vigi ran forth after Thore and straightway leaped upon him. Thore had to stop. The king shot a spear after him and Thore struck at the dog with his sword and gave it a great wound; but at that same moment the king's spear flew under Thore's hand, so that it went through him and stuck out on the other side. There Thore lost his life and Vigi was borne wounded to the ships. King Olav gave peace to all those men who asked for it and who would take up Christianity.

79. King Olav sailed with his army north along the land and baptised all the folk wherever he went. But when he came north into Salpti he wished to go into the fjord to find Raud, but stormy weather and a strong wind hung over the fjord and the king put in there for a week. The same stormy weather continued in the fjord, though outside there was a fresh wind for sailing north along the land. The king then sailed north as far as Amd and there all the folk took up Christianity. After this the king turned his journey to the south again, but when he came to Salpti, there was stormy weather and a rough sea in the fjord. He lay there some nights, but the weather was still the same. The king then spoke to Bishop Sigurd and asked if he could give any counsel as to how to counteract it. The bishop said he would try whether God would grant him help to overcome this work of the devil.

80. Bishop Sigurd now took all his mass ornaments and went forth into the stem of the king's ship; he had candles lighted and bore forth incense; he set up a rood cross in the stem and there read the gospel and many other prayers and he sprinkled holy water over the whole ship. He then bade them take down the awnings and row into the fjord. The king then bade them call to the other ships to row after

1 For *Vigi* cf. chapter 32.

them. And when the rowing began in the *Crane*, she went into the fjord and the men who rowed the ship felt no wind against them, and in the wake of the ship the sea was calm, but on both sides the sea foam rose so high that the fells on the side of the fjord could not be seen. Then every ship rowed after the other in calm weather and so they went the whole day and night and a little before day they came to the Godöyers. And when they came before Raud's house, his great dragon ship floated there near the land. King Olav with his men went straight up to the house and fell upon the loft where Raud slept, and his men broke the door down and rushed in. Raud was seized and bound, and of the other men who were inside some were slain and others taken prisoner. Thereupon the king's men went to the shieling where Raud's huscarls slept and there some were slain, some bound and others beaten. The king had Raud brought before him and bade him let himself be baptised: "I will not", said the king, "take from thee thy possessions, but rather will I be thy friend, if thou art worthy of it". Raud shouted against this and said that he would never believe in Christ, and he blasphemed against God. The king was wroth and said that Raud should have the worst of deaths. He had him taken and bound by the back to a pole, and he had a bit of wood set between his teeth and thus kept open his mouth. Then the king took a lingworm and put it to Raud's mouth; but the worm would not enter the mouth and turned away from it because Raud breathed against it. The king then got a hollow stalk of angelica and put it in Raud's mouth (though some say that the king took his horn and put it in Raud's mouth), and stuck the worm in it. He then brought a red-hot iron after it and the worm went into Raud's mouth, down his neck and bored itself out through his side: Raud lost his life. King Olav then took a great quantity of goods in gold and silver and other loose treasures, weapons and many kinds of costly things. He made all the men who had followed Raud be baptised, but those who would not, he caused to be slain or tormented. He then took the dragon which Raud had had and sailed it himself, for it was a much greater and finer ship than the *Crane*; at the bow there was a dragon's head, and in the stern a crook fashioned at the end like a dragon's tail, and both sides of the neck[1] and the whole stem were overlaid with gold. The king called the ship the *Serpent*, because

---

1 The O.S. name for this part of the stem is *sviri* = neck (in modern Scandinavian *nakke* or *hals*) and refers probably to the neck of the dragon head. In modern Scandinavian, nautical expressions in sailing ships are *bakbord* and *styrbord's halse*, meaning 'port' and 'starboard tack'.

when the sail was hoisted it was like the dragon's wing; it was the finest ship in the whole of Norway. The islands on which Raud dwelt were called Gylling and Hæring, but altogether they were called the Godöyers, whilst the Godöyström[1] was to the north between them and the mainlaid. King Olav christened the whole fjord and afterwards went his way to the south along the land, and on that journey much happened that is told of in folk tales, how trolls and evil sprites tempted his men and sometimes himself. But we will rather write about the things that befell when Olav christened Norway or those other lands to which he had brought Christianity. The same autumn King Olav came with his army to Trondheim; he steered to Nidaros and there he settled for the winter.

Now shall I next write down those things that are to be told about the Iceland men.

81. The same autumn there came to Nidaros from Iceland Kjartan, the son of Olav Hoskuldson and son of the daughter of Egil Skallagrimson. He has been called the most hopeful man of those who have been born in Iceland. There was also Haldor, the son of Gudmund of Mödruvellir,[2] and Kolbein, the son of Tord Freysgodi and brother of Flosi the Burner;[3] the fourth was Sverting, the son of Runolf the Good. These and many others, some mighty, others not, were all heathen. And then there also came from Iceland noble men who had taken Christianity from Tangbrand. One of them was Gissur the White, the son of Teit[4] Ketelbjörnson, and his mother was Alov, daughter of Bodvar the Herse, the son of Viking-Kari. Bodvar's brother was Sigurd, the father of Eric Bjodaskalli, the father of King Olav's mother Astrid. Another of the Iceland men was called Hjalti Skeggjason, who had wed Vilborg, the daughter of Gissur the White; Hjalti was also a Christian. King Olav greeted gladly his kinsmen, Gissur and Hjalti, and they stayed with him. And those Iceland men, who owned the ships and were heathen, sought to sail away as soon as the king came to the town, for they had been told that he would compel all men to take up Christianity; but the weather was against them and it drove them back under Nidarholm. These were the men who owned the ships: Toraren Nevjolvson, Halfred Ottarson the poet, Brand the Open-handed and Torleik Brandson.

1 *Godöyström* (or Godöystream) probably refers to a strong current passing between the islands and the mainland. The Saltenfjord is known for its strong currents. Cf. p. 33, note 4. Vadla stream is also thought to be a current between an island and the mainland. 2 *Mödruvellir* is situated in the Eyjafjord (North Iceland). 3 *Flosi the Burner* lived by Svinafell. About him has been written in the well-known Njal Saga. 4 This name is pronounced in the same way as the English 'Tate'.

King Olav was told that some Icelanders, who were all heathen, had come with some ships and would fly from a meeting with him, and he then sent men to them forbidding them to sail away and bidding them lie off by the town. They did so, but they bore nothing away from their ships.

82. Then came Michaelmas, which the king greatly upheld, and he had Mass sung solemnly. The Icelanders went to it and listened to the fair singing and the ringing of the bells. And when they came to their ships, each of them said what he thought of the way of the Christian men. Kjartan praised it, but most of the others jeered at it. And so it was, as is often said, that "Many are the ears of a king": the king was told. He straightway sent a man for Kjartan and bade him come to him. Kjartan went with some men to the king, who greeted him well. Kjartan was the biggest and finest of men and able of speech. And when the king and he had spoken a few words together, the king bade Kjartan take up Christianity. Kjartan said he would not say 'nay' to that if he should have the king's friendship. The king promised him his full friendship and the matter was now agreed upon between them. The next day Kjartan and Bolli Thorlakson his kinsman were baptised with all their following. Kjartan and Bolli were bidden to be guests of the king so long as they were in white clothes[1] and the king was very friendly towards them.

83. One day King Olav went out in the street and some men met him and he who was in front greeted the king, who asked him his name; he was called Halfred. Then said the king, "Art thou a poet?" "I can compose", he said. Then said the king, "Wilt thou take up Christianity and afterwards become my man?" He replied, "This shall be the condition of it: I will let myself be baptised, if thou, O king, thyself wilt stand for me in baptism; from no other man will I take it". The king said, "That will I do". Then Halfred was baptised and the king stood for him in baptism. After that, the king asked Halfred "Wilt thou now be my man?" Halfred answered, "I was formerly a guardsman of Hacon the Jarl; and I will not become thy man nor any other chief's, unless thou promise me that such a thing shall not befall me that thou drivest me away from thee". "So am I told about thee, Halfred", said the king, "that thou art not so wise or prudent but that I may expect thee to do those things which I will not brook." "Slay me then", said Halfred. The king said, "Thou art a troublesome scald, but thou shalt now be my man". Halfred

1 *White clothes* were worn for a week after the baptism.

answered, "What wilt thou give me, O king, for a name gift, if I am called the Troublesome Scald (i.e. Vandradascald)?" The king gave him a sword, but no sheath was with it. The king said, "Make now a verse about the sword and put *sword* in every line". Halfred quoth:

| | |
|---|---|
| Of all swords there is only one sword | Nothing will the sword lack, |
| That hath made me rich in swords, | My lord, if I could get |
| For the swinger of the swords | A sheath for my sword; |
| There shall now be swords in plenty. | I am worthy of three swords. |

The king then gave him the sheath and said, "But there is not a sword in every line". "Yes", answered Halfred, "there are three swords in one line." "That is right", said the king. From Halfred's poems we prefer to take our information and evidence about what is told therein of Olav Trygvason.[1]

84. The same autumn Tangbrand the priest came from Iceland to King Olav and told him that his journey had not been a happy one, for the Icelanders had been spiteful to him and some had wished to kill him; he thought that they could not hope for that land to be made Christian. King Olav became so heated and wroth that he had all the Iceland men, who were in the town, called together and then said that they should all be slain. But Kjartan, Gissur, Hjalti and the others who had taken up Christianity went to him and said, "Thou wilt not, O king, go from thy words, by which thou didst say that no man should do so much to make thee wroth but that thou wouldst forgive him when he let himself be baptised and give up heathendom. Now all these Iceland men who are here will let themselves be baptised, and we may well find a plan by which Christianity shall win entrance to Iceland; here there are from Iceland the sons of many mighty men and their fathers will grant good help in the matter. But Tangbrand treated everybody there as here with you, with haughtiness and manslaughter and folk there would not bear such things of him". The king began to listen to this talk and now all the Iceland men who were there were baptised.

85. King Olav was the greatest man in all kind of sports, of those that are told about in Norway. He was stronger and nimbler than any man, and there are many tales written about it. One was that he went up the Smalsarhorn and fastened his shield on the top, and another was that he helped a guardsman of his who had climbed up to the top so that he could get neither up nor down; but the king

---

1 It is considered historical that Halfred Vandradascald is buried at *Reilig Oiran* Cemetery in Iona (Hebrides). Macbeth is, according to tradition, also buried there, together with 48 Scottish, 8 Norse and 4 Irish kings.

went up to him and bore him down on his arm. King Olav also ran on the oars outside the ship when his men were rowing in the *Serpent*, and he played with three hand swords, so that one was always up in the air and he always had hold of another by the hilt. He smote equally well with both hands and shot two spears at one time. King Olav was the gladdest of all men and very playful, blithe and forgiving, very heated in all things, generous and prominent amongst his fellows, bold before all in battle, but very gruesome when he was wroth and his foes he tormented much; some he burned, some he let wild hounds tear asunder, and others he maimed or cast down from high mountains. Because of all these things his friends loved him, but his foes were afraid of him; his success was great because some did his will out of love and friendship, but others out of fear.

86. Leif, the son of Eric the Red, who first settled Greenland, came that summer from Greenland to Norway. He went to King Olav and took up Christianity and stayed during the winter with King Olav.

87. Gudröd, the son of Eric Blood-axe and Gunhild, had been harrying in the Westlands since he had fled from the land on account of Hacon the Jarl. But that summer, which has already been spoken of, when King Olav Trygvason had ruled four years in Norway, Gudröd came to Norway with many warships. He had sailed from England; and when he thought he was near Norway, he moved south along the land where he least expected to find King Olav; he sailed south to

King Gudröd's men harry in the Vik

the Vik. But as soon as he came to land he began to harry and subdue the folk and he craved of them to take him as king. And when the land folk saw that so great an army was come upon them they sought peace and terms and they offered the king that a thing bidding should go over the land, to give him homage rather than oppose his army, and a truce was arranged to last till the thing was called. Then the king craved money for food, whilst he waited. But the bonders chose rather to prepare feasts for the king the whole time he needed it and the king took that choice, so that he went through the land feasting with one part of his army, whilst the others watched his ships. But when King Olav's brothers-in-law, the brothers Hyrning and Torgeir, learned this, they gathered their folk and got themselves ships; they then went north to the Vik and one night came with their men to where King Gudröd was at a feast and fell upon them with fire and sword. There King Gudröd fell and the most part of his men; and of those who had been on the ships, some were slain, but others escaped and fled far away. Now were all the sons of Eric and Gunhild dead.

88. The winter after King Olav had come from Halogaland, he had a great ship built by the Ladehammers,[1] that was much bigger than the other ships which were then in the land and the ship stocks are still there to be seen. A man called Torberg Skavhogg was the stem shipwright, but there were many others on the work, some to fell trees, some to hew them and some to strike nails in and some to move the timber. All things in it were well chosen and the ship was both long and broad, of great timber and high bulwarks. And when they were planking the ship, Torberg had a needful errand to go home to his place and he was there a very long time. And when he came back the ship was fully timbered, and straightway in the evening the king and Torberg with him went to see how the work was done, and every man said that never had been seen so great or so fine a longship. The king then went back to the town, but early the next morning the king and Torberg came back to the ship; the wrights had already come, but they all stood there not at work. The king asked why they bore themselves in this manner. They answered that the ship was shamefully cut about and some man must have gone from stem to stern and have struck one deep notch after another down the one side of the planking. The king went to it and saw that this was true, and he straightway said and swore that the man who had damaged the ship from envy should die if the king could get him,

1 Outside the Lade estate. Cf. 'History of Harald Hairfair', p. 47, n. 3.

"And he who can tell me of it, shall have great reward from me". Then said Torberg, "I will tell you, O king, who has done this deed". "I might look to thee as much as to any man", said the king, "to be lucky enough and tell me." "I will tell thee, O king", he said, "who has done it—I have done it." Then answered the king, "Then shalt thou make it just as good as before and thy life shall be at stake for it". Torberg then went and chipped the planks, so that all the notches were smoothed and made even with the rest. Then said the king—and all the others too—that the ship was much finer looking after Torberg had made this alteration. The king then bade him do so on the other side and offered him great thanks therefor. Tor-

The *Long Serpent* (Ormrinn Langi)

berg was then the head wright of the ship till it was finished; it was a dragon ship and made after the model of the *Serpent*, which the king had brought from Halogaland. But the new ship was much bigger and in all things more splendidly fitted. This vessel he called the *Long Serpent*, and the other the *Short Serpent*. In the *Long Serpent* there were thirty-four rowing seats. The head and the crook at the stern were all gilded and the bulwarks were as high as an ocean-going ship. That was the best fitted and the most costly ship that was ever built in Norway.

89. Eric Haconson the Jarl and his brothers and many other noble kinsmen of theirs went away from the land after the death of Hacon the Jarl. Eric the Jarl went east into Sweden to Olav King of the Swedes, and was well greeted there. King Olav gave the jarl

peace land[1] and great land rents to keep himself and his men in the land. About it Tord Kolbeinson says:

Thou robber-foe, etc. (see chapter 51).

Many men from Norway who left the land on account of Olav Trygvason sought Eric the Jarl. Eric took counsel to get himself ships and to go raiding to win goods for himself and his men. He sailed first to Gotland and lay off there for a long time in the summer and waylaid either merchant ships which were sailing to the land, or viking ships; sometimes he went up on the land and harried far about the coast. Thus is it said in Banda drapa:

Many were the                  The time when the war-chief
Mail storms the jarl conquered.    Harried far and wide
That we have heard before       Over Gotland shores
(Eric wins the land).           (Did deeds of strength and peace).[2]

After that Eric the Jarl sailed south to Vendland, and outside Stauren[3] he met several viking ships and fell to battle with them. Eric had the victory and slew the vikings. Thus is it said in Banda drapa:

The stern steed's steerer        At the evil sword meet
Left lying by Staur            The ravens clawed at the bodies
The fallen fighters' heads      Of the vikings on the sands
(The jarl was always fight-glad).  (To rule the land).

90. In the autumn Eric the Jarl sailed back to Sweden and was there another winter. But in the spring he made his ships ready and sailed then to the eastern countries. And when he came to King Valdemar's kingdom he began to harry and slay folk and to burn everything wherever he went, and he laid waste the land. He came to Aldeigjaborg[4] and beset the town till he won it, slew many folk and broke down and burned the whole town; he then went far and wide in Gardarik with the shield of war. Thus is it said in Banda drapa:

The chieftain then went to waste    Thou didst break Aldeigja, O prince,
Valdemar's lands;              When thou camest east into Gardar.
With fire and sword            And grim was the strife between men
(Great waxed the sword-fight).    (We know it well).

1 The O.S. word is *fridland,* meaning that foreigners could live in freedom and peace in the land. The Norsemen who went to Normandy were granted *fridland* there by the Norman dukes on account of the same racial descent.    2 The lines in brackets are repeated in the verses as a refrain.    3 *Stauren* is supposed to be the most southerly point of the island Femern, now Staver, south of Staberdorp.    4 This town is Aldagen or Ladoga, which was situated on the River Volkhov, which flows into Lake Ladoga.

Eric the Jarl was altogether five summers on this expedition; and when he came from Gardarik, he went with the shield of war over all Adalsysla and Eysysla[1] and there he took four viking ships from the Danes and slew all the men on them. Thus is it said in Banda drapa:

| | |
|---|---|
| I have heard how the sword- | There, where the warriors ran |
| Swinging warrior made waste | To the town, thou hadst |
| Once more in the island sound | Strife with the Gauts, O warrior chief |
| (Eric wins the land). | (The jarl was always fight-glad). |
| The generous prince | He bore the shield of war |
| Reft from the Danes | Throughout all the Syslas, |
| Four viking ships | He went not with gentleness |
| (Did deeds of strength and peace). | (To rule the land). |

Eric the Jarl went to Denmark when he had been one winter in Sweden; he came to the Danish king Swein Forkbeard and wooed his daughter Gyda and their wedding was arranged. Eric the Jarl wedded Gyda and the next winter they got a son, who was called Hacon. In the winters Eric was in Denmark and sometimes in Sweden, but in the summers he was harrying.

91. Swein Forkbeard, the Danish king, had wed Gunhild, the daughter of Burislav, King of the Vends. But in those times which are now described it happened that Queen Gunhild fell sick and died,[2] but a little later King Swein wedded Sigrid the Strong-minded, the daughter of Skogul-Tosti and the mother of Olav the Swede, the Swedish king. Then with this new kinship there arose great friendship between the kings and between them and Eric Haconson the Jarl.

92. Burislav complained to his son-in-law Sigvaldi the Jarl that the agreement was broken which Sigvaldi the Jarl had made between King Burislav and King Swein; King Burislav was to wed Tyri, the daughter of Harald and the sister of King Swein; but the wedding had not been furthered, because Tyri had said 'nay' very curtly to being wed to a heathen old man. Now King Burislav said to the jarl that he wished to crave that the agreement be kept and bade the jarl go to Denmark and bring Queen Tyri to him. Sigvaldi the Jarl did not refuse to do this journey, but went to Swein, the Danish king, and laid the matter before him; by his persuasive talk the jarl at length influenced the king, so that Swein gave his sister Tyri into the jarl's

---

1 About this cf. 'Ynglinga Saga', p. 24, n. 2.    2 Other authorities assert that Gunhild was cast aside by Swein and sent back to Vendland, but was brought back to Denmark after the death of Swein in England in 1014.

hands. With her there went some women and her foster-father, who was called Assur Akason, a mighty man, as well as some other men. It was arranged between the king and the jarl that Tyri should have the properties in Vendland which Queen Gunhild had had, and thereto other great posses-sions as a dowry. Tyri wept sorely and went away most unwillingly. And when she and the jarl came to Vend-land, King Burislav made a bridal feast and wedded Queen Tyri. But so long as she was amongst the heathens she would take from them neither food nor drink, and so it went on for a week. But it so befell one night that Queen Tyri and Assur fled away in the dark to the wood. To speak shortly about their journey, they came

Tyri wept sorely when she left for Vendland

forth into Denmark; but Tyri dared nowise remain there for this reason that she knew if her brother King Swein learned of her being there he would straightway send her back to Vendland. Everywhere they went in secret till they came to Norway. Tyri did not stop her journey before she came to King Olav who greeted them well and they were there well kept. Tyri told the king all about her hard lot and from him she begged helpful counsel and peace for herself in his kingdom. She was a fair-spoken woman and the king liked well her talk; he saw that she was beautiful and it came into his mind that this would be a good marriage for him; he turned their talk in that direc-tion and asked her if she would be wedded to him. And placed as she was now, it seemed hard to escape her position; on the other hand she saw what a good wedding it would be to get so well-known a king, and she bade him decide for her and her wedding. And according to what was spoken of, King Olav took Queen Tyri to wife. Their wedding was held in the autumn, when the king had come from the north from Halogaland. King Olav and Queen Tyri were at Nidaros during the winter. But in the following spring Queen Tyri com-plained often before King Olav, and wept sorely, that she had had such great possessions in Vendland, but in this land she had no goods as beseemed a queen. Sometimes she begged the king with fair words to get her her own possessions and said that King Burislav was so good a friend of King Olav that as soon as they met the king would give Olav all he asked for. But when King Olav's friends were aware of these talks they all counselled him from this journey. And so it is said that one day in early spring the king was going along the street and near the market place a man met him with many sticks of angelica which were wondrous big for that time of the year. The king took a big stick of it in his hand and went home to Queen Tyri's bower. Tyri sat in her room weeping when the king came in. The king said, "See here a big stick of angelica which I give thee". She struck it away with her hand and said, "Greater gifts did Harald Gormson give me, and he

Olav gives Tyri a stick of angelica

was less afraid than thou art to go from his land and seek his possessions, and it is true that he came hither into Norway and laid waste the greater part of the land and possessed himself of all the scot and tribute. But thou darest not go through Denmark because of my brother, King Swein". King Olav leaped up at these words and shouted loudly and swore besides, "Never shall I go in fear of thy brother, King Swein; and if we meet, then shall he give way".

93. A little later King Olav called a thing in the town. Before all the throng he made it known that he would raise an army in the summer and he would have a certain number of both ships and men from every shire; he then said how many ships he would have from the fjord there. He then sent behest both north and south in the land and throughout the land within and without and had men called out. He then had the *Long Serpent* launched and all his other ships, both great and small; he himself commanded the *Long Serpent*.[1] And when the men were chosen for the crew, there was such a careful choice, that on the *Long Serpent* there were to be no men older than sixty or younger than twenty, all specially selected for action and

1 In O.N. *Ormrinn Langi,* i.e. the long orme.

courage. The first chosen were King Olav's bodyguard, for these were taken from all the strongest and bravest men, from both within the land and without.

94. Ulf the Red was the name of the man who bore King Olav's standard and he was in the stem of the *Serpent*; next were Kolbjörn the king's marshall, Torstein Ox-foot and Vikar of Tiundaland, the brother of Arnljot Gellina.[1] In the *rausn*[2] by the railings in the forecastle were Vak from the Elf, son of Rauma, Bersi the Strong, An the Shooter from Jämtland, Trand Rami from Telemark and his brother Utyrmir; the Haleygers Trand Squint, Agmund Sandi, Lodver the Long from Saltvik,[3] Harek the Keen and these Inner-Tronds, Ketel the High and Torfinn Eisli, Howard and his brothers from Orkedale. In the forehold were these: Björn of Studla,[4] Torgrim Tjodolvson from Kvin, Asbiorn and Orm; Tord from Mardarlag, Torstein the White from Oprostader, Arnor from Möre, Halstein and Hauk from the Fjords, Eyvind the Snake, Bergtor Bestel, Halkel of Fjalir, Olav the Dreng, Arnfinn of Sogn, Sigurd Bild, Einar of Hordaland and Finn, Ketel of Rogaland, and Grjotgard the Brisk. In the middlehold by the mast were these: Einar Tambarskelver—he seemed not to equal the others, for he was only eighteen winters old, Halstein Livson, Torolv, Ivor Smetta, Orm Skoganef; and many other noble men were on the *Serpent* if we could name them. There were eight men in every half division of the hold in the *Serpent* and they were all chosen one by one; there were thirty in the forehold. It was the talk of men that those men who were chosen to be on the *Serpent* stood as far above other men in good looks, strength and boldness as the *Serpent* did above other ships. Thorkel Nevja, the king's brother, commanded the *Short Serpent*, Thorkel Dydrill and Jostein, the king's uncles, had the *Crane* and both these ships had very good crews. Eleven large ships had King Olav from Trondheim, besides ships with twenty rowing seats and smaller crafts.

95. When King Olav had got his army ready in Nidaros, he set men over all Trondlaw in all districts. Then to Iceland he sent Gissur the White and Hjalti Skeggjason to bid them take up Christianity there and gave them a priest called Thormod and other holy men, but he kept back as hostages four Iceland men who seemed to him most outstanding: Kjartan Olavson, Haldor Gudmundson, Kolbein Tordson and Sverting Runolfson. And about the journey of Gissur

---

1 About *Arnljot Gellina* cf. 'History of St Olav', chapters 141, 215, 226.   2 Cf. 'History of Harald Hairfair', chapter 9.   3 *Saltvik* is situated on the south side of the Ofotenfjord (North Norway).   4 Now Stöle in South Hordaland.

and Hjalti it was said that they came to Iceland and went before the Althing, and at that thing Christianity was taken up by law in Iceland and that summer the whole folk was baptised.

96. The same spring King Olav also sent Leif Ericson to Greenland to bid them take up Christianity there, and he went that summer to Greenland. On the sea, he picked up a ship's crew which was lying helpless on a wreck, and after that he found Vinland the Good.[1] In the autumn he came to Greenland and he brought with him a priest and teachers. He took lodging at Brattalid with his father Eric. Afterwards he was called Leif the Lucky;[2] but his father said that the two things went against each other, one that Leif had saved the ship's crew, and the other that he had brought a hurtful person to Greenland and that was the priest.

97.[3] Herjulf was son of Bard Herjulfson, who was a kinsman of Ingolf who first settled Iceland.[4] Ingolf gave Herjulf land to farm between Vog and Reykjanes. Herjulf lived first at Drepstock. Thorgerd was his wife and Biarne was their son. He was a doughty youth full of promise. He had early a wish to go abroad, and he soon gathered wealth and got renown. He spent alternately a year abroad, and a year with his father. Biarne soon owned a trading ship. Herjulf arranged with Eric to go to Greenland the last winter he was in Norway, and sold his houses. A Christian man from the Hebrides came along with Herjulf. He made a poem called the "Hafgerdingar[5] Song", in which there is this refrain:

| He whose hand protects me | The heavens above us, |
| The simple monk in company | Will stand by us! |

1 The Norsemen called America *Vinland*, i.e. Wineland, because they found grapes near their settlements. Carlyle in *The Early Kings of Norway* states: "wild grapes still grow in Rhode Island and more luxuriantly further south". 2 *Lucky* in O.S. is *heppinn*, and 'luck' or 'good fortune' is called *happ*. These words must be closely connected with the English words *happy* and *happen*. The words used in M.S. for 'lucky' are *lykkelig* or *lycklig*. 3 As pointed out in the preface some historians consider that the following eight chapters are not part of Snorre Sturlason's work and that they are interpolations by Peringskiold. It is apparent that they are written in a different style and that they do not come up to Snorre Sturlason's standard of reliability in details; but it is most improbable that Peringskiold should *sans façon* have added these chapters to his book, which after all must be considered a faithful copy and translation of an Icelandic manuscript. It cannot make any difference, if, as some historians contend, Peringskiold's work is based on a copy of such a manuscript. There is more reason for thinking that Snorre Sturlason or his clerical assistants have added these chapters to the copies of the original work during Snorre's lifetime. This would account for the fact that the narrative does not appear to be a continuation of Snorre's first dictation and that it is of a somewhat different character and style. 4 The original settlers in Iceland were called *Landnam-men*. 5 *Hafgerding* means the circle of high waves raised by currents in particular spots in the ocean.

Herjulf lived at Herjulfsnes[1] and he was much respected. Eric the Red lived at Brattalid, and was most honoured by everybody. These were Eric's children: Leif, Thorvald, and Torstein; and his daughter was called Freydis, who married a man called Thorvald, and they lived at Garth, the present bishop's seat. She was a big and hefty woman, and he was a small man. She was anxious for possessions and wealth. The folks in Greenland were heathen in those days.

Biarne came in the summer with his ship to Eyrar[2] where his father had already left the previous spring. He was surprised at these tidings and stayed on board his ship. His men asked him what he wished to do; he replied that he preferred to do as before and stay with his father in the winter. "But I will go to Greenland, if ye will join me." They all agreed to go with him. Then Biarne said, "Our voyage will be considered unwise as we have not sailed in the Greenland sea before". All the same they proceeded to sea, when the ship was ready, and sailed for three days, when the land was lost sight of.

Then the wind eased and a north wind with fog commenced blowing, and they knew not where they were; and this continued for several days. Finally the sun appeared and they could discern the quarters of the heavens. They set their sail again, and proceeded for a night and a day, when they got sight of land. They took counsel as to which land this was and Biarne said he did not think it was Greenland. They then asked if he would sail nearer to it; he said, "I advise that we sail close up to it". This was done; and they saw that the land had no fells, but was well wooded, and had some small heights. They sailed away and had the land on the port side of the ship and their sheet pointed to the shore. They sailed another two days before they saw land again. They asked Biarne if this might be Greenland; but he said he thought that this land could no more be Greenland than the first they sighted. "For in Greenland, they say there are great snow-fells." They soon approached the land, and saw it was flat and widely clad with wood. As the wind dropped, the crew thought it would be best to land; but Biarne would not allow it. They said they needed wood and water; but Biarne said: "Ye need not either".

1 The first Norse settlers in Greenland were probably exterminated by the Eskimos. If they were continually attacked by the Eskimos they had in the long run no chance to stand against far superior numbers. Gunpowder was of course unknown to them.    2 *Eyrar* is situated on the south coast of Iceland. *Eyrar*, or *Ayre* (in the Orkneys) means 'a flat sandy beach', suitable for landing and hauling up ships. The Scotch town Ayr probably derives its name from its beach.

Biarne was much blamed for this. He then bade them set the sail, which they did. The ship's stem was now turned from the land and they sailed to sea for three days with a south-westerly wind. Then they saw land for a third time, which had high fells, and icebergs. They asked Biarne to land here; but he said, "Nay, for I think this land is not of any use". They kept the sail standing, and proceeded along the shore, and found that it was an island. Afterwards they steered away from the land, and stood out to sea with the same wind; but a gale came on and Biarne had the sail reefed, and told his men not to sail harder than the ship's rigging might stand. After three days land was sighted for the fourth time. They asked Biarne whether this was Greenland; Biarne replied, "This land is most like what I have heard of Greenland; and I will go ashore here". This was done and they landed in the evening by a ness, where a boat was found. Biarne's father Herjulf lived on this ness; and therefore it is called Herjulfsnes. Biarne went home to his father and gave up going to sea. He remained with his father, Herjulf, as long as he was alive; and still lived there after his father's death.

98. Now is to be told that Biarne Herjulfson came over from Greenland on a visit to Eric the Jarl[1] and the jarl greeted him well. Biarne told him of his voyage, when he saw afore-mentioned lands; and it was thought he had not been very anxious to know about things when he was unable to tell anything about these lands, and for this he was blamed. Biarne became the jarl's bodyguardsman, and the next summer he sailed for Greenland; and there they spoke much about finding new lands. Leif, son of Eric the Red of Bratta-lid, came to Biarne Herjulfson and bought the ship from him, and obtained a crew so that they were thirty-five men altogether. Leif asked his father Eric to be chief of the voyage. He excused himself, saying he was too old, and not so able to stand wet and cold weather as in former days. Leif replied that he among all their kinsmen would have the most luck on such a voyage. Eric finally gave way, and rode from home with Leif when they were ready for sea; but when they were a short distance from the ship the horse on which Eric was riding stumbled so that Eric fell to the ground and his foot was hurt. Then said Eric, "It is not fated that I shall discover more lands than Greenland, on which we live: and we ought not to proceed all together on this voyage". Eric now went home again to Bratta-

---

1 *Biarne Herjulfson's* visit to *Eric the Jarl* appears to conflict with events related in chapter 96. It is evident that the short and casual narrative in chapter 96 is enlarged upon with full details in chapters 98 and 99.

lid; but Leif, with his crew, in all thirty-five men, made their vessel ready for sea. On this voyage there was a man from a southern country and his name was Tyrker. The ship was made ready, and they proceeded to sea, and found first the land which Biarne and his men had found last. They sailed to it, dropped anchor, put out a boat, and went on land; but saw no grass. There were big snow-fells inland, but from the shore to the snow-fells the land was all stone, and they thought the land was of no use. Leif said, "Now we won't have it said of us, as it was of Biarne, that we did not go ashore. I will now give the land a name and call it Helluland".[1] Afterwards they went on board, sailed away and found another land and sailed near it and dropped anchor. They put out a boat, and landed. This land was flat and covered with wood; and wherever they walked the strand consisted of white sand, with a low beach. Leif said, "This land shall have a name according to its appearance, and we shall call it Markland".[2] They hurried afterwards to the ship and sailed away. It was blowing a gale from north-east, and they sailed for two days before they saw land. When they came near it, they saw it was an island which was situated on the north side of the land. There they landed in good weather, and found that there was some dew on the grass. It happened that they touched the dew with their fingers and put it to their mouths, and they thought they had never tasted anything so sweet before. Afterwards they went on board, and sailed into a sound situated between this island and a ness which projected northwards and they proceeded west past the ness. The water was very shallow at ebb tide, and their ship lay dry, so it was a long way from the ship to the sea. But they were so keen to get on land that they would not wait for flood tide, but leaped ashore and came to a small river which flowed from a lake. But when their ship was afloat, they went to their boat and rowed to the ship. They towed her up the river, and then into the lake. There they anchored and bore their belongings out of the ship and built some booths. They decided to settle there for the winter, and soon commenced building a big house. They had no shortage of salmon, either in the river or in the lake; and the salmon was larger than they had ever seen. The land was thought to be so fertile, that they needed not to store cattle fodder for the winter. There was no frost in the winter and the grass did not wither much. Day and night were more equally divided than in Greenland or Iceland. The sun was there in the position of

1 *Helluland* = a naked land of rocks; in O.S. = *hella*; probably Labrador or Newfoundland. 2 *Markland* = a forest land; probably Nova Scotia or New England.

eyktarstad[1] and dagmalastad[2] during the shortest winter days. When they were ready with their house-building, Leif said to his followers: "I will now divide the men into two parts, in order to explore the country; and half of you shall stay at home and the other half shall get to know the land, but nobody shall go farther away than that they can come back the same day, and you must not walk far apart from each other". This they did for some time. Leif changed about, sometimes he went with them, and other times he stayed at home. Leif was a big and strong man, and of manly looks; besides a wise and careful man in all things.

99. One evening it happened that a man of the party was missing; and it was the South-country man, Tyrker. Leif was very concerned about it; because Tyrker had lived with his father and fostered Leif in his childhood. Leif gave his men the blame, and arranged to go with twelve men and search for him; but they had come only a short way from the house when Tyrker came to meet them. He was joyfully greeted. Leif soon saw that his foster-father was merry. Tyrker had sharp eyes, and was little in size and ugly with a small face, but was very skilled in all kinds of sports. Leif said to him, "Why art thou so late, my foster-father? and why didst thou leave thy comrades?" At first he spoke in Turkish, rolled his eyes and frowned, but they could not understand what he said. After a while he said in Norse, "I did not go much farther than the others; but I have something new to tell, for I found vines and grapes". "Can that be true, my foster-father?" said Leif. "Yes, it is true", answered he, "for I come from a country where there are plenty of vines and grapes." They slept all night and the next morning Leif said to his men, "We have now two things to look after for each day, first to gather grapes and cut vines, and next to fell wood in the forest as cargo for our vessel". And this they did. It is told that their tender was fully loaded with grapes. Then a cargo of wood was cut for the ship. They found wheat fields which were self-sown and a tree which is called massur. Of everything they took some quantities, and the trees were so large that they could use them for building houses.

---

1 In O.N. *eykt* is considered the time of the day between 3.30 and 4.30 p.m. and *eyktarstad* is considered the end of the *eykt*, viz. 4.30 p.m.    2 *Dagmalastad* in O.N. is 7.30 or 8 o'clock in the morning. The Norsemen had of course no clocks. This description of the positions of the sun has led to many theories regarding the spot where Leif Ericson landed; but the information given can never lead to any satisfactory conclusion; besides a difference of opinion exists regarding the exact time of the day which the words *eyktarstad* and *dagmalastad* convey.

When spring came they made themselves ready and left the country. Leif gave the land a name after its products, and called it Vinland. They sailed out to sea and had a favourable wind all the way until they saw Greenland and the fells below the snow-covered peaks. One of the crew then said to Leif, "Why do you sail so close to the wind?" Leif answered, "I look after the tiller, but I see to other matters as well; do you not see anything unusual?" He replied that he saw nothing. Leif said, "I cannot say whether it is a ship or a skerry I see there". Now they all saw that it was a skerry. But Leif saw better than the others, and could recognise people on the skerry. "I will now bear away", said Leif, "so that we can get near to them, if they are folks who need our help; but if they are not peaceful men, it is for us to do what we like, and not as they should wish." They came up to the skerry, took the sail down and dropped anchor. They launched a boat which they had on board. Tyrker then called to them and asked for the name of their leader. He called himself Thorer, and said he was a Norseman. "And what is your name?" Leif said who he was. "Are you a son of Eric the Red of Brattalid?" Leif said it was so. "And now", said Leif further, "I ask you all to come on board to me with all your belongings and goods, if the ship has room for it all." They took this offer and the voyage was continued until they arrived at Ericsfjord and came to Brattalid, where they unloaded their cargo. Leif told Thorer and his wife Gudrid, and three others, that they could lodge in his houses, and found rooms elsewhere for the remainder of the crew, both Thorer's people and his own. Leif rescued fifteen men from the skerry, and was afterwards called Leif the Lucky. After this voyage Leif got both wealth and fame. In the winter many of Thorer's people became ill and a great part of them died. Eric the Red also died that winter. This voyage to Vinland was much talked of, and Leif's brother Thorvald thought that the land had not been sufficiently explored. Leif then said to Thorvald, "Thou shalt go, brother, to Vinland in my vessel if thou wishest; but I must first send the ship for the wood which Thorer left behind on the skerry". And this he did.

100. Later Thorvald made preparations for his voyage with thirty men, under the advice of his brother Leif. They put their tackle in order and left the land. Nothing is told of this voyage until they arrived in Vinland, to Leif's houses, where they hauled the ship on shore. They stayed there quietly the whole winter and went fishing. But in the spring Thorvald had his ship rigged and bade some

of his men sail westward and explore the land during the summer.
They found that the land was beautiful and well-wooded. The distance was short between the woods and the sea, and the beach consisted of white sand. There were many islands and shallow water.
No houses for man or cattle were found; but on an island away to the
west there was a corn-lathe made of wood. They found no other work
of man and came back in the autumn to Leif's booths. The next
spring Thorvald went with his ship eastwards and then northwards
along the land. Near a cape a sudden gale started blowing and they
drifted on to the shore and the ship broke her keel. They had to stay
there for a long time to repair the vessel. Thorvald said to his men,
"We shall raise the keel here on the ness, and call it Keelness":
which was done. Afterwards they sailed eastward along the land and
into the mouth of a fjord, which was near by, until they came to a
fell ridge which was all covered with wood. They made the ship fast
and laid out landing stages, and Thorvald and his men went ashore.
He said, "It is beautiful here and this is where I would like to build
my house". Later they went on board and saw three black spots on
the sand in the bay. They went to them and found three skin boats,
and there were three men under each boat. They separated their men
and caught all of them except one, who managed to get away in his
boat. The eight were killed and afterwards they went to the fell
ridge and had a look round. Inside the fjord they saw some raised
ground, which looked like some houses. Then they suddenly
became very tired and could not keep awake and they all laid down
to sleep. They had not been long asleep before a loud voice awoke
them and they thought the voice said, "Awake, Thorvald, with all
thy followers, if ye will save your lives. Go on board your ship and
leave this land as soon as ye can". Then rowed out of the fjord a
crowd of skin boats and came alongside their ship. Thorvald said,
"We shall put up our storm boards along the railings, and defend
ourselves; but we shall not trouble to use our weapons much against
them". This was done. The Skrælingers[1] shot at them for some time,
and then ran away as fast as they could. Thorvald asked them if anybody was wounded, and nobody happened to be hurt. He said, "I
have a wound above my hand. An arrow flew between the railing
and the shield and hit me above my hand; here is the arrow, and it
will be my bane. I will now advise ye to get away from here as soon as
possible; but first shall ye carry me to the fell ridge upon which I
liked so much to build a house. May be, it will come true what I

1 The Norsemen called the Red Indians *Skrælingar*, i.e. weak and powerless men.

said, that there I shall remain for some time. Ye shall bury me
there and place a cross by my head and another by my feet and call
the fell ridge Crossness". Christianity was then established in Greenland; but Eric the Red had died previous to Christianity. Thorvald
then died and everything was done as he had wished. Afterwards
they went away to look for their comrades, and when they met they
told each other the tidings. They stayed at their houses all the winter
and gathered vines and grapes with which they intended to load their
vessel. When spring came they made ready to go back to Greenland,
where they arrived safely and went ashore at Ericsfjord and told the
tidings to Leif.

101. It had meantime happened in Greenland that Torstein of
Ericsfjord had married and taken Gudrid for his wife. She was
Thorbjörn's daughter who had been married as told already to
Thorer the Norseman. Torstein Ericson now listed to go to Vinland
for his brother Thorvald's body. He made the same vessel ready
and chose a strong and well-waxen crew, in all twenty-five men,
besides his wife Gudrid. When he was ready they put to sea and
soon lost the land. They drifted about the whole summer and knew
not where they were; but in the first week of winter they got ashore
at Lysafjord in West Greenland. Torstein looked for quarters for his
men, and got them all housed; but not himself and his wife. For a
few nights they slept on board the ship. Christianity was still young
in Greenland at that time. Early one morning some men came to
their tent and asked who were in the tent. Torstein replied, "Two
persons. Who is asking?" "Torstein", came the answer, "and I
am called Torstein the Black and my errand is to offer thee and thy
wife lodging in my house." Torstein said he would speak with his
wife. She left it to him to decide and they agreed to go to Torstein
the Black. "Then I shall fetch you in the morning with my horse,
for I can well afford to house you; but it is not cheerful to live with
me, for I and my wife live alone, and I am very sad. I have a different
religion from yours, but I think yours is the best." The following
morning he came with his horse and they went with Torstein the
Black, who was very hospitable. Gudrid had good looks and was
wise and had good manners with strangers. Early that winter illness
broke out among Torstein Ericson's followers and many of them
died. He bade that coffins should be made for the dead and be
carried on board and stowed away with great care. "For I will convey
the bodies to Ericsfjord in the summer." Soon also illness broke out

in Torstein the Black's home and his wife, who was called Grimhild, became ill first. She was very tall, and strong as a man; but still the illness got the upper hand of her. Soon afterwards Torstein Ericson fell ill, and they both lay sick together; but Torstein the Black's wife Grimhild died first. When she was dying Torstein went outside for a fur to place over her body. Gudrid said, "My dear Torstein, stay not long away". He said he would soon be back. Torstein Ericson then said, "Our housewife is strange, she lifts herself with her arms, pushes herself forward over the bed and looks for her shoes". At this moment Torstein the Black returned and Grimhild fell back in her bed, so that every beam in the house shook. Torstein made a coffin for Grimhild's body and moved it outside the house. Torstein Ericson's illness got worse. He lay dying and his wife Gudrid sorrowed much. They were all in one room, and Gudrid was sitting on a stool in front of the bunk where her husband's body was lying. Torstein the Black then took Gudrid in his arms and set her on his lap and spoke much with her. He comforted her and promised to go with her to Ericsfjord in the summer, with her husband's body and those of his followers. "And", he said, "I shall bring with me many servants to help and console thee." She thanked him for that. Torstein Ericson now rose in the bed and said, "Where is Gudrid?" and he repeated it three times, and she did not answer. She said to Torstein the Black, "Shall I answer or not?" He advised her not to speak. Torstein the Black then walked across the floor and sat down on a stool, and Gudrid placed herself on his lap. Torstein the Black said, "What didst thou want to say?" After a while the dying man replied, "I want to tell Gudrid her fate, so that she may better bear my loss; I have now come to a good place of rest. This I must tell thee, Gudrid, that thou wilt marry a man from Iceland, and ye will long live together; and from ye will come many brave and wise men. Ye shall sail from Greenland to Norway and afterwards to Iceland, where ye shall settle down. Long will ye live there, but thou shalt survive him. Then thou shalt go to the southern lands and afterwards return to Iceland to thy home. There shall a church be built, and thou wilt remain there and become a nun and end thy days there". Torstein then sank back, and his body was laid out and taken to the ship. Torstein the Black kept his word. He sold his cattle and land in the spring in order to take Gudrid home. He made the vessel ready, shipped a crew, and proceeded to Ericsfjord. The body was buried in the church. Gudrid went to Leif's houses at Brattalid, and

Torstein the Black settled in Ericsfjord, and remained there for the rest of his life and was considered a brave man.

102. That summer a ship came to Greenland from Norway. The vessel was steered by a man called Thorfinn Karlsefni, who was son of Tord Hesthofda, the son of Snorre Tordarson of Hofda. Thorfinn Karlsefni was a very rich man, and stayed that winter at Brattalid with Leif Ericson. He fell in love with Gudrid and wooed her; but she told him to see Leif and get his answer. They got betrothed and their wedding was celebrated the same winter. As usual there was much talk about going to Vinland, and Gudrid and others advised Karlsefni to undertake this voyage. Finally this journey was decided upon and they collected a crew of sixty men besides five women. Karlsefni and his men agreed between themselves that they should have an equal share in all they won. They took with them many kinds of cattle,[1] intending to settle in the land if they could. Karlsefni asked Leif to let him have his houses in Vinland; but he said he would only lend them and not sell them. They put to sea and came safely to Leif's booths and brought their belongings ashore. Soon they got a valuable catch, for a big whale had drifted ashore. It was cut up, and now they had no shortage of food. When their cattle had got up into the land, it soon grew wild and unmanageable. They brought a bull with them. Karlsefni had trees felled and cut to load the ship, and the wood was dried on a rock. They gathered all the fruits of the land such as grapes and all kind of game and fishes. After the first winter, towards summer, they soon caught sight of the Skrælingers, and a great number of them came out of the forests. The cattle was near to the woods, and when the bull began to roar the Skrælingers were frightened and ran off with their sacks. These contained furs and sables and other skins. Then they went to Karlsefni's houses and wished to go inside; but Karlsefni guarded the doors. They could not understand each other's language. Then the Skrælingers took their sacks and opened them and offered their goods, but preferred to have weapons in exchange; but Karlsefni had forbidden the men to sell arms. Then he conceived this plan; he let the womenfolk carry out to them milk and dairy produce, and when they examined

---

1 Grass grows in Greenland to-day for cattle fodder and undoubtedly did so at the time of Eric the Red. Some writers, over-eager to depreciate these most important narratives, have asserted that no cattle fodder grew in Greenland and that Karlsefni's account is unreliable. This misconception has added to the existing disbelief in these voyages.

it, they would buy this and nothing else. The trade with the Skrælingers resulted in that they carried away their profits in their stomachs, whilst Karlsefni and his men kept their sacks full of fur. Now is to be told that Karlsefni made a great wooden fence round the houses and made it strong enough to defend himself. At that time Gudrid gave birth to a son, who was called Snorre. Next winter the Skrælingers came back and were much more numerous and with the same wares. Karlsefni said to the womenfolk, "Now ye shall bear out the same food as they liked last time, and nothing else". And when they saw that, they threw their sacks over the fence. Gudrid sat by the door with her son Snorre lying in the cradle. Then a shadow appeared outside the door and a woman entered dressed in a black narrow kirtle, rather short, and with a kerchief on her head. She had light yellow hair and her face was pale with large eyes, much larger than anybody had ever seen. She walked up to where Gudrid was sitting and said, "What is your name?" "I am called Gudrid; and what is your name?" "I am also called Gudrid", she said. Then the housewife Gudrid shook hands with her and bade her sit down. But at that moment Gudrid heard a loud sound and the woman had disappeared. At the same time one of the Skrælingers was slain by one of Karlsefni's huscarls, because he tried to steal a weapon. Then they ran away with all speed, whilst their clothes and sacks were left behind. Nobody had seen the woman except Gudrid. "Now we must be careful", said Karlsefni, "for I think they will come a third time with more people and they will then put up some fight. We shall make this plan that ten men shall proceed to that ness and be conspicuous there, and the rest shall go into the woods, and make a clearance for our cattle; and we shall take the bull with us, and let him go in front." At the place where they were to meet there was a lake on the one side and a forest on the other. The plan which Karlsefni had proposed was now carried out. The Skrælingers came to the very place where Karlsefni wanted to fight; and there was a sharp fight and many of the Skrælingers fell. There was a big and handsome man among the Skrælingers' people, and Karlsefni thought that he was their chief. One of the Skrælingers had taken up an axe and looked at it for a while and swung it against one of his fellowmen,[1] so that he fell down. Then the big man took the axe, looked at it, and threw it as far as he could into the sea. Then they fled to the

---

1 The O.N. text for 'fellow-man' is *felagi*, pl. *felagar*, from which originates the English word *fellow*.

forest with all speed and thus the fight ended. Karlsefni remained there with his men the whole winter; but in the spring he returned to Greenland. They prepared for their voyage, and had much goods with them, such as vines, grapes, and skin wares. They put to sea, and came safely to Ericsfjord, and they remained there that winter.

103. Then they again started talking about a Vinland voyage, as such a trip would give them both gain and honour. The same summer that Karlsefni came back from Vinland a ship arrived in Greenland from Norway, which was in charge of two brothers called Helgi and Finbogi, who remained that winter in Greenland. These brothers were Icelanders and hailed from the Eastfjords. Now our tale begins, when Freydis, Eric's daughter, left her home at Garth and went to see the two brothers Helgi and Finbogi. She asked them to go to Vinland in their ship and they would receive half the goods they won. They were agreeable to this arrangement. Afterwards she went to her brother Leif's houses and asked him to give her the booths he had built. But he replied as before that he would lend the houses and not sell them. The brothers and Freydis agreed that each of them should have thirty weaponed men, besides women. But Freydis broke this bargain and had five men more and hid them, so that the brothers did not notice it, till they came to Vinland. They sailed away to sea; but before leaving they agreed that they should sail together if possible. They kept fairly close to each other; but all the same the brothers arrived a little earlier and carried their belongings to Leif's houses. When Freydis afterwards arrived her men also brought her belongings to the houses. Then said Freydis, "Why did you bring your things here?" They said, "Because we thought that everybody would abide by what was agreed". "Leif has lent me the houses", she said, "not you." Then said Helgi, "We brothers will hardly be able to strive with thee". Afterwards the brothers bore out their belongings and built another house, further away from the sea, on the beach of the lake and had everything well done. Freydis started cutting trees for a cargo. Now winter came and the brothers spoke about playing some games in order to pass the time, which was also done until they started quarrelling. Then they gave up the games and did not visit each other, and thus things went on for some time. One morning Freydis got out of her bed, clad herself, but put on no shoes or socks. The weather was good and much dew was fallen. She put her husband's

cape over her shoulders and went to the brothers' house and up to the door. Just before that a man had gone out and left the door half open. She walked in and stood for a while without saying anything. Finbogi lay farthest away and was awake. He said, "What wilt thou here, Freydis?" She answered, "I want thee to get up and come out with me, for I have something to talk with thee about". So he got up, and they went together to a tree trunk, which was lying near the house, and sat down. "How dost thou like it here", she said. He answered, "The land is all right; but I hate that strife should have cropped up between us, for it seems to me that there is no ground for it". She said, "It is as thou sayest, and I have thought the same. My errand to thee is that I want to exchange my ship with ye brothers, as my ship is smaller than yours and I want to get away". "That I will do if it will please thee", he said. Then they parted. She went home; but Finbogi went back to his bed. When she got into bed with her cold feet Thorvald awoke and asked why she was so cold and wet. She answered angrily, "I went over to the brothers to buy their ship, which is bigger than ours; but they turned angry over it and struck and abused me, and thou, miserable wretch, wilt not avenge this insult. I am not any longer in Greenland, and I will separate from thee, unless thou dost avenge this". He could not any longer endure her scolding and reproaches, and bade his men get up and arm themselves. They did so and went at once to the brothers' house and found them asleep. They bound the men and brought them out of the house, and Freydis had all of them killed. Thus the men were slain but the women were still left, whom nobody would kill. Then said Freydis, "Let me have an axe". So it was done, and she struck at the five women, and did not leave off until they were all dead. Then they went back to their house after this evil act; and nobody could notice anything else than that Freydis thought she had done well; and she addressed her fellows thus: "If we come safely back to Greenland, I shall kill anybody who speaks of this happening; and we shall only say that they remained here when we left". Now early in spring they made ready the ship which was owned by the brothers and brought on board all the products which they found and the ship could carry. They sailed out to sea, and had a quick and safe passage, and arrived at Ericsfjord in the early part of the summer. At that time Karlsefni was there; he had his ship ready for sea and waited for a favourable wind. It was a general saying that hardly ever before had a ship left Greenland with a more costly cargo than the vessel which Karlsefni owned. Freydis went home to her garth, which was unscathed whilst she was away. She gave her followers goods and many gifts, so that they should be quiet about her evil deeds. After this she remained at her garth. But all her men did not keep quiet about their misdeed and it soon became known to her brother Leif, who thought these sayings were dreadful. Then Leif took three of Freydis' followers and tortured them in order that they should confess to him all that happened, and all their sayings agreed. "I do not like", said Leif, "to do to my sister Freydis what she well deserves; but this I can foretell of her and her husband, that their offspring will never thrive." Now it also happened that ill was thought of them ever afterwards.

104. We now come back to where we told of Karlsefni being ready to leave the land. He had a good passage and came safely to Norway and stayed there during the winter. He sold his wares and he and his wife were much honoured by the best people in Norway. And in the spring he made his ship ready to go to Iceland. When he was quite ready to sail and his ship was lying outside the jetty waiting for a good wind, there came to him a southern man who hailed from Bremen in Saxland and would buy from Karlsefni his broom-stick. "I will not sell it", he said. "I will give you half a mark of gold for it", said the man from the south. Karlsefni thought it was a good offer and they concluded the deal, and the man went away with the broom-stick; but Karlsefni did not know what kind of wood it was. It was massur wood brought from Vinland. Afterwards Karlsefni put to sea and came to land in the north of Iceland, at Skagafjord, where the ship was put on land for the winter. In the spring he bought Glaumbæjarland, where he built his houses and where he lived all his lifetime. He was a good man and much honoured. From him and his wife Gudrid are descended many men, and they were all a fine race. When Karlsefni died Gudrid took over the garth together with her son Snorre, who was born in Vinland. When Snorre took a wife, Gudrid went abroad and to the southern countries; but came back to Snorre's garth, and Snorre had a church built at Glaumbo. Gudrid afterwards became a nun and a hermit, and stayed there as long as she lived. Snorre had a son called Torgeir, who was father to Ingvell the mother of Bishop Brand. The daughter of Snorre Karlsefnison was called Halfrid. She was mother of Runolf, who was father of Bishop Thorlak. Karlsefni and Gudrid had a second son called Björn. He was father of Thorun, the mother of

Bishop Biarne. From Karlsefni a numerous race has descended and they are all noble men. Nobody has given a clearer account than Karlsefni of the happenings on these voyages, of which something has here been told.[1]

105. The winter after King Olav had baptised Halogaland, he and Queen Tyri were in Nidaros; and the summer before Queen Tyri had borne King Olav a boy-child, who was both stout and promising and was called Harald, after his mother's father. The king and queen loved the child very much and were always hoping that it would grow up and take the heritage after its father, but it only lived a year after its birth and both parents sorrowed much over it. During that winter were many Icelanders and other well-famed men with King Olav, as before mentioned. With him at that time was his sister Ingebjörg; she was very good-looking and had a good judgment of things and was well liked by the people. She liked the Icelanders that were there, but most of all she liked Kjartan Olavson, as he had been longer than the others with the king; he found it always pleasant to talk with her, for she had good understanding and was witty in her talk. The king was always glad and full of mirth in his manner and often asked about the doings of the great men and chiefs in the neighbouring countries, when people came from Denmark or Sweden to see him. The summer before Halfred Vandradascald had been with Ragnvald the Jarl, the son of Ulf, who had lately become the ruler of West Gautland. Ulf, Ragnvald's father, was a brother of Sigrid the Strong-minded, so that King Olav the Swedish king and Ragnvald the Jarl were first cousins. Olav Trygvason was told by Halfred many tidings about the jarl; Halfred said he was well fitted for ruling the country, generous with money, brave, and had many friends. He also said that the jarl much wanted the friendship of King Olav and had spoken of wooing Ingebjörg, Trygvi's daughter. The same

1 Samuel Laing, in his translation of the Norse Sagas, mentions in the preface that Columbus went to Iceland in 1477 in order to gain nautical information and that he there must have obtained information about Vinland from Bishop Magnus or others with whom he might have come in contact. He bases his assertion upon the memoirs of Fernando, the son of Columbus. This visit by Columbus to Iceland is also written about by a Peruvian scholar, Luis Ulloa, in his book *Christophe Colomb, Catalan*. The two old authorities for Columbus' voyage to Iceland are his son Fernando, who wrote *Historie del S.D. Fernando Colombo*, and Fray Bartolomé de Las Casas. The latter wrote *Historia de las Indias*. Fernando states that his father "visited *Tile* in February 1477, an island as large as England where the English, specially those of Bristol, have commercial relations". There can be little doubt that *Tile* is *Thule*, i.e. Iceland. He further describes certain climatic conditions when Columbus was in Iceland.

winter messengers came from the jarl in Gautland and met King Olav at Nidaros, and gave the message which Halfred had spoken of, that the jarl desired Olav's full friendship and wished to become his brother-in-law and marry his sister Ingebjörg. The messengers gave the king sufficient tokens to prove that they came from the jarl. The king listened to their speech, and seemed to approve of it, but said that Ingebjörg must herself decide about it. King Olav then talked to his sister to find out her opinion; she answered thus: "I have been with you now for some time; you have always shown me brotherly care ever since you came to Norway; I will therefore agree to the proposal of marriage, provided you do not marry me to a heathen man". King Olav said it should be as she wished. He then spoke to the messengers and it was settled before they left that in the summer the king should meet Ragnvald the Jarl in the eastern part of the country and become friends, and when they met they would arrange about the wedding. The jarl's messengers left with this reply, and King Olav remained all the winter in Nidaros, in great splendour and with many people around him.

106. In the summer King Olav went with his ships and men southwards along the land, past Stad. Queen Tyri and Ingebjörg, Trygvi's daughter, the king's sister, were with him. He was joined by many of his friends and other mighty chiefs who were willing to follow the king. The mightiest man of these was his brother-in-law, Erling Skjalgson, who had with him his great *skeid*[1] with thirty rowing seats well fitted out in every way. His brothers-in-law Hyrning and Torgeir were also with him and each commanded a large vessel. Many other mighty men followed him. With this war host he sailed southwards along the land, but when he came south to Rogaland he stopped there, for Erling Skjalgson was giving a great feast at Sola for the king. Ragnvald Ulfson the Jarl from Gautland came there to meet the king, in order to settle the matter which had been arranged in the winter through the messengers, namely, the marriage of Ingebjörg, the king's sister. He was well received by Olav, and when the matter came to be spoken of, the king said he would keep his word and marry his sister Ingebjörg to him, on condition that he would accept the true faith and make all his subjects in the land he ruled be baptised. The jarl agreed to this, and he and

---

1 A *skeid* was a vessel built on specially fine lines and therefore swifter than other ships. Erling's *skeid* had no dragon head and was therefore probably not intended for war.

all his followers were baptised. It now became a great feast, for at the same time the jarl held his wedding with Ingebjörg, the king's sister. King Olav had now married off all his sisters; the jarl now set off on his way home with Ingebjörg and the king sent learned men with him to baptise the people of Gautland, and to teach them the true faith and righteous living. The king and the jarl parted in great friendship.

107. After his sister Ingebjörg's wedding, the king made ready in great haste to leave the country with his army, which was both great and made up of fine men. When he left the land and sailed south he had sixty warships with which he sailed past Denmark, through the Sound and then on to Vendland. He arranged a meeting with King Burislav, and when the kings met they spoke about a property which King Olav craved and the meeting passed off peaceably, and it was satisfactorily arranged about the properties to which King Olav thought he had a right in this land. King Olav remained long during the summer in Vendland and met there many of his friends.

108. King Swein Forkbeard was then wedded to Sigrid the Strong-minded, as is written above (chapter 91). Sigrid was King Olav Trygvason's greatest foe, because King Olav had broken his troth with her and smacked her on the face, as is written above (chapter 61). She egged on King Swein very much to hold battle with King Olav and said that there was a strong enough case against King Olav in that he had wedded Swein's sister Tyri "without thy assent and thy forefathers would not have suffered such a thing". Such speeches Queen Sigrid often put in her mouth and she pressed her entreaties for so long that King Swein was quite willing to take counsel thereon. And early in the spring he sent men east into Sweden to his kinsman Olav the Swedish king and to Eric the Jarl to tell them that Olav, King of Norway, had gathered his fleet, and thought of going in the summer to Vendland. The behest added that the King of the Swedes and the jarl should call out their army and go to meet King Swein, and that when they were all come together they should lay to battle with King Olav. And the King of the Swedes and Eric the Jarl were quite ready for this journey and they drew together a great fleet in Sweden. With that army they went south to Denmark and came there at the time when King Olav Trygvason had sailed east. About this Haldor the Unchristian says, when he composed verses about Eric the Jarl:

The kings' battle-eager
Warriors bade forth from
Sweden the hosts.
(He went south to the strife.)

The ravens of the sea
Waited for food and
Every warrior then longed
To follow Eric to battle.

The King of the Swedes and Eric the Jarl sailed to meet the Danish king, and they had gathered a countless host.

109. When King Swein had called forth his army, he sent Sigvaldi the Jarl to Vendland to spy on King Olav Trygvason's journey and to plan so that King Swein and the others should meet with King Olav. Sigvaldi the Jarl went his way and came to Vendland; he went to Jomsborg and then to King Olav Trygvason. There was much friendship between them, and the jarl got into the greatest favour with the king; the jarl's wife Astrid, King Burislav's daughter, was a good friend of King Olav, mostly on the ground of their former kinship, when King Olav had wedded her sister Geira. Sigvaldi the Jarl was a wise and masterful man, and when he got into converse with King Olav, he delayed much his departure from the east and found for it many different reasons. But King Olav's men were little content with that, for they longed to go home; they were ready to sail and the wind was good. Sigvaldi the Jarl got secret word from Denmark that now the Danish and Swedish kings and Eric the Jarl were come together and were sailing east by Vendland; that they had agreed to wait for King Olav by an island called Svold,[1] and that the jarl should bring it about so that they might find King Olav there.

[1] The site of the battle of *Svold* has given rise to a certain amount of controversy, because the place does not exist in our times, and some accuse Snorre Sturlason of lack of geographical knowledge. This accusation is hardly just, as Snorre, considering the vastness of his work, shows remarkable knowledge of geography and rarely makes mistakes of any significance. It is therefore inconceivable that he should make a mistake about *Svold*, in view of the great importance of this battle, in which all the three Scandinavian nations partook, besides the Jomsvikings. The battle must have been known and talked about in all these countries. The general belief is that *Svold* was a holme or small island situated on the east or south-east coast of Rugen, separated from the main island by a sound, and as it probably consisted of sand or chalk (like the other islands in this neighbourhood), it disappeared in the fourteenth century, when many changes took place on the Baltic coast. The poems of the scalds are mostly responsible for the doubt that is thrown upon this matter; but Snorre had full knowledge of the scalds' poems, and if he has occasionally been misled by them, it is clear that he did not alter his opinion and knowledge about Svold being a holme, because Scald Skuli Torsteinson mentioned in one of his verses: "south by the mouth of Svold", thereby making it appear that Svold was a river. There is no river to be found near Rugen except a bay and river mouth south of Stralsund. The second Scald Haldor the Unchristian states: "the jarl won helmets near the holme", so Haldor is in agreement with Snorre. But in the big Olav Trygvason's Saga (for which Snorre is not responsible), Halfred Vandradascald (who was not present at the battle) in three

110. Then was it rumoured in Vendland that Swein, the Danish king, had an army out, and it was soon talked about that he wanted to meet King Olav. But Sigvaldi the Jarl said to the king: "It is not King Swein's plan to lay to battle against you with only the Danish army, so big an army have ye here. But if ye have some misthought that unrest might be at hand, I shall follow with my men; and it was always thought of great help when the Jomsvikings accompanied the sea kings. I will follow thee with eleven well-manned ships". The king accepted this offer. There was a light but favourable wind, so the king had the fleet unmoored and the signal blown for the start. The men then hoisted the sails and all the small ships went more swiftly and they sailed out to sea. But the jarl sailed near to the king's ship and shouted to them and bade the king sail after him. "I know well", he said, "where it is deepest in the island sounds and that will ye need with the big ships." The jarl then sailed before with his ships—he had eleven—and the king sailed after him with his big ships—he also had eleven—but all the rest of the fleet sailed out on the sea. And when Sigvaldi the Jarl sailed outside Svold, a small boat rowed out to meet them. They told the jarl that the Danish king's army lay there in the haven near by them. The jarl then ordered his sails to be struck and they rowed in by the island. Thus says Haldor the Unchristian:

| | |
|---|---|
| The Öyna folks'[1] noble king | When the jarl had drawn out |
| With one and seventy ships | The ships of the Scania men |
| Sailed from the south | To battle (abruptly was peace |
| (His sword he dyed in the fight). | Now broken between men). |

of his poems writes the following lines in O.N.: *Verkendr Heðins serkjar, bekkdom Heðins rekka* and *a viðu sundi vigðey Heðins meyjar*. The last-named line has by some historical writers been construed into: *a viðu sundi Heðins eyar* (by the sound of Hiddense). Hiddense is the long island situated north-west of Rugen. *Heðin* or *Heðinn* was the name of a sea king, and the meaning of these verses has no connection with Hiddense. Olav Trygvason's course from Wollin (or Swinemunde) was northwards and east of Rugen, and to get to Hiddense it meant bringing his ships through the long and narrow western sound which separates Rugen from the mainland. It seems hardly credible that Olav would have followed Sigvaldi the Jarl into this trap, besides it was entirely out of his way. It is just as unlikely that Olav's opponents would have chosen such an out-of-the-way waiting place for catching him. Erling Skjalgson and the other ships that did not take part in the battle must have headed north and east of Rugen, and Olav would not have taken a different course. Cf. also p. 211, nn. 1 and 2. In O.S. þ is capital letter for *Th* and ð for *th*. These letters do not exist any longer in the modern Scandinavian languages, but *th* instead of *d* was used by Peringskiold in the Swedish text of his translation of Snorre Sturlason printed at Stockholm in 1697. 1 *Öyna folk* = the inhabitants of Öyna shire (in North Norway).

It is said that King Olav and Sigvaldi the Jarl had seventy-one ships when they sailed up from the south.

111. Swein, the Danish king,[1] Olav, the Swedish king and Eric the Jarl[2] were there with all their army; it was fair weather and a clear sky. All the chiefs now went up on the island with a great following and they saw many ships sailing together out on the sea. And they saw where a very great and splendid ship was sailing. "That is a great and very fine ship; it must be the *Long Serpent*." Eric the Jarl answered and said, "That is not the *Long Serpent*". And so it was as he said; that ship was owned by Eindridi of Gimsar. A little later they saw where another ship was sailing, much bigger than the former. Then said King Swein: "Afraid is Olav Trygvason now; he dare not sail with the dragon head on his ship". Then said Eric the Jarl: "That is not the king's ship; that ship and that sail I know, for the sail is striped; it is owned by Erling Skjalgson. Let them sail; it is better for us that that ship be missing from Olav's fleet than that it be in it, so well armed it is". A little later they saw and knew Sigvaldi the Jarl's ships, which turned thither to the holme. Then they saw where three ships were sailing and one of them was great. Then King Swein spoke and bade them go to their ships; he said that the *Long Serpent* was sailing there. Eric the Jarl said: "Many other great and splendid ships are there besides the *Long Serpent*; let us still wait". Then said many men: "Eric the Jarl will not now fight and avenge his father. That is a great shame (for it will be learned over every land) if we stay here with so great an army and King Olav sails out on the sea just by the side of us". But when they had talked about it for a while, they saw where four ships were sailing and one of them was a dragon, very big and much gilded. Then King Swein stood up and said: "High shall the *Serpent* bear me to-night; I shall steer it". Then many shouted that the *Serpent* was a mighty great and fine ship and it was a noble work to have such a ship built. Then Eric the Jarl said so loudly that some men heard it: "Even if King Olav had no greater ship than that, never would King Swein get it from him with only the Danish army". The men then drew to their ships and struck their awnings. But whilst the chiefs were talking about this amongst themselves (as is now told), they saw where three great ships were sailing and a fourth last of all, which was the *Long Serpent*.

1 *Swein* Forkbeard, the father of King Canute.   2 *Eric the Jarl* was the son of Hacon the Jarl; he fled from Norway on the death of his father. Cf. chapter 89.

But of those ships which had sailed by before and which they had thought was the *Long Serpent*, the first was the *Crane* and the last was the *Short Serpent*. But when they saw the *Long Serpent*, they all knew—and no one said aught against it—that there Olav Trygvason must be sailing. They went to their ships and made themselves ready to row against him. It was agreed between the chiefs, King Swein, King Olav and Eric the Jarl, that each of them should have for himself a third part of Norway, if they slew King Olav Trygvason; and that one of the chiefs who first boarded the *Serpent* should have for

The kings get sight of Olav Trygvason's ships

himself all the booty that was taken there, and each of them was to have the ships he himself cleared. Eric the Jarl had a very great *bardi*[1] which he was wont to have on his viking raids; there was a 'beard'[2] uppermost on both stems (i.e. the stem and the stern); and underneath a thick iron plate which was as broad as the 'beard' and which reached down to the waterline.

112. When Sigvaldi the Jarl and his men rowed in under the holme, Thorkel Dydrill on the *Crane* and the steersmen on the other

1 A *bardi* was a big ship and called by this name on account of its iron fittings in the bow.   2 The *beard* consisted of one or perhaps several iron spikes fitted at the stem. When fighting, the stems of two opposing ships were often lashed together. The iron plate which reached down to the waterline would strengthen the stem, and the *beard* would cause damage to the opposing ship.

ships that went with him saw that the jarl was turning his ships in under the holme. They also dropped their sails, rowed after them and shouted to them, asking why they went in this way. The jarl said that he would wait for King Olav: "It seems most likely that there is trouble at hand". They let the ships drift until Thorkel Nevja came with the *Short Serpent* and the three ships which followed him, and the same tidings were told them; they, too, let their sails drop and their ships drift and they waited for King Olav. And when the king sailed towards the holme, all the hostile army rowed out into the sound before them. When they saw that, they bade the king sail away and not go to battle against so great a force. King Olav answered loudly and stood up on the quarterdeck: "Let the sail fall; no men of mine shall think of flight: I have never fled in battle; God may decide my life, but never will I take to flight". So was it done as the king bade. Thus says Halfred:

I wish to mention those words
Which Olav's warriors told
That the deed-strong sea king
Spoke to the carls before the fight.

The battle-eager king bade
His champions not to think
Of flight—those bold words
Of the people's darling still live!

113. King Olav had all his ships called together. His own ship was in the midst of the host and on the one side of him lay the *Short Serpent* and on the other the *Crane*. And when they began to tie together the *Long Serpent* and the *Short Serpent*, the king saw it and he shouted loudly, bidding them put the big ship more forward and not let it hang back behind all the ships in the fleet. Then Ulf the Red answered: "If we put the *Serpent* so much more forward, as it is longer than the other ships, then there will be hard work in the bow railings[1] this day". The king said: "I knew not that I had a forecastle man who was both red and afraid". Ulf answered: "Turn thou not thy back on the quarterdeck any more than I do, when I guard the stem". The king grasped a bow in his hand, put an arrow on the string and turned it at Ulf, who called out: "Turn it elsewhere, O king, where it is more needed; what I do, I do for thee".

114. King Olav stood on the quarterdeck of the *Serpent* and high over the others; he had a gilded shield and a gold-plated helmet; he was easy to know from other men. He had also a short red kirtle outside his brynie. And when King Olav saw that the ships divided themselves and the standards were set up for the leaders, he asked,

---

1 The O.S. word is *Sax*, pl. *Söx*, for the sides of the ship in the forecastle.

"Who is the chief of the fleet which is straight before us?" He was told that it was King Swein Forkbeard with the Danish host. The king answered: "We are not afraid of those cowards; there is no courage in the Danes; but what chief follows those standards which are on the right hand?" He was told that it was King Olav with the Swedish host. King Olav said: "It were better for the Swedes to stay at home and lick their blood bowls[1] than to attack the *Serpent* under your weapons. But who owns the great ship which lies out there on the port side of the Danes?" "That is", they said, "Jarl Eric Haconson." Then answered King Olav: "He may well think he has good grounds for meeting us and from that troop we can expect a sharp onslaught; they are Norsemen, as we are".

115. The kings then spread their ships and started rowing towards each other; King Swein brought his ship towards the *Long Serpent*; King Olav the Swede put farther out and struck his bow against King Olav Trygvason's outermost ship; and on the other side was Eric the Jarl. There was now a hard battle. Sigvaldi the Jarl let his ships row backwards and fell not into the strife. Thus says Skuli who was at that time with Eric the Jarl:

| | |
|---|---|
| The Frisians' foe I followed | When we bore the bloody swords |
| (I got honour in my youth) | South by the mouth of Svold[2] |
| And Sigvaldi, there where the spears | In the midst of the battle's storm |
| Sang out (now I am old). | To meet the battle hero. |

And further Halfred says of these matters:

| | |
|---|---|
| I believe I know that much | The bold king alone |
| Did the leader, who brought on the battle, | Fought against two kings |
| Miss the Tronds' following, | And the jarl for a third: of such things |
| For many men were put to flight. | Is it noble to speak of after. |

116. This fight was very sharp and very bloody. The forecastle men on the *Long Serpent* and on the *Short Serpent* and on the *Crane* cast anchors and grappling hooks on to King Swein's ships, and they could bear their weapons down upon them; they cleared all the ships they could hold fast; but King Swein and those who escaped fled into other ships and at last drew from reach of the shots; it befell this host as King Olav Trygvason had guessed. Then Olav the Swedish king came up instead, but as soon as they came near the great ships,

---

1 King Olav referred to the Swedes as still offering to Odin. Christianity came first to Denmark and Norway.   2 Cf. p. 205, n. 1. The scald's words are in O.N.: *sunnr fyrir svolldrar mynni*, but they should not be taken literally.

it went with them as the others, so that they lost many men and some of their ships and in this way they withdrew. But Eric the Jarl put his beard ship against King Olav's outermost ship; he cleared it and straightway struck it loose; thereupon he came up to the ship that was nearest and fought till that was cleared. The crews now began to leap from the smaller ships on to the great ships, but the jarl struck every ship loose when it was cleared, and the Danes and Swedes then came into shooting range and from all sides they lay against King Olav's ships. Eric the Jarl continually lay alongside the ships and fought with hand weapons; and as soon as men in his ship fell, Danes and Swedes came up in their stead. Thus says Haldor:

> The sweep of sharp swords
> Went over the *Long Serpent*;
> Where the golden spears sang
> The carls fought long
> In the fight with the foe;
> There went forth in the south
> Against him the Swedes
> And the Danish sword-fighters.

The fight was then very sharp and many folk fell; the outcome of it was that all King Olav's ships were cleared except the *Long Serpent*; and all his men who were yet able to bear weapons came up on it. Then Eric the Jarl lay his beard ship against the *Long Serpent* and there was now much fighting with hand weapons. Thus says Haldor:

> In so hard a handling
> The *Long Serpent* now fell
> (The shields were shorn asunder,
> And sword met sword),
> The high-prowed beard was brought
> Alongside of the *Serpent*.
> The jarl won helmets near the holme[1]
> By Fafniss side.[2]

117. Eric the Jarl was in the forehold of his ship and there were men lined up behind a wall of shields; there was fighting both with hand weapons and throwing of spears and the casting of all things that could be used as weapons, and some shot arrows with bows and some with their hands. There was then such a downpour of weapons on the *Serpent* that they could scarcely protect themselves with shields; so thickly did the arrows and spears fly, for warships lay on all sides of the *Serpent*. King Olav's men were now so maddened that they rushed up on the railings to get at their foes with sword-blows, as many had not laid themselves so near the *Serpent* that they could join in the hand-fighting. But many of Olav's men went overboard,

---

1 It will be noticed that Haldor mentions *the holme*. Cf. p. 205, n. 1.    2 The O.N. text reads: *Jarl vann hjalms at holmi hrið við Fafniss siðu*. There can be little doubt that Fafniss is a place name, and the only locality of similar name in Rugen is Sassnitz (on the east coast of the island). In copying the sagas the long *s* might have been mistaken for *f*. Cf. similar names: Balegard side (p. 222, 'History of St Olav') and Kinnlima side (p. 223, 'History of St Olav'), also Ambleside (in the Lake District).

for they thought no more than that they were fighting on a level field, and they sank down with their weapons. Thus says Halfred:

Down from the *Serpent* they sank,    Even if the noble king
Wounded in the fight.    Still steered the *Serpent*,
Never would they yield,    That gliding ship would miss
But fought to the last.    Such doughty carls as these.

118. Einar Tambarskelver was aft in the middle hold (by the mast) of the *Serpent*; he was shooting with his bow and shot harder than all others. He shot at Eric the Jarl and struck the tillerhead right above the jarl's head, and the arrow went as far in as its own bands. The jarl

"Too weak, too weak is the king's bow"

looked at it and asked if they knew who had shot it; but at the same time there came a second arrow so near the jarl that it flew between his side and his arm and struck so deeply into the headboard[1] that the point stuck out on the other side. Then the jarl said to a man who was called Finn and who was said by some to be a Finn—he was an outstanding bowman: "Shoot the big man in the middle hold". Finn shot and the arrow struck the middle of Einar's bow at the moment when he was drawing his bow for the third time. The bow burst into two parts. Then said King Olav, "What burst there so

[1] The board that protected the head of the man at the tiller.

loudly?" Einar answered: "Norway from thine hand, O king!" "So great a burst has not yet befallen," said the king; "take my bow and shoot with it", and he threw his bow to him. Einar took the bow and straightway drew it beyond the point of the arrow; he shouted, "Too weak, too weak is the king's bow". He threw the bow back, took up his shield and sword, and fought.

119. King Olav Trygvason stood on the quarterdeck of the *Serpent* and shot most oft that day, sometimes with bow, sometimes with spear and then always with two at a time. He looked forward on the ship and saw his men swinging their swords and striking fast, but he saw that they bit badly; he then shouted loudly, "Swing ye your swords so dully that they don't bite for you?" A man said: "Our swords are blunt and much broken". The king then went down into the forehold and unlocked the high-seat chest; he took out many keen swords and gave them to the men; but when he reached down with his right hand, the men saw that blood was running down from under his brynie sleeve; no man knew where he was wounded.

120. The greatest and the most man-killing fight on the *Serpent* came from the men in the forehold and the forecastle, for in both these places the choice of men was the best and the railings were highest. And when the men had first fallen amidship, and few men stood up round the mast, Eric and fourteen others tried to board the *Serpent*. Hyrning, King Olav's brother-in-law, met them with his following and there befell the hardest fight, and the outcome of it was that the jarl turned back on to his beard ship; but of those men who had followed him, some were killed and others wounded. About it Tord Kolbeinson says:

| | |
|---|---|
| The helm-dighted warriors | Guarded his lord with the sword; |
| Fought on the bloody thwarts | That was Hyrning. Heaven o'er the |
| Of the king's warship. | high fells |
| Fair praises he got who | Shall burst, ere that be forgotten. |

Now again was there the sharpest of fighting and many were slain on the *Serpent*; but when the crew which should guard the *Serpent* was diminished, Eric the Jarl tried once more to board it, and again he was hard withstood. And when the men in the forecastle of the *Serpent* saw this, they went aft of the ship, turned to protect themselves against the jarl and made a hard struggle. But now so many men on the *Serpent* were fallen that the railings were empty of men, and then the jarl's men began to come aboard on all sides. But all the men who were still standing to defend the *Serpent* sought aft of the ship where the king was. Thus says Haldor the Unchristian, that Eric the Jarl then egged on his men.

Across the aft thwarts,
Olav's men must yield;
The hard-striking prince
Egged on those heated carls.

When the warriors had locked
The bold king's ship ways,
The path of the weapons
Was turned against the Vends' slayer.

121. Kolbjörn the Marshal went to the king on the quarterdeck; they were much alike in clothes and weapons. Kolbjörn was a very big and handsome man. There was again the sharpest of fighting in

Eric the Jarl's men board the *Long Serpent*

the forehold; but as so many of the jarl's men as could find room on the ship had now come on board the *Serpent*, and because his ships lay on all sides of the *Serpent* and few folk were now left to defend it from so great a force, the greater number of these fell in a short time, although they were strong and bold men. King Olav and Kolbjörn then leaped overboard, on each side of the ship. The jarl's men had got out small boats, and slew those who leaped into the sea; and when the king himself leaped overboard, they wished to take him prisoner and bring him to Eric the Jarl. But King Olav held his shield over him and dived into the deep; Kolbjörn, however, shot his shield underneath him and protected himself thus from the spears thrown from the ships which lay nearest; he fell into the sea so that his shield was underneath him and he could not get under the water quickly enough, and he was taken prisoner and dragged up into a boat. They thought it was the king, so he was brought before the jarl. But when the jarl was aware that it was Kolbjörn and not King Olav, Kolbjörn got quarter. But at that moment all King Olav's men who were still alive on the *Serpent* were leaping overboard, and Halfred says that Thorkel Nevja, the king's brother, was the last man to do so:

| | |
|---|---|
| The strong-minded Thorketil | Ere he, wearer of the bracelet, |
| Saw the *Crane* | Holding out in battle, |
| And both the *Serpents* floating wasted | Cast himself in the sea, |
| (Cheerfully had he fought) | And sought his life by swimming. |

122. So is it written above (chapter 109) that Sigvaldi the Jarl came into the fellowship of King Olav in Vendland; the jarl had ten ships and likewise an eleventh, upon which his wife Astrid, the king's daughter, had her men. When King Olav had leaped overboard, the whole army shouted a cry of victory, and then first the jarl and his men put their oars in the sea and rowed to the battle. About it Haldor the Unchristian says:

| | |
|---|---|
| The Vends' ships gathered | There was the din of swords on the sea |
| From afar to the battle. | (The eagles were tearing the wolves' |
| The thinned sword-blade | food); |
| Sang with iron mouths. | The dear leader of the carls |
| | Fought, but many fled. |

But the Vend ship, on which were Astrid's men, rowed away back to Vendland, and it straightway became the talk of many men that King Olav must have drawn off his brynie under water and have dived down away from the longships and then swum thence to the Vend ship, and Astrid's men had borne him to land. And about King Olav's journeys there were afterwards many tales made by certain men, and in this wise Halfred speaks:

| | |
|---|---|
| I know not if he, who | For with truth men |
| Stilled the ravens' hunger, | Tell me both things |
| Shall by me be praised | (Dangerous is it to question it). |
| As living or dead. | The prince was anyhow wounded. |

But in whatsoever wise it was, King Olav never again came back to his kingdom in Norway; but still Halfred Vandradascald says in this manner:

| | |
|---|---|
| He who said | It is said that Olav was come |
| That the prince of men lived, | From that storm of steel; |
| Was for a long time with Trygvi's | 'Tis much worse than that; |
| Son, the steadfast warrior. | Many men speak far from the truth. |

And Halfred also said this:

When the land host, with masses
Of men, fell on the warriors'
Strife-wont lord, it would
(I have heard) hardly happen
That the dear king
Could come alive
Out of the fight (the folks
Seemed not to speak the truth).

Some swains still say
To the poet, that the king
Was wounded or came
Safely east from the stormy clash.
But truthfully told from the south
Is the Sikling's death in that
Great battle (I cannot trust
The uncertain tales of men).

123. Eric the Jarl got by that victory the *Long Serpent* and much booty, and he steered the *Long Serpent* far away from the battle. Thus says Haldor:

The *Long Serpent* had brought
The helm-dighted king
Thither to the great sword thing
(Then they decked the ships).

But south amid the war din
Gladly the jarl took the *Serpent*.
(Heming's noble brother
Dyed the swords in blood.)

Swein, Hacon the Jarl's son, had then wedded Holmfrid, the daughter of Olav the Swedish king. But when Swein the Danish king and Olav the Swedish king and Eric the Jarl shared Norway between themselves, King Olav had four folk districts in Trondheim, both the Mōres and Raumsdale, and East Ranrik from Gōta River to Svinasund; that kingdom King Olav handed over to Swein the Jarl on such conditions as in former times the tributary kings or jarls had held it of the over-kings. And Eric the Jarl had four folk districts in Trondheim, Halogaland and Naumadale, the Fjords and Fjalir, Sogn, Hordaland and Rogaland and Agder from the north right to Lidandisnes.[1] Thus says Tord Kolbeinson:

I know that many hersers
Were one time Eric's friends
Excepting Erling Skjalgson.
(I praise the generous chief.)
But since the battle Eric laid
Under his rule the northern land
From Veiga[2] south to Agder
And even farther.

The land was glad of the prince;
It pleased them to have it so.
He felt bound to rule
Over the men of Norway;
But Swein the prince in the south
Was said to be dead, and wasted
In sorrow were his houses;
The powers of the mighty fail.

Swein the Danish king[3] again had the Vik, as he had formerly had, but he gave Eric the Jarl in fief Raumarik and Hedemark. Swein Haconson took a jarldom of Olav the Swede. Swein the Jarl was the finest man that men have ever seen. Eric the Jarl and Swein the

---

1 *Lidandisnes*, now Lindesnes, the most southerly point of Norway.    2 *Veiga*, an island in the southern part of Halogaland (North Norway).    3 Swein Forkbeard.

Jarl both let themselves be baptised and took the true faith, but as long as they ruled over Norway they let every man do as he would about holding Christianity; but they kept well the old laws and the old land customs. They were well-befriended men and good rulers. Eric the Jarl had most to say of his brothers in all the ruling of the land.

The victorious host returns home after the battle of Svold

## CHRONOLOGY

### OLAV TRYGVASON.  968–1000

968.        Birth of Olav Trygvason.
985.        Death of Harald Gormson, King of Denmark.
            Swein Forkbeard becomes King of Denmark.
988–95.  Olav Trygvason in the Westlands.
995.        Death of Harald the Grenlander (St Olav's father).
            Birth of St Olav.
            Death of Hacon the Jarl.
            Olav Trygvason becomes King of Norway.
1000.      Death of Olav Trygvason at the battle of Svold.

# VIII

## THE HISTORY OF ST OLAV

1. Olav, the son of Harald the Grenlander, was brought up with his step-father Sigurd Syr and his mother Asta. Rani the Wide-faring was with Asta and he fostered Olav Haraldson. Olav was early a doughty man, fair to look upon, and of middle height. He had good sense, and was wise in his talk. Sigurd Syr was keen in the management of his estate and kept his men ever at work; he went often himself to see to the fields and meadows or livestock, or else to the smithy, or wherever his men had anything to do.

2. Once King Sigurd wished to ride from the house, and there was no one handy at home; so he bade his step-son Olav saddle a horse for him. Olav went to the goathouse, took the biggest buck goat, and led it home; he laid the king's saddle on it and told the king he had got his steed ready for him. Then King Sigurd went thither and he saw what Olav had done. He said: "It is easy to see that thou wilt ignore my behests; it will also seem right to thy mother that I bid thee nothing which is against thee. It is easy to see that we two shall not be of one mind; thou art more proud than I am". Olav answered but little, laughed and went away.

3. When Olav Haraldson grew up, he was not tall, but of middle height, thick set and strong, light-haired, broad-faced, bright and ruddy of face; he had wondrous eyes, fair and keen, so that men feared to look him in the eyes when he was wroth. He was skilled in all kinds of sports; he could handle well the bow and shoot marvellously with the hand bow; he swam well, was deft with his hands and had skill in all smith's work that he did for himself or others. He was called Olav Digre.[1] He was bold and wise of speech, and at an early age he was developed in both strength of body and mind. All his kinsmen and friends thought well of him. He wished to be the leader in all games and would always be before all others, as it ought to be because of his rank and birth.

4. Olav Haraldson was twelve years old when he stepped on board a warship for the first time. His mother Asta got Rani, who

---

1 *Digre* means thick set and stocky, but in this connection probably 'proud', 'haughty' or 'full of self-esteem'. Cf. chapter 59, when the Swedish messengers came to Olav.

was called the king's-fosterer, to be leader of the host and to be in the following of Olav, for Rani had often been on viking raids. When Olav took over the men and ships, his men gave him the name of king, as it was the custom that warrior kings of royal birth who were on a viking raid should straightway bear the name of king, even if they had no land. Rani sat by the tiller, and for that reason some

Olav's first voyage with his foster-father Rani

say that Olav was the rudder boy, although he was still king over his men. They sailed east along the land and first they came to Denmark. Thus says Ottar the Black in the poem he composed about King Olav:

Young didst thou thrust
The sea steed to visit
Denmark; thou wert wont to do
Daring deeds, O battle-bold prince!
Victorious, O king, was thy journey

(By such boldness art thou become mighty).
I have learned
How thou didst go from the north.

5. But in the autumn, he sailed east along Sweden and began to harry and burn the land, for he thought it his right to requite the

Swedes with great enmity for taking his father's life. Ottar the Black clearly says that he then went east from Denmark:

With oars drove ye the fair-decked
Ships east on the sea
From land to land (the shields,
O land-watcher, ye bore to the ships).
The sails ye used, and at times
Ye had to turn the tiller.

The great billows did slit
Many oars under you.
Feeder of ravens! Thy folk
Got mighty fear of thy journey;
Since then didst thou seek
To harry the headlands of Sweden.

6. That autumn Olav fought his first fight near the Sota Skerry,[1] that is amidst the skerries of Sweden.[2] There he fought against vikings, and Soti was the name of the man who led them. Olav had fewer folk but greater ships. He laid his ships between some rocks and it was hard for the vikings to lay to. Those ships which lay nearest to them Olav's men struck with grappling hooks, drew them in and cleared them. The vikings took to flight and they had lost many men. Sigvat the Scald tells about this fight in the poem wherein he tells of King Olav's battles:

The young noble heir
Brought the longship out
To the sea (the folk were since
Afraid of the prince's wrath);

And for the first time he dyed
The wolves' feet in blood,
In the east near Sota Skerry
(Much I can call to mind).

7. King Olav then steered east along by Sweden and lay in by Lögrinn,[3] harrying on both sides of it. He lay right up to Sigtun and lay in by Gamla-Sigtun.[4] The Swedes say that there are still the stone walls which Olav had caused to be made to support his gangway. But in the autumn, Olav got to know that the Swedish king Olav was gathering a great host, and likewise that he had borne iron chains across Stoksund[5] and had set men to watch it. But the Swedish king thought that King Olav would bide there whilst it was freezing; and King Olav's army seemed to him of little worth, for he had few men. King Olav then went out to Stoksund but could not get any farther. There was a fort on the west of the sound and a troop of men on the south. But when they learned that the Swedish king had come with ships and that he had a great host and many ships, King Olav had a channel dug through Agna-fet[6] out to the sea. There was heavy rain. Now in Sweden every running water falls into

---

1 *Sota Skerry* or O.S. *Sotasker* is the Sotholme near Närike in Södermanland.    2 *The skerries* are along the coast of Södermanland and Upland.    3 Lake Mälar.    4 Cf. 'Ynglinga Saga', p. 4, n. 4.    5 *Stoksund*, i.e. present Norrström on the north side of the old town of Stockholm.    6 *Agna-fet* is the flat land on the south side of the old town of Stockholm.

Lögrinn, and there is but one outlet from Lögrinn into the sea and that is so narrow that many streams are wider. And when there is much rain and when the snow melts, the water rushes so forcefully that there is a waterfall through Stoksund, and Lögrinn rises so much in the land that it floods it far and wide. When the channel got near the sea, the water and the stream rushed out, and then King Olav had all the rudders of his ships put aboard, and the sails hoisted to the top, for a high wind was blowing. They steered with their oars and the ships went speedily over the shallows and came out all sound to the sea. But the Swedes then went to Olav the Swedish king and told him that Olav Digre had gone out to sea. The King of the Swedes gave ill words to those who should have seen to it that Olav did not get out. It was afterwards called King's Sound,[1] and there men cannot go with big ships except when the water runs strong. But it is the tale of some men that when Olav's men had dug out the thwaite and the water began falling, the Swedes were aware of it and went there with a great force to hinder Olav from going out. But the water dug out the land on both sides so that the banks fell in and all the folk on them, so that many were drowned. The Swedes, however, deny this and say it is not true that any men were lost there. King Olav sailed in the autumn to Gotland,[2] and made himself ready to harry. But the Gotlanders held a gathering and sent men to the king to offer him the tribute of the land. The king agreed to it, took tribute of the land, and stayed there during the winter. Thus says Ottar:

Chief of the seamen! on the host
Of the Gots thou didst lay tribute.
The men vowed not to guard
The land with the sword.

Eysysla's[3] men ran; but in the east
The wolves' hunger was sated.
Many a man has less courage
Than this heir of Yngvi's race.[4]

8. Here is it to be told, that when spring came on, King Olav went east to Eysysla and harried there. He made a land raid, but the Eysysla men came down and held battle with him. King Olav had the victory, put them to flight, and harried and laid waste the land. So it is said that when Olav and his men first came to Eysysla, the bonders offered him tribute, but when the tribute was expected on the shore, he met them with a fully armed force and then things

1 Now Söderström in Stockholm. 2 The big island in the Baltic. 3 *Eysysla* or *Ösysla*: the island of Ösel; cf. 'Olav Trygvason's History', p. 184, and 'Ynglinga Saga', p. 24, n. 2. 4 *Yngvi's race*, a familiar expression among the scalds for the kings descended from the Ynglings. About Yngvi, which is another name for Frey, cf. 'Ynglinga Saga', chapter 10.

turned out otherwise than the bonders had thought, for they had gone down, not with tribute, but with war weapons, and fought with the king, as is already told. Thus says Sigvat the Scald:

> Yet it was that Olav should
> Hold another fight
> On Eysysla, which was wasted
> (The treachery was clear).
>
> When they ran thence,
> The bonders again took
> To their feet for their lives;
> Few stood there to be wounded.

9. Afterwards he sailed to Finland, harried there and went up on land, but all the folk fled to the woods and bore all their goods out of the houses. The king went far up into the land through certain woods, and there he came upon some dale districts, called Herdales. They got little goods, and took no men. The day went on, and the king turned about to go down to his ships. But when they came into the woods, the folk drew together against them from all sides and shot at them, and they beset them hard; the king bade his men shield themselves, and strike as occasion served, but that was difficult because the Finns let the wood ward them. And when the king came out of the wood, he had lost many of his men and many others were wounded; about evening they came to the ships. During the night the Finns by witchcraft made bad weather and storms on the sea. But the king had the anchors weighed and the sails hoisted, and they tacked to windward off the land, and once more (as often later) the king's luck availed more than the witchcraft of the Finns. During the night they tacked along Balegard side and from there out to sea. But the Finns' host followed the ships on land, as the king sailed outside. Thus says Sigvat:

> The prince's son's third battle storm
> Of steel was fought hardily
> At the meet of the Finlanders
> In the raid on Herdale.
>
> The eastern lode
> Loosed the viking ships.
> Balegard side sent out
> Billows against the ships' stems.

10. Then King Olav sailed to Denmark, and there he met Thorkel the High, brother of Sigvaldi the Jarl, and Thorkel joined company with Olav, for Thorkel lay ready to go a-raiding. They sailed south along the coast of Jutland to a place called Suderwick[1] and there took many viking ships. Those vikings who ever lay out on the sea and ruled over mighty hosts let themselves be called kings, even if they had no land to rule over. King Olav lay to battle; there was a great

---

[1] *Suderwick* or *Sudervik* is now Söndervig west of Ringkjöbing on the west coast of Jutland.

fight and King Olav got the victory and much booty. Thus says
Sigvat:

| | |
|---|---|
| Yet a fourth time the king | Whilst the firm peace |
| (They say) wielded the start | Between the king's hosts |
| Of the battle strife (he won honour | Was broken asunder out |
| Who warded himself well), | At Suderwick, well known by the Danes. |

11. Then King Olav sailed south to Friesland and lay outside
Kinnlima side[1] in bad weather. The king went on land with his
army, but the landsmen rode down upon them and fought against
them. Thus says Sigvat the Scald:

| | |
|---|---|
| O prince, so hard for the helmets, | The time when the bold host |
| Thou didst win the fifth fight | Rode down upon the sea king's ships, |
| (The ships encountered | Whilst strongly there fought |
| Storms by Kinnlima side), | The warrior's host against the landsmen. |

12. King Olav then sailed west to England.[2] The Danish king,
Swein Forkbeard, was at that time in England with the Danish
army; he had been settled there for a short time and had King Ethelred's land. Then the Danes went far and wide over England, and it
came about that King Ethelred fled from the land and went south to
France. This same autumn, when King Olav came to England, it
happened that King Swein Haraldson died suddenly in his bed one
night, and it is said by Englishmen that St Edmund slew him in the
same way as the holy Mercurius slew Julian the Apostate; but when
Ethelred, King of England, learned that, he turned straightway back
to England. But when he came back into the land, he sent bidding
to all those men who would get goods in order to win back the land
along with him. Then great troops came to him. King Olav went
into his service with a great army of Norsemen. They first lay in the
Thames near London,[3] but the Danes held the bourgh. On the
other side of the river there was a great market town, called Southwark, and there the Danes had a great host fitted out; they had dug
dikes and within they had set up a wall of trees and stones and turf,
and they had there a great army. King Ethelred made a mighty
attack upon it, but the Danes warded it, and King Ethelred won
nothing. There was a bridge over the river between the bourgh and
Southwark, and this bridge was so broad that two wagons could be

---

1 The west coast of Holland.  It was also called *Kinnheim* or *Kennemarland*.
2 Thorkel, Olav and Thorkel's brother Heming came to Sandwich soon after Lammas
in 1009, and attacked Canterbury, but the citizens sued for peace. Cf. Roger de Hoveden
and Florence of Worcester, who name these three leaders. *Anglo-Saxon Chronicle*
only mentions 'Thurkill's army'.   3 In O.S. *Lundunir* or *Lundunaborg*.

driven past each other over it. On the bridge there were built strong-holds, both castles and bulwarks, down towards the stream as deep as waist-high, but under the bridge there were piles which stood down in the bed of the river. But when the bridge was stormed, the army marched on to it and warded it. King Ethelred was very ill at ease as to how he should win the bridge. He called together all the army chiefs in talk and sought counsel with them, how they could take the bridge. Then King Olav said he would try to attack it, if other chiefs also would help. At this meeting it was agreed that they should place their armies under the bridge; each of them then fitted out his men and ships.

13. King Olav had great mats of willows and pliable wood made, taken from houses made of wicker work, and he had them placed over his ships so that they reached over the railings. Underneath

Olav's fight at London Bridge

he caused staves to be set so thick and high that there was room for using weapons and the screen was strong enough to withstand stones, if such were cast down upon it. And when the army was ready, they rowed up along the river to the bridge; and when they came near, there were shot down and thrown upon them stones so big that nothing could hold, neither helmets nor shields. And the ships themselves suffered great scathe. Then did many withdraw.

But King Olav and the Norsemen's army with him rowed right up under the bridge, put ropes round the piles which supported the bridge and fastened them; and all the ships rowed down stream with all their might. The piles were dragged along the ground until they were loosened under the bridge. And then an armed force was standing thickly on the bridge—and there were also many stones and many weapons; and when the piles were broken away, the bridge burst asunder and many men fell into the river; all the others fled from the bridge, some to the bourgh,[1] others to Southwark. Thereafter they made an inroad into Southwark and won it. And when the bourgh men saw that the River Thames was won so that they could not hinder the passage of ships up into the land, they were afraid of the ships passing through, and gave up the bourgh, and received King Ethelred. Thus says Ottar the Black:

Yet didst thou break, warrior chief,
The bridge in London, with boldness
(Thou hadst luck with thee
To win gold in battle);
The hard-pounded shields
Rang out, when the battle waved,
And the iron rings sprang asunder
In the old brynies.

And thereto he said this:

Land-warder. Thou camest into the
　　land
And didst set Ethelred therein;
Thou hast might, and thereof
The friend of men got heed.
The passage was hard, when thou
Didst bring Edmund's heir
To his own now peaceful land,
At one time ruled by his kin.

And thereto Sigvat says about it:

It is true that the sixth fight
Was, where the speedy prince
Offered the Angles battle and Olav
Went against London bridge.
The Welsh swords bit, but the vikings
Warded there the dike;
Some had their booths
In Southwark.

14. King Olav was during the winter with King Ethelred, and then they held a great battle on Ringmere Heath[2] in Ulfkel's land, which kingdom was at that time held by Ulfkel Snilling. There the kings had the victory. Thus says Sigvat the Scald:

Yet once Olav held
In Ulfkel's land
Sword thing the seventh
As I say here.
Round about on Ringmere's Heath
Stood Ælla's landsmen,
The troops fell; ill-luck
Did Harald's heir[3] have there.

Thereto Ottar the Black says about the battle:

I have heard that thy host
Piled the heavy heap of corpses
Far from the ships; red
With blood was Ringmere Heath.
The land folk fell
To the ground in the sword noise,
But many Angles
Took to flight.

1 I.e. City.　　2 *Ringmere*, East Wretham, Norfolk.　　3 *Harald's heir* = Harald Gormson's heir, Swein Forkbeard.

Then the land was again put under King Ethelred, but the Thingmen[1] and the Danes held many towns, and far and wide they still held the land.

15. King Olav was chief of the army when they drew near Canterbury, and fought there till they won the place, slew many folk there and burned the town. Thus says Ottar the Black:

O, Yngvi, against the Sikling's[2] kin
Thou didst make great onslaught;
Blithe prince, the great
Canterbury thou tookest one morning.

Fire and smoke fiercely
Lay about the houses.
Thou sentest many to their death:
The king's son won the victory.

Sigvat reckons this as King Olav's eighth battle:

I know that the viking prince,
That friend of the Vends,[3] here
His eighth battle wrought;
The warriors' guardian made progress.

The port-reeves could not
Hold the proud Olav
From the town, the fort of the Kentish men;
It brought sorrow to the ports.[4]

---

1 *Thingamen* or *Thingmen* are often referred to in English history. They were the bodyguard of the Danish kings in England beginning with Swein Forkbeard; but the name was no doubt used previously to signify enfranchised citizens and bonders. The old Norsemen and Danes who came to England had inherited their forefathers' custom of holding thing meetings, at which important questions and disputes were settled, at certain times of the year. This was the beginning of democratic government in the northern countries. The big thing meetings were held in the open, where people were collected from far and wide, and the local meetings were held under roof and were called in O.S. *husthings*. At the open thing meetings stones—some for sitting on—were placed in the locality of the meeting, and many places in Scandinavia and Great Britain bear witness to these gatherings. In Yorkshire we have the 'Morthing', the name of which may be connected with Morathing south-east of Upsala. Cf. p. 286, n. 2. Fingay in Yorkshire was another meeting place. The locality was often chosen so that it was easily accessible by land and sea. Maidstone (in Kent), meaning 'Meet Stone' (in O.S. *Motstein*), was an important meeting place, and Staines (on the Thames) was probably another. In King John's time, the adjoining Runnymede Island was chosen. In the Midlands and in Scotland such names as Thingwall or Dingwall are often met with (in O.S. *þing-vollr*, i.e. 'thing-wold' where the thing had meetings). In the Orkney Islands a remarkable group of stone circles is found, of which the 'Ring of Brogar' is the largest, having a diameter of 366 feet, and the 'Ring of Steinsnes' (Stennis) is the most monumental. Sir Walter Scott found that Stennis had a striking resemblance to Stonehenge and refutes the opinion that these monuments are druidical. He considers them places of public assembly. It is well known that Cumberland was overrun by the Norsemen and it is probably not a mere coincidence that another important stone circle is found near Keswick.     2 *Sikling*, i.e. sea king.     3 *Vends* from Vendland. In O.S. *Vindar* and *Vindland*.     4 Snorre must here refer to the five towns, Hastings, Romney, Hythe, Dover and Sandwich. William the Conqueror called them the Cinque Ports; but they existed as an institution for defence before the Conquest. Samuel Laing in his translation of Snorre curiously enough connects the inhabitants with Perthmen (men from Perth) and a Norwegian translator

King Olav was entrusted with the guarding of England; he went with warships along the coast and came to land at Nyja Moda. There he met the Thingmen, held battle with them and won the victory. Thus says Sigvat the Scald:

The young king oft gave
The Angles bloody foreheads.
Once more the brown blood came
Upon the swords, in Nyja Moda.

Now have I mentioned the
Ninth battle, which the king fought.
The Danish force must fall,
Whilst the spears drove against Olav.

King Olav then went far over the land and took tribute from the folk or else harried them. Thus says Ottar:

The Angles had no might
To withstand thee,
Renowned prince,
When thou didst crave tribute.

It was not seldom that the folk
Brought gold to the Dagling;
Great things sometimes
Were brought down to the shore.

This time King Olav stayed there three years.[1]

T. Schjött copies Laing and makes the same mistake. The Norwegian historian Gustav Storm considers that Snorre speaks of port-reeves in a general way, and calls port a sea town. In 'History of Sigurd, Inge and Eystein' (chapter 20) Storm again refers to "inhabitants of a coast town", ignoring the old institution—the Cinque Ports.

1  The events in England are told in their wrong sequence. Snorre has apparently been misled by the scalds' poems and specially by Sigvat, who enumerates each battle. Sigvat was not present with King Olav in England (cf. chapter 43). Although the chronicles do not give all the details of Olav and Thorkel's fighting, it may be considered established that they arrived at Sandwich soon after Lammas 1009 and that Canterbury was first attacked. They subsequently appear to have proceeded to the Isle of Wight, after which they landed in Hampshire. King Ethelred collected an army against which they did not seek battle, but turned back to Kent and took up winter quarters in the Thames, probably at Greenwich, within easy reach of London, which they endeavoured to take; but the English chroniclers state that they were repulsed by the citizens: "not without some loss to themselves". In 1010 it appears that they proceeded up the Thames—disembarking from their ships, they passed the Chiltern Hills and arrived at Oxford. During Lent 1010, they are again in Kent (probably Greenwich) where the ships were refitted. After Easter they proceeded up the River Orwell and on to Ipswich, and now we come to the battle of Ringmere Heath (in East Wretham) where Duke Ulfketel (Ulfkel Snilling) lay with an army. The battle took place on the 5th of May, 1010, and the men of East Anglia were routed and fled. There fell Ethelstan (son-in-law of King Ethelred); Oswy the Thane and his sons; Wulfric, son of Leofwine; Edwy, brother of Elfric; and many other noble thanes and a large number of common people. Snorre writes as if this battle was fought against the Danes, and the English chroniclers relate that Thorkel Myrhead, a Danish jarl, was one of the first to flee with his men, so many Danes must have been in the fight. The Norsemen and the Jomsvikings, remaining masters of the field, obtained possession of East Anglia and, mounted on horseback, scoured the whole province for three months. In the Fen district also the Norsemen did much damage and burnt Thetford and Cambridge. After these expeditions, King Olav and Thorkel the High returned to the Thames, the infantry in

16. In the third spring King Ethelred died, and his sons Edmund and Edward took the kingdom. Then King Olav went south over the sea and fought in Ringsfjord and won a castle on the hills which the vikings had; he broke the castle down. Thus says Sigvat the Scald:

In the fair Ringsfjord
The tenth battle was fulfilled;
The army sailed thither
As the noble king bade them.[1]

The high fortress on the hills,
Where the vikings held themselves,
He broke down; they did not wish
Such another fight.

their ships but the cavalry on their horses. In 1011, King Ethelred sued for peace; but it was not secured till Canterbury was again sacked and the Archbishop Alfhege killed, because he would not make terms with the Norsemen. Elmar, the abbot of Augustine's monastery, was, however, given his freedom. King Olav and Thorkel the High finally made peace with King Ethelred, and agreed to disperse their ships but consented to forty-five ships remaining with King Ethelred, the crews swearing fealty to him and under-taking to defend England against foreigners. The battle of *Nyja Moda* (O.N.) is not men-tioned by the chroniclers but might refer to Malden in Essex or New Malden near King-ston; but as Snorre states that King Olav proceeded with his army along the coast, Malden in Essex seems the most likely place, and the battle could have been fought on his way to Ring-mere. The peace between King Ethelred and Olav and Thorkel was made in 1012 and in the following year Swein Forkbeard landed in England, and encamped at Gainsborough. The whole of the north of England submitted to him, after which he proceeded south-wards, conquered Oxford and Winchester and attacked London. In the battle of London Swein was repulsed by Ethelred, assisted by Olav and Thorkel, and these are the events related by Snorre in chapters 12 and 13. Swein was forced back to Wallingford and Bath. King Ethelred, however, lost heart as such a large part of England had submitted to Swein. He sent Queen Emma and his sons to her brother Richard II, Duke of Normandy, but remained himself with the Norse fleet and sailed in these ships to the Isle of Wight, where he spent Christmas, and subsequently crossed to Normandy. King Olav must meantime have left England to engage upon his further expeditions related in chapters 17, 18 and 19, because Snorre states definitely that he arrived in Normandy in the autumn of 1013, where he remained till the spring of 1014, when he returned to England, with King Ethelred's sons. Here is another discrepancy in Snorre's narration, as Snorre was under the impression that King Ethelred was then dead. Swein Forkbeard died suddenly on the 2nd of February, 1014, and the English at once endeavoured to get King Ethelred back from Normandy. The chroniclers state that he first sent his son Edward to England and, according to Snorre, King Olav accompanied him. Ethelred came back to England from Normandy during Lent 1014, and the battle in which he defeated Canute in Lindsey (now part of Lincolnshire) is probably the same which Snorre calls Jungufurda. This fight must have taken place in the early summer of 1014. Snorre thought the battle was indecisive as Canute afterwards became King of England. The chroniclers subsequently relate that King Ethelred paid off the Norse warships lying at Greenwich, and we may assume that King Olav's work in England had now come to an end and that he left for Norway in the autumn of 1014. The citizens of London long remem-bered King Olav's help against the Danes, and after he was canonised in Norway he was also made a saint in England. Many churches in England were dedicated to him, of which several are still in existence.   [1] This fight is confirmed from French sources, which relate that Olav was requested by Richard II, Duke of Normandy, to help him against Eude of Chartres. They attacked Brittany and conquered the fortress of Dol which

17. King Olav sailed west with his army to Grislupollar and there he fought with vikings before William's[1] town; there King Olav got the victory. Thus says Sigvat:

Olav, thou didst win the eleventh
Fight, where the nobles fell,
In Grislupollar;[2]
Thou didst come young from that thing.

The strife, I have heard,
Was near the town
Of the trusty Jarl William
To the peril of their helmets.

Next he fought in the west in Fetlafjord,[2] as Sigvat tells:

The twelfth time the prince
In Fetlafjord dyed

The wolves' fangs in blood:
There the men fell.

From there King Olav went right south to Seljupollar[2] and there held battle. He won the town called Gunvaldsbourgh—it was great and ancient—and there he took the jarl who ruled over the town and who was called Geirfinn. King Olav then held talk with the men of the town; from the town he demanded as ransom for the jarl 12,000 gold shillings, and as much scot was paid him by the town as he demanded. Thus says Sigvat:

The Tronds' keen lord
Won his thirteenth victory
In Seljupollar in the south;
Those who fled got sorrow.

The grim man one morning
Went up to the old town
Of Gunvaldsbourgh and seized
The jarl: Geirfinn was his name.

18. Thereafter King Olav steered with his army west to Karlsá; he harried there and had great strife. But when he lay in Karlsá,[3] waiting there for a fair wind as he thought of sailing out to Norvasund,[4] and from there to Palestine, he saw in a mighty dream that there came to him a strange, strong man but equally fearsome and this man spoke to him and bade him give up the thought of going out to these lands: "get thee back to thy own land, for thou shalt become King of Norway for ever". He understood the dream to mean that he would become king of the land, and his kin would rule the land for a long time after.

19. After this vision he turned about on his journey and lay out-

is situated at the end of the bay between Cotentin and Brittany. This bay the Norsemen called Ringsfjord.   1 This William was William the fifth, Duke of Aquitania (990–1030), who fought against Norse vikings on the coast of Poitou.   2 Unknown places. Probably on the south-west coast of France or northern Spain.   3 *Karlsá* is supposed to be the River Guadalquivir.   4 *Norvasund* was the O.S. name for the Straits of Gibraltar. Cf. 'Ynglinga Saga', p. 1.

side Peitaland[1] and harried there and burned the market town called Varrande.[2] About this Ottar says:

Young battle-glad noble!   O prince, thou didst try the shields,
Thou didst lay Peita waste.   Stained in Tuskaland.[3]

And still further Sigvat says:

The king of the Mörers who sailed   Varrande (a town
From the south, made a raid   In that well-cultivated Peitaland,
There where the old spears   Far from the sea)
Were splintered up in Leira.[4]   Was burned by thy warriors.

20. King Olav had been on this raid to the west of France for two summers and one winter. Thirteen years had then passed since the fall of Olav Trygvason. There were in France two jarls, William and Robert;[5] their father was Richard, Jarl of Ruda,[6] and they ruled over Normandy. Their sister was Queen Emma, whom Ethelred, King of England, had married, and their sons were Edmund and Edward the Good, Edwig and Edgar.[7] Richard, Jarl of Ruda, was son of Richard, son of William Longspear, and he was the son of Jarl Rolf the Ganger, who had won Normandy; he was the son of Ragnvald the Mighty, Jarl of Möre, as is written above ('History of Harald Hairfair', chapter 24). From Rolf the Ganger are the jarls of Ruda descended, and long afterwards they claimed kinship with the chiefs of Norway and set great store by it for many years; they were always the Norsemen's best friends, and all Norsemen, who would have it, had peace land[8] with them. In the autumn King Olav came to Normandy and remained during the winter in Signa,[9] and there he had peace land.

21. After Olav Trygvason's fall, Eric the Jarl gave peace to Einar Tambarskelver, son of Eindridi Styrkarson. Einar went north with the jarl to Norway. It is said that Einar had been the strongest man and the best bowshot in Norway, and he shot more skilfully than other men. He shot an arrow without point through a raw, wet oxhide that hung from a pole. He was before all others at ski-ing and he was the greatest in all sports and the strongest; he was of noble stock and

1 *Peitaland* is Poitou.   2 *Varrande* is Guerande in South-west Brittany.   3 Touraine.   4 River Loire. *Leira* is 'clay' in O.S. Scandinavians settled in this district of France before Rolf the Ganger arrived in Normandy.   5 *Robert* the Magnificent (1028–35) and *William* of Arques were brothers. Another brother was Richard III (1026–28).   6 *Richard* II (996–1026). *Ruda* is O.S. for Rouen. Richard's sister Emma married King Ethelred and afterwards King Canute.   7 *Edmund, Edwig* and *Edgar* were Ethelred's sons by his first marriage. *Edward* the Confessor was Emma's son, but Snorre makes no distinction between half-brothers, and calls them all brothers. 8 Cf. 'History of Olav Trygvason', p. 183, n. 1.   9 *Signa* is the River Seine.

rich. Eric the Jarl and Swein the Jarl married Einar to their sister Bergliot, Hacon's daughter; she was a strong woman; their son was called Eindridi. The jarls gave Einar great land rents in Orkedale and he became the mightiest and most noble of men in Trondlaw, and he was the jarls' greatest help and their good friend.

22. Eric the Jarl liked it ill that Erling Skjalgson had so great might; and he took to himself all the king's land that King Olav had given Erling in land rents. But, just as before, Erling took all the land rents in Rogaland and the bonders had often to pay double the land rents or he laid waste the district. The jarl got little of this tribute, for his stewards could not maintain themselves there long and the jarl went there to feasts only when he had many men with him. About this Sigvat says:

Erling who had the upper hand
Of the jarls and who had such
Might that he roused fear,
Was the kinsman of Trygvason.

Afterwards the kinsman
Of the bonders' lord gave another
Of his sisters to Ragnvald;
It was luck for this father of Ulf.

Eric the Jarl would not fight against Erling on the ground that he had many mighty kinsmen and was himself mighty and well beloved, and he always sat with a great throng of folk as if it were a king's court. In the summer Erling was often on raids and won himself goods, for he kept up in his wonted wise his show and pomp, although he had fewer and less certain land rents than in the days of King Olav his kinsman.[1] Erling was the fairest and greatest and strongest of men, more skilful than others and in all sports most like Olav Trygvason. About it Sigvat says:

Of all the landlords
There was no other
Who had fought in
More fights than Erling.

The generous master showed
His courage in many a strife.
Most often he went first
Into battle and came out the last.

It has always been the talk of men that Erling was the most generous of all great landowners in Norway. These were the children of Erling and Astrid: Aslak, Skjalg, Sigurd, Lodin, Tore, as well as Ragnhild, whom Torberg Arneson wedded. Erling had always about him ninety or more free men, and in both winter and summer it was usual with him for the drink to be according to measure in the daytime, but at night it was unmeasured. But when the jarls were in the neighbourhood he had two hundred men or more. He never went

[1] Erling was Olav's brother-in-law.

to sea except with a fully manned twenty-seat boat. Erling had
a great *skeid*[1] of thirty-two seats, and yet roomy besides; he used it
on viking raids and on the calling up of men, and in it there were
two hundred (i.e. two hundred and forty) men or more.

23. Erling had always thirty thralls at home in his houses besides
other servants. He set his thralls to daywork and gave them time
afterwards, and allowed every man to work for himself at dusk
or in the night. He gave them acres to sow corn thereon for themselves and produce crops for gain. He set a price and ransom on

Erling set his thralls to daywork

every one of them, and many freed themselves the first year or the
second; all who were thrifty enough had freed themselves in three
years. With this money Erling bought himself other thralls. Some
of his free men he turned to herring fishing and some to other trades.
Some cleared woods and built themselves farms there, and to all
of them he gave a good start in one way or another.

24. When Eric the Jarl had ruled over Norway for twelve years,
word came from his brother-in-law Canute, King of the Danes, that
Eric the Jarl should go with him to England with an army, for Eric
was very renowned for his fighting after he had won the victory
in two of the sharpest battles in the Northlands: one was when
Hacon the Jarl and Eric fought against the Jomsvikings, and the

1 Cf. 'History of Olav Trygvason', p. 203, n. 1.

other when Eric fought against King Olav Trygvason. About this Tord Kolbeinson says:

Still do I praise this,
That the land's lord sent
Word, as I heard, to the jarl,
That fight-longing chief,

That Eric, most bounden, should
Come to him and there
Hold a meeting
(I understood what the king
    wished).

Eric the Jarl takes leave of his son Hacon

The jarl would not decline the king's bidding and went forth from the land, but to protect the land he set his son Hacon over Norway and handed him over to his kinsman Einar Tambarskelver who was to rule for Hacon, for the latter was then no more than seventeen winters old.

25. Eric came to the meeting with King Canute in England and was with him when he won London.[1] Eric the Jarl fought west of London and there Ulfkel Snilling fell.[2] Thus says Tord:

The prince stirred up strife
West of London,
The sea steed's bold steerer
Fought for possession of land.

Ulfkel, bold in battle, got
The most frightful of blows
From the Thingmen;
There shook the blue swords.

Eric the Jarl was in England one year and he had several battles, but the next autumn he wished to make a journey to Rome. But he died in England through blood-letting.[3]

26. King Canute had many battles in England against the sons of Ethelred, the King of England. They fought with varying luck. He came to England the summer Ethelred died.[4] King Canute then

1 King Canute won London in the autumn of 1016.   2 At the battle of Assington (Essex), St Luke's Day, the 18th of October, 1016 (according to Roger of Wendover). 3 Eric became Earl of Northumberland in 1017.   4 Canute was in England when his father Swein died in 1014, and fought against Ethelred in Lindsey (cf. p. 228). He returned to England with a great force in 1015, when King Ethelred was lying sick at Corsham, and Ethelred died the following year (23rd of April, 1016).

wedded Queen Emma and their children were Harold,[1] Hardicanute and Gunhild. King Canute came to terms with King Edmund: each of them was to have a half of England. The same month Edric Streona slew King Edmund.[2] Thereafter King Canute drove all King Ethelred's sons from England. Thus says Sigvat:

| And Canute then slew | Or else, |
| Every son of Ethelred, | He drove them from the land. |

27. King Ethelred's sons came from England to Ruda in Valland to their uncles, the summer when Olav Haraldson came from a viking raid in the west, and they were all the winter in Normandy; they bound themselves by an agreement that King Olav should have Northumbria if they won England from the Danes. Then in the autumn King Olav sent his foster-father Rani to England to get men there, and Ethelred's sons sent him with tokens to their friends and kinsmen; but King Olav gave him much money to win men for them. Rani was in England during the winter and got promises from many great men, for the men of the land would much rather have landsmen as kings over them, but still the Danes' might in England was now so great that all the land folk had submitted to them.

28. In the spring King Olav and Ethelred's sons all went together from the west. They came to England at a place called Jungfurda and there they went with their army up into the land to the bourgh. There were present many of the men who had promised them help; they won the bourgh, and slew many men. And when King Canute's men were aware of it they drew an army together and soon had such a force of men that King Ethelred's sons had not strength enough to meet them, and they saw there was no other choice for them but to flee and get back to the west, to Ruda. King Olav then parted from them and would not go back to Valland. He sailed north along the coast right to Northumbria; there he lay in a haven called Furovald,[3] fought with the men of the villages and there got the victory and much goods.

29. King Olav let the longships lie behind, and fitted out two small ships, and then had two hundred and twenty men,[4] clad in brynies and well chosen. In the autumn he sailed north on the sea;

1 *Harold* was Canute's son by Algiva.    2 Although the *Anglo-Saxon Chronicle* and Florence of Worcester are silent about the cause of Edmund's death, Henry of Huntingdon and Roger of Wendover assert that he was killed at the instigation of the infamous ealdorman Edric Streona, often mentioned by the chroniclers, and William of Malmesbury makes an allusion to the same effect.    3 *Furovald* (or *fyrir Valdi*) refers no doubt to a harbour off the Wolds in Yorkshire, at that time in Northumberland.
4 I.e. 260 men. A hundred was always reckoned to be 120 (a big hundred).

they met with a storm, so that they were in peril of their lives; but as they were doughty men and had the king's luck with them, all went well. Thus says Ottar:

O fight-eager king!
Thou didst man two ships
From the west. On Skjoldung's
    thwarts
Thou didst risk thy life.

The stirring stream on the billows
Would badly have broken up
The merchant ships, had not
The men aboard been bold.

And likewise thus:

Ye were not afraid of Ægir[1]
When ye went on the sea way.
No prince ever had a
Better following of men.

The steep billows often shot
The ship from themselves,
Till thou, Harald's son, landed
On Norway's Midland.

Here it is said that King Olav came to the middle of Norway, and the island where they came ashore is called Sæla,[2] outside Stad. The king said it was a day of luck when they had landed at Sæla, and thought that it would be a good token that it had happened. Then they went up into the island; the king stepped with one foot into some mire, and sank to the knee with the other, and then he said: "Now I fall". Rani then said: "Thou dost not fall, O king; now dost thou set thy feet firm in the land".[3] The king laughed and answered: "So may it be, if God will". Thereafter they went down to the ships and sailed to Ulvasund. There they got to hear about Hacon the Jarl, how he was in the south in Sogn, and how they expected him in the north as soon as he got a fair wind; he had one ship only.

30. King Olav steered his ships in from the lode[4] when he came south by Fjalir; he turned into Saudungsund[5] and put in there. They laid a ship on either side of the sound and between them they had a thick rope. At the same time Hacon the Jarl rowed into the sound with a fully manned cutter; his men believed that it was two merchant ships which lay there and so they rowed forth into the sound between the ships. King Olav's men now drew up the rope in the middle under the cutter's keel and heaved it up with windlasses. When the rope was tight, the ship rose in the water and dipped forward so that the sea rushed into the prow and filled the cutter, which capsized. King

---

1 *Ægir* was the God of the Ocean.    2 *Sæla* in O.S. means 'luck'. The island's present name is Selja.    3 It may be recalled that William the Conqueror met with a somewhat similar accident, when he set foot on English soil, according to the chroniclers. 4 The M.S. word is *led*, in O.S. *leid*; both resembling the English *lode* or fairway. 5 Now Sauasund east of Atleöy in the Askvold district. Cf. 'History of Harald Hairfair', chapter 12.

Olav then took up Hacon the Jarl from the water and all the men they seized, but they slew some and others sank. Thus says Ottar:

Feeder of the ravens! thou who
Camest home with rich tributes,
Didst take Hacon's cutter
With its men and noble fittings.

Young man, thou didst seek
Thy kinsmen's lands that were thine;
The jarl had no might to withstand thee.

Hacon the Jarl was led up on the king's ship. He was the most handsome man to behold; he had much hair, as beautiful as silk. About his head there was bound a gold band. He was in the forehold. Then said King Olav: "No lie is said of you kinsmen, when it is told that you are handsome men to look upon, but gone is now your good luck". Then said Hacon: "It is not a misfortune that has befallen us. So has it long been that now one and now the other has lost; so has it gone with you and your kinsmen that now one and now the other has come on top, but I am newly come out of my childhood, and we were not ready just now to protect ourselves and we expected no hostility. It may be that another time we shall have better luck than now". Then answered King Olav: "Dost thou not expect, jarl, that this has befallen so that from now thou wilt get neither victory nor defeat?" The jarl said: "Thou must rule matters this time, O king". Then said King Olav: "What wilt thou do, jarl, if I let thee go whole and unscathed wherever thou wilt?" The jarl asked what he would demand, and the king answered: "Nothing more than that thou goest from the land, givest up thy kingdom and swearest oaths that hereafter thou wilt not hold battle against me". The jarl answered that he would do so. Now did Hacon the Jarl swear King Olav oaths that he would never afterwards fight against him, nor protect Norway with war against King Olav, nor seek after him. King Olav then gave peace to him and all his men, and the jarl got back the ship he had formerly had. They now rowed off on their way. About this Sigvat the Scald says:

The mighty battle-eager king
Said that in the old
Saudungsund he must
Fall upon Hacon.

The strong young prince
There found the jarl,
Who was of the best
And the noblest kin of the Danish tongue.[1]

31. After that the jarl went from the land as soon as possible. He sailed west to England and found his uncle, King Canute, who greeted Hacon very well, set him in his court and gave him great power in his kingdom. Hacon the Jarl now stayed there a long time

1 Cf. Snorre Sturlason's preface about the Danish tongue.

with Canute. Whilst Swein and Hacon were ruling over Norway, they made an agreement with Erling Skjalgson and it was thereby made binding that Erling's son Aslak should wed Gunhild, the daughter of Swein the Jarl; Erling and Aslak were to have all the land incomes that King Olav Trygvason had given Erling. Erling then became a full friend of the jarl and they bound their friendships with oaths to one another.

32. King Olav Digre now steered eastwards along the land, and far and wide held things with the bonders. Many now gave him allegiance, but others, who were friends or kinsmen of Swein the Jarl, spoke against it. King Olav, therefore, went hastily east to the Vik, brought his army into the Vik, drew up his ships and went up on land. And when he came to Vestfold, many men, who had been acquaintances and friends of his father, greeted him well; in Fold there were also many men of his family. In the autumn he went up into the land to his step-father, King Sigurd, and he came thither early one day. And when King Olav came into the neighbourhood of the house some servants ran before to the house and into the room. Therein sat King Olav's mother, Asta, and some women with her. The lads told her about King Olav's journey and that he could be expected there at once. Asta straightway stood up and bade the men and women make everything ready as best they could. She charged four women with the adornment of the room to array it quickly with hangings and place benches round about. Two men carried straw on to the floor and two set up the sideboard and the ale cask, two set up the table, two brought in the meat; two she sent away from the place and two brought in the ale. And all the others, women and men, went out into the yard. Messengers went to King Sigurd, where he was, and brought him his kingly clothes and his steed with the gilded saddle. The bit, too, was set with enamelled stones and all gilded. Four men she sent away to the four corners of the district, and bade all the great men come to the feast when she made the ale of welcome for her son. All others who were present she caused to put on the best clothes they had, and to those who had no good clothes themselves she lent some.

33. King Sigurd Syr stood outside in the field when the messengers came to him and told him all these tidings and likewise everything that Asta was taking in hand at home. He had there many men, some cutting corn, some binding it, some carting it home, others loading it in stacks or barns. But the king and two men with him went sometimes to the field, and sometimes where the corn was being

stacked. Thus it is said about his garb that he had a blue kirtle and blue hose, high shoes bound to the leg, a grey cape, and a grey, wide hat with a peak for the face; in his hand he had a staff with a silver-gilt socket at the top and therein a silver ring. Thus it is said about his character that he was a very enterprising man and eager for his goods and his estate, and he himself managed the business of the place. He was not fond of display and he was rather a man of few words. He was the wisest of all the men then in Norway and very wealthy. He was peaceful and not aggressive. Asta, his wife, was

Asta's messengers come to Sigurd Syr

generous and noble-minded. These were their children: Guthorm was the eldest, then Gunhild and Halvdan, then Ingerid and Harald. The messengers said: "These words did Asta bid us bring to thee that now it seemed to her an exceedingly great thing for thee to do, to bear thyself like a great man, and she bade that thou shouldst be more like Harald Hairfair's family in thy character than thy mother's father Rani Narrow-nose or Jarl Nereid the Old, even though they had been great men of wisdom". The king said: "Great tidings ye tell and moreover ye put them forth eagerly. Asta has said great words before about those men and more than was necessary to do; and I see that she still has the same mind and she takes this up with great eagerness. I hope she can attend her son out with as great pomp as she now escorts him in; but so it seems to me if this shall be, that they who take part in this matter must neither regard their goods nor their lives. This man, King Olav, is fighting against great odds, and upon him and his plans lie the wrath of the King of the Danes and the King of the Swedes, if he continues with this".

34. When the king had said this he sat down and had his shoes drawn off and put on his feet cordovan hose and bound to them a pair of gilded spurs. Then he took off his cape and his kirtle and clad himself in fine clothes and over all a scarlet cape; he girded himself with a costly sword, set a gilded helm upon his head and mounted his horse. He sent the workpeople out into the district and took thirty men well arrayed who rode home with him. But when they rode up to the house he saw where on the other side of the house King Olav's flag waved forth; Olav himself was there, and with him there were a hundred men all well clad. There were also men lined up everywhere between the houses. From his steed King Sigurd greeted his step-son King Olav and his men and bade him to drink with him; and Asta went out and kissed her son and bade him stay with her, and said that everything was at his service, land and men, that she could grant him. King Olav thanked her well for her words. She took him by the hand and led him after her into the rooms up to the high-seat. King Sigurd got men to attend to their clothes and give corn to their horses, and he went to his high-seat and the feast was given in plenty.

35. But when King Olav had been there a short while it happened one day that he called to him for talk and counsel King Sigurd, his kinsman, Asta his mother, and Rani his foster-father. King Olav began with these words: "So it is", said he, "as ye know, that I have come hither to this land and that I have been a long time beforehand in foreign parts. All these years I and my men have had nothing else for the upkeep of our life than what we have got in war, and in many places we have had to risk both body and soul. Many men who have been blameless have had to give up their goods and some their lives as well; but foreign men sit over the land which my father had and his father and one after the other of our kinsmen to whom I am heir; and they are not content with that, for they have taken the possessions of all our kinsmen who in direct line are come from Harald Hairfair. To some they give a little, but others get nothing. Now I shall reveal to you that which for a long time has been in my mind: I am thinking of craving my father's inheritance, and I will go to neither the Danish king nor the Swedish king to ask them for anything, although they have for a time called that inheritance theirs

which was Harald Hairfair's patrimony. Rather am I thinking to tell you the truth of winning my inheritance by spear and sword, and of seeking help for that from all my kinsmen and friends and all those who will agree to that plan with me. And in this way I shall take up the matter so that one of two things shall happen; either I shall possess myself of all that kingdom from which they drove my kinsman King Olav Trygvason, or else I shall fall in fight for my inheritance. Now I expect of thee, kinsman Sigurd and of those other men in the land who are rightly born here to the kingdom, according to those laws which Harald Hairfair set up, that ye will not fail to rise and avenge this shame on our family, and that ye will set everything up to strengthen the man who will be the leader in raising up our family. But whether ye will now show some manliness in this matter or not, I know the common mind, that all men will be glad to be free from thraldom under foreign rulers as soon as they have someone to trust themselves to. I have not brought this matter forward to anyone before thee because I know that thou art a wise man and understand well how this plan should be taken in hand from the first; whether it should be spoken about in secrecy to a few men or whether it should forthwith be brought before the common people at an open meeting. I have to some degree now shown them my teeth when I took Hacon the Jarl prisoner; he has now fled from the land and he gave me with oaths that part of the kingdom which he had formerly had. Now I think that it will be easier for us to have to do with Swein the Jarl alone than if both were there to protect the land". King Sigurd answered now, "There dwell no little things in thy mind, King Olav. This plan according to my meaning bears evidence more of lust for power than of foresight; after all it was to be expected that there would be a wide gap between my small circumstances and the great strength which thou must have, for when thou wast but come a little while from thy childhood thou wast straightway full of rivalry and wouldst be master in everything thou couldst. Now also thou art much proven in battle and thou hast framed thyself after the custom of foreign rulers. Now I know that thou hast taken this up so eagerly that it will be of no use to counsel thee from it. One can hardly be astonished that such things should strongly strike the minds of those who are somewhat jealous that the whole kin and kingdom of Harald Hairfair is fallen. But I will not bind myself with any promise till I know what the other kings in the Uplands think or choose. But thou hast done well in that thou didst let me know about this plan before thou didst bring it in open talk

before the common people. I will vow thee my help along with the
kings and other chiefs and the rest of the land folk. Likewise shall
my goods, King Olav, be ready for thy support; but first do I wish
to bring this before the common folk when I see that something can
come of it, or that we can get some support for this great plan, for
thou must understand clearly that thou hast taken much into thy
hands when thou wilt raise up strife with Olav the Swedish king and
with Canute who is now king both in England and in Denmark, and
strong enough supports must be raised against them if this is to be

Sigurd Syr, Asta, Olav and Rani

of avail. But it does not seem to me unlikely that thou wilt get much
help from the folk, for they are eager for changes. Thus it happened
before when King Olav Trygvason came to power in the land, that
all were glad of it, but he did not enjoy the kingdom long". When
the talk was gone so far, Asta took up the word: "Thus it is with me,
my son; I am glad over thee and I should be most glad if thy might
could be the greatest. For that I will spare nothing that I have means
for, but here where I am there is little help in counsel; but if I were to
choose I would rather that thou didst become king over all Norway,
even if thou didst live no longer in the kingdom than Olav Trygvason, rather than that thou shouldst become a king no greater than
Sigurd Syr and die of old age". And after these words the meeting

ended. King Olav stayed there a while with all his men. King Sigurd gave them at table every other day fish and milk, and every other day meat and the best ale.

36. At this time there were many Upland kings who ruled over the folk districts and most of them were come from the family of Harald Hairfair. Over Hedemark there ruled two brothers, Rörik and Ring, and in Gudbrandsdale Gudröd ruled. There was also a king in Raumarik. There was also a king who had Tote and Hadeland, and in Valders there was also another king. Sigurd Syr had a meeting with the folk kings up in Hadeland, and Olav Haraldson was at that meeting. Sigurd then put before the folk kings with whom he had made the meeting his kinsman Olav's plan, and begged them to help it with both men and counsel and their assent. He then reckoned up how needful it was for them to cast off the yoke that the Danes and Swedes had put upon them. He said that they would now get the man who could go forward with that plan, and thereafter he reckoned up the many doughty deeds which King Olav had done on his travels and raids. Then said King Rörik: "True it is that the kingdom of King Harald Hairfair has fallen very low if none of his kin is king over Norway. We have now experienced changing fortunes in the land. Hacon, the foster-son of Athelstan, was king and all men liked it well; but when the sons of Gunhild ruled the land, all men were so loath of their might and unrighteousness that they would rather have foreign kings over them and be more independent, for the foreign rulers were always far from them and broke little into the customs of the folk if they could get such tribute from the land as they craved. But when Harald, King of the Danes, and Hacon the Jarl were not united, the Jomsvikings harried in Norway. Then the common folk and crowd gathered together against them and drove this unrest away. The men then egged on Hacon the Jarl to keep the land against the Danish king and ward it with spear and sword. But when he seemed to rule the kingdom fully with the help of the men of the land, he was so hard and forceful towards the folk that no man would bear it from him; the Tronds slew him and then raised to the rule Olav Trygvason who was nobly born and in all ways well fitted as a ruler. All the folk were eager to have him as their king and in such a way to raise up anew that kingdom which Harald Hairfair had owned. But when Olav was fully lord over the kingdom no man was independent because of him. He went hard upon us small kings to exact for himself all the incomes that Harald Hairfair had taken here, and in certain ways he was still harder. But

so much less freedom had the folk because of him, for no one could say in what god he could believe. But after he was taken from the land we have held friendship with the Danish king and we have had from him much help in all those things which we have had need to crave, and have had independence and peace in the land but no downtreading. Now I may say about my own wish that I am well content with things as they are. I know not, though my kinsman be king over the land, if my right will in any measure be bettered by it, and in any case I will have no share in this plan". Then said his brother Ring: "I will lay bare my wish; if I still have the same kingdom and possessions it seems to me still better that my kinsman is king over Norway rather than foreign rulers, and that he could still raise up our family in the land. It is my thought about this man, Olav, that his fortune and luck may decide whether he shall get the kingdom or not. But if he should become sole king over Norway, then it seems that he will have the best things who has the greatest claims to his friendship. Now he has no greater chance than any of us, but rather much less, as we have some land and kingdom to rule over, but he has nothing at all. We are also as well born to the kingdom. Now we shall be his good helpers if we grant him the greatest position in this land and support him with all our strength. Why should he not reward us well for it and long remember it with joy if he is so great a man as I believe and as all say? Now if I may give counsel we shall run the risk of binding our friendship with him". After that one after the other stood up and spoke, and it appeared that most of them had a wish to make an alliance with King Olav. He promised them his full friendship and better rights if he became sole king over Norway. They now bound this agreement with oaths.

37. After that the kings called things. Then King Olav drew up before the folk his plan and the claim he had to the kingdom. He bade the bonders take him as king over the land, and in return he promised them to keep the old laws and to guard the land against

King Olav rides to a thing meeting with the Uplanders

foreign armies and rulers. About that he spoke long and well and got good cheers for his speech. Then the kings stood up and spoke one after the other, and all spoke to the folk about this matter and business. The end of it was that Olav was given the name of king over the whole land, and they granted him the land according to the Upland laws.

38. Then King Olav began his journey and had feasts ordered for himself where there were king's garths. He went first over Hadeland and thereupon he went north to Gudbrandsdale. Then it happened, as Sigurd Syr had said, that so many men came to him that he did not seem to need half of them, and he had then almost three hundred (three hundred and sixty) men. Then the feasts as arranged did not suffice, for it had been a custom that the kings went over the Uplands with sixty or seventy men but never more than one hundred (one hundred and twenty). The king then went over the land quickly and was but one night in each place. And when he came north to the fell[1] he went on his way over the fell till he came down on the north side. King Olav came down into Opdale and stayed there for the night. After that he went over Opdale Wood and came forth into Medaldale;[2] there he summoned a thing and called the bonders to him. The king spoke at the thing, and craved that the bonders should choose him as their king, and in return offered them rights and laws as King Olav Trygvason had done. The bonders had no strength to hold battle with him, and the end of it was that they acknowledged him as king and bound it with oaths. But they had before sent word down into Orkedale and likewise to Skaun[3] telling all they knew about King Olav's journey.

39. Einar Tambarskelver had a house and seat in Skaun, but when news came to him about King Olav's journey he straightway had the arrow of war cut and sent out in all directions. He called together every man fully weaponed, and the bidding was followed by the words that they should ward the land against King Olav. The bidding went to Orkedale and then to Guldale, and from all over an army drew together.

40. King Olav went with his army down to Orkedale. He proceeded quietly and in peace. But when he came out to Grjotar he met there a gathering of bonders and they had more than seven hundred (eight hundred and forty) men. The king drew up his force because he thought the bonders would fight, and when they saw it

1 Dovre-fell.    2 Now Meldale in Upper Orkedale.    3 Now Börseskogn, between Orkedale and Guldale.

they also began to line up. But it was hard for them because they had not decided beforehand who should be their chief, and when King Olav saw how confused the bonders were he sent Tore Gudbrandson to them. And when Tore came he said that King Olav would not fight with them. He called up twelve men who were the most noble in their flock to come and meet King Olav. The bonders did so and went over a hill which was there to the spot where the king's lines stood. Then said King Olav: "Ye bonders have now done well, so that now I get a chance of speaking to you, for I will tell you this about my business here in Trondheim. Firstly, I know ye have heard before that I and Hacon the Jarl met in the summer and our meeting ended in such way that he gave me all the kingdom he had here in Trondheim, and, as ye know, that is the land of the folks of Orkedale, Guldale, Strind and Öyna. And here I have witnesses who were there, who saw my handshake with the jarl, and who heard the words, oaths, and promises which the jarl gave me. I will offer you laws and peace such as King Olav Trygvason offered you before me". He spoke long and boldly, and at last it came about that he offered the bonders two things to choose between. One was to put themselves in his hands and promise him obedience, but the other was to hold battle with him. Then the bonders went back to their army and told their message. They sought the counsel of all the folk as to which they should choose; but even if they split for a while between themselves, they chose, however, to put themselves in the king's hands. It was then bound with oaths on behalf of the bonders. The king now arranged for his journey and the bonders made feasts for him. The king then went out to the sea and there got himself ships. He had a longship, a twenty-seater, from Gunnar of Gelmin;[1] another ship, also a twenty-seater, he had from Lodin of Vigg; a third ship, a twenty-seater, he had from Angrar[2] of Nes; Hacon the Jarl had owned this place, but a bailiff called Bard the White now ruled there. The king had four or five ships. He went speedily and steered in along the fjord.

41. Swein the Jarl was then in Trondheim at Steinker[3] and had a Yule feast made ready there. It was a market town. Einar Tambarskelver learned that the men of Orkedale had put themselves in King Olav's hands. He then sent men to Swein the Jarl. They went first to Nidaros and there they took a rowing boat which Einar had. They went in along the fjord and came later in the day to Steinker;

---

1 Now Gjölme near the Orkedale's Oss.  2 *Angrar*, now Hangran at Bynes.  3 Now the town of Steinkjær.

they brought their message to the jarl and told all about King Olav's journey. The jarl had a longship which was afloat outside the town. Straightway in the evening he had his treasures, and people's clothes and drink and food brought into the ship, as much as it could hold. And they rowed forthwith in the night and came at dawn to Skarnsund.[1] There they saw King Olav rowing in along the fjord with his army. The jarl then turned to the land outside Masarvik[2]—there was a thick wood. They drew so near the cliff that the leaves and branches stretched out over the ship. Thereupon they cut great trees and set them outside the railings right down into the sea so that they could not see the ship for leaves, and it was not quite light when the king rowed by them. It was calm weather and the king rowed by the island;[3] but when they were no longer in sight the jarl rowed out of the fjord right out to Frosta[4] and came to land there. It was in his country.

42. Swein the Jarl sent men out to Guldale for his kinsman Einar. And when Einar came to the jarl, the jarl told him all about how things had passed between him and King Olav, and likewise that he would gather men to go and fight against King Olav. Einar answered thus: "We shall now go with counsel and spy out what King Olav is thinking of doing. We will only let them learn about us that we are keeping quiet. If he does not learn that we are collecting folk, then it may be that he will settle down at Steinker over Yule, for everything is now made ready there for it. But if he learns that we are gathering folk he will straightway sail out of the fjord and then we shall not get hold of him". So it was done as Einar said; and the jarl went feasting with the bonders up in Stjordale. When King Olav came to Steinker he took all the festive goods and had them borne on to his ship; he got freight ships besides and took with him both food and drink. He made himself quietly ready and sailed right out to Nidaros. There King Olav Trygvason had had a market town built, as is written above ('History of Olav Trygvason', chapter 70). But when Eric the Jarl came to the land, he settled at Lade where his father had had his chief estates. But he had neglected the houses which Olav had had made at Nid;[5] some of them were then fallen down, but some still stood and were almost uninhabitable. King Olav sailed his ships up into Nid and straightway had those houses mended which still stood, and he had those raised up which were fallen down;

1 *Skarnsund* is situated west of Inderöy.    2 *Masarvik*, now Mosviken, south-west of Skarnsund.    3 I.e. Inderöy.    4 The peninsula Frosta on the east side of the Trondheimsfjord.    5 *Nid*, i.e. Nidaros.

and for that he used a great number of people. He also had both drink and food brought up into the houses, and he settled there for Yule. When Swein the Jarl and Einar learned that, they changed their plan.

Swein the Jarl and his men hide their ship, when King Olav passed up the fjord

43. Tord Sigvaldi's Scald is the name of an Icelander. He had been for a long time with Sigvaldi the Jarl and afterwards with Thorkel the High,[1] the jarl's brother; but after the jarl's death, Tord became a merchant. He met King Olav when he was on a viking raid in the west; he became his man and followed him afterwards. He was with the king when this happened. Tord's son was called Sigvat and he was being fostered with Thorkel from Apavatn.[2] But when he was almost grown up he went out from Iceland with merchants; in the autumn the ship came to Trondheim and these men got themselves quarters there in the lordship. The same winter King Olav came to Trondheim, as is written above (chapter 38). But when Sigvat learned that his father Tord was there with the king, Sigvat went to the king, met his father Tord and stayed there a while. Sigvat was a good poet early in life. He had composed a poem about King Olav, and he asked the king to listen to it. The king said that he would

1 *Thorkel the High* and King Olav ranged themselves on King Ethelred's side and defended London against the Danes under Swein Forkbeard, the father of King Canute. Cf. chapters 12 and 13.  2 *Apavatn* was a farm in Iceland, north-west of Skalholt.

have no poem composed about him, and that he did not understand how to listen to verse. Then quoth Sigvat:

Thou who didst curb the murky steed
'Neath the awning, hear my song.
One scald mayest thou own,
Noble-born chieftain.

Even if thou deniest other scalds
Thy leave to compose lays,
I bring thee in any case,
O prince, enough of praise.

King Olav gave Sigvat as a reward for his poem a gold ring which weighed half a mark. Sigvat became one of King Olav's bodyguard. Then he quoth:

Gladly I took thy sword
(Afterwards I shall not censure it),
O hero of war!—An honourable pursuit
It is, and it is my desire.

Gold-giving prince!
Good have we both got:
Thou dost get a true huscarl,
And I get a noble master.

Swein the Jarl had taken half the land dues[1] of the Iceland ships as was formerly the custom, for Eric the Jarl and Hacon had half of these incomes, as of others in Trondheim. But when King Olav came thither he sent his men to demand half the land dues of the Icelanders. But they went to the king and asked Sigvat for help. He then went before the king and quoth:

Persistent in pleas
I now become known
If I beg for the skins.[2]
Once I got gold from the prince.

Generous king, grant me
That half of the land dues
May go back to the ship.
For this I earnestly pray.

44. Swein the Jarl and Einar Tambarskelver drew a large army together and went out to Guldale by the upper way, and then turned out to Nidaros; they had nearly two thousand men.[3] King Olav's men were out on Gaularas[4] and kept watch on horseback. They were aware of the army going down from Guldale, and they then bore news of it to the king at midnight. King Olav straightway stood up and had the army wakened. They went straight to the ships and bore out all their clothes and weapons and everything they could come upon; so they rowed out of the river. At the same time the jarl's men came to the town and they took all the Yule provisions and burnt all the houses. King Olav went out along the fjord to Orkedale and there went from the ships. He went up through Orkedale right to the fell

1 This tax was paid by the men from Iceland when they landed in Norway. It was rescinded in 1262, when Iceland definitely became a Norwegian dependency.   2 The land dues were often paid by the Icelanders in skins.   3 I.e. 2400 men.   4 Now Byasen in Trondheim.

and east over the fell to the Dales. About Swein the Jarl's burning of Nidaros, it is said in the poem composed about Klong Bruceson:[1]

| | |
|---|---|
| They burnt the king's half-built Houses by the Nid. | Fire, I believe, felled the hall;[2] Ashes fell upon the army. |

45. King Olav then went south along Gudbrandsdale and from there on to Hedemark; in the midst of the winter he went about feasting, but in the spring he drew an army together and went out into the Vik. He had from Hedemark a great force which the kings gave him. Many district chiefs went from there with him and amongst them was Ketel Kalv of Ringanes.[3] King Olav also had men from Raumarik. King Sigurd Syr, his kinsman, came to help him with a great troop of men. They now made for the sea, got themselves ships and fitted themselves out in the Vik; they had fine and numerous folk. And when they had fitted out their men, they made for Tunsberg.

46. Straightway after Yule Swein the Jarl gathered folk from all over Trondheim; he called out the army and also fitted out the ships. At that time there were many district chiefs in Norway. Many of them were mighty and of such great family that they came from king's or jarl's kin, and had few ancestors to reckon back to them; they were also very rich. All the strength of kings or jarls, if they ruled over the land, lay in the district chiefs, for so it was in every folk district that they ruled over the bonders. Swein the Jarl was friendly with the district chiefs, and he found it easy to get folk. Einar Tambarskelver, his kinsman, and many other chiefs were with him, and there were many of them, both district chiefs and bonders, who had sworn oaths to King Olav the previous winter. As soon as they were fitted out they went out of the fjord and sailed to the south along the coast and drew to themselves men from every folk district. And when they came south by Rogaland Erling Skjalgson came to meet them, and he had many folk and with him were many chiefs. They sailed east with all the army to the Vik. It was late in Lent when Swein the Jarl came to the Vik. The jarl brought the army past Grenmar[4] and lay in by Nesjar.[5]

---

1 *Brusi* (or *Bruce*) is a name often met with in the sagas.    2 *Hall* is used by the Norsemen for the king's habitations. In mythology Odin's house was called Valhall and to-day the name exists in Hacon's Hall (at Bergen) and Oscar's Hall (near Oslo). In England *Hall* is often used in connection with country houses, such as Haddon Hall, Hardwicke Hall, Kepwick Hall, Nesham Hall, etc.    3 Now Ringnes in Ottestad district (Hedemark).    4 In the fjord of Langesund.    5 *Nesjar* is the peninsula between the Langesund and Tönsberg fjords.

47. Then King Olav sailed with his army out along the Vik, and now there was only a short distance between them. And they knew of each other on the Saturday before Palm Sunday. King Olav had the ship which was called *Carlhead*; there was carved on the prow a king's head; he had carved it himself. Such a head was for a long time afterwards used in Norway on those ships which kings commanded.

48. As soon as dawn came on Sunday morning, King Olav got

up and clothed himself; he went up on land and had the horn blown for the whole army to make a landing. Then he made a speech to the army and said that he had now learnt that there was only a short distance between them and Swein the Jarl: "We shall now arm ourselves", he said, "for it will be but a short time till we meet. Now shall ye prepare yourselves and every man shall make himself ready at such part of the ship as he has been given so that all are ready when I have the horn blown to put out to sea. Let us afterwards row together, no one going before the whole fleet, and no one staying behind when I row out of the harbour; for we cannot know if we shall meet the jarl there where he lies or if they

King Olav had the horn blown
for the whole army

will make towards us. But if we meet and there is battle, then our men must bring the ships together and be ready to rope them. We shall protect ourselves first with our shields and take care of our weapons, so that we do not throw them in the sea or cast them away. But when the strife begins and the ships are bound together, then must ye make as hard an attack as ye can, and then must every warrior do his manliest".

49. King Olav had on his ship one hundred men who all had ring-armour and French helms;[1] most of his men had white shields whereupon lay the Holy Cross in gold; on others it was painted in

1 The O.N. text has *Valska hialma*, meaning 'helmets from *Valland*' (North of France). Cf. also 'History of Harald Hairfair', chapter 18.

red or blue. A white cross he had also caused to be painted on the front of all the helmets. He had a white standard and on that was a dragon. Mass was held and afterwards he went on his ship and bade the men get enough food and drink. He then had the war blast blown and they put out of the harbour. But when they came before the harbour where the jarl had lain, the jarl's men were armed and wished to row out of the harbour; but when they saw the king's army they began to rope their ships; they set up the standard and made themselves ready. And when King Olav saw that they rowed towards them, the king lay to by the jarl's ship; then began the battle. Thus says Sigvat:

| | |
|---|---|
| When he made for Swein | The bold king, who brought about |
| In the harbour, the prince | The battle, held on |
| Made a sharp onslaught. | Without mercy, whilst Swein's men |
| The blood fell red in the sea. | Bound their ships together. |

Here it is said that King Olav drew forth to battle, and Swein lay before him in the harbour. Sigvat the Scald was with him in the battle. In the summer after the battle he straightway composed the poem which is called "the Songs of Nesjar" and therein he speaks truly of these tidings.

| | |
|---|---|
| I know that in the east | Had the *Carlhead*[1] lying |
| Of Agder, the battle-storm maker | Near by the jarl. |

The battle was very sharp and it was a long while before they could make out how it would go. Then many fell on both sides and many were wounded. Thus says Sigvat:

| | |
|---|---|
| No man says of Swein | For the friends of both chiefs, |
| That his courage in battle betrayed him, | Wherever they met, dealt out |
| Nor of the fight-happy Olav | The wounds. No army |
| In the gust of the sword din, | Ever came to a worse spot. |

The jarl had the greater army, but the king had on his ship chosen men, who had followed him on raids and who were so well armed (as was said before) that every man had a suit of ring-mail; they were not wounded. Thus says Sigvat:

| | |
|---|---|
| Gladly I saw in the king's | But during the downpour of arrows |
| Brave host the cool brynies | I hid my swarthy locks |
| Covering our shoulders; | Under the Welsh helmet. |
| Hard did the swords sound. | Such was then our battle outfit. |

But when the men began to fall dead on the jarl's ships and some were wounded, the crew in the railings began to thin.

---

1 *Carlhead*, i.e. the name of King Olav's ship.

50. Then King Olav's men made themselves ready to board. The standard was borne up on the ship that was nearest the jarl's and the king himself followed the standard forward. Thus says Sigvat:

The gilded staff moved forward,
When the angry warriors
Went up under the standard
On the ship with the noble king

During the clash of swords.
On the ship, it was not indeed
As when the maid bears the mead
To the men in the king's halls.

There the fight was hard and Swein's men fell in crowds, and some leaped overboard. Thus says Sigvat:

There where we could hear
The loud din of weapons—
Blades cleaving shields—
We clambered on to the ships.

But the wounded bonders
Went overboard where they fought.
Not a few bodies floated out
By the shore and the ships were seized.

And likewise this:

Dyed red in the strife
We got our shields,
Which came thither white;
It was easy to see it.

I know that the grim young man
Went up on the ship and we
Followed him there, where our swords
Were blunted. The ravens got drink.

Then the loss of men began to turn against the jarl's army. The king's men made for the jarl's ship and they almost came up on it. But when the jarl saw into what a bad position they were come, he shouted to the stem men to cut the ropes and loosen the ships. They did so. Then the king's men hooked grapples on to the ship's stemhead, and held it fast. Then the jarl told the stem men to cut the stemhead off. They did so. Thus says Sigvat:

Bersi the Scald in prison

Swein himself bade them
Sharply cut the stem heads;
He was just before then almost
Fallen into our hands,

The time when the host
In the ship's prow struck for
The good of the ravens. We eagerly
Got food for Odin's birds.

Einar Tambarskelver had drawn his ship up by the side of the jarl's and his men cast an anchor on to the bow of the jarl's ship; in that way they all came together out in the fjord. After that all the jarl's army fled and rowed out in the fjord. Bersi Scaldtorfuson was in the forehold of Swein the Jarl's ship, but when the ship glided forth from the fleet King Olav said aloud when he saw Bersi—for Bersi was easily recognised as he was a handsome man and well fitted with weapons and clothes: "Farewell, Bersi". He answered: "Live well, King". Thus says Bersi in a poem he composed when he was come into King Olav's power and sat in chains:

Thou badest this eager
Worshipper of poetry farewell,
And we could answer
The same, O strife-wont warrior!
It listed me not to be delayed
Longer; therefore I sold
To the noble-born giver of gold
Those words as I bought them.

I have seen the great fights
Of Swein; we fared together
Once when the cool blades
Afterwards sang loudly;

Never again hereafter
Shall I follow in a host,
O king, any chieftain
More glorious than he.

This year I lie in chains
For a long while in the great ship.
O swinger of the sword! I humble
Myself never so lowly,
That I betray, O wise war king,
My loyal friends or be loath
To have them. In my youth
Among my friends I found thy foe.

51. Some of the jarl's men now fled up on the land, and some got quarter. Then Swein the Jarl and his men rowed out of the fjord and brought their ships together, and the leaders talked amongst themselves; the jarl sought counsel with the district chiefs. Erling Skjalgson counselled that they should sail north, gather men, and again fight against King Olav. But as they had lost many men, most of them rather wished the jarl to go out of the land to his kinsman, the Swedish king, and get help of men from him. And that plan Einar supported, for it seemed to him as if they had no strength to fight against King Olav. They dispersed their army. The jarl sailed south by Fold and with him was Einar Tambarskelver, but Erling Skjalgson and many other men besides, who would not flee from their lands, went home to the north. Erling had a crowd of men with him during the summer.

52. King Olav and his men saw that the jarl had drawn his ships together. Then King Sigurd Syr egged them on to draw up to the jarl and so force battle with him to the uttermost. King Olav said that he would first see what plan the jarl was taking, whether he held his host together, or whether the army should be parted from him. Sigurd said that he could decide: "But it is my thought that with thy temper and lust for power thou wilt be late making these great bucks true men, as they are wont to go fully against their leaders". There

was then no battle. They saw that the jarl's men were parting. King Olav then let them ransack the fallen. They lay there some nights and shared the booty. Then Sigvat the Scald quoth this verse:

I guess that many a man
Who sailed from the north
To the battle will not turn
Home from the hard fight.
From the steed of the fjords have many
Sunk down to the ground;
It is true that out at sea
We met Swein the Jarl.

This year shall the fair
Trond maids taunt us not,
For we fought well,
Though the king's host was less.
Rather will the bride scoff,
If she will choose, the other host
Which came not forth to battle;
Red was the sea dyed.

And likewise this:

The king's might is now greater
(As thou didst find, Swein),
For the men of the Uplands will
Help this dear sea king.

It is now true that, as they swung
The swords, the Hedemark men
Could do much more
Than drink ale with the king.

When they parted King Olav gave gifts to King Sigurd Syr, his kinsman, and likewise to the other chiefs who had granted him their help. To Ketel of Ringanes he gave a great rowing-boat of fifteen benches, and Ketel took the boat up the Raumelv[1] right to the Mjöse.[2]

53. King Olav sent spies to find out about the jarl's journey; but when he learned that the jarl had gone out of the land, he went west along the Vik. Then people drew to him and he was taken as king at things. Then he went right to Lidandisnes. He learned then that Erling Skjalgson had a great gathering of folk. He did not stay in North Agder, for he got a good wind and went north as speedily as possible to Trondheim to put the land under him whilst the jarl was out of the land, for all the strength of the land seemed to him to be there. But when King Olav came to Trondheim no rising was made against him and he was taken as king there. He stayed in Nidaros during the autumn and made everything ready for wintering there; he had houses built there in the king's enclosure and raised the Klemenskirk[3] on the place where it now stands. He marked out building ground and gave it to bonders and merchants and others whom he chose, who wished to build houses. He stayed there with many men, for he had no faith in the trustiness of the Tronds if the jarl came back into the land. Ample evidence of this came from the Inner Tronds, and from them he got no scot.

1 *Raumelv*, i.e. River Glommen.  2 *Mjöse*, the great lake in East Norway.  3 The *Klemenskirk* was situated in the Strandgate.

54. Swein the Jarl went first to Sweden to his kinsman Olav, the Swedish king, and told him all about his meeting with Olav Digre, and then sought counsel from him as to what he should do. The king said that the jarl should be with him if he liked and have there such a kingdom to rule as he thought fitting: "Or else", he said, "I will give you enough help of men to get the land from Olav". The jarl chose the latter, for all his men wished it, as many of them who were with him had great possessions in Norway. But whilst they sat at this counselling, they were agreed that the next winter they should make themselves ready to go overland through Helsingeland and Jämtland and thence down into Trondheim, for the jarl had most faith in the Inner Tronds for support and help with men if he came to them. But they agreed, first, to go raiding in the summer in the Baltic to win goods.

55. Swein the Jarl went east with his men to Gardarik[1] and harried there. He stayed there during the summer, but about harvest time he turned back with his army to Sweden. There he got a sickness which brought on his death. After the jarl's death the men who had followed him went back to Sweden, but some turned to Helsingeland, from there to Jämtland and so west over the Kjöl[2] to Trondheim, and there they told the tidings of what had happened on their journey. Then was the death of Swein the Jarl truly learned.

56. Einar Tambarskelver and the army which had followed him went in the winter to the Swedish king and were well greeted by him. There were also many other men who had followed the jarl. The Swedish king was very ill-pleased with Olav Digre, for he had set himself in his tributary land and had driven Swein the Jarl away. The king therefore threatened Olav with the hardest punishment if he got the power to do it. He said that Olav should not be so bold as to take to himself the power the jarl had had, and all the Swedish king's men agreed that it was so. But when the Tronds learned for a truth that Swein the Jarl was dead and they could not expect him in Norway, all the common folk turned in obedience to King Olav. Many men then went from Trondheim to King Olav and became his men, and some sent word and token that they would serve him. In the autumn Olav went to Trondheim and held a thing with the bonders. He was taken as king in every folk district. He then went out to Nidaros; he had all the royal rents brought thither and made himself ready to settle there for the winter.

1 In O.S. *Gardariki*, i.e. Russia.  2 The frontier between Sweden and Norway.

57. King Olav had his house set in the king's garth in Nidaros. There a great hall was built with doors at both ends. The king's high-

seat was in the middle of the room, and next to him sat Grimkel, his bishop, and then his other priests, and outside sat his counsellors. In the other high-seat opposite to him sat his marshal Björn Digre and next to him the guests. When noble men came to the king they were greeted well. At that time they drank ale by the fires. He told off men to their duties, such as was the custom of kings. He had with him

The king's garth at Nidaros being built

sixty guardsmen and thirty guests [1] and he paid them wages and made laws for them. He had thirty huscarls who were to do such work in the garth as was needful and bring goods thither. He had also many thralls. In the garth there was a great shieling in which the bodyguard slept, and there was also a great room wherein the king held his counsel meetings.

58. It was the wont of King Olav to get up early in the morning, clothe himself and wash, then to go to Church and hear Matins and Morning Mass, and then go to meetings either to reconcile men or to say what seemed right to him. He called to him the great and the small and all those who were wise. He often had the laws told him which Hacon, the foster-son of Athelstan, had made in Trondheim. He made laws according to the counsel of the wisest men and added to them or took away from them wherever it seemed advisable. And the Christian law he set up according to the advice of Bishop Grimkel and other teachers; and set his mind on taking away heathendom and those customs which seemed to him to be opposed to Christianity. And it came about that the bonders agreed with the laws which the king set up. Thus says Sigvat:

Thou who sittest in the lofty poop        Which amongst all men
Can set up the law of the land            Shall stand with might.

1 'Guests' in this connection were a special élite corps of the king's huscarls or guards.

King Olav was an upright man, sober, and of few words, generous, but lusty for wealth. At that time, Sigvat the Scald was with the king—as was said before (chapter 43)—and many Iceland men too. King Olav asked closely as to how Christianity was held in Iceland. Then it seemed to him that it was far from being well, for they told him that in the way Christianity was held they were allowed according to the laws to eat horseflesh and to cast out children as heathen men did; and still more things they told him wherein there was harm to Christianity. They also told the king about many great men who were then in Iceland. Skafti Toroddson was then the lawman in the land. Much of other lands he learned from these men who knew most about it, as about their customs; but mostly he led his questions to Christianity and how it was held both in the Orkneys and in the Shetlands and in the Faroes, and he seemed to perceive that it must fall far short of being good. He often had such words in his mouth or else he was speaking about the law and the rights of the land.

59. The same winter messengers came west from Sweden from King Olav the Swede. Their leaders were two brothers, Torgaut the Harelip, and Asgaut the Steward, and they had twenty-four men. And when they came west over the Kjöl to Værdale, they called things with the bonders and talked with them; there they demanded taxes and dues in the name of the Swedish king. But the bonders took counsel with one another and they were of one mind in that they would grant what the Swedish king would have if King Olav did not demand land dues of them in his own name; they would not pay land dues to both of them. The messengers went away out along the dale and at every thing they held they got the same answer from the bonders, but no money. They then went out into Skaun; there they held a thing and also demanded dues, but everything went in the same wise as before. Then they went to Stjordale and there demanded a thing, but the bonders would not come. Then the messengers perceived that nothing was coming of their errand and Torgaut then wished to turn home to the east. "It does not seem to me", said Asgaut, "that we have carried out the king's errand; I will go to King Olav Digre, as the bonders will put their case to him." His decision now prevailed, and so they went out to the town and there took lodging. The day after they went to the king—he was then sitting at table—they greeted him and said that they came on the business of the Swedish king. The king bade them come back to him next day. Next day when the king had heard Mass, he went to his husthing; he had the Swedish king's men called thither and

bade them bring forth their business. Then Torgaut spoke and said first on what business they came and had been sent, and then how the Inner Tronds had answered them. Thereafter he bade the king give his finding as to what should become of their business. The king said: "Whilst the jarls were ruling here over the land it was not strange that the men of the land showed them obedience rather than bow themselves under foreign kings, for they had a birthright title to their lands; but it would have been most right if the jarls had

granted obedience and service to those kings who had a right to the kingdom, rather than to foreign kings, and rather than raising themselves up with unrest against the right kings and driving them from the land. But when King Olav the Swede makes demands on Norway, I know not what fair claim he can have, but we are minded what scathe we have got from him and his kinsmen". Then Asgaut said,

The Swedish king was very wroth when he heard the news

"It is not strange that thou art called Olav Digre, for with haughty words dost thou answer such a chieftain's message.[1] Thou knowest not rightly how heavy it will be for thee to bear the king's wrath; for so has it gone with them who had greater might than thou dost seem to me to have. But if thou wilt hold fast to thy kingdom, then will it be best for thee to go to him and be his man. Then will we pray with thee that he give thee this kingdom in fief". Then the king spoke quietly these words: "I will tell thee another plan, Asgaut. Go ye now back east to your king and tell him that early in spring I will make myself ready to go east to the boundary which has aforetime parted the kingdoms of the Kings of Norway and Sweden. He can come there, if he will, so that we can agree that each of us may have the kingdom which is his birthright". Then the messengers turned away and went back to their lodging. They now made themselves ready to go away and the king went to table. But the messengers then went into the king's garth, and when the door watchers saw it they told the king. He bade them not to let the

1 Cf. p. 218, n. 1, about King Olav's nickname *Digre*.

messengers in, "I will not speak with them", he said; then the messengers went away. Torgaut said that he and his men would turn home, but Asgaut said that he would carry out the king's errand. Then they parted. Torgaut went into Strind, but Asgaut and his twelve men turned up into Guldale. He thought of going south on to Möre and carrying out there the Swedish king's errand. But when King Olav was aware of it he sent guests[1] out after them and they found them out on Nes[2] near Stein. They took them prisoner and led them to Gaularas; there they raised up a gallows and hanged them so that they could be seen from far out in the fjord and in the fairway. Torgaut learned these tidings as he was going out of Trondheim; then he went his way till he met the Swedish king and told him what had happened on their journey. The king was very wroth when he heard the news. There was then no shortage of strong words.

60. The next spring King Olav called an army out from Trondheim and made himself ready to go east in the land. At that time an Iceland ship was to sail from Nidaros. King Olav sent bidding and tokens to Hjalti Skeggjason and called him to him; he sent greeting to Skafti the Lawman and the other men who counselled most for the laws in Iceland, that they should take from the laws all that seemed to him to be most against Christianity. Thereto he sent friendly words to all the men of the land. The king then went south over the land, and he stayed in every folk district and held things with the bonders. At every thing he had the Christian laws read out and the bidding which followed thereto. He then straightway did away with many ill habits amongst the folk and much heathendom, for the jarls had kept well the old laws and rights of the land, but about the holding of Christianity they had let everyone do as he would. At that time things were gone so far that folk in the districts by the sea were christened but Christian laws were unknown to most. But round about in the upper dales and in the fell districts they were heathen everywhere; for as soon as folk could rule themselves, that faith clung most in their minds which they had learnt in childhood. But hard conditions he promised those men who would not right themselves according to the king's words about Christianity, both great and small. King Olav was taken as king over the whole land at every law thing and no one spoke against him. When he was in Karmtsund[3] bidding went between him and Erling Skjalgson that they

should be reconciled, and a meeting was arranged in Hvitingsöy.[1] And when they met, they spoke together about being reconciled. It seemed to Erling that there was something else in the king's words than he had been told about, for Erling said that he would have all the land rents which Olav Trygvason and later the jarls, Swein and Hacon, had given him. "Then will I be thy man and true friend", he said. The king answered: "It looks to me, Erling, as if it is no worse for thee to take from me as great land rents as thou didst get from Eric the Jarl, the man who had done thee the greatest scathe. I will let thee be the most noble man in the land, although I will give out the land rents according to my own will. But I will not let it be as if the district chiefs are the heirs to my inheritance and that I should buy thy service for many times its worth". Erling had no mind to pray the king to change in this, for he saw that the king would not be led. He also saw that two choices were open to him: the one was not to make any agreement with the king and to let things go in whatever way they would; and the second was to let the king have his own way. He chose the latter, though it seemed much against him, and he said to the king: "This service will seem to be of most avail to thee as I grant it thee freely". They ended their talk. Thereafter Erling's kinsmen and friends went to him and bade him give in and act with wisdom but not with haughtiness. "Thou wilt always be", they said, "the most noble district chief in Norway both in doughtiness, kinship and wealth." Erling found that it was a good plan and that they who said this were acting with good will. Therefore he did so. And he put himself in the king's hands in this manner, that the king should make the choice. After that they parted and were, so to speak, reconciled. Olav then went farther east through the land.

61. As soon as King Olav came into the Vik and that was learnt, the Danes, who had offices there from the Danish kings, went away. They made for Denmark and would not wait for King Olav. But King Olav went in along the Vik and held a thing with the bonders. There all the folk of the land put themselves under him, and he took all the royal rents and stayed in the Vik during the summer. From Tunsberg he sailed east over Fold right by Svinasund. There the Swedish king's lordship began, and he had set sheriffs over it. In the north part was Eiliv the Gaut, and Roe Skjalgi was over the east part

---

1 The O.N. name for this island was *Hvitingsey*, meaning 'Hviting's island'. The name is equivalent to the English 'Whiting'. The island is situated on the coast close to the entrance of the Stavangerfjord.

right to the Elv.[1] Roe had his family on both sides of the Elv, and great houses in Hising.[2] He was a mighty man and very rich. Eiliv was also a man of great family. When King Olav came with his army to Ranrik he called there a thing with the land folk, and to the thing there came the men who lived on the isles or near the sea. And when the thing was sitting, Björn the Marshal spoke and bade the bonders greet King Olav in the same way as he had been received in other places in Norway. There was a noble bonder named Brynjulv Ulvaldi. He stood up and spoke: "We bonders know what has been of old time the right land boundary between the kings of Norway, Sweden, and Denmark; the Gautelv has formed the boundary from Väner[3] to the sea, and then the boundary goes north of the Marks to Eidaskog, and thereafter it is the Kjöl right away north to Finmark. So also it is that at different times

King Olav and Brynjulv speak alone

each has gone on the other's lands, and for a long time the Swedes have had power right to Svinasund, but—to tell you the truth—I know that it is the wish of many men to serve the King of Norway, as this seems better to them, but they have not courage enough for that. The kingdom of the Swedish king is both to the east of us and to the south of us, and it can be expected that the King of Norway will soon go north in the land where the strength of the land is greatest, and then shall we have no might to hold battle with the Gauts.[4] Now the king might find a good plan for us, if we wish to become his men". In the evening after the thing Brynjulv was the guest of the king and likewise the next day too; and they spoke much between themselves in a room. After that the king went east along the Vik; and when Eiliv learned that the king was there, he sent men to spy on his journey. Eiliv had thirty men; they were his swains. He was in the upper part of the settlement near the woods and he had there a gathering of bonders. Many bonders went

1 I.e. Göta River by Gothenburg.　2 *Hising* is the island by the mouth of the Göta River.　3 *Väner*, i.e. Lake Väner.　4 The men of Götland in Sweden.

to King Olav, and others sent words of friendship to him. Now men went between King Olav and Eiliv and for a long time the bonders bade each of them to call a thing between themselves and arrange peace in one way or another. They said to Eiliv that if they did not set themselves right according to the king's words they must expect hard dealing from him, and they said that Eiliv should not lack help. It was then arranged that Eiliv and his men should come down and hold a thing with the bonders and the king. The king sent Tore the Long, his guest-chief,[1] with eleven men to Brynjulv. Under their kirtles they had mail-coats, and hats over their helms. The day after the bonders came down in crowds with Eiliv. In his troop there was Brynjulv, and in Brynjulv's following there was Tore. The king brought his ships to the edge of a cliff which jutted into the sea. There he went up with his men and sat on the cliff, but farther up there was a flat piece of ground and there was the troop of bonders. But Eiliv's men stood in a rampart of shields before him. Björn the Marshal talked long and wisely on the king's behalf; and when he sat down, Eiliv stood up and was about to speak, but at that moment Tore the Long raised himself up, drew his sword, and struck Eiliv in the neck so that his head fell off. Then the whole host of the bonders leapt up, but the Gauts fled thence and Tore and his men slew some of them. But when the army stopped and the uproar ceased, the king stood up and said that the bonders should sit down. They did so, and now there was talk for a long time. The end of it was that the bonders put themselves in the hands of the king and promised him obedience, and in return he promised them not to part from them but to be with them till he and Olav, the Swedish king, could end their strife one way or another. After that King Olav put the northern district under him and in the summer he went east right to the Elv. He now got all the royal rents along the sea coast and on the islands. When summer was nearly gone, he turned back north into the Vik and went up the Raumelv.[2] Here is a great waterfall which is called Sarp. A ness reaches out in the river from the north towards the waterfall. King Olav had a wall of stone and turf and timber set up across the ness and ditches dug outside, and he made there a great earthwork; and within the bourgh he laid the foundations of a market town.[3] There he had a king's garth built and a church built

---

1 I.e. chamberlain.   2 I.e. Glommen.   3 *Sarpsborg*, i.e. the bourgh of Sarp, was called by this name at the beginning of the thirteenth century. Borregard, west of the Sarp waterfall, was another fortress or bourgh built by King Olav. The old fortress disappeared through a landslip in 1702, but part of 'St Olav's wold' still remains.

to St Mary. He had tofts marked out for other houses and he got men to build houses. In the autumn he had such wares brought thither as would be needed for wintering, and he settled there in the winter with a great assembly of men, but he had his own men in all the shires. He forbade the carrying of goods from the Vik up to Gautland, both herrings and salt, which the Gauts could ill be without. He held a great Yule feast, and bade to it many great bonders from the lordships.

62. There was a man called Eyvind Urarhorn whose kin came from East Agder. He was a great man and of good family. Every summer he went harrying, sometimes west across the sea, sometimes in the Baltic, or south to Frisia. He had a twenty-bencher, a well-fitted craft. He had been at the battle of Nesjar with King Olav and had given him help. When they parted there the king vowed him his friendship, and Eyvind vowed the king his help wherever he would crave it. In the winter Eyvind was at the Yule feast with King Olav and there he got gifts from him. Brynjulv Ulvaldi was also there with him, and he got as a Yule gift from the king a gold-dight sword and thereto the garth called Vettaland, which is a great manor farm. Brynjulv composed a poem about these gifts and it is quoted here:

Sikling[1] gave me
Sword and Vettaland.

Then the king gave him the name of landed man (or lenderman[2]) and Brynjulv was all his life the king's good friend.

63. That winter Trand the White went east from Trondheim to Jämtland to demand tribute in the name of King Olav Digre. But when he had got together the tribute the Swedish king's men came thither, and slew Trand and eleven men with him, took the tribute and bore it to the Swedish king. King Olav learned that and liked it little.

64. King Olav had Christian laws enforced throughout the Vik in the same way as he did in the north, and all went well, for the men of the Vik knew Christian customs better than the folk in the north of the land, because there were in the Vik both in winter and in summer many merchants, both Danes and Saxers. The men of the Vik also went much on trading journeys to England, and Saxony, Flanders and Denmark, and some went on viking raids and had winter settlements in Christian lands.

1 *Sikling*, i.e. the sea king.    2 *Lenderman* (in O.S. *lendr-maðr*) was a title given by the king to a person to whom the king had given lands and property.

65. In the spring King Olav sent bidding for Eyvind to come to him. They talked for a long time in a room. Straightway after that Eyvind went on a viking raid. He sailed south along the Vik and lay in by the Eikeröyer outside Hising.[1] There he learned that Roe Skjalgi had gone north to Ordost[2] and there had drawn together a troop and collected land dues, and he was then expected in the south. Eyvind then rowed into the Haugesunds[3] and Roe then rowed to the south, and they met in the sound and fought. There Roe fell, with nearly thirty men, and Eyvind took all the goods that Roe had had with him. Eyvind then went to the Baltic and was there on viking raids during the summer.

66. There was a man called Gudleik, the Gardariker,[4] whose kin were from Agder;[5] he was a seafarer and a great merchant; he was rich and went on trading journeys to many lands. He often went east to Gardarik. King Olav sent word to him that he wished to speak with him; and when Gudleik came, the king said to him that he would form a partnership with him and bade him buy for him such costly things as were hard to get in Norway. Gudleik answered that it should be according to the king's wish. Then the king handed over to him as much money as seemed right. In the summer Gudleik went to the Baltic. For a while he lay by Gotland;[6] then it was, as often happens, that not all his men held their tongue, and the folk on the land got news that a man on the ship was in partnership with Olav Digre. During the summer Gudleik went to the Baltic to Holmgard[7] and there bought fine skins which he procured for the king for his high robes of state, and besides he bought costly skins and an excellent table service. In the autumn when Gudleik went to the west he got contrary winds and for a long time he lay in by Öland.[8] Torgaut the Harelip had during the autumn spied on Gudleik's journey. He came upon his followers with a longship and fought with them. For a long time they warded themselves, but as the folk against them were too numerous, Gudleik and many of his shipmen fell and many were wounded. Torgaut took all their goods and King Olav's costly things. He and his men shared the booty equally, but he said that the Swedish king should have the costly things: "It is", he said, "a part of the dues that he has to take from Norway". Torgaut went east to Sweden

1 The island by the mouth of the Göta River.    2 Now Orust, a big island north of Hising.    3 Now Högasund, on the north side of the Göta River.    4 The Russian. 5 *Agder* is a shire in the south of Norway.    6 The island of Gotland in the Baltic. 7 *Holmgard*, i.e. Novgorod.    Many Scandinavians, principally Swedes, settled in Russia.    8 The island of Öland in the Baltic.

and there these tidings were quickly learnt. A little later Eyvind Urarhorn came to Öland, and when he learned this he came east after Torgaut and they met amid the Swedish skerries and fought. Torgaut fell and so did most of his men, or else they leaped into the sea. Then Eyvind took all the goods they had taken from Gudleik and likewise King Olav's costly things. Eyvind went back in the autumn to Norway and he then brought King Olav his costly goods. The king thanked him well for his journey and vowed him his friendship anew. At that time, King Olav had been king in Norway for three winters.

67. The same summer King Olav made his warships ready and he went back east to the Elv and stayed there for a long time during the summer. Messages went between King Olav and Ragn- vald the Jarl and Ingebjörg, Trygvi's daughter, the jarl's wife. She wished to help King Olav with all her might, and was very eager in this matter. Two things brought her to this: one was that there was kinship between her and King Olav; and the other was that she could not forget that the Swedish king had been party to defeating and causing the death of her brother

King Olav's meeting with Ragnvald the Jarl by the Göta River

Olav Trygvason, and she thought he had for this reason no claims on the rule of Norway. Through her prayers the jarl was well disposed to friendship with King Olav, and it came about that the king and the jarl called a meeting between themselves and met near the Elv. There they spoke of many things and especially about the enmity between the Kings of Norway and Sweden, and both of them said—as was true—that for both the men of the Vik and the Gauts it was the greatest harm that there should be no free trade between the lands; and at last they made peace between the districts till the next summer. At their parting they gave each other gifts and agreed to friendship. The king thereafter went north to the Vik, and he had then all the royal rents right to the Elv and all the land folk had put themselves under him. For days King Olav the Swede laid up so great enmity against Olav Haraldson that no man dared call him by his proper name in the king's hearing. They called him 'the proud man',[1] and they always had much ill to say of him if he were spoken of.

68. The bonders in the Vik said amongst themselves that the only end to the matter was for the kings to make peace and reconciliation between themselves, and they said that they were ill-placed if the kings warred against each other, but no one dared boldly bear this speech to the king. They bade Björn the Marshal put the matter before the king, that he should send men to the Swedish king to ask for peace on his own behalf. Björn was anxious to make objections, but through the entreaties of many of his friends he at last promised to speak about it to the king, though he said it foreboded him that the king would not take it well to yield to the Swedish king in anything. That summer Hjalti Skeggjason came to Norway from Iceland through a message of King Olav. He went straight to King Olav and the king greeted him well. He asked Hjalti to be with him and showed him to a seat at table near Björn the Marshal. They were table-mates and there was soon good friendship between them. Once when King Olav had a meeting with his men and the bonders and was holding counsel about the affairs of the land, Björn the Marshal spoke: "What plan hast thou, O king, about this enmity which is between Olav the Swedish king and thee? Now each of you has lost men against the other, but it is no more decided than before what part each shall have of the land. Thou hast now been here in the Vik one winter and two summers and hast turned thy back on the land in the north. There are men tired of staying here who have their lands and possessions in the north of the land. Now the landed men and other warriors, and likewise the bonders, wish the matter to be ended one way or another. And now when peace has been made with the jarl and the West Gauts who are nearest here, it seems best to the folk that thou shouldst send men to the Swedish king in thine own name. And many men there are indeed with the Swedish king who will support it, for it is to the gain of all those who inhabit the land both here and there". At Björn's speech the men made a great applause. Then the king said: "This plan, Björn, which thou hast brought forward is the best thou hast made for thyself and thou shalt go on this errand. Thou wilt have the advantage if thou hast counselled well, but if there is loss of life thou thyself hast most blame therein. It is also thy office to say at these meetings what I wish to have brought forward". Then the king stood up, went to church, and had High Mass sung before him. He then went to table. The next day, Hjalti

[1] In O.S. *hinn digra mann.*

said to Björn: "Wherefore art thou not glad, man? Art thou sick, or wroth with anyone?" Björn then told him about his talk with the king and called this a fatal errand. Hjalti said: "So it is in following kings that such men have great honour and are exalted before other men, but often they come in peril of their lives and with both lots they should be well content. Great is the king's good luck, and great honour will be won on this journey if it goes well". Björn answered: "Thou makest light of the journey. Perhaps thou wilt go with me, for the king said that I should have my own following of men on the journey". Hjalti said: "Certainly shall I go with thee if thou wilt, for hardly shall I get a better fellow if I part from thee".

69. A few days after, when King Olav was at the meeting, Björn came there with eleven men. He told the king that they were ready to go on their errand and their steeds stood outside saddled. "I now wish to know", said Björn, "with what message I shall go, or what counsel thou wilt give us." The king said, "Ye shall bear these my words to the Swedish king, that I will make peace between our lands according to the boundaries which Olav Trygvason had before me, and let it be bound with agreements that neither of us goes beyond them. But no one need speak of the loss of men if this shall be agreed upon, for the Swedish king cannot with goods requite the loss of men we have had through the Swedes". Then the king stood up and went out with Björn and his men; he then took up a gold-decked sword and a gold finger-ring and gave them to Björn: "This sword I give to thee which Ragnvald the Jarl gave to me in the summer. To him shalt thou go, and bear to him these my words that he grant thee counsel and help so that thou mayest carry out this errand; and to me it will seem well done if thou hearest the Swedish king's words whether he say yea or nay. But this ring shalt thou bear to Ragnvald the Jarl: this token will he know".

Hjalti went before the king and greeted him: "We now need much that thou givest us thy good luck on this journey", and he added that he hoped they might meet again with luck. The king asked whether Hjalti was going thence. "With Björn", he said. The king said: "It will help them on this journey if thou goest with them, for thou hast often been proved to have luck. Know this for certain that I shall put my whole mind on it, if that counts anything, and give my good luck to thee and all of you". Björn and the others now rode their way and came to the household of Ragnvald the Jarl. There they were greeted well. Björn was a famous man and known both by his appearance and his speech by all who had seen King Olav, for at every thing Björn stood up and spoke the king's messages. Ingebjörg, the jarl's wife, went up to Hjalti and talked to him. She knew him because she was with her brother Olav Trygvason when Hjalti was once in their company; and she claimed kinship between the king and Vilborg, Hjalti's wife, for Eric Bjodaskalli (father of Astrid, King Olav Trygvason's mother) and Bodvar (father of Alov, the mother of Gissur the White, Vilborg's father) were brothers, both sons of Viking-Kari, a landed man of Voss.[1] And now they

Björn the Marshal shows Ragnvald the Jarl King Olav's tokens

were there in good cheer. One day Björn and his men went to talk with the jarl and Ingebjörg. Then Björn brought forth his errand and showed the jarl his tokens. The jarl asked: "What has happened to thee, Björn, that the king wishes thee dead? So little success wilt thou have with this message that no one who speaks these words before the Swedish king will come away without punishment. Olav, the Swedish king, is more arrogant than to allow men to bear in his presence such talk as is against him". Then said Björn: "Nothing has happened for which King Olav has got wroth with me, but there are many of his plans, both for himself and for his men, which for anxious men seem daring whatever the outcome. But all his plans have as yet turned out lucky and we hope that it will do so even now. Now, to tell you the truth, jarl, I will go to the Swedish king and not

1 *Voss*, near Bergen.

turn back before I have let him hear all those words that King Olav bade me bring to his ears, unless death hinders me, or I am fettered so that I cannot come forth. I will do this whether you act upon the king's words or not". Then said Ingebjörg: "I will straightway lay bare my mind, jarl; thou shalt put all thy strength in furthering King Olav's message, so that this errand shall come before the Swedish king whatever he may answer to it, even if we should draw upon ourselves the wrath of the Swedish king or should lose all our possessions and wealth; I would far rather risk that, than that it should be learnt that thou didst put aside King Olav's message for fear of the Swedish king. Thou hast thy birth and strength of kinship and every claim to be so free here in Sweden that thou canst say what well beseems and which all can hear, either many or few, great or small, or even the king himself". The jarl answered: "I can see clearly enough what thou art egging me on to. Now it may be that thou dost counsel me to promise the king's men to help them, so that they can manage to carry out their errand before the Swedish king, whether the king likes it well or ill. But according to my own plan will I let it go forward as to what way the matter shall be taken in hand. I will not run after the headstrong ways of Björn or any other man in so hard a matter. I wish them to stay with me till the time comes when it seems to me somewhat better that this errand can go forward". And when the jarl had laid bare to them that he would support them in this matter and give his help, Björn thanked him well and said that he would follow his counsel. Björn and his following now stayed a long time with the jarl.

70. Ingebjörg was very friendly towards them. Björn often spoke with her about the matter and it seemed ill that the journey should be put back so much. Hjalti also often talked together with them about it. He said: "I can go to the king if you wish. I am not a Norseman, and the Swedes will not be prejudiced against me. I have learned that with the Swedish king there are Iceland men in his favour, Gissur the Black and Ottar the Black, the king's scalds, and they are known to me. From them I can get to know what to believe about the Swedish king, whether in this matter there is so little prospect as it now appears, or whether there are other possibilities. I shall find for my errand such reason as seems fitting to me". That seemed to Ingebjörg and Björn a very clever plan and they were quite united about it. Ingebjörg now fitted out Hjalti's journey. She got him two Gauts and bade them follow him and be his helpers both for service and if he wished to send them anywhere. Ingebjörg gave him

twenty marks of silver as spending money. She sent word and tokens by him to Ingegerd, King Olav's daughter, to put her whole mind to this matter in whatever he might have need to crave her help. Hjalti left as soon as he was ready. And when he came to King Olav, he straightway found Gissur and Ottar, the scalds; they greeted him with joy and went with him at once before the king; they told the king that the man who was come thither was their countryman; and was a very much honoured man in the land. They bade the king greet him well. The king bade them take Hjalti and his followers with them in their troop. And when Hjalti had stayed there some time and was well known amongst the men, all liked him well. The scalds were often with the king, for they were bold of speech. They often sat in the daytime before the king's high-seat and Hjalti with them; they esteemed him most in all things. He was then well known also to the king, who often talked with him and asked tidings of Iceland.

71. Before Björn had gone from home he had asked Sigvat the Scald to go with him, for Sigvat was at that time with King Olav, but men were not wishful to go on that journey. There was good friendship between Björn and Sigvat. Sigvat quoth:

Always have I had a good time / O Björn, for me thou hast often
From all the battle-bold / Done much with our prince;
Warrior's good marshals / O swinger of the sword, thou givest
Who go before the king's knee. / Good counsel, as thou canst.

And when they rode up to Gautland, Sigvat quoth these verses:

Sigvat recites for his companions

Oft was I glad out in the storm,
When the hard wind strained
The sails of the king
In the blasts out on Strind's fjords.

The steed of the deep trotted on
And the keels had cleft the waves at
Lister
Where through the sound
We let the ships go.

The bold king's ships
We let ride all tilted
Outside the good land
By the island early in summer.

But when the sea kings' steeds
In autumn are drawn upon land,
I take the task of riding,
I choose changing pursuits.

And when they rode up through Gautland late one evening, Sigvat quoth:

The lean steed trots
In the dusk on the long ways.
His hoof may tear up the turf.
(We have now little daylight.)

Now my dun horse bears me
Over the streams far from Denmark.
The steed slipped with his foot
In the ditch, in the twilight.

Then they rode into the market town of Skara[1] and forth through the street[2] to the jarl's dwelling. He quoth:

The proud girls shall peep out.
They shall see by the reek
How fast we ride
Through Ragnvald's town.

Let us drive on the horses
So that the good-hearted women
In the houses shall hear
The tramp of our steeds a long way off.

72. One day Hjalti and the scalds went before the king. Hjalti then spoke these words: "It is, O king, as you know, that I have come hither to you and have been travelling a long and dangerous way. Since I have come over the sea and have got to know of your great name, it seemed foolish to me to go home without having seen you and your glory. But there is a law between Iceland and Norway that when Iceland men come to Norway they pay the land dues. When I came over the sea I took the land dues from all my shipmates; but when I knew it to be right that you had power over Norway I came to you to bring you the land dues". He showed the king the silver and poured ten marks of it into Gissur the Black's lap. The king spoke: "Few have brought such to us from Norway for some time. I will grant you thanks and favour, Hjalti, for thou hast shown much eagerness in bringing the land dues to us rather than in paying them to our foes. But yet I wish thee to take this money from me and therewith my friendship". Hjalti thanked the king with many words and from that time Hjalti came into the greatest favour with the king and was often talking with him. It seemed to the king, as was true, that Hjalti was a wise man and of good words. Hjalti told Gissur

---

1 *Skara* is the most important town in Vestergötland.   2 The Scandinavian word *stræde* or *stræte* = street (both originating from the Latin *strata*) is not so frequently seen in Norway as in Denmark. In Sweden and Norway the word *gate* or *gata* is used and it is probably not a mere coincidence that, for instance, in York, where the Norsemen had great influence, the designation *gate* is often met with, whilst in the south of England, where the Danes were powerful, *street* is used everywhere. Bishopsgate, Ludgate, Newgate, etc., in London derive their names from the gates which existed in the London Wall, and the word in this instance has a somewhat different meaning from the Scandinavian *gate*. In O.S. the word *gatt* means 'door opening'. These names are cognate with O.E. *geat*.

and Ottar that he had been sent with tokens to Ingegerd the king's daughter to get her help and friendship, and he asked them to help him speak with her. They said that that was not hard, and one day they went to her house where she sat drinking with many men. She greeted the scalds well, for she knew them. Hjalti brought greetings to her from Ingebjörg, the jarl's wife, and said that she had sent him thither to get her help and friendship, and he brought out the tokens. The king's daughter greeted him, and said that he had a right to her friendship. They sat there for a long time during the day and drank. She asked Hjalti of many tidings and bade him come there often to talk with her. He did so; he often came there and talked with the king's daughter. He told her in secrecy about Björn and his journey and asked what she thought about how the Swedish king would take the matter, that peace should be made between the kings. The king's daughter said that she believed that it was useless to try and get the king to make peace with Olav Digre. She said that the king was so wroth with Olav that he would not hear him named. One day Hjalti sat before the king talking with him; the king was then very merry, for he had drunk much. Then Hjalti said to the king: "Much glory of all kinds can be seen here and now I have seen what I have often heard tell, that no king in the north is so noble as thou art. It is very awkward that we have come here on so long and so perilous a journey; first there is the great ocean and then it is not peaceful to go through Norway for those men who will come hither in friendship. But why do folk not seek to bring words of peace between you and Olav Digre? Much talk about it have I heard in Norway and likewise in West Gautland that all were wishful that peace be made, and it was told me with truth about the King of Norway's words that he had a wish to be reconciled with you. I know it will come to this, that he will understand that he has much less might than you have. It is also told that he is thinking of wooing thy daughter Ingegerd, and such a thing would give hope of lasting peace. He is also an outstanding man according to all that I have heard truthful men say about him". Then the king answered: "Such things thou shalt not say, Hjalti, but I will not take these words ill of thee, for thou knowest not what has to be considered: the haughty man shall never be called king at my court, and he is of much less worth than many say; and thou wilt understand, when I tell thee, that such a relationship cannot be fitting, for I am the tenth king in Upsala, and each of us has taken the kingdom one after the other and been sole king over Sweden and many other great lands; and all have been kings over the other kings in the north.[1] But Norway is little inhabited and the dwellings are spread apart. They have been small kings there, though Harald Hairfair was the mightiest king in that land, and he had battles with the kings of the folk districts and broke them down under him. He understood what his own share was, not to be greedy after the power of Sweden, and so the Swedish kings left him in peace; and besides, it came about that there was kinship between them. But when Hacon, the foster-son of Athelstan, was in Norway, he stayed there in peace until he made war in Gautland and Denmark; but afterwards there rose an army against him and he was driven from the land. Gunhild's sons were likewise cut off from life as soon as they became disobedient to the Danish king. Then Harald Gormson added Norway to his own kingdom and made it liable for taxes; but still it seemed to us that King Harald Gormson stood far behind the Upsala king, for our kinsman Styrbjörn cowed him and Harald became his man. But yet my father, Eric the Victorious, stepped over the head of Styrbjörn when they tried their strength against each other. But when Olav Trygvason came to Norway and called himself king, we did not let him fulfil it, for Swein the Danish king and I went and deprived him of his life. Now I have possessed myself of Norway and with no less might than thou now hearest of, and with no less claim than that I sought it in battle and overcame the king who formerly ruled there. As a wise man thou mayest understand that it must be far from me to give that kingdom freely to the haughty man. And it is strange that he remembers not that he hardly came out of Lögrinn[2] when we had shut him in, for I think that he had other things in his mind—if he could only get away with his life —than to hold battle with us Swedes more often. Now, Hjalti, thou shalt not again have words in thy mouth to talk about this before me". Hjalti found there was little prospect of the king's listening to any attempts at peace. He left it and began to talk about something else. Somewhat later when Hjalti was talking with Ingegerd, the king's daughter, he told her all his talk with the king. She said that she had expected such an answer from the king. Hjalti bade her put in some word to the king and said that that would soon be of avail. She said that the king would not listen to what she said: "but I may talk about

1 The succession of kings, which Snorre here refers to, commences with (i) Sigurd Ring (cf. 'History of Harald Hairfair', chapter 13); (ii) Ragnar Lodbrok (cf. *ibid.*); (iii) Björn Ironside; (iv) Eric; (v) Björn of Hauge; (vi) Björn's brother, Emund; (vii) Eric Emundson (cf. *ibid.*); (viii) Björn Gamle (or the Old) (cf. *ibid.* chapter 29); (ix) Eric the Victorious (cf. 'History of Olav Trygvason', chapter 43); (x) Olav. 2 Lake Mälar.

it if thou wishest", she said. Hjalti answered that he would be thankful for it. One day Ingegerd, the king's daughter, was in talk with her father, and when she found that the king was in good spirits she said: "What intention have you about the hostility between you and Olav Digre? Many men are now lamenting this strife: some say that they have lost goods and some have lost kinsmen through the Norsemen, and none of your men can go into Norway under these conditions. It was very unlucky that you laid claim to the kingdom of Norway. That land is poor, and bad to cross, and the folk not to be trusted: the men in that land would rather have any one for their king than you. Now if I might counsel, you should leave off claiming Norway and rather push yourself in the Baltic, for that kingdom the earlier Swedish kings had and Styrbjörn[1] put it under himself. But let Olav Digre have the land of his inheritance, and make peace with him". The king answered wrathfully: "It is thy counsel, Ingegerd, that I shall give up the kingdom of Norway and wed thee to Olav Digre. No," he said, "something else shall happen instead. Rather shall it come about that in the winter at the Upsala thing, I shall make known before all the Swedes that all the folk shall be called up before the ice is gone from the waters. I shall go to Norway and lay waste that land with spear and sword, and burn everything: and in that way pay them for breaking their troth". The king was now so raging that she could not answer him a single word. She then went away. Hjalti was looking out and straightway went to meet her. He asked her how her errand had sped with the king. She answered that it had gone as she had expected: no one could come with such words to the king unless he held out threats in return. She bade Hjalti never mention the matter to the king. When Ingegerd and Hjalti talked together they often talked about Olav Digre. He often spoke to her about him and his ways; and he praised him as he knew how to, and what he said was true. All that seemed good to her. And once when they were talking together Hjalti said: "May I, O king's daughter, with thy leave talk about that which lies in my heart?" "Speak", she said, "so that I alone hear it." Then said Hjalti: "How wouldst thou answer if Olav, the King of Norway, sent men to thee to woo thee for him?" She blushed and answered slowly and coolly: "I am not steady in my mind to answer that, for I think I shall have no need to give answer to it; but if Olav is such a man of parts as you say about him, then could I not wish my husband

---

1 *Styrbjörn* was the son of the brother of Eric the Victorious. He harried in the Baltic Provinces and conquered Jomsborg on the island of Wollin, at the mouth of the River Oder.

otherwise, if it be not so that thou hast praised him too highly in many things". Hjalti said that in nothing had he spoken better of the king than was true. They often talked of this matter between themselves. Ingegerd bade Hjalti beware of speaking about it in the presence of others—"because the king would be wroth with thee if he got to know". Hjalti told it to Gissur and Ottar, the scalds; they said that it would be the happiest plan if it could be put forward. Ottar was bold of speech and beloved by royalty. He was soon talking about it with the king's daughter and, like Hjalti, he reckoned up for her the king's good qualities. She and Hjalti and Ottar often talked together about this matter; and when Hjalti had now got full knowledge as to the outcome of his errand, he sent away the Gautish men who had followed him thither and he let them go back to the jarl with the letters which Ingegerd, the king's daughter, and Hjalti were sending to the jarl and Ingebjörg. Hjalti also let fall a hint about the matters he had mentioned to Ingegerd and likewise about her answer. The messengers came to the jarl somewhat before Yule.

73. When King Olav had sent Björn and his following east to Gautland, he sent other men to the Uplands for the purpose of ordering feasts for him; that winter he would go feasting through the Uplands; for it had been the wont of former kings to go feasting through the Uplands every third winter. The king began his journey from Borg in the autumn. He went first to Vingulmark; he so arranged his journey that he began feasting in the neighbourhood of the forest dwellings, and called to him all the men of the dwellings and especially all those who dwelt farthest from the lordships. He asked them closely about the upholding of Christianity in those parts, and where improvements seemed needful he taught them the right ways and laid great penalties upon them, if there were people who would not give up their heathen ways. He drove some away from the land, some he caused to be maimed either in hand or foot, or to have their eyes plucked out, and some he caused to be hanged or beheaded; and no one he let go unpunished who would not serve God. In such wise he went over the whole district. He punished the mighty with like strength as he punished the poor. He gave them priests and put as many of them in the lordships as he thought needful. He had three hundred (three hundred and sixty) warriors when he went up to Raumarik. He soon found that Christianity was upheld less and less the farther he went up into the land. He continued still in the same wise and turned the whole folk to the right faith, and gave heavy punishments to those who would not listen to his words.

74. When the king who ruled over Raumarik learned this, it seemed to him to be a very difficult matter, for every day there came to him many men, many rich, others poor, who complained of such things to him. The king took the plan of going up to Hedemark to King Rörik, for he was the wisest of the kings who were there. And when the kings had spoken together, they agreed to send word north to the Dales[1] to King Gudröd, and likewise to Hadeland to the king who was there, bidding them come to Hedemark to meet them. They did not withhold themselves from the journey, and in such wise the

The Upland kings went to a room
to take counsel

five kings met in Hedemark at a place called Ringsaker; Ring was the fifth king, the brother of King Rörik. The kings went first into a room to talk. He who was from Raumarik began first and spoke about Olav Digre's journey and about the trouble he made both by slaying men and by maiming them; some he drove from the land, and took to himself the goods of all those who in any wise spoke against him. He went about in the land with a whole army, but not with the

number of men the law allowed. He also said that because of this trouble he had fled thither and that likewise many other great men from Raumarik had fled from their inheritances. "But even if this trouble is now nearest us, it will not be long before you come in for the same thing; and it is therefore best that we should all take counsel together what plan we shall take up." And when he had finished his speech the kings turned to Rörik for an answer. He said: "Now has that come about which I guessed would happen—when we held the meeting in Hadeland and ye were all eager to raise him up over our heads—that he would be 'hard to take by the horns', when he had the power over the land. Now there are two choices at hand; one is that we all go to him and leave it to him to 'shear and shape' everything between us—and I think that is the best we can do. The second is that we rise up against him whilst he has not yet gone far through the land. And even if he had three hundred or four

1 Gudbrandsdale.

hundred men he would not overpower us if we all took one plan. But it is often harder for those to win amongst whom there are many of equal might than where one only is the leader of the army. My counsel is rather that we do not venture to try our luck with Olav Haraldson". After that each of the kings spoke as seemed best to him; some warned, others egged on, and nothing was settled. They held that in both plans there were difficulties. Then Gudröd, King of the Dales, began and spoke thus: "It seems strange to me that ye waver in settling this matter; also that ye are thoroughly afraid of Olav. We are here five kings and none of us is of lower birth than he. We granted him strength to fight against Swein the Jarl and by our power he has possessed himself of this land. But if he will now forbid each of us the little kingdom that we have hitherto held and practise pains and compulsion against us, then I will say for my part that I will not find myself in subjection to this king, and I call each of you a poor man who is afraid of taking Olav's life when he comes hither into our lands in Hedemark; for this may be said to you that never shall we bear a free head so long as Olav is alive". After being egged on thus they all turned to this counsel. Then said Rörik: "It seems to me about this plan that we must needs strengthen our ties so that none of us wavers in faith with the others. Now ye are thinking that when Olav comes hither to Hedemark ye will fall upon him at a place arranged, but then I should have no trust in you if some of you were north in the Dales and others were far out in Hedemark. If this plan shall be ratified between us I wish us all to be together day and night till this plan is brought forth". The kings agreed to that, and now they all went off together. They bade a feast be made ready for them out on Ringsaker. They had drinks all round. They sent spies out in Raumarik; some of the spies they bade go out straightway, and others they bade turn back, so that they knew every day and night how things went with King Olav's journeys and the number of his men. King Olav went feasting in Raumarik and everywhere he did in the same wise as was told before. But when the food did not last out because of the crowd of men, he requested the bonders to increase the feasts where it seemed necessary for him to stop. In some places he stayed a shorter time than was previously arranged, and therefore his journey to the water[1] was quicker than was agreed upon. And when the kings had confirmed the plan between themselves, they sent bidding and called to them the landed men and mighty bonders from all those folk districts. When the latter came,

1 I.e. Lake Mjöse.

the kings held a meeting with them in a room and laid bare to them this plan; they decided a day when this plan should be furthered, and they agreed that each of the kings should have three hundred (three hundred and sixty) men. They then sent the landed men back, to gather men and then come to the kings there as it was arranged. Most men liked this plan well, but yet it was as is always said, that "every man has a friend amid his foes".

75. Ketel of Ringanes was at that meeting. When he came home in the evening he got food for his night meal and then he and his huscarls clad themselves. He then went down to the water and took the vessel which he owned and which King Olav had given him, and thrust it into the water. All the tackle was in the boathouse. They took that and set themselves at the oars, and rowed out along the water. Ketel had forty men, all well armed. Early in the morning they came out to Vasenda;[1] from there Ketel went with twenty men, and the other twenty he left to guard the ship. King Olav was then at Eid[2] in Upper Raumarik. Ketel came there when the king was coming from Matins; he greeted Ketel kindly. Ketel said that he must straightway speak with the king, and so the two of them went together to talk. Then Ketel told the king what plan the kings had on hand, and all the plan of which he had got knowledge. And when the king was aware of it, he called men to him; some he sent out into the farms and bade them bring horses to him; others he sent to the water to take such rowing boats as they could get hold of, and keep them in readiness for him. Thereupon he went to church and had Mass sung before him. After that he went to the table. When he had taken food he quickly made himself ready and went to the water; there the ships came to meet him. He himself stepped into the big vessel and with him as many men as the vessel had room for; all the others got themselves ships as best they could. When it was evening they put out from land. It was calm weather and they rowed up along the water. The king had nearly four hundred (four hundred and eighty) men. Before dawn he came up to Ringsaker, but the watchmen were aware of nothing till the army came up to the farm. Ketel and his men knew exactly in what houses the kings slept. King Olav had all these houses taken and watched so that no man should come out, and so they waited for daylight. The kings had no might of men to protect them and they were all taken prisoner and brought before the king. King Rörik was a very wise man and hard of counsel; King Olav thought that he could not trust him, even if he made

1 Vassenden by Minne.    2 *Eid*, by Eidsvold (on the south shore of Lake Mjöse).

terms with him, and so he had Rörik blinded in both eyes and took him with him. He made them cut off the tongue of Gudröd the Dale king. He caused Ring and two others to swear oaths to him that they would go away from Norway and never come back. And of the landed men and bonders who were guilty of this treachery, he drove some from the land, others he maimed and with some he made terms. About this Ottar the Black says:

Gold-giving prince!
Thou hast paid in full
With ill the evil plots
Of all the landed men.
Army leader, thou didst once
Let the kings of Hedemark
Who used treacherous plans
Have fitting reward.

Warrior prince! Thou hast driven
The Dagling kings away from the land.
Swinger of sword! Thy strength
Was greater than theirs.

Each of the kings fled far
From thee, as all men know.
And then thou tookest the tongue
Of him who ruled farthest north.

Now thou rulest over
All that realm which five kings
Formerly owned. God hath
Given thee great victories.
The broad family lands
East to Eid lie under thee.
No swinger of sword ever
Owned such a land.

King Olav put under him the kingdoms which these five kings had had, and took hostages from the landed men and the bonders. He took feast money from Dale in the north and from far about in Hedemark. He then turned back to Raumarik, and thereafter went west to Hadeland. That winter Sigurd Syr, his step-father, died. King Olav then turned to Ringerik, and his mother Asta made a great feast for him. Olav then bore the name of king of all Norway.

76. It is said that when King Olav was at the feast with Asta, his mother, she led forth her children to show him. The king set his brother Guthorm on his knee, and on the other knee he set his brother Halvdan. The king looked on the boys, then he frowned and looked wrathfully at them; the boys were afraid. Then Asta brought to him her youngest son who was called Harald and who was three years old.[1] The king frowned at him, but the boy looked straight back at him. Then the king took the boy by the hair and pulled it, but the boy took the king by the beard and tugged it. Then said the king: "Vindictive wilt thou be later on, my kinsman". The day after the king went out in the village with Asta his mother. They went to a tarn where the boys, Guthorm and Halvdan, Asta's sons, were playing. They had made great farms and great lathes with many cows

[1] The later Harald Hardrade who fell at Stamford Bridge (in Yorkshire) against Harold Godwinson in 1066.

and many sheep; for that was their game. A short way along the tarn there was a muddy creek, and there was Harald, and he had chips of wood which were floating in great numbers near the shore. The king asked him what that was for. They were, he said, his warships.

King Olav and his half-brothers

Then the king laughed at it and said: "It may be, my kinsman, that thou wilt sometime command ships". Then the king called Halvdan and Guthorm to him, and he asked Guthorm: "What wouldst thou have most of, my kinsman?" "Fields", he said. The king said: "How great fields wouldst thou have?" He answered: "I would that all this ness that reaches out into the water were sown every summer". At that time there were ten farms on it and so the king answered: "Much corn might grow thereon". Then the king asked Halvdan what he would have most of. "Cows", he said. The king asked him: "How many cows wouldst thou have?" Halvdan said: "So many that when they go to the water they stand as thickly as possible round the water". The king answered: "Great possessions wilt thou have. That is like thy father". Then the king asked Harald: "What wouldst thou have most of?" "Huscarls", he answered. The king said: "How many wilt thou have?" "I would like so many that at one meal they would eat my brother Halvdan's cows." The king laughed at that and said to Asta, "Here, mother, thou art certainly bringing up a king". Nothing more is told of them at that time.

77. In Sweden there was an age-old custom whilst they were still heathen that there should be a blood offering in Upsala during Goodmonth.[1] Then they would sacrifice for peace and victory for their king. And thither would they come from all over Sweden. There also were all the Swedish things. There was besides a market and a fair, and it lasted a week. But when Christianity came to Sweden they still kept the law thing and the market there. And when Christianity prevailed throughout Sweden and the kings no longer sat in Upsala,

1 *Goodmonth* lasted from the middle of February until the middle of March.

the market was shifted and held at Candlemas. It has always been held then ever since, but now it does not last more than three days. The thing of the Swedes is there and to it they come from all over the land. Sweden lies in many parts. One part is West Gautland with Värmland and Markerland, and all that belongs to it; and it is so great a district that under the bishop who is over it there are eleven hundred churches. The second part of the land is East Gautland where there is a second bishop's see. Gotland and Öland belong to this see now, and all together it is a much greater bishopric. In Sweden itself there is a part called Södermanland, and that is a bishopric. Then there is a part called Vestmanland or Fjadrundaland, and that too is a bishopric. Then there is the third part of Sweden called Tiundaland,

Map of Sweden at the time of Snorre Sturlason

and the fourth part called Attundaland.[1] Then there is a fifth called Sjaland and all that belongs to it lies east along the sea coast. Tiundaland is the wealthiest and best peopled part of Sweden. The whole kingdom turns towards it; for in it is Upsala, the king's seat and the

1 Vexiö bishopric is not mentioned, but it probably did not exist at that time.

archbishop's see; and from that the Upsala Öde[1] takes its name. The Swedes call the Swedish king's wealth the Upsala Öde. Each of these districts has its own law thing and its own laws on many questions. Over every law district there is a lawman and he rules mostly over the bonders; for what he utters shall be law. But if king or jarl or bishops go through the land and hold things with the bonders, then the lawman answers on the bonders' behalf. But they all support him so that the mightiest men dare hardly come to their *Althing*[2] if the bonders and lawman do not let them. But if the laws are different at the district things, then shall they go by the Upsala law, and all the other lawmen shall be under the lawman who is in Tiundaland.

78. At that time there was in Tiundaland a lawman who was called Torgny; his father was called Torgny Torgnyson. His forefathers had been lawmen in Tiundaland in the time of many kings. Torgny was old, he had a great bodyguard and he was called the wisest man in Sweden. He was the kinsman and foster-father of Ragnvald the Jarl. Now we are going to tell how there came to Ragnvald the Jarl the men whom Ingegerd, the king's daughter, and Hjalti had sent from the east. They put forth their errand to Ragnvald the Jarl and Ingebjörg his wife, and said that the king's daughter had often talked to the Swedish king about peace between him and King Olav Digre; she was King Olav's best friend, but the Swedish king was wroth every time she mentioned Olav. And there seemed to her under such circumstances to be little hope of peace. The jarl told Björn what he had learned from the east. But Björn still said the same: he would not turn back before he had met the Swedish king and said that the jarl had promised him to go with him to the Swedish king. It was now getting well on in winter and straightway after Yule the jarl made himself ready for the journey and he had sixty men; in his following there were Björn the Marshal and his companions. The jarl went straight east into Sweden. When he got up into the land he sent his men beforehand to Upsala with bidding to Ingegerd, the king's daughter, to come out to Ullaraker to meet him; she had great estates there.[3] And when the jarl's word came to the king's daughter, she did not forgo the journey but made herself ready with many men. Hjalti wished to go with her. But before he went away, he went to

---

1 *Upsala Öde* or the Swedish king's Crown property; cf. 'Ynglinga Saga', chapter 10.
2 A thing held for the whole country.   3 *Ullaraker* was a district on the west side of the Fyris River, near the present Upsala, whilst Old Upsala was situated to the north on the east side of the river in the district of Vaxhalda (now Vaksala)—Ullaraker's thing place was situated near the present Bondkyrka (Farmer's Church) at Upsala.

King Olav and said: "Farewell, O king; it may be truly said that nowhere have I seen such great glory as here with you. I shall bear the word forth wherever I come hereafter. For that I will ask you, O king, to be my friend". The king answered: "Wherefore dost thou talk as if thou hadst a wish to go away? Where shalt thou go?" Hjalti answered: "I shall ride out to Ullaraker with Ingegerd, thy daughter". The king said: "Then farewell. Thou art a wise man and of good manners, and thou understandest well how to bear thyself amongst kings". Thereafter Hjalti went away. Ingegerd, the king's daughter, rode out to her place at Ullaraker and had a great feast made ready there for the jarl. So the jarl came thither and was greeted well. He stayed there some nights. After that, he and the king's daughter talked much together, but mostly about the Swedish king and the King of Norway. She told the jarl that there seemed to her to be little hope of peace. Then the jarl said: "How wouldst thou be minded, kinswoman, if Olav, King of Norway, were to woo thee? It seems to us that the outlook for peace would be nearest if such kinship could be made between the kings. But I will not take up this matter if I know that it is against thy will". She answered: "My father will decide about my marriage, but among my kinsmen I would sooner take counsel from thee on such things as seem weighty to me. But how wise a plan does this seem to thee?" The jarl urged her much and reckoned up in King Olav's praise many things which were very honourable, and told her truly about that which had happened fairly recently, that King Olav had in one morning seized five kings, taken the kingdoms from them all, and put their possessions and riches in his own power. Much they talked together about this matter, and they were agreed about everything between themselves. The jarl went away when he was ready, and Hjalti with him.

79. One day towards evening Ragnvald the Jarl came to Torgny the Lawman's stead[1] where there were great and splendid houses and many men standing outside. They greeted the jarl well and took care of the horses and belongings. The jarl went into the hall and there was a great crowd of folk within. On the high-seat there sat an old man, and Björn and his men had never seen such a big man. His

---

1 The O.S. word *staðr* meaning 'stead' does not exist any longer in the northern countries and the words *sted* and *stad* have taken its place. These words are cognate with O.E. *stede* and modern *stead* used in place names such as Hampstead, Banstead, East Grinstead, Halstead, Horstead, Oxted, etc. etc. In Ireland the ending *-ster* in Ulster, Leinster and Munster is connected with O.N. *staðir*, plur. of *staðr*.

beard was so great that it lay in his lap and spread all over his chest. He was a fine and noble man. The jarl went to him and greeted him, and Torgny welcomed him and bade him go to the seat in which he was wont to sit. The jarl sat down in the middle on the other side opposite Torgny. They were there for some nights before the jarl laid bare his business. He asked Torgny to go into the dinner-hall with him. Björn and his men went there with the jarl. The jarl began

his words and told how Olav, King of Norway, had sent his men east to him to make peace, and he talked for a long time about how hard it was for the West Gauts with this unrest between them and Norway. He also told how King Olav of Norway had sent men thither —and the king's messengers were here now—and how he had promised them to go with them to the Swedish king. He said that the Swedish king took this matter so heavily that he said it would be to no man's good to come with this matter to him. "Now it is, foster-father", said the jarl, "that I alone am not enough in this matter. I have therefore

Torgny the Lawman speaks against the Swedish king at the Upsala thing

sought thee and I hope for good counsel and thy help." But when the jarl had ended his speech Torgny was silent for a while. But when he began, he said: "Strangely thou bearest thyself in this. Thou longest to take the name of jarl, but thou understandest not how to rule nor how to counsel when thou comest upon a difficulty. Why shouldst thou not have thought before thou didst promise to make this journey that thou hadst no power to speak to King Olav? It seems to me no less honourable to be reckoned amongst the bonders; and to have freedom to say what one will even if the king is present. I shall now come to the Upsala thing and grant thee such help that thou canst say without fear before the king such things as thou hast a mind to". The jarl thanked Torgny much for this promise and stayed with him. He then rode with him to the Upsala thing. A great crowd of folk was there and King Olav was there with his bodyguard.

80. The first day the thing sat, King Olav sat on his seat and his bodyguard sat about him, and on the other side of the thing Ragnvald the Jarl and Torgny sat on a seat, and in front of them sat the jarl's bodyguard and Torgny's huscarls. Behind the chair and round about, all the bonders stood; some went up on to hillocks and howes to listen from there. And when the king's business, such as was wont to be talked about at the thing, was spoken about and they were through with it, Björn the Marshal stood up near the jarl's seat and said aloud: "King Olav sent me hither on this errand that he will bid the Swedish king make peace and agree about the land boundaries which have from old time been between Norway and Sweden". He spoke loudly so that the king heard it clearly. But at first when the Swedish king heard "King Olav" named, he thought that the man was bringing some message for him. But when he heard him talking about peace and the boundaries between Sweden and Norway, he understood where it came from. Then he leaped up and shouted loudly to the man to be quiet. Then the jarl stood up and spoke. He spoke about Olav Digre's message and words of peace to Olav the Swedish king, and that the West Gauts were all sending word to King Olav that peace should be made with the men of Norway. He mentioned how hard it was for the West Gauts to feel the want of all those things from Norway which they needed for their upkeep, and yet, on the other hand, to lie open to onslaught and harrying if the King of Norway gathered an army together and warred upon them. The jarl also said that Olav, King of Norway, had sent men thither with the message that he would ask for the Swedish king's daughter, Ingegerd. But when the jarl stopped speaking, the Swedish king stood up. He answered wrathfully about the peace, and he gave the jarl a severe talking to for his boldness in having made a truce and peace with the proud man and in having made friendship with him. He called the jarl guilty of planning against him and found it right that Ragnvald should be driven from the kingdom. "All that", he said, "he has got from the egging on of Ingebjörg, his wife, and it was a most unwise plan that he should have followed his lust in taking such a woman." He spoke long and hard and then turned his talk against Olav Digre. And when he sat down, there was stillness at first, but then Torgny stood up. And when he stood up, the bonders who

before had been sitting all got up, and all who had been in other places pressed towards him to hear what Torgny said. There was much din from the swarming of men and from their weapons. And when it was still, Torgny spoke. "The Swedish kings are now otherwise minded than they formerly were. Torgny, my grandfather, remembered the Upsala king, Eric Emundson, and said this about him that so long as he was in his most active years he led an army out every summer and went to many lands; he put under himself Finland and the Kirialers' land,[1] Estland and Kurland, and many of the Eastlands, and still could men see the earthworks and other great works which he had made. He was not so haughty that he would not listen to folk when they would talk with him about anything. Torgny, my father, was for a long time with King Björn and knew his ways. In Björn's time his kingdom stood with great might and lost nothing through his being gentle towards his friends. I can remember King Eric the Victorious, and I was with him on many raids. He increased the kingdom of the Swedes and warded it by fighting. It was easy for us to give him counsel. But he who is king now lets no man dare say to him anything except the one thing which he himself will have, and to this end he lays all his might; but he lets his tax lands slip from him through weakness and treachery. He yearns to hold the realm of Norway under him, which no Swedish king has yearned for before, and it causes trouble to many a man. Now we bonders wish thee to make peace with Olav Digre, King of Norway, and wed thy daughter Ingegerd to him. And if thou wilt win back to thyself the kingdoms in the Baltic which thy kinsmen and forefathers have had there, so will we all follow thee there. But if thou wilt not have it as we say, then shall we go against thee and slay thee, and endure no more unrest and lawlessness of thee. Thus have our forefathers done before. At the Mula[2] thing, they pitched down into a well five kings who had been too haughty as thou art now to us. Say now at once what choice thou wilt make." Then the crowd straightway clanged their weapons and made a great din. The king then stood up and spoke; he said that he would let everything be as the bonders wished. "Thus have all Swedish kings done: they have let the bonders counsel with them in everything they wished." Then the bonders' shouting stopped. And thereafter their chiefs, the king and the jarl,

---

1  The *Kirialers* lived in the eastern and north-eastern part of Finland, towards the White Sea.    2  Snorre here mentions *Mula thing*. Another name for it was *Mora* thing. The field of Mora with Mora Stones is situated by Lagga, south-east of Upsala, on the border between Tiundaland and Attundaland.

and Torgny spoke together, and they made peace and terms on the Swedish king's behalf, according to what the King of Norway had sent word about beforehand. At that thing it was arranged that Olav's daughter, Ingegerd, should be married to King Olav Haraldson. The king entrusted the jarl to arrange this betrothal and to make all arrangements about the wedding. They parted at the thing when the matter had gone thus far. And when the jarl went homeward he met Ingegerd, the king's daughter, and they talked together about the matter. She sent King Olav a fur cape, gold-embroidered and trimmed with silk. The jarl went back to Gautland, and Björn went with him. Björn stayed a short time there and then went back to Norway with his following. And when he met King Olav and had told him what outcome his business had had, the king thanked him well for the journey and said, as was true, that Björn had had good luck to be able to fulfil his errand amid such unrest.

81. When spring came, King Olav went out to the sea, had his ships made ready, called men to him and then went out along the Vik as far as Lidandisnes and then went north to Hordaland. He sent bidding to the landed men and called out all the mightiest men from the lordships. He prepared magnificently for this journey to go and meet his bride. The bridal feast was to take place in the autumn near the Elv[1] in the east near Land's End.[2]

King Olav had with him King Rörik the Blind. When Rörik's wounds were healed, King Olav set two men to serve him and let him sit on the high-seat with him; keeping him in drink and in clothes as well as Rörik himself had formerly done. Rörik said little and answered sharply and shortly when he was spoken to. It was his wont to let his shoe boy lead him out during the day away from other men; he then beat the boy. And when the boy ran away from him, Rörik told King Olav that the boy would not serve him. King Olav then changed his serving-men for him, but so it went as before, that no serving-boy held out with King Rörik. Then Olav set the man called Swein to follow and serve Rörik, and this man was King Rörik's kinsman and had formerly been his man. Rörik kept in his wonted wise to surliness and likewise to his lone journeys, but when he and Swein were alone together, Rörik was happy and talkative. He remembered many things which had formerly been, and which had happened in the days when he was king. He remembered his former power and likewise who had brought about the change in his might and luck,

---

1 Göta River by Gothenburg.  2 In O.S. *Landsendi* (or *Land's End*) was the boundary between Norway and Sweden, by the Göta River.

and who had made him a beggar. "But it seems yet heaviest of all to me", he said, "that thou and my other kinsmen who gave such hope of becoming manly are now so fallen that they avenge not the shame which is done to our kin." Such harmful talk he often brought to his lips. Swein answered and said that they would have to fight against great odds, whilst they themselves had little power. Rörik

said: "Why shall we live long with shame and maiming, except that it may happen that I, a blind man, get the victory over him who won the victory over me when I slept? Let us try our luck and slay Olav Digre. He fears nothing now. I shall lay down a plan for it, neither would I spare my hands if I could have the use of them. But I cannot because of my blindness, and thou therefore shalt bear thy weapon against him. And when Olav is slain I know and I can foretell that the kingdom will come under his foes. Then it may be that I

King Rörik goes walking with his kinsman Swein

shall be king, and then shalt thou be my jarl". His words so worked that Swein promised to follow that foolish plan. Then it was agreed that when the king went to Evensong, Swein should stand outside in the porch before him and have a drawn sword under his cape. But when the king came out of the church, he came faster towards Swein than Swein had expected, and he looked at the king's face. Then he paled and went white as a corpse and his hands fell. The king noticed his fear and said: "What is it now, Swein? Wilt thou betray me?" Swein cast the cape and sword from him, fell at the feet of the king, and said: "All is in the power of God and you, O king". The king bade his men take Swein, who was then set in irons. Then he had Rörik's seat shifted to the second bench[1] and he gave Swein peace, and Swein went away from the land. The king now gave Rörik another house to sleep in, other than that which he himself slept in, and in that house many of the bodyguard slept. He set two

---

1 The second bench was opposite the bench upon which the king's throne stood. Rörik had previously sat on the king's bench.

of the guard to follow Rörik day and night. These two had long been with King Olav and they had proved their trustiness to him. It is not said that they were men of great family. King Rörik now bore himself in such a way that he was silent for many days so that no one could get a word out of him; but sometimes he was so happy and glad that there seemed fun in every word he said. And sometimes he talked much, but of evil only. So it was also that sometimes he drank every man off the bench and made all who were near him good for nothing; but most often he drank little. King Olav gave him much spending-money. Often when he came to the bedroom and before he laid himself down to sleep, he made them bring in several butts of mead and gave it to all his room-mates to drink. From that he was well liked.

82. There was from the Uplands a man called Finn the Little, and some say that he was Finnish by birth. He was smaller than most and so very fleet of foot that no steed could overtake him. He was before all men skilled in ski-ing and shooting with the bow. He had long been King Rörik's serving-man and had often gone on such errands of his as demanded trustiness. He knew the ways over all the Uplands and he was also known to all the great men there. And when Rörik was put in the custody of certain men, Finn got into their company, and often he went in the following of swains and servants. And every time he could he came and served King Rörik and talked to him. But the king would not talk with him long at a time and so let folk think ill of their talk. As spring passed, and they went out to the Vik, Finn went away from the army for several days. Then he came back and stayed there for a time. And so it was often, but no one took any notice of it, for there were many stragglers with the army.

83. King Olav came to Tunsberg before Easter[1] and stayed there a long time during spring. And to the town there came many merchant ships, both Saxers[2] and Danes, and folk from the east of the Vik and from the north of the land; and there was a very great crowd of folk. At that time it was a good season and there was much drinking. One evening it happened that King Rörik had come to his bedroom rather late; he had drunk much and was then very merry. Thither came Finn the Little with a butt of mead, and the mead was spiced

1 On the 6th of April, 1018. 2 The inhabitants of Old Saxony were called in O.S. *Saxar*, whilst the East Germans were called *Vindar*. Old Saxony embraced the largest part of the present North-west Germany, whilst Denmark extended south to Altona (near Hamburg).

and very strong. The king had it given to all there to drink, even till every man fell asleep in his place. Finn had then gone away, but the light was still burning in the bedroom. Rörik then woke the men who were wont to follow him and said that he wished to go out into the yard. They had a lighted lamp with them, for outside it was pitch dark. There was in the yard a great outhouse, built on stocks, with steps up to the door. Whilst Rörik and his men sat there, they heard a man shouting: "Strike the devil down!" After that they heard a crash and a thud as if something had fallen. King Rörik said: "They

King Rörik's men leaped ashore; but Rörik sat up in the poop

who are striking each other there have drunk enough. Go at once to them and part them". They made themselves ready and ran out, and when they came out on the steps the last man was struck down first, and both were slain. King Rörik's men had then come there; there was Sigurd Hit who had been his standard-bearer, and eleven others, and there was Finn the Little. They dragged the bodies up between the houses, and they took the king with them, leaped on a boat they had, and rowed away. Sigvat the Scald was sleeping in King Olav's house. He got up in the night and his shoe boy with him, and they went out to the great outhouse. And when they were coming back and were going down the steps, Sigvat slipped and fell on his knee; he thrust his hands down and he felt that it was wet underneath. He said: "I think that the king has made many of us unsteady on the feet to-night", and laughed at it. But when they came back into the room where the light was burning, the shoe boy asked: "Hast thou grazed thyself, or why art thou bloody all over?" He answered: "I have not grazed myself, but this must be a sign of tidings". He then woke Tord Folason the standard-bearer, his bedfellow, and they went out, having with them a lighted lamp, and straightway found the blood. Then they looked for and soon found the bodies, and recognised them. They also saw a great tree trunk lying there which was much struck, and they learned afterwards that this had been done as a feint to bring out those who were slain. Sigvat and Tord said to themselves that it was needful for the king to know these tidings as soon as possible. They straightway sent the boy to the room in which King Rörik had been; all the men there were sleeping, but the king was gone. He woke the men who were in there and told them the news. They stood up and went out into the yard at once to where the bodies lay. But though it seemed needful that the king should know of these tidings as soon as possible, no one dared wake him. Then said Sigvat to Tord: "What wouldst thou rather do, my friend, waken the king or tell him the news?" Tord said: "Not at any price dare I waken him, but I will tell him the news". Then said Sigvat: "There is still much of the night left and it may happen that before dawn Rörik will have found himself a hiding-place, so that afterwards he will not be easily found. But they cannot yet have gone far, for the bodies are warm. Never shall such shame befall us that we did not let the king know of this treachery. Go thou into the room, Tord, and wait for me there". Then Sigvat went into the church, woke the bell-ringer and bade him toll for the souls of the king's guards, and he named the men who were slain. The bell-ringer did as Sigvat bade him, but on the ringing of the bell the king awoke, and sat up. He asked if it was time for Matins. Tord answered: "There is a worse thing afoot; great events are befallen. King Rörik has gone away, and two of your bodyguard are slain". Then the king asked what had happened. Tord told him such as he knew. Then the king stood up and called up the bodyguard. And when the guard came together the king chose men to go on all the ways from the town to look for Rörik on sea or land. Tore the Long took a cutter and went with thirty men, and when it became light they saw two small cutters going before them. When they saw each other, all rowed their best. King Rörik was there and he had thirty men. And when they came nearer together, Rörik's men turned towards land and they all leaped ashore. But the king sat up in the poop and wished them all farewell and hoped to meet again unscathed. Then

Tore's men rowed to land, but Finn the Little shot an arrow and it hit Tore in the middle of the body. He got his death from it. Sigurd and his men ran to the wood, but Tore's men took his body and King Rörik and brought them to Tunsberg. The king then took King Rörik into his own keeping. He had him watched and took great heed of his treachery; he got men to mind him day and night. King Rörik was then very happy and no one noticed in him that he liked things not as well as he might.

84. It happened on Ascension Day[1] that King Olav went to High Mass. The bishop went in a procession round the church leading the king. And when they came back to the church, the bishop brought the king to his seat in the north of the choir. King Rörik sat next to him as was his wont and had a hood over his face. When King Olav sat down, King Rörik put his hand on his shoulder and felt about. Then he said: "Fine clothes thou hast now, my kinsman". King Olav answered: "Yes, a great high festival is held in memory of Christ's rising from earth to Heaven". King Rörik answered: "I do not understand what thou tellest me about Christ so as to hold it fast in my mind. Much of what thou sayest seems to me somewhat unbelievable, but however, many strange things happened in former times". And when Mass was on, King Olav stood up and lifted his hands up over his head and bowed towards the altar, and his cloak hung down from his shoulders. King Rörik sprang up quickly, and struck at King Olav with such a knife as is called a dagger. The blow fell on the cape near his shoulders when the king had bowed down. The clothes were much cut but the king was not wounded. And when King Olav noticed his intention he leaped forth on the floor. King Rörik struck at him a second time with the knife, but reached him not; he then said: "Dost thou now flee, Olav Digre, before me, a blind man?" The king bade his men take Rörik and lead him out of the church. And so it was done. After these happenings they egged on King Olav to let Rörik be killed. "It is", they said, "trying your luck, O king, to have him about you, and to spare him whatever evil he may yet do. He watches day and night to take your life, but as soon as you send him away from you, we see no one who can mind him so well that we do not expect him to slip away. But if he gets loose he will straightway raise an army and do great evil." The king answered: "Ye are right, in that many a man has got his death for less ill-doing than Rörik. But I like not to mar the victory I won over the Upland kings when I took all five

1 15th of May, 1018.

of them in one morning, and so got all their kingdoms without having to be the slayer of any of them, for they were all my kinsmen. But still I cannot well see whether Rörik should make me have him killed or not". Rörik had put his hand on King Olav's shoulder for this reason: he wished to find out if King Olav had a brynie[1] on.

85. There was a man called Toraren Nevjolvson. He was an Icelander and his kin were from the Northland.[2] He was not of great family, but he was wise and clever of speech, and bold in talk with princes. He was a great traveller and was abroad for long stretches of time. Toraren was an ugly man, and especially so because he was ill-shaped in the limbs. He had great ugly hands, but his feet were very much uglier. Toraren was present in Tunsberg when these things happened which have been told of before. He was acquainted with King Olav. Toraren made ready the merchant ship he owned

Toraren shows his uglier foot to King Olav

and would go to Iceland in the summer. King Olav had Toraren as a guest for some days and talked much with him. Toraren slept in the king's room. Early one morning the king lay awake, but the other men in the room were asleep; the sun had just risen, and there was much light within. The king saw that Toraren had stretched one foot forth from the bedclothes. He looked at the foot for a time; then they woke up in the room. The king said to Toraren: "I have been awake some time and I have seen a sight which seems of great worth; it is a man's foot, so ugly that I believe there will not be one uglier in the whole town", and he bade the others look and see whether it seemed the same to them. And all who saw it said truly that it was so. Toraren understood then what they were talking about and answered: "There are few things so odd that you cannot expect to find the like to them, and it is most likely that it is so now". The king said: "I will not hold with it that you can find so ugly a foot, even if I should bet on it". Then Toraren answered: "I am ready to bet you that here in this house I can find an uglier foot".

1 *Brynie* is coat of mail.    2 I.e. the northern part of Iceland.

The king said: "Then shall the one of us who is right crave a boon of the other". "So shall it be", said Toraren; he stuck forth from the bedclothes the other foot, and it was no whit fairer and the big toe was off too. Then said Toraren: "Look here, O king, at another foot which is so much uglier as there is a toe off. I have won the bet". The king said: "The first foot is so much uglier as there are five ugly toes on it, but on this only four. I have the right to crave a boon of thee". Toraren said: "Costly are the king's words, but what boon wilt thou crave of me?" He said: "This, that thou dost take Rörik to Greenland and bring him to Leif Ericson".[1] Toraren answered: "I have not been to Greenland". The king said: "For such a traveller as thou it is now time thou didst go to Greenland, if thou hast not yet been there". At first Toraren answered little to this matter, but when the king held on to getting the thing done, Toraren did not turn it from him altogether, and so he said: "I shall let you hear, O king, the boon which I had thought of asking for, if I had won. It is that I would ask to become one of your guard. If you grant it, then· I shall have less power to deny what you crave" The king agreed to it and Toraren became one of his guard. When Toraren had fitted out his ship and was ready he took charge of King Rörik. And when King Olav and Toraren parted, Toraren said: "If it now turns out, O king, as is not unlikely, and as often might happen, that we come not to Greenland, but are driven to Iceland or some other land, how shall I part with this king to your liking?" The king said: "If thou comest to Iceland, thou shalt give him to Gudmund Eyolfson[2] or Skafti the Lawman or any other chief who will have my friendship and my tokens. But if thou comest to other lands which are nearer here, see to it that thou art certain Rörik will never again come back alive to Norway. But this thou mayest do only if thou seest no other way out". And when Toraren was ready and there was a fair wind he sailed on the fairway outside the isles and north-west by Lidandisnes and so out to sea. He did not soon get a fair wind, but he took most heed not to come to land. He sailed south of Iceland and he knew the land. And thereafter he went west along the land into the Greenland Sea. There he had stormy weather and high seas. When summer was ending he landed in Breidafjord in Iceland. Torgils Arason[3] was the first chieftain to come to them.

---

1 *Leif Ericson* was the discoverer of North America. Cf. 'History of Olav Trygvason', chapters 96 and 98.  2 *Gudmund* the Mighty of Mödruvellir, chief of the northern part of Iceland (died 1024).  3 *Torgils* lived at Reykholar in Bardastrand district, on the north side of the Breidafjord (Western Iceland).

Toraren told him about King Olav's words and his promise of friendship and showed him the tokens regarding the taking over of King Rörik. Torgils answered in a friendly way and bade King Rörik go with him, and Rörik was with Torgils Arason during the winter. He liked it not there, and bade Torgils give him a following to go to Gudmund. He said that he seemed to have heard that with Gudmund there was the greatest magnificence in Iceland, and he wished to be sent to him. Torgils did as he wished and got men to follow Rörik to Gudmund of Mödruvellir. Gudmund greeted Rörik well because of the king's messages, and Rörik was with Gudmund during the second winter. Then he liked it no longer. Gudmund then got him lodging in a little place called Kalvskin[1] where there were few folks. Rörik was there during the third winter, and then he said that since he had lost his kingdom he liked being there best, for he sat the highest of all. The next summer Rörik got an illness which brought him to his death. So it is said that he is the only king who rests in Iceland. Toraren Nevjolvson was afterwards on sea journeys for long stretches of time, but sometimes he was with King Olav.

86. The summer that Toraren went with Rörik to Iceland, Hjalti Skeggjason also went to Iceland, and King Olav sent him away with friendly gifts when they parted. The same summer Eyvind Urarhorn went on a viking raid to the west, and in the autumn he came to Ireland to King Konofogor. The King of the Irish and Einar the Jarl from the Orkneys met in the autumn in Ulvreksfjord[2] and there was a sharp battle. King Konofogor had a much greater army and won the victory, whilst Einar the Jarl fled with only one ship and came back to the Orkneys in the autumn, and he had then lost almost all his men and all the booty he had taken. The jarl was ill at peace with his army and blamed the Norsemen who had been with the Irish king in the battle for causing his defeat.

87. Now we may take up the matter from which we turned before, how King Olav Digre went on his wedding journey to fetch his betrothed Ingegerd, the daughter of Olav, King of the Swedes. The king had many men and they were well chosen. All the great men he could get followed him, and each of these mighty men had with him men well chosen both in kinship and doughtiness. All the army was fitted out with the best ships, weapons and clothes.

---

1 *Kalvskin* is situated on the west side of the Eyjafjord (North Iceland).   2 Now Lough Larne, a narrow fjord in Co. Antrim, north of Belfast. The Irish king Konofogor is probably the O.S. form for the Irish Conchobhar. Several kings of this name are mentioned in the Irish Annals. Norse burial places have been found at Larne.

They steered their ships east to Konungahella.[1] But when they came there, they heard nothing of the Swedish king, nor had any men come there on his behalf. King Olav stayed a long time during the summer at Konungahella and asked much what men could tell him about the Swedish king's journey or intentions, but no one could tell him anything certain. He then sent his men up into Gautland to Ragnvald the Jarl to ask him if he knew the reason why the Swedish

King Olav fares on his wedding journey to Land's End

king had not come to the meeting place as was arranged. The jarl said that he did not know, "but if I find out", he said, "I shall straightway send my men to King Olav to let him know what grounds there are for it; and whether this delay comes of anything else than the many matters which may often happen to delay the Swedish king's journey more than he expected beforehand".

88. The Swedish king, Olav Ericson, first had a mistress called Edla, the daughter of a jarl in Vendland. She had formerly been taken prisoner and had been called the king's thrall woman. Their children were Emund, Astrid and Holmfrid. But afterwards he got a son by the queen and he was born on St James' Day. When the child was to be christened the bishop had him called Jacob. The Swedes did not like that name, and said that never had a Swedish king been called Jacob. All King Olav's children were handsome, and had good understanding. The queen was haughty and was not

---

1 Now Kungälf, on the north side of the Göta River (by Gothenburg).

friendly towards the step-children. The king sent his son Emund to Vendland, and he was brought up with his mother's kinsmen and did not keep long to Christianity. Astrid, the king's daughter, was brought up in West Gautland with a nobleman called Egil; she was a beautiful woman and well spoken, happy in talk, humble and generous. When she was grown up she was often with her father, and was well liked by all. King Olav was haughty and unfriendly in talk; he was very wroth that the army had clamoured against him at the Upsala thing and threatened him with hard choice, and he mostly blamed Ragnvald the Jarl for that. He did not make himself ready for the wedding journey, as had been arranged in the winter, that he should wed his daughter Ingegerd to Olav Digre, King of Norway, and should go now in the summer to Land's End. But when time passed men became very anxious to know what the king intended, whether he would hold to the agreement with the King of Norway, or whether he would break the treaty and likewise the peace. Many were troubled over it, but none was so bold that he dared ask the king about it. Many complained about it to Ingegerd, the king's daughter, and asked her to get knowledge of what the king would do. She answered: "I have no wish to speak with the king about the difference between him and Olav Digre, for neither of them is the other's friend. The one time I spoke about the matter of Olav Digre, he answered me ill". This matter gave Ingegerd, the king's daughter, much thought. She was sick at heart and unhappy, and she would eagerly know what the king would do. She doubted that he would keep his word to the King of Norway, all the more when they noticed that the king was wroth every time Olav Digre was called king.

89. It happened early one day that the king rode out with his hawks and hounds, and with him were his men. And when they loosed the hawks the king's hawk slew in one swoop two black-cocks. And after that it swooped again and slew three black-cocks. The hounds ran along and picked up each bird as it fell to earth. The king rode after them and he himself took his own catch; he boasted much about it and said: "Most of you will go a long time before you make such a kill". They said it was true, and they said they thought that no king could have such good luck in his hunting. The king afterwards rode home with his men and was very happy. Ingegerd, the king's daughter, was then going out of her bower, and when she saw the king riding into the garth, she turned towards him and greeted him. He greeted her with a laugh and straightway brought out the

birds; he told her about his catch and said: "Where dost thou know a king who has got so great a catch in so short a time?" She answered: "It is a good morning's catch that you have taken five blackcocks, but more it was when Olav, King of Norway, took five kings in one morning and got all their kingdoms". When the king heard that he leaped from his steed, turned towards her and said: "Thou shalt know, Ingegerd, that much love as thou hast given the proud man, thou shalt never get him, nor he thee. I shall wed thee to some other chief with whom I may have friendship. But never can I be the friend of a man who has taken my kingdom as war booty and done me great scathe in robbery and manslaughter". Thus they ended their talk, and they each went their own way.

90. Ingegerd, the king's daughter, had now got to know the truth about her father's mind, and straightway sent men down into West Gautland to Ragnvald the Jarl to let him know how matters were with the Swedish king and that all the agreement with the King of Norway was broken. She bade the jarl and the other West Gauts be careful, for they could not now expect peace from the men of Norway. And when the jarl learned these tidings, he sent word over all his kingdom bidding them beware lest the men of Norway should make war on them. The jarl also sent men to King Olav Digre to let him know what he had heard, and likewise that he himself would keep the agreement and friendship with King Olav. He also begged the king not to make war upon his kingdom. And when this message came to King Olav he was very wroth and sick at heart, and for some days no man could get a word out of him. After this he had a husthing with his men. Björn the Marshal stood up first and mentioned at the beginning of his speech that in the winter before he had gone east to make peace. He told how Ragnvald the Jarl had greeted him well; he also said how crossly and heavily the Swedish king had taken this matter at first: "but the agreement which was made", he said, "came about more through the help of the crowd and Torgny's might and Ragnvald the Jarl's help than through the good will of the Swedish king. For this reason we think we know that it is certainly the king who has brought about the breaking of the agreement, and we put no blame for it on the jarl. In him we found a true friend of King Olav. Now the king wishes to know from his chiefs and other warriors what plan he shall take up, whether he shall go up into Gautland and harry there with the army we now have, or whether it seems better to you to choose another plan". He talked

both long and wisely. After him others spoke and nearly all ended their speeches with the same; they counselled against making war and said: "Even if we have many men, yet are there gathered here only mighty and noble men; but to go a-warring is likewise fitting for young men to whom it seems good to win wealth and honours. It is also the way of great warriors when they go into the fight that they have with them many men to go in front and protect them, and often those men who have little wealth fight better than those who are brought up in riches". According to their proposals the king

Björn the Marshal speaks to King Olav at a husthing

took up the plan of breaking up the meeting and gave every man leave to go home, but he said that the next summer he would lead out an army from the whole land and then go against the Swedish king to avenge his broken agreement. This pleased them all. After that King Olav went north into the Vik and stayed in the autumn at Borg; he had all the things brought there that he needed for wintering, and he stayed there during the winter with many men.

91. Men talked very diversely about Ragnvald the Jarl. Some said that he was King Olav's true friend, but to others he did not seem trustworthy, for they said that he could well have worked it with the Swedish king so that he held his word and agreement with King Olav Digre. Sigvat the Scald was Ragnvald the Jarl's friend, and he often talked about it to King Olav. He offered the king to go to Ragnvald the Jarl to find out what he could get to know about the Swedish king, and to try to bring about the agreement. That pleased the king, for it seemed good to him to talk often with his trusted men about Ingegerd, the king's daughter. At the beginning of the winter Sigvat the Scald went with two men from Borg east

over Marker[1] and then to Gautland. And before King Olav and Sigvat parted, Sigvat quoth this verse:

Now sit thou unscathed,
King Olav, till I come back
Hither to this hall,
And here we meet again.
The scald's wish is this:
That luck and life may the king have
And may he rule this land
With honour. Now ends my verse.

Now are the words said
That are weightiest for all for us.
But, O king, we have insight
Into many things besides;
O strong-hearted prince, let
God keep thy land for thee,
For thereto wert thou born.
That is ever my wish.

After that they went east to Eid[2] and they had a poor craft to ferry them over the river; it was an oak trunk, and it hardly got across. Sigvat quoth:

Wet, I let the faltering skiff
Draw to Eid; I feared
To have to turn back.
We were in danger in that boat.

Would that the witches
Had the ship—the worst I know.
In peril was I on that boat;
But it went better than I thought.

After that they went through Eidaskog.[3] Sigvat quoth a verse:

It was not joyful to go
From Eid, for much-harmed
I went thirteen miles through woods:
Heavy hurts we met with!

The king's men bore blisters
Under their sore feet.
But still we went thither
Quickly throughout that day.

After that they went through Gautland and in the evening they came to a place called Hov.[4] There the door was locked and they could not get in. The folk said that it was hallowed. They went away from there. Sigvat sayeth:

Sharply to Hov I hurried
But locked was the door,
And pleading without, I asked things
Whilst I pushed my nose in the place.

Few words I got, but the folk
Said it was hallowed.
Heathens thrust me away,
But I bade the devil take them.

After that he came to another garth, where the housewife stood in the doorway, and bade him not come in: "they are holding an offering to the elves", she said. Sigvat quoth:

"Go no further in,
Thou wretch", said the woman.
"Heathen are we, and we fear
The enmity of Odin."

They were holding an elf offering,
The old hag said.
She thrust me out of the garth,
As if I had been a wolf.

1 I.e. Aremark in Smalenene (Norway). 2 I.e. Stora Ed between Trollhättan and Vänersborg by the Göta River. 3 The forests east of Stora Ed. 4 Now Stora Hof, south-west of Skara in West Gautland.

The next evening he came upon three bonders who were all called Ölvir, and they all drove him out. Sigvat said:

Now have three of a name,
Who turned their backs on me,
Driven me out; they are
Hardly eager for honour.

Now I fear that all men
Who bear the name of Ölvir
Hereafter will drive out
Their guests from the garth.

After that they went farther that evening and came upon a fourth bonder. He was said to be the best of them, but he drove them out. Sigvat quoth:

After this I hoped for peace
And went to find a bonder
Whom they all called
The best of all men.
The bonder merely looked at me;
If this is the best
Then the worst must be bad.
Reluctant I blame these folk.

To the east from Eidaskog
On my journey I found not
Shelter, which I craved.
Lodging with the unchristian
I did not find the son
Of mighty Saxi, and welcomes
Within were lacking. In one
Evening I came out four times.

And when they came to Ragnvald the Jarl, the jarl said that they had had a hard journey. Sigvat composed the following:

The lord of the Sognings'
Messengers, who came
Hither with the king's errands,
Have had so hard a journey.
We spared ourselves least, but much
Must we struggle on the journey.
The king of Norway planned
That we should go hither from the
north.

Hard it was for the men
To go over Eidaskog
On the way east to the jarl.
Still I praise the king.
The chieftain's men would not
Have driven me away
Ere I came to meet
My good lord there.

Ragnvald the Jarl gave Sigvat a gold ring. A woman said that he had yet come for something with those black eyes of his. Sigvat quoth:

These black eyes of Iceland
Have brought us, O woman,
To this bright ring,
By the long steep ways.

O maid of the mead! These feet
Of mine have gone
Bravely on the ancient ways
Which thy husband knows not.

And when Sigvat came home to King Olav and had gone into the hall he quoth as he looked on the walls:

Those guards who feed the eagles
Adorn the hall of the king
With helms and brynies; I see
The walls full of both.

Hardly any young king
Can boast himself of better
House ornaments, it is certain.
The hall is noble to behold.

After that he told about his journey and quoth this verse:

I bid the great-hearted guard
Of the mighty king hear
Of what I have suffered.
I made these verses.

In autumn I was sent up
From the skis of the sea
Far east to Sweden.
Little have I slept since.

And when he talked with the king he quoth:

Uprightly for thee, King Olav,
I voiced my errand,
When I met the bold
And mighty Jarl Ragnvald.
Many words with the noble
Warrior I got,
And never in the halls of counsel
Had I heard clearer talk.

O foe of the gold, the jarl's kin
Begged thee to greet well
Each of his huscarls
Who might come hither.
And it is likewise certain
That each of thy men
Who will journey east
Will Ragnvald help.

When I came from the west
Many men thought
That Eric's kin
Were working treachery.
But thou, who alone hast won
The jarls' lands from Swein,
Wilt with Ulf's kinsmen
Find brotherly help.

O Olav, the son of Ulf said
That between you both
A peace was newly made.
You lay down your complaints.
Ragnvald said that it was
Easy for thee to hinder
The rising anew of enmity.
Thou slayer of bands of thieves!

Sigvat the Scald came to Ragnvald the Jarl, and was in good cheer there for some time. Then he learnt by letters from Ingegerd, the king's daughter, that messengers had come to Olav, the Swedish king, from King Jarisleiv[1] from Holmgard[2] to woo Ingegerd, the daughter of Olav, the Swedish king, on Jarisleiv's behalf, and that King Olav took this in a very friendly way. At that time also Astrid, King Olav's daughter, came to Ragnvald the Jarl's household. A great feast was then made there. Sigvat the Scald soon got to know the king's daughter; she also was acquainted with him and his kin, for Ottar the Scald, the son of Sigvat's sister, had for a long time been friendly with Olav, the Swedish king. There were now many talks. Ragnvald the Jarl asked if Olav, King of Norway, would marry Astrid: "and if he will", he said, "I think we should not ask the Swedish king about the marriage". Astrid, the king's daughter, said the same. After that Sigvat and his following went home and a little before Yule they came to King Olav in Borg. Sigvat straightway told King Olav the tidings he had learnt. At first the king was very unhappy when Sigvat told him about King Jarisleiv's wooing,

---

1 Jaroslav, son of Vladimir (cf. 'History of Olav Trygvason', p. 118, n. 2). He was Grand Duke in Kiev and Novgorod (1016–54). 2 I.e. Novgorod.

and Olav said that he did not expect anything but ill from Olav, the Swedish king: "if we can now avenge it, then he will remember it". But as time wore on the king asked Sigvat about many things from the east in Gautland. Sigvat told him much about the beauty and good talk of Astrid, the king's daughter, and likewise that all men said that she in no wise stood behind her sister Ingegerd. This fell well on the king's ears. Sigvat told him of all the talks Astrid and he had had between them; the king listened carefully to it and then said: "The Swedish king thinks not at all that I perhaps dare wed his daughter without his will". This matter was not brought forward before many men, but King Olav and Sigvat the Scald often talked about it. King Olav asked Sigvat what he had got to know about Ragnvald the Jarl: "whether he is our friend", he said. Sigvat answered that the jarl was King Olav's best friend, and Sigvat then quoth:

Thou shalt hold fast, mighty prince,     Worthy king, I know not
The treaty with Ragnvald                A better friend than he
The Mighty. He will watch well          That thou hast in the Eastway,
For thee by night as by day.            All along the green sea.

After Yule, Tord Skotakoll, the son of Sigvat the Scald's sister, went secretly from the court and with him Sigvat's shoe boy. They went east to Gautland. In the autumn before they had been east there with Sigvat. And when they came to the jarl's court they brought forth before the jarl the tokens which King Olav himself had sent the jarl in trust. Straightway the jarl made himself ready to go and with him Astrid, the king's daughter, and they had nearly one hundred (one hundred and twenty) men, folk chosen both from the bodyguard and from the sons of the great bonders; their array was splendid both in weapons and in clothes and in steeds. They rode north to Norway to Sarpsborg and came thither at Candlemas.[1]

92. King Olav had caused everything to be made ready. There were all kinds of drink—the best to be got—and all other things there were also of the best; he had also called to him many great men from the lordships. And when the jarl came thither with his men, the king greeted him very well, and the jarl got great and goodly rooms, richly fitted out, and thereto servants and men who were to see to it that nothing was short which could enrich a feast. And when the feast had been on for some days, the king and the jarl and the king's daughter met in talk together, and the outcome of their talk was that Ragnvald the Jarl should betroth Astrid, daughter of Olav

1 2nd of February, 1019.

the Swedish king, to Olav King of Norway, with the dowry which it had been formerly agreed upon that her sister Ingegerd was to have from home. This feast now continued, and the bridal of King Olav and Queen Astrid was drunk with great honour. Thereafter Ragnvald the Jarl went back to Gautland and at their parting the king gave him great and goodly gifts; they parted the dearest of friends, and they held to that friendship as long as they both lived.

Ragnvald the Jarl and Astrid, the king's daughter, meet King Olav at Sarpsborg

93. The spring after, King Jarisleiv's messengers came from the east from Holmgard to Sweden to settle the matter that King Olav the summer before had promised, to wed his daughter Ingegerd to King Jarisleiv. King Olav talked about this matter with Ingegerd and said that it was his wish that she should be married to King Jarisleiv. She said: "If I wed King Jarisleiv I will have as my dowry Aldeigjaborg[1] and the jarldom which goes with it". The Holmgard messengers promised that on their king's behalf. Then said Ingegerd: "If I go east into Gardarik[2] I will choose from Sweden the man who seems to me best fitted to go with me. I will also have it settled that there in the east he shall have no less a title than here; and in no way fewer rights or less honour than he has here". The king assented to that and likewise the messengers; the king gave promises about it and so did the messengers. Then the king asked Ingegerd who the

1 I.e. the town Aldagen or Ladoga; 'History of Olav Trygvason', p. 183, n. 4.　2 I.e. Russia.

man was in his kingdom whom she would choose to follow her. She answered: "The man is Jarl Ragnvald Ulfson, my kinsman". The king answered: "I have thought that Ragnvald the Jarl should pay otherwise for his treachery to his king[1] in that he went to Norway with my daughter and gave her as mistress to the proud man whom he knew to be our worst foe; and for that thing he shall be hanged in the summer". Ingegerd bade her father keep the promise he had given her, and by her prayers it came about that the king said that Ragnvald the Jarl should go away in peace from Sweden, but never come into the king's sight and not into Sweden as long as Olav was king. Ingegerd then sent men to the jarl to let him know these tidings, and set him a place where they should meet. And the jarl straightway made himself ready for the journey and rode up to East Gautland. There he got ships and after that he brought his men to the meeting with Ingegerd, the king's daughter. They then went east together to Gardarik in the summer. After that Ingegerd was wedded to King Jarisleiv. Their sons were Valdemar,[2] Vissavald[3] and Holte the Courageous. Queen Ingegerd gave Ragnvald the Jarl Aldeigjaborg and the jarldom which went with it. Ragnvald the Jarl was there a long time; and he was an outstanding man. The sons of Ragnvald the Jarl and Ingebjörg were Ulf the Jarl, and Eiliv the Jarl.

94. Emund of Skara was the name of a man. He was lawman there in West Gautland, and a very wise and smooth-tongued man; he was of good kin, had many kinsmen and was very rich. He was reckoned as an underhand man and but little trustworthy. He was the mightiest man in West Gautland when the jarl had gone away. In the spring when Ragnvald the Jarl went from Gautland, the Gauts held a thing amongst themselves and they murmured often with each other as to what the Swedish king would now take upon himself to do. They learned that he was wroth with them because they had made friendship with Olav, the King of Norway, instead of bringing strife against him. He also put the blame on those men who had followed his daughter Astrid to Norway. Some said that they should seek help from the King of Norway and offer him their service, but others counselled against that and said that the West Gauts had no strength to fight against the Swedes. "And the King of Norway is too far away from us," they said, "for his main strength is too remote from us; the first thing we have to do is to send men to the

1 Treachery to the king was in O.S. called *drottins-svik*.    2 In Russia his name was Vladimir.    3 Vsevolod, Grand Duke from 1078 to 1093.

Swedish king to ask if we can come to terms with him. But if that does not succeed, then we have the choice of seeking help from the King of Norway." The bonders then bade Emund make this journey and he said yea to it; he went with thirty men and came forth into East Gautland. Many of his kinsmen and friends were there and he had a good welcome. There he had talks with the wisest men about this difficult matter, and he was agreed with them; to the men it did not seem customary and lawful to do as the king did to them. Emund now went up into Sweden and there held talks with many great men, and they were fully agreed. He went farther on his

The Swedish king's counsellors

journey till he came one evening to Upsala. There he got himself a good room and was there for the night. Next day, Emund went to the king when the king sat in his court with many folk about him. Emund went forth before him, bowed and greeted him. The king saw him, greeted him, and asked for news. Emund answered: "There is but little news from us Gauts; but it seems news to us that Atti in Värmland went up into the woods during the winter with his skis and bow; we call him the greatest of hunters. He had got so many squirrel skins on the fell that he had filled his sleigh with as many as he could bring with him. Then he turned homewards from the wood. Now he saw a squirrel in a tree, shot at it, but did not hit it. He then grew wroth, left the sleigh and ran after the squirrel, but the squirrel always went where the wood was thickest, sometimes in the tree roots, sometimes up in the branches; it swung amongst the branches to another tree, and whenever Atti shot at it, the arrow always flew above or below; but the squirrel never leaped so that Atti did not see it. He then became so eager for this catch that he chased it the whole day. But for all that he couldn't catch the squirrel. When it became dark, he threw himself down in the snow as he was wont, and lay there during the night in snow drifts. Next day Atti went to look for his sleigh, but he never found it, and so he had to go home. Such are my tidings, my lord". The king said:

"There is little news in that, if there is no more to tell". Emund answered: "A short time ago something else happened which might be called news: Gauti Tofason went with five warships out along the Gautelv, and when he lay in by the Eikeröyer the Danes came there with five great trading ships. Gauti soon took four of the trading ships without losing one man, and got many goods. But the fifth got away on the sea, and they got under sail. Gauti went after them with one ship and at first came near them, but then the weather began to be rough so that the trading ship went better and got away out to sea. Gauti then wished to turn back. A storm came on and his ship was stranded on Lesö. There all the goods and the greater part of his men were lost. His other men were to wait in the Eikeröyer. The Danes then came upon them with fifteen trading ships and slew them all and took all the goods which they had won before. That they got for their greed". The king said: "That is great news and worth telling. But what is thy errand here?" Emund answered: "I came to seek an explanation of difficult matters, how our law differs from the Upsala law". The king asked: "What is it you wish to complain of?" Emund said: "There were two noble-born men alike in kindred, but unlike in possessions and mind. They quarrelled about lands and did each other scathe and most of all he who was mightiest, until their quarrel was ended and judgment given at the thing. He who was formerly the mightiest had to pay, but at the first payment, he paid a gosling for a goose, and a young pig for an old sow; for a mark of burnt gold he yielded one half-mark in gold, but the other half in clay and mud; and even also he threatened with hard dealing him who took these goods as his right. What do you judge thereof, my lord?" The king said: "He shall pay fully what he was judged to pay and to the king three times as much; but, if it is not paid within a year, he shall be outlawed from all his possessions and half the goods shall fall into the king's power and half to him to whom he should make amends". Emund craved as witness to that decision all the mightiest men who were present and put the case before the thing which was held at Upsala. After that he took leave of the king and went away; and then other men brought their complaints before the king. And when the king came to table, he asked where Emund the Lawman was. It was told him that Emund was at home in his room. Then said the king: "Go after him; he shall be my guest to-day". Thereupon the food came in and after that players came in with harps and fiddles and other musical instruments; and then came the drink servers. The king was very merry and had many great men at the feast; he then forgot Emund. All the day the king drank and then slept the night after. But in the morning when the king awoke he remembered what Emund had said the day before. When he was clad he had his wise men called to him. King Olav had twelve wise men who sat over judgments with him and counselled in difficult matters; but it was not easy work, for the king liked it not that a judgment went against his rights, and it was no use to gainsay him. At the meeting the king began the talk and bade Emund the Lawman be called thither. When the messenger came back, he said: "My lord, Emund, the Lawman, rode away yesterday, as soon as he had taken food". Then said the king: "Tell me, ye good chieftains, what meaning there was in the law question Emund came with yesterday?" They answered: "Lord, you must have made something more out of it if it signified anything else but what he said". The king answered: "The two noble-born men who he said had been unfriendly and the one the mightier, and each of whom did the other scathe—by them he meant Olav Digre and me". "So it is, lord, as you say." The king said: "Our case was judged at the Up-sala thing, but what does it mean, as he told, that it was ill-paid when a gosling came for a goose, a young pig for an old sow, and half clay for gold?" Arnvid the Blind answered: "My lord, unlike are red gold and clay, but more unlike are king and thrall. You promised to Olav Digre your daughter Ingegerd who is kingly born on all sides of the Upsala race which is the uppermost in the northern lands, for this stock is come from the gods themselves. But now has King Olav got Astrid; and even though she is a king's daughter, yet her mother was a thrall woman and a Vendish one besides. Great difference there is between kings when one takes such a thing thankfully, and it is to be expected that a Norseman cannot be equal to the Upsala king. Let us be thankful that it will be so, for the gods have long taken great care of their offspring, even though many now neglect that faith". There were three brothers present. The first was Arnvid the Blind who saw so little that he could hardly be in any fighting, but who was very wise. The second was Torvid the Stammerer—he could not say more than two words together, but he was the boldest and the most trusted. The third was called Fröivid the Deaf—he heard badly. These brothers were all mighty and rich men, of great family, wise, and held highly by the king. Then said King Olav: "What does that mean which Emund said about Atti?" Then no one answered, but each looked at the other. The king said, "Say it now". Then Torvid the Stammerer answered: "Atti, quarrelsome, greedy, ill-minded, foolish, dumb". Then said the king: "Who shall take this to himself?" Then answered Fröivid the Deaf: "We shall speak more clearly if it be by your leave". The king said: "Thou hast my leave thereto, Fröivid, to say what thou wilt". Fröivid then began: "My brother Torvid, who is called the wisest of us, calls it all the same thing: Atti, quarrelsome, foolish and silly; so he calls him who is loath to have peace so that he strives after small things which he does not get, and misses thereby great gains. Now I am somewhat deaf but still many have spoken in such a way that I can see that folks, both mighty men and common men, like it ill that you, my lord, keep not your word to the King of Norway. But it is worse that you break common judgments which are adjudged at the Upsala thing. No need have you to fear the King of Norway, or the King of the Danes, or any other, so long as the army of the Swedes will follow you. But if the folk of the land turn against you, all as one, then we your friends see no plan at hand which we know can avail". The king asked: "Who is leader in betraying the land from me?" Fröivid answered: "All Swedes will have their own laws and full rights. See to it now, my lord, how many of your chiefs are sitting here in council with you. I think it is true that we six are here whom you call your counsellors, but all the others, I think, have ridden away and gone out into the lordship and there are holding things with the folk; it is a thing of escheat. All we brothers have been asked to take part in that council, but none of us wish to be called by the name of king-traitor, for our father was not that". The king then took up the talk: "What way out shall we now find? A great difficulty is now at hand. Give good counsel, ye good chiefs, so that I may hold the kingdom and my father's inheritance; but I do not wish to fight against the whole Swedish army". Arnvid the Blind answered: "My lord, it seems best to me that you ride down to Aros[1] with the men who will follow you and take there your ships and go out into Lögrinn; then call the folk to you. Go not with strife, but offer the men laws and land rights; strike down the war arrow; it has not yet gone far about in the land, for the time has been short. Then send your men whom you trust well to meet the men who have this plan in their hands, to try if this unrest can be damped". The king said that he would follow that counsel. "I wish you brothers to make this journey," he said, "for I trust you best of my men." Then said Torvid the Stammerer: "I will stay behind, but Jacob shall go; it is needful". Then said Fröivid: "Let us do, my lord, as Torvid says. He will not be parted

1 *Aros* was the name of the present Upsala.

from you in this journey; but Arnvid and I will go". That plan went forward so that King Olav went to his ships and sailed out into Lögrinn, and he soon had a strong body of men. But Fröivid and Arnvid rode out to Ullaraker and took with them the king's son Jacob, but they kept it secret. They soon became aware that there was a great gathering and running of troops in that the bonders held things day and night. And when Fröivid and Arnvid came together with their kinsmen and friends they said that they would join their troop, and they took it gladly. Straightway all plans were passed over to them and a great crowd gathered around them; but all, however, said the same thing, that they would no longer have King Olav over them, and that they would not thole his lawlessness and such over-might that he would not hear any man's talk, even though great chiefs told him the truth. When Fröivid saw the crowd's heatedness he understood how far the matter had gone. He then held meetings with the land chiefs and talked to them and spoke thus: "If this great plan to drive Olav Ericson from the kingdom goes forward it seems to me as if we Up-Swedes will go in the fore. It has always been so here that the other men of the land have followed the plan which the Up-Swede chiefs have bound amongst themselves. Our fathers had no need to seek counsel from the West Gauts about the rule of the land. Now we will not be so faithless to our forefathers that Emund need give us counsel. I will that we, kinsmen and friends, bind our counsel together". To that they all said 'yea', and it seemed well spoken. After that the whole crowd turned to the bond which the Up-Swede chiefs had agreed to; Fröivid and Arnvid were now leaders of the army. And when Emund noted that, he could understand what outcome this plan would have. He then went to meet the brothers and they held talk. Then Fröivid asked Emund: "What is your thought about Olav Ericson losing his life? What king will ye have?" Emund said: "He who seems to us best fitted whether he be of high family or not". Fröivid said: "We Up-Swedes do not wish the kingdom to go out of the family of the old kings in our days so long as there are so many to choose between as now. King Olav has two sons; we will have one of them for king, and there is still great difference between them; one is noble-born and Swedish in all his ancestry, but the other is a thrall woman's son and half Vendish by race". On that speech there was a great shout and all would have Jacob as king. Then said Emund: "Ye Up-Swedes have might to settle this time, but I will tell you what will happen, that some of those who now will hear of nothing else than that the kingdom in Sweden should go by lineage, will themselves live to agree that the kingdom should come into other families and it would be of greater benefit".[1] After that the brothers Fröivid and Arnvid let Jacob the king's son be led forth in the thing and let him be given there the name of king; thereby the Swedes gave him the name of Anund, and so he was afterwards called as long as he lived. He was then ten or twelve years old. After that King Anund took himself a bodyguard and chose himself chiefs; and they had altogether as great an army as it seemed to them he needed. But he gave the whole body of men leave to go home. Thereafter messengers went between the kings and thereupon it came about that they themselves met and made terms between them: Olav was to be king of the land as long as he lived, and he was to keep peace and terms with the King of Norway, and likewise with all the men who had been in that undertaking; Anund was also to be king and to have as much of the land as his father and he were agreed upon, but he was to be bound to go with the bonders if King Olav did such things as the bonders would not thole of him. After that messengers went to Norway to King Olav with these errands that the king should go to a meeting at Konungahella to meet the Swedish king, and likewise that the Swedish king wished them to bind their agreement. And when King Olav heard this message he was ready for peace, even now as before, and he went with his men as had been arranged. The Swedish king came there; and when he met his son-in-law, they bound between themselves terms of peace. Then was Olav, the Swedish king, pleasant to talk with and meek of mood. Torstein the Wise says that there was a district in Hising, which sometimes had gone with Norway, sometimes with Gautland.[2] Then the kings said to each other that they would cast lots with dice for that possession; he who threw the highest number was to have it. Then the Swedish king threw two sixes and said that King Olav had now no need to throw. The latter said whilst he shook the dice in his hands: "There are still two sixes on the dice and for the Lord my God it is an easy thing to let them turn up". He threw and two sixes came up. Then Olav the Swedish king threw and again two sixes turned up. Thereupon Olav, King of Norway, threw and there was a six on one dice but the other broke in bits and it became seven. He won the district. We have not

1 This was a prophecy about Steinkel's dynasty, which came to the throne of Sweden in 1056. 2 The two southern districts in Hising, Lundby and Tuve, belonged from olden times to Gautland, whilst the four others, Bakke, Bjorlande, Sæve and Thorslanda, belonged to Norway.

heard many tidings told of that meeting. The kings now parted as the best of friends.

95. After these tidings which have just now been told, King Olav went with his men north into the Vik. First he went to Tunsberg, and stayed there for some time; he then went north through the land and in the autumn he came right north to Trondheim, and had his winter quarters made ready there, where he sat through the winter. Then was Olav sole king over the whole kingdom which Harald Hairfair had had, and so much better in that he was the only king in the land. In peace and by terms he had got the part of the land which Olav the Swedish king had formerly had. But that part of the land which the Danish king had had he had taken by might and ruled over it in the same way as other places in the land. Canute the Danish king at that time ruled over both England and Denmark, and was most of the time in England; but he set chiefs to rule the land in Denmark, and at that time he made no claim upon Norway.

96. It is said already that the Orkneys were settled in the days of King Harald Hairfair, but formerly they had been a viking haunt. Sigurd was the first jarl of the Orkneys and he was the son of Eystein Glumra and brother to Ragnvald the Jarl of Möre; after Sigurd, Guthorm his son followed for one year; after him Ragnvald the Jarl's son, Turf-Einar, took the jarldom and was jarl for a long time, and a mighty man. Halvdan Highleg, Harald Hairfair's son, went against Einar the Jarl and drove him away from the Orkneys. Einar thereafter came back and slew Halvdan on Rinansöy.[1] After that King Harald went with his army to the Orkneys and Einar fled to Scotland. King Harald made the Orkney men swear to him all their *odal* lands. The king and the jarl came to terms thereafter; the jarl became his man and held his land of the king, but he was not to pay tribute thereon because it lay exposed to foes. The jarl paid the king sixty marks of gold. Then King Harald harried in Scotland, as is told in Glymdrapa. After Turf-Einar, his sons Arnkel, Erlend and Torfinn Hausakljuv[2] ruled over the land. In their days, Eric Bloodaxe came from Norway and the jarls submitted to him. Arnkel and Erlend fell in a fight, but Torfinn ruled over the land and grew old. His sons were Arnfinn, Howard, Lodver, Ljot and Skuli, and their mother was Grelad, daughter of Dungad (i.e. Duncan), Jarl of Caithness; her mother was Groa, daughter of Torstein the Red. In the later days of Torfinn the Jarl, the sons of Eric Blood-axe came from

1 Ronaldsey.   2 The ancestor of Torfinn, the great Earl of Orkney. Cf. 'History of Harald Hardrade', p. 536, n. 1.

Norway after they had fled on account of Hacon the Jarl; their dealings in the Orkneys were very fierce. Torfinn the Jarl died in his bed.
After him his sons ruled and about them many things are told. Lodver
lived longest of them and at last he ruled alone. His son was Sigurd
Digre who took the jarldom after him; he was a great and mighty
warrior. In his days, Olav Trygvason went with his army from a
viking raid in the west and lay in by the Orkneys; he took Sigurd the
Jarl prisoner on Rinansöy; the jarl had been there with one ship. Olav
offered him his freedom on condition that he should be baptised and
take the true faith, become his man, and bid all the Orkney men become Christian. As hostage, King Olav took the jarl's son who was
called Hound or Whelp. From there Olav went to Norway and became
king. Hound was with King Olav some years and died in Norway.
But afterwards Sigurd the Jarl showed no loyalty to King Olav; he
then married a daughter of Melkolm the Scottish king[1] and their son
was Torfinn. Sigurd the Jarl's elder sons were Sumarlide, Bruce and
Einar Wrymouth. Four or five years after the fall of Olav Trygvason, Sigurd the Jarl went to Ireland and set his elder sons to rule the
land. Torfinn he sent to the Scottish king, his wife's father. On that
journey, Sigurd the Jarl fell in the Brian battle.[2] And when this was
learnt in the Orkneys the brothers Sumarlide, Bruce and Einar were
taken as jarls and they divided the land into three shares amongst
themselves. Torfinn Sigurdson was five years old when Sigurd the
Jarl fell. And when Sigurd's death was learnt by the Scottish king,
he gave Torfinn, his kinsman, Caithness and Sutherland with the
name of 'jarl', and set men to rule the land for him. Torfinn the Jarl
was, in growing up, soon strongly developed in all bodily accomplishments. He was big and strong and unsightly, and as he grew
up it was seen that he was greedy, hard, grim and cunning. About
it Arnor Jarlascald says:

No man under the heaven      Is said to be more active
As young as Einar's brother      In guarding the land and harrying.

97. The brothers Einar and Bruce were unlike in mind. Bruce
was calm and peaceful, clever and wise of speech and well befriended;
Einar was stubborn, reserved and unfriendly, greedy and grasping
and a great warrior. Sumarlide was like Bruce in mind; he was the

1 Malcolm MacKenneth ruled from 1005 to 1034. 2 *The Brian battle* was the Norsemen's name for the famous battle of Clontarf (near Dublin) which took place on the 23rd
April, 1014. Sigurd the Jarl here referred to was Sigurd the Stout, father of Torfinn, the
great Earl of Orkney, who married Ingebjörg, the daughter of Jarl Finn Arneson. Torfinn
died at Birsay (Mainland) in 1064.

eldest, and lived shortest of the brothers. He died in his bed. After his death, Torfinn claimed his share of the Orkneys. Einar answered that Torfinn had Caithness and Sutherland, the kingdom which their father Sigurd the Jarl had formerly had, and Einar reckoned that to be much greater than a third share of the Orkneys. He would not therefore share with Torfinn, but for his part Bruce allowed the sharing; "I will not", he said, "claim to have more of the land than the third share which I have free". Then Einar put under himself two-thirds of the isles and he now became mighty and had a great strength of men; in the summer he was often raiding and had great gatherings from the land, but his winning of booty on viking raids was very uneven. The bonders began to be tired of that toil, but the jarl upheld with hardness all that was laid upon them and suffered no man to speak against it. Einar was a very haughty man; dearth now arose in his kingdom from all that toil and the cost that the bonders had to bear. But in that part of the land which Bruce had, the bonders had good seasons and happiness. Bruce was well befriended.

98. There was a rich and mighty man called Amund who lived on Rossöy[1] in Sandvik[2] on Laupandanes. His son was called Thorkel and he was the doughtiest man in the Orkneys. Amund was very wise, and one of the noblest men on the islands. It happened, one spring, that Einar the Jarl again called up men as usual, but the bonders murmured and brought the matter before Amund, and bade him speak to the jarl for help for them. He answered: "The jarl is not willing to hear objections", and meant that it was no use asking the jarl any boons about that; "the friendship between the jarl and me is good for the present, but if we disagree it seems dangerous to me according to both our moods. I will have nothing to do with it". Then they talked with Thorkel about it; he was not willing, but promised it, when they had begged him much. Amund thought that Thorkel had given the promise too rashly. But when the jarl held a thing Thorkel spoke on the bonders' behalf and bade the jarl give the folk a little relief from their burdens and mentioned their need. The jarl answered in a friendly way, and said that he ought to lay much weight on Thorkel's words: "I had wished to have six ships from the land, but now I will take no more than three, for thou, Thorkel, dost not often beg such a boon". The bonders thanked Thorkel much for his help. The jarl went on his viking raid and came back in the autumn. But the spring after, the jarl had the same

1 Now Mainland, the largest island in the Orkneys.    2 *Sandwich* is situated on the Deerness peninsula.

bidding out as was his wont and held a thing with the bonders. Then Thorkel spoke again and bade the jarl spare the bonders. The jarl then answered wrathfully and said that the bonders' lot should now be worse after his boon; he was then so wroth and frantic that he said that next spring both of them should not be alive at the thing, and with that the thing ended. When Amund got to hear what Thorkel and the jarl had said against each other, he bade Thorkel go away, and Thorkel went over to Caithness to Torfinn the Jarl. Thorkel was there a long time, and became a friend of the jarl whilst he was young; he was afterwards called Thorkel Foster-father, and he was an outstanding man. There were many great men who fled from their *odal* lands in the Orkneys because of Einar the Jarl's might. Most of them fled over to Caithness to Torfinn the Jarl; some fled from the Orkneys to Norway; and some to other lands. And when Torfinn the Jarl was grown up he sent bidding to his brother Einar the Jarl and claimed from him the land which he thought he had a right to in the Orkneys, and that was a third share of the isles. Einar was not willing to lessen his realm. When Torfinn learned that, he called out an army from Caithness and went out to the isles. And when Einar the Jarl got to know of it, he gathered his army and would guard his lands. Bruce the Jarl also gathered an army, and went towards them and bore words of peace between them. Terms were then made between them that Torfinn was to have a third share of the land in the Orkneys, as he had a right to. But Bruce and Einar put their shares together, and Einar was to have the sole rule over them; but if either died before the other, he who lived the longer of them was to own the lands after the other; but this arrangement did not seem right, for Bruce had a son who was called Ragnvald, whilst Einar was without son. Torfinn the Jarl then set his men to rule the land he had in the Orkneys, but he was most often in Caithness. Einar the Jarl was most often about in the summer on raids in Ireland and Scotland and Wales. One summer when Einar the Jarl was on a raid in Ireland he fought in Ulvreksfjord against the Irish king Konofogor as is before written about; and Einar the Jarl had a great defeat and loss of men (chapter 86). The summer after, Eyvind Urarhorn came west from Ireland and wished to go to Norway, but when the weather was stormy and the tide against him, he lay at Osmondwall[1] for some time weatherbound. And when Einar the Jarl learned that, he sailed there with a great army, took Eyvind and had him slain. But to most of his men he gave peace and they went east to Norway

1 *Asmundvag.* Cf. 'History of Olav Trygvason', p. 153, n. 1.

in the autumn; they came to King Olav and told him of Eyvind's death. The king answered little thereto, but this they found out from him, that he thought it a great scathe and that it was done to spite him; he spoke little about most things which he thought were against him. Torfinn the Jarl sent Thorkel Foster-father out to the isles to gather his taxes. Einar the Jarl gave Thorkel most blame for the uprising when Torfinn the Jarl had laid claim on the isles. Thorkel went speedily from the isles over to Caithness. He told Torfinn the Jarl he was sure that Einar the Jarl had wished to slay him if his kinsmen and friends had not given him news thereof; "Now have I this to choose from," he said; "to let the meeting between me and the jarl be such as was arranged between us; but the other choice is that I go farther away to where he has no might". The jarl wished Thorkel to go east to Norway to King Olav: "Thou wilt", he said, "be reckoned highly wherever thou comest amongst princes, and I know both thy mind and the jarl's to be such that ye two within a short time will meet to fight". Then Thorkel made himself ready and went in the autumn to Norway and afterwards to King Olav with whom he was in great favour during the winter. The king took Thorkel very much into counsel in his affairs. He thought as was true that Thorkel was a wise and goodly man. The king gathered from his talk that he spoke very differently about the jarls, that he was a good friend of Torfinn but that he had much to say against Einar the Jarl. Early in the spring the king sent a ship west over the sea to Torfinn the Jarl with the behest that the jarl should come east to the king. The jarl did not delay the journey, for a promise of friendship came with the message.

99. Torfinn the Jarl went east to Norway and came to King Olav; he was greeted well and stayed there long during the summer. And when he was to go back west, King Olav gave him a great and goodly longship, well fitted out. Thorkel Foster-father also made himself ready for the journey, and the jarl gave him the ship which he had had when he came from the west in the summer. The king and the jarl parted with great love. Torfinn the Jarl came in the autumn to the Orkneys. But when Einar the Jarl learned that, he called up a great strength of men, and lay aboard ship. Bruce the Jarl then went to meet his brothers and bore words of peace between them; it then came about that they made peace and bound it with oaths. Thorkel Foster-father was to be in peace and friendship with Einar the Jarl, and it was agreed that each of them should invite the other to a feast, and the jarl should first visit Thorkel at Sandwich. When the jarl was at the feast, strong drink was served, but the jarl was not happy. There was a great shieling with doors at both ends. The day

when the jarl was to go away, Thorkel was to go with him to the other feast; but Thorkel sent spies to find out their intentions on that day; and when the spies came back they told Thorkel they had found three ambushes of armed men, "and we believe", they said, "that treachery is certain". When Thorkel learned that, he put off making himself ready and called his men to him. The jarl bade him make himself ready and said that it was now time to ride. Thorkel said that he had much to put in order; sometimes he went out, sometimes came in. A fire was burning on the floor. Then he came in at one door and after him came a man called Halvard, who was an Icelander from the Eastfjords; he locked the door again. Thorkel went towards the fire and the place where the jarl sat. The jarl asked: "Art thou still not ready?" Thorkel answered: "I am ready now", and so he struck the jarl on the head; the jarl fell down on the floor, and then the Icelander said: "Here I see the worst absent-mindedness in that you do not drag the jarl out of the fire". He drove a battle-axe in under the nape of the jarl's neck and pulled him up on to the bench. Thorkel and his followers went quickly out by the opposite door from that that they had gone in by. There outside stood Thorkel's men fully weaponed. Inside, the jarl's men attended to the jarl, but by then he was dead. All of them lost heart, so that this was not avenged; that was because it happened so quickly and no one expected such work from Thorkel, for they all thought that there was friendship between the jarl and Thorkel as had been agreed upon before; most of the men within were also without weapons and many were already good friends of Thorkel. Besides, it was Thorkel's luck that he should have a longer life. When Thorkel came out his men were no fewer than the jarl's men. Thorkel went to his ship and the jarl's men went their way. Thorkel sailed away that day, and went east on the sea. That was after Winter's Night and he came unscathed to Norway, and straightway went speedily to King Olav and there had a good greeting. The king uttered his praises over that deed and Thorkel was with him during the winter.

100. After the fall of Einar the Jarl, Bruce the Jarl took that share of the lands which Einar the Jarl had formerly had, for it was known by many men by what arrangement the brothers Einar and Bruce had gone into fellowship. But it seemed most right to Torfinn that each of them should have a half share of the isles; Bruce, however, this winter had two-thirds of the land. The next spring Torfinn laid claim to this land from Bruce, namely that he should have half share with Bruce; but Bruce denied that. They now held a thing and met about these matters; their friends sought to settle the affair, and it

then came about that Torfinn would have nothing but a half share; he said, however, that Bruce had no need of more than a third share with the ambition he had. Bruce said: "I was happy in having the third share which I took in succession to my father; nor has any man claimed it of me. And now have I taken the second third share in succession to my brother according to our just arrangement. But even though I have no might to bear strife against thee, my brother, yet will I try anything rather than give away my realm under such circumstances". In that way they ended their meeting. And when Bruce saw that he had no might to stand up to Torfinn (for Torfinn had a much greater realm and help from the Scottish king, his mother's father), Bruce took the plan of going east from the land to King Olav; he had with him his son Ragnvald who was then ten years old. And when the jarl came to the king, he was greeted well. The jarl put forth his errand and told of the whole matter which stood between the brothers, and he bade the king grant him help to keep his realm and offered his full friendship in return. The king then first began to talk about the fact that Harald Hairfair had possessed himself of all the *odal* lands in the Orkneys, whilst the jarls had ever afterwards held the land in fief, but never in true possession; "and there is proof of this when Eric Blood-axe and his sons were in the Orkneys the jarls were subject to them; and when Olav Trygvason, my kinsman, came thither, thy father, Sigurd the Jarl, became his man. Now have I taken all the inheritance after King Olav; I will give thee the choice that thou becomest my man and I shall then give thee the isles in fief. If I grant thee my help, we two shall try if it be not of more avail than the Scottish king's help to thy brother Torfinn. But if thou wilt not have this, then will I myself seek after the possessions and *odal* lands which our kinsmen and forefathers have had there in the west". This talk the jarl now fixed in his mind and brought it before his friends and sought counsel as to what he should do, whether he should come to terms on those conditions with King Olav and become his man; "but if I say nay, it is not clear to me what my lot will be on our parting, for the king has laid bare the claim he has on the Orkneys; but because of his great plans and likewise because we are now come hither, it will be easy for him to do with us as he will". But even though the jarl saw much to find fault with on both sides, he took the choice, however, of laying all in the king's power, both himself and his realm. Thereafter King Olav took from the jarl power and lordship over all the jarl's inheritance; the jarl became his man and bound it with oaths.

101. Torfinn the Jarl learned that his brother Bruce had gone east to King Olav to seek help from him. But, as Torfinn had formerly been with King Olav and won his friendship, he thought that his affair stood well and he knew that many would be there to bear out his case. And he expected that there would be still more if he himself went again. Torfinn the Jarl then chose this plan and made himself speedily ready and went to Norway; he thought that there should be as little difference as possible between the times of their leaving and that Bruce's errand should not be over before Torfinn met the king. But it went otherwise than the jarl had thought, for when Torfinn the Jarl came to King Olav the agreement was fully made between the king and Bruce the Jarl; nor did Torfinn know it before he came to King Olav that Bruce the Jarl had given his kingdom up. And as soon as Torfinn the Jarl and King Olav met, King Olav came forth with the same claim on the realm of the Orkneys as he had laid before Bruce the Jarl, and bade Torfinn likewise give over to the king that share of the land which he had before. The jarl answered well and coolly to the king's words and said that he laid much weight on the king's friendship. "And if you, my lord, think you need my help against the chiefs, then have you every claim to it, but I cannot submit to you, for I am already jarl of the Scottish king and owe him loyalty." And when the king found from the jarl's answer that he would withdraw the claims he had formerly set forth, the king said: "If you will not be my man, then have I the power of setting over the Orkneys what man I will; and I wish thee to swear oaths that thou wilt not claim those lands and wilt let him be in peace whom I set over them. But if thou wilt have none of these lots, then it will seem to him who rules over the land that enmity might be expected of thee; and then it will not seem strange to thee if dale follow upon hill". The jarl answered and bade him give him time to think over the matter. The king did so, giving the jarl time to take counsel on this choice with his friends. Then he bade the king let him have time till the next summer, so that he could then first go west over the sea, for his counsellors were at home and he himself was still a child in years. But the king bade him choose now. Thorkel Foster-father was then with King Olav, and he secretly sent a man to Torfinn the Jarl, bidding him not to think—whatever he had in his mind—of parting this time from King Olav in such a way that they were not agreed, inasmuch as he was now in the king's hands. With such reminders the jarl seemed to see that his only choice this time was to let the king's will prevail; it did not seem to him desirable

that he himself should lose every hope of his inheritance and make oaths that they who were not born to the kingdom should have it in peace. But when he seemed uncertain of getting away he chose to put himself into the king's hands and become his man, just as Bruce had done. The king found that Torfinn was much more haughty than Bruce, and he consented less willingly to this restraint. The king trusted Torfinn less than Bruce, and he saw that Torfinn would seem able to expect help from the Scottish king if he broke this treaty. With his good understanding the king saw that Bruce went into the agreement slowly, and promised no more than what he thought of keeping; but when Torfinn had first decided what he would choose, he went gladly into every term and made no objection to what the king demanded in the beginning. But the king doubted whether the jarl would go back on some of the terms or not.

102. When King Olav had thought out with himself all this matter, he had a large meeting summoned and had the jarls called thither. Then said the king: "I will now lay bare before all of you the agreement between me and the jarls of the Orkneys. They have now accepted my claim to the possession of the isles and both are become my men; they have bound it with oaths. Now I will give it to them in fief, a third share to Bruce, and the second third share to Torfinn; but the third share which Einar Wrymouth held, has, I judge, fallen into my possession, for Einar slew Eyvind Urarhorn, my counsellor, fellow and dear friend; I will take care of that share of the land in such manner as I list. This also will I claim of you my jarls that ye come to terms with Thorkel Amundson for the death of your brother Einar; I will that the judgment hereof shall lie with me if ye will abide by it". And it was, like everything else, that the jarls agreed to all which the king said. Thorkel then went forth and bound the king's judgment in this matter, and in this way the thing ended. King Olav laid as great fines for the death of Einar the Jarl as on three landed men. But the third part of the fines should fall away because of his guilt. Torfinn the Jarl then bade the king give him leave to go home, and as soon as he had got it he speedily made himself ready. But when he was almost ready it happened one day when the jarl was drinking on the ship that Thorkel Amundson suddenly came before him and laid his head on the jarl's knee, bidding him do with it as he liked. The jarl asked why he did so. "We have indeed already come to terms according to the king's judgment; stand thou up, Thorkel." He did so and said, "This agreement which the king has made, I will abide by in the matter between me and

Bruce, but in that which is between thee and me thou alone shalt rule. Even though the king has granted me my possessions and a right to live in the Orkneys, I know thy mind so well that it would not be feasible for me to be in the isles unless I have thy promise of trustiness, O jarl. I will promise thee never to come to the isles whatever the king says to it". The jarl was silent and took long to answer. He said: "If thou, Thorkel, wouldst rather that I judge in the matter between us than follow the king's judgment, the first condition of our agreement must be that thou shalt go with me to the Orkneys and be with me and not part from me without my leave or assent, and be bound to guard my land and carry out all that which I will demand so long as we are both alive". Thorkel said: "Like everything else in which I have a say this shall be in thy power, jarl". Thorkel then stepped forward and confirmed all that the jarl had claimed. The jarl said that he could settle afterwards as to fines, and he straightway took oaths from Thorkel. Thorkel at once made himself ready to go with the jarl. As soon as the jarl was ready he went away, and he and King Olav never saw each other again. Bruce the Jarl stayed longer and took good time to make himself ready. But before he went away King Olav held a meeting with him and spoke thus: "It seems to me, jarl, that I might have in thee a trusty man there in the west across the sea. My will is that thou shalt have the two third shares of the lands to rule, which thou hast had before. I will that thou shalt be no less a man and no less mighty when thou hast submitted to me than thou wast before. But I will bind thy trustiness herein that thy son Ragnvald shall stay here with me. When thou hast my help and two third shares of the land, I think that thou mayest well hold fast to thy possessions against thy brother Torfinn". Bruce thanked him for receiving two third shares of the lands. Bruce afterwards stayed but a short time before he went away; he came west in the autumn to the Orkneys. Ragnvald, Bruce's son, remained in the east with King Olav. He was very fair, had long hair, golden like silk, and he grew big and strong at an early age, the goodliest of men in wisdom and modesty. He was a long time afterwards with King Olav. About this Ottar the Black says in a poem which he composed about King Olav:

It is known that the Shetlanders
Have done thee homage as lord.
Thou holdest strongly to the whole
Might of the folk kings.

Before thou camest,
No warrior Yngling[1]
Existed on earth who could
Cow the isles in the west.

1 I.e. of the Yngling race. Cf. 'Ynglinga Saga', chapter 10.

103. When the brothers Torfinn and Bruce came west to the Orkneys, Bruce took two-thirds of the land to rule over and Torfinn one-third. Torfinn was always in Caithness or Scotland, but he set his men over the isles, and at that time it was unlucky, for Norsemen and Danes harried the Orkneys much on their western viking raids, and they often came there when they went west or east and robbed on the nesses. Bruce complained then to his brother Torfinn that the latter had no troops out for the Orkneys or Shetlands, and only took full taxes and duties for his share. Torfinn then offered Bruce the choice that Bruce should have one third share of the lands and Torfinn the two, and then he alone should have the warding for them both. But though this sharing was not at once sanctioned, it is said in the Jarls' Sagas that this sharing—that Torfinn should have two shares and Bruce one share—came about when Canute the Mighty had taken Norway to himself and King Olav had gone from the land. Jarl Torfinn Sigurdson had been the noblest jarl in the isles and had the greatest realm of the Orkney jarls; he possessed himself of Shetland, the Orkneys and Hebrides; he had also a great kingdom in Scotland and Ireland. About this Arnor Jarlascald says:

> From Thurso Skerries to Dublin     The ringleader; truly I tell
> The drengs must obey               What might Torfinn had.

Torfinn was the greatest of warriors; he took the jarldom when five years old; he ruled more than sixty years and died in his bed[1] in the last days of Harald Sigurdson's reign.[2] But Bruce died in the days of Canute the Mighty, a little while after the fall of St Olav.

104. Now we go on with two narratives and we shall now take up what we turned from, namely that Olav Haraldson had made peace with Olav the Swedish king and that King Olav had gone north that summer to Trondheim (chapter 95). He had then been king for five years. That autumn he made himself ready for winter quarters in Nidaros, where he stayed during the winter. That winter Thorkel Amundson the Foster-father was with King Olav, as is written before (chapter 98). King Olav then brought up the question as to how Christianity was upheld in the land, and he got to know that as soon as one came north to Halogaland it was hardly kept at all, and it fell very short of being kept well in Naumadale and in Inner Trondheim. There was a man called Harek, son of Eyvind Scalda-

---

1 *Torfinn* died in 1064, and as the King of the Scots gave him the title of earl when he was five years old, Snorre is right in saying that he ruled for more than sixty years. Orkneyinga Saga states that he was earl for seventy winters and he was therefore seventy-five years old when he died.     2 Harald Hardrade.

spiller; he lived in an island called Tjotta, which is in Halogaland. Eyvind had not been a very rich man, but he was of good kin and very doughty. In Tjotta there dwelt not a few small bonders. Harek first bought there a farmstead not very big and settled down there. But in a few years he had driven away all the bonders who lived there, so that he owned the whole island and then built great houses. Harek now became very rich. He was clever and enterprising and he reckoned himself in kinship with the kings of Norway; for these reasons Harek had enjoyed great honour among the chiefs of the land. Harek's father's mother, Gunhild, was daughter of Halvdan the Jarl and Ingebjörg, Harald Hairfair's daughter. When these events happened, Harek was somewhat old; he was the most important man in Halogaland, and for a long time he had had the sole rights of Finnish trade and the king's business in Finmark. Sometimes he had it alone, and sometimes others had a share in it with him. He had not come to King Olav, but words and messengers had gone between them and everything was friendly; and the winter when King Olav was in Nidaros men went backwards and forwards between him and Harek of Tjotta. The king wished to go north the next summer to Halogaland, right north to the end of the land, but the men of Halogaland thought very differently about that journey.

105. King Olav made himself ready in the spring with five ships and nigh on three hundred (three hundred and sixty) men. When he was ready he started on that journey north through the land, and when he came to the Naumadale folk district he called a thing; there as in other places he had those laws read out wherein he bade the men in the land keep to Christianity and set loss of life or limbs or possessions on every man who would not submit to Christian laws. The king punished many men heavily and judged equally over the mighty as well as the small. He only left every lordship after all the folk had undertaken to keep the Holy Faith. Most of the chiefs and many great bonders made feasts for the king and in such a way he went right north through Halogaland. Harek of Tjotta also made a feast for the king; there was a great crowd at it and it was the finest of feasts. Harek then became a district chief; King Olav gave him land rents such as he had had of the former rulers.

106. There was a man called Grankel or Granketel, a rich bonder, who was then somewhat old. But in his youth he had been on viking raids and was at that time a great warrior. He was a very doughty man in all accomplishments and sports. His son was called Asmund and he was in all things like his father, or even doughtier. It was

the talk of many men that he was the third best endowed man in Norway in good looks, strength and sports.[1] The first mentioned were Hacon, Athelstan's foster-son, and Olav Trygvason. Grankel bade King Olav to a feast and it was the costliest of banquets; Grankel let him go away with great gifts of friendship. The king bade Asmund go with him and talked him into it with many words; Asmund could not resist this honour and went on the journey with the king, he afterwards became his man and fell into great friendship with the king. King Olav stayed the greatest part of the summer in Halogaland and went to all the things and baptised all the folk there. At that time Tore the Hound dwelt in Bjarköy;[2] he was the mightiest man there in the north, and he then became a district chief for King Olav. The sons of many mighty bonders went on that journey with King Olav. When it got late in the summer, the king proceeded to the south and sailed in by Trondheim to Nidaros where he settled the winter after. That winter Thorkel Foster-father came from the west from the Orkneys after he had slain Jarl Einar Wrymouth (chapter 99). That autumn there was a dearth of corn in Trondheim, but for a long time before this there had been good seasons. And there was dearth right north in the land and so much more so the farther north it was; but the corn was good in the east of the land and likewise in the Uplands; in Trondheim they had less need because there they had much old corn.

107. That autumn King Olav was told these tidings from Inner Trondheim that the bonders had a crowded feast on Winter's Night. There was great drinking and it was told the king that they blessed all the bowls to the gods, after the old custom; tales also followed that cows and horses were struck down and the stalls were dyed with blood, and that a blood offering was made. And there followed also such talk that the offering was made for better seasons. News also followed that all men saw clearly that the gods were wroth that the men of Halogaland had turned to Christianity. And when the king learned these tidings he sent men into Inner Trondheim and called to him those men whom he thought fit to name.

There was a man called Ölvir of Egge. He was called after the place he dwelt in. He was a mighty man, of great kin, and leader on the bonders' behalf of the journey to the king. And when they came to the king the king brought the mentioned charges against the bonders. But Ölvir answered on the bonders' behalf and said that they had no feast that autumn except their guild feasts and friendly

---

1 The O.N. name for sport is *iþrott*. In M.S. *idræt* and *idrott*.

2 *Bjarköy* is situated to the north-east of Hinnöy (in Tromsö) folk district.

drinkings, and also some feasts among friends; "but if what is told you about us Tronds when we drink, be true, then may all wise men beware of such talk, but I cannot answer for what witless and drunken men say". Ölvir was wise and bold of speech and defended the bonders against all this talk. And at last the king said that the Inner Tronds themselves would bear witness as to what they had for a faith. The bonders got leave to go home; they also went as soon as they were ready.

108. Later in the winter the king was told that the Inner Tronds were holding a gathering at Mæren[1] and that there was a great blood offering at midwinter, when they were sacrificing for peace and good winter weather. And when the king thought of knowing the truth about it, he sent men and messengers into Inner Trondheim and called the bonders to the town; he again called up the men who seemed to him wisest. The bonders then held a meeting and talked amongst themselves about this bidding; then were all those who had gone previously that winter least happy about that journey. But through the entreaties of all the bonders, Ölvir undertook the journey. And when he came out to the town, he went straight to the king and talked with him. The king brought this charge against the bonders that they had held a midwinter sacrifice. Ölvir answered and said that the bonders were blameless in that; "we had", he said, "a Yule feast and drinkings together far about in the lordships; the bonders do not prepare themselves so scantily for the Yule feast that there is not much left over; what was left they drank up a long time after, my lord. In Mæren there is a great garth and great houses and great buildings round about, and there folks find gladness in drinking when many are together". The king answered little and was somewhat wroth. He seemed to know truer things than that which was now said about it. The king bade the bonders go home; "but even if ye deny it and do not stand up to it, I shall still get to know the truth; but however it has been till now, do such things no more". The bonders then went home and told about their journey and how the king was rather wroth.

109. King Olav held a great feast at Easter[2] and had bidden to it many townsmen and likewise bonders; and after Easter the king had his ships set forth and told men to bear tackle and oars to them; he had the floorboards and awnings laid and the ships floated ready for sea. After Easter the king sent men to Værdale. There was a man called Torald, the king's steward, who ruled the king's estate at

1 Cf. 'History of Hacon the Good', chapter 18.    2 2nd of April, 1021.

Haug.[1] To him the king sent word that he should come speedily to him. Torald did not delay that journey, but went straightway out to the town with the messengers. The king called him to a talk in a small room and asked whether there was truth in what was told him about the customs of the Inner Tronds. "If it is that they are turning to blood offering, I wish", said the king, "that thou wilt tell me as it

is and as thou knowest to be true. Thou art bound to do that, for thou art my man." Torald answered: "My lord, I wish first to tell you that I have moved here to the town, my two sons and my wife and all the loose treasures I could bring with me. And if thou wilt have the truth about this from me, it shall be at thy service. And if I

The king's men bring their booty on board

say as it is, thou must take care of my lot". The king said: "Tell the truth about that which I ask thee and if I take care of thee thou shalt have no scathe from it". "It is true to tell thee, O king, if I shall tell thee what is, that in Inner Trondheim almost all the folk are heathen in their faith, even though some men there are Christians. And it is their custom to hold a blood offering in the autumn and then bid winter welcome, another at midwinter, and the third on Summer's Day and when they bid summer welcome; together in that place are the Öyner, and the Sparbyggjer, the Værdöler, and the Sköyner. Twelve men there are who understand the blood offerings, and this spring Ölvir will undertake the feast. He has now much work in Mæren and thither are moved all the goods which will be needed for holding the feasts."

When the king got to know the truth, he bade them summon his men together and let them be told to go to the ships. The king named men as helmsmen and likewise as leaders of the crews, and settled how every crew should be shipped. They soon made themselves ready; the king had five ships and three hundred (three hundred and sixty) men, and he sailed in along the fjord. There was a good wind and the ships lost no time pushing forth before the wind. But no one expected that the king would come there so quickly. He came in the

1 In Western Værdale, between Værdalsöra and Stiklestad.

night into Mæren where he straightway threw a ring of men around the houses. Ölvir was taken prisoner and the king had him and many others slain and the feast goods he seized and shipped out to his ships; likewise he took all the goods, both house wares and clothes and treasures, which they had brought thither and let them be shared as booty amongst his men. The king also told them to seek out the bonders who seemed to him to have had the greatest share in this plan; some were taken prisoner and set in irons, some got away in flight and many were deprived of their goods. The king then called a thing with the bonders; and when he had taken many great men and had them in his power, their kinsmen and friends agreed to promise the king loyalty, and this time no rising was made against the king. He there turned all the folk to the right faith and set priests there and had churches built and hallowed. The king deemed that no fines should be paid for Ölvir and drew into his own possession all the goods Ölvir had had; but of all the others who seemed to him most guilty he had some slain, some maimed, some he drove from the land, and from some he took their goods. Thereafter the king went back to Nidaros.

110. There was a man called Arne Armodson who was married to Thora, daughter of Torstein Galga. Their children were Kalv, Finn, Torberg, Amund, Kolbjörn, Arnbjörn, Arne, and Ragnhild who was married to Harek of Tjotta. Arne was a landed man, mighty and noble, and a good friend of King Olav. His sons, Kalv and Finn, were then with King Olav and they were there in great honour. The woman whom Ölvir of Egge had had was young and beautiful, and of great kin and rich. She seemed a good match, but the king had now to decide about that. She and Ölvir had two young sons. Kalv Arneson bade the king wed him to the woman whom Ölvir had had, and, for the sake of their friendship, the king granted him that, and thereto all· the possessions which Ölvir had had. The king then made him a landed man and gave him charge of the Inner Tronds. Kalv now became a great chief and he was a very wise man.

111. Then King Olav had been seven years in Norway. That summer Torfinn and Bruce, the Jarls of the Orkneys, came to him. King Olav took to himself the lands in such a manner as is written about before (chapter 102). That summer King Olav went over both North and South Möre and in the autumn to Raumsdale; there he went from his ships, went to the Uplands and came forth into Lesjar.[1] He bade his men take all the best men in both Lesjar and Dovra,[2]

1 The present Lesjaskogen and Lesja districts.    2 Dovre district between Lesja and Sel.

and they had to take Christianity or suffer death, or those who could had to flee thence. But those who took Christianity gave the king their sons as hostages for their trustiness. In the night the king was at a place called Borar in Lesjar and he set priests there. After that he went over Orkedale and then along Ljardale[1] and came down to a place called Stavabrekka.[2] A river called the Otta runs through the dale, and there on both sides of the river is a fair district called Loar,[3] and the king could see down upon it: "Great scathe it is", said the king, "that so fair a place should be burnt", and he went down into the dale with his men. They were in the night at the place called Nes[4] and the king took as his room a loft which he himself slept in; it is still standing to-day—it has had nothing done to it since. The king was there five nights and sent out a thing bidding and summoned folk both from Vaga, Loar and Hedale;[5] and he let it be said that they should either hold battle with him and suffer burning of their farms, or take up Christianity and bring him their sons as hostages. They afterwards came to the king and put themselves in his hands; some fled south to the Dales.

112. There was a man called Dale Gudbrand. He was as a king over the Dales, but was a herse[6] by rank; Sigvat the Scald put him in the same rank as Erling Skjalgson for might and possessions. About Erling, Sigvat says:

Only one warrior          Gold-hater! Ye both
I knew to be great as thee.   Seem equally big, I say;
Gudbrand was his name; wide   He who calls himself better,
Over lands the chieftain ruled.  Only lies about himself.

Gudbrand had a son who is later told about here. When Gudbrand got these tidings that King Olav was come to Loar and had made the folk take up Christianity, he cut up the war arrow and called all the Dale men to meet at the place which is called Hundtorp.[7] There they all came and there was a great crowd of men, for it was near by the

---

1 *Ljardale* is Lordale, a dale adjoining Lesja.  2 *Stavabrekka* is a mountain road from Lesja to Skjak.  3 Now Lom.  4 Now Sönste Nes in Upper Lom. The house where the king slept was shown right up to the beginning of the nineteenth century. It was moved to Ekre about 1830 and rebuilt.  5 An annex of Vaga, by Sjoa.  6 *Herse* (in O.N. *hersir*) was a military district chief or prefect, who supplied the king with men for his ships and army and also collected the king's scot, of which he was entitled to retain a portion. In Harald Hairfair's time each jarl had four hersers under him. Erling Skjalgson of Sola was the mightiest *herse* in Norway (cf. 'History of Olav Trygvason', chapter 58). Landed men (in O.N. *lendir-menn*) was a title bestowed by the kings on landed proprietors who had rendered the king services and were given land.  7 Now Hundorp in Southern Fron.

water which hight Lögr and they could come there on ships as well as by land. Gudbrand held a thing with them and said that "the man who is called Olav is come to Loar and will offer us another faith than we formerly had and break all our gods asunder, and he says that he has a much greater and mightier God. It is strange that the earth does not break asunder under him when he dares talk of such things or that our gods let him live longer. I expect that if we bear out of our temple Thor, who stands in this place and who has always helped us, and if he sees Olav and his men, then will Olav's God, Olav himself, and his men melt and become as nothing". Then they all shouted out at once and said that Olav should never go from there if he came to meet them, "and he will not indeed dare to go farther south through the Dales", they said. They afterwards chose eight hundred (nine hundred and sixty) men to go spying north to Breida.[1] Over this troop Gudbrand's son was leader; he was eighteen years old and many noble men followed him. They came to a garth called Hov and were there three nights; thither came to them many men who had fled from Lesjar and Loar and Vaga and who would not take up Christianity. But King Olav and Bishop Sigurd set priests over Loar and Vaga; they then went over the Urgoröst[2] and came down to Usa and were there during the night; there they heard the tidings that a great army was gathered against them. The bonders who were in Breida also got to know this and made themselves ready to fight against the king. When the king stood up he put on his war clothes and went south along the Su-wolds,[3] and did not stop before he reached Breida, where he saw before him a great army ready for battle. The king then drew up his own army and he himself rode before and talked to the bonders, bidding them take Christianity. They answered: "To-day thou mayest well do otherwise than mock us", and they shouted their war cry and struck their weapons on their shields. The king's men then leaped forth and shot their spears; but the bonders turned straightway in flight, so that only a few withstood them. Then Gudbrand's son was taken and King Olav gave him peace and kept him with him. The king was there four nights and then he said to Gudbrand's son: "Go thou back to thy father and say to him that I shall come there speedily". He afterwards went back home and told his father the hard tidings that they had met the king and gone into battle with him—"but our men fled straightway in the beginning and I was taken", he said; "the

1 Breida, in Sel district. 2 O.N. *Urgoröst*, now Vagarusten between Vaga and Sel.
3 Now Selsvolds (Selvoldene).

king gave me peace, and bade me go tell thee that he was coming here speedily; we have here now no more than two hundred (two hundred and forty) men of all the army which we had when we met him. Now I counsel thee, father, not to fight against this man". "I can hear", said Gudbrand, "that all thy courage is knocked out of thee, in an ill moment thou went from home and that journey will long be remembered of thee. Thou believest straightway in all that wild talk which this man goes about with and which has done thee and thy men such shame." In the night Gudbrand dreamt that there came to him a fair man of whom there was great awe, and he said to Gudbrand: "Thy son had no journey of victory against King Olav, but much less wilt thou get if thou thinkest of holding battle against the king; thou thyself and all thine army will fall and wolves will drag thee and all of you and ravens will tear at you". Gudbrand was much afraid at this sight and told it to Tord Bigmaw who was chief over the Dales. He said: "The same thing came before me". In the morning they had a thing called and said that it seemed advisable to them to hold a thing with this man who came from the north with new words of bidding and get to know with what truth he fared. Then Gudbrand said to his son: "Thou shalt now go to the king who gave thee peace, and twelve men with thee"; and so it was done. And they came to the king and told him their errand that the bonders would hold a thing with him and make peace between the king and the bonders. The king said it seemed a good thing to him, and they now bound it with terms between themselves for as long as the meeting should last. After that they went back and told Gudbrand and Tord that peace was made. The king then went to the place which was called Lidstader[1] and was there five nights. Thereupon the king went to meet the bonders, and held a thing with them, but there was much rain that day. When the thing was set the king stood up and said that the folk in Lesjar and in Loar and in Vaga had taken Christianity and broken down their temples of blood offerings, "and now they believe in the true God who shaped heaven and earth and knows all things". After that the king sat down and Gudbrand answered: "We know not of whom thou talkest. Thou callest by the name of God Him whom neither thou nor anyone hast seen. But we have a god whom we can see every day; he is not out to-day, because the weather is wet. He will seem awe-inspiring and mighty to thee and I think that fear will come upon thee when he comes to the thing. But since thou sayest that thy God can do so much, let Him now do so

1 Now Listad.

that the weather to-morrow be cloudy but without rain, and let us then meet here". The king then went home to his room, and Gudbrand's son went with him as hostage, but the king gave them another man in return. In the evening the king asked Gudbrand's son how their god was made. He answered that "he is marked like Thor and he has a hammer in his hand, is big of build and is hollow inside, and there is a stand on which he rests when he is outside. There is no shortage of gold or silver on him, four loaves of bread are brought to him, and meat withal". After that they went to bed, but the king awoke in the night and was at his prayers. But when it was day the king went to Mass and then to food and so to the thing; the weather was now such as Gudbrand had wished for. Then the bishop stood up in his Mass cape, wearing his mitre[1] on his head and with his staff in his hand, and he spoke of the faith to the bonders and told of many tokens which God had made, and so he ended his speech well. Then Tord Bigmaw answered: "Much doth this man of the horns[2] say who hath in his hand a staff which is crooked like a ram's horn; but since thou and he say that your God can make so many tokens, then say thou to Him that in the morning before sunrise He let the weather be clear with sunshine, and then let us meet here and do one of two things, either agree about this matter, or hold battle"; and thereupon they parted for the time being.

113. Kolbein the Stark[3] was the name of a man who was with King Olav and who hailed from the Fjords.[4] He always went about armed with a sword in his belt and in his hand a great wooden stake such as is called a club.[5] The king said that Kolbein should stand next to him in the morning, and he then said to his men: "Go ye in the night to where the bonders' ships are and bore holes in them all and drive their nags away from the garths in which they are"; and so it was done. But the king was all night at prayers and bade that God would loosen this difficulty with His mildness and loving-kindness. And when the king had heard Mass and it was getting towards day he went to the thing; and when he came there only a few bonders had come. And then they saw a great crowd of bonders coming to the thing and bearing amongst themselves a man-like object all shining with gold and silver. When the bonders who were at the thing saw that, they all leaped up and bowed themselves before the monster. It was afterwards set in the middle of the

---

1 In O.N. *mitr* from the English *mitre*.  2 *The man of the horns* = the bishop, on account of his mitre, the points of which stand out like two horns.  3 In O.N. *Sterki* = the strong or stark.  4 The Fjords = Söndfjord and Nordfjord.  5 In O.N. *klubba*

thing field; on one side sat the bonders, and on the other side the king and his men. Then Gudbrand of the Dales stood up and said: "Where is thy God now, O king? I think that he now weareth his beard somewhat low. And it seems as if thou art not so forceful as yesterday, nor is that man of the horns whom thou callest bishop and who sits there with thee—for now is come our god who rules over all things and he looks on thee with keen eyes, and I see that thou art now full of fear and dare hardly look up with thine eyes. Cast away thy cant and believe in our god who has thee in

The king speaks to the bonders at the thing at Hundorp

his hands"; and thus his speech ended. The king spoke to Kolbein so that the bonders heard not: "If it so goes in my speech that they look away from their god, give thou him as great a blow as thou canst with thy club". The king then stood up and spoke: "Much hast thou said to us this morning. Thou dost wonder that thou dost not see our God, but we expect that He will soon come to us. Thou frightenest us with thy god who is both blind and deaf, who can help neither himself nor others and who can come nowhere unless he is borne; and I expect now that in a short while he will get an unlucky blow. Look ye now towards the east; there goes our God now with much light". The sun then rose and all the bonders looked towards the sun. But at the same moment Kolbein struck at their god so that he burst all asunder and from him there leaped out mice as big as cats, and adders and serpents. And the bonders were so afraid that they fled, some to their ships; but when they shot their ships out, the water rushed into them and filled them, and they could not go in them. And they who ran to their nags found them not. The king then let the bonders be called and said that he would have a meeting with them; the bonders now turned back and held a thing. The king stood up and spoke: "I know not what is the cause of this tumult and rush which ye make. But now ye can see what might your god has to whom ye bore gold and silver and food, and just now ye saw who it was who got good from it, mice and serpents, adders and toads; and it is worse now for those who believe in such things and will not give up such folly. Take ye your gold and wealth which lies here over this field and bear it home to your women, but never again hang them on stocks and stones. Here now are two lots to choose between, either that ye now take up Christianity or this day ye hold battle with me, and let them win the victory whom the God we believe in will give it to". Then Gudbrand stood up and said: "Great scathe have we got for our god, but since he could not help us we will now believe in the God whom thou believest in"; and then they all took up Christianity. The bishop christened Gudbrand and his son and left priests there. They who before were foes parted as friends, and Gudbrand had a church built in the Dales.[1]

114. King Olav then went out to Hedemark and christened there, for at that time when he had taken the kings he was not ready to go farther about the land after such a mighty deed; Hedemark therefore was not widely Christian. But on this journey he did not stop until Hedemark had become fully Christian, churches hallowed and priests set in them. After that he went out to Tote and Hadeland and there taught men the true faith, and only stopped when it was fully Christian. From there he went to Ringerik and there all the folk undertook Christianity. Then the Raumer heard that King Olav would come up to them, and they gathered a great army together and said amongst themselves that they well remembered his journey when he had come there before. The gathering of bonders came to him by the river which is called Nitja.[2] The bonders had a great army; and when they met, they streamed forth to battle, but they speedily got great scathe. They straightway gave way and were "beaten for their bettering", for they took up Christianity. The king

1 The church stood at Listad until 1787, when it was moved to the spot where Söndre Fron church now stands. 2 *Nitja*, now Nitelven, in the Nittedale (Lower Raumarik).

went over the district and did not part from them until all men had become Christian. Thither he went east to Solör and christened the settlement. There Ottar the Black[1] came to him and offered to put himself in King Olav's hands. In the winter before, Olav the Swedish king had died and now Anund Olavson was king in Sweden. King Olav then turned back to Raumarik, and winter was almost over. King Olav called a crowded thing in the place where Heidsævi thing[2] has since been held. He then set up the laws that all the Uplanders should come to that thing and the Heidsævi law should hold over all the Upland districts and in other places as far as it has since been held. And when it was spring he went out to the sea, had his ship made ready and went out to Tunsberg, where he stayed in the spring whilst it was crowded, and heavy wares were brought to the town from other lands. It was a good year over all the Vik and it was likewise good right north to Stad, but in the north there was dearth.

115. In the spring King Olav sent word west over Agder and right north through Rogaland and Hordaland that he would not let either corn or malt or meal be sold from there, and that he would come there with his men and go feasting, as was his wont. That word now went through all these districts, and in the summer the king stayed in the Vik and then went right east to Land's End.

Einar Tambarskelver had been with Olav, King of Sweden, since the death of his brother-in-law, Swein the Jarl; he had become the Swedish king's man and had got there a great grant of land from him. But when the king was dead, Einar wished to seek peace with Olav Digre and in the spring messages had gone between them. And when King Olav was by the Elv,[3] Einar Tambarskelver came with some men; he and the king then talked about their agreement. They settled that Einar should go north to Trondheim and have all his possessions and likewise the lands which Bergliot had brought as her dowry. Einar then went his way to the north, but the king stayed in the Vik and was a long time in Borg[4] in the autumn and the beginning of the winter.

116. Erling Skjalgson so held his lands that he ruled in all things over the bonders as far north as the Sognsjö and east to Lidandisnes.[5] But he had fewer land rents from the king than before. There was so much fear of him that no one did otherwise than what he wished. It

---

1 Cf. chapter 70. 2 By Eidsvold. Cf. 'History of Hacon the Good', p. 84, n. 1. 3 Göta River, by Gothenburg. 4 Sarpsborg, in East Norway. 5 *Lidandisnes*, i.e. Lindesnes, the most southerly point of Norway.

seemed to the king that Erling's might was too big. There was a man called Aslak Fitjaskalli, a mighty man and of great family; Erling's father Skjalg and Aslak's father Askel were the sons of brothers. Aslak was a good friend of King Olav and the king let him settle in South Hordaland, gave him a great grant of land and big land rents and bade him hold out against Erling. But nothing came of it as soon as the king was not near by; Erling alone ruled between them just as he would. He was no meeker because Aslak wanted to be equally powerful as Erling; their difference ended in Aslak not holding to his district. He went to the king and told him of his conflicts with Erling. The king then bade Aslak be with him "until I and Erling have met". The king then sent word to Erling that he was to come in the spring to the king in Tunsberg. And when they met they held a meeting and the king said: "Thus is it told me of thy might, Erling, that there is no man north from Sognsjö to Lidandisnes who can have freedom because of thee; there are many men who deem themselves *odal* born, and who should get their rights from men of equal birth as themselves. Here is Aslak, thy kinsman, who thinks he has suffered coldness enough from thee in thy dealings. Now I know not whether it comes from any guilt he might have in this or whether he should pay for my setting him to look after my interests there. But though I mention him in that connection, there are many others who complain of such things to us, both those who are in the lands I have granted them and stewards who look after our garths and make feasts for me and my men". Erling answered: "I shall answer at once; I deny that I have given Aslak or other men cause, because they are in your service. But I will stand by it, that it is now as it long has been, that each of us kinsmen wishes to be greater than the others. I will also agree that I gladly bow my head to thee, King Olav; but it will seem hard to me to bow it to Sel-Tore who is thrall-born on all sides, even though he is now thy steward, or to other such men who are his like in kinship even though thou givest them honours". Then the friends of both of them began to speak and bade them be reconciled; they said that no man could be of such great help to the king as Erling, "if he can be your true friend". On the other side they said to Erling that he should give way to the king; if he would only hold himself in friendship with the king, it would be easy for him to bring about what he would with the other men. Thus the meeting ended, that Erling should have the same land rents as he had had before, and all the charges which the king had made against Erling were dropped; further, Erling's son Skjalg was to come to the king and be with him. Aslak then went back to his garths and they were now reconciled, so to speak. Erling also went home to his garths and kept his might as before.

117. Sigurd Toreson was the name of a man who was the brother of Tore the Hound of Bjarköy; Sigurd was married to Sigrid Skjalg's daughter, the sister of Erling. Their son was called Asbiorn, and as he grew up he gave great promise. Sigurd lived in Trondenes[1] in Amd; he was a rich man of great worth. He was not in the king's service, so that Tore, his brother, was the better known of the brothers because he was a landed man of the king. But at home in his district Sigurd bore himself with no less state. As long as heathendom lasted he was wont to hold three blood offerings every winter, one on Winter's Night, a second at midsummer, and the third towards summer. But when he took up Christianity he kept up in the same way with the feasts: in the autumn he had a great feast of friends, then in winter a Yule feast, when he bade many men come to him again, and the third he had at Easter, when he had also a great crowd of guests. He kept this up as long as he lived. Sigurd died in his bed, when Asbiorn was eighteen winters old, and the latter took the inheritance after his father. He held to the old custom and had three feasts every winter, just as his father had done. A short while after Asbiorn had taken his inheritance the seasons began to grow worse and the crops failed. Asbiorn still kept on with the feasts in the same way, and it stood him in good stead that there was old corn and old supplies, which were needed. But when that year passed and the second came, the corn was no better than in the former years, and then Sigrid wished the feasts to be laid aside, either some or all. But Asbiorn would not. He went out in the autumn to find his friends and he bought corn where he could, and from some of them he got it given. And so in that winter it happened that he held all the feasts. But in the following spring they had but little sowing, for no one was able to buy seed corn. Sigrid said that they should have fewer huscarls, but Asbiorn would not agree, and he kept to it throughout the summer. It looked like another bad corn year. News followed upon this from the south of the land that King Olav had forbidden corn and malt and meal to be shipped from the south to the north of the land, and then it seemed to Asbiorn to be difficult to get what was needful for the house. His plan was then to have a trade ship he owned put forth; it was a seagoing craft of goodly size, it was strong and its tackle well chosen, and it had a striped sail. Asbiorn and twenty

1 *Trondenes*, in Hinnöy (Tromsö) folk district.

men made themselves ready for the journey, and in the summer they went towards the south, but nothing is told of their journey until they came one afternoon into Karmtsund[1] and lay in by Agvaldsnes. A little way up in the island of Karmt there stands a great house called Agvaldsnes, a king's garth and a good one, over which Tore Sel ruled and was steward. Tore was of lowly family but had raised himself up in life; he was a very enterprising man, wise of speech, and had a good appearance; he was forceful and strong headed, and this he could do since he had the king's help; he was sharp and great of speech. Asbiorn and his men lay there during the night. In the morning when it was light Tore and some of his men went down to the ship. He asked who commanded that fine ship. Asbiorn said his name and mentioned his father. Tore asked how far he was going and what was his business. Asbiorn said that he wished to buy corn and malt, and, as was true, that there was much dearth in the north of the land; "but", he said, "it has been told us that here they have a good season. Wilt thou, bonder, sell us corn? I see here great barns; it would be a help to us to have to go no farther". Tore answered: "I will give thee help so that thou wilt need go no farther buying corn here or farther about in Rogaland. I can tell thee that thou mayest well turn back and go no farther, for thou wilt get no corn either here or in any other places, as the king has forbidden us here to sell corn to the north of the land. Go thou home again, thou man of Halogaland; it is best for thee!" Asbiorn said: "If it is, bonder, as thou sayest, that we cannot buy corn, it is still my business to go as a guest to Sola and see the home of my kinsman Erling".[2] Tore said: "How near kin art thou to Erling?" He said: "My mother is Erling's sister". Then Tore said: "Then it may be that I have not spoken warily if thou art the nephew of the king of Rogaland". Asbiorn's men then threw off the awning and brought the ship out. Tore shouted to them: "Fare ye well and come here when ye go back home", and Asbiorn said that it should be so.

They now went their way and in the evening they came to Jadar.[3] Asbiorn went up with ten men, whilst the other ten watched over the ship. When Asbiorn came to the house he was greeted well and Erling was very glad about his coming. Erling gave him a seat next to him and asked him about many tidings from the north of the land. Asbiorn told him all about his errand. Erling said that it was not lucky then, inasmuch as the king had forbidden the sale of corn; "I

1 By the island Karmt or Karmöy (near Haugesund).   2 Erling Skjalgson.   3 *Jadar* (modern Norwegian Jæderen) is the flat coast land between Stavanger and Egersund.

do not think that men are to be found here", he said, "who are ready to break the king's word; I find it hard to keep myself in friendship with the king, for there are many who seek to break our friendship". Asbiorn said: "The truth may be learned later; I have learned in my youth that my mother was free-born on all sides and likewise that Erling of Sola was the noblest of her kinsmen. But now I hear thee say that thou art not so free as the king's thralls because thou canst not do as thou likest with thy corn". Erling looked at him, laughed and said: "Ye Halogalanders know less of the king's might than we here in Rogaland. Great of speech thou art at home and that is in thy blood. Now let us drink first, kinsman, and then to-morrow see what can be done about thy errand". They did so and were merry during the evening. The day after Erling and Asbiorn talked together and Erling said: "I have now thought about thy buying of corn, Asbiorn. But art thou particular as to from whom thou buyest corn?" He said he laid no weight upon whom he bought corn from if it were sold rightly. Erling said: "It seems likeliest to me that my thralls have corn so that thou mayest buy fully enough. They are not subject to the law or land right as other men". Asbiorn said he would take that offer and the thralls were then told about the buying, so that they brought forth corn and malt and sold it to Asbiorn, who loaded his ship as he would. And when he was ready to go away, Erling let him leave with many gifts and they parted in friendship. Asbiorn got a good wind and in the evening lay in by Agvaldsnes in Karmtsund, where they were during the night. Tore called men to him during the night so that before daybreak he had sixty men. As soon as it was daybreak he went to Asbiorn; they went straightway out to the ship. Asbiorn and his men were then clad, and Asbiorn greeted Tore. Tore asked what goods Asbiorn had on his ship, and Asbiorn said that it was corn and malt. Then said Tore: "Then Erling is doing as is his wont by making small the king's words, and he is still not loath to go against the king in everything; strange it is that the king puts up with everything from him". Tore spoke frantically for a while, but when he stopped, Asbiorn said that Erling's thralls had owned the corn. Tore answered sharply that he did not mind his and Erling's tricks: "Now it is, Asbiorn, that thou must go on land or we shall throw thee overboard, for we will not be too crowded whilst we are clearing the ship". Asbiorn saw that he had no strength of men to meet Tore, and so Asbiorn and his men went on land and Tore had all the cargo shifted from the ship. And when it was cleared, Tore walked alongside the ship and said: "An exceeding good sail have these Halogalanders; fetch our old ship sail and give it to them; it will be good enough for them when they are sailing home with an empty keel". And so it was that the sail was taken away. After that Asbiorn went his way, sailing northwards along the coast and stopping not before he came home in the beginning of the winter; that journey was much talked about.

Then all the trouble of making feasts ready was spared from Asbiorn that winter. Tore bade Asbiorn and his mother to a Yule feast with such men as they could bring with them, but Asbiorn would not go, and sat at home. It was found out that Tore thought Asbiorn had treated his bidding lightly and Tore mocked at Asbiorn's journey: "there is great difference of standing between us kinsmen of Asbiorn, and he is causing it; look at what trouble he went to in the summer to visit Erling in Jadar, whilst he will not now come to the next house to me; I do not know if he thinks he will meet a Sel-Tore in every holme". Such words and others like them did Asbiorn hear from Tore. Asbiorn was ill-pleased with his journey and still more so when he heard that it was looked on with laughter and mockery. He was at home during the winter and went nowhere to any feast.

118. Asbiorn had a longship; it was a cutter with twenty seats and it stood in a great boathouse. After Candlemas[1] he had the ship put in the water, its tackle taken to it and the ship made ready. He then called to him his friends and he had nigh on ninety men, all well armed. And when he was ready and a good wind blew he sailed south along the coast; and they went on their way but had only a slow wind. When they came to the south of the land they went in the outer fairway more than in the sheltered waters. There is nothing to tell about that voyage until they came to land in the evening of the fifth day after Easter[2] on the outside of Karmt. This is a big island, long, but for the most part not broad, and it lies on the outside of the main fairway. There is a great settlement there, but it is widely unsettled on the side which faces the sea; Asbiorn and his men came to land on this side where it was not inhabited. And when they had fixed the awning, Asbiorn said: "Now shall ye stay here and wait for me. I will go up into the island and spy out what is going on, for we have not heard anything yet". Asbiorn had rough clothing and a low hat; he had a fork in his hand, but under his clothes he was girt with a sword. He went up on land and crossed the island. And when he came to a height from where he could look down on the houses at

1 2nd of February, 1023.   2 18th of April, 1023.

Agvaldsnes and farther out over Karmtsund, he saw many men going about both on sea and land, and all these folk were coming to the houses of Agvaldsnes, and this seemed strange to him. He then went into the place where the serving-men were setting out the food. Straightway he heard and gathered from their talk that King Olav was come there for a feasting and likewise that the king had gone to table. Asbiorn then turned to the hall; and when he came into the ante-room one man went out and another went in, but no one gave

Asbiorn goes into the island to spy what is going on

heed to him. The hall door was open and he saw that Tore Sel was standing before the table by the high-seat. The evening was then drawing on. Asbiorn heard folk asking Tore about his meeting with Asbiorn, and likewise he heard Tore telling a long tale about it, and to Asbiorn it seemed that he clearly stressed one side in the telling of it. He then heard a man say: "How did Asbiorn bear up when ye cleared the ship?" Tore said: "He bore himself fairly well, when we cleared the ship, but when we took the sail from him, he wept". When Asbiorn heard that, he drew his sword, hard and sharp, rushed into the hall and struck Tore at once. The blow fell on the back of the neck; the head dropped on the table before the king, but the body fell at his feet. The table cloth was bloody all over. The king straightway bade them take him, and so it was that Asbiorn was taken prisoner and led out of the hall. Then the costly things and the table cloths were taken out and Tore's body was likewise borne away, and the blood was all washed away. The king was very wroth, but guarded well his words, however, as he was usually wont to do. Skjalg Erlingson stood up, went before the king and said: "Now it may be as often happens, O king, that we must seek help from you. I will offer to pay fines for this man, so that he may have his life and limbs, but you, O king, may 'shape and shear' as in all else". The king said: "Is it not a matter of death, Skjalg, if a man break the Easter peace? And moreover if he slay a man in the king's hall, and again (as may well seem of little worth to

Asbiorn is kept a prisoner

thee and thy father), that he had my feet as a chopping block?" Skjalg answered: "Ill it is, O king, that you like it not, for otherwise the deed would be well done. But if this deed, O king, seems against you and hurts you, yet may I expect something from you for my service; many will say that you may well do it". The king said: "Even if thou art worth much, Skjalg, yet not for thy sake will I break the law and lay down my kingly honour". Skjalg then went away out of the room; twelve men who had been there with Skjalg all followed him and many others went away with him. Skjalg said to Toraren Nevjolvson: "If thou wilt have my friendship, give thy whole mind to it that this man, Asbiorn, be not slain before Sunday". After that Skjalg and his men went away; they took a rowing boat which Skjalg had, and they rowed southwards as quickly as they could until they came at daybreak to Jadar; they went straight to the house and to the loft in which Erling slept. Skjalg ran at the door so that it burst off the nails. On that, Erling and the others who were inside awoke. Erling was quickest to his feet, grabbed at his shield and sword, and ran to the door asking who went so violently there. Skjalg gave his name and bade him open the door. Erling said: "It was most likely to be thee if anyone went about so foolishly. Or are folk coming after thee?" The door was then unlocked and Skjalg said: "Even though it seems to thee that I come violently I do not think thy kinsman Asbiorn will think it too quickly where he sits in chains in the north in Agvaldsnes. And it would be more manly to go and help him". Father and son then spoke together and Skjalg told Erling all that had happened at the slaying of Tore Sel.

119. King Olav sat down in his seat when all was made straight in the hall and he was very wroth; he asked what had been done with the slayer, and was told that Asbiorn was outside in the passage and being kept under watch. The king asked: "Why has he not been slain?" Toraren Nevjolvson said: "My lord, do you not call it murder to slay a man during the night?" Then said the king: "Set him in chains then and slay him in the morning". Then was Asbiorn set in chains and shut in the house during the night. The day after, the king heard Matins; he then went to his meetings and sat there till High Mass, and when he left Mass he said to Toraren: "Has the sun now risen high enough for thy friend Asbiorn to be hanged?" Toraren bowed before the king and said: "My lord, last Friday the bishop said that the King Who is Almighty had to endure great trials, and he is blessed who likens himself to Him rather than to those who condemned Him to death or to him who brought about His death. It is not long now till to-morrow when it is a weekday". The king looked at him and said: "Thou shalt have thy say in this, that he be not slain to-day. Thou shalt now take him thyself and watch over him, and know it for a truth that thy life shall answer for it if he gets away by any means". The king then went away, and Toraren went to where Asbiorn sat in irons. Toraren had the chains taken off him and he followed him to a little room where he gave him food and drink and told him that the king had threatened him if Asbiorn got away. Asbiorn said that Toraren had no need to fear that. Toraren sat for a long time with him during the day and he likewise slept there during the night. On Saturday the king got up and went to Matins; he then went to his meetings, for many of the bonders were come there and they had much to complain of. He sat there a long

time and so they went somewhat late to High Mass, after which the king went to table. When he had had food, he drank for a while, whilst the tables were not taken away. Toraren went to the priest who saw to the church and gave him two silver coins to ring the bells for a holy day as soon as the king's table was moved. And when the king had been drinking as long as he wished, the table was taken away, and then the king said it was now time the thralls went away with the murderer and slew him   At that moment the bell was rung for a holy day and Toraren went before the king and said: "This man shall have peace over the holy day, even though he has sinned"; the king said: "Watch him, Toraren, so that he does not escape". The king then went to church to afternoon Mass (Nones), but Toraren still sat with Asbiorn the whole day. On Sunday the bishop went to Asbiorn and shrived him, giving him leave to hear High Mass. So Toraren went to the king and bade him set men to watch the murderer: "now will I have no more to do with his case". The king thanked him for what he had done and then got men to watch over Asbiorn; he was then set in chains again. And when they went to High Mass Asbiorn was led to the church; he stood outside the church with those two who were watching him whilst the king and the whole gathering were at Mass.

120. Now shall we tell what we have before turned aside from: Erling and his son Skjalg took counsel together about this difficulty, and through the egging on of Skjalg and Erling's other sons it was at last agreed that they should gather men and cut up the war arrow. A great army soon came together, and they got ships. A count of the men was held and there were nigh on fifteen hundred (eighteen hundred) men. They went with this army and on Sunday they came to Agvaldsnes in Karmt; they went up to the stead with the whole troop and got there when the gospel was being read. They went straightway up to the church and took Asbiorn, and the chains were broken off him. But at this din and clattering of weapons all who were then outside ran into the church; but of those who were in the church all looked round except the king, who stood still and did not look about. Erling drew up his army on both sides of the way which led from the church to the hall. And when the whole of the Mass was sung, the king went straightway out of the church; he went first through the lines of men and then came his men one after the other. As soon as he came forth to the door, Erling went before the door, bowed before the king, and greeted him. The king answered and bade God help him. Then Erling began to speak: "It is told me that

my kinsman Asbiorn has done a great misdeed, and it is ill, O king, if it is come about that you are ill pleased. I am now come, therefore, to offer terms and such fines for him as you yourself will have in return for his life and limbs and right to be in the land". The king answered: "It seems to me, Erling, as if thou thinkest thou hast power in Asbiorn's case. I know not why thou pretendest as if thou

King Olav walks from church towards Erling Skjalgson, through the lines of
Erling's huscarls

shouldst offer terms for him; I think that thou hast now drawn together an army of men because thou now wishest to decide between us". Erling said: "You shall decide, and decide so that we part in peace". Then said the king: "Dost thou think of frightening me, Erling? Is it for that thou hast so great a strength of men?" "Nay", said he. "But if anything else lies beneath it all, I shall not flee", said the king. Erling said: "Thou hast no need to remind me that our meetings hitherto have been such that I have had few men against thee. But what I have in my mind shall not be hidden from thee; it is, that we shall part in peace. Otherwise, I shall risk no more meetings between us". Erling's face was then as red as blood. Bishop Sigurd then went forth and said to the king: "My lord, for the sake of God I bid you obey and make peace with Erling as he bids, namely, that this man may have life and limb, and that you alone decide on all the terms". The king answered: "You shall decide".

Then said the bishop: "Erling, give the king such surety as he wishes; then shall Asbiorn go in peace and put himself into the king's power". Erling gave his surety and the king took it. Asbiorn then received peace, put himself in the king's power and kissed the king's hands. Erling thereupon turned away with his men; there was no bidding farewell. After this the king went into the hall with Asbiorn and then the king arranged terms and said: "This is the first of the conditions, Asbiorn, that thou shalt put thyself under this law of the land, that he who slays a king's serving-man shall take on himself the same service if the king wishes. Now I bid thee take over the position of steward which Tore Sel held and rule over my place here in Agvaldsnes". Asbiorn said that it should be as the king wished; "but may I first go to my own garth and put it in order". The king was agreeable to this and went thence to another feast, which was made ready for him; Asbiorn made himself ready to go with his followers, who had lain in secret creeks all the time Asbiorn was away. They had spied out as to what had befallen him, and would not go away until they knew what might come of it. Asbiorn then went on his journey and did not stop until he came north to his garth. He was called Asbiorn Selsbane. And when he had been at home a short while, he and his kinsman Tore met and they talked with each other. Tore asked Asbiorn carefully about his journey and what had befallen him, and Asbiorn told how everything had gone. Then said Tore: "Thou seemest well to have avenged the shame of being robbed in the autumn?" "So it is," said Asbiorn, "but what thinkest thou, kinsman?" "I shall say quickly", answered Tore, "that the former journey thou madest to the south was shameful, but it was possible to avenge it; but this journey is a shame both on thee and on thy kinsmen if it ends in thee becoming the king's thrall and the equal of Tore Sel, the worst of men. Be now so manly as rather to stay here in thy possessions; we, thy kinsmen, shall grant thee such help that thou shalt never again come into such a scrape." Asbiorn found this fitting, and before he and Tore parted the plan was fixed that Asbiorn should stay in his garth and not go back to the king or go into his service. And so he did, sitting at home in his garth.

121. After King Olav and Erling Skjalgson had met in Agvaldsnes, discord arose between them afresh, and it grew until there was open enmity between them. King Olav then went feasting through Hordaland in the spring, and afterwards he went up to Voss, for he learned that the folk there did not keep up Christianity. There

he held a thing with the bonders at a place called Vang[1] and thither the bonders came in crowds and fully armed. The king bade them take up Christianity, but the bonders offered him battle and it came about that both sides drew up their men. Then it happened with the bonders that fear fell on their hearts and no man would stand to the fore; the end of it was, as served them best, that they put themselves in the king's hands and took Christianity. The king did not part from them until they were all fully christened. One day it befell that the king was riding on his way singing psalms; and when he came before the howes he stopped and said: "Man shall tell man these words of mine, that I call it advisable that never hereafter shall a King of Norway go between these howes". It is also the talk of many men that most of the kings since have guarded against it. The king then went out to Osterfjord[2] where he came to his ships; he went north to Sogn and held feasts there during the summer. And when autumn came he went into the fjord and thence up to Valders, which was still heathen. The king went as speedily as possible up to the lake, where he came suddenly upon the bonders, and there he took their ships. He himself went out on them with his whole troop. He afterwards sent out a thing bidding; the thing was held so near the water that the king had power over all the ships if he should need them. The bonders came to the thing in great crowds and fully weaponed. The king bade them take up Christianity, but the bonders shouted against it and bade him be quiet; they straightway made a great din and clattering of weapons. When the king saw that they would not listen to what he taught them and likewise that they had so great a crowd of men that no one could withstand them, he turned his talk to other things and asked if at the thing there were men who had such matters against one another that they wished him to settle them. It was soon found from the bonders' words that many of them who had come together to oppose Christianity were not at peace with one another. And as soon as the bonders began to complain of their troubles, each of them got witnesses to back up his own suit. With this the whole day went and in the evening the thing was disbanded. As soon as the bonders learned that King Olav had come over Valders and to the peopled parts, they had the war arrow sent out and called all men together; with this army they went to meet the king so that far about the district there were rather few men. The bonders had kept their men together after the thing had ended, and this the king got to know. When he came to his ships he had them rowed across the water in

1 Now Vossevangen.    2 By the big island called Oster.

the night; he made his men go up into the district and burn and rob. The day after they rowed from ness to ness, burning the district everywhere. And when the bonders who were in the gathering saw the smoke and fire in the homesteads they began to part from the troop. Each then went away homewards to see if he could find his household. But as the breaking away of the army came about, one went after another until all were separated in small troops. The king rowed over the water, burning on both sides. The bonders then came to him and asked for mercy and offered to put themselves in his hands. He gave peace to every man who came to him and asked for it, and he likewise granted them their goods. No man then spoke against Christianity; the king had all the folk baptised and took hostages from the bonders. He stayed there a long time during the autumn and he had the ships dragged up on the necks of land between the two lakes. He did not go far away from the lakes, for he ill-trusted the bonders. He had churches built and hallowed and set priests over them. And when the king expected it to freeze he went up on land and then came forth into Tote. About the burning King Olav did in the Uplands, Arnor Jarlascald says in the verse he composed about his brother Harald:

| It goes in the kin, that Yngvi[1] | The bonders would not obey |
| Burnt the Uplanders' houses; | The victorious prince, |
| The folk felt the wrath of the prince | Ere ill-luck befell them; |
| Who is foremost of all men. | The foes ended on the gallows. |

Afterwards King Olav went north through the Dales right to the fell and did not stop till he came to Trondheim and right to Nidaros, where he got ready his winter quarters and stayed during the winter. That was the tenth year of his reign.

The previous summer, Einar Tambarskelver had gone from the land and he had first gone west to England. There he met his brother-in-law Hacon the Jarl, with whom he stayed for a while. After this Einar went to King Canute and got great gifts from him. Einar then went south over the sea right to Rome and he came back the next summer. He then went to his estates, but that time he and King Olav did not meet.

122. There was a woman called Alvhild, who was called the king's serving-maid; she was come, however, of good kin and was a beautiful woman; she lived at King Olav's court. And that spring news came that Alvhild was with child, and the king's trusted friends knew that he was the father of the child. So it befell one night that

1 I.e. Harald Hardrade.

Alvhild fell sick, and there were few folk present—some women, a priest, Sigvat the Scald, and a few others. Alvhild suffered greatly and was nigh unto death; she bore a son and there was a time when they did not know for sure if the child was alive. But when the child drew breath—very weakly however—the priest bade Sigvat go and tell the king. He answered: "For no price dare I waken the king, for he has forbidden any man to disturb his sleep ere he wakes himself". The priest answered: "It is needful that the child be baptised; it does not seem to me that the child can live". Sigvat said: "I would dare counsel thee to christen the child rather than that I should wake the king; I will take any ill words for it, but give the child a name". This they did, and the child was baptised and called Magnus. The morning after when the king was awake and clad, all was told him of what had befallen. He then had Sigvat called to him and said: "Why wast thou so bold as to have my child christened ere I knew about it?" Sigvat answered: "Because I would rather give two men to God than one to the devil". The king said: "Why should that be at stake?" Sigvat answered: "The child was nigh unto death and he would be a man of the devil if he died a heathen; but now is he a child of God. There is also another thing: I knew that even if thou wert wroth with me there would still be nought to pay but my life. And if thou wilt that I lose it for the sake of this matter, I hope I shall become God's man". The king said: "Why didst thou have the boy called Magnus? It is not a name in our race". Sigvat answered: "I called him after King Karlamagnus,[1] whom I knew to be the best man in the world". Then said the king: "Thou art a man of great luck, Sigvat. It is not strange that luck goes with wisdom, but strange it is, as sometimes can happen, that luck goes to the foolish man so that witless counsels turn out luckily". The king was very glad then. The boy grew up, and as he advanced in age he soon gave good promise.

123. The same spring King Olav gave Asmund[2] Grankelson a district in Halogaland, half of which was held together with Harek of Tjotta; Harek had formerly had the whole, partly as a land grant and partly in fief. Asmund had a cutter and on it were nearly thirty men, well weaponed. And when Asmund went north he met Harek; Asmund told him how the king had settled about the district and produced the king's token. Harek said that the king must decide who should have the district; "but the former princes never did such

---

1 Emperor Carolus Magnus (Charlemagne).    2 *Asmund* is in English *Osmond*: in a similar way *Asbiorn* has become *Osborn*. Cf. p. 730, n. 4.

things as to lessen the rights of us who are noble-born to our power, nor did they ever give this power to bonders' sons who never before have had such power in their hands". But even if it was clear to Harek that this was not to his liking, yet he let Asmund take the district just as the king had sent word. Asmund then went home to his father, stayed there a short time and then went north to his district to Halogaland. And when he came north into Langöy,[1] there were two brothers living there, one called Gunstein, the other Karli; they were wealthy and outstanding men. Gunstein dealt with most of the business of the stead and was the elder of the brothers; Karli was a handsome man and loved much fine clothing; and both were great in all manner of sports. Asmund was well greeted, and he stayed there for a time; he gathered from his district such incomes as he could get. Karli told Asmund that he would go south with him to King Olav and try to get into the king's court. Asmund encouraged the plan and promised to put in a good word with the king so that Karli should accomplish the errand he wished for. He put himself in Asmund's following. Asmund learned that Asbiorn Selsbane had gone south to the Vaga meeting[2] and had a trading ship he owned with nearly twenty men on board, and that he was now expected in the north. Asmund and his following went their way to the south along the land and they had a favourable wind though not strong; they met the ships which were of the Vaga fleet. They heard secretly about Asbiorn's journey and they were told that he would soon be coming north. Asmund and Karli were bed-fellows and there was great friendship between them. It befell one day when Asmund and his men were rowing forth along a sound that a trading ship came towards them; the ship was easy to recognise, for it was light of colour on the sides, painted with white and red; it had a striped sail. Then said Karli to Asmund: "Thou hast often said that thou art very curious to see Selsbane; I know not that ship if it is not he who sails there". Asmund answered: "Be so good, fellow,[3] and tell me if thou dost recognise him". The ships went near each other and Karli said: "There sits Selsbane at the helm in a blue kirtle". Asmund answered: "I shall give him a red kirtle". Asmund then shot a spear at Asbiorn Selsbane; it struck him in the middle and flew straight through him so that it stood fast in the head-plank; Asbiorn fell dead from the helm. Each ship then went its own way. They brought Asbiorn's body north to Trondenes. Sigrid then had word

1 The most westerly island in Vesteralen.   2 The fishing meeting at Vaagen.   3 In O.N. *felagi*, from which *fellow* originates.

sent to Tore the Hound in Bjarköy and he came where Asbiorn's body was laid out according to their custom. And when they went away, Sigrid chose gifts for her friends. She accompanied Tore to the ship, but before they parted she said: "So it is now, Tore, that Asbiorn my son listened to thy friendly counsel. Now he did not live long enough to reward it as it was worth, but though I am less doughty to do it than he would have been, I still have the will to do it. Here now is a gift I will give thee, and I hope it may be of good use to thee";—it was a spear—"here now is the spear that went through Asbiorn my son, and his blood is still on it; then wilt thou sooner remember that it fits the wound thou sawest on Asbiorn, thy brother's son. Thou wouldst be manly if thou lettest it go from thy hands in such a way that it stood in the breast of Olav Digre. Now I tell thee this", she said, "that thou wilt be a coward before all men if thou dost not avenge Asbiorn". She then went away. Tore was so wroth at her words that he could not answer; he heeded not that he had let the spear slip; he heeded not the pier and he would have gone into the sea if his men had not taken him and helped him when he went on to the ship. It was a graven spear

Tore the Hound went down to the pier with the spear

and not big, and the shaft socket was inlaid with gold. Tore and his men rowed away home to Bjarköy.

Asmund and his following went their way till they came south to Trondheim to King Olav. Asmund told the king tidings of what had befallen on his journey. Karli became one of the king's bodyguard, and he and Asmund kept their friendship well. And the words which Asmund and Karli had said to each other before Asbiorn was slain they did not hide, for they told the king about it. But there it was as is said, that "every man has a friend amid his foes"; there were a few men who kept such things in mind and from them it came to Tore the Hound.

124. When spring was drawing to an end King Olav made himself ready and fitted out his ships. In the summer he went south-

wards along the coast, held things with the bonders, mediated between men and set customs in the land. He also gathered the king's land rents wherever he went. In the autumn he went east to Land's End. King Olav had then made the land Christian where the great lordships were, and he had then set laws throughout the land. He had also subjected the Orkneys to his rule, as was told before (chapter 102). He had also sent out messages and gained many friends in Iceland and Greenland and likewise in the Faroes. He sent wood for a church to Iceland and the church was built on the Thingvold,[1] where the *Althing* is held; he also sent a great bell which is still there. That was after the Icelanders had changed their law and set up the Christian faith as King Olav had sent word. Afterwards there came from Iceland many outstanding men who became the handmen of King Olav; there were Thorkel Eyolfson,[2] Torleik Bollason,[3] Tord Kolbeinson,[4] Tord Barkson,[5] Torgeir Howardson[6] and Tormod Kolbrunarscald.[6] King Olav had sent many gifts to many chiefs in Iceland and they sent him such things as were found there and which they expected he would reckon as worthy greetings. But in these tokens of friendship which the king showed to Iceland there were hidden many other things which were to be laid bare later.

125. This summer King Olav sent Toraren Nevjolvson to Iceland with his messages, and Toraren sailed his ship out from Trondheim at the same time as the king left and followed him southwards to Möre. Thereupon Toraren sailed out to sea and he got a fair sweeping wind so that he was sailing only four whole days before he reached Eyrar[7] in Iceland. He went straightway to the *Althing* and came there when the people were on the Lawhill,[8] whither he went forthwith. And when they were done with the law matters, Toraren began to speak: "Four nights ago I left King Olav Haraldson, who sends here the greetings of God and himself to all the land chieftains and rulers, and withal to the common folk, men and women, young men and old, and rich and poor. And thereto he sends word that he will be your lord if ye will be his men, and all be friends and helpers in all good things". They answered his speech well; all

---

1 In O.N. *Thingvellir*, some thirty miles east of Reykjavik, the principal town in Iceland. 2 Lived at Hvamm; cf. Laxdale Saga. 3 Eyolf's step-son, son of Bolli, mentioned in the 'History of Olav Trygvason', p. 178. 4 *Tord Kolbeinson* was a scald. 5 Son of Bark Digre and first cousin of Snorre Godi. 6 Two foster-brothers told about in Foster-brothers' Saga. 7 *Eyrar* is the present Eyrarbakki, on the western coast of Iceland, south of Thingvold. Eyrar is also mentioned in 'History of Olav Trygvason', p. 189. 8 *Lawhill* was the rock ridge in Almannagja, where proclamations were made by the *lögsögumann*, meaning the law-speaking man or the 'speaker'.

said that they would with gladness be the king's friends if he would be the friend of the men in the land. Then Toraren went on: "This follows herewith, that he will beg of the Northlanders to give him an island or a skerry which lies without Eyjafjord and is called Grimsey; in return for this he will send such goods from his land as the men may wish of him. And he sends word to Gudmund of Mödruvellir to help in this matter, for the king has heard that Gudmund rules most there". Gudmund answered: "I am eager for King Olav's friendship and I reckon it of much more use than the skerry he wants. But the king has not heard the truth about my having more might here than others, for this island is now common property. Now shall we who have most gain from the island hold a meeting about it". The men then went to their booths, and after that the Northlanders met and talked about the matter; each also said what he thought. Gudmund helped the matter on and many others followed his lead. Men then asked why his brother Einar had said nothing about it; "he seems to us to be able to see most clearly through most things", they said. Einar answered: "I have spoken little about this matter, for none has asked me. But if I shall say my thoughts, I believe it would be best for folk here in the land not to submit to being taxed by King Olav or to such burden as he has put on the men of Norway. But this loss of freedom is not only brought upon us, but also upon all our sons and upon all our kin, who dwell in this land, and that serfdom will never leave the land. And even if this king is a good man, as I well believe he is, it may befall hereafter when there are changes in kings, that they will be unequal, some good, some bad. But if the men of the land will keep the freedom they have had since the land was settled, then the way out is not to show the king loyalty so that he will get a hold on us, either by getting possessions here or by giving him a fixed scot such as can be reckoned as an obligation. But I call it very fitting that they who wish may send the king friendly gifts of hawks or horses, ship covers or sails or other things which can be sent; it is worth while if friendship comes in return. But as to Grimsey, it is to be said that though nothing can be brought thence which might serve as food, yet an army can be fed there; and if there is on this island a foreign army and it sends out from there its longships, then will many small bonders think the doors are being thronged". And as soon as Einar had said that and made clear the way through it, the whole people were agreed in thinking that this should not be done. Toraren then saw the outcome of his errand in this matter.

126. Toraren went next day to the Lawhill and then again held speech, saying: "King Olav sent word to his friends here in the land, and he named Gudmund Eyolfson, Snorre Godi, Thorkel Eyolfson, Skafti the Lawman and Torstein Hallson.[1] He sent you word to go to him and get a friendly welcome from him. He said ye should not delay this journey if ye laid any weight on his friendship". They answered this matter, thanking the king well for his invitation, and said that they would speak later to Toraren about their journey, when they had taken counsel with themselves and friends. And when the chieftains talked among themselves, each said what seemed right to him about this journey. Snorre Godi and Skafti warned them against setting faith in the men of Norway by letting all the men who had most rule in the land go at one time from Iceland thither. They said that from this message it seemed clear that there was some reason for the misgiving which Einar had guessed, and that the king had some constraint to bring upon the Icelanders if he could plan it. Gudmund and Thorkel Eyolfson spoke much in favour of following King Olav's wish and thought that it would be a journey of great honour. And when they had considered the matter amongst themselves, they were agreed that they should not go themselves, but rather that each of them should send a man on his behalf, who seemed best fitted for it—and with such an arrangement they parted at the thing, and there was no journey to Norway that summer. And Toraren went back in the summer and came in the autumn to King Olav, to whom he told the outcome of his journey and likewise that the chieftains to whom he had sent bidding or their sons would come from Iceland.

127. The same summer Gilli the Lawman, Leif Assurson, Toralv[2] of Dimun,[3] and many other bonders' sons came to Norway according to King Olav's message to the Faroes. Trand of Gata[4] made himself ready to go, but when he was almost ready, he got such a sickness that he was not strong enough to go and stayed at home. And when the Faröymen came to King Olav, he called them to a meeting; he laid bare to them the object of their journey and told them that he would have scot from the Faroes and likewise that the Faröymen should have the law which King Olav set over them. And at the same meeting it was clear from the king's words that he would take security for this matter from the Faröymen who were come thither if

1 Son of Hall of Sida (cf. 'History of Olav Trygvason', p. 171, n. 3). 2 Son of Sigmund Brestison. 3 Now Great Dimun, one of the most southern islands in the Faroes, between Sandöy and Suderöy. 4 A farm on the east side of Österöy.

they would bind this agreement with oaths; he offered the men who seemed noblest to him that they should submit to him and take honours and friendship from him. The Faröymen set much worth on the king's words because it could not be certain how their case would go if they would not submit to everything the king demanded of them. And though many meetings were held on this matter before it was decided, the upshot was, however, to grant what the king demanded. Leif, Gilli and Toralv put themselves in the king's hands and came into his bodyguard, and all their followers swore oaths to King Olav to keep in the Faroes the law and land rights which he set for them, and the tax-paying he decided. After that the Faröymen made themselves ready for the homeward journey, and on their parting the king gave them friendly gifts; those who had submitted to him then went their way when they were ready. The king had a ship fitted out and men too, and he sent them to the Faroes to gather scot which the Faröymen were to pay him. They were slow in getting ready, and about their journey it is to be told that they came not back. The next summer there came no scot, for they had not come to the Faroes and no man had claimed scot there.

128. King Olav went in the autumn into the Vik and sent word before him to the Uplands that feasts should be ordered, and that he thought of going through the Uplands in the winter. Afterwards he began his journey and went to the Uplands, where he stayed that winter, going to feasts and putting right those things that seemed to him to need bettering. He strengthened Christianity where it seemed to him to demand it. When the king was in Hedemark, tidings came that Ketel Kalv of Ringanes[1] had begun his courtship and asked for Gunhild, the daughter of Sigurd Syr and Asta; Gunhild was King Olav's sister, and the king had to answer for and decide in this. He was willing, because he knew that Ketel was of great kin and rich, a wise man and a great chief. He had also long before been a good friend of King Olav, as is told before (chapter 75); through all these things together it came about that the king allowed Ketel's wedding, and the end was that Ketel got Gunhild as wife; King Olav was there at the banquet. King Olav then went north into Gudbrandsdale and held feasts there. A man called Tord Guthormson dwelt there, in a stead called Steig,[2] and Tord was the mightiest man in the northern part of the Dales. And when he and the king met, Tord began his courtship and asked for Isrid, Gudbrand's daughter, King Olav's mother's sister; the king had to answer in this matter. And

1 Cf. chapter 45.     2 In Southern Fron.

when they had pondered on it, it was agreed that the wedding should be made ready and Tord got Isrid to wife; he afterwards became one of the trustiest of King Olav's friends, and likewise there were many others of Tord's kinsmen and friends who followed his lead. Thereafter King Olav went back to the south through Tote and Hadeland and then to Ringerik, and from there out into the Vik. In the spring he went to Tunsberg and stayed there a long time whilst there was a great market and coming in of wares. He had his ship fitted out and with him was a great crowd of men.

129. This summer there came from Iceland, in compliance with King Olav's message, Skafti the Lawman's son Stein, Snorre Godi's son Torodd, Thorkel's son Gelli and Hall of Sida's son Egil, the brother of Torstein.[1] Gudmund Eyolfson had died the winter before. These Iceland men went to King Olav as soon as they could. And when they met the king they got good greeting and were all with him. The same summer King Olav learned that the ship was lost which he had sent to the Faroes for scot the summer before, and it had not come to land anywhere, such as had been heard of. The king then fitted out another ship and men, and he sent them to the Faroes for the scot. These men went and put to sea but afterwards nothing more was learned of them than of the others, and there were many guesses as to what had become of these ships.

130. Canute the Mighty, whom some call Old Canute, was at that time king over England and Denmark. He was the son of Swein Forkbeard, the son of Harald. His forefathers had for long ruled over Denmark. Harald Gormson, Canute's grandfather, had possessed himself of Norway after the fall of Harald Gunhildson; he had taken scot therefrom and had set Hacon the Jarl to rule the land. Swein the Danish king, Harald's son, also ruled over Norway and set Jarl Eric Haconson over it. He and his brother Swein Haconson ruled over the land until Eric the Jarl went west to England after the message sent by his brother-in-law Canute the Mighty. And to rule over Norway he set his son Hacon, the son of Canute the Mighty's sister. And when Olav Digre came to Norway he first took Hacon the Jarl prisoner and then outlawed him from the kingdom, as is written before (chapters 30 and 31). Hacon then went to his uncle Canute and remained with him all the time since and until where the story has now come. Canute the Mighty had won England by war; he had fought for it and had had long strife before the land folk were obedient to him. And when he thought he had come fully into the

[1] Cf. chapter 126.

rule of the land there, he called to mind what right he thought he had
to the kingdom which he himself had not ruled over, and that was
Norway; he thought he had hereditary rights to the whole of Norway, but his sister's son Hacon thought he had a right to a share of
it, and likewise he deemed he had lost it with shame. One reason
why Canute and Hacon had kept quiet about their claims on Norway
was that at first when Olav Haraldson came into the land all
the common folk and crowd had rushed to him and would hear
nothing else than that Olav should be king over the whole land.
But now afterwards when the men thought that they could not rule
themselves because of Olav's might, many went away from the land.
Many great men and mighty bonders' sons had gone to King Canute
and given themselves different errands. And each man who came to
King Canute and would join with him got his hands full of goods
from him. There could they also see greater splendour than in other
places, both as to the number of folk who were daily there and in all
costly fittings which were in the rooms he owned and lived in himself.
Canute the Mighty took scot and taxes from those lands which were
richest in the Northlands, and in the same proportion as he had more
to receive than other kings he also gave away more than any other
king. In the whole of his kingdom there was such good peace that
no one dared break it, and the landsmen themselves had peace and
the old land rights. By such things he got great honour through all
lands. Many of those who came from Norway complained over their
loss of freedom; they brought it before Hacon the Jarl, and some
before the king, that the men of Norway would now be ready enough
to submit to King Canute and the jarl and get their freedom back from
them. These talks struck the jarl's mind well and he complained to the
king, bidding him try if King Olav would give up the kingdom to them
or share it by agreement; there were many who helped the jarl in this.

131. Canute the Mighty sent men east from England to Norway
and they were splendidly fitted out; they had letters and seals from
Canute, the King of England. In the spring they came to Tunsberg
to Olav Haraldson, King of Norway. But when it was told the king
that Canute the Mighty's messengers were come thither, he became
very wroth thereat and said that Canute would send no man with
such messages unless there would be gain therein either for himself
or his men; several days went by before the messengers could come
before the king. And when they got leave to speak to him they went
before the king, gave up King Canute's letter and delivered the message
which went with it that "King Canute claims the whole of Norway

as his own possession and maintains that his forefathers have had the kingdom before him. But because King Canute will offer peace to all lands, he does not wish to go with the shield of war against Norway if there is anything else to choose. And if King Olav Haraldson will be king over Norway, let him go to King Canute and take the land in fief of him and become his man and pay him such dues as the jarls have paid before". Then they gave up the letters, which contained the same message. King Olav then answered: "I have heard it said in olden tales that Gorm the Danish king was thought to be an excellent folk king, and he ruled over Denmark only, but the Danish kings who have been since do not seem to have been content with it. Now it has come about that Canute rules over Denmark and England and thereto he has subdued a great part of Scotland. Now he claims my inheritance from me.

King Canute's messengers come to King Olav in Tunsberg

He should, however, learn to hold this greed in check, or does he think he will have sole rule over all the northern lands? Or does he think of eating up alone all the cabbages in England? He must first have the might to do it, ere I should bring him my head or show him any obedience. Now shall ye tell him these words of mine, that I will protect Norway with spear and sword as long as life is granted me, and I will pay no man scot from my kingdom". After that answer King Canute's messengers made themselves ready to go away, and they were not happy over the outcome of their errand.

Sigvat the Scald had been with King Canute, and King Canute had given him a gold ring which weighed half a mark. At that time Bersi Scaldtorfuson was there with King Canute, and King Canute gave him two gold rings, each weighing half a mark; and besides these he had given him a gold-chased sword. Thus says Sigvat:

O Bersi, the time we both
Had found Canute,
This noble king had
Proudly decked our hands.

To thee the king gave a mark
Or more in gold and a sword,
And as a gift I got half a mark.
God ruleth wholly in all things.

Sigvat got into talk with King Canute's messengers and learned many tidings. They told him such as he asked after about their dealings with King Olav and the outcome of their errand. They said he had taken their case heavily "and we know not", they said, "how he has got courage to refuse to become King Canute's man and not to go to him; it would be his best choice, for King Canute is so mild that however much the chiefs do against him, he forgives them all as soon as they go to him and grant him obedience. It was but lately that two kings came to him from the north from Fife in Scotland, and he withdrew his wrath against them, and let them have all the lands they had had before, and thereto he gave them great gifts of friendship". Then said Sigvat:

| | |
|---|---|
| The doughty kings from Fife | Often won he victories; |
| In the north have borne | But here in this world |
| Their heads to Canute; | King Olav Digre hath never |
| It was a good bargain for peace; | Sold his head to any man. |

King Canute's messengers went their way back and they had a fair wind over the sea. They then went to King Canute and told him the outcome of their errand and likewise the words which King Olav had last said to them. King Canute answered: "Olav guesses not rightly if he thinks that I alone shall eat up all the cabbages in England; I should rather wish him to find that within my ribs there is something more than cabbage only, for hereinafter there shall come from every rib of mine a cold plan against him". The same summer there came to King Canute from Norway Aslak and Skjalg, the sons of Erling of Jadar; they were well greeted, for Aslak had wedded Sigrid, the daughter of Jarl Swein Haconson; she and Jarl Hacon Ericson were the children of brothers. King Canute gave the brothers Aslak and Skjalg great land rents with him.

132. King Olav called to him his landed men and had many folk with him during the summer, for word had come that Canute the Mighty was coming east that summer. Men seemed to hear from trade ships which came from the west that King Canute had drawn together a great army in England. And when summer went on some believed that an army would come, but others denied it. King Olav was in the Vik during the summer and he kept folk out to spy if King Canute came to Denmark. In the autumn King Olav sent men east to Sweden to King Anund his brother-in-law to tell him King Canute's message and the claim he had to Norway. He also sent word that he believed that if Canute put Norway under himself, Anund would keep Sweden in peace but a short while

thereafter; he therefore thought it advisable that they should bind an agreement together and rise up against Canute; he said that they were not short of might to hold battle with King Canute. King Anund took King Olav's message well and sent word back that he would join hands with King Olav in agreement so that each should grant the other help from his kingdom whoever first needed it. It was also arranged between them that they should meet and take counsel together. The next winter, King Anund would go through West Gautland, and King Olav then made himself ready for wintering in Sarpsborg. Canute the Mighty came that autumn to Denmark and stayed there during the winter with a great host of men. He was told that men and messages had gone between the Kings of Norway and Sweden and that under it all there certainly lay great plans. In the winter, King Canute sent men to Sweden to King Anund, with great gifts and friendly words, and said that Anund could well sit at rest during the strife between himself and Olav Digre, "for King Anund", he said, "and his kingdom shall be in peace for me". And when the messengers came to King Anund they delivered the gifts which King Canute had sent him and thereto his words of friendship. King Anund did not take their talk in a friendly way, and the messengers seemed to find in him that he leaned most to King Olav; they went back and told King Canute the outcome of their errand, and likewise that he must expect no friendship from King Anund.

133. That winter, King Olav sat in Sarpsborg and he had many folk there. He sent Karli the Halogalander north in the land on his errands. Karli first went to the Uplands and then north over the fell, coming forth into Nidaros, whence he took from the king's goods as much as he had sent word about, and thereto took a good ship which seemed to him well fitted for the journey on which the king had sent him, namely to go north to Bjarmaland. It was arranged so that Karli should be in partnership with the king, and each of them was to have one-half of the goods with the other. Early in spring, Karli sailed with his ship north to Halogaland, where his brother Gunstein came with his following and trading goods of his own; there were then twenty-five men aboard. They went straightway north to Finmark. Tore the Hound learned that, and he sent men with word to the brothers that he thought of going to Bjarmaland in the summer and wanted them to sail together and have like shares in the booty they won there. Karli and Gunstein sent word that Tore should have twenty-five men as they had, and they agreed

that the goods which were won should be shared equally between the ships, apart from the trading goods they had with them. But when Tore's messengers came back, he had a great longship he owned put on the water and made ready. He took to the ship his huscarls and there were in it nearly eighty men. Tore alone had the lead of this troop and likewise he would have all that was won on the journey. And when Tore was ready he sailed his ship northwards along the coast and met Karli in the north in Sandsvær.¹ They then went on together and had a fair wind. Gunstein told his brother Karli as soon as they and Tore had met that Tore seemed to have too great a strength of men; "and I believe", he said, "that it would be more advisable for us to turn back and not go on so that Tore would have us altogether in his might, for I trust him not". Karli said: "I will not turn back; true it is, however, that had I known when we were home in Langöy that Tore the Hound would come on this journey with us with so great a crew as he has, then would we have had more men with us". The brothers talked about it to Tore and asked why it was that he had many more men than they had sent word about. He answered thus: "We have a great ship which needs many men; it seems to me that in so perilous a journey one cannot have enough good men". In the summer they proceeded as ships do; when there was little wind Karli's ship went faster and sailed away, but when it was blowing harder Tore's ship came up; they were seldom together, but they always knew of each other. When they came to Bjarmaland they lay in to the market town, where there was at that time a market and the men who had money with them all got wares in plenty. Tore got many fur wares, beaver and sable; Karli had also much goods with which he bought many skins. And when the market was at an end, they sailed out along the River Vina,² and the peace with the men of the land was then ended. And when they came out to sea they held meetings with the ship crews. Tore asked if the men were eager enough to go up on land and win goods for themselves; they answered that they were eager to do it if there was a good chance of booty. Tore said that goods could be won there if the journey went luckily; "but it is to be looked for that the journey will entail risk of life". All said that they would try if booty could be won. Tore said that here the custom was that when rich folk died the money was shared between the dead man and his heirs; the former would have a half or a third or sometimes less, and

¹ *Sandsvær* was a fishing centre outside Ringvassöy (Tromsö folk district).　² The River Dvina.

the wealth would be borne out into the woods, sometimes to howes, and they would cast earth over it, and sometimes they built a house over it. He said they should make themselves ready for the journey that evening. So it was arranged that no one should run from the others and no one should stay behind when the helmsmen said they should be off. They left men behind to watch the ships, and went up on land. At first there were flat fields and then a great wood. Tore went foremost and the brothers Karli and Gunstein last. Tore bade the men go quietly and take bark off the trees "so that we can see from each tree to the next". They came forth into a great clearing and in the clearing there was a high faggotgarth, with a door in front which was locked. At that faggotgarth six of the local men were to watch every night, two at a time. When Tore and the others came to the garth the watchmen had gone home and they who should keep watch next had not yet come on the watch. Tore went to the fence, hooked his axe on it and hauled himself up; he then went over the fence to the one side of the doorway; Karli had also come over the garth on the other side of the doorway. They came at the same time to the door, drew the bolts and opened the door. The folk then went into the stead. Then said Tore: "In this stead there is a howe wherein gold and silver and earth are mixed together; thither shall the men go; but in the stead stands the Bjarmers' god which is called Jomale; none must be so bold as to rob him". They then went to the howe and took as many goods as they could and bore them away in their clothes; much earth came therewith, as was to be expected. Then Tore said that the men should go away, and he also said: "Now shall ye brothers Karli and Gunstein go first and I will go last". They all returned to the doorway. Tore went back to the Jomale and took a silver bowl which stood on his knees, and it was full of silver pennies. He poured the silver into his cloak and put his arm within the handle of the bowl, and then went out of the doorway. The folk were then all come outside the garth, and they were then aware that Tore had stayed behind—Karli turned back to look for him and they met by the doorway; Karli saw that Tore had the silver bowl. Karli then ran towards the Jomale and saw that there was a thick collar on his neck. Karli swung his axe at it and struck the cord asunder, by which the collar was fastened behind the neck. The blow was so mighty that the Jomale's head flew off; there was so great a crash that all thought it strange. Karli then took the collar and they went away. But at the same moment as the crash befell, the watchmen came forth into the clearing and straightway blew their horns.

They then heard horns being blown from all sides. They went forth to the wood and ran into it, and behind them in the clearing they heard shrieks and shouts; the Bjarmers had come thither. Tore the Hound was last of all his men; two men were before him bearing a sack, wherein was something like ashes. Tore took it in his hand and strewed it on their tracks; sometimes he cast it forth over the men. Thus they went forth from the wood out on to the fields. They heard the Bjarmers' army coming after them with shouting and hideous yells. They rushed forth after them from the wood on both sides of them; but in no place did the Bjarmers or their weapons come so near them that they got harm from them; therefore they perceived that the Bjarmers had not seen them. And when they came to the ships, Karli and Gunstein went first on board, for they were foremost on the way, but Tore was farthest back in the land. As soon as Karli and his men came on their ship, they tore off the awning and cast off the moorings; they hoisted their sail and the ship went quickly out to sea. But everything went more slowly with Tore and his men, for their ship was not so easy to manage, and when they had got under sail Karli's ship had gone far from the land. They both sailed over Gandvik;[1] the night was light. They sailed night and day until Karli one evening lay in by some islands, where they dropped the sails and cast anchor, waiting for the tide, for there was a strong whirlpool before them. Tore and his ship came up, and they also rested on the anchor. Then they thrust a boat off and in it went Tore and a few men, and they rowed to Karli's ship. Tore went up into the ship. The brothers greeted him in a friendly way. Tore bade Karli give him the collar; "it seems right to me that I should have the treasures which were taken there, for it was thanks to me that we got away without loss of men; and thou, Karli, seemest to me to lead us into the worst misfortunes". Then said Karli: "King Olav owns half the goods I win on this journey; I mean him to have the collar. Go thou to him if thou wilt; it may be that he will give thee the collar if he does not wish to have it because I took it off Jomale". Then Tore answered and said that he wanted them to go up on the island to share the booty. Gunstein said that now the tide was turning it would be time to sail. After that they hauled up their anchor ropes. And when Tore saw that, he went down into his boat, and they rowed to his ship. Karli's men had then hoisted their sail and had gone far before Tore's men had got their sail up. And now they went so that Karli's ship sailed foremost all the time, and on both ships they sailed

1 The White Sea.

as fast as they could. Thus they went until they came to Geirsvær,[1] where is the first jetty when one comes from the north. There both ships came one evening and moored at the pier. Tore's ship lay in the inner harbour, but Karli's was in the outer part of the harbour. And when Tore's men had put up the awnings, Tore went ashore together with many of his men, and they went to Karli's ship, which was then put straight. Tore shouted out to the ship and bade the steersmen come on land. The brothers then went ashore with some of their men. Tore began the same talk as before, bidding them come ashore and bring the goods they had taken as booty to be shared. The brothers said that there was no need for that before they came to their homesteads. Tore said it was not their wont to leave the sharing till they got home and in that way try folks' honesty. They said several words thereon and each held to his own view. Tore then went away, but when he had gone but a short way he turned round and said that his men should wait for him there. He shouted to Karli. "I wish to speak alone with thee", he said. Karli went to him. And when they met Tore thrust a spear into the middle of his body so that it passed through him. Then said Tore: "There thou mayest know a Bjarköyman, Karli; I also thought that thou oughtest to know the spear called Sel's Avenger".[2] Karli died immediately, and Tore and his men went back to their ship. Gunstein and his men saw the fall of Karli, and they rushed there at once, took the body and bore it to their ship. They straightway took down the awning, pulled away the gangways, and put out from land; then they hoisted the sail and went their way. Tore and his men saw this, and they straightway cast off the awning and speedily made themselves ready. But when they hoisted the sail, the stay broke asunder and the sail fell down across the ship; it took Tore's men a long time before they could get the sail up again, and Gunstein's ship had gone a long way ere Tore's ship could get under way. Tore's men both sailed and rowed, and Gunstein's did the same thing. They both went as fast as they could, both day and night. They drew together but slowly, for as soon as the island sounds began it was easier to steer with Gunstein's ship, yet Tore's ship overhauled them so much that when Gunstein's men came past Lengjuvik[3] they turned to land and rushed from the ship up on land; a little later Tore's men came there, sprang up on land and pursued them. A woman got help for Gunstein and hid

1 Now Gjesvær, a fishing centre north-west of the Mageröy (outside Finmark).
2 Cf. chapter 123. Asbiorn Selsbane was killed by Asmund Grankelson. 3 Now Lenvik on the peninsula west of Malangen.

him, and it is said that she was very troll-wise. Tore's men went back
to the ship and took all the goods which were on Gunstein's ship and
bore stones on to it instead. They shifted the ship out into the fjord,
struck holes in it and sank it. Tore and his men then went home to
Bjarköy. At first Gunstein and his men went very secretly; they
moved out in small boats and sailed during the nights, but lay still in
the daytime; thus they travelled until they got past Bjarköy and out
of Tore's district. Gunstein first went home to Langöy and stayed
there but a short while. Then he went to the south, and did not stop
until he came to Trondheim where he met King Olav and told him
such tidings as had happened on the journey to Bjarmaland. The
king was ill pleased with their journey, but bade Gunstein stay with
him and said that he would put his case right as soon as he could do
so. Gunstein accepted that behest and remained with King Olav.

134. It has been said before (chapter 133) that King Olav was in
the east in Sarpsborg the winter when Canute the Mighty was in
Denmark. Anund the Swedish king rode this winter through West
Gautland with more than three hundred (three hundred and sixty)
men. Men and messages passed between him and King Olav.
They agreed between themselves upon a meeting in the spring
at Konungahella; they delayed their meeting for this reason,
that they wished to know ere they met what King Canute had taken
upon himself to do. And as spring was passing, King Canute
made himself ready with his men to go west to England. In Denmark he left his son Hardicanute and with him Ulf the Jarl, son of
Torgils Sprakalegg. Ulf was married to Astrid, daughter of King
Swein and sister to Canute the Mighty; their son was Swein who was
afterwards king in Denmark. Ulf the Jarl was a very remarkable
man. Canute the Mighty went west to England. And when the
Kings Olav and Anund learned that, they went to their meeting, and
met on the Elv near Konungahella. This was a happy meeting and
there was much friendly talk, as was clear to all men; but they talked
between themselves, however, about many things of which they two
alone knew, and some of these things afterwards leaked out and
became known to all. On their parting, the kings gave each other
gifts and parted as friends. King Anund then went up into Gautland, and King Olav went north into the Vik and then out into Agder
and from there north along the coast; for a long time he lay in Eikundasund[1] waiting for a fair wind. He heard that Erling Skjalgson
and the Jadar men with him were gathered together with a great

---

1 Now Egersund, south of Stavanger.

army. One day the king's men were talking amongst themselves about the wind, whether it was a south or a south-west wind and if the weather was good for sailing along Jæderen or not; most of them thought that they could not sail with it. Then Haldor Brynjulvson answered: "I should think that you would find this weather good enough to sail along Jæderen if Erling Skjalgson had made ready a feast for us in Sola". Then King Olav said that they should take down the awnings and put the ships out. They did so; that day they sailed past Jæderen and the wind proved to be very good. In the evening they lay in Hvitingsöy.[1] The king then went north to Hordaland and there went feasting.

135. That spring a ship had gone from Norway out to the Faröys and on that ship word had gone from King Olav that one of his bodyguard, Leif Assurson, Gilli the Lawman or Toralv of Dimun, should sail to him from the Faröys. And when this message came to the Faröys and was told them there, they talked amongst themselves as to what might lie behind the message, and they agreed in believing that the king wished to learn tidings of what some men thought had happened in the isles, namely about the ill-fated journey of the king's messengers and the two ship crews of which not one man had come back. They agreed that Toralv should go; he made himself ready for the journey, fitted out a trading ship he owned and got his men for it; there were ten or twelve men on the ship. But when they were ready and awaiting a fair wind, it befell at Trand's house in Gata in Österöy one fine day that Trand went into a room. There on the benches lay his brother Torlak's sons, Sigurd and Tord, and the third was Gaut the Red who was also a kinsman of theirs.[2] All Trand's foster-sons were doughty men. Sigurd was the eldest and the foremost in almost all things. Tord had a by-name and he was called Tord the Low; he was, however, very tall and moreover he was stout and of great strength. Then said Trand: "Much may change in a man's lifetime. When we were young it was not usual for young and doughty men to sit or lie down on fine days. Nor would it have seemed fitting to the men of former days that Toralv of Dimun should be a stronger man than ye. The trading ship I own which stands here in the boathouse is now, I think, so old that it rots under the tar. Here is every house full of wool, and it is not offered

---

1 Outside Stavanger.  2 The O.N. text reads: *frændi þeirra*. *Frændi* is pronounced similar to the English *friend*, but in O.N. *frændi* is only used in connection with *kin* and *kinship*. The O.N. *kyn* is generally used for more distant relatives. *Kynstorr* means 'of great and noble descent'.

for sale; such would not have happened if I were some years younger ".
Sigurd leaped up and called upon Gaut and Tord, and said he would
not thole such mocking words from Trand. They went out to where
the huscarls were; they came to the ship and set it out on the water.
They had a cargo brought to it and loaded the ship. There was no
shortage of cargo at home, nor likewise of tackle for the ship.
They got it ready in a few days and on the ship there were ten or
twelve men. They and Toralv all sailed out in the same weather and
they always knew of each other on the sea. They came to land one
evening in Hernar.[1] Sigurd and his men lay to farther out along
the shore, but there was only a short distance between them. In
the evening when it was dark and Toralv's men were making ready
to go to bed, it befell that Toralv and another man went ashore to find
a place they were in need of. And when they were ready to go back
again, he who followed him said that a cloth was cast over Toralv's
head, and he was lifted up from the ground. At that moment he heard
a great noise; then he was borne away and put down. Afterwards he
was cast into the sea but managed to get ashore again. He then went to
the place where he and Toralv had parted, and there he found Toralv;
he was cloven down to the shoulders and was then dead. And when the
crew were aware of this, they bore Toralv's body out to the ship and
laid it there for the night. King Olav was then feasting in Lygra[2] and
word was sent thither. An arrow bidding and thing was called, and
the king was at the thing. Thither he had the Faröymen of both ships
called and they were to come to the thing. And when the thing was
gathered the king stood up and spoke: "Such tidings have befallen
and it is best that they seldom happen. Here a good dreng has lost
his life and we believe he was blameless. Is there any man at the
thing who can say who brought about this deed?"—but no one came
forth. Then said the king: "What my thoughts are about this deed
shall not be hidden; I believe it is the Faröymen. It rather seems to
me that Sigurd Torlakson has slain the man and that Tord the Low
cast the other into the sea. And moreover I will guess that the reason
might be found, for these men did not wish Toralv to report about
their evil doings which he would have known were true, and of which
we have had misgivings, namely that my messengers were murdered ".
And when the king stopped talking, Sigurd Torlakson stood up and
said: "I have not spoken at things before and I do not think that you
will find me wise of speech, but still I think that it is needful enough

---

1 Now Hennöyerne, outside Manger in North Hordaland.    2 *Lygra* in Lindas district, east of Manger.

to answer something. Now I will guess that the words the king has said must have come from the tongue roots of men who are much less wise and who are worse than he, and it is quite clear that they will be our foes. It is an unfitting speech to say that I should wish Toralv harm, for he was my foster-brother and my good friend; and if there was some ground for it and if there were matters between Toralv and me, I am wise enough to know that I would rather risk such a deed in the Faröys than here under your arm, O king. Now I wish to deny this charge for myself, and all us sea men; I will offer you such oaths as your laws demand, and if it seems better to you in aught, I will bear the hot irons, and I wish you yourself to be present at the ordeal". And when Sigurd ended his talk there were many to take up his cause, and they bade the king that Sigurd should have leave to free himself; Sigurd seemed to them to have spoken well and they thought that he was guiltless of that which was said against him. The king said: "About this man we have to choose between two extremes. If they have lied about him in this matter he must be a good man; but otherwise he must be much bolder than a man cares to be and that is rather my thought; but I guess that he will himself bear witness of that". And through the boons of the men the king took surety of Sigurd for the ordeal of hot irons—he was to come the day after to Lygra and the bishop should make the ordeal—and thus the thing came to an end. The king went back to Lygra, and Sigurd and his followers to their ships. It soon began to grow dusk and then said Sigurd to his men: "To tell the truth we are come into a great difficulty and we are faced with a great lie; this king is crafty and treacherous and it is easy to see our fate if he shall rule, for first he had Toralv slain, and now he will make us felons. It is an easy matter for him to misuse this ordeal of irons. And now I think that he will get the worse who risks it with him. Now there is a breeze blowing from the fell out along the sound; I counsel that we hoist our sail and sail out to sea. Trand can go another summer with his wool if he will have it sold. But if I get away I think it may be expected that I shall never again come to Norway". That seemed to the shipmen to be a wise plan; and then they hoisted their sail and let the ship go out to sea during the night as fast as they could. They did not stop ere they came to the Faröys and home to Gata. Trand took their journey ill; nor did they answer him well, but they stayed at home with him.

136. King Olav heard at once that Sigurd and his men were gone away, and a hard judgment was then pronounced on their case. Many

who had formerly denied the charge and spoken for Sigurd now found it likely that Sigurd and his men were truly guilty. King Olav said little about the matter, but now he seemed to know the truth where before he had only had misgivings. The king now went on his journey and held feasts where they were made ready for him. King Olav then summoned to talk to him the men who were come from Iceland: Torodd Snorrason, Gelli Thorkelson, Stein Skaftason, and Egil Hallson. The king then began his words: "This summer ye have called to my mind the matter that ye would make yourselves ready for your journey to Iceland, but in this matter I have not given ye any final answer. Now I will tell ye what I intend to settle. I wish thee, Gelli, to go to Iceland if thou wilt bear my errands there, but of the other Iceland men who are here now, none shall go to Iceland until I learn how they take the matters which thou, Gelli, shalt bear thither". And when the king had made this known, it seemed to those who had a wish to go and had been forbidden, that there was a certain unfriendliness towards them, and reckoned they were kept there for ill-luck and compulsion. But Gelli made himself ready for the journey and went in the summer to Iceland; he had with him the messages which he delivered the next summer at the thing. And this was the king's message, that he claimed of the Icelanders that they should take the laws he had set in Norway, and grant him from the land thane gild[1] and nose gild,[2] for every nose a penny—there should be ten to one ell of homespun. Thereto he promised the men his friendship if they would enter into this agreement, but otherwise he promised hardships to those he could come upon. Upon this matter men sat for a long time, and counselled about it amongst themselves, but at length they were agreed with the assent of all to refuse the taxes and impositions he had claimed. And that summer Gelli went to Norway to King Olav whom he met in the east in the Vik during the autumn, when he was come down from Gautland, which I expect to tell of later in King Olav's saga. When autumn was passing, King Olav went north to Trondheim and sailed with his army out to Nidaros, where he had his winter quarters made ready for him. The winter after King Olav sat in Kaupang.[3] That was the thirteenth year of his reign.

137. There was a man called Ketel Jämte, son of Jarl Anund of Sparabu in Trondheim; he had fled before King Eystein Illrade east over the Kjöl; he had cleared the woods and settled the land now

---

1 *Thane gild* was a fine for killing a king's subject.   2 *Nose gild*, meaning 'nose scot', was a poll tax.   3 I.e. Nidaros.

called Jämtland. Thither to the east there also fled a crowd of men from Trondheim because of unrest, for King Eystein had put taxes on the Tronds and set as king there his hound which was called Saur.[1] Ketel's grandson was Tore the Helsing; Helsingeland, which he settled, is called after him. And when Harald Hairfair cleared the kingdom for himself, there also fled before him from the land a crowd of men, Tronds and Naumadale-men, and then were new settlements made in the east in Jämtland; some of these men went right to Helsingeland east along the sea and they submitted to the Swedish king. And when Hacon, Athelstan's foster-son, was King of Norway, peace was settled and trading journeys made from Trondheim to Jämtland; and because the king was friendly the Jämters came west to him, promised him loyalty and paid him scot; he set up laws and land rights for them; they would rather put themselves under his kingdom than under the Swedish king, for they were come of Norse stock. So also did the Helsingers whose kin came from the north of the Kjöl, and thus they remained for a long time after until Olav Digre and Olav the Swede quarrelled over the land boundaries; then the Jämters and the Helsingers put themselves under the Swedish king, and then Eidaskog was the eastern land boundary and afterwards the Kjöl right north to Finmark. The Swedish king then took scot from Helsingeland and likewise from Jämtland. But King Olav thought that by the treaty between him and the Swedish king the scot from Jämtland should go another way than it had formerly gone. It had happened, however, for a long time that the Jämters had paid scot to the Swedish king and that the sheriffs had come throughout the land from him; nor would the Swedes hear of aught else than that the whole land which lay east of the Kjöl should go under the Swedish king. Then it was, as often may happen, that, even though there was kinship and friendship between the kings, each of them would have all the kingdom upon which he thought he had some claim. King Olav had sent word to Jämtland that it was his will that the Jämters should show him loyalty—otherwise he promised them hardship. But the Jämters had taken counsel to show the Swedish king loyalty.

138. Torodd Snorrason and Stein Skaftason were ill pleased that they could not counsel for themselves. Stein Skaftason was a fair man and doughty in all kinds of sports; he was also a good poet, bore himself showily and was full of arrogance. His father Skafti had made a poem about Olav and had taught it to Stein, for it was his

---

1 Cf. 'History of Hacon the Good', chapter 12.

intention that Stein should bring it before the king. Stein did not keep himself from using words and making jests against the king, both in loose words and in verse. Both he and Torodd were very reckless in talk; they said that the king should have it worse than they, who in trust had sent him their sons whom the king had put in bondage. The king was wroth. One day Stein Skaftason stood before the king and asked him if he would hear the poem his father Skafti had composed about the king. He answered: "First it must be, Stein, that thou dost recite that which thou hast made about me". Stein said that there was nothing he had composed: "I am no poet, O king," he said, "but if I could compose, it would seem, like everything else about me, of little weight to you". Stein went away and thought he perceived what the king aimed at. Torgeir was the name of the king's steward who looked after the king's garth in Orkedale; he was then with the king and heard the talk between the king and Stein. Torgeir went home a little later. One night, Stein ran from the garth with his shoe swain; they went up over the Gaularas and farther out until they came to Orkedale; in the evening they came to the king's garth, which Torgeir looked after; Torgeir bade Stein stay there the night and asked what was the reason for his journey. Stein bade him get him a steed and sleigh, for he saw that the corn was being brought home on sleighs.[1] Torgeir said: "I know not how it stands with thy journey, whether thou goest with the king's leave or not. It seemed to me the other day that there were no meek words between thee and the king". Stein said: "Even if I cannot decide for myself in aught before the king, I shall not bear such from his thralls". He drew his sword and then slew the steward; he took a horse and bade the lad jump on its back, and Stein sat in the sleigh. They then left the place and drove all the night, and went on farther until they came down to Syrnadale[2] in Möre; afterwards they got a ferry over the fjords. Stein went as quickly as he could. Wherever they came they did not mention anything about the murder but said that they were the king's men; wherever they went they got help. One day in the evening they came to Giske[3] to Torberg Arneson's garth; Torberg was not at home; but his wife Ragnhild, Erling Skjalgson's daughter, was at home. Stein was well greeted by her, for they were well known to each other. It had befallen

1 The corn was evidently brought home to be thrashed in the winter, from corn ricks in the fields. Ricks for corn and hay are nowadays seldom used in Scandinavia; but they are still employed in England, Belgium and elsewhere.  2 Now Surnadale in North Möre, west of Orkedale.  3 *Giske* is an island north-west of Alesund (in South Möre).

formerly when Stein had come from Iceland—he owned the ship himself—and came to land by Giske where he lay in by the isle, that Ragnhild lay heavy with child and was in sore need, but there was no priest in the isle and none in the neighbourhood. Folk then came to the trading ship and asked if there was some priest there; there was on the ship a priest called Bard from the West Fjords, but he was young and little learned. The messengers bade the priest go with them to the house; it seemed to him to be a difficult matter when he thought of his lack of learning, and he would not go. Then Stein gave word to the priest and bade him go. The priest answered: "I will go if thou wilt go with me; it will seem safe to have thee with me to counsel me". Stein said that he would readily do that. They went to the garth, where Ragnhild was. A little later she bore a child; it was a girl and seemed rather weak. Then the priest baptised the child and Stein held her at the font; she was named Thora. Stein gave the child a finger-ring of gold. Ragnhild promised Stein her full friendship and bade him come there to her if he seemed to be in need of her help. Stein said that he would not come to hold more children at the font, and thereafter they parted. And now it came about that Stein claimed fulfilment of these promises of friendship made by Ragnhild, and told what had befallen and likewise that he was come away on account of the king's wrath. She said that her help would answer to her might and she bade him wait there for Torberg; she gave him a seat next to her son Eystein Orre who was then twelve years old. Stein gave gifts to Ragnhild and Eystein. Torberg had heard all about Stein's journey before he came home and he was rather unfriendly. Ragnhild went to talk to him, and told him about Stein's journey and bade him greet Stein and see to his business. Torberg said: "I have heard that the king has called a war thing about Torgeir, that Stein is outlawed and likewise that the king is very wroth. I know better than to take a foreign man on my hands and thereby bring the king's wrath on me. Let Stein go away from here as soon as he can". Ragnhild answered that she and Stein would both go away or both stay there. Torberg bade her go if she wished; "I expect", he said, "that even if thou goest thou wilt soon come back, for here thou wilt have most to say". Then their son Eystein Orre came forth and he spoke, saying he would not stay behind if Ragnhild went away. Torberg said that they showed much stubbornness and wilfulness in this; "It looks", he said, "most likely that ye two must counsel in this since ye lay so great weight on it, but all too much dost thou take after thy kin, Ragnhild, in reckoning King Olav's word so small". Ragnhild said: "If it is getting too much for thee to keep Stein, then go thou thyself with him to my father Erling, or give him such a following that he can come there in peace". Torberg said that he would not send Stein thither: "Erling has enough to answer for such as the king is ill-pleased with". Stein was there during the winter. After Yule messengers came from the king to Torberg with word that Torberg should go to him before Mid-Lent, and a strong bidding went with the message. Torberg brought it before his friends and sought their counsel as to whether he should risk going to the king under such circumstances. Most of them counselled against it and found it most advisable first to send Stein away and then go to the king. But Torberg most wished not to delay the journey. A little later Torberg went to his brother Finn and put the matter before him, bidding him go with him. Finn answered and said that such rule by women seemed bad to him if for his wife's sake he dared not be trusty to his right chief. "Thou canst choose if thou wilt not go", said Torberg; "I believe, however, that thou leavest the matter alone more through fear than through allegiance to the king." They parted wrathfully. Then Torberg went to his brother Arne Arneson, told him how things stood with him and bade him go with him to the king. Arne said: "It seems strange to me that such a wise and wary man as thou should have come into such great ill-luck and have got the king's wrath when there was no need; there might be some excuse if thou had kept thy kinsmen or foster-brothers, but there is no excuse that thou hast taken on thy hands an Iceland man and one who is outlawed and now brings thee and all thy kinsmen in peril". Torberg said: "So it is as is said: 'One man is outcast in every family'. It is easy to see my father's ill-luck in getting sons and that he should get him last who has no likeness to our kin and is deedless; and it might be found true, if it did not seem to be shameful talk against my mother, that I should not call thee our brother". Thereafter Torberg turned away and went home; he was somewhat unhappy. After this he sent word north to Trondheim to his brother Kalv and bade him come to Agdenes to meet him. And when the messengers met Kalv he promised to go and made no objection. Ragnhild sent men south to Jæderen to her father Erling and bade him send her help. From there came Erling's sons Sigurd and Tore, and each of them had a twenty-bencher and on each were ninety men. And when they came north to Torberg he greeted them well and with great gladness. Torberg made himself ready for the journey and he, too, had a twenty-bencher. They went their way to the north, and when they came to Trondheim's Minne,[1] Finn and Arne, Torberg's brothers, lay ready there with two twenty-benchers. Torberg greeted his brothers with friendliness and said that the whetting had helped; Finn said that there was seldom need of that with him. They then went with all their army north to Trondheim and Stein was with them on the journey. And when they came to Agdenes Kalv Arneson lay by there, and he had a well-fitted-out twenty-bencher. With this army they went into Nidarholm and lay there during the night. The morning after they held a meeting. Kalv and Erling's sons went with the whole army into the town and then let matters go as fate would. But Torberg wanted them first to go warily and have terms made, and therein Finn and Arne agreed. It was then arranged that Finn and Arne should first go to King Olav with few men. The king had by then learned about the crowd of men they had and he was very harsh in his talk with them. Finn offered terms for Torberg and likewise for Stein—he offered that the king might claim as big fines as he would, but that Torberg should have his right to be in the land and to his land rents, whilst Stein should have life and limb. The king said: "So it seems to me as if this journey is such that ye well think ye can rule me half or more; but I should least think of you brothers that ye would come with an army against me. I know the Jadar men have put forward this plan, but it does not avail to offer me fines". Then said Finn: "Not for that reason have we brothers gathered an army, that we should offer you unrest, O king. The reason is rather that we will first offer you our service. But if you refuse and offer Torberg a hard lot, then shall we all go with the army we have to Canute the Mighty". Then the king looked at him and said: "If ye brothers will swear oaths that ye will follow me inland and abroad and not part from me without my leave and permission, and that ye will not hide from me any treachery ye know is being laid up against me, then I will make terms with ye brothers". Finn then went back to his brothers and told of the choice the king had given them. They now held counsel. Torberg said that he would take the choice for himself. "I have no wish", he said, "to flee from my possessions and seek foreign chiefs; I think it will always be to my honour to follow King Olav and be where he is." Then said Kalv: "No oath will I swear to the king, but I will be with him whilst I can have my land rents and other power and the

---

[1] In the O.N. text *þrandheims mynni*, i.e. Trondheim's Minne, which is supposed to be Krakevad, south of Storfosna.

king will be my friend; and it is my wish that we shall all do so". Finn answered: "I will advise that we leave to King Olav the sole settlement of the choice between us". Arne Arneson said: "If I were sure of wishing to follow thee, brother Torberg, even if thou wilt fight against the king, I would not part from thee if thou were to choose a better plan, and I will follow thee and Finn and take the lot ye choose to take into your hands". Thereafter the three brothers, Torberg, Finn, and Arne, went on one ship and rowed to the town and thence they went to the king. And then the agreement came about that they swore the king oaths. Torberg asked the king for terms for Stein: the king said that Stein should go in peace for him: "but he shall not be with me hereafter", he said. Torberg and his brothers then went out to their folk. Kalv went to Egge, and Finn went to the king, but Torberg and their other men went home to the south. Stein went south with Erling's sons and early in the spring he went west to England; he put himself in Canute the Mighty's hands and was with him for a long time in good favour.

139. When Finn Arneson had stayed a short time with King Olav, the king one day called Finn and several other men whom he was wont to have with him in his councils to talk with him. The king began his words and spoke thus: "This plan I have now decided in my mind: this spring I will call an expedition out from the whole land, both of men and ships, and then go with all the host I can get against Canute the Mighty, for I know of the claim on the kingdom which he has set up against me, and he does not intend to let it be only idle talk. Now I will tell thee, Finn Arneson, that I wish thee to go as my messenger to the north to Halogaland, and hold there a levy and call out a force of men and ships, and lead the army to meet me in Agdenes". The king then named the other men and some he sent into Trondheim and some south in the land, so that his bidding went through the whole land. Finn's journey will now be told of: he had a cutter and on it nearly thirty men; when he was ready he went on his journey until he came to Halogaland. He then called a thing of the bonders, made known his errand and demanded a levy. In the land there the bonders had great ships and on the bidding of the king they fitted themselves and made their ships ready. And when Finn went farther north to Halogaland he held things, and he sent men to Bjarköy to Tore the Hound and there claimed a troop as in other places. And when the king's behest came to Tore, he made himself ready for the journey and took his huscarls to the ship which the summer before he had had in Bjarmaland; he fitted it out

at his own cost. Finn called together at Vagar[1] all the Halogaland men who were from the north and in the spring a great strength of men gathered there, and all bided there till Finn came north; Tore the Hound had also come there. And when Finn came, he had all the men of the force called together to a husthing, and at this thing the men showed their weapons and then a muster was made of the men from each *Skipreide*.[2] And when that was done, Finn said: "Tore the Hound, I will ask thee about this: what offer wilt thou make King Olav for having slain Karli, his bodyguard, or for the robbery by which thou didst take the king's goods in the north in Lengjuvik?[3] Now the king has charged me to deal with this case; but I wish to know thy answer at once". Tore looked about and noticed that on each side of him there stood many fully weaponed men; and there he recognised Gunstein and many others of Karli's kinsmen. Then said Tore: "My offer is soon said, Finn; I will set my case for the king's judgment, to do what he demands of me". Finn answered: "It is most likely that thou wilt gain less honour by it, but now it is necessary that thou settlest the case according to my judgment if thou wilt have peace". Tore said: "Then I also think that my case has come into good hands, and I shall stand by it". Tore then went forward to offer surety, and Finn gave out his findings in everything. Finn then set out the peace terms, that Tore should pay the king ten marks of gold and to Gunstein and his kinsmen another ten marks, and for robbery and damage to goods a third ten marks;[4] "And thou shalt pay forthwith", he said. Tore said: "That is a big fine". "There is the other choice", said Finn, "that the peace proposal is at an end." Tore said that Finn must let him have time to see if he could get loans from his followers. Finn bade him pay there on the spot and mentioned besides that Tore should bring forth the great collar which he had taken from the dead Karli. Tore said that he had not taken any collar. Then Gunstein came forth and said that Karli had the collar round his neck when they parted, "but when we took his body it was not there". Tore said that he had not noticed the collar, "but if we have taken any collar it may well be at home in Bjarköy". Finn then put the spear's point before Tore's breast and said that he should now produce the collar. Tore took the collar from his neck and gave it to Finn. Tore then went away to his ship; Finn followed him to the ship with many men. Finn walked on board and his men filled the ship rooms. And near the mast they

---

1 Now Vaagen (North Norway).      2 Cf. 'History of Hacon the Good', chapter 20.
3 Cf. p. 363, n. 3.      4 A gold mark was worth eight silver marks.

saw down under the floors two tuns so great that it seemed strange to them. Finn asked what was in the tuns, and Tore answered that his drink was in them. Finn said: "Why doest thou not offer us drinks, good friend, with so much drink as thou hast?" Tore told one of his men to tap off the tun into a bowl. It was then given to Finn and his men to drink, and it was the best drink. Finn then bade Tore bring out the money. Tore went fore and aft on the ship and talked to various men. Finn shouted and bade him bring forth the money. Tore bade him go up on land and said that he would bring it. Finn and his men then went up on land and Tore came there and paid silver; from one bag he produced ten marks by weight. He then took out many purses: in some there was one mark by weight, in others half a mark, or some *örer*.[1] Then said Tore: "These are loans which different men have lent me, for all the loose money I have now is, I think, come to an end". Tore then went out on the ship, and when he came back he paid out silver little by little. The day was then passing, and as soon as the thing was ended folk went to their ships and made themselves ready to put off; as soon as they were ready they began to sail, and then it came about that most of the men had sailed away. Finn then saw that the folk were thinning about him, and his men were shouting to him, bidding him get ready. Not a third of the fine was yet paid. Then said Finn, "The payment goes very slowly, Tore. I see that it goes hard with thee to pay the money. This may now do for the first, and what is left thou shalt pay the king". Then Finn stood up. Tore said: "It seems well to me, Finn, that we are parting. But I shall have the will to pay this fine in such a way that neither the king nor thou wilt find it to be a bad payment". Finn then went to his ship and sailed forth after his men. Tore was late in getting ready to leave the haven, and when the sail was hoisted they sailed across the West Fjord [2] and then out to sea, south along the coast, so far out that the sea was sometimes on mid-mountain and sometimes the land was under the water. He went on southwards until he sailed into the England sea and came forth into England. He then went to King Canute who greeted him well. Then it came out that Tore had much wealth, for he had there all the goods which he and Karli had taken in Bjarmaland; and in those great tuns there was a second bottom a short way from the outer one, and between these there was drink, but the tuns themselves were both full of furs, beaver and sable. Tore was then with King Canute. Finn Arneson

1 In a mark there were eight *örer*.    2 The wide bight between the Lofoten Islands and the mainland.

meanwhile drew near King Olav with a great strength of men, and told him all about his journey; he said likewise that he believed Tore to have left the land and gone west to England to Canute the Mighty, "and I think he will do us great scathe". The king said: "I believe that Tore will be our foe, but it has always seemed better to me to have him farther off than nearer".

140. Asmund Grankelson had that winter been in his district in Halogaland and was at home with his father Grankel. Out towards the sea there was an outlying fishing place where there was the catching of both seal and bird, an egg lair, and a fish lair, and it had from olden times belonged to the garth which Grankel owned. But Harek of Tjotta made claim on it, and it came about that for some years he had had all the catches of this place. But now Asmund and his father thought they had the king's help in all rightful matters; so father and son both went in the spring to Harek and told him King Olav's words and showed his token that Harek was to give up his claim to the place. Harek thereupon answered wrathfully and said that Asmund had gone to the king with this and other slanders: "I have all the right on my side: thou, Asmund, shouldst understand how to keep within measure, even though now thou thinkest thou art a great man since thou hast the king's help. Thou mayest need it, too, if it shall be granted thee to slay sundry chiefs and make them felons, and rob from us who aforetime seemed to be able to hold our rights ourselves, even though we had to do with men of equal birth; but now it is far from thee being equal to me in kinship". Asmund answered: "There are many that feel about thee, Harek, that thou art strong in kinship and hast over-stepped thy might; many have lost their rights because of thee, but it is likeliest now, Harek, that thou shouldst seek another place than here with us in order to go on with thy wrongfulness or act so lawlessly as this". They then parted. Harek sent away his huscarls, ten or twelve, with a great rowing ferry-boat. They went to the fishing spot, took every kind of catch and loaded the ferry-boat. And when they were ready to go away, Asmund Grankelson came upon them with thirty men and bade them give up all their catch. Harek's huscarls answered somewhat slowly; then Asmund and his men took hold of them and the advantage in numbers soon told. Some of Harek's huscarls were beaten, some wounded, and some driven overboard, and all the catch was borne away from the ship; Asmund and his men took it with them. After that Harek's huscarls came home and told Harek about their journey; he answered: "These tidings seem to be a new attempt; it has not befallen before

that my men have been beaten''. The matter was left thus. Harek did not say a word about it and he was very merry. In the spring Harek had a twenty-bench cutter made ready and on it he took his huscarls; this ship was well fitted out with both men and tackle. Then Harek went harrying, and when he found King Olav, Asmund Grankelson was also there. The king then brought about a meeting between Asmund and Harek and made peace between them, and the matter was left to the king's judgment. Afterwards Asmund brought forth witnesses that Grankel had owned the fishing place, and the king gave his judgment according to that. The outcome of the affair was unsatisfactory, for Harek's huscarls got no award, whereas the fishery was accorded to Grankel. Harek said that it was no shame to him to accept the king's judgment, however the matter might turn out afterwards.

141. Torodd Snorrason had stayed on in Norway at King Olav's wish when Gelli Thorkelson got leave to go to Iceland, as is written before (chapter 136). He was with King Olav and was ill pleased at his loss of freedom, whereby he could not go travelling where he would. At the beginning of the winter when King Olav was in Nidaros, he wanted to send men to Jämtland to demand scot; but folk had little wish to make that journey, for the messengers Trand the White and eleven men whom the king had sent there before had lost their lives, as is written above (chapter 63), and the Jämters had since held themselves loyal to the Swedish king. Torodd Snorrason offered himself for the journey, for he laid little weight on what became of him if he could only decide for himself. The king accepted that and Torodd went with eleven men. They came forth east into Jämtland and sought the house of the man called Torar; he was the lawman there and a man of high rank, and there they were well greeted. And when they had been there a short while they made known their errand to Torar. He said that the other landed men and chiefs could decide the answer no less than he, and added that he would call a thing about it. So it was done; the thing bidding was sent out and an ordinary thing called. Torar went to the thing, but meanwhile the messengers stayed at his house. Torar then put the matter before the people, but they were all agreed that they would pay the King of Norway no scot; some would have the messengers hanged, others would have them for a blood offering, but it was arranged that they should be kept there until the Swedish king's sheriffs came, and that with the assent of the men of the district the sheriffs should settle what they would about them. But they

were to keep the messengers well and make it seem that they were being kept back to wait for the scot, and they were to separate them in their lodgings, two and two together. Torodd was with another man at Torar's house. There was a great Yule feast and great ale drinkings. In the village there were many bonders and they all drank together during Yule. Another village was a little way from there, and there dwelt Torar's brother-in-law, a rich and mighty man who had a grown-up son. Each of these kinsmen were to drink half of the Yuletide at each other's, and first at Torar's. The brothers drank with each other and Torodd with the bonder's son; they had a drinking match and in the evening there was still much drinking with each other and comparing of Norsemen and Swedes and then of their kings, of those who had formerly been and of those who were now, and likewise of the dealings of each land in slaughter and robbery. Then said the bonder's son: "If our kings have lost more men, the Swedish king's sheriffs will balance it with the lives of twelve men when they come from the south after Yule, and ye do not know rightly, ye wretched men, why ye are being kept back". Torodd took note of that but many laughed at it and uttered words of shame against them and their king. Now when the ale made the Jämters talk, what Torodd had not before thought about was no longer hidden. The day after Torodd and his followers took all their clothes and weapons and laid them so that they could easily get them; the night after when the folk had gone to sleep they ran away to the wood, and next morning when the Jämters were aware that these men had run away they went after them with bloodhounds and came near them in the wood where they had hidden themselves; they took them back home into a booth, where there was a deep pit, into which they were dropped, and then the door was locked. They had little food and no other clothes than those they were wearing. And when the middle of Yuletide came, Torar and his freemen went to his brother-in-law's, where they were to drink the second half of the Yuletide. Torar's thralls were to watch the pit. They had drink enough but they kept little check on the drinking of it and so they got themselves dead drunk the first evening. And when they had drunk well, they who were to bear food to the men in the pit talked amongst themselves and said that they should not lack aught. Torodd sang songs and rallied the thralls, and they said that he was their good friend and so they gave him a great candle and lit it. Then the thralls who had been in came out and they shouted eagerly for the others to go in. But both parties were so drunk with ale that they did not lock either the pit or the booth. Torodd and the other man then cut their capes asunder into strips and tied them together; they made a loop at one end, and cast it up on to the floor of the booth. It twisted round the foot of a chest and held fast. They then tried to get up; Torodd heaved his fellow up until he stood on his shoulders; the man then hauled himself up through the hole. There was no lack of ropes in the booth and he let one down to Torodd; but when he would draw Torodd up, he could not lift him. Torodd then said he should cast the rope over a balk which was in the booth, make a loop at one end and tie therein so much wood and stone that it was more than his weight. He did so, and as the weight sank down into the pit, Torodd rose up. In the booth they got themselves the clothes they needed. There were also reindeer hides and from these they cut off the hoofs and bound them back to front under their feet. But before they went away they set fire to a great corn lathe which was there and then ran away into the darkness. The lathe burned and so did many other houses in the village. Torodd and the other man went the whole night through the wastes and hid themselves in the daytime. In the morning they were missed; and men went with bloodhounds to look for them on all the ways leading out from the garth, but the hounds followed the tracks back to the garth, for they followed the reindeer hoofs the way the clefts showed. They then searched no more for them. Torodd and the other men went a long time through the wastes and one evening they came to a little garth and there they went in. A man and woman were sitting there near the fire; the man called himself Tore and said that she who sat there was his wife; he also said that he owned the cottage. He bade them stay there and they accepted. He then told them that he was come thither because he had fled from the town because of a murder. Torodd and his follower were well looked after and they all had food by the fire. A bed was made for Torodd and the other man on the bench and they lay down to sleep, but there was still some light from the fire. Torodd saw then a man from another house going in and never had he seen so great a man; he wore scarlet clothes inset with gold bands and looked stately. Torodd heard him blaming them for taking in guests when they had hardly food enough to keep themselves alive. The housewife said: "Be thou not wroth, brother, for seldom indeed has this happened; rather give them a helping hand, for thou art more fitted to do it than we". Torodd heard that the big man was called Arnljot Gellina and likewise that the housewife was his sister; Torodd had heard the name Arnljot and also that he was a great highwayman and evil doer.

Torodd and his follower slept well during the night, for they were weary from the journey. But when there was yet only a third of the night gone Arnljot came and bade them get up and make themselves ready for the journey. Torodd and the other man straightway got up and clad themselves and then had breakfast. Tore then gave each of them skis, and Arnljot got ready to go with them; he stepped into his skis, which were both broad and long. And as soon as Arnljot had set his ski-staff to the ground he was a long way in front of them; he waited for them and said that in that way they would get no distance and bade them step on to his skis. They did so: Torodd stood next to him and held on to Arnljot's belt and Torodd's follower held on to him. Arnljot slid forward as fast as if he were going alone. Late that evening they came to a wayside house where they made a fire and got food ready. As they were eating the food, Arnljot bade them not to cast down any of it, neither bones nor bits. Arnljot then brought forth from under his shirt a silver bowl and he put the food therein. And when they had fed, Arnljot hid their leavings. They then made themselves ready to go to rest. At one end of the house there was a loft upon two cross balks, and to this loft Arnljot and the other two went and laid themselves down to sleep. Arnljot had a great spear with a gold inlaid socket; he was also girded with a sword. They had both their weapons and their clothes up in the loft with them. Arnljot bade the others keep still and he lay foremost in the loft. A little later twelve men came to the house; they were merchants who were going to Jämtland with their wares. And when they came into the house they made much din and were very merry, and they made themselves great fires. And when they had had food, they cast out all the bones, and then they made themselves ready for rest and lay down on the benches near the fire. When they had slept there a short while a great troll woman (witch) came to the house, and when she came in she swept quickly about her, took the bones and everything that she thought eatable and thrust them into her mouth. She then grabbed the man nearest her, tore him and slit him in half and cast him on the fire. Then the others awoke as from an evil dream and leaped up, but she sent one after another to hell, so that one alone was alive. He ran farther under the loft and shouted for help, if such there was in the loft to help him. Arnljot stretched down to him, took him by the hands and drew him up into the loft. The witch then went to the fire, and began to eat the men when they were cooked. Arnljot stood up, grabbed his spear and struck it between her shoulders so that the point came out through her breast; she jumped up, shrieked hideously and rushed out. Arnljot let the spear slip and she took it off with her. Arnljot went forward, cleared out the bodies and set up the door and the door-post of the room, for she had broken it all down when she rushed off. They then slept the rest of the night. And when it was light they got up and first ate their breakfast, and when they had had food Arnljot said: "Now we must part here. Ye shall now go on the sleigh path where the merchants came yesterday. I will look for my spear. As my wages I will have the goods these men owned, which seem to be my money's worth. But thou, Torodd, shalt bear my greeting to King Olav and tell him this, that he is the man whom I have the greatest desire to meet; but he will deem my greeting of little worth". He took up his silver bowl, dried it with a cloth and said: "Bear thou this bowl to the king and say that it is my greeting". Then they all made themselves ready for the journey and parted. And Torodd, his fellow, and that merchant who had escaped, went each his own way. Torodd went until he found King Olav in the trading town[1] and told him all about his journey. He told him Arnljot's greeting and brought forth the silver bowl. The king said it was ill that Arnljot had not been to see him, "and it is great scathe that so much bad luck should fall on so good a dreng and such a noteworthy man". Torodd was then with the king for the rest of the winter and then got leave of him to go to Iceland the next summer. He and King Olav parted as good friends.

142. In the spring, King Olav made himself ready to go from Nidaros, and there was a gathering of many folk both from Trondheim and from the north of the land. And when he was ready, he first went south with his army to Möre and there gathered his levy men and likewise from Raumsdale. He then went to South Möre. For a long while he lay in the Heröys[2] awaiting his men, and he often held husthings, for there much came to his ears which seemed to him to demand attention. At one husthing he held he brought forth this matter: he told about the loss of men he had had in the Faröys; "but of the scot they have promised me", he said, "nothing has come forth. Now shall I again send men there for the scot". The king broached this matter to sundry men and said that they should undertake this journey. But answers came back that all men excused themselves from the journey. Then a great and active-looking man stood up at the thing; he wore a red kirtle, a helm on his head, and had a great spear in his hand and was girt with a sword; he began to speak: "To tell the truth, here is a great variety of folk. Ye have a good king, but he has bad drengs. Ye withhold yourselves from the errand he

1 I.e. Nidaros.　2 The *Heröys* are west of Hareidland.

bids you, and ye have before taken friendly gifts and many good things from him. Hitherto, I have not been a friend of this king; he, too, has been my foe, and he thinks he has good grounds for it. Now, O king, I will offer you to go on this journey if there is no better choice". The king said: "Who is this manly carl, who answers my speech? There is a great difference between thee and the other men who are here, when thou dost offer thyself for the journey and they excuse themselves whom I thought would have answered it well. But of thee I know nothing, not even thy name". He answered: "My name offers no difficulty, O king, I expect thou hast well heard me mentioned; I am called Karl Mærski". The king said: "So it is, Karl, that I have heard thee mentioned, and to tell thee the truth, there have been times whereof thou wouldst not have been able to tell tidings if we had met. But now I will not be worse than thou who dost offer me thy help, in that I will in return give thee my thanks and favour. Thou shalt come to me, Karl, and be my guest to-day; we two shall talk further on this matter". Karl said that it should be so.

143. Karl Mærski had been a viking and a great robber, and very often the king had sent men after him to deprive him of his life. Karl was of good stock and very enterprising, skilled in sports and doughty in many things. And when Karl had promised to make this journey the king came to terms with him and showed him friendliness; he caused him to be fitted out with the best for the journey. On his ship there were nigh on twenty men and the king sent word to his friends in the Faröys—they were Leif Assurson and Gilli the Lawman—to help and aid Karl, and thereto he sent his tokens. Karl went as soon as he was ready; they had a good wind, came to the Faröys and lay in by Torshavn in Strömöy.[1] A thing was called and many men came to it. Thither came Trand of Gata with a great troop; thither, too, came Leif and Gilli, and they also had a great crowd. And when they had set up their awnings and made themselves ready, they went to meet Karl Mærski, and there were good greetings. Karl then put forward King Olav's words and tokens and his friendly message to Leif and Gilli. They took it well, bade Karl go with them, and promised to further his errand and give him such help as they had might for. He took it with thanks. A little later Trand came there and greeted Karl well. "I am glad", he said, "that such a man is come here to our land with our king's errands which we are bound to further; I wish for naught else, Karl, than that thou wilt go and spend the winter with me and bring so many of thy men that thine honour will be greater than before." Karl said he had already promised to

1 The biggest island in the Faroes, of which Torshavn is the capital.

go to Leif, "but otherwise", he said, "I would accept thy invitation gladly". Trand said: "Then will Leif alone get honour for that. But are there other things I could do, so that it would be of some help to thee in this?" Karl answered that it would seem to him to be a great help if Trand would gather the scot throughout the Eastern Isles and likewise through all the Northern Isles. Trand said that he was bound as well as willing to grant this furtherance of the king's business. Trand then went back to his booth. Nothing more happened at that thing. Karl went to stay with Leif Assurson and he was there the winter after. Leif gathered the scot in Strömöy and in all the isles to the south. In the spring after, Trand fell into bad health; he had pains in his eyes, besides other sicknesses. But he got ready to go to the thing, as was his wont. And when he came to the thing and his booth was covered, he had it lined inside with a black cloth so that the light should be less bright. And when some days of the thing were gone, Leif and Karl went to Trand's booth with a great following, and as they came to the booth there stood some men without. Leif asked if Trand was in the booth and they said he was. Leif said they should ask Trand to come out; "Karl and I have business with him", he said. But when they came out they said that Trand had such eye ache that he could not come out, and "he bade thee, Leif, to go in". Leif told his followers to go warily when they went into the booth and not to throng each other—"he shall come out first who goes in last". Leif went in first, Karl next, and then his followers, and they went fully weaponed as if they were ready to fight. Leif went farther in towards the black cloth and then asked where Trand was. Trand answered and greeted Leif. Leif accepted his greeting and asked if he had gathered any of the scot from the Northern Isles and how he had managed with the silver. Trand answered and said that what he and Karl had talked about had not gone from his mind, and that the scot should be paid readily; "Here is a bag, Leif, which thou shalt take, and it is full of silver". Leif looked about him and saw few men in the booth, some lay on the benches; others were sitting up. Leif then went to Trand and took the bag and carried it farther out of the booth where it was light; he poured the silver out on his shield, stirred it about with his hand and told Karl to look at the silver. They looked at it for a moment and then Karl asked Leif how the silver seemed to him. He said: "I believe that here has surely come every single bad penny which there is in the Northern Isles". Trand heard that and said: "The silver seems bad to thee, Leif?" "So it is", he said. Trand then said: "Then those kinsmen of mine are real villains since one can trust them in naught. This spring I sent them to gather the scot in the north of the isles, when I was good for nothing myself. But they have had gifts from the bonders to take such false money as will not pass in payment. It is best, Leif, for thee to look at this silver which has been paid me for my land dues". Leif bore the silver back, took out another bag and brought it to Karl. They searched through this money and Karl asked how this lot seemed to Leif. He answered that the money seemed bad, but good enough to be taken in payment of which there was no precise arrangement, "but I will not take this money to the king". Then a man who lay on a bench cast his skin cape from his head and said : "There is the old saying that every man grows worse as he grows older. So is it also with thee,

Leif is called to Gilli the Lawman's booth

Trand; thou wilt let Karl Mærski reject money for thee the whole day". It was Gaut the Red. Trand leaped up on Gaut's words, grew mad and talked very hard against his kinsman, but at last he said that Leif should give him back the silver: "and take this bag which my tenants have brought home to me this spring, and though I do not see clearly, one's own hand is, however, the most trustworthy". A man lying on the bench raised himself up on his elbow: it was Tord the Low. He said: "No more injurious charges will we have from Karl Mærski; he should have it in payment". Leif took the bag and bore it to Karl. They looked at the money and Leif said: "There is no need to look long at this silver. Here is every penny better than the others and this money will we have. Get thou a man, Trand, to see to the counting". Trand said he would like it best if Leif would see to it on his behalf. Leif and the others then went out a short way from the booth and there they sat down and weighed the silver. Karl took his helm off his head and poured in the silver when it was weighed. They saw a man going by, who had in his hand a pike-axe and on his head a hat and was wearing a green cape; he was barefoot and had linen breeches laced round his legs. He set the pike-axe down in the field and went away saying: "Look thou to it, Karl

Mærski, that thou gettest no hurt of my pike-axe". A little later a man came rushing up and shouted heatedly to Leif Assurson, bidding him go to Gilli the Lawman's booth as quickly as he could: "Sigurd Torlakson has rushed in through the cover and has wounded a man to death in the booth". Leif and all his men straightway leaped up and went away to meet Gilli in his booth; but Karl sat behind and his Norsemen stood round him. Gaut the Red rushed up and struck with a hand-axe over the men's heads and the blow fell on Karl's head, but the wound was not great. Tord the Low grabbed up the pike-axe which stood on the field and with it he struck at the axe hammer so that the latter went down into Karl's brain. At the same moment a crowd of folk rushed out of Trand's booth. Karl was borne away dead. Trand was ill pleased with this deed and he offered money as fines for his kinsmen. Leif and Gilli brought up the case of man-slaughter and the fines were not taken. Sigurd was outlawed for the scathe he had done Gilli's boothman, and Tord and Gaut were out-lawed for Karl's murder. The Norsemen got the ship ready which Karl had brought thither and went east to King Olav. He was very wroth over that deed, but it was not possible for King Olav to take vengeance on Trand or his kinsmen because of the unrest which then arose in Norway and which shall be told of hereafter. And now is ended the tale of the tidings which came of King Olav demanding scot from the Faröys. But later there was great strife in the Faröys over the murder of Karl Mærski, and Leif Assurson fought against Trand's kinsmen; thereof there are great tales.

144. Now shall we tell where we before left off (chapter 142) that King Olav went with his army and took a levy out from the land. All the landed men of the north followed him, except Einar Tambar-skelver; he had sat at home on his estates in peace since he came into the land and he served not the king. Einar had no rents of the king's land. King Olav sailed with the army to the south by Stad; and there many men of the lordships gathered to him. King Olav then had the ship he had had built the winter before, a very big ship which bore the name of *Visund*[1]; on the prow was a bison's head all covered with gold. About this Sigvat the Scald says:

The Ling Fish[2] which bore
The flight-shy son of Trygvi,
Carried its gold-decked snout
Till all was lost as God willed.

Olav Digre then had
Another ship to tread the billows.
'Twas the *Bison*, whose horns
The sea oft fiercely laved.

---

1 *Visund* means 'Bison'.    2 *The Ling Fish* is an allusion to Olav Trygvason's ship the *Long Serpent*.

Thereafter the king went south to Hordaland. He got tidings that Erling Skjalgson had gone out from the land with a big army, and four or five ships; Erling had the great vessel, and his sons three twenty-bench crafts; they had sailed west to England to Canute the Mighty. King Olav then went eastward along the coast and got a great army. He asked carefully whether men knew aught of Canute the Mighty's journey, but all they could say was that he was in England. It was also said that he had levied troops and would come to Norway. But because King Olav had a great army and could not get to know the truth as to whether he were to meet Canute, and because his men thought it of ill-service to lie still in one place with so great a force, he took up the plan of sailing southwards with his army to Denmark; he took with him all the folk who seemed most doughty for fighting and best fitted out, and the rest he gave leave to go home. Thus it is said:

| | |
|---|---|
| The word-wise Olav drove | But another grim warrior was ploughing |
| The *Bison* with oars from the north. | The billows from the south with the *Dragon*. |

And now the folk whom he deemed he had least use for went home, and King Olav had there a great and fine army; in it were most of the landed men of Norway, except those who had fared from Norway, as is already told, and those who sat at home.

145. When King Olav sailed to Denmark he steered to Zealand, and when he came thither he began to harry and made landings; then were the folk of the land robbed, some slain, some seized and bound and thereafter brought to the ships, but all who could flee did so and there was no withstanding; King Olav there made a great harrying. And when King Olav was in Zealand, he learned tidings that King Anund Olavson had called out a levy and was going with a great army from the east along Scania and harrying there. Then the plans were clear which King Olav and King Anund had made on the Elv when they settled their terms and friendship, that they should both withstand King Canute. King Anund now went on till he found his brother-in-law King Olav. And when they met, they made it known both to their own armies and to the folk of the land that they would subdue Denmark and demand loyalty from the men of that land. And it was then as we see it often is, that, when the folk of the land were harried and had no help to withstand, most of them submitted to the burdens by which they bought peace for themselves. It then befell that many men put themselves in the kings' hands and promised them obedience; the kings subdued the lands far and wide wherever they went,

or otherwise they harried. Sigvat the Scald says about this war in
the poem he made about King Canute the Mighty:

| | |
|---|---|
| Canute was under the heavens[1]; | As was seen, the cold keels |
| Harald's kinsman | Sailed from the north |
| Set his mind | To the plains of Zealand |
| On the fight. | With the grim warrior. |
| The victorious king | And Anund the king |
| Olav made the army | With another host |
| Go from Nid | Of Swedes fared forth |
| On the fishes' ways. | Against the Danes. |

146. In the west, in England, King Canute had learned that
Norway's king, Olav, had a levy out and likewise that he had gone
with this army to Denmark, and that there was unrest in his kingdom.
Canute then began to gather men. He soon drew to him a great
army and a great number of ships. Hacon the Jarl was the second
leader of that army. This summer, Sigvat the Scald came to England
from the south from Rouen in Valland with a man called Berg; the
summer before they had gone there on a trading journey and Sigvat
composed the *flokk* which is called "Songs of the Western Journeys"
—this is the first verse:

| | |
|---|---|
| We called to mind, Berg, | On a trading journey |
| Many a morn, how in Rouen | I moored the ship in the western fairway. |

And when Sigvat came to England he went straightway to meet
King Canute and would ask him for leave to go to Norway. But King
Canute had forbidden the passage of all trading ships ere he had got
his army ready. But when Sigvat came to him, he went to the room
the king was in; the room was locked and he stood a long while
without. When he at last had talk with the king he got leave for that
which he asked. Then he quoth:

| | |
|---|---|
| Ere I could get talk | But in the hall Gorm's kinsman |
| With the king of the Jutes | Would eagerly answer |
| I had to wait outside the house-door, | Our errand. On my arms |
| For the house was locked. | I oft wear armlets of iron. |

And when Sigvat was aware that King Canute was fitting out an
expedition against King Olav and he knew how great a strength
King Canute had, he quoth:

| | |
|---|---|
| King Canute who hath the might | Even if Canute and the jarls wish |
| And Hacon both yearn | Otherwise, yet may he live! |
| To take Olav's life. | Then shall I be more glad |
| I forebode the king's death. | Than at the first meeting on the fell. |

1 This is a split-up refrain completed by the last line of the verse on p. 394: 'The
noblest king'.

Besides this Sigvat composed many verses about the journey of Canute and Hacon. Then he quoth:

The bold jarl ought to bear
Words of peace between
Olav and the old bonders
Who began the strife.

They have parted chiefs
With greater scathe before
Than Hacon the Jarl has suffered;
Eric's race is valiant.

147. When Canute the Mighty had fitted out his army, he had a great crowd of men and very big ships. He himself had a Dragon which was so big that it counted sixty benches, and on it were gold-decked heads. Hacon the Jarl had another Dragon on which there were forty benches, and on it too there were gilded heads. The sails of both were striped with blue and red and green. The ships

King Canute the Mighty prepares for war

were all painted above the water and the whole rigging of the ships was of the best. Many other ships they had, big and well fitted out. About this Sigvat the Scald says in the Canute poem:

Canute was under the heavens[1];
The bright-eyed leader
Of the Danes heard
Of the army from the east.
From the west there shot
The ship which bore
Ethelred's foe
Out of the land.

Dear was the prince's journey.
The king's Dragons
Bore in the fair wind
Blue sails on the sail-yards.
And those keels
Which came from the west
Were borne o'er the sea
Forth to the Limfjord.

So it is said that King Canute sailed with this great army from the east from England and came unscathed with all his men and lay in by the Limfjord; there was present a great gathering of the men of the land.

148. Jarl Ulf Sprakaleggson had been set to ward the land when Canute went to England, and Canute had given over to Ulf his son who had the name of Hardicanute. That was the summer before, as is written of above (chapter 134). And the jarl said straightway that King Canute on their parting had bidden him with these words, that he willed they should take his son Hardicanute as king over Den-

mark: "for that reason he gave him into our hands; I and many others of this land's men and chiefs have complained to King Canute that it seems difficult for men to sit here in the land without a king whilst former Danish kings had their hands full to keep the Danish kingdom alone for themselves, for in former times many kings ruled over this kingdom. It is, however, much more difficult now than it has been formerly, for hitherto we have managed to live at peace with foreign chiefs. But now we learn that Norway's king is thinking of warring on us and moreover we have misgivings that the Swedish king will also make ready for the journey. And King Canute is now in England". The jarl then brought forth King Canute's letter and seal which confirmed all the jarl had said. Many other chiefs furthered that business. And with the agreement of all of them they assented to taking Hardicanute as their king, and so it was done at the same thing. But at the head of this plan was Queen Emma;[1] she had had the letter written and the seal set thereto, for by guile she had got at the king's seal; and all this was hidden from the king. And when Hardicanute and Ulf the Jarl were aware that King Olav was come from the north from Norway with a great army, they went to Jutland, for there was Denmark's chief strength. They sent out the arrow of war and a great army was gathered. But when they heard that the Swedish king was also come there with his army, they did not think they had strength to lay to battle with both of them. They then kept the army together in Jutland, intending to ward the land against the kings; all their fleet drew together in the Limfjord and waited for King Canute. And when they heard that King Canute was come east to the Limfjord, they sent messengers to him and to Queen Emma and bade her get to know if the king was wroth with them or not, and so let them know. The queen spoke about this matter to the king and said that their son Hardicanute would forfeit all the king would wish if he had done such things as might be against the king. He answered and said that Hardicanute had not gone forth after his own counsels: "it has gone", he said, "according to what might be expected, as he is a witless child and wanted to be called 'king'; and then the trouble fell into his hands when the shield of war was going throughout the land and the land would submit to foreign chiefs unless our help came. Now if he will come to terms with me, let him come to me and throw down this empty name, whereby he has had himself called

[1] The sister of Richard II, Duke of Normandy. She was first married to Ethelred the Unready and afterwards to Canute. Hardicanute was her son by Canute. Edward the Confessor, who built Westminster Abbey, was her son by Ethelred.

'king'". The queen then sent these same words to Hardicanute and withal she bade him not delay his journey; she said, as was true, that he would have no strength to withstand his father. And when that behest came to Hardicanute, he sought counsel with the jarl and the other chiefs who were with him. And they soon saw that, as soon as the folk of the land learned that Old Canute was come, the whole people would draw to him and put all their trust in him. The jarl and his other followers then saw that there were two choices in their hands: either to go to the king and lay everything in his power, or else leave the land; but all of them bade Hardicanute go to his father. He did so. And when they met he fell at his father's feet and laid on his knee the seal which went with the kingship. King Canute took Hardicanute by the hand and set him in as high a seat as he had sat in before. Ulf the Jarl sent his son Swein to the king; Swein was King Canute's sister's son. Swein asked for peace and terms for his father and offered to give himself up as a hostage on the jarl's behalf. Swein and Hardicanute were of the same age. King Canute bade them tell the jarl to gather the army and ships and come to the king, and then they could talk about terms afterwards. The jarl did so.

149. And when King Olav and King Anund heard that King Canute was come to the east, and that he had a mighty army, they sailed east along Scania and began to harry and burn in the lordships. In that way they went farther east along the coast towards the Swedish king's realm. But as soon as the folk of the land knew that King Canute had come east, no man would any longer assist the kings. About that Sigvat the Scald says:

| | |
|---|---|
| The swift kings | Then the slayer |
| Did not put | Of the Danes sharply |
| Denmark under them | Harried Scania. |
| On their war-journey. | Noblest king! |

The kings then went east along the coast to the place called Helgáin[1] and stayed there a while. They then heard that King Canute was coming east with his army after them. They took counsel together and decided that King Olav with some of his men should go up on land right through the woods to the water from which the River Helgáin ran down. There at the outlet of the river they made a dam of trees and turf and so stemmed the water; besides this they cut big ditches and brought many waters together, so that there was a great flood. But into the river bed they felled great trees. They kept

[1] *Helgáin* = the Holy River, is in Eastern Scania. The English chroniclers call it the Holy River.

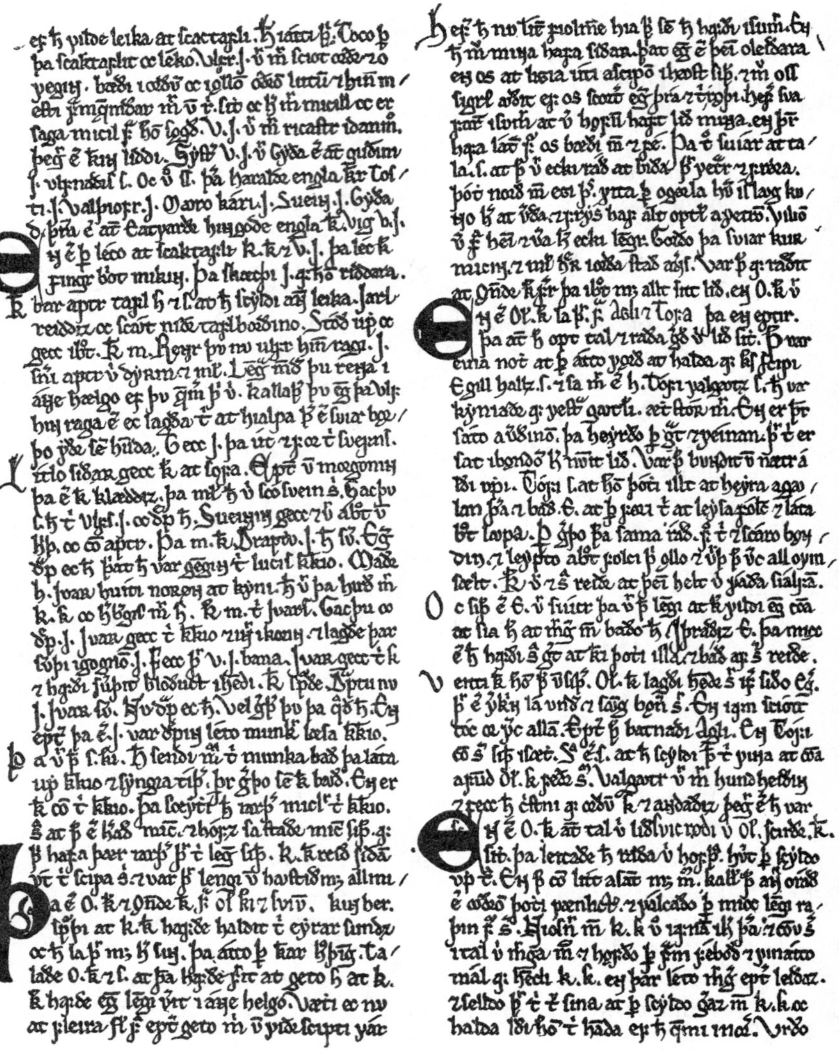

The only extant leaf of the earliest known copy of Snorre

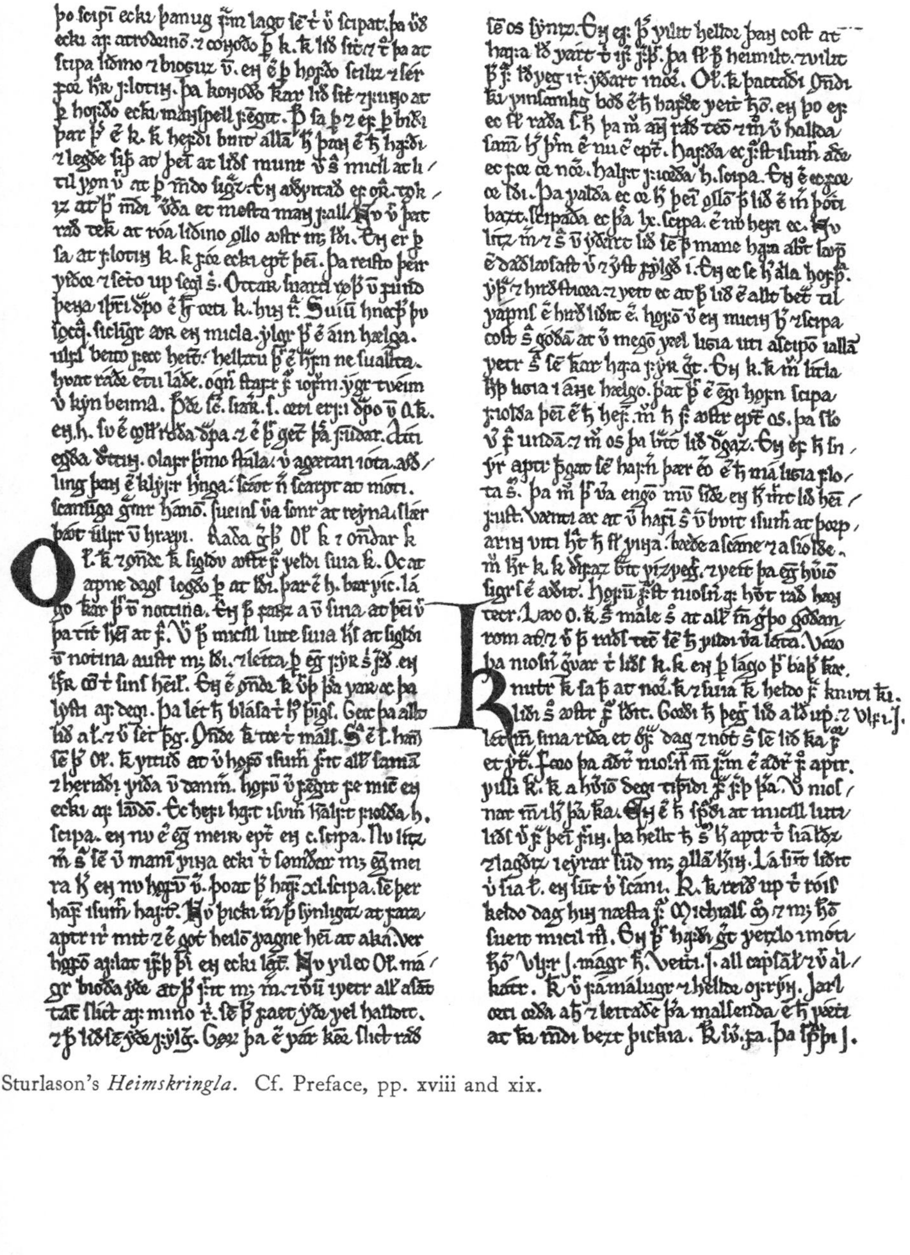

Sturlason's *Heimskringla*. Cf. Preface, pp. xviii and xix.

up with this work for many days and King Olav had the ordering of these plans, whilst King Anund was leader of the fleet. King Canute heard of the journey of the kings and likewise of all the scathe they had done in his kingdom. He sailed to meet them where they lay in Helgáin; he had a great army, double as big as both theirs. About them Sigvat says:

When the ruler of Jutland    The warder of the Danes
Was turned homewards    Would not
He did not let his heritage    Lose his homeland.
Be taken from him.    The noblest king.

150. One day towards evening King Anund's spies saw King Canute's sail and he was not far away—King Anund had the war blast blown. The men then cast off the awnings and armed themselves; they rowed out of the harbour along the coast, laid their ships together, lashed them and made themselves ready for the fight. King Anund sent spies up into the land and they went to King Olav and told him these tidings. King Olav then had the dam broken down and so brought the river into its former course, and in the night he went down to his ships. King Canute came outside the harbour and he then saw where the kings' fleet lay ready for battle; but it seemed to him that it would be too late in the day to fall to battle and for all his army to be ready, for his fleet needed much sailing room on the sea. It was far between the first ship and the last, as well as between that which went farthest out and that which sailed nearest land. There was little wind. And when King Canute saw that the Swedes and Norsemen had left the haven, he went in with those ships which could get berths; the chief force, however, lay out at sea. In the morning when it was light, many of their men were up on land, some talking, others playing games. They had word of nothing ere the waters were rushing down on them in torrents. Withal there followed great trees which drove out against their ships, and the ships were damaged by them; the waters flooded all the meadows. The folk who were on land were drowned and likewise many who were on the ships; but all who could manage it cut their ropes and let themselves loose, and now the ships were driven against each other. The great *Dragon*, on which the king himself was, was driven out by the stream; it was not easy to turn it with oars, so that it was driven out to King Anund's and Olav's fleet. And when they recognised the ship, they straightway lay to around it; but it was not easy to attack, because the ship had tall bulwarks like a castle and it had a great crew of men aboard, chosen men, well weaponed and very

valiant. It was also but a short while before Ulf the Jarl came up with his men, and then the battle began. Thereupon King Canute's army drew up from all sides. When the Kings Olav and Anund saw how this time they had won as much as they could, they let their ships go back and cast themselves loose from King Canute's army; the fleets then parted. But because this onset had not been made as King Canute intended and because the ships had not gone forth where it had been arranged, there was no pursuit. King Canute's men looked over their army, began to draw up the men and made themselves ready. And when they had parted and each fleet had gone its own way, the kings looked over their host and found that they had had little loss of men. But they also saw that if they waited until King Canute had drawn up all the host he had and until he came against them, his advantage in numbers was so great that there would be little hope of winning, and it was easy to understand that there would be a great loss of men if there was a battle. And now they took up the plan of rowing with the whole army eastward along the coast. And when they saw that King Canute's host was not following them, they raised their masts and hoisted their sails. Ottar the Black says about this meeting in the poem he composed about Canute the Mighty:

| | |
|---|---|
| O king, who art wont to fight, | Hardy warrior! Thy land |
| The Swedes hast thou broken | Thou didst keep against the two kings, |
| By the Helga-river, | Where the raven starved not. |
| Where the wolf got food. | Quick-minded thou art in battle. |

The Scald Tord Sjarekson composed a dirge on King Olav: it is called Rodadrapa and there he, too, speaks of this meeting:

| | |
|---|---|
| Olav, the lord of the Agder men, | The lord of the Scania men |
| Had a clash of steel | Shot sharply enough against him. |
| With the noble prince of the Jutes, | This son of Swein was not dull,[1] |
| That cleaver of rings. | When the wolf was howling. |

151. King Olav and King Anund sailed eastwards along the Swedish king's realm and towards evening they came to land at a place called Barvik,[2] where they stayed during the night. But it was noticed that the Swedes had a longing to go home; there was a great part of the Swedish army which sailed eastwards along the coast during the night and it did not stop until each one of them came to his home town. When King Anund was aware of this and dawn was breaking, he had a husthing called. The whole army went ashore and the thing was set. King Anund then began to speak:

1 Canute's father was Swein Forkbeard.     2 *Barvik* is a harbour in Blekinge (East Sweden).

"So it is", he said, "as you know, King Olav, that we have this summer gone together and harried far and wide in Denmark; we have won many goods but no land. This summer I have had three hundred and fifty ships (four hundred and twenty), but now there are no more left than one hundred (one hundred and twenty). Now it looks to me as if we shall not win honour with no greater host than we have now, even if you have the sixty ships which you have had through the summer. It seems best to me to go back to my kingdom, for 'it is good to drive the wagon home whole'. We have won something on this journey and have lost nothing. Olav, my kinsman, I will bid you go with me, so that we be together this winter. Take what you will in my kingdom so that you can keep yourself well and likewise the men who follow you. When spring comes we can make such an arrangement as we wish. But if you would rather choose to go through our land and go by land to your kingdom in Norway, then you shall have the right to do it". King Olav thanked King Anund for the friendly offer he had made him. "And if I may counsel", he said, "another plan shall be made and that is to keep together this army which is still left. At the beginning of the summer before I went from Norway, I had three hundred and fifty ships, but when I left the land I chose from that army the men who seemed best to me. These I set on the sixty ships I have now. It also looks to me as if those men of yours have run away who were deedless and who were of the least help; but here I see your bodyguard and counsellors and I know that the bodyguard are the best skilled with weapons. We have still a great army and ships so good that we can stay out in them the whole winter, as kings have done in olden times. King Canute will stay but a short while in the Holy River, for there is no haven for such a crowd of ships as he has. He may wish to pursue us, and then we shall go hence and folk will straightway gather to us. But if he turns to where there are such havens as he can stay in with his fleet, then many of his army will long for home, there no less than here. I think that this summer we have settled it in such a way that the villagers both in Scania and in Zealand know what they will have to deal with. Canute's army will soon scatter and then I know not to whom the victory will be granted. Let us then send spies out to get to know what his plans are." King Olav ended his speech so that all cheered him, and the counsel he would have was taken up. Spies were sent to King Canute's army and both kings lay where they were.

152. King Canute saw that the Kings of Norway and Sweden had sailed eastwards along the coast with their army. He straightway

sent men up on land and ordered them to ride day and night on the landways, and follow the movement of the kings' army. Some spies went away when the others came back. Then King Canute had tidings each day about their journey and his spies were in the kings' army. And when he learned that a great part of the army had left them, he sailed back with his army to Zealand and lay with the whole force in the Sound; part lay off Zealand and part off Scania. King Canute then rode up to Roskilde, the day before Michaelmas, with a great troop of men, for there his kinsman, Ulf the Jarl, had made a great feast for him. The jarl was eager to entertain him and was very happy, but the king was silent and not at all friendly. The jarl talked to him and sought topics of conversation which he thought the king would like best, but the king answered little. Then the jarl asked if he would play chess. He said 'yes' to that, and they then took out the chessmen and played. Ulf the Jarl was quick in his words and daring both in speech and in all other things; he was an active man in his land and a great warrior; about him a long saga is told. Ulf the Jarl was the mightiest man in Denmark next after the king. Ulf the Jarl's sister was Gyda whom the Jarl Gudine Ulvnadson[1] had wed; their sons were Harold, King of England, Tosti the Jarl, Valtjov[2] the Jarl, Mörukare[3] the Jarl and Swein the Jarl, and their daughter was Gyda who was wed to Jatvard the Good,[4] King of England.

153. And when King Canute and Ulf the Jarl were playing chess, the king made a bad move and the jarl then took a knight from him. The king put his men back and said he should play another move. The jarl grew angry and threw down the chessboard; he stood up and went away. Then said the king: "Runnest thou off, Ulf the Coward?" The jarl turned round near the door and said: "Farther wouldst thou have run in the Holy River if thou hadst been able. Thou didst not call me Ulf the Coward when I came to thy help when the Swedes were beating you like dogs". Thereupon the jarl left and went to sleep. A little after the king went to bed. Next morning when the king was clad, he said to his shoe-lad: "Go thou to Ulf the Jarl and slay him". The lad went, was away some time, and then came back. Then said the king: "Hast thou slain the jarl?" He answered: "I have not slain him, for he was gone to St Luke's Church". There

1 Earl Godwin of Wessex, the father of Harold Godwinson, the last of the Old English kings. 2 Earl Waltheof. 3 Earl Morcar. Waltheof and Morcar were not Harold's brothers. (Cf. 'History of Harald Hardrade', p. 561, n. 3.) 4 Edward the Confessor.

was a man of Norse stock, called Ivor the White, who was at that time in King Canute's bodyguard and slept in the king's house. To him the king said: "Go thou and slay the jarl". Ivor went to the church into the choir and there he struck a sword through the jarl, whereby Ulf the Jarl met his bane. Ivor then went to the king with his bloody sword in his hand. The king asked: "Hast thou slain the jarl?" Ivor answered: "I have slain him now". "Thou hast done well then", said the king. But after the jarl had been slain, the monks had the church locked. This was told the king, who then sent a man to the monks, bidding them unlock the church and sing Mass, and they did as the king bade. And when the king came to the church, he granted it great lands so that it became a big lordship and this church has since grown greatly. King Canute rode out afterwards to his ships, and there he lay a long time in the autumn with a great host.

154. When King Olav and King Anund heard that King Canute had sailed to the Sound and that he lay there with his army, they held a husthing. King Olav spoke and said that matters had gone as he had guessed, namely that King Canute would not stay long in Helgáin: "I expect now that many of the things we shall have to do will turn out as I guess. He has now a much smaller number of folk than he had this summer and later he will have still fewer, for they are no happier than we are in staying out in ships late in the autumn, and we shall win the victory if there is no lack of endurance and boldness. So it went in the summer that we had fewer men, but through us they lost both men and goods". The Swedes then began to talk and said it was not advisable to wait there for winter and frost, "even if the Norsemen egg us on to it; they do not know exactly how it can be here, for the sea often freezes in the winter. We will go home and be here no longer". The Swedes murmured much and they talked one with another; it was then arranged so that King Anund went away with all his men, but King Olav remained there.

155. At this time when King Olav lay there, he often held meetings and took counsel with his men. One night Egil Hallson was keeping watch on the king's ship with a man called Tovi Valgautson, who was of good family from West Gautland. Whilst they sat on watch, they heard weeping and wailing where the prisoners of war sat in bonds, for they were bound on shore during the nights. Tovi said it seemed evil to him to hear their howls and bade Egil that they should go loose the folk and let them run away. They did it; they went and cut the bonds and let all those men run away. This deed was ill spoken of and the king was so wroth that they were in

peril of their lives. And afterwards when Egil was sick, it was a long while before the king would go and see him, although many men bade him do so. Then Egil rued it much that he had so acted that the king thought ill of it and he bade the king forgive him; the king granted him this, and he laid his hands on the side where the pain was and sang his prayers, and in that moment all the aching stopped and thereafter Egil was better. Afterwards Tovi also came to terms with the king. So it is said that he agreed to get his father to come to King Olav. Valgaut was a hound-heathen, but on the king's words he became a Christian and died soon after he had been baptised.

Wailing was heard from the prisoners who sat in bonds

156. When King Olav held talks with his men he sought counsel with the leaders as to what should be done. And there was little unity amongst them; one man would call ill-counselled what others found useful, and now they talked a long time backwards and forwards about what should be done. King Canute's spies were always in their army and got much into talk with many men, and they brought forth offers of money and friendship on King Canute's behalf. And many were enticed and sold their trust so as to become King Canute's men and help him to win the land if he came to Norway. Later this clearly became known of many, even if it was hidden in the beginning. Some straightway took gifts of money, and others got promises of money later. But there were very many who had formerly had from him great gifts, for it is true to say of King Canute that every man who came to him who seemed to have some doughtiness and who sought his friendship, had his hands full of goods from the king. Thereby King Canute was well befriended. His generosity was

shown especially to foreign men and most of all to those who had come from most distant lands.

157. King Olav often had talks with his men and asked their counsel. But when he found that every man had a different opinion, the king had misgivings that there were some who said other than they would really hold advisable, and it could not be certain if all were wholly loyal in their trustiness to him. Many urged that they should use the favourable wind and sail to the Sound, and then north to Norway; they said that the Danes would not dare fall upon them, even if they lay there with a great army. But the king was so discerning that he saw that such a thing could not be done. He also knew that when Olav Trygvason lay to battle with a small strength, it had not happened that the Danes were afraid to fight. He also knew that there were many Norsemen in King Canute's army and he had misgivings that they who counselled such a thing as this were more loyal to King Canute than to himself. King Olav then decided that they who would follow him should make themselves ready and go by the landways through Upper Gautland and thereafter to Norway, "and our ships and all the heavy things which we cannot move with us I will send east into the Swedish king's realm and let them be watched over there for us".

158. Harek of Tjotta answered King Olav's speech and said: "It is easy to see that I cannot go on my feet to Norway; I am old and heavy and little used to walking. Also I will only part with my ship when need be; I have taken such care of this ship and its fitting-out, that it will go ill with me to leave my ship to the hands of my foes". The king answered: "Go thou with us, Harek; we will carry thee with us, if thou canst not walk". Harek then quoth a verse:

Foe of the gold! I took the plan
Of riding on the long ways
From here on a steed of the sea
Rather than walk,
Even though the generous king,
Canute, lay with his warships
Out in the Sound.
All men know of my boldness.

King Olav now got ready for the journey. The men had their walking clothes on and their weapons, and on the pack-horses they could lay packs of clothes and valuables. The king then sent men to take the ships east to Kalmar, where they had the ships drawn up and all the tackle and other goods put under watch. Harek did as he had said: he bided a good wind and then sailed to the west by Scania until he came to Holane;[1] it was then evening and there was a strong wind from aft. He then had the sail taken down and

1 The bight inside Skanör.

likewise the mast and the weather-vane, and had the whole ship above the waterline covered with a grey awning; he let men row fore and aft, but most of the men he ordered to sit low in the ship. King Canute's watchmen saw the ship and talked amongst themselves as to what ship it might well be; they guessed that it would be carrying salt or herring when they saw few men and little rowing; and the ship seemed grey and untarred and it looked as if the sun had blistered it, and they saw that it was heavily laden. But when Harek came forth into the Sound past the army he hoisted his mast and drew up the sail and set up the gilded weather-vane; the sail was as white as snow with red and blue stripes. Then King Canute's men saw it and told the king that King Olav had probably sailed by. But King Canute said that King Olav was a clever enough man not to go with one ship through King Canute's army, and he said that he found it more likely to have been Harek of Tjotta or his like. The men then held it for a truth that King Canute had known of Harek's journey and that this man would not have gone in such a way if friendly words had not passed between King Canute and him; this seemed clear afterwards when the friendship between King Canute and Harek was fully known. When Harek sailed north past Vedröy,[1] he composed this verse:

I let not the widows of Lund
Or the maids of Denmark laugh
Thereat (when we brought
The boat forth outside the isle),

That this autumn I dare not
Fare back with the ship
Over the flat watery ways
Of Frode, fair ladies!

Thereafter Harek went on his journey and did not stop before he came north to Halogaland to his stead in Tjotta.

159. King Olav then went on his journey. He first went up through Smaland and came forth into West Gautland. He went quietly and peacefully and the men of the land gave him good help. The king then went on until he came down into the Vik, and thence northwards until he came to Sarpsborg, where he stayed and got ready to spend the winter. He then gave the greatest part of the army leave to go home, and kept with him those whom he wanted of the landed men. There were with him all the sons of Arne Armodson, who were much honoured by the king. Gelli Thorkelson who the summer before had come from Iceland, then came to King Olav, as is before written (chapter 136).

160. Sigvat the Scald had been a long time with King Olav, as is here written, and the king had made him his marshal. Sigvat the

Scald did not talk quickly in ordinary language, but scaldship came so naturally to him that he talked in rimes as easily as if he were talking in the ordinary way. He had been on a trading journey to Valland and on that journey he had been to England and found King Canute the Mighty, from whom he had got leave to go to Norway, as is written before (chapter 146). And when he came to Norway he went straightway to King Olav and found him in Borg. He went before the king when the latter was at table. Sigvat greeted him, but the king looked at him and was silent. Sigvat said:

Hear thou me, my war king!　　　Tell me where the folk king
Home is come thy marshal;　　　Hath granted me a seat
May the men mark　　　　　　　Amongst his bodyguard. To behold
The song I sing!　　　　　　　Thy hall is dear to me.

Then it was true, the old saying, that "the king's ears are many"; King Olav had heard all about Sigvat's journeys and that he had been with King Canute. King Olav said to Sigvat: "I know not if thou wilt now be my marshal or if thou hast become King Canute's man". Sigvat said:

Canute, the giver of good rings,　　One lord, I said, is enough
Asked me if I　　　　　　　　For me to have at a time.
Would have his friendship　　　　And I believed I answered the truth,
As the keen-minded Olav's.　　　As every man may witness.

Then King Olav said that Sigvat should go to the seat which he was wont to have before, and Sigvat soon came back into the same favour he formerly had.

161. Erling Skjalgson and all his sons had been that summer in King Canute's army in the following of Hacon the Jarl; Tore the Hound was also there, and he was much honoured. When King Canute heard that King Olav had gone by the landway to Norway, King Canute released his troops and gave all men leave to take winter quarters. There was then in Denmark a great host of foreigners, both Englishmen and Norsemen and men from several other lands, who had brought men to the army in the summer. In the autumn Erling Skjalgson went with his men to Norway and on parting he got great gifts from King Canute. Tore the Hound was left behind with King Canute. King Canute's messengers went with Erling to Norway, and they had many valuables. During the winter they went far about the land and paid out the money which King Canute had promised men in the autumn, to win their adherence. And they gave money also to others and bought their friendship for King Canute; the messengers had Erling's help on the journey. So it happened

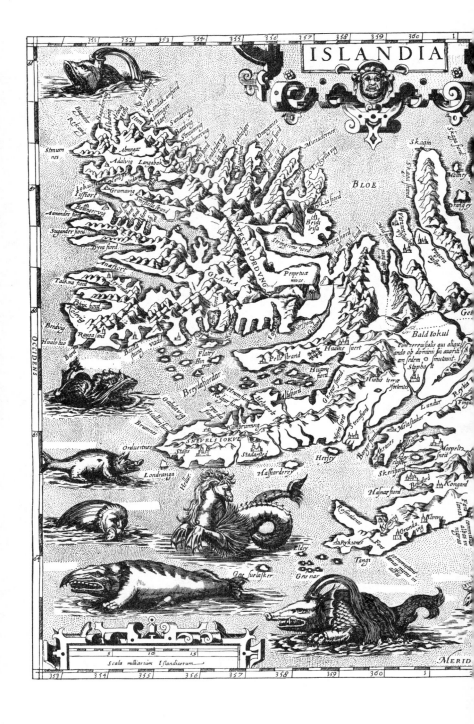

that a great crowd of men turned to friendship with King Canute and promised him their service and likewise their opposition to King Olav; some men made it known, but there were many who hid it from the common folk. King Olav learned these tidings, for many could tell him of them and at the king's court there was much on men's lips. Sigvat the Scald then quoth thus:

There go the prince's foes
Bringing their open purses.
Many bid dearly in metal
For the head of our king.

Everyman knows that he who sells
His own good lord for gold
Will end in black hell,
And of such is he worthy.

And Sigvat quoth still further:

Thronged was the way to heaven
Against those who betrayed their lord,

And they who worked the treason
Will seek Hel, the fire's deep home.

It was often spoken about, how it ill beseemed Hacon the Jarl to bring an army against King Olav, since the latter had given him his life when the jarl had fallen into his power. But Sigvat the Scald was a very good friend of the jarl's, and when he heard him ill spoken of, he quoth:

Then would the huscarls
Of the Hordaland king be too much
The jarl's friends if they
Took money for Olav's life.

It honours not the bodyguard
That such should be heard of them.
Better it were for us
That all were clean of treason.

162. King Olav had a great Yule feast and many great men were come to him. And on the seventh day of Yule the king went out with a few men; Sigvat followed the king day and night, for he was then with him. They went into a house where the king's valuables were hidden. He had then arranged things beforehand, as was his wont, and had gathered his valuables together to give friendly gifts on the eighth day of Yule. There were in the house not a few gold-embellished swords. Then quoth Sigvat:

There stand gorgeous swords
Chased in gold, and we praise
These blood-tinglers.
Honour from the war king is our joy.

For some time have I followed thee,
Gold-giver, and if, O mighty prince,
Thou wilt give thy scald a gift,
I will take it from thee.

The king took one of the swords and gave it to him; the handle was bound with gold and the hilt was gold-chased. It was a noble gift. But the gift excited envy, as was afterwards heard of. Straightway after Yule King Olav began his journey to the Uplands, for he had a great crowd of folk and no land rents were come to him from the north of the land, in that there had been a levy in the summer and the king had spent on it all the incomes which were available. Nor had he ships then to go with his men to the north of the land. Besides, he had learned naught from the north but that which did not seem to him to be peaceful, if he did not go with a great army. Therefore the king took the plan of going through the Uplands. But it was not so long before that he had gone there feasting as the law bade or as the kings were wont to do. And when the king came up into the land, the landed men and mighty bonders bade him to their homes and in this way lightened his expenses.

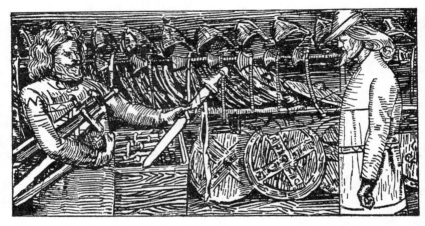

King Olav gives a sword to Sigvat the Scald

163. There was a man of Gautish stock called Björn and he was a friend and acquaintance of Queen Astrid and somewhat related to her. She had got him a stewardship and district chief's position in Upper Hedemark, and he had also some rule in the East Dales. The king held naught by Björn, who was not liked by the bonders either. It had also befallen that a great many cows and swine had been lost sight of in the town which Björn ruled over. Björn, therefore, had called a thing and sought after the thieves; he called those men most likely to do such evil things, who lived in the forest settlements far from other men. He accused those who lived in the East Dales of this matter; the settlement was very scattered and built near waters or in forest clearings, and in few places did great buildings lie together.

164. There was a man called Raud, who lived there in the East Dales. His wife was called Ragnhild and his sons Sigurd and Dag;

they were men of great promise. They were present at the thing and answered on behalf of the Dalesmen and said they were not guilty of the charges. Björn thought they bore themselves with great show and boast and were well arrayed with both clothes and weapons. Björn turned his speech against the brothers and said it was not unlikely that they should have done this; they denied it and thus the thing ended. A little later, King Olav came to Björn the Steward's with his men and was his guest. The matter which had been brought before the thing was complained of to the king, and Björn said that Raud's sons seemed to him most likely to have brought about such scathe. Bidding was therefore sent to Raud's sons. And when they came before the king he did not think they looked like thieves and freed them from these charges. They bade the king come to their father to spend three nights guesting there with all his men. Björn counselled against the journey, but none the less the king went. At Raud's the feasting was of the finest. Then the king asked who Raud was, and his wife. Raud said he was a Swede, rich and of good stock; "but I ran from there", he said, "with this woman, whom I have since wed; she is the sister of King Ring Dagson". The king then straightway knew the kinship of both of them; and he found now that both father and sons were very clever, and asked after their accomplishments. Sigurd said he could read dreams and tell the time of day, though he could not see the sun. The king tested this accomplishment and it was true as Sigurd had said. Dag gave out as his accomplishment that he could see the virtues and vices in every man who came before his eyes, if he could take note of it and think about it. The king then bade him tell the vice he could see in him, and Dag found out what the king deemed right. The king then asked about Björn the Steward, what fault he had. Dag said that Björn was a thief and moreover he said that Björn had hidden in his garth both bones and horns and hides of the cattle he had stolen this autumn; "he is the leader of all the robberies which have befallen this autumn and for which he has given other men the blame". Dag told the king all the marks as to where he should seek. And when the king went away from Raud, he received great and friendly gifts; Raud's sons went with him. The king went first to Björn, and now knew everything to be as Dag had said. Afterwards the king sent Björn away from the land, and it was for the queen's sake that his life and limbs were spared.

165. Tore, the son of Ölvir of Egge, the step-son of Kalv Arneson and son of Tore the Hound's sister, was a handsome man, and big

and strong; he was eighteen years old. He made a good marriage, and got wealth and land in Hedemark; he was a well-befriended man and hoped to become a district chief. He bade the king home to a feast with his men; the king took the invitation and went to Tore and was well greeted. It was a noble feast, and the waiting and all the food were very good. The king and his men talked amongst themselves and said that all the things seemed to fit together and they knew not what might be the best, either Tore's house or house adornments or table deckings or drink, or the man who was the host. Dag did not speak greatly about it. King Olav was often wont to talk with Dag and ask him about many things, for the king found all that Dag said to be true, whether it were of the past or the future, and the king set great store by his words. The king then called Dag to talk with him alone and mentioned many things to him; the king ended by remarking how noble a man Tore was who made so stately a feast for them. Dag uttered little thereto, but said all was true that the king said. The king then asked Dag what fault of mind he saw in Tore. Dag said he believed that Tore would surely enough be well-minded if he were really such as all men could see. The king then bade him say what he asked about and said he was bound to do so. Dag answered: "Then wilt thou, O king, also promise me that I decide the vengeance if I find out the fault". The king said he would not hand his judgment over to other men and bade Dag tell him what he asked about. Dag answered: "Dear is the lord's word. I find that Tore's weakness, as might befall many a man, is that he is too greedy". The king answered: "Is he a thief or a robber?" Dag answered: "He is not". "What is it, then?" said the king. Dag answered: "In order to get goods, he has become a king's traitor. He has taken money from Canute the Mighty to take thy life". The king answered: "How wilt thou show it?" Dag said: "On his arm he has above the elbow a thick gold ring, which King Canute has given him and which he lets no man see". With that the talk between Dag and the king came to an end, and the king was very wroth. The king sat at table; they had drunk for some time and the men were very merry, whilst Tore went about seeing that the waiting was properly done. The king had Tore called to him, and he came to the table and rested his hands on it. The king asked: "How old a man art thou, Tore?" "I am eighteen years old", he said. The king said: "Big thou art and bold, Tore, for so young a man". The king then took him by his right arm and stroked it above the elbow. Tore said, "Go warily there, for I have a boil on my arm". The king held on to his arm and felt that it was somewhat hard underneath. The king said: "Hast thou not heard that I am a leech? Let me see the boil". Tore saw that it could be of no use hiding anything, and he brought the ring forth. The king asked if it were King Canute's gift, and Tore said that he could not hide that. The king had Tore taken prisoner and set in irons. Kalv then went up and asked for peace for Tore and offered fines for him; many men furthered the matter and offered their goods thereto. The king was so wroth that no man could get a word with him; he said that Tore should have such judgment as he had thought of for the king. The king then had Tore slain. But that deed worked the greatest harm both there round about the Uplands and no less in the north in Trondheim where most of Tore's kinsmen were. Kalv took this man's death very near to himself, for Tore in his childhood had been his foster-son.

166. Grjotgard, the son of Ölvir and brother of Tore, was older than Tore. He was a doughty man and had his own following. He also at that time stayed in Hedemark. When he heard of Tore's death, he made raids wherever he found the king's men or goods, but otherwise he kept to the woods or other hiding places. And when the king heard of this unrest he had men to spy on Grjotgard's journey and got to know much thereof; Grjotgard had taken nightquarters not far from the place where the king was. Straightway in the night, King Olav went and got there at dawn; he drew a ring of men round the dwelling wherein were Grjotgard and his men. Grjotgard and his men woke up at the noise of

Tore shows King Olav the ring given him by King Canute

the men and the clashing of weapons; they leaped straightway to their own weapons and Grjotgard rushed out into the porch. Grjotgard asked who led this army, and he was told that King Olav was come there. Grjotgard asked if the king could hear his words. The king stood before the door and said that Grjotgard could say what he wished to say: "I hear thy words", said the king. Grjotgard said: "I will not ask for peace!" Grjotgard then rushed out; he had over his head a shield and in his hand a drawn sword. It was not very light and he did not see clearly; he struck the sword at the king, but it pierced Arnbjörn Arneson. The blow went under his brynie into his maw. There Arnbjörn got his bane, and Grjotgard was also slain at once, and so were most of his men. After these happenings the king turned back and again drew towards the south to the Vik.

167. And now when King Olav came to Tunsberg, he sent men to all the districts to call up men for a levy. He got but few ships, for there were no other ships than bonders' crafts. Many folk came to him from the lordships round about but few came from far away, and it was soon noticed that the folk of the land had now turned from their trustiness towards the king. King Olav sent his men east to Gautland for his ships and the possessions which they had left behind the autumn before. But this journey went slowly, for it was then no better to go through Denmark than in the autumn, in that King Canute called out his army in the spring throughout Denmark and he had no fewer than twelve hundred (fourteen hundred and forty) ships.

168. Tidings were learned in Norway that Canute the Mighty had drawn a great army together and likewise that he would go to Norway with all his army and subdue the land. And when such was heard, the men were still worse to rule for King Olav and later he got little help from the bonders. His men often talked about this amongst themselves. Then Sigvat quoth this:

| | |
|---|---|
| The lord of England bid out | Mean it is, if the men of this land |
| His host, but we ourselves | Leave our king |
| Got few men and small ships. | Without help. For money |
| But little did I see our king afraid. | Have the men betrayed their trust. |

The king held meetings with his bodyguard and sometimes he held husthings with all his men and asked their counsel as to what seemed best for them to take up: "We need not hide from ourselves", he said, "the fact that King Canute will come to seek us at home this summer, and he has a great army as ye have well heard, but we have a small strength under these circumstances to meet his host; and the folk of the land are not now to be trusted". But those men to whom the king spoke his words answered the king differently. About this it is said as Sigvat quoth:

| | |
|---|---|
| Flee we must before the king's | Every counsellor shall now |
| Foes. They mock us, | Keep himself longest, even if the following |
| But these foes pay out money. | Of the king's friends are traitors; |
| I get to hear these words of scorn. | This treason is laid open. |

169. The same spring it befell in Halogaland that Harek of Tjotta called to mind that Asmund Grankelson had robbed and beaten his huscarls. The ship which Harek owned, a twenty-bencher, was floating before his garth, with her awnings and floors fitted. He said he would go south to Trondheim. One evening Harek went to the ship with his huscarls and he had nigh on eighty men. They rowed during the night and towards morning they came to Grankel's garth and drew a ring about the house. They then went forth and set fire to it. Grankel and his men were burnt within and some were slain outside; in all thirty men fell. After this deed Harek went home and sat in his garth. Asmund was then with King Olav. And of the men who were in Halogaland there was not one who demanded fines from Harek for this deed, and neither did he offer any.

170. Canute the Mighty drew his army together and sailed to the Limfjord. And when he was ready he sailed thence with all the army to Norway; he went speedily and did not anchor east of the

Tunsberg in St Olav's reign

fjord but sailed across the Fold[1] and lay in by Agder and there demanded a thing. The bonders came and held a thing with King Canute, who was then taken as king over the whole land. There he set men in the districts and took hostages of the bonders. None spoke against him. King Olav was then in Tunsberg and so Canute went northwards along the coast. Men came to him from the lordships and all promised him their loyalty. King Canute lay for some time

1 Oslofjord.

in Eikundasund[1] and thither Erling Skjalgson came to him with many men. He and King Canute then bound their friendship anew. It was amongst King Canute's promises to Erling that he should have all the land between Stad and Rygjarbit[2] to rule over. King Canute then went farther north; and to speak shortly of his journey, he did not stop before he came north to Trondheim and sailed into Nidaros. In Trondheim he called a thing of eight folk districts, and at that thing Canute was taken as king over all Norway. Tore the Hound had come with King Canute from Denmark and was there with him. Harek of Tjotta was also come there. He and Tore then became landed men of King Canute and bound it with oaths. King Canute gave them great land rents and made over to them the Finnish trade rights; besides this he gave them great gifts. To all the landed men who would turn to him he gave richly both in land rents and in valuables; he let them all have greater might than they had had before.

171. King Canute had now laid all Norway under him. He then held a thing where there were present many men both of his own army and of the men of the land. King Canute then listed to give his kinsman Hacon the Jarl all that land to rule over which he had won on this journey; thereto it followed that he led his son Hardicanute to the high-seat beside him and gave him the name of king over the realm of Denmark. King Canute took hostages of all the landed men and the great bonders; he took their sons or brothers and other near kinsmen, or the men who were dearest to them or who seemed fittest for it. In such way as is now spoken of did the king secure the men's trustiness to himself. As soon as Hacon the Jarl had taken over the realm of Norway, his kinsman, Einar Tambarskelver, went into fellowship with him; he then got all the land rents which he had had before at the time when the jarls ruled over the land. King Canute gave Einar great gifts and bound him in great friendship to himself; he promised that Einar should be the greatest and uppermost of the commoners in Norway so long as his might held in the land, and he added thereto that Einar or his son Eindridi seemed to him most fitting to bear the name of prince on account of their kinship, if the jarl was not there. Einar set great store by these promises and in return he promised his trustiness. Then arose anew Einar's leadership.

172. There was a man called Toraren Praisetongue; he was an Icelander by kin and a great scald, and he had been much with

---

1 I.e. now Egersund (cf. chapter 134).    2 The frontier between Nedenes and Bratsberg.

kings and other chiefs. He was with King Canute the Mighty and had composed a *flokk*[1] about him. And when the king heard that Toraren had composed a flokk about him he was wroth and bade him bring forth a *drapa* for him next day when the king sat at table; unless he did so, said the king, Toraren should be hanged for his boldness, in that he had composed but a *drœpling*[2] about him. Toraren then indited a refrain and set it in a song and shaped some verses thereto. This is the refrain:

> Canute wards the land, as Christ,
> The shepherd of Greece, doth the heaven.

King Canute rewarded the poem with fifty marks of silver; the drapa was called "The Head-Ransom". Toraren composed a second drapa about King Canute which was called *Tög-drapa*, in which he tells of King Canute's journey when he went from the south from Denmark to Norway, and this is in stanzas:

> Canute is under the sun
> Better than any lord.
> My great-minded friend
> Went with many men
> Up to this place.
> This prince of the sea
> Did bring out
> From the Limfjord
> A mighty fleet.
>
> Though skilled in fight,
> The men of Agder
> Were much afraid
> Of this warrior's journey.
> The grim man's ship
> Was gold bedecked;
> To me such appeared
> Much more than a tale.
>
> And on past Lister
> These black ships
> Glided forth
> Over the sea.
> Eikundasund was full within,
> South from the ocean,
> Of the skis of the sea.

> And the truce-seeking
> Peace men glided
> On past Hjornaglen's[3]
> Ancient howe.
> The prince's journey
> Was full of glee
> When on past Stad
> The sea steeds drove
> This mighty host.
>
> Blown by the strong winds
> These beasts of the sea
> Bore their long sides
> Along by Stim.[4]
> These falcons of the sea
> Glided from the south
> So that the king
> Neared Nid[5] in the north.
>
> Then the wise king
> Of Jutland gave Norway
> To his sister's son.
> Then, as I say it,
> He gave to his son
> Denmark, those dim
> Halls of the sea.

1 A short poem (without a refrain). 2 *Drœpling* means a 'small *drapa*'. A *drapa* was a poem with a refrain. 3 *Hjornaglen*, now Tjörnaglen, in the most southern part of Söndhordaland. 4 *Stim*, now Stemshesten by Hustadvik, on the frontier between Raumsdale and Nordmöre. 5 River Nid (Trondheim).

Here it is to be told that he who quoth this had seen for himself
King Canute's journey, for Toraren praises himself for being in
King Canute's following when he came to Norway.

173. The men whom King Olav had sent east to Gautland for his
fleet took the ships which seemed best to them but burned the others.
They took with them the tackle and the other possessions which the
king and his men had there. They sailed from the east when they
heard that King Canute had gone north in Norway. They sailed
west through the Sound and thereafter northwards to the Vik,
to King Olav, and brought his ships to him; he was then in Tunsberg. And when King Olav learned that King Canute was going
with his army northwards along the coast, King Olav sailed into Oslofjord and up into the water which is called Dravn,[1] and kept there
until King Canute's army had gone by towards the south. And on
this journey when Canute was going south along the coast, he held
things in every folk district; at every thing they swore him the land
and gave him hostages. He went east through the Fold to Borg and
there had a thing; there they swore the land to him as in other places.
King Canute then went south to Denmark and he had then possessed
himself of Norway without battle; he now ruled over three lands.
Thus spoke Halvard Hareksblesi when he spoke of King Canute:

The strong warrior, the battle-glad        Now hath the warrior chief
Yngvi, rules alone                          Subdued Norway to himself.
Over England and Denmark;                    This strife-eager man has stopped
Thereby peace waxeth.                        The hawk's dire hunger.

174. King Olav sailed out with his ships to Tunsberg, as soon as
he learned that King Canute had gone south to Denmark. He then
fitted himself out to go with the army that would follow him, and he
then had thirteen ships. Afterwards he sailed out along the Vik and
got but little goods and few men. Only they would follow him who
dwelt on the isles and distant nesses. The king did not go up on
land but took such goods and men as lay in his path. He found that
the land had now turned from him. He then went as the wind blew.
That was in the beginning of the winter. They waited long for fair
wind and lay for a very long time in the Sel-isles,[2] and learned from
traders tidings from the north of the land. It was told the king that
Erling Skjalgson had an army gathering in Jæderen;[3] his ship lay
ready fully manned along with many other ships which the bonders

---

1 *Dravn* or *Dramm*, the inner part of the Drammensfjord, between the present Svelvik
and Drammen.     2 On the west side of Lindesnes, the most southerly point of Norway.
3 The flat land south of Stavanger.

owned; there were barks and fishing boats and rowing ferryboats. The king sailed westward with his army and lay some time in Eikundasund. Then the men on both sides learned of each other's presence. Erling then gathered as many folk as possible.

King Olav's ships leave Tunsberg

175. On Thomas-Mass before Yule,[1] at dawn, the king straight way sailed out of the haven. There was a very good wind but somewhat strong. He sailed north past Jæderen. The weather was wet with some fog drifts. Word went forthwith throughout Jæderen, when the king left. When Erling was sure that the king was sailing westward he had all his army called to the ships. All the men went out on the ships and made themselves ready for battle. But the king's ships sailed speedily to the north past Jæderen. Thereafter he turned into the inner lode, for he wished to go into the fjords and there get himself men and goods. Erling sailed after him with a great army and many ships. And their ships glided on well, for they had nothing on board but men and weapons. Erling's longship went on faster than the others, and then he reefed his sail and waited for his men. When King Olav saw that Erling's men were coming up quickly, for the king's ships were very heavy and swollen since they had been afloat all the summer, through the autumn, and now through the winter, he realised that there would be great odds of folk against him if he should meet the whole of Erling's army at one and the same time. He then had the order shouted from ship to ship that they should

1  21st of December, 1028.

lower the sails, but very slowly, and reef the sails. And so it was done. Erling and his men noticed that. Erling then shouted to his men and bade them sail faster. "You see", he said, "that now their sails are lower and they are drawing away from us." He then had the reefs taken out of the sail of his longship and it went speedily forward.

176. King Olav sailed inside Bokn[1] and they were then not within sight of each other. The king

The king struck the point of his axe in Erling's cheek

bade them take the sails down and row forth into a narrow sound which was there. They then laid their ships together; outside of them was a rock ness. All the men were fully weaponed. Erling sailed towards the sound and they did not notice an army lying there ere they saw the king's men rowing all their ships together against them. Erling's men let their sails fall and took to their weapons, but the king's men lay on all sides around the ship. There was now a fight, and a very hard one; the fall of men soon turned against Erling's men. Erling stood on the quarterdeck of his ship, with his helm on his head, a shield before him, and his sword in his hand. Sigvat the Scald had been left behind in the Vik and he learned these tidings; he was a good friend of Erling's, had had gifts from him and had been with him. Sigvat composed a flokk about Erling's fall, and this verse is in it:

Erling let his cutters
Shoot forth against the king;
He who dyed red
The pale foot of the eagle.

The longship lay side by side
With the ship of the king
In the great host; the quick
Warriors then fought with swords.

1 Inside Bokn means sailing eastward in the southern part of Boknfjord, situated north of Stavangerfjord. The battle took place in Soknarsund (now Soknsund), between the islands of Bru and Omöy (cf. chapter 250).

Erling's men began to fall as soon as the strife started, and when Olav's men boarded the longship every man fell in his place. The king himself went forth hardily. Thus says Sigvat:

| | |
|---|---|
| The chief struck at the men; | The sea king dyed red |
| With wrath he boarded the longship. | The broad Jadar sea, |
| Thickly they fell to the floors, | Down in the wide water |
| Hard was the fight near Tungur.[1] | The warm blood poured. |

Erling's army fell to the last man, so that no one stood up on the longship but Erling alone. The reason was that they did not ask for quarter and no one would have got it even if he had asked, and no one could turn in flight, for the ships lay all round Erling's longship. It is also said with truth that no man tried to flee. Even so Sigvat says:

| | |
|---|---|
| All Erling's shipmen | Long did Skjalg's sharp son |
| Were slain out by Bokn; | Stand up, far from his friends, |
| The young Skjoldung | Alone in the poop |
| Cleared the ship north of Tungur. | On his wasted ship. |

They then set upon Erling both from the forehold and from the other ships. There was good room on the quarterdeck, and it lay high above the other ships, and no one could get to it except with shots and partly with spear thrusts; but he struck them all from him. Erling warded himself so nobly that no one can mention any other man who stood alone for so long against so many. But never did he try to escape or ask for quarter. Thus says Sigvat:

| | |
|---|---|
| Skjalg's hard-minded | There never has been |
| Avenger would not seek | Nor will there ever be, |
| Peace from the king's friends, | On the sea-surrounded earth, |
| Though the fight waxeth. | A chief more brave. |

King Olav went aft of the forehold and saw what Erling was doing. The king spoke to him and said: "To-day thou turnest thy face towards us, Erling". He answered: "Face to face shall eagles strike". Sigvat mentioned these words:

| | |
|---|---|
| Erling, who guarded the land | When he spoke to Olav |
| And did not betray the ward thereof, | Words which were true |
| Bade the eagles | In the fight near Utstein,[2] |
| Fight face to face. | Erling was ready for battle. |

Then the king said: "Wilt thou put thyself in my hands, Erling?" "That I will", he said. Then he took his helm off his head, laid down

---

1 *Tungur* means 'Tungenes', by the entrance of the Stavangerfjord. 2 *Utstein*, an island north of Soknsund, where existed an old monastery, the church of which still remains.

his sword and shield and went forth from the quarterdeck to the fore-hold. The king struck the point of his axe in Erling's cheek and said: "Marked shall be the king's betrayer". Aslak Fitjaskalli then suddenly ran up and struck his axe into Erling's head so that it stood deep down in his brain. That was at once a deadly wound, and Erling lost his life. Then said King Olav to Aslak: "May thou yet get ill-luck for thy blow; now hast thou struck Norway from my hands". Aslak said: "Ill it is then, O king, if thou gettest hurt from this blow; I thought I struck Norway into thy hands. But if I have done thee

Erling Skjalgson's body comes home to Sola

harm, O king, and thou art not thankful to me for this deed, I shall have no avail therefrom, for I shall get no thanks and so much enmity for the deed that I must rather need your help and friendship". The king said that it should be so. The king then bade every man go to his ship and make himself ready as soon as possible; "we will not rob the fallen; each of us may have what he has got". The men went back to their ships and made themselves ready as speedily as they could. And when they were ready the ships sailed into the sound towards the bonders' army. Then it was as often happens when a great army comes together and they have lost their chief, that they show no eagerness to attack, having no leader. None of Erling's sons was there, and nothing came of the bonders' attack. The king sailed his way northwards, and the bonders took Erling's body and laid it out and brought it home to Sola, as they did with all the fallen. They sorrowed much over Erling, and it has since been the talk of many men that Erling Skjalgson was the noblest and mightiest man in Norway amongst those who did not bear the name of prince. Sigvat the Scald composed this besides:

| | |
|---|---|
| Erling fell, and | I know no other man |
| No better man awaits death, | Who more fully held |
| Caused by the deed | All his honour in life, |
| Of the mighty king. | Even though he suddenly lost it. |

Besides, he also says that Aslak had brought about the slaying of a kinsman which was untimely:

| | |
|---|---|
| Kin-guilt has Aslak | Kin-slaughter he cannot |
| Increased; few should do | Deny; the words |
| Such deed; the chief | Of old are true, that kinsmen |
| Of the Hordamen is now dead. | Born should keep from anger. |

177. Of Erling's sons some were north in Trondheim with Hacon the Jarl, some in the north in Hordaland, and some in the Fjords, and they went on gathering men. And when Erling's fall was heard of, news followed that there was a calling up of men from the east through Agder and Rogaland and Hordaland; an army was gathered and a great crowd came together; this army went north with Erling's sons to find King Olav. When King Olav went from the fight with Erling he sailed north through the sounds, and by then the day was almost ended; so it is said that he composed this verse:

| | |
|---|---|
| Little will the pale dead men | Sorely hath his treason |
| Be joyful in Jadar to-night, | Scathed him for ever, |
| For the ravens are eating the bodies; | For with wrath I boarded his longship; |
| I did win the victory. | This land hath wrought the fall of men. |

The king then went northwards with his men along the coast, and he then learned the truth of the bonders' gathering. There were at this time many landed men with King Olav, and with him were all the sons of Arne. About this Biarne Gullbrarscald speaks in the poem he made about Kalv Arneson:

| | |
|---|---|
| Thou wast there where Harald's | Ill the folk got from the strife, |
| Weapon-bold offspring | Erling there was taken. |
| Offered battle in the east, | The black boards swam |
| O Kalv, near Bokn itself. | In blood north by Utstein. |
| A good catch didst thou give | It is easy to see that the king |
| The grey wolf for Yule. | Was betrayed of his land. |
| Foremost thou wentest in the fight | The realm fell under the Agdermen, |
| Between the spears and the stones. | For their troop was the greatest. |

King Olav went on until he came north of Stad, and lay in by the Heröys[1] and there heard the tidings that Hacon the Jarl had a great army in Trondheim. The king then sought counsel with his men; Kalv Arneson urged much that they should seek Trondheim and fight with Hacon the Jarl, even though the odds of men were great. Many supported that plan, but some counselled against it. It was left to the king's decision.

178. Afterwards King Olav sailed into Steinavag[2] and lay there the night. But Aslak Fitjaskalli sailed with his ship into Borgund[3] and lay there the night, and there Vigleik Arneson was present. In the morning when Aslak would go to his ship, Vigleik fell upon him and would avenge Erling; Aslak fell. Then men came to the king from Freköysund[4] in the north; they were his bodyguard who had sat at home during the summer, and they told the king the tidings that Hacon the Jarl and many landed men with him had come in the evening to Freköysund with a great army; "and they will take thy life, O king, and thy army's, if they have the might to do it". The king sent his men up on the fell which is there, and when they came on to the fell[5] they saw north towards Bjarnöy[6] that a great army with many ships was coming southwards; they went down again and told the king that the army was coming towards the south, and the king lay there with twelve ships. Then he gave the signal and the awnings were taken off his ships and they took to the oars. But when they were ready and had put out of the haven, the bonders' army was going southwards past Tjotande[7] and they had twenty-five ships. The king then sailed into Narve[8] and in past Hundsver.[9] But when King Olav came just outside Borgund, there was also the ship which Aslak had had coming towards him. When they met King Olav they told their tidings that Vigleik Arneson had taken Aslak Fitjaskalli's life because he had slain Erling Skjalgson. The king was ill pleased with these tidings, but he could not stop his journey for the sake of this unrest, and so he went in through Vegsund[10] past Skot.[11] Some of his men then left him; Kalv Arneson and many other landed men and helmsmen went from him and sailed to meet the jarl. But King Olav continued his journey and did not stop until he came to Todar-

---

1 West of Hareidland.     2 Between Hessöy and Aspöy, now the western part of the town Alesund.     3 On Oxenöy.     4 The sound between Freköy and the mainland. 5 Now Sukkertoppen on Hessöy.   6 *Bjarnöy*, in Borgund district.   7 I.e. Kverven, the most western ness at Ellingsöy.   8 Farm by the Narvesund.   9 I.e. some small islands outside Borgund.   10 Between Sula and Oxenöy.   11 Now Skottet, where Storfjord turns southwards.

fjord,[1] and lay in by Valldale where he left his ships. He had there five ships; he set them up on land and left his sails and tackle to be guarded. He then set up his tent on the island which is called Sult,[2] where there are fair meadows. He raised a cross there on the island. There lived a bonder called Bruce of Möri[3] and he was a chief in the dale. Bruce and many other bonders came down to King Olav and gave him a friendly welcome as was fitting; he showed himself happy at the friendliness. The king then asked if they could travel from the dale up through the country to Lesjar. Bruce told him that there was a ravine in the dale called Sevsurd,[4] "which neither man nor steed can pass". King Olav answered him: "We must now try it, bonder; it shall go as God wills. And come here tomorrow with your nags and your men and let us then see how it is when we come to the ravine, if we can find out any trick for getting over with steeds and men".

179. And when day came the bonders went down with their nags as the king had told them. On the nags they moved all their possessions and clothes, but the whole troop and the king himself walked. And he walked to where it is called Krossbrekka[5] and rested when he came up to the brink, sitting down for a while. He looked into the fjord and said: "My landed men, who have betrayed their trust and who were lately my friends and liegemen, have given me a hard journey". Two crosses now stand on the brink where the king sat. The king then mounted a horse and rode up along the dale, and he did not stop until he came to the ravine. The king then asked Bruce if there was some hut or other where they could live. He said there was. The king pitched his tent and was in it during the night. And in the morning the king bade them go to the ravine and try if they could get wagons over it. They went and the king sat at home in the tent. And towards evening the king's bodyguard and the bonders came back, and said that they had taken much trouble but had got nowhere; they said that a way would never be laid over it. They remained there another night and the king was at prayers all night. And as soon as the king found it was day he bade his men go to the ravine and try again if they could get over with wagons. They went unwillingly and said that they could do nothing.

---

1 I.e. Tafjord, the inner parts of Storfjord.   2 Now Sylte by the Tafjord, on the east side of the river running through the Valldale.   3 On the west side of the same river.   4 Now Skjærsuren, on the north side near Gröning.   5 *Krossbrekka* is O.N. In modern Norwegian Kross has altered to Kors. The present name of the place is Langbrekka, meaning 'a long ravine' or 'scree'.

And when they had gone away, the man who saw to the foodstuffs came to the king and said that there were no more than two pieces of beef; "and thou hast four hundred men of thine own and one hundred bonders". Then the king said he should open all the kettles and slip a little of the flesh into each kettle—and so it was done. And the king went up and made the sign of the cross over them, and bade them get the food ready. Thereafter the king went to Sevsurd where they were to clear the way. And when the king came there, they were all sitting down tired of the work. Then said Bruce: "I told you, O king, but you would not believe me, that the ravine could not be passed over". The king then put his cape down and said that they should all go and try again. So it was done. And now twenty men brought where they wished the stones which beforehand not a hundred men had been able to stir in any way, and by midday the way was cleared so that there was a passage for men and pack-horses, and it was not much worse than the level field. The king went down again to where the food was and where it is now called Olavshellar.[1] There is a spring near the cave and in it the king washed himself; and if cattle are sick in the dale and drink of that water they are cured. The king and all his men then had their meal, and when the king had eaten he asked if there was some hut in the dale above the ravine where they could stay during the night. And Bruce said: "There is a shieling called Gröninger [2] but there no man can be at night because of the trolls and wicked wights which haunt the shieling". Afterwards the king said they should get ready and that he would stay during the night in the shieling. Then the man who saw to the foodstuffs came to him and said that there was enough food: "and I know not from where it has come". The king thanked God for His gift; he then had loads of food made for the bonders who went down the dale; he himself was in the shieling during the night. And at midnight when the men lay asleep, a horrible shriek was heard outside the milking-place, and a shout: "King Olav's prayers are now burning me so that I cannot be in my home; now must I flee and never again come to the milking-place". And in the morning, when the folk awoke, the king went to the fell and said first to Bruce, "Here shall a stead be built and the bonder who lives here will always have success, and his corn shall never freeze, even though it freezes hard above and below the stead". Thereafter King Olav went over the fell and came forth into Einbu [3] where he was during the

[1] The place still bears this name.　[2] Now the farm of Gröning.　[3] *Einbu* is situated at the top of the Lesja forest.

night. King Olav had been king in Norway for fifteen winters including the winter when he and Swein the Jarl were both in the land to the winter which has now been spoken of for a while. It was past Yule when he left his ships behind and went up on land, as is now told. This division of his reign was first written about by the priest Ari Torgilson the Wise, who was both truthful and of good memory, and who was so old a man that he remembered the men and had tales from those who were so old that on account of their great age they could call to mind these tidings, as Ari himself has told of in his books, where he has named the men from whom he had learned this. But it is generally believed that Olav was king in Norway for fifteen winters before his fall; but they who say so reckon until Swein the Jarl's reign the last winter he was in the land, for after that Olav was king and lived for fifteen winters.

180. After King Olav had been all night in Lesjar, he went on with his men day after day, first to Gudbrandsdale and from there out to Hedemark. It was then seen who were his friends, for they followed him now, whereas the others who had served him with less trustiness now parted from him; some of them turned out unfriendly even to enmity, and this soon became apparent. It was especially noticed of many Uplanders that Tore's death galled them, as is mentioned above (chapter 165). King Olav gave home leave to many of his men who had garths and children to look after, for they did not seem to know with any certainty what peace there would be for the possessions of those men who would go from the land with the king. Then the king laid it bare to his friends that it was his thought now to go from the land, first east to Sweden where he would lastly take counsel as to where he should be or where he should go thence. And he bade his friends believe that he still thought of seeking the land and his kingdom again if God gave him his life; he said that he had a presentiment that all the folk in Norway would again be bound in service to him; "and I should think", he said, "that Hacon the Jarl will have power over Norway but for a short while, and that will not seem strange to many, for Hacon the Jarl has previously been short of good luck when he has been against me. But few men will believe, though I say it, what I fear about Canute the Mighty: within a few winters he will be dead and all his kingdom will vanish, and there will be no rising up of his kin, if it so comes to pass as my words point to". And when the king ended his speech, the men got themselves ready for the journey and the king turned east to Eidaskog with the men who were following him. There were with him Queen Astrid, their

daughter Ulvhild, King Olav's son Magnus, Ragnvald Bruceson and Torberg, Finn and Arne, the sons of Arne, besides other landed men; he had a good choice of men; Björn the Marshal got leave to go home; he went back home to his garth and by the king's leave many others of the king's friends went home to their garths. The king bade them let him know if such tidings befell in the land as it was needful for him to know. The king then went on his way.

King Olav fares to Sweden

181. To tell of King Olav's journey, he first went from Norway eastward through Eidaskog to Värmland, then out to Vatsbu[1] and from there through the wood where the way leads and so forth into Närike.[2] There lived a rich and mighty man called Sigtrygg; his son was called Ivor and he afterwards became a renowned man. King Olav stayed there with Sigtrygg during the spring. And when summer came, the king made himself ready for his journey and got himself ships. He fared during the summer and did not stop until he came east to Gardarik[3] to King Jarisleiv and Queen Ingegerd.

1 The most northern district in West Gautland, south of Tiveden.    2 Cf. chapter 77.
3 I.e. Russia.

Queen Astrid and the king's daughter Ulvhild were left behind in Sweden, but the king took his son Magnus to the east with him. King Jarisleiv greeted King Olav well and bade him stay with him and take such land there as he needed for the upkeep of his men. King Olav accepted it and stayed there. So it is said that King Olav was good and diligent in praying to God throughout his life, and after he had noticed that his might lessened and his opponents grew in strength, he set his whole mind to the service of God and the other cares and the troubles he had had on his hands hindered him not therefrom, for during the time he had sat in his realm he had struggled with that which seemed to him most needful, first to make peace and free the land from thraldom under foreign chiefs and afterwards to turn the folk of the land to the true faith, and thereafter to set up laws and land rights. And this he did for the sake of righteousness and in order to punish those who desired lawlessness. It had often been the wont in Norway for the sons of landed men or mighty bonders to go on warships and get themselves goods by harrying both within the land and without. But since Olav had been king, he had freed the land by forbidding all robbery there. And if the sons of mighty men broke the peace or did things which seemed to the king to be unlawful, so far as he could get at them with punishment, he contented himself with nothing less than that they should lose life or limbs, and neither prayers nor offers of money availed. Thus says Sigvat the Scald:

They who broke the peace
Oft offered gold to buy themselves
From punishment. But the great-
    minded
Ruler took no fines thereof.
The heads of these men he bade
Be struck off—for so shall the land
Be guarded. For robbery
They had to suffer fitting pains.
The dear lord who fed
The wolves full, lessened
The race of thieves and robbers:
Robbery he stopped.

The strong king ordered
Every bold thief to lose
Hands or feet. Thus he got
Peace for the land folk.
It is most proof of his might
That many vikings lost
Their heads through the keen
Weapons of the land's watcher.
The generous father of Magnus
Hath done much good;
Most of Olav Digre's victories
Hath furthered his honour.

He dealt out the same punishments to the mighty and the poor alike. But it seemed to the men of the land like arrogance and they were filled with enmity against it when they lost their kinsmen through the righteous judgment of the king, even though the case were true. This was the beginning of the uprising which the men of the land made against King Olav that they would not suffer his righteousness; but he would rather give up his kingdom than forgo to rule it with justice. Wrongfully was the complaint made against him that he was miserly with goods to his men, for he was generous to his friends. But one reason why they showed enmity towards him was that he seemed hard and strong in punishing, whereas King Canute offered many goods. The great chiefs had, however, been tempted by his promising each of them great might and a princely name, and likewise by offering the people of Norway Hacon the Jarl as their lord, for he had been much loved by the folk of the land when he had ruled the land before.

182. Hacon the Jarl had sailed from Trondheim with his army

and had gone against King Olav in the south by Möre, as is written above (chapter 178). And when the king sailed into the fjord the jarl went after him. Then Kalv Arneson and the other men who had left King Olav came to meet him, and Kalv was well greeted there. The jarl then sailed into Todarfjord to Valldale where the king had drawn up his ships. The jarl took the ships the king had had, drew them out and made

Jökul sat down on a bank and a man
stood ready to strike him

them ready, and then lots were cast among the men for helmsmen. There was with the jarl an Iceland man called Jökul, the son of Bard Jökulson of Vatsdale.[1] It fell to Jökul's lot to steer the *Bison*, King Olav's ship. Jökul then indited this verse:

From Sult I got the ship
To steer which Olav Digre
Had owned. Late shall the women
Hear that I was afraid.

Ill weather I expect on this steed
Of the sea, O ye women.
In the summer the grim man
Himself lost the victory.

Here may be told in short what befell much later: Jökul fell in with King Olav's men in Gotland and was taken prisoner. The king had him led away to be executed, and a stick was twisted in his

1 In North Iceland. He was descended from Ingemund the Old (cf. Vatsdölasaga).

hair and a man held on to it. Jökul sat down on a bank. Then a man made himself ready to strike him. But when Jökul heard the whiz of the blow, he raised himself up and the blow fell on his head, so that there was a great wound. The king saw that it was a death wound and bade them stop. Jökul sat up and then composed a verse:

| | |
|---|---|
| My sores smart with pain; | The blood pours out from the wound; |
| I have oft sat better. | To sorrow I am hardened. |
| Wounds I have, wherefrom | The helm-covered, honoured king |
| The red stream warmly gushes. | Casts on me his wrath. |

Jökul then died.

183. Kalv Arneson went north with Hacon the Jarl to Trondheim and the jarl bade him be with him and become his man. Kalv said that he would first go to Egge to his garth and then at length give his answer; Kalv did so. And when he came home, he soon noticed that his wife Sigrid was very agitated, and she reckoned up all the sorrows she said she had got from King Olav; the first was that he had had her husband Ölvir slain; "and now since then my two sons", she said, "and thou Kalv wast present at their death; that I should least have expected of thee". Kalv said that it was much against his will that Tore had lost his life; "I offered fines for him," he said: "and when Grjotgard was felled I lost my brother Arnbjörn". She said: "It is well that thou hast suffered this from the king, for maybe thou wilt avenge thy brother if thou wilt not avenge my sorrow. Thou sawest when Tore thy foster-son was slain, how much the king minded thee". Such harmful talk she was ever putting before Kalv. Kalv often answered wrathfully, but it came about at last that he let himself be led by her words and promised to put himself in the jarl's hands if the jarl would increase his land rents. Sigrid sent word to the jarl to tell him how far it had gone with Kalv. And as soon as the jarl was sure of it, he sent word to Kalv to come to the town to him. Kalv did not delay the journey, and a little later he went out to Nidaros and there found Hacon the Jarl; he was well greeted and had talk with him. They came to an agreement and arranged that Kalv should submit to the jarl and get great land rents from him. Kalv then went home to his garth, and now he had most say of all in the rule of Trondheim. As soon as it was spring, Kalv fitted out a ship he owned, and when he was ready he sailed out to the sea and steered his ship westwards to England, for he had heard that King Canute had sailed west from Denmark to England earlier in the spring. Canute had then given a jarldom in Denmark to Harald, son

of Thorkel the High. Kalv Arneson went to King Canute as soon as
he got to England. Thus says Biarne Gullbrarscald:

| | |
|---|---|
| The princely Olav let his ships | And when ye parted |
| Shoot east o'er the sea. | Soon thou wentest to Canute; |
| Harald's fight-bold brother[1] | It lists me not to gather |
| Had to go to Gardar. | Lies about the deeds of men. |

And when Kalv came to King Canute he had an exceedingly
friendly welcome and had talks with him. It was amongst King
Canute's talks that he bade Kalv bind himself to make an uprising
against Olav Digre, if he came back to the land. "And I will give
thee a jarldom", he said, "and let thee rule over Norway; and my
kinsman Hacon shall come to me as he is best fitted for it, for he is
so noble-minded that I believe he would not throw so much as a shaft
against King Olav if they met."[2] Kalv listened to what King Canute
said and was now eager for the name of jarl; this arrangement was
now bound between Kalv and King Canute. Kalv then made himself ready for his journey home, and at their parting King Canute gave
him gifts. About this Biarne the Scald speaks:

| | |
|---|---|
| O fight-bold jarl's son, | The Lord of London |
| Thou hast England's king | Let land be promised thee, ere thou |
| To thank for thy gifts. Truly | Wentest from the west. The matter |
| Thou wentest far with thy case. | Was delayed, but thy honour was great. |

184. That summer Hacon the Jarl left the land and went west to
England; and when he came there, King Canute greeted him well.
The jarl was betrothed in England and now he went to get his bride,
for he would make his wedding in Norway; he gathered in England
the objects which seemed to him hard to get in Norway. In the
autumn the jarl made himself ready to go home, but he was very late
getting ready. He then sailed out to sea. And about their journey
it is to be said that the ship was lost and no man came back from
it; it is the talk of some men that the ship had been seen north of
Caithness one evening in a great storm when the weather was bad
off Pentland Firth; they who believe this say that the ship was driven
into the Svelg;[3] it is, however, known for a truth that Hacon the Jarl
was lost at sea and that none of those who were on the ship came to
land. The same autumn merchants told that tidings were spread about
the lands that they believed the jarl was lost at sea. And all men knew

---

1 I.e. King Olav.     2 Olav had given Hacon peace under promise that he would not
fight against him (cf. chapter 30).     3 In O.N. *Svelgr* = the strong current sometimes
prevailing in the Pentland Firth, which is still called *Swelchie*.

that this autumn he had not come to Norway and so the land was without a chief.

185. Björn the Marshal sat at home in his garth after parting with King Olav. Björn was a renowned man and it was soon known far and wide that he had settled down in peace. Hacon the Jarl and the other chiefs heard this and then they sent men and messages to Björn. And when the messengers came forth to him he greeted them well. Björn called the messengers to a talk and asked them their business, and he who was their leader spoke and bore forth greetings to Björn from King Canute and Hacon the Jarl—even from other chiefs; "and thereto", he said, "King Canute has heard much of thee and that thou hast long followed Olav Digre, and hast been a great foe of King Canute; it seems ill to him, for he will be a friend of thine as of all other doughty men, as soon as thou wilt leave off being his foe. And for thee there is no other choice than to turn thyself

King Canute's messengers visit
Björn the Marshal

for trust or friendship where it is best to seek it and where all men in the northern parts of the world consider it an honour to win it. Now ye, who have followed Olav, can see how he has left you; ye are all without help against King Canute and his men, although ye harried in his land last summer and slew his friends. Thou mayest take it thankfully when the king offers his friendship, and it would be more fitting if thou prayest for it or dost offer goods for it". And when he had ended his speech, Björn answered and said: "I will now sit happily at home in my garth and serve no lords". The messenger answered: "Such men as thou are the king's men. I can tell thee now that thou hast two choices in thy hands. One is to be outlawed from thy possessions, just like Olav, your fellow-man. The other choice which may seem most useful is to take the friendship of King Canute and Hacon the Jarl, and become their man, and put thy faith therein and here take thy reward"—and he held forth English silver from a great bag. Björn¹ was a man greedy for money, and when he saw the silver he grew sick at heart and silent. He then thought to himself what he should do: he thought it hard to lose his possessions and uncertain that there would be an uprising for King Olav in Norway. And when the messenger found that Björn's heart was set on the money, he cast forth two thick gold rings and said: "Take thou the money now, Björn, and swear oaths. I promise thee that of little worth are these goods compared to those which thou wilt get if thou seekest King Canute in his home". And with these rich goods and fair promises and great gifts of money he was enticed by greed; he took up the money and afterwards submitted and swore trust to King Canute and to Hacon the Jarl. Thereupon the messengers went away.

186. Björn the Marshal heard the tidings, which were told, that Hacon the Jarl was drowned. Then his mind turned and he rued breaking faith with King Olav. He now thought himself free of his promises that he had vowed Hacon the Jarl his allegiance. Björn thought that there was some hope of success for King Olav's kingship if he came to Norway when it was leaderless. Björn therefore speedily made himself ready to go, and he had a few men with him; he went on his journey day and night, on horse when he could or on ship where he could travel by sea, and he did not stop till he came east to Gardarik and to King Olav. It was then winter towards Yuletide. The king was very glad when Björn came, and he asked of many tidings north from Norway. Björn said that the jarl was lost at sea and the land was now leaderless. At these tidings the men were glad who had followed King Olav from Norway and had great possessions and kinsmen and friends there, and they now yearned for the journey home. Björn also told the king many other tidings from Norway such as he was curious to hear of. The king then asked after his friends, and how far they kept their trust to him. Björn said it was very indifferently done and then he stood up and fell at the king's feet, and clasping the king's feet he said: "All is in God's power and in thine, O king. I have taken money from Canute's men and sworn them oaths of faith, but now I will follow thee and not part from thee as long as we both shall live". The king answered: "Stand up at once, Björn. Thou shalt be at peace with me. Pray forgiveness of God. I may well know that there will be few men in Norway who have kept their

---

1 In O.N. *Biörn*, but also *Bjørn* as in modern Scandinavian. The English chroniclers mention the names Biorn and Beorn, and in *Diplomatarium Norvegicum* many variations of the name are given, such as Beorn, Byrn, Biron, Birun, Byærn, Biern, Born and Berno. The families of Byron and the French Marshal Biron (1524–92) came from Normandy.

trust to me, when such as thou turnest from me. It is also true that they are sitting in a hard position there when I am far away and they are exposed to the unrest of my foes". Björn told the king who had most bound themselves to raise up enmity against the king and his men; thereto he mentioned the sons of Erling of Jadar and others of their kinsmen, besides Einar Tambarskelver, Kalv Arneson, Tore the Hound and Harek of Tjotta.

187. After King Olav had come to Gardarik he had had much to think of, and he pondered over what plan he should take up. King Jarisleiv and Queen Ingegerd bade Olav stay with them and take the kingdom which was called Vulgaria;[1] it was a part of Gardarik and the folk in that land were heathen. King Olav weighed up this offer in his mind, but when he put it before his men all of them counselled against fixing their homes there and urged the king to go north to his kingdom in Norway. The king had also had it in his thoughts to lay down his kingly honour and go out in the world to Jerusalem or to other holy places and there become a monk. But it came most often to his mind, to think how he could manage to get to his realm in Norway. And when he fixed his mind thereon, he remembered that in the first ten years of his rule all things were to his use and honour, but afterwards all his plans were heavy and difficult and everything he tried his luck at went always against him. For this reason he had doubt as to whether it could be a wise plan to try his luck and go with a small force against his foes when all the people had agreed to withstand King Olav. Such troubles he often bore; he put his case before God and prayed to Him to guide him so that he could see more clearly what would be of most help. Olav thought much upon this and knew not what to do, for ill-luck seemed certain to him in anything that he might choose.

188. One night, King Olav lay in his bed and was awake long into the night; he thought of his plans and he had great cares on his mind. But when his mind was grown weary, sleep fell upon him and so lightly did it come that he thought he was awake and saw all that was going on in the house. He saw a man standing before the bed, a great and noble man, who was finely clad. And it most struck the king's mind that Olav Trygvason must be come there. The man spoke to him: "Art thou sick at heart over thy plans as to what counsel thou shalt take up? It seems strange to me that thou art pondering much, and likewise that thou thinkest of laying down thy kingdom which God has given thee, and moreover that thou thinkest of staying here

1 Greater Bulgaria by the Rivers Volga and Kama, the capital of which was Bolghar.

and taking a kingdom from kings who are foreign and strangers to thee. Go thou rather back to thy kingdom which thou hast taken as thy inheritance and hast long ruled over with the strength God gave thee, and let not thy underlings make thee afraid. It is to a king's honour to win victories over his foes, and an honourable death to fall in battle with his men. Or dost thou doubt whether thou hast the right in thy struggle? Thou shalt not do so as to deny thy true right. Thou canst boldly seek the land, for God will bear thee witness that it is thine own possession". And when the king awoke he seemed to catch a glimpse of the man when he went away; and from that moment he hardened his heart and set himself to go back to Norway just as he himself formerly had most wished to, and just as he had noticed his men most wished. He fixed it in his mind that the land would be easy to take when it was leaderless, as he had then heard it was. He believed that if he himself came there, many would even then be ready to help him. When the king laid this plan before his men, they all took it thankfully.

189. It is said that it befell in Gardarik when King Olav was there that the son of a noble widow had a boil in his throat, and it grew so big that the boy could get no food down and they thought that he must die. The lad's mother went to Queen Ingegerd, for she was an acquaintance of hers, and she showed her the boy. The queen said she had no leechcraft for that; "but go thou", she said, "to King Olav— he is the best leech here—and ask him to run his hands over the boy's sore, and if he will not, bear these words of mine to him". She did as the queen said. When she found the king she said that her son was nigh unto death through a throat boil and bade him run his hands over it. The king said he was not a leech and bade her go where leeches were. She said that the queen had sent her there, "and she bade me bear her words to you, that you should use the remedy which you understand; she told me that you were the best leech in this town". Then the king began to run his hands round the boy's neck and rubbed long at the boil until the lad opened his mouth. The king then took a loaf and broke it up and laid the bits in a shape of a cross in his hand; he then put it in the boy's mouth and he swallowed it down. After that all the ache went out of the boil and in a few days he was quite well. His mother was very glad, as were the boy's other kinsmen and acquaintances. At first it was held that King Olav had good leech hands, as they say of those men who have great skill, that they have good hands. But afterwards when his miracles were commonly known, it was reckoned as a true miracle.

190. It befell one Sunday when the king sat in his high-seat at table that he fell into deep thought and heeded not the hours. He had a knife in his hand and held a stick from which he was cutting shavings. A lad waiting on him stood before him holding a table dish. He saw what the king was doing and perceived that he was thinking of other things; he said: "To-morrow is Monday, my lord!" The king looked at him when he heard that and then it struck his mind what he had been doing. He bade them bring him a lighted taper and he swept into his hand all the shavings he had cut; he set light to it and let the shavings burn in the hollow of his hand. Thereby it might be noticed that he would hold fast by God's law and com-

"To-morrow is Monday, my lord"

mandment and would not set aside what he knew to be right.

191. After King Olav had taken up the plan of turning on his homeward journey, he put it before King Jarisleiv and Queen Ingegerd. They counselled him against the journey and said that in their kingdom he should have such power as seemed fitting to him, and bade him not get within reach of his foes with such small strength as he had there. Then King Olav told them his dreams and likewise that he believed that it was God's will. And when they found that the king had taken up the plan of going back to Norway, they offered him all the help he would take of them for the journey. The king thanked them with fair words for their good will and said that with gladness would he take from them all that he needed for his journey.

192. Straightway after Yule the king made himself ready; he had nigh on two hundred (two hundred and forty) of his own men and King Jarisleiv gave them all the steeds and everything which was needful. And when he was ready, he went off. King Jarisleiv and Queen Ingegerd saw him depart with great honour, and with them King Olav left his son Magnus. He then went westward, first over frozen waters right down to the sea. And when spring came and the ice melted, he put his ships in order; and when they were ready and a

fair wind blew they sailed forth and had a good journey. King Olav came with his ships to Gotland,[1] and there he heard tidings both from Sweden and from Denmark and right from Norway. It was then learned for a truth that Hacon the Jarl had been drowned and that the land of Norway was leaderless; the king and his men then had hopes for their journey. When the wind was fair they sailed thence and steered to Sweden. The king and his men lay in by Lögrinn[2] and steered up through the land to Aros.[3] Olav then sent men to Anund the Swedish king and made a meeting with him. King Anund was glad of his brother-in-law's message and went to meet King Olav, just as King Olav had requested. Queen Astrid also came to King Olav with the men who had followed her. There was a happy meeting between them all, and the Swedish king greeted King Olav, his brother-in-law, well, when they met.

193. Now shall be told about what they were doing in Norway in these days. Tore the Hound had had the Finnish trade these two winters, and each winter he had been a long time up in the fells and had won many goods. He had many kinds of trade with the Finns. He had made there twelve reindeer cloaks for himself with such wizardry that no weapon could pierce them; they were stronger than a ring-brynie. And the last spring Tore had fitted out a longship he owned and manned it with his huscarls. He had called the bonders together and had demanded a levy to the northernmost thing district; he had thus drawn together a great number of folk and in the spring he had gone southwards with this army. Harek of Tjotta also gathered men and got a great army. On that journey there were also other great men, though these were the most famous. They wished this army to go against King Olav and guard the land against him when he came from the east.

194. Einar Tambarskelver had most say in Outer Trondheim after Hacon the Jarl's death was known; he and his son Eindridi thought they had the best rights to inherit the possessions and wealth the jarl had had, and Einar now called to mind the friendly speeches and promises which King Canute had given him at their parting. Einar had a good ship he owned made ready, and he himself went aboard with a great following; and when he was ready he sailed south along the coast and then west over the sea, and he did not stop till he came to England; he went straightway to King Canute, and the king greeted him well. Einar then put his business before the king and said that he had now come to get fulfilment of the promises which the

1 The island of *Gotland* in the Baltic.    2 Lake Mälar.    3 I.e. Upsala.

king had given him, that Einar should have the name of jarl over Norway if Hacon the Jarl was not there. King Canute said that the matter now stood quite otherwise; "I have now sent men with my tokens to Denmark to my son Swein", he said, "and thereto I have promised him the kingdom of Norway. But I will keep my friendship for thee and thou shalt have such titles from me as thou mayest have by thy birth, and be a landed man with land rents as much greater than those of other landed men as thou art doughtier than the other landed men". Einar then saw what outcome his errand would have, and so he made himself ready to go home. And when he knew the king's plans and likewise that it might be expected that if King Olav came from the east there would be no peace in the land, it occurred to Einar that there were no grounds for hastening his journey any more than necessary if they should have to fight against King Olav, and then have no more increase of power than before. Einar now sailed out to sea when he was ready, and came to Norway when those tidings had already befallen which were the weightiest that summer.

195. The chiefs in Norway kept spies in the east towards Sweden and in the south towards Denmark to get to know if King Olav had come from the east from Gardarik; and straightway they heard, as quickly as folk can fare, that King Olav was come to Sweden, and as soon as that was known to be true the war call went through the whole land; all the men were called out and an army was gathered. And then the landed men who were from Agder and Rogaland and Hordaland parted; some went north and others east, and they all thought that in these two places a strength of men was needed. The sons of Erling of Jadar with all the men who hailed from the east turned eastwards, and the sons of Erling were leaders of this army; and to the north went Aslak of Finnöy[1] and Erlend of Gerde[2] and the landed men who dwelt to the north of them. These men who are named here had all sworn oaths to King Canute to take King Olav's life, if the chance were given them.

196. And when they heard in Norway that King Olav was come from the east to Sweden, his friends who would give him help gathered together. The foremost man in that troop was Harald Sigurdson,[3] King Olav's brother; he was then fifteen years old, tall and full-grown to look upon. Many other noble men were also there. In all they had six hundred (seven hundred and twenty) men when

---

1 *Finnöy* is an island in the Ryfylkefjord near Stavanger.    2 A farm in Etne district in South Hordaland.    3 The later Harald Hardrade.

they went from the Uplands, and they made east with that army through Eidaskog to Värmland. Then they moved east through the woods to Sweden, and then they learned about King Olav's journey.

197. King Olav was in Sweden during the spring and had spies in the north in Norway, but all he learned from them was that it would be unpeaceful to go there, and the men who came from the north counselled him much against going into the land; he had however but one thought in his mind and that was to go on, as he had decided before. King Olav asked King Anund what strength he would grant him to seek his land. King Anund answered and said that the Swedes had little desire to go to war in Norway; "we know", he said, "that the Norsemen are hard and great warriors and ill is it to seek them in their homeland with warfare. I shall not be slow to tell thee what I shall give. I will let thee have four hundred (four hundred and eighty) men, good warriors, chosen from my bodyguard and well fitted out for battle. Then I will give thee leave to go through my land and gather all the men thou canst get and who will follow thee". King Olav took the offer and made himself ready for his journey. Queen Astrid stayed behind in Sweden with Ulvhild, the king's daughter.

198. When King Olav began his journey there came to him the troop which the Swedish king had given him and there were four hundred (four hundred and eighty) men. The king now went on the ways which the Swedes could show him. They went up the land to the woods and came forth into a district called Jarnberaland.[1] There the army which had gone from Norway to meet him, as is already spoken of, came to the king. He met his brother Harald and many other kinsmen and it was the gladdest of meetings. They had now altogether twelve hundred (fourteen hundred and forty) men.

199. There was a man called Dag of whom it is said that he was the son of the Ring Dagson who had fled the land because of King Olav; and they say that Ring was the son of Dag, the son of Ring, the son of Harald Hairfair. Dag was, therefore, King Olav's kinsman. He and his father Ring had settled in Sweden and had there got a district to rule. In the spring, when King Olav was come from the east to Sweden, he sent word to Dag his kinsman to come into his following with all the strength of men he had. And if they won the land in Norway Dag should have there no less land than his forefathers had. When this message came to Dag, it fell well to his mind, for he had a great longing to go to Norway and win the land his kinsmen formerly had. He answered the matter at once and

1 Dalarne in Sweden.

promised to go with him. Dag was quick in word and counsel, very eager and very bold, but not a wise man. He then gathered folk and had nearly twelve hundred (fourteen hundred and forty) men, and with this army he went to King Olav.

200. King Olav sent word into the districts that those men should come to him and follow him, who would win goods by gathering booty and taking the garths wherein the king's foes sat. King Olav then moved his army forward and went through the forest districts, sometimes through wastes and often over great stretches of water; they dragged or carried their ships with them between the waters. A crowd of men came to the king; they were wood dwellers and some of them were highwaymen. Many of the places where he lay for the night have since been called Olav's booths. He did not stop until he came forth into Jämtland, whence he went north to the Kjöl.[1] His men scattered themselves about in the districts and were much spread about so long as they did not expect trouble. But always when they were scattered, the Norsemen followed the king, whilst Dag went another way with his men and the Swedes and their folk another way.

201. There were two men, one called Gauka Tore and the other Afrafasti; they were the greatest of robbers and they had with them thirty men like themselves. These brothers were bigger and stronger than the others and they were not short of boldness and courage. They heard about the army which was going through the land, and said amongst themselves that it would be a stout plan to go to the king, follow him to his land and go there into a real battle with him and try themselves in that way, for they had not before been in a fight where armies were drawn up. They were very curious to see the king's battle line. This counsel pleased their followers well, and they set out on the way to meet the king. And when they came there, they went with their following before the king, and their men were fully weaponed. They greeted the king and he asked what men they were. They gave their names and said that they were men of the land. Thereafter they put forward their business and offered to go with the king. The king said that it looked to him as if there was a good following in such men: "I have a great wish to take such men; but are ye Christian men?" Gauka Tore answered and said that he was neither Christian nor heathen; "we and our men have no other faith than that we believe in ourselves and our strength and our good luck in victory, and by this are we well served". The king

---

[1] *Kjöl* (or *Kjölen*) is the frontier between Sweden and Norway.

answered: "It is a great scathe that men who look such fine warriors should not believe in Christ, their leader". Tore answered: "Is there any Christian man in thy following, O king, who has grown more in one day than we two brothers?" The king bade them let themselves be baptised and take the true faith with it, "and then can ye follow me," he said; "I shall make ye into very great men. But if ye will not, then go ye back to your work". Afrafasti answered and said

The king meets Gauka Tore and Afrafasti

that he would not take up Christianity. They then turned away. Then Gauka Tore said: "It is a great shame that this king throws away our help. Never before have I been anywhere where I was not good enough to go in fellowship with other men. I will never turn back in this way". Afterwards they cast themselves in with other wood-dwellers and followed the troops. King Olav then went westward to the Kjöl.

202. And when King Olav went from the east over the Kjöl and turned westward down from the fell, so that the land was lower in the west towards the sea, they had a wide view over the land. Many went before the king and many behind him. He rode where there was most room, and he was quiet and talked not with the others. He rode a long time in such a way that he saw little about him. And then the bishop rode up to him and asked him what he was thinking of since he was so quiet, for the king was always happy and talkative with his men on a journey and thus made all who

were near him happy. The king answered seriously: "Strange things have come before me for a while. I looked out over Norway, when I saw westwards from the fell just now. It came into my mind that many a day had I been happy in that land. I then had a vision that I saw right out through all Trondheim and then over all Norway, and the longer the vision was before my eyes, the farther I saw, until I looked upon the whole world, over both land and sea. I clearly knew again the places I had been to and seen before, and just as clearly I saw the places which I had not seen before, and I saw some such places I had heard of as well as those which I have not before heard spoken of, both settled and unsettled alike, all over the world". The bishop said the vision was a holy one and very remarkable.[1]

203. After the king had turned down from the fell, they came to the garth which is called Sula[2] in the uppermost part of the districts in Værdale. And when they came to the garth there were tilled fields by the wayside and the king bade his men go soberly and not spoil the bonder's crop. This they did so long as the king was near, but the followers who came up later gave no heed thereto and they ran over the field and the crop was quite trodden down. The bonder who lived there was called Torgeir Flekk and he had two sons, almost grown up. Torgeir greeted the king and his men well and offered him all the help he could grant. The king thanked him well and thereafter he asked Torgeir for tidings of what was afoot in the land or what gathering of men they were making against him. Torgeir said that a great army had drawn together in Trondheim and that landed men were come there both from the south of the land and from the north from Halogaland, "but I know not", he said, "whether they will lead this army against you or go elsewhere". He then complained to the king of the scathe he had suffered and of the carelessness of the king's men in breaking down and treading over all his fields. The king said it was ill that harm was done him. He then rode to where the crop had stood and saw that the corn was all laid down to the ground. The king rode round it and said: "I expect, bonder, that God will right thy scathe and this field will be better in a week"—and it turned out the best field, as the king had said. The king stayed there for the night and in the morning he made himself ready to go. He said that Torgeir the Bonder should go with him, but he offered his two sons for the journey. The king said that they should not go with him, but the boys would go, however. The king

---

1 St Olav evidently had then a vision of the Nordic races settling in all parts of the world.  2 Now Sulstuen, at the upper reach of Værdale by the Sul River.

bade them stay behind; and when they would not listen to this, the king's bodyguard wished to bind them. When the king saw that, he said: "Let them go! They will soon come back!" And so it came to pass with the lads as the king had said.

204. They moved their army out to Stav;[1] and when the king came to the Stav-marshes, he rested for a while. He then learned for a truth that the bonders were coming with an army against him and that he would soon have to fight. The king then mustered his army and took the numbers; he had more than thirty hundred (thirty-six hundred) men. Amongst these were nine hundred (ten hundred and eighty) heathen men; and when the king got to know this, he bade them be baptised and said that he would have no heathen men with him in the fight; "we do not wish to put our trust in strength of numbers," he said; "in God shall we set our trust, for with His strength and mercy can we get the victory; but I will not mix heathen men with my men". And when the heathens heard this, they took counsel together and at last four hundred men let themselves be baptised, but five hundred denied Christianity and these men turned back to their own land. Then the brothers, Gauka Tore and Afrafasti, went with their men and again offered the king their following. The king asked if they had now been baptised. Gauka Tore said that it was not so. The king then bade them take baptism and the right faith, but otherwise go away. They turned away from him then and talked amongst themselves and took counsel as to what plan they should take. Then Afrafasti said: "I may say what is in my mind, that I will not turn back. I will go to the battle and help one or the other of the fighting sides, for it is all the same to me which army I am in". Then Gauka Tore answered: "If I go to the battle, I will grant the king my help, for he is most in need of help. And if I am to believe in any God, how can it be worse for me to believe in Christ than in any other God? It is my counsel that we let ourselves be baptised if the king sets so great store by it, and let us then go to the battle with him". They all agreed, and then went and told the king that they would now take baptism. They were baptised by the priests and then by the bishop. The king took them with him in the fellowship of his bodyguard and said that they should stand under his standard in the battle.

205. King Olav had learned for a truth that it would be but a short time ere he would come to battle with the bonders. And after he had mustered his army and the men were counted, he had now more

1 A farm in Værdale, which no longer exists.

than thirty hundred men, and it seemed to be a great army in one field. The king then talked to the army and spoke thus: "We have a great army and fine men. And now I will tell my men how the army shall be drawn up. I will have my standard go forth in the middle of the army and thereafter shall follow my bodyguard and my guests and the men who have come to us from the Uplands, and likewise those who have come to us here in Trondheim. And to the right of the standard shall be Dag Ringson with the army which he brought to follow us; he shall have the second standard. To the left of my line shall be the army which the Swedish king gave us and all the men who came to us in Sweden; they shall have the third standard. I will that you are divided into small bands, and kinsmen and friends shall stand together, for then each will help the other and each will know the other. We shall mark all our army; we shall make a sign on our helmets and shields and paint thereon the holy cross in white. And when we come into battle we shall have one war cry: 'Forward, forward, Christ's men, cross men, king's men'. We must have thin lines if we have fewer men, for I do not wish them to surround us with their host. Scatter the men now in small bands, and let these bands then be gathered in lines; each must get to know his place and give heed how far he is from the standard he is to follow. We shall now keep together in our lines and the men shall be fully weaponed night and day until we know where we shall meet the bonders". After the king had spoken they drew up the army and ranked it in the way the king had ordained. Thereafter the king held meetings with the leaders of the troops. Then the men were come there whom the king had sent out into the lordship to demand men of the bonders. They brought tidings from the district that everywhere they had been there was a lack of fighting men, and the folk had gone to the bonders' gathering; and where they met men few would follow them and many answered that they sat at home because they would follow neither side: they would fight neither against the king nor against their own kinsmen. The king's men had, therefore, got few folk. Then the king asked his men what counsel it were best to follow. Finn answered the king's words: "I will say how it should be done, if I could decide. We should go with the war shield through all the district, robbing all the goods and burning all the settlements so thoroughly that not a cottage should be left standing, and in that way punish the bonders for their treason; I think that many would break loose from the bonder's troop if they saw smoke or flames at home in their houses and did not rightly know how matters were with their children or women or old folk, their fathers or mothers or other kinsmen. I expect", he said, "that if any of them contrive to break away from the gathering their lines will soon be thinned, for it is the way of the bonders that the last counsel is dearest to them". And when Finn ended his speech they all gave him a good cheer; many liked it well to seek for booty and all found that the bonders deserved scathe, and it was likely, as Finn said, that many bonders would get away from the gathering. Tormod Kolbrunarscald then quoth a verse:

Let us burn all the garths, The Inner Tronds should have
And all we find within. Nothing but ashes left of their houses,
Let all ward the land If I might counsel.
And the king's estates.

And when King Olav heard the eagerness of his men he demanded quietness and spoke thus: "The bonders deserve well enough that it should be done as ye wish. They know that I have burned their houses for them and given them other great punishments. But when I burnt them before, I did it then because they had gone from their faith and taken up blood offerings and would not better themselves according to my words. We then had God's right to avenge. But now when they do not keep faith with me, their treason is a much smaller crime, even though it does not appear to be seemly for those who would be manly men. I have a somewhat greater right to show some mildness here when they do wrong against me than when they showed hate to God. I will now that my men go peacefully and make no war here. I will first go to meet the bonders, and if we come to terms all will be well; but if they fight against us there are two choices in our hands. If we fall in the fight then it will have been a good counsel that we did not go robbing their goods. And if we win, then shall ye be the heirs of those who are now fighting against us, for some of them will fall and others flee, and all these will have forfeited all their possessions. Then it will be good to go to great houses and noble garths, whereas no one can enjoy well what has been burned. In such a way, too, it goes with stolen goods, that many more are spoiled than are put to any use. We shall now scatter out in the district and take with us all the weapon-bearing men we can get; we shall also strike down cattle or take other goods as far as we need to feed ourselves withal; but ye shall make no other raids. It seems well to me that the bonders' spies should be slain if ye take them. Dag and his men shall go by the north way down through the dale, and I will go out by the main road, and we will meet at eventide and all have one night place".

206. So it is said that when King Olav drew up his army he placed men in a rampart of shields which they should hold before him in the battle, and for that he chose the men who were strongest and boldest. Then he called his scalds to him and bade them go in the shield rampart. "Ye shall", he said, "be here and see what befalls; then it will not be needful for men to tell you thereof, for you yourselves can tell and sing of it hereafter."[1] There were Tormod Kolbrunarscald and Gissur Gulbra, the foster-father of Hofgard

King Olav's army

Rev, and the third was Torfinn Munn. Then said Tormod to Gissur: "Let us not stand so thronged, good friend, so that Sigvat the Scald cannot get his place when he comes; he will stand before the king and naught else will please the king". The king heard that and answered: "There is no need to sneer at Sigvat, even though he is not here. He has often followed me well and he will now pray for us, and that we shall yet need".[2] Tormod said: "It may be that thou wilt now have most need for prayers; but the men would be thinned around thy standard shaft if all thy bodyguard were now on the way to Rome; it was true also when we complained that no one could get a place anywhere if Sigvat would talk with you".

1 This shows the important position held by the scalds.   2 Sigvat the Scald was blamed for having left Norway and gone on a voyage to Rome.

They talked amongst themselves and said it would be fitting to compose some verses about the events which would soon be taking place. Then quoth Gissur:

The word is heard, and never shall
The bonder's daughter call me
Unhappy; we will fit ourselves
For the throng at the shield thing.

The war maids themselves
Await the bold warriors;
In the fight in the east[1]
Let us keep our trust to the king.

Then Torfinn Munn quoth a second verse:

It darkens towards the keen rain
In the hard weather of the shield storm.
The Værdale men will fight
Against the wise king.

Let us feed the raven gladly
And ward the generous prince.
Let us fell the Tronds
In this storm of Odin.

Then quoth Tormod:

Warriors! Now we come
To the great fight.
The noble fighters shall not pale nor
    quake
Now the sword time grows.

Let us fit ourselves for fight
When the battle-glad Olav,
The warrior, goes to the spear
    thing.
The name of coward must be shunned.

The men learned these verses at once by heart.

207. The king then went on his journey and turned out of the dale; he took himself night quarters and there all his army came together; they lay out in the night under their shields. And as soon as it was light, the king had his army made ready, and when they were armed, they moved farther along the dale. Many bonders then came to the king and most of them joined his army, and all of them could say only one thing, that the landed men had drawn a mighty army together and would hold battle with the king. Then the king took many marks of silver and gave them into a bonder's hand, saying: "This money shalt thou watch and afterwards share out: some thou shalt give to the churches, some thou shalt give to the priests and some to almsmen, and it shall be given for the lives and souls of those men who fall in battle fighting against us". The bonder answered: "Shall this money be given for the souls of your men, O king?" Then the king answered: "This money shall be given for the souls of the men who are with the bonders in the battle and fall through the weapons of our men; but the men who follow us to battle and fall there shall all with us be saved together".

208. That night when King Olav slept with the army, as has

---

1 The scald evidently continued to visualise events that happened *in the east* (i.e. Norway) as if he were in Iceland. This circumstance should not lead us to assume that the poem was written later on in Iceland or by others.

already been spoken of, he was awake for a long time and prayed to God for himself and his army, and he slept little. Towards day a heaviness fell on him and when he awoke the day broke. It seemed to the king rather early to awaken the army and then he asked where Tormod the Scald was. He was near by and answered by asking the king what he would of him. The king said: "Say before us a poem!" Tormod sat up and quoth very loudly so that he was heard all through the army. He recited the old Bjarkamal, and this is the beginning of it:

| | |
|---|---|
| The day is sprung up, | Har the Quick, |
| The cock's feathers rustle; | The hard-shooting Rolf,[1] |
| It's time for thralls | Ye men of good kin, |
| To tread to their toil. | Who never flee. |
| Awake, awake, | I wake you not for wine, |
| Dear friends, | Or the chatter of women, |
| All ye noble | But rather for battle, |
| Guests of Adils![1] | For the hard sport of Hild.[2] |

Then the army awoke, and when the poem was ended the men thanked him for it and thought well of it. They thought it well chosen and called it "the egging on of the huscarls". The king thanked him for his banter; he afterwards took a gold ring which weighed half a mark and gave it to Tormod. Tormod thanked the king for his gift and said: "A good king have we, but hard it is to say how long he will live. It is my boon, O king, that thou lettest us not part either in life or death". The king answered: "We shall now all go together, as long as I can decide it, unless ye part from me". Tormod said: "I hope, my king, whether the peace be better or worse that I may stand by thee as long as I can choose, whatever we hear of Sigvat's faring with 'The Golden Hilted'".[3] Tormod afterwards quoth:

| | |
|---|---|
| Fight-bold king, still will I | Even though we grant the raven |
| Go before thy knee | The corpses of the fallen, we shall |
| Until thou wishest for other | Get hence or lay here; |
| Scald; when expectest thou such? | It cannot be altered. |

209. King Olav now moved his army out through the dale. Dag still went another way with his men. The king did not stop his journey till he came out to Stiklastader.[4] Then they saw the bonders' army; it was much spread about and it was so great a crowd that men went on every footpath and the places were thick with men where great

1 Cf. 'Ynglinga Saga', chapters 28 and 29.   2 *Hild* was a Valkyrie. *Hild's sport* = fighting.   3 Sigvat the Scald was given a *golden-hilted* sword, which roused the envy of the other scalds (cf. chapter 162).   4 Now Upper Stiklestad, above Stiklestad Church.

troops went together. They saw where a band of men were going over from Værdale; they had been out spying and went near where the king's men were; they did not notice it until there was but a short way between them so that the men could recognise each other. It was Rut of Vigg with thirty men. Then the king said that his foreign guests should go against Rut and take his life, and for that deed the men were eager. Then the king said to the Icelanders: "It is told me that there is a custom in Iceland whereby in autumn the bonders are bound to give their huscarls a buck[1] for slaughter; I will now give you a buck to slay". The Icelanders were easy to egg on to that deed and straightway went against Rut with the other men. Rut was slain and all the troop which followed him. The king made a halt and let his army stop when he came to Stiklastader. He bade his men get off their horses and make themselves ready there; the men did as the king said. The lines were drawn up and the standards set up. Dag and his men were not yet come back and they lacked that wing of the army. The king then said that the Uplanders should go forth and take up the standards. "It seems advisable to me", he said, "that my brother Harald[2] be not with us in the fight, for he is a child in years." Harald answered: "I shall indeed be in the fight; but if I am not so strong that I can swing a sword, I know a good plan for that, and it is that my hand shall be bound to the handle; no one shall have a better will to do the bonders scathe than I; I will follow my men". So men say that Harald then quoth this verse:

That wing shall I ward
In which I shall stand;
In blood shall we dye the shields,
And thereof shall the widow be glad.

The young fight-glad prince
Will not turn from the spears
When in battle the sword
Is swung; their men will meet us.

Harald got his wish to be in the battle.

210. Torgils Halmason was the name of a bonder who dwelt at Stiklastader, and he was the father of Grim the Good. Torgils offered the king his help and asked to be with him in the battle. The king thanked him for his offer; "but I will", said the king, "that thou be not in the strife, bonder. Promise us rather to save after the battle our men who are wounded and give a grave to those who are fallen; likewise if it befalls, bonder, that I fall in this fight, grant thou my body the service which is needful, if thou art not forbidden". Torgils promised the king what he craved of him.

211. And when King Olav had drawn up his army he spoke to his men; he said that they should harden their hearts and go boldly

1 The word *hrutr* in O.N. means a 'buck' or 'he-goat'.　　2 King Harald Hardrade.

forth when the strife began. "We have", he said, "a good army and strong, but even though the bonders have somewhat more men, fate will, however, decide the victory. I will make clear that I shall not flee from this fight, whether I win the victory over the bonders or fall in the strife. I will pray for it to happen as God sees it to be to my best advantage. We will put our trust in that we have a better case than the bonders, and that God will save us our possessions after the battle or else, for the loss we get here, give us greater rewards than we ourselves may wish. And if I am to rule after the battle I will reward each of you according to his worth and according as each goes forth in the strife. If we win the victory there will be enough of both land and valuables to share amongst you, that which our foes now have. Let us go forth as hardily as possible in the beginning, for it will soon change if there are great odds against us. We can expect the victory if we act swiftly. But it may fall heavily upon us if we fight until we are weary, so that for this reason men become weak in the fight. We have fewer men than they, so that they can let some go forth while others guard themselves and rest. But if we throng forth so hard that they who are foremost turn away, then will one fall upon the other, and their ill-luck will be so much the greater as they are the more numerous". And when the king ended his speech, his men gave a great cheer and each egged on the other.

212. Tord Folason bore King Olav's standard; and thus says Sigvat the Scald in the poem which he composed about King Olav and made in the manner of the story of the Resurrection:

| | |
|---|---|
| The battle throve and I heard | There Agmund's brother loftily |
| That Tord hardened | Bore the fair golden standard |
| The strife with Olav; | Before the valiant king, |
| There the brave hearts met. | And there this bold man fought. |

213. King Olav himself was so armed that he had a golden helm on his head and a white shield whereon was painted the holy cross in gold. In one hand he had the spear which now stands in Christ Church above the altar; he was girded with a sword which is called *Hneitir*, the sharpest of swords, whereof the handle was bound with gold; he had also a ring-brynie. About this Sigvat says:

| | |
|---|---|
| Olav felled many; | And the Swedes who wandered |
| Often did Digre win | Westward with the mild king, |
| The victory; forward the Sinjor[1] | Waded forth on the bloody |
| Went with his brynie in the strife. | Ways, when the battle waxed. |

1 I.e. the French *Seigneur*. Sigvat the Scald had been to Normandy (cf. chapter 160).

214. And when King Olav had drawn up his army, the bonders were yet come nowhere near them, and then the king said that the army should sit down and rest. The king himself sat down with his army and they sat at their ease. The king leaned over and laid his head on Finn Arneson's knee; sleep fell upon him and some little time went by. Then they saw the bonders' army which was coming against them with their standards raised; there was a mighty host of men. Finn then awoke the king and told him that now the bonders were coming against them. And when the king awoke, he said: "Why dost thou waken me, Finn, and let me not enjoy my dream?" Finn answered: "Thou hast not dreamt such things that it would not be better for thee to wake and make ready for the army which comes against us. Or dost thou not see how far the bonders' troops are now come?" The king answered: "They are not yet so near us that it would not be better that I had slept". Then said Finn: "What didst thou dream of, my king, since thou thoughtest it so great a loss that thou didst not awaken by thyself?" Then the king told his dream; he thought he had seen a high ladder and that he went up it so far that the heavens opened and thither the ladder led: "I was come to the uppermost rung", he said, "when thou wakenedst me". Finn answered, "The dream does not seem so good to me as it does to thee; I think it forecasts thy death, if that which came before thee were aught but the bewilderment of a dream".

215. After King Olav had come to Stiklastader it befell that a man came to him. But it was not strange, for many men came to the king from the lordships, but this man seemed an exception because he was not like the others who had come to the king. He was so tall a man that none of the others came farther than his shoulders; he was very handsome to look upon and had fair hair; he was well-weaponed, having a fine helmet and ring-brynie, and a red shield, and he was girded with an ornamented sword; he had also in his hand a great, gold-bound spear, the shaft of which was so thick that it filled the hand. The man went before the king, greeted him and asked if the king would take his help. The king asked him his name and race and from what land he was. He answered: "I take my stock from Jämtland and Helsingeland, and I am called Arnljot Gellina; but rather would I tell thee that I helped thy men whom thou didst send to Jämtland to gather scot there; I gave them a silver bowl, which I sent thee as a token that I would be thy friend".[1] Then the king asked if Arnljot was a Christian man or not.

1 Cf. chapter 141 about Arnljot Gellina's meeting with the king's messengers.

He said about his faith that he believed in his might and strength. "This faith hath been enough for me up till now; but now I rather think of believing in thee, O king." The king answered: "If thou wilt believe in me, then thou shalt believe in what I teach thee; thou shalt believe that Jesus Christ has shaped heaven and earth and all men, and that after death all men who are good and of true faith shall go to him". Arnljot answered: "I have heard of Christ, but I know not anything of what he hath taken upon himself to do nor where he ruleth. Now will I believe in all that thou tellest me. I will put all the decision into thy hands". Arnljot was afterwards baptised; and the king taught him as much of the faith as seemed to him most needful; he let him stand foremost in the line and before his standard. There also were Gauka Tore and Afrafasti and their followers.

216. Now must we tell about that from which we have turned before, that the landed men and bonders had gathered a mighty army as soon as the king had gone east from Gardarik and was come to Sweden (chapter 195). And when they learned that the king had come west into Jämtland and would go westward over the Kjöl to Værdale, they led their army into Inner Trondheim and there gathered a whole crowd both of freemen and thralls; they went into Værdale and they had there so great an army that there was no man who had ever seen so great a host gathered in Norway before. But it was there, as it always must be in a great army, that the men were of varied worth; there were many landed men and a crowd of mighty bonders, but most of them were small bonders and workmen. The whole body of men was gathered in Trondheim and the troops were hot in their hostility to the king.

217. Canute the Mighty had taken to himself all the land of Norway, as is written about (chapter 171), and thereto he had set Hacon the Jarl over the kingdom. He gave the jarl the court bishop who was called Sigurd, who was of Danish birth and had long been with King Canute. The bishop was a strong-minded man and of fair words; he always supported King Canute in his speeches as much as he could and he was a great foe of King Olav. The bishop was there in the army and often talked to the bonders, egging them on much to withstand King Olav.

218. Sigurd the Bishop spoke at a husthing where a great crowd was present; he began thus: "Here is now come together so great a host that in this poor land it might never befall to see a greater army of countrymen. This great strength should now be to your advantage, for it is needful enough if this Olav does not yet leave off his harrying

you. From his youth he was wont to rob and slay folk and for that he went far about in the lands; but at last he turned hitherwards to this land and began to make himself the foe of those who were the best and the mightiest, and first of all King Canute, whom all who can are most bound to serve. He set himself in Canute's tax lands, and the same he did to Olav the Swedish king; and the jarls Swein and Hacon he drove away from their patrimony. But against his own kinsmen he was, however, most gruesome, for he drove all the kings away

The Danish Bishop Sigurd speaks to the bonders at a husthing

from the Uplands; this, however, was in some measure well done, for they had beforehand broken their faith and their oaths to King Canute and had followed this Olav in every ill-counsel he took up. Their friendship now ended in a fitting manner; he maimed them and took to himself their realms and in that way he cleared all the princely men out of the land. And afterwards ye know well how he bore himself towards the landed men; the best are slain and many have fled the land because of him. He has also gone far about in the land with bands of robbers, has burned the lordships and slain and robbed folk. Who is there here amongst the great men who has not good reason to take vengeance on him? Now he goes with an army of foreigners, and most of them are woodmen and highwaymen and robbers. Think ye that he, who makes such war when all who followed him counselled him from it, will be merciful to you with such evil men? I call it advisable for you to call to mind King Canute's word whereby he counselled you if Olav again sought to come back to the land how ye should hold fast your freedom which King Canute promised you. He bade you withstand and drive from you such wicked bands of men. Now may ye choose to go against them and slay these evil men for the eagles and wolves and leave each man to lie where he is struck down, unless ye would rather drag their bodies out into the holts and cairns; let no man be so bold as to move them to churches, for they are all vikings and evildoers". And when he ended his speech they gave a great cheer and all promised to do as he said.

219. The landed men who were come together there held a meeting and they spoke as to how they should draw up their lines and who was to be leader of the army. Kalv Arneson then said that Harek of Tjotta was best fitted to be leader of this army, "for he is of Harald Hairfair's race; the king bears hatred against him because of Grankel's death, and Harek will be subjected to the greatest hardship if Olav comes back into his might; Harek is well tried in battle and eager for honour". Harek answered that the men were better fitted who were now at their best age; "and I am now old," he said, "and tottering and not well fitted for battle; there is also kinship between me and King Olav, and although he has done little for me, it does not beseem me to go farther in this unrest than any other in our troops. Thou, Tore, art well fitted to be leader when we fight against King Olav; thou hast also matters enough against him: thou hast to avenge on him the loss of thy kin and also that he outlawed thee from all thy possessions. Thou hast indeed promised King Canute and likewise thy kinsmen to avenge Asbiorn. Or dost thou think a better chance than now will be given thee to avenge once and for all these many insults?" Tore answered this speech: "I do not trust myself to bear the standard against King Olav or be the leader of this army. The Tronds have here the greatest strength in men; I know their haughtiness, that they will not obey me or any other Halogaland man. But I do not need to call to my mind the matters for which I seek vengeance. I remember the loss of men, whereby Olav has taken the lives of four men, all noble in honour and kinship: my brother's son Asbiorn, my sister's sons Tore and Grjotgard and their father Ölvir, and each of them I am bound to avenge. And to

speak of myself I may say that I have chosen eleven of the boldest men from my huscarls, and I think we shall not leave it to others to deal King Olav blows, if we get the chance".

220. Kalv Arneson then took up the word: "In the plan we have taken up it is needful for us not to put to ill use this army which has come together. If we hold battle with King Olav, we shall need other things than each man drawing back from taking up responsibility, for we may well think that, although Olav has not many men when put beside this army that we have, their leader cannot, however, be shaken and all his men will be true to him in following him. But if we who should rather be the leaders of our army now waver somewhat and will not strengthen and egg on the army and go in the forefront, then a great number of our men will become uneasy and each will decide for himself. And although a great host is gathered here, we may, however, come into such a test when we meet King Olav and his army that loss of the victory will surely betide us, unless we, the leading men, be hardy and the host move forward all together. But unless this is done, it would be better for us not to risk a fight, and then the easiest choice would be to seek Olav's mercy, even though he seemed hard in smaller matters than will now appear to him. I know, however, that there are such men in his army of whom I shall get quarter if I ask it. Now if ye wish as I do, thou, Tore my kinsman, and thou, Harek, shall go under the standard which we shall all raise up and then follow. Let us all be bold and hardy in this plan we have taken up, so that they shall not find weakness in us, and it will egg the people on if we gladly go to draw up the battle line and urge on the host". And when Kalv had ended his speech, all agreed with his words and said they would have it all as Kalv had counselled them; they all wished Kalv to be leader of the army and divide the men into what troops he would.

221. Kalv set his standard up and placed there under it his own huscarls and likewise Harek of Tjotta and his men. Tore the Hound with his following was at the head of the army before the standards; there also was a chosen troop of bonders who were boldest and best weaponed on both sides of Tore. The line was made both long and thick and in that line were Tronds and Halogalanders.[1] On the right side of this line was a second line, and on the left of the head line the men of Rogaland, Hordaland, Sogn and the Fjords[2] had their line and the third standard.

1 Also called *Haleygers* from Halogaland (North Norway).    2 Nordfjord and Sönd-fjord.

222. There was a man called Thorstein the Shipwright who was a merchant and a good wright, a big and strong man, hardy in all things and a great slayer. He had come into strife with the king, and the king had taken from him a big new trading ship which Thorstein had built; that was as a punishment for Thorstein's violence and also for a thane gild[1] which the king had a right to. Thorstein was there in the army, and he went forth before the line to where Tore the Hound was standing, and he spoke thus: "I will be here in this following with you, Tore, for if Olav and I meet I mean to be the first to bear weapons on him if I can get near enough, and settle with him that ship theft when he robbed me of the ship which was one of the best in the merchant fleet". Tore and his men took Thorstein, and he then went into their following.

223. And when the bonders' line was fixed, the landed men spoke and bade the men of their army give heed to the spot where each man had to stand and under or near which standard each man should be, and how far he should stand from the standard. They bade the men be bold and sharp in going into the lines when the horns sounded and the war blasts were heard, and then go forth in battle formation, for they had still a long way to lead the army forward and it was to be expected that the lines would slacken on the march. Then they egged on the men. Kalv said that all the men who had wrongs and vengeance to give back to King Olav should now go forth under those standards which would make for King Olav's standard, and now call to mind the harm he had done them. They would, he said, have no better chance again for avenging their wrongs and freeing themselves in such a way from the constraint and thraldom which he had laid on them; "he will be a wicked fellow," he said, "who does not fight like the boldest, for ye have matters enough against those who will fight against you; they will not spare you if they can get at you". There was a great cheer raised for his speech, and now a great din and egging on was heard through all the army.

224. The bonders afterwards moved their army to Stiklastader; and thither was King Olav also come with his army. Foremost in the army Kalv and Harek went forth with the standard. And when the armies met, they did not straightway fall to battle, for the bonders waited to go in, because their men had not gone forward alike and they waited for those who came up later. Tore the Hound had gone last of all with his following, for he had to see that the men did not

---

1 In O.N. *þegngildi*, i.e. compensation or fine to the king for killing a *þegn* or king's subject (cf. also chapter 136).

fall behind when the battle cry went up or when the foe was seen; Kalv and Harek waited for Tore. To urge on their men in the strife, the bonders had as their war cry "Forward, forward, bonders". King Olav did not go forward either, because he was waiting for Dag and the strength of men which followed him. But then the king's men saw where Dag's troop was. It is said that the bonders had no fewer than a hundred hundred men,[1] but thus quoth Sigvat:

Sore is my sorrow that the king,  
Who swung the gold-decked  
Sword handle, brought  
Little gathering from the east.

Therefore the bonders won:  
They were double as many:  
It was to Olav's scathe.  
I charge no man with cowardice.

The bonders' army

225. When the two armies stood still and men recognised each other, the king said: "Why art thou there, Kalv? We parted friends in Möre in the south. Ill it beseems thee to fight against us or shoot hostile shots into our army, for here are thy four brothers". Kalv answered: "Many things now go otherwise than best beseems; ye left us in such a way that it was needful to seek peace with those who came after. Now each must be where he stands. But we might still come to terms if I were to decide". Then Finn answered: "It is to be noted of Kalv that if he speaks well he has it in his mind to do ill". The king spoke: "It may be, Kalv, that thou wilt come to terms, but

1 I.e. 14,400 men.

it does not seem to me that ye bonders act peacefully". Then Torgeir of Kviststader ¹ answered: "You shall now have such a peace as many have before had from you, and that will you now have to atone for". The king answered: "Thou needest not to be so eager to meet us, for thou wilt not get the victory over us this day. I have raised thee to power from being a small man".

226. Then Tore the Hound went forth with his following before the standard and shouted: "Forward, forward, bonders!" They set up their war cry and shot with both arrows and spears. The king's men now shouted their war cry and when it was ended they egged each other on as they had been taught beforehand; they said: "Forward, forward, Christ's men, cross men, king's men!"² And when the bonders heard that, they who stood in the wings of the line shouted the same as they had heard the king's men shout. And when the other bonders heard it they thought it was the king's men and they bore down with their weapons upon them; they fought against each other and many fell ere they knew. The weather was fair and the sun shone clearly. But when the battle began a redness came over the heavens and likewise over the sun, and before it ended it grew as murk as night.³ King Olav had drawn up his lines where there was a hill, and his men stormed down on the bonders' army and thronged forth so hardily that the bonders' line bent so that the van of the king's line now stood where beforehand the rearguard of the bonders' army had stood. Many of the bonders were ready to flee, but the landed men and the landed men's huscarls stood firm and there was now a very sharp battle. Thus sayeth Sigvat:

| | |
|---|---|
| The earth lay wide spread | When the bowmen |
| Under the feet of the men. | With their bright helms |
| The brynied troops burst | Early rushed down. Great |
| Abruptly forth into battle, | Was the fight at Stiklastader. |

1 *Kviststader*, now Kvistad on the Inderöy.   2 In O.N. *Fram, Fram, Kristsmenn, Krossmenn, Konungsmenn.*   3 According to the Norwegian Professor Hansteen's calculations, made about a hundred years ago, the eclipse of the sun visible at Stiklestad occurred a month later, viz. the 31st of August. This has given rise to a certain amount of controversy and some contend that the battle was fought on the 31st of August instead of the 29th of July, 1030. The weight of evidence is, however, strongly against this theory. Others contend that Snorre must have been misled by Sigvat the Scald about the light vanishing. This is also unlikely because Snorre could not have attached so much importance to what Sigvat wrote after he came back to Norway from Rome, where he was when the battle was fought. Snorre has written so fully about this battle that he no doubt had information from other sources about everything that happened, including the alleged eclipse of the sun, and he had certainly good knowledge of the land at Stiklestad and its surroundings. The battle must have been greatly talked about and have excited everybody's imagination

The landed men egged on their men and thronged forth. About this Sigvat speaks:

| | |
|---|---|
| In the midst of the folk lines | There the bold men met; |
| The Tronds' standard fared forth, | The bonders rued that deed. |

Then the bonders' army came forth on all sides; they who stood foremost struck blows, they who were next thrust with spears, and all who came up behind, shot with spears or arrows or cast stones or hand axes or javelins. The battle soon grew bloody and many fell on both sides. In the first spell there fell Arnljot Gellina, Gauka Tore, and Afrafasti and all their following; but each of them had felled one man or two and some several. Therefore the troop before the king's standard was thinned. The king then bade Tord bear the standard forth, and the king himself followed the standard with the troop of men whom he had chosen to be near him in the strife; the men who were in his following were the boldest with weapons and the best fitted out. About this Sigvat says:

| | |
|---|---|
| My liege, I heard, | His standard; forward rushed |
| Went to the fore nearest | The staff; the strife was strong. |

King Olav went forth from his wall of shields and foremost in his line, and when the bonders beheld his face they were afraid and their hands fell down. About this Sigvat says:

| | |
|---|---|
| 'Twas grim, indeed, I trow, | The Trondmen dared not |
| For those fighting men | To look at his serpent-gleaming |
| To look into the keen eyes | Eyes. The lord of the hersers |
| Of the battle-happy Olav. | Seemed terrifying to them. |

Then the strife grew very hard and the king himself went forth hardily into the thick of the fight. Thus sayeth Sigvat:

| | |
|---|---|
| With shield in his hand he dyed | And the prince who was eager |
| His sword in the blood of the men, | In the hard play of the irons, |
| When the troops of the bonders | Let the red brown swords |
| Made for the dear king. | Fall on the crowns of the Tronds. |

227. King Olav now fought very boldly; Torgeir of Kviststader, the landed man who is mentioned above (chapter 225), he struck across the face, cutting asunder the nose guard of his helmet and cleaving his head down by the eyes so that it almost fell off. And when he fell, the king said: "Is it not true, as I told thee, Torgeir, that thou shouldest not win in thy meeting with me?" At that

at the time, and it is highly probable that certain exaggerations about the sun vanishing and that "it grew as murk as night" found favour with the ecclesiastics and populace and became general knowledge which everybody believed.

moment Tord thrust the staff of the standard down so hard that it stood upright; Tord had then got his death wound and he fell there under the standard. There also Torfinn Munn and Gissur Gulbra fell; two men had come upon Tord, but he had slain one and wounded the other before he fell. Thus sayeth Hofgard Rev:[1]

| | |
|---|---|
| Against two fast fighters | A death blow he dealt one; |
| The warrior had to strive: | The other one he wounded. |

It befell then, as is mentioned above, that the heavens cleared, but the sun went out of sight and it grew dark. About this Sigvat says:

| | |
|---|---|
| It is called no little | Strange signs befell |
| Wonder, that the sun | That day before the king: |
| Though unclouded could not | The light vanished; |
| Shine warmly on the men. | I heard it in the east. |

At this time Dag Ringson came up with the troop he had, and he began to draw up his army and raise the standard. But, because it was very dark, this was not done speedily, for they knew not surely who stood against them. They turned, however, to where the men of Rogaland and Hordaland stood opposite them. Many of these happenings befell about the same time, though some were a little before or after.

228. Kalv and Olav were the names of two kinsmen of Kalv Arneson; they stood on one side of him and were big strong men. Kalv was the son of Arnfinn Armodson, whose brother was Arne Armodson. On the other side of Kalv Arneson, Tore the Hound went forth. King Olav struck Tore the Hound over the shoulders; the sword did not bite, but it looked as if smoke came out of the reindeer skin coat. About this Sigvat speaks:

| | |
|---|---|
| The mild king himself best | When the battle leader |
| Noticed that the strong spell | Struck the Hound over the shoulders |
| Of the troll-wise Finns | With his gold-decked sword |
| Strengthened the big Tore, | (Blunt, it would not bite). |

Tore struck at the king and they exchanged blows, but the king's sword would not bite when it struck the reindeer skin coat; Tore, however, was wounded in the hand. Again Sigvat quoth:

| | |
|---|---|
| I heard this from home: | When that warrior who went forth |
| The man who said that Tore | Dared to lift his sword |
| Was lacking in courage, denied | Against the king. Who might have |
| The deftness of the hard-striking Tore, | Seen a greater deed? |

---

[1] *Hofgard* is a farm by Snefjeldnes (Iceland).

The king said to Björn the Marshal: "Slay thou the Hound, as this iron bites not". Björn turned the axe in his hand and struck with the hammer end of it; the blow fell on Tore's shoulder and was very mighty so that Tore staggered under it; and at the same moment the king turned against Kalv's kinsmen, Kalv and Olav, and gave Olav his death wound. Tore the Hound then struck with his spear at Björn the Marshal in his middle and gave him his death wound. Then Tore said: "Thus we stick bears". Thorstein the Shipwright

King Olav's death

struck with his axe at King Olav and the blow fell on his left leg above the knee. Finn Arneson straightway slew Thorstein. But after that wound, the king leaned up against a stone, cast away his sword and bade God help him. Then Tore the Hound struck at him with his spear and the thrust went under the brynie up into his maw. Kalv then struck him and the blow fell on the left side of his neck, though men are not agreed which Kalv it was who wounded the king.[1] These three wounds brought about King Olav's fall. And after his death most of the followers fell who had gone

1 Whether it was Kalv Arneson or his kinsman Kalv Arnfinnson.

forth with the king. Biarne Gullbrarscald quoth this about Kalv Arneson:

Thou, battle-happy, wouldst ward
The land in fight against Olav.
Thou didst strive with the noble
King (I have heard it for a truth).

To the fore thou wentest in
Stiklastader underneath the standard.
It is true that thou didst fight
Till the king was fallen.

Sigvat the Scald quoth this verse about Björn the Marshal:

I know that Björn as well as
Marshals of olden times knew
How it was good to keep
Their hearts full towards their liege.

With the faithful men
In the host he fell
Near the head of the king,
The honoured ruler; I praise such death.

229. Dag Ringson now upheld the strife and made the first onset so hardily that the bonders turned back and some turned in flight. A great crowd of bonders fell, besides these landed men, Erlend of Gerde and Aslak of Finnöy, and the standard they had held was now struck down. Then was the battle very fierce; it was called *Dag's Spell*. Kalv Arneson, Harek of Tjotta and Tore the Hound then turned against Dag, with the line which followed them. Dag was overpowered and he turned in flight with all the men who were left behind. Where the crowd of men fled there is a dale road and here many fell and the men were scattered on both sides. Many men were badly wounded, and many were so tired that they were fit for nothing. The bonders pursued the fleeing but a short way, for their leaders soon turned to the place where the fallen lay, as many of them would there see to their friends and kinsmen.

230. Tore the Hound went to where King Olav's body lay and attended to it: he laid the body down, straightened it and spread a sheet over it, and when he dried the blood off the face, the king's countenance was—he said afterwards—as red in the cheeks as if he were asleep; and it was much brighter than before when he was alive. The king's blood came on Tore's hand and trickled to the palm where he had been wounded, and from that moment there was no need to bind up the wound, so quickly did it heal. About this happening Tore himself bore witness to each and all when the holiness of King Olav was known. Tore the Hound was the first to uphold the holiness of King Olav of all the great men who had been in the host which withstood him.

231. Kalv Arneson searched for his brothers who were fallen there. He found Torberg and Finn, and it is the tale of men that Finn cast a sword after him and would slay him; he spoke hard words to

him and called him a peace dastard and a king betrayer. Kalv gave no heed to this, but had Finn and likewise Torberg borne away from the field of battle. Their wounds were then looked over, but they had no deadly wounds; they had fallen down from the burden of their weapons and from weariness. Kalv then sought to move his brothers down to a ship and he himself went with them. And as soon as he turned away, all the bonders whose homes were in the neighbourhood also turned away, except those who were busying themselves with their kinsmen or friends who were wounded or with the bodies of those who were fallen. The wounded men were moved home to the garths so that every home was full of them, and over some a tent was pitched outside. And strange as it seemed that so many had gathered in the bonders' army, it seemed to men even stranger that the gathering broke up so speedily; the reason for this was that most of the host had gathered there from the lordships and were yearning for home.

232. The bonders who had their homes in Værdale went to meet their leaders, Harek and Tore, and complained to them of their troubles; they said: "These men who have fled hence will go up through Værdale and will deal ill with our garths; and we dare not go home so long as they are here in the dale. Now do ye so well that ye go after them with an army and let no man escape, for such a fate would they have thought of for us if they had won in the meeting with us, and so may they still do, if we meet them later and if they have a greater might than we. It may be that they will stay in the dale if they expect they have nothing to fear. Then will they straightway go wildly through our settlement". The bonders spoke with many words about this, and with great eagerness they egged on their leaders to go and slay the men who had escaped. And when the leaders talked about it amongst themselves they thought there was much truth in what the bonders said. They agreed that Tore the Hound and his men should go on the journey with the Værdale men; he had six hundred (seven hundred and twenty) men who were his own. They went when night began to fall. Tore did not stop his journey until he came to Sula during the night, and there he heard tidings that Dag Ringson and many bands of King Olav's men had come there that evening. These men had stayed there for their night meal and had afterwards gone up the fell. Tore then said he would not run after them over the fells; he turned back down the dale and they had but few men slain. The bonders then went to their homes, and the day after Tore and his men went out to their ships. And the king's men

who were able saved themselves by hiding in the woods, and some by getting help from the men in the neighbourhood.

233. Harald Sigurdson[1] was sorely wounded; but Ragnvald Bruceson brought him in the night after the battle to a certain bonder, who received him and secretly healed his wounds. Afterwards the bonder got his son to follow him. They travelled unnoticed over the fells and waste lands and came forth to Jämtland. Harald Sigurdson was fifteen winters old when King Olav fell. Harald found Ragnvald Bruceson in Jämtland, and they travelled together to Gardarik[2] to King Jarisleiv, as is mentioned in Harald Sigurdson's History.

234. Tormod Kolbrunarscald was in the battle under the king's standard. And when the king was fallen and the strife was most furious the king's men fell one after another and most of those who stood were wounded. Tormod was sorely wounded; he then did like all the others and turned back from the place where the peril of their lives was greatest; some ran. Then the struggle which is called *Dag's Spell* came on and the king's men who could handle their weapons went thither, but Tormod went not into the fight, for through wounds and weariness he was then too weak to fight. He remained with his comrades, however, although he could do nothing. He was wounded in the left side by an arrow; he broke off the shaft and went off from the battle and got to the houses and to a lathe; it was a big building. Tormod had a sword in his hand, and when he went in a man came out to meet him, saying: "It is grievous, so horrible a din there is inside, with anguish and howling. It is a great shame that great fellows cannot thole their wounds. It may be that the king's men went forth well, but they do not bear their sores like men". Tormod answered: "What is thy name?" He called himself Kimbi; and Tormod asked: "Wert thou in the battle?" "I was with the bonders, as was best". "Art thou wounded?" said Tormod. "A little," said Kimbi; "and wast thou in the fight?" Tormod answered: "I was with those who had it best". Kimbi saw that Tormod had a gold ring on his arm, and said: "Thou art a king's man, well enough; give me the ring and I will hide thee. The bonders will slay thee if thou comest in their path". Tormod said: "Take thou the ring, if thou canst; now have I lost more." Kimbi stretched his hand forward to take the ring, and Tormod swung his sword and struck off his hand; and it is said that Kimbi bore his wound no better than those whom he had before carped at. Kimbi went away and Tormod sat down in the lathe; he sat there for a while and

1 The later Harald Hardrade (cf. chapter 196).  2 I.e. Russia.

listened to the talk of the men. Their talk was mostly about what each had said whom they had seen in the battle; they talked about the attacks of the men. Some praised most King Olav's courage, but some named others no less. Then quoth Tormod:

| | |
|---|---|
| Olav's heart was fiery; | I saw all the warriors |
| The bloody steel did bite. | Spare themselves but the king, |
| Forth he hied to Stiklastader, | In the fast downpour of arrows; |
| Where his men fought. | Yet most were hard in strife. |

235. Tormod then went away to a little room which he entered. Many were already there, sorely wounded men, and there was present a woman[1] who bound up their wounds. A fire was burning on the floor and she warmed water wherewith to wash their wounds; Tormod sat down by the door. One came out and the other went in of those who were busying themselves with the wounded men. One of them turned to Tormod, looked at him and said: "Why art thou so pale? Art thou wounded and why dost thou not ask for a leech?" Then Tormod quoth a verse:

| | |
|---|---|
| I have no fresh hue, | Generous woman! The wound |
| But the fair, slim woman | In me was caused by |
| Herself hath a ruddy husband.[2] | The deep track of Dag's Spell |
| Few bother about my wounds. | And the Danish weapons' smart. |

Tormod then stood up and went to the fire where he stood for a while. The leech said to him: "Thou, man, go out and fetch me the wood which lies outside the door!" He went out, brought in an armful of wood and cast it down on the floor. The leech looked at his face and said: "Strangely pale is this man. Why art thou so?" Then quoth Tormod:

| | |
|---|---|
| The noble woman wonders | Through me the curved steel |
| That we are so wan. | Went, mightily driven. |
| Few grow fair of wounds; | Keenly hath the perilous iron |
| I found them in the arrow-fall. | Pierced near my heart, I think. |

Then said the leech: "Let me see thy wounds and I will attend to them". He sat down and took off his clothes. When the leech saw his wounds, she looked carefully at the wound in his side; she noticed that therein stood a bit of iron but knew not for sure what path the iron had taken. In a stone kettle she had put leeks and other

---

1 It is interesting to note that the Old Norsemen had women to attend to their wounded.
2 *Husband* in O.S. is *husbondi*. *Husbonde* in M.S. is not used in the same sense as the English *husband*.

grass,[1] and cooked them together; she gave it to the wounded men to eat and so tried to find out if they had deep wounds, for she could notice the smell of the leek coming out of a deep wound. She brought it to Tormod and bade him eat. He answered: "Take it away; I have not groats-sickness". She took a pair of tongs to draw out the iron, but it was fast and would not come out; it stood but a little way out, for the wound was swollen. Then said Tormod: "Cut the flesh away down to the iron, so that thou canst get at it well with the tongs; then give them to me and let me wrench it". She did as he said. Then Tormod took the gold ring off his hand and gave it to the leech, bidding her do with it what she would; "a good possession it is," he said, "King Olav gave me this ring this morning". Tormod afterwards took the tongs and wrenched the arrow out; there were barbs on it and on these lay the fibres of the heart, some red, some white. And when he saw it, he said: "Well hath the king fed us; fat am I still about the roots of the heart!" He then fell back and was dead. Here ends the tale of Tormod.

236. King Olav fell on a Wednesday *quarto kalendas Augusti* (29th July); it was near midday when they met, and they came into battle before the afternoon;[2] the king fell before nones and the darkness lasted from early afternoon till nones. Sigvat the Scald tells about the outcome of the battle:

Hard is the loss of the foe
Of the Angles,[3] since
The warriors slew our king,
When the hard shields were broken.

The sword time robbed
Olav's life, where the host cleft
The shields; only Dag
Was able to flee.

Also he quoth this:

Folk had not before
Known of such a strength
Of bonders or hersers.
They brought about the king's death.

Hard it is to hear
That sword-swingers could fell
Such a mighty king as Olav.
Many drengs lost their lives.

The bonders robbed not the fallen, but straightway after the battle it rather happened that fear fell on many who had been against the king. They held fast by their ill will, however, and decided amongst themselves that the men who had fallen with the king should not get such attentions or such graves as beseemed good men; they called them all robbers and outlaws. But the men who were mighty and

1 In O.N. *lauk oc önnor grös*. In M.S. onions are called *lök*, whilst leeks are called *purre*.
2 *Midmunde*, midway between midday (12 noon) and nones (3 p.m.).    3 Sigvat the Scald must mean the Anglo-Danes, as King Olav made peace with King Ethelred and supported him against the Danes in England (cf. p. 223).

who had kinsmen there amongst the fallen gave no heed to this; they moved their kinsmen to the churches and had them buried.

237. Torgils Halmason and his son Grim (chapter 210) went to the field of battle in the evening when it was dark; they took King Olav's body and bore it away to where there was a little empty shed on the other side of the garth. They had light and water with them; they took the clothes off the body, washed it and swathed it in linen cloths; they laid it out there in the house and hid it with wood so that

Torgils and Grim bore away King Olav's body

no one could see it, even if people came into the house, and afterwards they went home to the garth. With both armies there had followed the men many tramps and such poor folk who asked for food. And in the evening after the battle many of these kinds of folk had stayed behind, and when it was night they sought lodging for themselves in all the houses, both great and small. There was a blind man, of whom may be told; he was poor and his lad went with him and led him. They went round the garth, looking for lodging. They came to the same empty shed, and the door of it was so low that they had almost to creep in. And when the blind man came into the house, he groped about on the floor, seeking for what he might lie down on. A hat he had on his head and the hat had slipped down over his face when he bent down. He felt with his hands that there was water on the floor. Thereafter he raised his wet hand to put his hat straight and his fingers passed over his eyes. He forthwith got so strong an itching in his eyelids that he rubbed the eyes himself with his wet fingers; he then crawled out of the house and said that they could not lie there, for it was all wet. And when he came out of the house he straightway saw first his hands and then all that was near him—that is all he could see in the darkness of the night. He went home to the garth at once and into the hall and there told all men that he had recovered his sight and was now a sharp-sighted man. Many men there knew that he had long been blind, for he had been there before and had gone about the houses. He said that he first saw when he came out of a little, poor house, "and therein it was all wet," he said; "I groped there with my hands and rubbed my wet hands over my eyes"; he also told where the house stood. And the men who were there and saw these things wondered much at this happening and talked amongst themselves as to what could be in the house. But Torgils the bonder and Grim his son thought they knew how this thing might have come about. They feared much that the king's foes should go and ransack the house. They then slipped away and went to the house and took the body. They moved it out into the garden and hid it there. Afterwards they went to the garth and slept through the night.

238. On the Thursday[1] Tore the Hound came from Værdale to Stiklastader and many folk followed him; many of the bonders' men were still there, too. The battlefield was again cleared and they moved away the bodies of their kinsmen and friends and helped the wounded whom they would heal. A great number of them were now dead after the battle was ended. Tore the Hound went to where the king fell and looked for the body. And when he found it not, he asked if any man could tell him where the body had gone; but no one could say. Then Tore asked Torgils the bonder if he knew anything about where the king's body was. Torgils answered thus: "I was not in the battle and got few tidings from it. Many tales are going round now; it is said that King Olav has been seen in the evening near Stav[2] with a troop of men. But if he is fallen, then your folk have hidden his body in the holts or cairns". But although Tore seemed to know truly that the king was fallen, many, however, held little to it and set out the rumour that the king had gone away from the battle and that it would be but a short while ere he got an army and came against them. Tore then went to his ships and sailed out along the fjord. All the bonders' army began to scatter and they carried away all the wounded men who could be moved.

239. Torgils Halmason and his son had King Olav's body in their keeping and were very sick at heart as to how they should manage things so that the king's foes should not mishandle the body, for they heard such talk from the bonders that if the king's body were found they would bring about the plan of burning it or taking it out to the sea and sinking it. In the night they had both seen something like a taper burning over the place where King Olav's body lay on the battlefield, and likewise afterwards wherever they hid the body they always saw a light at night towards where the king was resting. They

---

1 30th of July.    2 This farm has since been demolished.

were afraid that if the king's foes could see these signs they would look for the body where it was; Torgils therefore wished to move the body away to a place where it would be well hidden. Torgils and Grim made a chest and attended to it very carefully, and therein they laid the king's body. Thereafter they made a second coffin and put straw and stones therein, so as to be the weight of a man, and they carefully locked the chest. And when all the bonders' army had left Stiklastader, Torgils and Grim made themselves ready to go. They took a rowing boat, and in it there were altogether seven or eight men, all kinsmen or friends of Torgils. They secretly moved the king's body to the ship and set the chest down under the floors. The chest with stones in it they also had with them and they placed it on the ship so that all men could see it. Then they went out along the fjord; they had a fair wind and in the evening when it was dark they came out to Nidaros and lay to near the king's jetty. Torgils then sent men up to the town to tell Bishop Sigurd they had come with King Olav's body. And when the bishop heard these tidings he straightway sent his men down to the jetty, where they took a rowing boat, came up by Torgils' ship and asked for the king's body. Torgils and his men then took the chest which stood on the floors and bore it to the boat. These men then rowed out into the fjord and sank the chest there. The night was then dark. Torgils and his men then rowed up the river to the end of the town and lay to by the place called Saurli, which was above the town. They bore the body up into an empty shed, which stood there above the other houses, and there they watched over the body during the night. Torgils went down into the town and got into talk with the men who had been the king's best friends there; he asked them if they would take the king's body, but no man dared do it. Torgils and his men then moved the body up the river and buried it in a sandhill which was there; afterwards they levelled all round it so that folk should not see that the work was new; then they went to their ship, and at once rowed out of the river. They continued their journey until they came home to Stiklastader.

240. Swein, the son of King Canute, and of Algiva, the daughter of Alfrim the Jarl,[1] had been set to rule over Jomsborg in Vendland. But at that time word came to him from his father, King Canute, that he was to go to Denmark, and afterwards to Norway and there take over the rule of the realm of Norway and have the name of King of Norway. Swein went to Denmark and from there he took many

1 Alfhelm, the ealdorman.

men; with him there went Harald the Jarl[1] and many other great men. About this Toraren Praisetongue speaks in the poem which he composed about Swein Algivason and which is called "The song of the Sea-calm":

It is not hidden  
That the Danes gave  
A doughty following  
To the Dagling's prince.  
There was the jarl  

Greatest of all,  
And each man, too,  
Who followed him,  
One dreng better  
Than the other.

Swein then went to Norway and with him went his mother Algiva; he was taken as king at every law thing. He had then come from the south-east to the Vik when the battle took place at Stiklastader and King Olav fell. Swein did not stop his journey until he came north in the autumn to Trondheim where he was taken as king, as in other places.

King Swein brought new laws into the land about many things; they were made after the law of Denmark, though some were much harder. No man was to leave the land unless the king allowed it; and if he went, then all his possessions were to fall to the king. Whoever slew a man was to lose land and valuables. If a man was outlawed and an inheritance fell to him, the king was to have the inheritance. At Yule every bonder was to give the king a measure of malt for every hearth and half a hind quarter of a three-year-old ox— it was called 'garth due'— and a pail of butter, and every housewife was to give him 'housewife's wool', that is, as much unspun flax as could be held between the thumb and the long finger. The bonders were bound to build all the houses which the king would have in his garths. Every seven men should fit out one man for the levy and all males over five winters old were to be reckoned, and to provide oarsmen according to the numbers. Every man who rowed on the sea[2] was to pay the king *landvörðr*[3] wherever he rowed from; and that was five fishes. Every ship which went away from the land was to keep a room for the king. Every man who went to Iceland was to pay land dues, whether he were a native of Norway or of Iceland. Thereto it followed also that Danish men were to be of such worth in Norway that the witness of one of them should over-ride the witness of ten Norsemen. And when these laws were made known to the people, men forthwith began to turn their minds against them and murmured

---

1 Son of Thorkel the High (cf. chapter 183).    2 I.e. in order to fish.    3 *Landvörðr* was a tax paid to the king for warding the land.

amongst themselves; they who had not been planning against King Olav spoke thus: "Now ye men of Inner Trondheim, take friendship and reward from these Danish *Knytling*[1] princes for fighting against King Olav and depriving him of his land. You were promised peace and betterment of your rights, but now ye get constraint and thraldom and great shame and scorn withal". And it was not easy to speak against this. All now saw that they were ill advised, but they had, however, no courage to make a rising against King Swein and mostly because they had given their sons or near kin as hostages to King Canute; and besides, there was no leader for an uprising. They soon had much to say against King Swein; and they gave Algiva most blame, however, for all that they disliked, and then many a man understood the truth about King Olav.

241. This winter the talk arose amongst many men in Trondheim that King Olav was a holy man, and that many tokens witnessing his holiness occurred. Many began praying to King Olav about matters which seemed weightiest to them. Many got help from these prayers, some got their health and some had good luck on their journeys or in other matters as they thought needful.

242. Einar Tambarskelver had come home from the west from England to his garths and he had the land rents which King Canute had given him when they were together in Trondheim; it was almost a jarl's domain. Einar Tambarskelver had not been active in the opposition to King Olav, whereof he praised himself. Einar called to mind that Canute had promised him a jarldom in Norway, and likewise that the king had not kept his promises. Einar was the first among the great men to uphold the holiness of King Olav.

243. Finn Arneson stayed but a short while in Egge with Kalv, for he was very wroth that Kalv had been in the battle against King Olav and for that reason Finn was always speaking hard words to Kalv. Torberg Arneson reined himself in much better than Finn; but Torberg wished to go away home to his garth. Kalv gave his brothers a good longship with all the tackle and other fittings and a good following. Then they went home to their garths. Arne Arneson lay wounded for a long time, but he was healed and free from maiming; in the winter he went south to his garth. All these brothers made peace with King Swein and sat quietly in their homes.

244. The summer after there was much talk about King Olav's holiness, and quite differently did folk speak about the king. Of those who had before gone against him in full enmity and had no

1 *Knytlings* = King Canute's children or descendants.

wish to own the truth about him there were many now who believed it true that the king was probably holy. They then turned their reproaches against the men who had most egged them on to withstand the king. Bishop Sigurd got much blame for that, and they became such great foes to him that he found it advisable to go away westward to England to King Canute. Afterwards the Tronds sent men with word to the Uplands that Bishop Grimkel should come north to Trondheim. King Olav had sent Bishop Grimkel back to Norway when the king went east to Gardarik; since then Bishop Grimkel had been in the Uplands. And when this message came to the bishop he forthwith made himself ready for the journey. The reason the bishop went was also very much that he believed it was true what was told of King Olav's miracles and holiness.

245. Bishop Grimkel went to meet Einar Tambarskelver, who greeted the bishop gladly. They afterwards talked about many things and especially about the great events which had there befallen in the land. They were agreed between themselves in all matters. The bishop then went into the market and the whole crowd greeted him. He asked carefully about the miracles which were told of King Olav and he got to hear much thereof. The bishop afterwards sent word to Stiklastader to Torgils and his son Grim calling them out to meet him in the town. Torgils and his son did not delay that journey, and they went out to the town to the bishop. Then they told him all the remarkable things of which they knew and likewise where they had hidden the king's body. The bishop then sent word for Einar Tambarskelver and Einar came to the town. Einar and the bishop then had a talk with the king and Algiva and bade the king give them leave to take up King Olav's body from the earth. The king gave leave for that and bade the bishop do with it as he would. There was then a great crowd of men in the town. The bishop and Einar and men with them now went to where the king's body was buried and had it dug up. The chest had then almost come up out of the earth. It was the counsel of many men that the bishop should have the king buried in the ground by St Clement's Church; and this was done. Twelve months and five nights[1] were gone when his holy relics were taken up and the chest had almost come out of the earth, and the king's coffin was as new to look upon as if it were newly planed. Bishop Grimkel went to where King Olav's chest was unlocked, and there was a precious fragrance. The bishop then uncovered the king's face, and his countenance was in no wise changed; the

---

[1] 3rd of August, 1031.

cheeks were red as if he had just fallen asleep. They who had seen King Olav when he fell found a great difference in that his hair and nails had grown almost as much as they would have done if he had been alive in this world all the time since his fall. King Swein and all the chiefs who were there then went to see King Olav's body. Then said Algiva: "Very slow doth a body rot in sand; it would not have been so if he had lain in mould". The bishop then took a pair of scissors and cut off some of the king's hair and likewise some of his beard; he had had a long beard, as was the wont of men at that time. Then the bishop said to the king and Algiva: "Now are the king's hair and beard as long as when he died, and since then they have grown as much as ye now see here shorn off". Then Algiva answered: "This hair will seem a holy relic to me if it does not burn in the fire; we have often seen whole and unscathed the hair of men who have been longer in the earth than this man". The bishop then had fire brought in on a censer; he crossed it and put incense therein. He then laid King Olav's hair in the fire. And when all the incense was burned the bishop took up the hair from the fire and it was not burned. The bishop let the king and the other chiefs see it. Then Algiva bade them lay the hair in unhallowed fire. But Einar Tambarskelver bade her be silent and spoke many hard words to her. Then the bishop declared and the king agreed and the folk deemed that King Olav was truly holy. The king's body was then borne into St Clement's Church and placed over the high altar. The coffin was wrapped in a pall[1] and over it was cast a cover of goodly web.[2] And then many kinds of miracles befell at the holy remains of King Olav.

246. On the sandhill wherein King Olav's body had lain in the earth there came up a fair spring and men got their ills healed by that water. The spring was built over and they have always carefully taken heed of it.[3] A small church was first built and the altar set where the king's grave had been, and in that place there now stands Christ Church. Archbishop Eystein had the high altar set in the same place as the king's grave had been, when he raised up the great minster[4] which is now there; in that place also the altar had been in the old Christ Church. So it is said that St Olav's Church now stands where the empty shed had stood in which Olav's body was

1 In O.N. *pell*, an expensive cloth woven in silk.    2 In O.N. *gudvefr*, a costly woven material (cf. 'History of Harald Hairfair', chapter 25).    3 In the cathedral of Trondheim, under the high choir, a spring was found, which is supposed to be connected with the spring found at St Olav's grave.    4 The celebrated cathedral of Trondheim, which was built on the site of Christ Church.

placed in the night; it is now called Olavsli and is in the middle of the town. The bishop took care of King Olav's relics and he cut his hair and nails, for both these grew as they did when he was alive in the world. Thus says Sigvat the Scald:

I lie if Olav had not
Like quick men
Sharp servants.
But I praise most
The waxing of his hair.

Just as his hair grew
On his fair head in Gardar
Where he gave Valdemar[1]
    his sight,
So still grows it now.

Toraren Praisetongue composed about Swein Algivason the poem which is called "The song of the Sea-calm" and therein are these verses:

Now the folk king
Hath got
A seat for himself
In Trondheim.
There he will
His whole life long
Fully rule
O'er his realm.

There, where Olav
Owned his land,
Until he went
Up to heaven.
And there he,
Who before as king
As all men know,
Was living.

Hardly had
Harald's son
Got a home
In the heavenly realm
Ere he became
A mighty man of peace.

There he lies
Whole and pure,
The high-praised king,
With his body,
And there may
Hair and nails
Grow on him
As when he lived.

There the bells
May ring aloud
By themselves
Above the shrine,
For every day
The folk to hear
The clanging bells
Above the king.

And up there
From the altar
Candles burn
Which do please Christ.
So hath Olav
Until his death
Saved his soul
Free from sin.

A host of men
Where the holy
King doth lie
Kneel for help.
Blind and dumb
Seek the king,
And home they go,
Their sickness healed.

Pray thou to Olav,
The man of God,
That he grant thee
His holy spirit;
With God himself
He seeks

1 It is told of St Olav, that he gave back his sight to Valdemar (Vladimir), the eldest son of King Jarisleiv of Russia.

| | |
|---|---|
| Success and peace | Thy own boons |
| For all men, | Before the altar |
| Where thou dost bear | Of the holy scriptures. |

Toraren Praisetongue was then with King Swein and heard of these great signs of King Olav's holiness, that they could hear sounds by heavenly powers above his relics, such as the ringing of the bells and the candles over the altar lighting themselves by heavenly fire. And when Toraren said that, there came to King Olav a crowd of men, halt, or blind, or in any other way sick, and that they went away sound, he did not speak of or mention otherwise than that there must have been a great crowd of men who got their health in the beginning of the working of miracles by St Olav. But only the greatest of King Olav's miracles which have since befallen have been written or told about.

247. Thus say men who reckon carefully that St Olav was king over Norway for fifteen years after Swein the Jarl had left the land; but the winter before that he had taken the name of King of the Uplanders. Sigvat the Scald speaks thus:

| | |
|---|---|
| Olav's proud head | What worthier prince |
| Ruled over this land | Won the world's northern |
| Full fifteen years | End? The king lived |
| Until he found death. | A shorter time than he should. |

According to the saying of the priest Ari the Wise, St Olav was thirty-five years old when he fell. He had then fought twenty great battles. Thus sayeth Sigvat the Scald:

| | |
|---|---|
| Some men did believe in God | On his right hand the bold man |
| ('Twas easy to see the difference). | Bade the Christian men stand. |
| Folk-battles twenty | I pray God to embrace |
| Did the bold king have. | The flight-shy father of Magnus. |

Now have we told a part of King Olav's history about some of the things which befell while he ruled over Norway and likewise about his fall and the revealing of his holiness. Nor shall that be left out which is to his greatest honour—that is, the story of his miracles, even though it is written later in this book.

248. King Swein Canuteson ruled over Norway for some winters. He was childish both in years and counsel. His mother Algiva had most rule in the land, and the men of the land were in many things her foes, both then and ever after. Danish men then had much might over Norway and the men of the land liked it ill. When such talk was brought up, the other men of the land gave the Tronds the blame for having mostly brought it about that King Olav lost the

land and that the men of Norway were come under that evil rule, when constraint and loss of freedom over-ran all the folk, both mighty men and small men and the common people; they said that the Tronds were bound to withstand it, "for they can free us from this kingship". It was also the belief of the men in the land that the Tronds then had the greatest help in Norway from their rulers and from the great crowds of folk who were there. And when the Tronds heard that the men of the land directed this talk against them, they also knew that it was true speech and that they had acted badly in robbing King Olav of life and land; and they also took it for a truth that they had got ill reward for their ill doing. The chiefs now met and held counsel amongst themselves, and Einar Tambarskelver was the leader in these counsels. Thus it was also with Kalv Arneson, that he now found in what a snare he had let himself be caught by the egging on of King Canute. The promises Canute had given Kalv were now all broken, for King Canute had promised Kalv a jarldom and might over the whole of Norway, and Kalv had therefore been head man in holding battle with King Olav and depriving him of his land. But Kalv got no greater name than before and now it seemed that he had been well hoodwinked. Messages now passed between Kalv and his brothers Finn, Torberg and Arne, and their relations were now bettered again.

249. When Swein had been king in Norway for three winters tidings were learned in Norway that a troop was gathered west over the sea, and the leader thereof was one who bore the name of Trygvi; he called himself the son of Olav Trygvason and the English woman, Gyda.[1] And when King Swein heard that a foreign army would come to the land, he bade out men from the north of the land, and most of the landed men went with him from Trondheim. Einar Tambarskelver sat at home and would not go with King Swein. And when King Swein's word came to Kalv in Egge that he should row out to the levy with the king, Kalv took a twenty-bench bark he owned; he went on board with his huscarls, fitted it out as quickly as he could, then sailed out along the fjord, and waited not for King Swein. Kalv sailed south to Möre and did not stop until he came to Giske to his brother Torberg. All these brothers, the sons of Arne, met and held counsel together. After this, Kalv went home to the north. And when he came to Freköysund,[2] King Swein was come there, too, and he lay in the sound with his army. And when Kalv rowed from the south into the sound, they shouted to each other; and the king's men

---

1 Cf. 'History of Olav Trygvason', chapter 32.   2 Cf. p. 418, n. 4.

bade Kalv lay to and follow the king and guard his land. Kalv answered: "I have done enough, if not too much, fighting against my countrymen to win this kingdom for the Danish Knytlings". Kalv's men then rowed on their way northwards, and he went on still farther till he came home to Egge. None of the sons of Arne rowed to that levy with the king. King Swein sailed southwards by the land with his army. And when he did not hear anything about the army that was come from the west, he sailed south to Rogaland and right on to Agder, for folk guessed that Trygvi would first make eastward for the Vik, where his forefathers had been and had had most power and where he had a great many kinsmen.

250. When King Trygvi sailed from the west he came with his fleet to Hordaland. He then heard that King Swein had sailed south and so King Trygvi also sailed south to Rogaland. And when King Swein got news about Trygvi's arrival, he turned northwards with his army and he and Trygvi met in Bokn in Soknarsund[1] near the spot where Erling Skjalgson fell. There was a great and hard struggle. Men say that Trygvi shot spears with both hands at a time; he said: "Thus my father taught me to chant!" His foes said that he might be the son of a priest, but he praised himself that he was more like King Olav Trygvason; Trygvi was also the doughtiest of men. In that struggle, King Trygvi and many of his men fell; some fled and some got quarter. Thus it is said in Trygvi's flokk[2]:

Eager for honour, Trygvi
Hied to battle from the north;
But King Swein sailed
To meet him from the south.

There I was near the strife;
It was a fight-meeting.
Many a man there lost
His life when the sword clang was heard.

It is also told about this strife in the flokk[2] which was composed about King Swein:

Woman! It was not like Sunday
When the maid in the morn
Bears ale or leek to the man
(Many swains were wounded).

When King Swein bade
His drengs to lash
The stems together and the raven
Got raw flesh to eat.

King Swein still ruled over the land after this battle, and there was good peace. The next winter King Swein stayed in the south of the land.

---

1 Cf. p. 414, n. 1, regarding *Soknarsund*.    2 In O.N. *flokkr* was a short poem without a refrain. It was considered disrespectful to offer a flokk to a king. It was good enough for a jarl or an untitled chief.

251. This winter Einar Tambarskelver and Kalv Arneson had meetings and took counsel together; they met in Kaupang.[1] A messenger then came from King Canute to Kalv Arneson and he brought King Canute's word that Kalv should send him three dozen axes and they were to be chosen of the best. Kalv answered: "No axe will I send to King Canute; but tell him that I will get his son Swein so many axes that he shall not be thought to lack them".

252. Early in spring Einar Tambarskelver and Kalv Arneson prepared for their journey; they had a great band of men, the best chosen of all who were in Trondlaw. In the spring they went east over the Kjöl to Jämtland, then to Helsingeland, and so they came forth into Sweden where they got themselves ships. In the summer they went east to Gardarik and in the autumn they came to Aldeigjaborg.[2] They sent messengers up to Holmgard[3] to King Jarisleiv with word bidding Magnus the son of St Olav, that they would welcome him and follow him to Norway, that they would grant him help so that he could win his father's inheritance and that they would make him king over the land. And when this message came to King Jarisleiv, he held counsel with the queen and his chiefs. They then agreed to send bidding to the Norsemen, and they were called to meet King Jarisleiv and Magnus; they got leave for their journey. And when they were come to Holmgard they all swore allegiance so that the Norsemen who were come submitted to Magnus and became his men, and Kalv and all his men who had been against King Olav at Stiklastader were also bound with oaths. Magnus gave them promises of peace and bound it with oaths that he would be true to them if he got the rule and the kingdom of Norway; he was to be the foster-son of Kalv Arneson, and Kalv was obliged to do everything which Magnus thought would increase his power in the kingdom.

1 I.e. Trondheim.   2 *Aldeigjaborg* was the town Aldagen or Ladoga, situated by the River Volkhov, which flows into Lake Ladoga.   3 I.e. Novgorod.

## CHRONOLOGY

ST OLAV. BORN 995. KING OF NORWAY 1015–30

1007. St Olav leaves Norway and harries in Denmark, Sweden and Finland.

1008. St Olav in Denmark and Friesland.

1009. Arrival of St Olav and Thorkel the High at Sandwich (in Kent).
Attack on Canterbury and Hampshire.

1010. St Olav goes to Oxford, and returns to the Thames during Lent. After Lent, St Olav and Thorkel proceed up the River Orwell and fight against Ulfkel Snilling at Ringmere Heath (in East Wretham), afterwards returning to the Thames.

1011. King Ethelred sues for peace.
Canterbury again attacked and Archbishop Alfhege executed.

1012. St Olav and Thorkel the High make peace with King Ethelred.

1013. In the spring, Swein Forkbeard lands in England and encamps at Gainsborough.
Swein attacks London and is repulsed by King Ethelred assisted by St Olav and Thorkel.
In the autumn, St Olav leaves England at the request of Richard II, Duke of Normandy, and helps him to conquer Brittany. Afterwards St Olav goes south to Aquitania and Spain.

1014. St Olav returns to Normandy (in the spring).
Death of Swein Forkbeard (on the 2nd of February).
St Olav returns to England with King Ethelred's son Edward (the later Edward the Confessor).
St Olav fights against the Danes in England, and leaves for Norway in the autumn.
Arrival in Norway at the island of Sæla (outside Stad).

1015. Battle of Nesjar.
St Olav elected King of Norway.

1016. Death of King Ethelred.
St Olav goes to the Vik, conquers Ranrik and builds the merchant town of Sarpsborg.

1017. St Olav treats with Ragnvald the Jarl about the marriage of the daughter of the King of Sweden.

1019. St Olav marries Astrid, the daughter of the Swedish king.
1021. Bruce, Earl of Orkney, and his son Ragnvald and Earl Torfinn arrive in Norway.
The Orkneys again become tributary to the Crown of Norway.
The Upland people are baptised.
1024. Birth of Magnus the Good.
1025. King Canute's messengers come to St Olav.
1026. King Canute goes back to England from Denmark.
1027. King Canute returns to Denmark and fights St Olav and King Anund of Sweden at the Holy River.
Birth of William the Conqueror at Falaise.
1028. King Canute subjugates Norway and appoints Hacon the Jarl regent.
1029. St Olav sails north along the coast and meets Erling Skjalgson in Soknarsund, where Erling falls after a fierce fight.
St Olav leaves Norway for Russia.
1030. Björn the Marshal visits St Olav in Russia, and St Olav returns to Norway.
Battle of Stiklastader, and death of St Olav (29th of July).
Swein (King Canute's son) becomes King of Norway.
1031. Harald Hardrade in Russia.
St Olav's relics interred in Trondheim.
1035. Magnus the Good returns to Norway and Swein Canuteson leaves the country.

# IX

# THE HISTORY OF MAGNUS THE GOOD

1. After Yule, Magnus Olavson went west from Holmgard down
to Aldeigjaborg. There he and his men began to fit out their ships
when the ice thawed in the spring. About this Arnor Jarlascald says
in Magnus' drapa:

| | |
|---|---|
| Now I believe that he who swung | This foe of the gold was not |
| The sword in bloody battle | Eleven winters old, |
| Bade his men, as indeed I | At the time when the Horders' lord |
| Knew, make themselves ready; | Brought the warship from Gardar. |

In the spring King Magnus sailed west to Sweden. Thus sayeth
Arnor:

| | |
|---|---|
| The young sword-swinger | The king on his ice-covered ship |
| Called men out to the meeting. | Cut through the sea from the east; |
| The bold bodyguard bore | Mighty winds bore |
| Their war clothes to the ship. | The prince to Sigtun. |

Here it should be said that when King Magnus went from the
east he sailed first to Sweden and up to Sigtun.[1] At that time
Emund Olavson was king in Sweden, and there too was Queen
Astrid whom King Olav, his father, had had. She greeted her step-
son Magnus exceedingly well and she had a numerous thing called
forthwith in the place which is called Hangrar.[2] And at that thing
Astrid spoke and said: "Here is come to us now the saintly King
Olav's son, who is called Magnus: he will go now to Norway to seek
his father's inheritance. I have great grounds for strengthening him
for this journey, for he is my step-son as is well known to all, both to
Swedes and to Norsemen. Neither men over whom I have power
nor goods shall I spare, so that his strength may be great, and all
those who make ready to go on this journey with him shall have my
full friendship. I will also make it known that I myself will go on this
journey with him. Then it will be clear to all that for his help I do
not spare anything which I can grant him". She talked long and
wisely, and when she ended, many answered and said that the Swedes
had gone to Norway on a journey of little honour when they followed
his father, King Olav: "and there is nothing better to be expected

1 Cf. 'Ynglinga Saga', p. 4, n. 4.    2 Unidentified.

with this king", they said, "and so the men have little wish for this journey". Astrid answered: "All those who will pass for bold men will not fear such. But if any man has lost his kinsmen or himself got wounds with King Olav, then it is a manly deed to go to Norway to avenge them". Astrid went so far with her words and her help that a great crowd of men gave themselves up for the journey with Astrid in order to follow Magnus to Norway. About this Sigvat the Scald says:

Highly with our vows
For rich gifts we will pay.
The daughter of Olav
Whom Digre King had,
A numerous host of Swedes
Held a thing out on Hangrar,
At that time when in the east
Astrid spoke for Olav's son.
She could not have given
The good Swedes better counsel
Even if the very manly
Magnus was her own son.

Next after mighty Christ
She most brought it about
That Magnus might embrace
The whole of Harald's kingdom.
The mild Magnus may thank
Astrid for such mighty help:
The friend of the men left it
In her hands; it gladdened us;
The wise woman has thus
Helped her step-son with counsel,
As few others did: the truth
I tell to her honour.

Thus sayeth Tjodolv the Scald in Magnus' flokk:

At this time thou didst let out
The speedy cutter and the ship with
    thirty
Rowing benches to glide on the sea:
The sailyard hummed in the blast.

On the way the mighty gusts
Spared not to strain the mast;
In Sigtun the proud bodyguard
Lowered the striped sail.

2. Magnus Olavson went on his journey from Sigtun and he then had many men whom the Swedes had got for him. They went on foot through Sweden and so to Helsingeland. Thus sayeth Arnor Jarlascald:

Axe-bearer! In the Swedish home-
    steads
Thou didst since bear the red shields.
Thou didst get great help,
For the landsmen gave themselves to
    thee.

The wolf-feeder was widely known!
From the east the chosen troops
    streamed
With white shields and seasoned
    spears
To the thing and the king's following.

Magnus Olavson then went west through Jämtland, and over the Kjöl and down into Trondheim, and straightway all the land folk greeted him well. And as soon as King Swein's men learned that King Olav's son Magnus was come thither into the land, they all fled far and wide and saved themselves. No opposition was then offered to King Magnus. King Swein was in the south of the land. Thus sayeth Arnor Jarlascald:

| | |
|---|---|
| Thou camest from the east into the Trondsteads. | Bold prince, thy foes Did feel ill-luck a-coming; |
| With the most dreaded helm of all. | Thy foes affrighted must save |
| Friend of the ravens! Thy foes | Their lives by fleeing thence. |
| Fled afeared—so it is told. | |

3. Magnus Olavson went out with his men to Kaupang[1] and there he was well received. He then had the Örething[2] summoned; and when the bonders came to the thing Magnus was taken as king over all the land, even as far as his father King Olav had had it. King Magnus afterwards took himself a bodyguard and chose the landed men; everywhere in the lordships he set men as stewards and sheriffs. Forthwith in the autumn King Magnus called out a levy of troops from all over Trondheim; it went well with him in gathering men and with this army he afterwards went south in the land.

4. King Swein Algivason was in South Hordaland when he heard of this talk of war. He forthwith had the war arrow cut up and sent forth from him to the four corners of his land. He called to him the bonder folk and bidding followed therewith that all the common folk and their ships were to come out and guard the land with him. All the men who were in the king's neighbourhood came to him. The king then held a thing and talked with the bonders; he put before them his business and said that he would go against King Magnus, the son of King Olav, and hold battle with him, if the bonders would follow him. The king spoke somewhat short and the bonders made little cheering at his speech. Afterwards the Danish chiefs who were with the king held long and wise talks, but the bonders answered and spoke in reply; many said that they would follow King Swein and fight with him, but some declined; others said nothing at all and some said they would go to King Magnus as soon as they could. Then King Swein answered: "It seems to me that here are come few of those bonders to whom we have sent bidding; but these bonders who are here tell us themselves that they will follow King Magnus. These men seem to me as if they will be of as much help as those who say they will sit at home and as those who are silent. And of those who they will follow us it may well be that every other man, if not more, will not be of use to us if we come to battle with King Magnus. It is my counsel that we do not put our trust in these

1 I.e. Trondheim.   2 *Örething*, situated in Trondheim by the mouth of the River Nid, was generally used for doing homage and swearing fealty to the king.

bonders, but rather that we go where all the folk are trusty and true to us; there we have strength enough to win this land for ourselves". And as soon as the king had uttered this opinion, all his men followed his counsel. They turned their ships about and hoisted sail; King Swein then sailed east along the coast and he did not stop until he came to Denmark, where he was welcomed heartily. And when Swein met his brother Hardicanute[1] the latter bade King Swein have rule with him in Denmark, and Swein accepted it.

5. In the autumn King Magnus went right east to Land's End and everywhere in the land he was taken as king; all the land folk were glad that Magnus had become king. The same autumn Canute the Mighty died in England *idus Novembris* (13th of November) and he was buried at Winchester; he had then been king of Denmark for twenty-seven years, and king of both Denmark and England for twenty-four years,[2] and king of Norway for seven years. Canute's son Harold was then taken as king in England. The same winter Swein Algivason died in Denmark. About King Magnus Tjodolv spoke thus:

Feeder of the eagles, thou didst ride    And, betrayed by all, Swein
Over the wastes from Sweden;    Then fled from the land.
Bold warriors followed thee,    Exiled from here, as I heard,
My lord, from the east to Norway.    The son of Algiva fled.

Biarne Gullbrarscald composed this about Kalv Arneson:

Thou didst vow the young king    Kalv, thou didst let Magnus,
The inheritance he claimed.    Eager for battle, come to the land
True it is that Swein must    From Gardar, for thou didst bring it about
Sit alone in Denmark.    That the prince should get his realm.

That winter King Magnus ruled in Norway and Hardicanute in Denmark.

6. The following spring both kings levied troops and word was told about them that they would come to battle on the Elv.[3] And when both armies went against each other, the landed men of both hosts sent bidding to their kinsmen and friends, and along with the messages of both sides there followed word that they should make peace between the kings. And as both kings were young and child-like, the rule of their lands was held by the mighty men who were chosen for it in both lands; the matter went so far that a peace meeting was arranged between the kings. They met, and peace was

---

1 *Hardicanute* was King of England from 1040 to 1042.    2 Canute was King of England from 1016 to 1035.    3 I.e. Göta River by Gothenburg.

discussed; they agreed that the kings should swear brotherhood and

make peace between themselves, so long as they were both alive; and if one of them died without son, the one who lived longer should hold the other's lands and people after him. Twelve men who were the uppermost in either kingdom swore the kings that this peace should be kept so long as any of them were alive. Thereupon the kings parted and each of them went home to his kingdom, and this peace was kept as long as they lived.[1]

Magnus the Good meets Hardicanute

7. Queen Astrid whom St Olav had wed had come to Norway with her step-son King Magnus, and she was with him in such good cheer as was due to her position. Then Magnus' mother Alvhild also came to the court, and the king straightway welcomed her with great love and gave her an honourable place there. But with Alvhild it went, as it may go with many who get power, that pride soon grew within her, and she liked it ill that Queen Astrid was somewhat more highly honoured than she was, in seat or in other service. Alvhild wanted to sit nearer the king, and Astrid called her her serving-woman, as it had formerly been when Astrid was queen over Norway during the time King Olav ruled over the land. Astrid would not on any account have a seat with Alvhild, and they could not be in one house together.

Sigvat the Scald had gone to Rome when the battle took place at Stiklastader. And when he was on his way to the north, he learned of King Olav's death. It was a great sorrow to him. He then quoth:

On the Mount[2] near the forts I stood          I thought of the king who long
One morning and remembered               Had happily ruled the land
The land where they split                 When Torrad[3] my father was
Many a shield and broad brynie.           There with him in his youth.

1 Under this treaty King Magnus claimed the crown of England when Hardicanute died in 1042; cf. chapter 37.     2 Probably Monte Pincio or another of the heights in Rome.     3 *Torrad*, i.e. Tord. Cf. 'History of St Olav', chapter 43.

One day Sigvat went through a village and heard a husband wailing much because he had lost his wife; he struck himself on his breast, tore off his clothes and said he would gladly die. Sigvat said:

| | |
|---|---|
| When he loses the maiden's embrace | But the flight-hating king's man |
| The man longs for death. | Who has lost his lord |
| Too dearly bought is love | Sheds tears for his slaying, |
| If we weep the lost one. | The loss is worse for us. |

8. Sigvat came home to Norway; he had a house and children in Trondheim. He went northwards along the coast in a trade ship, and when they lay in Hillarsund[1] they saw many ravens flying by. Sigvat said:

| | |
|---|---|
| I see the ravens hastening | Every day outside Hillar |
| To the harbour where the good | There screech the greedy eagles |
| Prince of Norsemen once had | Whom Olav formerly |
| His ships: they remembered the corpses. | Oft called to the plunder. |

And when Sigvat came north to Kaupang, King Swein was there and he bade Sigvat go to him, for Sigvat had formerly been with King Swein's father Canute the Mighty. Sigvat said he would go home to his house. And one day it was that Sigvat went out in the street and he saw where the king's men were holding games. Sigvat said:

| | |
|---|---|
| I turn away from the king's swains, | Then I remember how formerly |
| From the bodyguard's games, | My far-famed lord |
| For I feel ill in my heart, | Oft played with his men |
| And I grow pale at seeing it. | In their *odal* fields.[2] |

He then went to his house. He heard that many men reproached him and said that he had run away from King Olav. Sigvat said:

| | |
|---|---|
| May the White Christ give me | I have from others' witness |
| The hot fire of Hel, | To overflowing for that. |
| If I wished to betray | I went to Rome in mortal sin; |
| Olav: I am guiltless; | It is far from me to deny it. |

Sigvat liked it not at home, and one day he went out and said:

| | |
|---|---|
| The high, bending fells | Since then, the sorrow is my own |
| In the whole of Norway seemed | And the hillsides seem to me |
| To laugh, when Olav lived: | To be much less happy: |
| I used to be known on the warships. | Favour I had with the king. |

At the beginning of winter Sigvat went east over the Kjöl to Jämtland and thence to Helsingeland; he then came forth into

---

1 *Hillarsund* is the sound between Hillöy and the mainland south-west of Mandal.
2 The Norsemen were fond of playing games in the fields. In the West Riding in Yorkshire there still exists a game called *Knur and Spell*, the name of which is no doubt of O.S. origin.

Sweden. He went straightway to Queen Astrid and was with her in good cheer for a long time. He was also with her brother, King Anund, and from him he got ten marks of burned silver, as it is said in Canute's drapa. Sigvat often asked when he found merchants who went into Holmgard what they could tell him about Magnus Olavson; he said:

Yet I long to learn
News from the east, from Gardar.
About the young prince I oft
Hear praises, and not sparingly.

Little I learn, though the small,
Creeping birds of love
Fly between us. The journey
Here, I fear, is hopeless.

9. And when Magnus Olavson came from Gardarik to Sweden, Sigvat was with Queen Astrid and they were all very glad. Then said Sigvat:

Thou didst seek home with thy faring
And it may be well that thou,

King Magnus, wilt greet thy men
And thy land; I praise thy might.

Afterwards Sigvat went on the journey with Queen Astrid to follow Magnus to Norway. Sigvat said:

I tell the men my mind,
Magnus, that I greet
Thy life with welcome;
There is promise of good luck.

Few folk might be alive
Who will have such a king,
If the son is to liken
His dear father.

And when Magnus was king over Norway, Sigvat the Scald followed him and was very dear to the king. When Queen Astrid and Alvhild the king's mother had had a bout of words with each other he quoth this:

Alvhild, let thou Astrid
Sit uppermost before thee,

Even if thy standing hath grown
Much, as God willed it.

10. King Magnus had a shrine made; he had it decked with gold and silver and had costly stones set therein. And both in size and in other respects the shrine was made like a coffin, but with arches below and with a cover above shaped like a roof with gables and ridges; on the back of the lid there were hinges and on the front there were hasps whereby it was locked with a key. King Magnus then had the holy relic of King Olav laid in the shrine. Many miracles happened there before the holy relic of St Olav, and about it Sigvat the Scald says:

For him a golden shrine
Is made, which holds his bold heart.
The king's relic I praise;
He went to God.

From the king's tomb
Many a man, who came
There blind, now goes away
With his sight all restored.

Then it was made law over all Norway to keep St Olav's festival day. The day was forthwith held to be as holy as the greatest of festivals. About this Sigvat the Scald quoth:

| | |
|---|---|
| Free from harm we ought | It beseems me to keep holy |
| To observe the Mass of Olav, | The festival of the king we miss, |
| Magnus' father, in my house. | Who hath bedecked |
| God gives the king power. | My hands with red gold. |

11. Tore the Hound went away from the land a short while after King Olav's death. Tore went out to Jerusalem and it is the tale of many men that he came not back. Tore the Hound's son was called Sigurd, and he was the father of Rannveig who was married to John, the son of Arne Arneson; their children were Vidkunn of Bjarköy, Sigurd the Hound, Erling and Jardtrud.

12. Harek of Tjotta sat at home in his garths until Magnus Olavson came into the land and became king. Harek then went south to Trondheim to King Magnus. At that time Asmund Grankelson[1] was with King Magnus. And when Harek went from his ship he came to Nidaros, and Asmund was standing on a balcony with the king; they saw Harek and recognised him. Asmund said to the king: "Now will I pay Harek back for the slaughter of my

"Take my axe rather"

father". He had in his hand a little, thinly hammered broad-axe. The king looked at him and said: "Take my axe rather"; for it was forged broad and thick; the king said besides: "I think, Asmund, that there are rather hard bones in that fellow". Asmund took the axe and went down and out from the garth; and when he came down to the cross-road Harek and his men were coming up towards him. Asmund struck Harek on the head so that the axe sank straightway down to his brain, and that was Harek's bane. Asmund went back into the garth to the king and the whole edge was bent through the blow. Then said the king: "What use would the thin axe have been to thee? It seems to me as if this is now useless". Afterwards King Magnus

1 Cf. 'History of St Olav', chapter 169.

gave Asmund a county and shire in Halogaland, and there are many great tales about the strife between Asmund and Harek's sons.

13. In the beginning Kalv Arneson had most power with King Magnus for some time. But then some folk reminded the king how Kalv had been at Stiklastader[1] and it was harder then for Kalv to get round the king's mood. Once it befell when there were many folk with the king and they were bringing forward their matters that a man called Torgeir, of Sula in Værdale, came forth before the king with his rightful business. The king gave no heed to his words, but listened to those who were nearer to him. Then Torgeir spoke loudly to the king so that all who were near heard it:

> Speak thou with me,
> Magnus my king;
> I was in the following
> Of thine own father.
>
> I brought from there
> A blow on my head
>
> When they were stepping
> Over the dead prince.
>
> But thou lovest
> The evil folk,
> Those king-betrayers,
> Who gladdened the devil.

Then men made great din at that, and some bade Torgeir go out. The king called him to him and did his business so that Torgeir was at peace, and the king promised him his friendship.

14. It was a little later that King Magnus was at a feast at Haug in Værdale, and when the king sat down at table Kalv Arneson sat on one side of him and Einar Tambarskelver on the other. Then things had gone so far that the king was unfriendly to Kalv and esteemed Einar most. The king said to Einar: "We two shall ride to-day to Stiklastader; I want to see signs of what befell there". Einar answered: "I can tell thee nothing thereof; let thy foster-father Kalv go; he will be able to tell thee tidings of what befell there". And when the tables were taken away the king made himself ready to go; he said to Kalv: "Thou shalt go with me to Stiklastader". Kalv said that it was not needful. Then the king stood up and said rather wrathfully: "Go thou shalt, Kalv!" Afterwards the king went out. Kalv clothed himself quickly and said to his lad: "Thou shalt ride out to Egge and bid my huscarls take all my belongings on to the ship before sunset". The king rode to Stiklastader and Kalv went with him; they got off their horses and walked to where the battle had taken place. Then said the king to Kalv: "Where is the place where the king fell?" Kalv answered, pointing with his spear shaft: "Here he lay fallen", he said. Then the king said: "Where wast thou, then, Kalv?" He answered: "Here, where I am standing now". The king

---

1 The battle of Stiklestad, where St Olav fell.

answered, and he was as red as blood: "Then could thine axe have reached him". Kalv answered: "My axe came not near him"; he then went away to his horse, leaped on its back and rode on his way with all his men, whilst the king rode back to Haug. In the evening Kalv came to Egge and his ship then lay ready by the gangways; all his valuables had been carried therein and his huscarls were aboard. Straightway that night they sailed out along the fjord and afterwards Kalv went on day and night, as there was a fair wind. So he sailed

King Magnus and Kalv Arneson at Stiklastader

west over the sea and stayed there a long while, harrying in Scotland and Ireland and the Hebrides. About this Biarne Gullbrarscald speaks in Kalv's flokk:

Torberg's brother, I heard
That Harald's nephew showed thee
Friendship, whereof thou wast worthy.
It lasted till others spoilt it.

Thy enviers aroused
Always the split between
Thee and Olav's offspring;
Unfortunate it seemed to me.

15. King Magnus possessed himself of Vigg which Rut[1] had owned, and Kviststader which Torgeir had owned, as well as Egge

1 *Rut*, in O.N. *hrutr*, means a 'ram' or 'he-goat'. In Scotland, the name Ross-shire probably comes from O.N. *hross*, meaning 'horse', the O.N. *hors* being also used. 'Sutherland' derives its origin from O.N. *Suðrland* (the land to the south) and Rutland may likewise be connected with O.N. *hrutr*.

and all the goods which Kalv had left behind him. And into his crown property he took many other great possessions which had been owned by the men who had fallen at Stiklastader in the bonders' army. He punished heavily many of the men who had been against King Olav in that battle; some he drove from the land, and from some he took many goods; for others he had their cattle struck down. The bonders then began to murmur and talk amongst themselves: "What might this king be thinking of, when he breaks the laws which King Hacon the Good set up? Does he not remember that we have never endured unfairness? He will go the same way as his father and other such chiefs whom we have deprived of their lives when we were weary of their overbearing and lawlessness". This complaining went far and wide in the land. The men of Sogn held an army gathering and word went round that they would meet King Magnus in battle if he went there. At that time King Magnus was in Hordaland where he had many men and he let it seem that he would go north into Sogn. The king's friends were aware of this and twelve men then held a meeting; they agreed to decide by casting lots which of them was to tell the king about this discontent. And so it happened that the lot fell to Sigvat the Scald.

16. Sigvat composed a flokk which was called the "Bare Truth Songs", and first he says that they thought the king too much delayed the set plan of being at peace with the bonders when the latter were threatening to raise up strife against him. He said:

There is trouble in the south with the
    Sognings.
Sigvat hath warned the king
Against attempting a folk-fight;
I shall go, if we fight, however;
Let us take weapons and ward
Our king well with our swords;
I am eager for that meeting;
How long shall the land sorrow.

In the same poem there are these verses:

Hacon, who did fall
At Fitjar, was called the Good.
He punished the foes' harrying,
And the men loved him.
Long afterwards did the land
Hold fast the laws, which the blithe
Foster-son of Athelstan had given;
The bonders forget him but slowly.

Rightly, I think, did the carls
Choose, as well as the jarls:
Therefore to the bonders' goods
The two Olavs gave peace;

Harald's trusty offspring
And Trygvi's son had
The good laws kept which the land
Got in gift from both of them.

Hear without wrath thy counsellors
Who speak out so clearly,
My lord! it will afterwards clear
The path to the king's glory.
The bonders bewail that they
Have other and worse lots
Than thou didst vow them in Ulvasund,
Unless the land warriors lie.

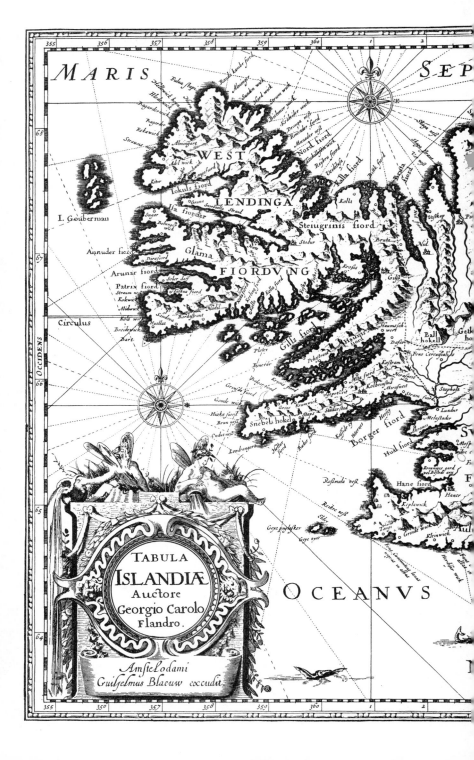

MARIS

SEP

Fulta Stap

Fulta knate fiord
Almingia
Sunden wick
Sorl wick
Derum wick

Rieltnec wick
Drong nefs
Rimmaker fiord
Manador nefs
Nord fiord
Iselhope wick
Reijbra fiord
Vestilofe

Kalla fiord

WEST

Flot wick

Helencot by
Hagardenwick
Hagarda
Relewick

Straung wick

Almingart

Sibur

Iokuls fiord

LENDINGA

Kalla

Steiugrinis fiord

Bruta

Nid

Vestkar

I. Goubernan

Sugar

Bolunga wick

Gruna
Snerpaalta Strand

Ila fioyder

Studur

Krofes

Gilfs

Annuder fiord

Glama

Difrafiore

FIORDVNG

Arunar fiord

Solar darf

Patrix fiord

Saltna fiord

Sialua fiord

Kalla fiord
Fyla

Straum nefs
Rokewie

Midwick

Kadil

Circulus

Kols wick
Breidewick

Bart.

Sandra
Bardiftrand
Hullal

Plates

Gills fiord

Hanmasch
wick

Dafen

Ball
hokell

Geth
ho

Bmefar

Fons Cercushaln

Vastbur fiord

Roxua fiord

Grind Krummuck

Popotleit

Mia fiord
Kolbemsta
Mirafiuel
Straun fiord

Kostram
Norafhett

Staphofe

OCCIDENS

Greyda fiord

Gomle wick

Stadur stad

Kaffil ef
Stadur

Haters

Hirfs

Landur
Melaftader

Regem

S

Huka fiord

Brun nefs

Snebels hokel

Ofapa

Borger fiord

Cudut nefs

Leandranger

Miltur
fiorg

Thuler fiord

Hudl fiord

Hane fiord

Haner

Rofimala nefs

Kennians gard
vel Biffuls are

Keplawick

Reikre nefs

Tlong
Grinde wick

Kleinwick

Au

Elu

Geye gnafasker

Aula

Geye gnar

Helie wick

TABULA
**ISLANDIÆ**
Auctore
Georgio Carolo
Flandro.

OCEANVS

Amstelodami
Guilielmus Blaeuw excudit.

Grims ey.

N TRIONALIS      PARS

68

neß
Sigla fiord
Heidis fiord
Rolskey
Olais fiord

Lundey
Ranghayger
Brau hopa

Fulminga wich

Langa neß

Katr
Hitidlia fiord
Hrtidlis fiord
Platey

Ramgar hopa

Solungs wick

belle fiord

Pistils fiord

Gunolps pial

Suhardt
lur

Brisey

Hanoska

Tiar neß
Huswick

Pistils

Heßtuncik

Faga neß

Gunolps pial

Modrueseller
x sedes
spatus et
Holgurdalur
aslat

Eya fiord

Skalanda fiord

Rokta
heide

Ald fiord
Peva fiord

Dyra neß

NORD

Greynastari
Naki

i Hop

Hopna fiord

67

NGA      FIORDVNG

Alumbaguera

Mokrufeld
Reikiadalur

Alincth

Kurbar

Tabei bus onare in higto arenas
sobis inscripta sunt

Burgar fiord

Aincopelts
hokell
Sandt
hokell

Hver Skin natsfell
Sunndirt

Snattarnoti

Ikrida Closter

Helles fiord

Arcticus

66

Aradal
AVST   LENDINGA

Fliotzdal

Reidt

Reidt fiord

holt Episcopalis
es et. schola

Hnappa
dalr hokel

Bern

wick

Bern fiord

Papey

VNG
gdaler

Hekli pial
Hekla mons
perpetuo ardens

Poma
Gunpur

FIORDVNG

Efte fiord

Kunareper

Midals
hokel

Purdun
gamitt
Kirkeba closter

Hierskeid
closter

Ituga hilbi

Lonn

Papi fiord

Plee
ina harge
per

Solheima
hokel

Breide

Skua

Eirar

Hopdi

Horn

Branslabol fluder

DVNG
Oldts

Tunga

Gnut

Medallende

Hollanass
eyor

Hopdi

ba
Erapialla
hokel

Efa

Picknekop

Horna fiord

65

Kiapial Ia. his
nombus sunt coru et solen ates albi

Nimkaks

orlarks
basin

Hafke

Eldor

Ingolyß hopdi

Hekla prom.

Weftmanna vel
Pisthlia eyar

DEVCALE      DO

54

Miliaria  Germanica  communia
2      4      6      8      10      12      14

Miliaria  Gallica  communia
2    4    6    8    10    12    14    16    18

ORIENS

Vengeance-wreaking lord!
Who now eggs thee on
To turn from thine own words?
Oft thou triest the steel.
Bound to his own word should the chief
Always be. Victorious
Warrior, thou oughtest not
To break thine own promises!

Leader of the host, who eggs thee on
To strike down the bonders' cattle?
To waste thus in the land
Is overbearing in a king;
No man has hitherto thus
Counselled a young prince;
Thy bodyguard hate robbery,
And the army is threatening.

Mighty slayer of thieves!
Thou oughtest to show heed
To the rumour about the men,
Which is heard here; hold thyself in
    check!

Thy friend bids thee be
Wary, feeder of the ravens!
He bids thee listen
To what the bonders will ask.

Ill it is when all
Older men trust
And are vexed at their prince;
It should be stopped beforehand.
Heavy it is when the thingmen
Put their heads together
And stick their noses in their pelts
And stillness falls on their talks.

One thing there is they say:
My lord puts his hand
On the men's *odal* lands;
The noble bonders rise up;
The men will count it as robbery
To lose their fathers' heritage
Which an unfair judgment
Can give to the king's stewards.

After this warning the king changed his temper and many others also brought such words of warning to the king. Thus it came so far that the king had talk with the wisest men and they then agreed upon their laws. Afterwards King Magnus had the law book written which is still in Trondheim and which is called *Grey Goose*. King Magnus was then well befriended and loved by all the land folk; for that reason he was called Magnus the Good.

17. Harold, King of England, died five years after the death of his father, Canute the Mighty, and he was buried with his father at Winchester. After his death the kingdom of England was taken by Harold's brother Hardicanute, another son of Old Canute; Hardicanute was King of both England and Denmark, and he ruled the kingdom for two years; he died in his bed in England and was buried at Winchester with his father. After his death, Edward the Confessor, son of Ethelred, King of England, and of Queen Emma the daughter of Richard, Duke of Normandy, was taken as King of England. King Edward was brother to Harold[1] and Hardicanute by the same mother. Gunhild was the name of a daughter of Old Canute and Emma, and she was married to the Emperor Henry of Saxony, who was called Henry the Generous. Gunhild was three

1 Harold was not Emma's son. There is some uncertainty about his parentage; but it is thought that he was Canute's son by his mistress Algiva of Northampton.

years in Saxony before she fell sick; she died two years after the death of her father, King Canute.[1]

18. King Magnus Olavson learned of Hardicanute's death; he straightway sent men south to Denmark and gave messages to the men who had bound themselves to him with oaths when terms of peace were made between Magnus and Hardicanute, and he reminded them of their words. He also sent word that he himself would come at once in the summer to Denmark with his army; lastly he sent word saying that he would possess himself of all Denmark according to their agreement and their oaths or else he would fall in battle with his army. Thus says Arnor Jarlascald:

The lord of the jarls had
A mighty store of words;
Deeds followed on the words
Which the wolf-feeder spoke:

He would fall dead
Under the raven's claw
In the grim din of the shields
Or own Denmark as king.

19. King Magnus then gathered an army together, called to him the landed men and mighty bonders and got himself longships. And when the force came together, it was a fair host of men and well fitted out; he had seventy ships when he sailed from Norway. Thus says Tjodolv:

Victorious king, boldly
Didst thou steer the longships,
Where thy men sailed
With seventy ships to the east.

The keel glided to the south,
And the sail strained the ropes.
The high-masted ship cut through the creeks,
The *Bison* swayed with the stem.

Here it should be said that King Magnus had the great *Bison*[2] which King Olav had had built; it had more than thirty seats; in the prow there was a bison's head and aft there was a tail; the head and the tail and both necks[3] were overlaid with gold. About this Arnor Jarlascald says:

From outside, the ugly sea-foam squirted
Against the quarterdeck; the rudder shook,
The wind bent the red-fir timbers
All bedecked with the red gold.

From the north thou didst steer southwards
The fir stems past Stavanger
To Denmark; the tops of the masts
There gleamed like fire.

1 The English chroniclers, Matthew of Westminster, William of Malmesbury and Roger of Wendover relate that Gunhilda or Gunhild was given in marriage by her brother King Hardicanute to the Emperor Henry, and they give details of the splendid marriage ceremony in London, which took place in 1041. Other sources state that Gunhild was married in 1036 and died in 1038 or three years after her father King Canute.    2 Cf. 'History of St Olav', chapter 144.    3 Cf. 'History of Olav Trygvason', chapter 80. The O.N. text in this chapter reads *svirarnir badir*, literally 'both necks', *sviri* being used in the plural sense, and applies probably both to the stem and stern.

King Magnus put to sea from Agder across to Jutland. Thus says Arnor:

> I will tell how the sharp lord
> Of the Sognings was borne
> South on the rime-covered *Bison*:
> The wind blew to leewards.

> The strife-starter steered
> His stems out to the broad
> Jutland, where the men
> Eagerly greeted him.

20. And when King Magnus came to Denmark he was well received there; he straightway held things and meetings with the men of the land and demanded to be taken as king as the agreement stood. And since the chiefs of the land, who were thought most of in Denmark, were bound with oaths to King Magnus and wished to keep their word and oaths, they helped much in putting this before the folk; moreover they put forward also that King Canute the Mighty and all his descendants were dead; the third reason was that King Olav's saintliness and his miracles were then known all over the land.

21. Afterwards King Magnus had a thing summoned at Vebjorg[1] where the Danes elected their kings in the olden times as now. And at that thing the Danes took Magnus Olavson as king over all Denmark. King Magnus stayed a long time in the summer in Denmark, and all the folk greeted him well and showed him obedience. He then set men over all the land, in shires and lordships, and gave land rents to the great men. And in the autumn he sailed with his army to Norway and stayed some time by the Elv.

22. Swein was the name of a man; he was the son of Ulf the Jarl, who was son of Torgils Sprakalegg; Swein's mother was Astrid, the daughter of King Swein Forkbeard; she was sister by the same father to Canute the Mighty and sister by the same mother to Olav Ericson, the Swedish king; their mother was Queen Sigrid the Strongminded, daughter of Skogul Tosti. Swein Ulfson had then lived a long time with his kinsmen, the Swedish kings, ever since his father, Ulf the Jarl, had fallen, whereof it is written in the History of Canute the Old ('History of St Olav', chapter 153) that he had his brother-in-law, Ulf the Jarl, slain at Roskilde. For that reason Swein was not afterwards in Denmark. Swein Ulfson was the fairest of men; he was very big and strong, a great man in all sports, and very wise. It was the talk of all men who knew him that he had all the qualities which a good chief has. Swein Ulfson came to King Magnus when he lay in the Elv as is written above, and the king greeted him well. There were also many men who brought forward their case, for

1 Viborg in Jutland.

Swein was the most befriended of men. He himself also told his case fairly and wisely to the king and it came about that Swein submitted to King Magnus and became his man. Afterwards the king and Swein talked much together in private.

23. One day when King Magnus sat in his high-seat, and there were many folk around him, Swein Ulfson sat on the footstool before the king. The king began to speak: "I will make known to the chiefs and the whole people a plan that I have; here is come to me a man, excellent both in lineage and in person, Swein Ulfson. He has now made himself my man and sworn me his troth thereon. And as I know that all the Danes have made themselves my men this summer, so the land is now without a chief when I am away, and it is much laid open to harrying by Vends and Kurlanders and other men from the easterway as well as by Saxers.[1] Also I promised to give them a leader to ward and rule the land. I see no man who is so well fitted for it in every way as Swein Ulfson; he has the kinship to be a chief. Now I will make him my jarl and give into his hands the rule of Denmark when I am in Norway, in the same way as Canute the Mighty set his father Ulf the Jarl as chief of Denmark when he was in England". Einar Tambarskelver said: "Too great a jarl, too great a jarl, my foster-son!" The king said wrathfully: "Little does it seem to you that I am able to understand; it looks to me as if you think that some are too great jarls and that others are fit for nothing". Then the king stood up, took a sword, and fastened it to Swein's belt; he then took a shield, and fastened it to his shoulder; he set a helm on his head and gave him the name of jarl, together with such land rent in Denmark as his father Ulf the Jarl had formerly had there. Then a shrine with holy relics was brought forth, and Swein laid his hands thereon and swore trustiness to King Magnus. After this the king led the jarl to the high-seat next to him. Thus says Tjodolv:

| | |
|---|---|
| By the Elv in the east | Olav's son wished |
| Ulf's son placed with fair vows | To decide about the oaths; |
| His hands on the shrine; | The treaty lasted not |
| Swein would swear oaths there. | As long as it should. |

Thereupon Swein the Jarl went to Denmark and was well received by the common people. He took himself a bodyguard and was soon a great chief. In the winter he went far about the land and made himself the friend of the great men; he was also well befriended by the common folk.

24. King Magnus went northwards with his army to Norway and

[1] *Saxers*, men from Saxony, North-west Germany.

stayed there during the winter. When spring came King Magnus called up a great host and with it he went south to Denmark. And when he came thither he had tidings from Vendland that the Vends in Jomsborg[1] had fallen from lealty to him. The Danish kings had had a great jarldom there; they had founded it first in Jomsborg and it was now become a great stronghold. But when King Magnus heard such talk, he called out a great fleet from Denmark and in the summer he sailed with all the host south to Vendland; he had a great army. Thus says Arnor Jarlascald:

| | |
|---|---|
| In this verse, you shall hear How the chief bore the war shield Into Vendland; with gladness didst thou Draw the frosted keels from the smooth rollers. | Never before have I heard tell That any prince brought out More ships to his *odal* land; My lord, thou broughtest the Vends sorrow. |

And when King Magnus came to Vendland, he lay into Jomsborg and straightway won the stronghold; there he slew many men, burned the town and land far and wide and made there the greatest war-havoc. Thus says Arnor Jarlascald:

| | |
|---|---|
| Skjoldung,[2] thou broughtest fire upon The monsters; they found death. South in Jomsborg, thou foe of thieves Didst kindle the fire's bright light. | In that broad fortress the heathen men Dared not ward their halls. O king, with the bright fire thou gavest Fearful hearts to the townsmen. |

Many folk in Vendland submitted to King Magnus, but many there were who fled away. Thereafter King Magnus went back to Denmark and made himself ready for wintering there. He sent away from him both the Danish army and many of those who had followed him from Norway.

25. The same winter that Swein Ulfson had got the rule of Denmark and had made himself the friend of many great men and secured the favour of the common folk, he had himself called 'king', and in that counsel many chiefs took part. But when in the spring he learned that King Magnus was coming from the north with a great army, Swein went to Scania[3] and from there up into Gautland and so to Sweden to his kinsman King Emund; he stayed there during the summer, but kept spies in Denmark to get news of King Magnus' journey and the number of his men. And when Swein learned that King Magnus had let a great part of his army go from him and like-

---

1 *Jomsborg* was a fortified town on the east side of the island of Wollin at the mouth of the River Oder, now part of Prussia.    2 *Skjoldung*, the name of the Danish royal family.    3 The south part of Sweden.

wise that he was south in Jutland, Swein rode down from Sweden
and he had with him then a great army which the Swedish king had
given him. And when Swein came down to Scania the men of Scania
greeted him well and took him as their king; many men then drew
to him. Afterwards he went over to Zealand and there they received
him well and he laid the land under him. Thereafter he went to Fyn
and subdued all the isles and the folk submitted to him; Swein had
a great army and many ships.

Swein Ulfson rides from Sweden with a great army

26. King Magnus learned these tidings and likewise that the
Vends had an army out. After this King Magnus called folk to him
and a great host from all over Jutland soon drew to him. Then Duke
Otta of Saxony came to him from Brunswick; he had wed Ulvhild, daughter of St Olav, and sister of King Magnus; Otta had a
great troop of men. The Danish chiefs egged King Magnus on to go
against the Vends and not let the heathens go over the land and lay it
waste; the plan was taken that the king should turn his army south
to Hedeby.[1] And when King Magnus lay by Skotborg River[2] in
Lyrskogsheath[3] word came to him about the Vends' army and
likewise that they had so great a host that no man could count it,

---

1 *Hedeby* was the old name for the present town of Sleswick.　2 The *River Skotborg*
runs into the sea to the north of the town of Ribe.　3 *Lyrskogsheath*, where King
Magnus fought his celebrated battle, is situated to the north-west of the town of Sleswick.

and that King Magnus could not deal with so great an army and that there was naught else to do but flee thence. King Magnus, however, wished to fight if his men thought it was at all likely that he could win the victory; but most of them counselled him from it and all said the same that the Vends had a mighty host. But Duke Otta had much desire to fight. The king then had the whole host called together and all the men put on their armour; during the night they lay out under their shields, for it was told them that the Vends' army was near by and the king was very sick at heart; he thought it ill if he had to flee, for never had he done that before; he slept little during the night, but sang his prayers.

27. The next day was Michaelmas Eve. And when it neared dawn, the king slept and dreamt that he saw the saintly King Olav, his father, who said to him: "Thou art now much sick at heart and full of fear, because the Vends come against thee with a great army. But thou shalt not fear this heathen host, even though they are many together. I shall follow thee in this battle; make yourselves ready for battle with the Vends when ye hear my horn". And when the king awoke, he told of his dream. The day then began to dawn and all the folk heard the sound of bells in the air, and King Magnus' men who had been in Nidaros knew that it was as if they were ringing with *Glad*, the bell which King Olav had given to St Clement's Church in Kaupang.[1]

28. Then King Magnus stood up and shouted that the war blast be blown. And at that moment the Vendish army was coming against them from the south over the river. All the king's army leaped up and made for the heathens. King Magnus cast off his ring-brynie and he wore uppermost a red silk shirt; he took in his hand the axe, Hel, which King Olav had had. King Magnus ran before all the other men against the army and forthwith struck down one man after another with both hands. Thus sayeth Arnor Jarlascald:

With the broad-axe the prince
Unwearily rushed onward;
He cast off his brynie; swords
Were swung against the Horders' king.

He gripped both hands
About the shaft, and the axe Hel
Cleft the skulls; but the Creator
Of Heaven decided the victory.

The battle was not long; the king's men were very eager, and wherever they came together the Vends fell as thickly as when the sand is cast up by the billows; they who stood behind turned in flight and were then struck down like cattle. The king himself drove the

---

1 I.e. Trondheim.

fleeing men east over the heath and all over the heath they fell in heaps. Thus sayeth Tjodolv:

Foremost amongst the men, I believe,
Harald's brother's son stood forth.
The raven knew its hunger
Would be sated.

Far about lay the fleeing Vends;
It was known that where Magnus won
The fallen men could cover
The mile-broad heath.

It is the talk of all men that there has never been in Christian times so great a fall of men in the northern lands as that which the Vends

The battle of Lyrskogsheath

suffered at Lyrskogsheath. Among King Magnus' men not many fell, but a great number were wounded. After the fight King Magnus had his men's wounds bound up. But there were not as many leeches in the army as were needed, and then the king went to the men who seemed suitable and felt their hands; and when he had taken them by the palms of their hands and felt them, he chose twelve men who seemed to him to have the softest hands and said that they should bind up the men's wounds. None of them had bound up wounds before, but all these men were the best leeches. There were two Icelanders, one being Thorkel Geirason from Lyngar,[1] the other being

[1] A farm in Medalland in West Skaptafells district on the south-east coast of Iceland.

Atle, the father of Bard the Black of Selardale,[1] and from these two men many leeches have since sprung.

After this battle the miracle which St Olav had done became very renowned far and wide in other lands, and it was the saying of all men that no man need fight against King Magnus Olavson, for his father, King Olav, stood by him, so that for this reason his foes could not oppose him at all.

29. King Magnus now straightway turned with his army against Swein, whom he called his jarl, even though the Danes called him king. King Magnus got himself ships and fitted out his army; both now got many men. There were then many chiefs in Swein's army, Scania men, Halland men, and Fyn dwellers, but King Magnus had most Norsemen and Jutes; he now sailed with his army to meet Swein. They met off the Westland on Re[2] and there was a great battle which so ended that King Magnus had the victory and Swein fled and lost many men; he fled back to Scania, for he had a hiding-place up in Gautland if he needed to take to it. But King Magnus then went back to Jutland and stayed there with many men during the winter and kept watch with his ships. About this Arnor Jarlascald says:

> On Re the quick king had            The Welsh swords he dyed
> A hard fight-thing held.            In blood off the wide Westland.

30. Swein Ulfson went out on his ships as soon as he learned that King Magnus had gone ashore. Swein drew to him all the men he had and in the winter he went through Zealand and Fyn and the isles. And when it drew towards Yule, he sailed south to Jutland and first lay in by the Limfjord; there many folk submitted to him and from some he took money; others went to King Magnus. And when King Magnus heard what Swein had taken upon himself to do, he went to his ships and had with him the Norsemen who were then in Denmark and some of the Danes; he then sailed northwards along the coast. Swein was then in Aros[3] and he had many men, and when he learned of King Magnus' journey he brought his men out of the town and arrayed them for battle. When King Magnus had learned where Swein was, and when he knew that there would now be but a short distance between them, he held a husthing and spoke in this way to his men: "We have now learned that the jarl with his men will soon be before us here. I am told that they have a great

---

1 *Selardale*, on the south side of Arnarfjord, in Bardastrand district, on the north-west coast of Iceland.    2 *Re* was the old name for the island of Rugen.    3 *Aros*, now Aarhus in Jutland.

army. I will now make known to you my thoughts: I will go against the jarl and fight with him, even though we have somewhat fewer men. Now as before we must always have our trust in God himself and the holy King Olav, my father. Several times before has he given us the victory when we have fought and when we have often had a smaller army than our foes. Now I will that my men arm themselves so that we may seek for them, and as soon as we meet, we shall row to them and straightway fall to battle; let all my men then be ready to fight". Afterwards they put on their armour and every man made himself ready. Magnus' men rowed forward until they saw the jarl's host and then they rowed against them. And Swein's men armed themselves and roped their ships together. There was soon a hard fight. Thus says Tjodolv:

A short while since the king
And the jarl brought their shields
Together against each other;
Sword play there was for the men,

So that the warriors
No greater battle ever
Called to mind; the host
Could make din with the spears.

They fought about the stems and they alone who were in the stems could get near with their blows. Those who were in the forehold thrust with their spears, and all those who were farther aft shot with barbed spears or gavelocks or darts. Some cast stones and shaft flints, and they who were abaft the mast shot with bows. About this Tjodolv says:

I heard that in the strife
They shot shaft flints and many
A spear against the broad shields;
Straightway the ravens got food.
The men as best they could
Cast stones and darts
In the weapon fight, and the wounded
They sank down on the floors.

The bowmen could never shoot
More shots with their bows.
That day the Tronds grew
Not tired of shooting.
So thickly did the barbed spears
Fly through the battle
That no man saw the others;
Everywhere the arrows rained.

Here it is to be told how heated was the shooting. King Magnus at the beginning of the battle was in the cover of shields; but when things seemed to him to go slowly he leaped forth from the shield cover, and rushed along the ship, shouting loudly, and egging on his men, and he went right forward to the bow to the hand-to-hand fight. And when his men saw that, each egged the other on; there rose then a great shout through the whole army. Thus sayeth Tjodolv:

Mightily did Magnus' men
Egg each other on

To thrust forth their shields;
The shouts waxed wilder.

This then became the hottest of battles. In the fight Swein's ship was cleared about the stem[1] and the bow railings. King Magnus himself and his following then went up on to Swein's ship and so did his men, one after another. It went so hard that Swein's men retired and King Magnus cleared the ship, and so he did one ship after the other. Then Swein and a great part of his army fled, but a goodly number of his men fell and many got quarter. Thus says Tjodolv:

> Magnus, watcher of the ships,
> To the fight went boldly
> Forth in the ship's bow;
> It was nobly done.
> So strongly did the king
> Fight there, that the jarl's
>
> Huscarls dwindled;
> The host cleared the ships.
> The jarl's folk went off
> In flight, ere the dear
> Giver of gold could grant
> Quarter to the sword-fighters.

This battle befell the last Sunday before Yule.[2] Thus quoth Tjodolv:

> Grim was the fight then
> When the great gold-giver fought;
> The victory was won on Sunday;
> Swiftly the host went to fight.
>
> There where the warriors
> Fought with death and the
> Folk sank down, the bodies
> Floated on every billow.

King Magnus there took seven ships from Swein's men. Tjodolv quoth:

> The son of Olav Digre
> Cleared seven ships.
>
> The king won the victory; in Sogn
> Such will gladden the women.

And besides, he said:

> Swein's men, his sword-bearers,
> Have lost their home-coming;
> The journey of the warriors
> Has grown hard enough.
>
> The billows, stirred by the storm,
> Beat their legs and skulls
> To the edge of the sea;
> The ocean howls about the corpses.

Straightway in the night Swein fled to Zealand with the men who had got away and who would follow him; but King Magnus brought his ships to land and straightway at night he let his men go ashore. Early in the morning they came down with great booty. About this Tjodolv the Scald sayeth:

> Yesterday I saw great stones
> Cast with strength, and the skulls
> Were cleft. Their battle lines
> Stood not fast in the fight.
>
> We brought down a shore raid;
> In the midst of the land the ship
> Is moored. With words alone
> Swein will not ward the land.

31. King Magnus sailed straightway with his army to the north to Zealand after Swein. And as soon as Magnus' army arrived,

1 *Stem* can also be called forecastle, and the stem men, forecastle men.     2 18th of December, 1043.

Swein and all his host fled up on land. But King Magnus followed them, put them to flight, and slew such as he could get near. Thus says Tjodolv:

True it is that many
Maids from Zealand heard
Who bore the standard;
Blood-red shields they had.
The women must hasten
In through the woods;
Their feet carried many
Refugees to Ringstader.[1]

The Scania men's swift lord
Wore his neckcloth bespattered.
I wonder if Lund's[2] noble
Chieftain is not betrayed.
Yesterday over earth and mire
Did the spears fly.
The strong jarl's standard
Sped o'er hills to the sea.

Swein then fled over to Fyn, and King Magnus went with the shield of war through Zealand and burned far and wide amongst those who in the autumn had gone into Swein's host. Tjodolv quoth:

The jarl must turn
In winter from the king's seat.
Thou hadst to do no little
Warding of the land.
Many a fight mightest thou,
Generous Magnus, get 'neath the
        shield.
Canute's goodly nephew
Seemed to lose all.

Lord of the Tronds! The shields
Thou didst strike; in wrath
Didst thou bid every house
To be burned to fire and ashes.
Friend of the princes! Thou wouldst
With might avenge on the jarl's
Followers their perilous
Enmity; they fled away.

32. As soon as King Magnus had learned news of Swein, he went with his army over to Fyn. And when Swein heard that, he went on to his ships and sailed and came forth into Scania; from there he went to Gautland and after that to the Swedish king. King Magnus went up into Fyn and he had many houses robbed and burned. All Swein's men who were there fled by wide paths. Tjodolv sayeth:

From the oaken walls in the south
The wind sent the embers
Up into the sky; the tindered
Fire played eagerly.
The houses in Fyn flamed
Still higher; over the dwellers
The bark thatch suffered scathe;
The Norsemen burned the halls.

The king's men will not mind
To court the fair maids,
Since they have won
Three fights against Swein's men.
In Fyn we can find
Fair women; we won.
Let us be foremost in the troop
In the clash of the weapons.

After this all the folk in Denmark submitted to King Magnus. Then there was good peace through the latter part of the winter. King Magnus set his men to rule everywhere in Denmark. And

---

1 Now Ringsted in the middle of Zealand.    2 The town of Lund (in Scania).

when spring was passing he went northwards with his army to Norway and stayed there a long time during the summer.

33. And when Swein learned that, he straightway rode down to Scania and he had a great army from Sweden. The Scania men greeted him well and he got more men. After that, he went across to Zealand and laid it under him, as well as Fyn and all the isles. And when King Magnus heard of this, he gathered his army and ships and then sailed south to Denmark. He learned where Swein lay with his army and went against him. They met towards evening at a place called Helganes.[1] And when the battle began King Magnus had fewer men but bigger and better-fitted ships. Thus quoth Arnor Jarlascald:

| | |
|---|---|
| Heard have I far and wide | At first the Rygers'[2] chief |
| About Helganes, where the king, | Made his men gather |
| The far-famed feeder of wolves, | Their shields together. All |
| Destroyed many a steed of the sea. | That autumn night the battle lasted. |

The fight was sharp and when the night was passing there was a great fall of men. King Magnus shot hand-shots all night; about this Tjodolv says:

| | |
|---|---|
| Yonder by Helganes | The blithe prince of the Möre men |
| Swein's men have fallen | Sent many a barbed spear. |
| Before the spears. The wounded | The point of the ashen dart |
| Swains sank in death. | The lord dyed in blood. |

To speak briefly about this battle: King Magnus won the victory and Swein fled. His ship was cleared and all his other ships were cleared too. Thus sayeth Tjodolv:

| | |
|---|---|
| Out of his wasted ship | The war king steeped the keen edge |
| The jarl hastened from battle, | Of his sword in blood. |
| When Magnus boldly | The biting sword swished |
| Barred Swein's path. | With blood; he won the land. |

And further Arnor says:

| | |
|---|---|
| The bold king of Scania | From Björn's brother, |
| Took all the ships | When the men rowed thither. |

There many of Swein's men fell, and King Magnus and his men got much booty. Tjodolv quoth:

| | |
|---|---|
| A Gautish shield I bore | Fair weapons I got— |
| From the strife and a brynie, | (I foretold this to the woman). |
| Which I got in the south this summer; | There I won a helm when the hard |
| The sword din was heated. | War king beat the Danes. |

1 *Helganes* is on the east coast of Jutland near Aarhus.    2 *Rygers*, i.e. the men from Rogaland, the district round Stavanger.

Swein fled up into Scania with all his men who had got away, and King Magnus and his men followed them far up into the land, but little opposition was then made by Swein's men or by the bonders. Thus says Tjodolv:

| | |
|---|---|
| Olav's son bade the men | The prince bade them harry in Scania; |
| Go up into the land. | Here in Denmark is trouble. |
| Magnus went with a mighty | The horse is hurrying |
| Strength of men from the ships. | Fiercely over the howes from the west. |

Afterwards King Magnus bade them go with the shield of war through all the districts. Tjodolv sayeth:

| | |
|---|---|
| Now the Norsemen bear forth | The warrior through Scania |
| Magnus' standard; nearer | Hastens on fast feet |
| The staff we seldom go. | South to Lund. Few ways |
| I bear my shield on my arm. | Have I found fairer. |

Afterwards they began to burn the districts and all the folk fled away thence by wide paths. Tjodolv quoth:

| | |
|---|---|
| The ice-cold iron we bore | Over the heaths of Denmark |
| Full well against the jarl's troops. | The warrior bore the shields. |
| Speedily fell the Scania men's | We won the victory and Swein's |
| Beautifully decked houses. | Wounded men ran. |
| The red fire played | The prince spurred his steed |
| Over the broad garth | In Fyn over the old moors; |
| According to our plan, and many | A short way there was |
| Brought help to that work. | Between the host of the Skjoldungs.[1] |
| The clear fire burned | Now Swein's fleeing troops |
| Over the men's houses | Will not deny the great deeds |
| In Denmark; the leader | Of Magnus; many standards |
| With his host laid waste the towns. | That morning went up. |

Swein fled east in Scania, and then King Magnus went to his ships and afterwards sailed east along the coast of Scania; he had hurriedly made himself ready. Then Tjodolv quoth this:

| | |
|---|---|
| I have naught else to drink | The Swedes I fear little; |
| Excepting sea water, | Toil we have had for the king. |
| When I follow the prince; | Here before us we look at |
| Swallow I do the salt sea. | The broad side of Scania. |

Swein fled up into Gautland and then sought the Swedish king. There he stayed the winter in good cheer.

34. King Magnus turned about on his journey when he had subdued Scania. First he sailed to Falster[2] where he went up and harried.

---

1 *Skjoldungs* here means the Danes.    2 The island situated between Zealand and Laland.

## THE GOKSTAD SHIP

O. Væring, Oslo

Found in 1880 at Gokstad near Sandefjord and now exhibited at the Sjöfartsmuseum at Oslo. The picture shows the port stern view. Built of oak, her dimensions are: length over all 78 ft, waterline 73 ft. 3 in., beam 16 ft. 7 in., draft 3 ft. 7 in.

Some human remains were found within which are supposed to have been those of a sea king. The ship was buried with all her equipment of oars, spars, etc., and dates from the latter part of the ninth century. A bedstead was found in the burial chamber, upon which the body was placed, and the picture shows the well-preserved wooden structure raised above the burial chamber. Skeletons of twelve horses and six dogs were discovered near the vessel's burial-place. One of the king's peacocks was however buried inside the ship. The clay soil had pre-served all the woodwork except the upper part of the stem and stern, which reached above the clay. Nothing therefore remained of the dragon head and tail, with which warships were usually ornamented.

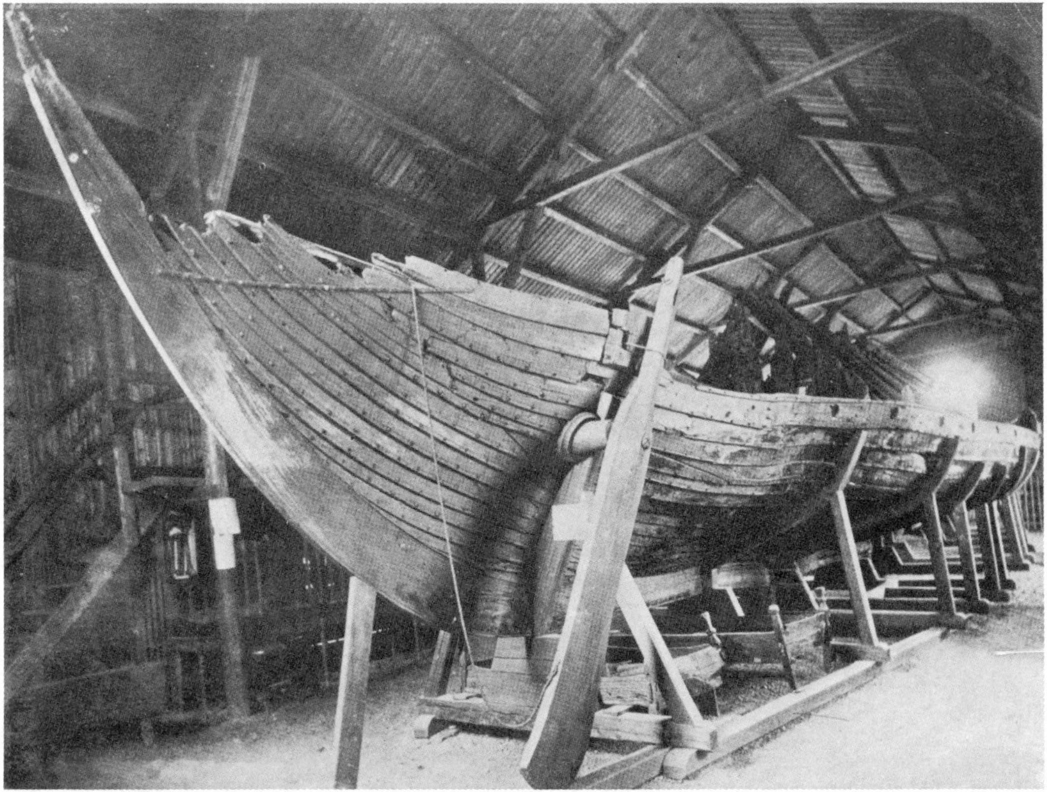

*O. Væring, Oslo*

THE GOKSTAD SHIP

This picture shows the starboard stern view, and the rudder

There he slew many folk who had before submitted to Swein. About this Arnor says:

| | |
|---|---|
| The king bade them avenge | The young warrior offered |
| The Danes' treason with hardness. | To the eagles heavy heaps |
| The bold prince caused | Of corpses, and the bodyguard nobly |
| The Falster dwellers to fall. | Helped the eagles' feeder. |

After this King Magnus sailed with his army to Fyn, where he harried and won much booty. Thus sayeth Arnor Jarlascald:

| | |
|---|---|
| The king in Fyn dyed | Let many mind which warrior |
| The fair standards bloody. | Filled another ten years of life |
| They rushed forth in the land; | To the ravens' joy. |
| The host was robbed by him. | The prince had the boldest heart. |

35. King Magnus sat that winter in Denmark and then there was good peace. He had had many battles in Denmark and won the victory in all of them. Odd Kikinascald quoth:

| | |
|---|---|
| Before Michaelmas | But just before Yule |
| A metal-grim strife arose. | Another cheerless strife |
| The Vends fell; those folks | Broke out near Aros; |
| Were used to the din of weapons. | The fight was mighty amongst the men. |

Arnor sayeth further:

| | |
|---|---|
| Olav's avenger! thou gavest stuff | Thou ready shield-bearer! Thou hast |
| For my work; I choose to praise thee. | Won fair battles amidst the arrows |
| Thou didst let the ravens drink | In one single winter; my lord, |
| Of the blood. Now must my song wax. | Thou shalt ever be called victorious! |

Three battles did King Magnus hold with Swein Ulfson. Thus says Tjodolv:

| | |
|---|---|
| With good warnings the fight | The prince of the Tronds dyed |
| Broke out, as Magnus would, | His sword red and always |
| For speaking about his victories | After in three battles |
| The warrior gives me topics. | Victory won he, and booty. |

36. When King Magnus the Good, the son of St Olav, ruled over Norway, Jarl Ragnvald Bruceson, as before related, stayed with him. Jarl Torfinn Sigurdson,[1] the uncle of Ragnvald, ruled over the Orkneys. King Magnus sent Ragnvald west to Orkney and ordered that Torfinn should let him have his father's heritage. Torfinn let Ragnvald have a third part of the land with him, for so had Bruce, the father of Ragnvald, had it at his death. Jarl Torfinn was married to Ingebjörg, the earl-mother, who was a daughter of Finn Arneson. Jarl Ragnvald thought he should have two-thirds of the land, as

---

1 The great Earl Torfinn of Orkney.

St Olav had promised to his father Bruce, and which Bruce had enjoyed as long as Olav lived. This was the beginning of a great strife between these kinsmen, concerning which a long saga is written. They had a great battle in Pentland Firth, in which Kalv Arneson was with Torfinn. About this Biarne Gullbrarscald quoth:

Kalv, we have heard why
Thou followed Finn's kinsman
And launched thy ships
To aid Jarl Torfinn.
Then the sword-eager warrior
Destroyed Bruceson's bold attacks.
Glad in strife thou wast,
But more out of hate
Thou went to Torfinn's help.

37. King Magnus now ruled over both Denmark and Norway. And after he had possessed himself of Denmark, he sent his messengers west to England. They went to King Edward and brought him King Magnus' letters and seal. And besides King Magnus' greetings the letter ran: "You must have heard of the agreement which Hardicanute and I made between us, that if one died without son the other who lived after him should take the lands and subjects the former had. Now has it so befallen, as I know you have heard, that I have taken the whole of Denmark in succession to Hardicanute. At his death he had England no less than Denmark, and I contend that I have a right to England according to our just agreements. I will that you give up the kingdom to me or otherwise I shall seek it with forces from both Denmark and Norway; then shall he have the rule of the land who wins the victory".

38. And when King Edward had read this letter he answered thus: "It is known of all men in this land that my father, Ethelred, was born to the inheritance of this kingdom both from old time and from new. We were his four sons, but when he had fallen from his possessions my brother Edmund took the rule and kingship, for he was the eldest of us; thereat I was well pleased, as long as he lived. But after him my step-father Canute took the realm and it was not easy to claim it so long as he was alive. And after him my brother King Harold was king, as long as he might live: And when he died, my brother Hardicanute ruled over Denmark, and the only sharing between brothers that seemed right to him was that he should be king over both England and Denmark, and I had nothing to rule over. Then he died, and it was the counsel of all the men of the land to take me as king in England. And as long as I did not bear the name of king I did not serve my chieftains more haughtily than the men who had no claim for the rule here. Now I have here taken the consecration as king and the name of king as fully as my father had

before me, and I will not give this name up as long as I live. But if King Magnus comes here with his army I will not gather a host against him and he will be able to possess himself of England, but before that he must take my life. Tell him my message in such a way". The messengers then went back and came to King Magnus and told him all their business. The king was slow in answering, and then he spoke thus: "I think it is most right and fitting for me to let Edward have his realm in peace, and to hold fast to the kingdoms which God has let me win".[1]

1 The English chroniclers are silent about this treaty between Magnus and Hardicanute. The *Anglo-Saxon Chronicle* states: "In the summer of 1045 King Edward went out with his ships to Sandwich, and there so great a force was gathered, that no man had seen a greater fleet in this land". No reason is given for this assembly of the fleet. Florence of Worcester mentions in the year 1045 "Edward, King of England, assembled a very powerful fleet at the port of Sandwich to oppose Magnus, King of Norway, who threatened to invade England". Roger of Wendover, Matthew of Westminster and Roger de Hoveden make a similar reference to an invasion by Magnus.

Harald Hardrade, when he invaded England (cf. 'History of Harald Hardrade', chapters 83 to 93), no doubt felt that the treaty made by his nephew Magnus, although not applicable to himself, gave him a certain justification for attacking England. When Earl Tosti came to Norway (cf. 'History of Harald Hardrade', chapter 79) he reminded him of King Magnus' treaty with Hardicanute, but King Harald still held back as he saw the enormity of the task. However, Tosti's arguments and Harald's ambitious nature had the better of him. It should be borne in mind that Harald Hardrade had from his early youth been fighting abroad and had for several years been the leader of the Værings (the Nordic warriors of the Greek Emperors at Constantinople). He was a born ruler of men, full of ambition, and an opportunity to seize the crown of England, which was left without an heir, must have appealed strongly to his aspiring nature.

## CHRONOLOGY

### MAGNUS THE GOOD. BORN 1024. KING OF NORWAY 1035–47

1035. Magnus becomes King of Norway.
   Death of King Canute at Shaftesbury, and burial at Winchester.
   Harold Harefoot becomes King of England.
1036. Death of King Swein Canuteson in Denmark.
1040. Death of Harold Harefoot.
   Hardicanute becomes King of England.

1042. Death of Hardicanute, who is succeeded by Edward the Confessor.

Magnus elected King of Denmark.

1043. Battle of Lyrskogsheath.

1044. Battle near Aarhus.

1045. Battle of Helganes.

1047. Death of Magnus the Good. His uncle Harald Hardrade succeeds him.

Swein Ulfson becomes King of Denmark.

# X

# THE HISTORY OF HARALD HARDRADE[1]

1. Sigurd Syr's son Harald, who was half-brother of St Olav on his mother's side, was at the battle of Stiklastader, when King Olav fell. Harald was wounded and escaped with the others who fled. Thus quoth Tjodolv:

| | |
|---|---|
| I heard that the keen storm of battle | Forced from the fallen Olav, |
| Drove against the king near Haug.[2] | The prince parted and saved |
| And the burner of the Bulgars[3] | His head when he was |
| Helped his brother well. | But fifteen years old. |

Ragnvald Bruceson brought Harald away from the battle and took him to a bonder who lived in a wood far from other men, and there Harald lay until he was better. Afterwards the bonder's son followed him east over the Kjöl and all the time they went by the forest paths, where they could, and not by the highways. The bonder's son knew not whom he followed, and when they were riding between certain waste woods, Harald quoth this:

| | |
|---|---|
| Now I must crawl from wood | Who knows if I shall not |
| To wood with little honour. | Become famous far and wide?[4] |

He went east through Jämtland and Helsingeland and so on to Sweden, where he found Ragnvald Bruceson and many others of King Olav's men who had escaped from the battle.

2. The following spring they got ships and in the summer they went east to Gardarik[5] to King Jarisleiv; there they were during the winter. Thus says Bolverk:

| | |
|---|---|
| Mild king, thou didst dry the mouth | And the next year thou wast |
| Of the sword when thou didst leave | In the east in Gardarik. |
| the strife. | Strong warrior! I have not heard |
| Thou gavest the raven food to eat, | Of a war-wager better than thou. |
| And the wolf howled on the hills. | |

1 *Hardrade* means 'hard to *rede*' (O.E.) or 'counsel'.    2 The farm *Haug* in Værdale, near Stiklestad.    3 Harald Hardrade helped the Greek Emperor in 1041 to subdue the Bulgars, who had revolted against the Emperor.    4 Harald says of himself in a poem he composed that he knew eight accomplishments and sports: he was a smith, he could ride, swim, run on skis, shoot, throw javelins, play the harp and compose poetry. 5 Russia.

King Jarisleiv greeted Harald and his men well, and Harald then became leader of the king's land guards (country militia) together with Eiliv, son of Ragnvald the Jarl.  Tjodolv quoth:

| | |
|---|---|
| In their war lines | They drove the East Vends |
| The brave leaders | Into such a tight corner. |
| Went forth | The law of these warriors |
| Where Eiliv stood. | Was not easy for the Lesjar.[1] |

Harald stayed some years in Gardarik and went far about in the easterway (Baltic). Afterwards he began a journey to Greece, and he had a great troop of men with him.  He drew near to Miklegarth.[2] Thus sayeth Bolverk:

| | |
|---|---|
| The cold shower drove forward | The prince saw Miklegarth's |
| The black bows of the ship, | Iron towers before his bows. |
| And the barks, nobly brynied, | The fair-hulled ships were borne |
| Bore their sails along the coast. | To the stronghold's lofty walls. |

3. Queen Zoe the Mighty[3] then ruled over Greece and with her Michael Katalaktus. And when Harald came to Miklegarth to the queen he went into her service for pay, and forthwith in the autumn he went on board galleys with the warriors who were going out into the sea of Greece.  Harald kept a number of his own men. The leader of the army was called Gyrge[4] and he was a kinsman of the queen. Harald had been but a short while in the army when the Værings[5] made an alliance with him and they went together in one troop when there was a fight; then it came about that Harald became chief over all the Værings. Gyrge and his army went far about in the Isles of Greece and harried much there in their corsairs.[6]

4. Once when they had gone overland and were to take their night quarters by some woods, it happened that the Værings came first to the night halt and they chose for themselves such places for their tents as they saw were best and lay highest. For there the land so lay that as soon as it rained it would be ill to rest where the land lay low. Then Gyrge, the Værings' leader, came up, and when he saw where the Værings had pitched their tents he bade them go away

---

1 Lesjar. This name is unknown. As Tjodolv speaks of the East Vends it might refer to the people of Poland.    2 Miklegarth (the big garth or town) was the Norsemen's name for Constantinople, the capital of the old Greek Empire.    3 The Empress Zoe ruled from 1028 to 1052 and was married from 1028 to 1034 to the Emperor Romanos Argyros, from 1034 to 1041 to the Emperor Michael Katalaktus (as mentioned by Snorre), and her last husband was the Emperor Konstantin Monomachos (1042 to 1054)    4 Gyrge, i.e. Georgios.    5 Væring was the name of the Nordic warriors who fought in the service of the Greek Emperors. The town of Warwick was in O.E. called Wæring wic, meaning a fortified garrisoned town.    6 I.e. the Greek warships.

and pitch their tents in another spot; he said that he would pitch his tents there. Harald said: "If ye come first to the night quarters then ye take your right place, and we must pitch our tents in some other spot which we like; now do ye so also, pitch your tents where ye will in another spot. I thought that it would be the right of the Værings here in the realm of the Queen of Greece to be independent and free in all things before all men and be liable for service to the king and queen alone". They quarrelled about it with great heat until both sides armed themselves; they nearly came to blows, but the wisest men came up and parted them; they said it would be more fitting to come to terms on this matter and make a clear arrangement between themselves about it, so that there should be no need of strife about it hereafter. Then they agreed upon a meeting, and the best and wisest men had charge of it. And at that meeting they so counselled that all agreed to cast lots together in a sheet, and the Greeks and the Værings should draw lots as to who should ride first or row and come to harbour or choose tent grounds: each of them should now be at peace according to what the lot said. After this they made and marked the lots. Then said Harald to Gyrge: "I will see how thou hast marked thy lot so that we shall not mark both lots in the same way". He did so. Harald then marked his lot and threw it into the sheet, and so did Gyrge. And the man who was to take out the lot, took one up and held it between his fingers, lifted his hand and said: "This man shall ride first and row and lay to harbour and choose his tent ground first". Harald grabbed at it with his hand, took the lot and cast it into the sea; then he said: "That was our lot". Gyrge said: "Why didst thou not let more men see it?" "See now", said Harald, "the lot which is left; thou knowest well thy mark." Then they all looked at the lot and all knew Gyrge's mark. It was adjudged that the Værings should have the choice in all they had quarrelled over. Other things befell too which they·did not agree about, and it always ended in Harald having his own way.

5. They all went together in the summer and harried. When the whole host was together Harald kept his men away from the fighting, also from where there was any risk for his men; he said that he was anxious not to lose his warriors. But when he was alone with his men he went into battle so hotly that he must get either the victory or his death. So it often befell that when Harald was leader of the men he won the victory, whilst Gyrge did not win. The warriors perceived this and said that their affairs would go better if Harald was sole chief over the whole army, and they blamed the leader

that he and his men were of no use. Gyrge said that the Værings would not grant him their help and he bade them go elsewhere whilst he went with the rest of the army and harried separately. Harald then left the army and with him went the Værings and Latins;[1] Gyrge went with the army of the Greeks. Then it would be shown what each could achieve. Harald always won victory and goods, but the Greeks went home to Miklegarth excepting the young men who would win themselves goods; they gathered to Harald and had him as their leader. He then went west with his army to Africa, which the Værings called Serkland,[2] and then he got a great many more men. In Serkland he won eighty strongholds; some gave themselves up and others he took by force. Afterwards he went to Sikiley.[3] Tjodolv quoth:

| | |
|---|---|
| Eighty strongholds in Serkland, | This was before the warrior, the foe |
| I say, were taken; the young hater | Of the Serks, went to rouse up |
| Of the serpents' bed[4] | The war-play of Hild[5] with the shield |
| Placed himself in danger. | On the level plains of Sikiley. |

Thus sayeth Illugi Bryndalerscald:[6]

| | |
|---|---|
| Harald, under Michael thou brokest | The son of Budli, as we have heard, |
| The southlanders with thy war shield; | Bade his sons-in-law to the feast.[7] |

Here it should be said that Michael was at that time King of the Greeks. Harald stayed many years in Africa and got many valuables, gold and all kinds of costly things. And all the goods which he took and did not need for his own costs he sent by his trusted men to Holmgard[8] into King Jarisleiv's power and keeping; and there he gathered a great many goods, for which he had the best opportunity, as he was harrying in that part of the world which was richest in gold and costly things. He had done great deeds and possessed himself of eighty strongholds, as has already been told.

6. And when Harald came to Sikiley he harried there, and then lay with his army near a great and well-peopled town. He surrounded the town, for the walls were so strong that he did not think he could force them. The townsmen had food enough and were well

---

1 I.e. warriors from the Latin countries, France or Italy.    2 The name *Serkland* was used both for Asia Minor and the north coast of Africa.    3 I.e. Sicily. 4 The expressions "hater of the serpents' bed" and "hater of gold" are often used by the scalds. In the Norse mythology the serpents' bed was gold, and its hater—who parts with it, as with a thing he hates—was the generous giver.    5 *Hild* was one of the Valkyries. *The play of Hild*=fighting.    6 I.e. the scald from Brynjedal in the south-western part of Iceland.    7 This refers to Atle, who according to the Elder Edda invited his wife's friends to a feast and killed them.    8 I.e. Novgorod, about 100 miles south of Leningrad.

armed to guard the town. Then he thought of this plan: his fowlers caught small birds which had nests in the town and which flew out into the woods during the daytime to get food. On the backs of the birds Harald let his men bind fir chips; melted wax and brimstone were poured thereon and fire set to it. As soon as they were free the birds flew together straight back to the town to seek their young in the nests which they had under the house roofs; they were thatched with reeds or straw. Then the house thatches caught fire from the birds. And although each bird only bore a little burden of fire, there was soon a great blaze when all the birds came to the thatches all over the town; and then one house burned after another until the town was on fire. All the folk then went out of the town and asked for mercy, the same men who many a day before had spoken haughtily and mockingly about the Greeks' army and their leader. Harald gave quarter to all who asked for it and afterwards he had power over this town.

7. There was another town which Harald came to with his army. It was both well-peopled and strong so that they did not expect to win it; there were hard flat wolds round the town. Harald then had a pit dug where a stream flowed, and it had a deep bed so that they could not be seen from the town. They threw the earth into the water and let the stream bear it away. They were at that work day and night, and they worked in shifts. Every day the army went towards the town and the townsmen went to the battlements, and they shot at each other. But at night both sides slept. And when Harald perceived that the tunnel was so long that it must come in past the town walls, he bade his men arm themselves, and it was towards day when they went into the tunnel. And when they came to the end they dug up over their heads until they came to stones set in lime; it was the floor of a stone hall. Afterwards they broke through the floor and went up into the hall. There many of the townsmen sat, eating and drinking, and for them it was the most unexpected ill-luck, for the Værings went forth with drawn swords and slew some, but others who could get out fled. The Værings went after them, but some seized the town gates and unlocked them; then the whole host went in. And when they came into the town the townsmen fled, but many asked for quarter and all who gave themselves up got it. In this way Harald possessed himself of the town and huge booty besides.

8. They came to a third town which was the greatest and strongest and mightiest in wealth and folk. Round this town there were great dikes so that they saw they could not win it with such tricks

as they had won the others. They lay there a long while and they could achieve naught. And when the townsmen saw that, they grew bold thereby. They set their men upon the town walls; then they unlocked the gates and shouted to the Værings, egging them on and bidding them come into the town; they taunted them for their lack of boldness and said they were no better than hens for fighting. Harald bade his men act as if they did not understand what they were saying; "we achieve nothing if we run to the town; they will bring their weapons upon us from under their feet, and even if we get into the town with some troops they have the power to lock in those they wish and keep out others, for they have set watch over all the gates. We will mock them no less and let them see that we fear them not. Our men shall go forth in the fields as near the town as possible but watch, however, that they do not go within range of shot. All our men shall go without weapons and play games and let the townsmen see that we heed not their lines of men". Thus it went on for some days after.

9. Iceland men are mentioned who went there with King Harald: one was Haldor, son of Snorre Godi, who brought this report to Iceland, and the other was Ulf, the son of Ospak, son of Osvifer the Wise. They were both very strong, bold men with weapons, and dear friends of Harald; they both joined in the games. And when things had gone on in this wise for some days the townsmen wished to show still greater boldness: they went without weapons on the town walls and still let the gates stand open. And when the Værings saw that, they went one day to their games with swords under their capes and helms under their hats. And when they had played a while they saw that the townsmen were off their guard; they quickly took their weapons and then ran to the gates. And when the townsmen saw it they went boldly against them, and all had their weapons. Then a fight began at the gate. The Værings had no armour to protect themselves except their capes which they wrapped round their left arms. Some were wounded, some fell and all were in sore need. Harald and the men with him who were in the camp came up to help his men. But the townsmen were then come up on to the walls and shot at them and cast stones on them. It was a hard fight, and it seemed to those who were at the gate that the others were too slow in bringing them help. And when Harald came to the gate, his standard-bearer fell. Then said Harald: "Haldor, take up the standard!" Haldor took up the standard, but answered and spoke unwisely: "Who wishes to bear the standard for thee when thou followest so weakly

as thou hast done this while?" These were more words of anger than words of truth, for Harald was the boldest of men with weapons. They then went into the town and the fight was hard, but it ended with Harald getting the victory and winning the town. Haldor was badly wounded, for he got a great wound on his face and there was a scar all the time he lived.

10. The fourth town which Harald came to with his army was greater than all those which have been spoken of before and it was so strong that there was no hope of taking it by storm. They then surrounded the town so that no goods could be moved into it. But when they had stayed there a short while Harald fell sick so that he lay in his bed; he had his tent pitched away from the other tents, for it seemed to give him rest not to hear the turmoil and noise of the army. His men often came to and fro in bands to ask his counsel. The townsmen saw that something had happened amongst the Værings, and they sent spies out to get to know what it might be. And when the spies came back to the town they could tell the tidings that the Værings' leader was sick and that they could not attack the town for that reason. And when things went on thus for a while, Harald's strength lessened and his men then grew sick at heart and sorrowful. All this the townsmen learned. It then came about that his sickness grew daily worse and one day his death was told through the whole army. The Værings then went to talk with the townsmen, and told them of the death of their leader and bade the priests grant him a grave in the town. And when the townsmen heard these tidings (there were many who ruled over the cloisters and other big churches in the town), each of them wished to have the body for his church, for they knew that great offerings would result. Then the whole crowd of priests clad themselves in shrouds and went out of the town with shrines and relics, and made a fair procession. And the Værings also made a great funeral procession. The coffin was carried high in the air and was covered with a pall, and before it many standards were carried. And when the coffin was borne in through the gates they set it down across the gates in front of the opening. The Værings then blew a war blast with all their horns and drew their swords. The whole Væring army rushed out of the camp with their weapons and ran to the town with shrieks and shouts. But the monks and other priests who had come to this funeral procession and striven with each other to be the first to receive the corpse, now struggled as hard as ever to get away from the Værings, for the latter slew everyone who was nearest to them, whether he were clerk

or layman. The Værings went through the whole town and slew the menfolk and robbed all the churches in the town and took much booty.

11. Harald was many winters on this journey, which is now spoken of, both in Serkland and Sikiley. He afterwards went back to Miklegarth with this army and stayed there a short while, until he set out on a journey to Jerusalem.[1] He left behind him the gold he had got in payment from the Greek king, and so did all the Værings who went on this journey with him. So it is said that in all these journeys Harald had eighteen battles. Thus quoth Tjodolv:

Every man knows that Harald
Hath held eighteen grim
Battles. Oft hath the peace
Been broken by the prince.

The grey eagle's keen claws,
O king, thou didst dye in blood,
And the wolf was always fed,
Ere thou didst go homeward.

12. Harald went out with his men to Palestine and afterwards he went to Jerusalem. Wherever he went in Palestine, all the towns and castles were given into his power. Thus sayeth Stuf the Scald, who had heard the king himself tell these tidings:

The sword-bold, great-minded
Warrior subdued
Jerusalem; the land was
Friendly to him and the Greeks.

And with full might
The land fell unburned
Into the warriors' hands.—
*Let the soul of mighty Harald*[2]

Here it should be said that the land fell unburned and unharried into Harald's power. He then went out to the Jordan and bathed himself where other palmers[3] are wont to bathe. Harald gave many things to the Lord's grave and to the Holy Cross[4] and other holy relics in Palestine. He freed the way right out to the Jordan and slew robbers and other unpeaceful folk. Stuf quoth:

The counsel and wroth words
Of the Agder-king[5] acted,
On both banks of the Jordan,
Against men's treachery.

And for true sinfulness
They must bear hard fines:
They suffered ill from the prince.—
*Abide eternally with Christ.*

Thereafter he went back to Miklegarth.

13. When Harald had come back to Miklegarth from Palestine, he wished to go to his *odal* lands in the north; he had then learned

1 The Greek Emperor concluded a treaty with the Caliph of Egypt in 1036, which allowed the Emperor to restore the church erected on the grave of Christ. The Emperor sent his workmen to Jerusalem and soldiers to protect them. Harald Hardrade was the leader of this regiment.    2 This line should be read in conjunction with the last line of the verse below: "Let the soul of mighty Harald Abide eternally with Christ". 3 *Palmers*, i.e. pilgrims to the Holy Land.    4 The Holy Cross Church.    5 *Agder*, the district of Agder in the south of Norway.

that Magnus Olavson, his brother's son, had become King of Norway as of Denmark, and then Harald withdrew from service with the Greek king. But when Queen Zoe got to know of this, she was very wroth and brought up charges against Harald; she said that he had been dishonest with the Greek king's goods, which had been taken on raids when Harald was leader of the army. But there was a fair young maid called Maria, who was Queen Zoe's brother's daughter. Harald had asked to wed her but the queen had refused. The Værings who had been in service in Miklegarth have told it here in the north that the tale went round amongst men who knew, that Queen Zoe herself wanted Harald as her husband. And that was in all likelihood the greatest reason for what befell Harald, when he would go away from Miklegarth, even though other things were put before the folk. The Greek king had Harald seized and borne off to prison. At that time the Greek king was called Konstantin Monomachos, and he ruled the kingdom with Queen Zoe.

14. But when Harald came near to the prison, the saintly King Olav showed himself to him and said that he would help him. In that street there was afterwards a chapel consecrated to King Olav and the chapel has stood there ever since.[1] The prison was so built that there was a high tower, open above, and a door led from the street into the tower. Harald was put in there and with him were Haldor and Ulf. The next night a mighty woman came to the top of the prison and went up the steps; with her went two serving-men. They let a rope down into the prison and drew them up. St Olav had formerly healed this woman and had now shown himself to her and said that she should free his brother from prison. Harald then went straightway to the Værings and they all got up and greeted him with welcome. The whole army then armed themselves and went to where the king was sleeping. They seized the king and blinded him in both eyes. Thus sayeth Toraren Skeggjason in his poem:

The noble king got
The gold, but the crowned king
    Of Greece went stone blind
    With hard wound marks.

Thus also sayeth Tjodolv the Scald:

The destroyer of the wolf's sorrow
Had both eyes of the crowned
King struck out.
There was strife on the journey.
    In the east the Agder prince
    Left a grisly mark on the
    Noble king, and gruesomely
    Was the Greek king stricken.

In both these poems on Harald and in many others it is said that Harald himself blinded the Greek king. Instead of him they could

1 This chapel no longer exists.

have mentioned a duke or a count or some other such princely man if they knew it was more correct, but Harald himself and the other men who were there with him came with this story.[1]

15. The same night Harald and his men went to the tower where Maria slept and took her away by force. They then went to the Værings' galleys, of which they took two, and rowed to Sævidar-sund.[2] And when they came to where iron chains lay across the sound, Harald said that the men should fall to their oars on both galleys and that the men who were not rowing should run aft in the galleys and each should have his sack with him. Thus they ran the galleys on to the iron chains; and as soon as the ships were fast and their movement stopped, he bade all his men run forward. Then the galley Harald was on plunged forward, and after swinging on the chain, slipped off, but the other galley stuck fast to the iron chain and broke its back, and many were drowned, though some were picked up from the water. In this way Harald came out from Mikle-garth and thus went into the Black Sea. But before he sailed away from land he put the girl ashore and gave her a good following back to Miklegarth. He bade her ask her kinswoman Zoe how much might she now had over Harald and whether the queen's might could have hindered him from getting hold of the girl. Thereupon Harald sailed north into Ellipallta[3] and therefrom farther through the East Realm.[4] On that journey Harald composed some humorous verses of which there are sixteen in all in the same poem; this is one:

The ship cut along by wide
Sikiley, where we were proud.
The boat merrily glided
With the joyful swains.

I do not expect that a laggard
Will ever come there.
Still, the gold-decked maid in Gardar
Will say that she scorns me.

By this he meant Ellisiv, daughter of King Jarisleiv in Holmgard.

16. And when Harald came to Holmgard, King Jarisleiv greeted him exceedingly well, and he stayed there during the winter. He then took into his own keeping all the goods and many kinds of costly things which he had before sent out there from Miklegarth. There was so much wealth that no man in the Northlands had ever seen so much in the possession of one man. Harald had three times come

---

1 The Greek Emperor Michael Kalafates who ruled together with the Empress Zoe was blinded in the street by his bodyguard, and Harald Hardrade was the leader of this troop. Snorre apparently is misinformed in mentioning Konstantin who succeeded Michael; cf. p. 506, n. 3.    2 I.e. the Golden Horn, the bay between Constantinople and Galata. In troublesome times iron chains were fastened across this bay.    3 The mouth of the River Dnieper in the Black Sea.    4 I.e. Russia and the Baltic Provinces.

into palace spoils whilst he was in Miklegarth. There exists a law that every time a Greek king dies the Værings shall have the palace spoils; they shall go through all the king's palaces where his taxes are hoarded and each shall then take freely what he can get hold of with his hands.[1]

17. This winter King Jarisleiv wedded his daughter to Harald; she was called Elizabeth, but the Norsemen called her Ellisiv. About this Stuf the Blind witnesseth:

The Agder prince won
Such kinship as he would.

The friend of the men got gold
In plenty and the king's daughter.

In spring he began his journey from Holmgard and then went to Aldeigjaborg,[2] where he got himself ships and whence he sailed west in the summer. He turned first to Sweden and he lay in by Sigtun. Thus quoth Valgard of Vellir:

Harald, thou broughtest out
On thy ship the fairest lading;
Gold thou broughtest west
From Gardar; honour was
    shown thee.

Great-minded king, strongly thou
Didst sail in hard sea weather.
And the ships were rolling.
Then thou sawest Sigtun,
When the sea spray ceased.

18. There Harald found Swein Ulfson; in the autumn he had fled before King Magnus at Helganes. And when they met, they greeted each other well. The Swedish king, Olav, was grandfather to Ellisiv, Harald's wife, and Swein's mother Astrid was King Olav's sister. Harald and Swein promised each other friendship and bound it with secret agreements. All the Swedes were Swein's friends, for he had great kinship in the land; all the Swedes, too, were Harald's friends and helpers; many great men were also bound to him by kinship. Thus Tjodolv quoth:

The oak keel cut through the sea
To the west from Gardar.
Afterwards, wise land-ruler,
The Swedes gave thee help.

Harald's cutter, which bent
Leewards, went with much
Gold 'neath the broad sail,
When the storm raged.

19. Harald and Swein then got themselves ships and soon a great army gathered to them; and when the men were ready they sailed west to Denmark. Thus says Valgard:

The oak keel glided under thee,
Fight-happy prince, to the sea
From Sweden. Fate gave
Thee thy *odal* lands with right.

The cutter was reefed
To the top, when it tacked
Along Scania's flat coast
And scared the Danish women.

1 As Harald came into three palace spoils, he must have arrived in Constantinople before 1034, when Romanos Argyros' reign ceased.    2 Cf. 'History of Olav Tryg-vason', p. 183, n. 4.

They came first to Zealand and harried and burned far and wide there. Afterwards they sailed to Fyn where they went up and harried. Valgard quoth:

Harald, thou didst harry
All Zealand; the wolf
Hied there to find the fallen.
The prince threatened the foe.
The folk-strong king went
To Fyn and gave the helmets
Hard work to bear;
The shields burst asunder.

Grimly the fire burned
In the garth south of Roskilde;
The warrior king made
The fallen houses glow.

The landsmen lay fallen,
Hel[1] robbed them of freedom;
The house folk, bent with anguish,
Fled hastily to the woods.

Sorrowfully they left their homes,
And the Danes who lived
Thereafter fled away;
The fair women were seized.
The lock held the maiden's body;
Before thee thou didst send
Many a loath woman to the ships.
The fair-skinned bore the chains.

20. In the autumn after the battle of Helganes[2] Magnus Olavson went north to Norway. Thereafter he learned the tidings that his kinsman Harald Sigurdson had come to Sweden and that he and Swein Ulfson had made a pact, had gathered a great army and thought besides of subduing Denmark and then Norway. King Magnus called out a levy from Norway and soon a great host gathered to him. He then heard that Harald and Swein had come to Denmark and were burning and setting fire to everything, and that all the men of the land were submitting to them far and wide. It was likewise said that Harald was a greater and stronger man than others and he was so wise that nothing was impossible to him, and that he always got the victory. He was also so rich in gold that no man could be compared with him. Thus sayeth Tjodolv:

Now can the seafarers
Scarcely hope for peace.
The bodyguard fear to go,
For his fleets are off the land.

Eager for battle Magnus sails
With his ships from the north,
And Harald brings other steeds
Of the sea from the south.

21. Those of King Magnus' men who were his counsellors told him that they would deem it unlucky if he and his kinsman Harald were to bear the spears of death against each other; many men offered to go and make terms between them. And after these counsels the king agreed to it. Men were then sent in a cutter and they came as quickly as they could to Denmark. They got Danish men who were good friends of King Magnus to bring this message before Harald. The business was dealt with quietly. And when Harald

1 *Hel,* i.e. goddess of death. She ruled over those who died of sickness and old age.
2 Cf. 'History of Magnus the Good', chapter 33.

heard it said that King Magnus his kinsman would offer him peace and pact and that he should have half Norway with Magnus but that each of them should have half their joint store of valuables, he agreed to it, and the secret messengers returned to King Magnus.

22. One evening a little later Harald and Swein talked over their drink. Swein asked what treasures Harald had that he set most store by. He answered that it was his standard, the Land-Waster.[1] Swein then asked what went with the standard since it was so great a treasure. Harald said it had been foretold that he who went behind that standard would always have victory, and he also said that it had happened so ever since he had had it. Swein answered: "I will believe that the standard has this quality if thou holdest three battles against King Magnus, thy kinsman, and gettest the victory in them all". Harald then said wrathfully: "I know there is kinship between me and Magnus even if thou dost not remind me of it, and though we now go against each other with the shield of war, that does not mean that other meetings between us might not be more fitting". Swein changed colour and said: "Some will guess, Harald, that thou hast so done before as to keep only to those agreements of thine which thou thinkest will best further thy own affairs". Harald answered: "Thou must know of fewer times that I have not kept my agreements than I know that Magnus will say thou hast not kept thine to him". Thereafter each of them went his way. In the evening when Harald went to sleep in the quarterdeck of his ship, he said to his shoe lad: "I will lie down in this resting-place to-night, for I have misgivings that all will not be free from treachery; this evening I found that my kinsman Swein grew very wroth at my straight speaking; thou shalt keep watch if anything befalls here in the night". Harald then went to another place to sleep in, and in his own place he put a tree log. In the night a boat rowed up to the stern, and a man went on board and cut open the quarterdeck cover; he then went in and struck at Harald's bed with a mighty axe, so that it stuck fast in the tree. The man leaped straightway into the boat— it was pitch dark—and forthwith rowed away. But the axe was left as a witness where it stood fast in the tree. Afterwards Harald woke his men and let them know what treachery they were come upon:

1 In O.N. *Landeyda* means 'a country's destruction' or 'killing of its inhabitants'. It was a white standard with a raven on it. The Normans at Hastings had a standard, which they called *Gonfanon*, from O.N. *Gunnfani* (meaning something that blinks or glistens in the battle). Cf. p. 99, n. 6. The Italian word *gonfalone* (i.e. *gonfanon*) derives its origin from the Normans in Italy; also *gonfaloniere* (i.e. the standard-bearer); in French *gonfalonier*.

"We can now see", he said, "that here we have no power against Swein as soon as he strikes with treachery against us; it may be the best choice to go from here whilst it is possible; let us now loosen our ships and row secretly away". So they did; they rowed in the night north along the coast and they went day and night until they found King Magnus where he lay with his host. Harald then went to meet his kinsman King Magnus and it was a glad meeting, as Tjodolv says:

Wide-famed prince, thou didst cut
Through the water under thy keels,
Where thou drewest west to Denmark;
Thy dragon ships cleft the billows.

And Olav's son afterwards
Offered thee half his land
And men. There the kinsmen
Met each other gladly.

After this the kinsmen talked with each other and everything passed in a friendly way.

23. King Magnus lay by the land and he had his tent pitched on shore. He then bade his kinsman Harald to his table and Harald went to the feast with sixty men; it was a fair banquet. And when the day was passing, King Magnus went into the tent where Harald was sitting; men went with him carrying weapons and clothes. The king went to the man who sat lowest and gave him a good sword, to the next a shield, and thereafter clothes or weapons or gold, and to the more noble he gave greater gifts. At last he came before Harald, his kinsman, and in his hand he had two canes; he spoke thus: "Which of these two canes wilt thou have?" Harald answered: "That which is nearer to me". Then said Magnus: "With this cane I give thee half of Norway with all the dues and taxes and possessions that pertain thereto, with the agreement that thou shalt be king everywhere in Norway with the same right as myself. When we are both together I shall be first in greeting and service and seat; if there are three princely men together I shall sit in the middle and I shall have the king's berth and the king's jetty. Thou shalt also help and strengthen our kingdom in return for my having made thee such a man as I never thought there would be in Norway whilst my head was above the ground". Harald then stood up and thanked him for the name of king and for the honour. They both sat down and were very joyful that day; in the evening Harald and his men went to their ships.

24. Next morning King Magnus had the whole army called to a thing, and when the thing was sitting King Magnus made known to all men the gift he had given his kinsman Harald. Tore of Steig[1]

---

[1] Son of Tord Guthormson of Steig and Isrid Gudbrand's daughter. Cf. 'History of St Olav', chapter 128.

gave Harald the name of king at the thing. That day King Harald bade King Magnus to his table and Magnus went with sixty men to Harald's tent, where he had made ready the feast. Both kings were on the same seat and it was a fair banquet and choice food, and both the kings were glad and merry. And when the day was passing, King Harald had many bags brought into the tent, and there his men also bore in clothes and weapons and all kinds of costly things; he dealt out the things he gave and shared them amongst King Magnus' men who were at the feast. Afterwards he had the bags undone and then said to King Magnus: "Yesterday thou gavest us a great kingdom, which thou hast formerly won from our mutual foes, and thou tookest us into fellowship. It was well done, for thou hast fought much for it. It is in different ways that we have been abroad. We have both, however, had many trials ere I gathered this gold which thou canst see now. I will share this with thee. We two shall have all these treasures with equal right, even as we two each have half the kingdom of Norway. I know that our minds are unlike. Thou art more open-handed than I; we will then share these goods equally between us, so that each can do what he will with his share". Harald then had a great ox-hide spread out and poured thereon the gold from the bags; they then took scales and weights, dealt out the gold and shared it all by weight. To all men who saw it, it seemed wonderful that so much gold should have come together in one place in the northern lands. In reality, it was the Greek king's possession and wealth, for, as all men said, the houses there are full of red gold. The kings were now very merry. Then a stoup,[1] as big as a man's head, was brought in and King Harald took it up and said: "Where now is thy gold, Magnus my kinsman, to come up to this knop-head?" Then King Magnus answered: "There has been so much unrest and so many levies of men that almost all the gold and silver which was in my keeping is used up. There is now no more gold in my possession except this ring". He took off the ring and handed it to Harald, who looked at it and said: "That is little gold, kinsman, for a king who has two kingdoms, and yet there may be some men who doubt if thou ownest this ring". Then said King Magnus sadly: "If I do not own that ring rightfully, then I know not what I have got rightfully, for my father, King Olav, gave me this ring on our last parting". Then King Harald answered, laughing: "Thou sayest the truth, King Magnus; thy father gave thee the ring; this ring he took from my father for some small cause. It is also true that it was not easy

1 The O.N. text is *staup*, in M.N. *stöp*, from the verb *stöpe* = to cast or to found by melting.

for small kings in Norway when thy father was at his mightiest".
King Harald at this feast gave Tore of Steig a mazer; it was girt with
silver and had a silver handle above, and both were gilded; it was
full of cut silver pennies. There were also two gold rings which together weighed one mark. Harald also gave him his cape which was
of brown purple with white skins; he promised Tore great honour
and his friendship. Torgils Snorrason[1] said that he had seen the
altar cloth which had been made of the cape; and Gudrid, daughter of
Guthorm, son of Tore of Steig, said that she had seen her father
Guthorm with the mazer. Thus sayeth Bolverk:

| | |
|---|---|
| As I have heard, O warrior, | The pact between the kinsmen |
| Thou hadst title after this | Ended in peace and joy, |
| To the green earth when thou didst meet | And afterwards Swein had |
| Magnus and thou gavest him gold. | Sharp strife to expect.. |

25. King Magnus and King Harald both ruled over Norway the
next year according to their agreement and each had his own court.
In the winter they went round feasting in the Uplands and sometimes they were together, but sometimes each went by himself. They
went right north to Trondheim and on to Nidaros. King Magnus
had watched over King Olav's holy relics since he came into the land,
clipping his hair and nails once a year, and he himself kept the key
by which the shrine might be unlocked. Then many kinds of miracles
took place at the relics of King Olav. Soon there arose some discord
between the kings, and many men were so ill-minded that they went
between them with evil.

26. When Harald had gone away, Swein Ulfson lay behind asleep.
He afterwards asked carefully about Harald's journey. And when
he got to know that Harald and Magnus had made a treaty and now
had one great host together, he sailed east with his army off Scania
and stayed there until he learned in the winter that Magnus and
Harald had gone north to Norway with their army. Swein then
sailed south with his host to Denmark, and that winter he took all
the king's dues.

27. When spring came King Magnus and King Harald called
out a levy from Norway. Once it befell that King Magnus and King
Harald lay in the same haven, and next day Harald was ready first
and sailed forthwith; in the evening he came into the haven where he
and King Magnus had thought of being that night. Harald laid

---

1 *Torgils Snorrason* was son of the lawman Snorre Hunbogason (died 1170). Torgils
was a clergyman and lived at Skard by the Breidafjord in the western part of Iceland: he
died in 1201.

his ship in the king's berth and fitted his awnings. King Magnus sailed out later in the day and he came into the haven when Harald's men had finished raising their awnings. They saw that Harald had drawn up in the king's berth and that he meant to lie there. And when King Magnus' men had let their sails down, King Magnus said: "Now shall our men get ready to row and sit along the bulwarks, and others shall undo their weapons and arm themselves; if they will not move off, then we shall fight". And when King Harald saw that King Magnus would come to blows with them, he spoke to his men: "Cut now the ropes and let the ships be shifted from the berth. Magnus, my kinsman, is wroth". They did so; they shifted their ships from the berth, and King Magnus hauled his ships to it. When both had then made themselves ready, King Harald went up with some men on to King Magnus' ship. The king greeted him well and bade him welcome. Then King Harald answered: "I thought that we were come amongst friends, but I lately had some doubt if thou wouldst let it be so. But it is true that youth is hot; I will not count it other than the deed of a child". Then said King Magnus: "It was the deed of kinship, not of childhood. I can remember well enough what I agreed to and what I refused. If this little matter was taken without our notice, another would soon follow. We will keep the treaty we made in every way and we will have the same of thee as we have settled". Then said King Harald: "It is also an old saying that the wiser man gives way"—and he then went back to his ship. In such dealings between the kings it was found hard to keep measure; King Magnus' men asserted that he was right, but they who did not understand maintained that Harald was made to look somewhat small. And King Harald's men said that it should not be otherwise than that King Magnus should have the berth if they both came to it at the same time, but King Harald was not bound to move out of the berth if he lay there first; they maintained that Harald had acted well and wisely. But they who would make the worst of it said that King Magnus wished to break the agreement and that he had been wrong and unjust to King Harald. About these quarrels witless men soon talked so much that there was a split between the kings. Much also befell so that the kings went their own ways, even though little is written about it here.

28. King Magnus and King Harald sailed south with their host to Denmark. And when Swein heard of this he fled thence to Scania. King Magnus and King Harald stayed a long time in the summer in Denmark and subdued it all. In the autumn they were in Jutland.

One night when King Magnus lay in his bed he dreamed and thought he was where his father, King Olav, was, and the latter seemed to be talking to him: "What lot, my son, wilt thou choose: to go now with me, or become the mightiest of kings and live long but do such evil that thou mayest hardly or even not at all atone for it?" And he seemed to answer: "I will that thou choose for me". Then he thought that the king answered: "Thou shalt go with me". King Magnus told his men this dream. And a little later he fell sick and lay at a place called Sudertorp.[1] And when he was nigh dead he sent his brother Tore[2] to Swein Ulfson to say that he should grant Tore the help he needed. Word followed that King Magnus gave Swein the Danish kingdom after his death. He said that it was fitting that Harald should rule over Norway and Swein over Denmark. Then King Magnus the Good died and the whole people sorrowed over his death. Thus quoth Odd Kikinascald:

| | |
|---|---|
| Men shed many tears | Sore were the huscarls' hearts; |
| When the generous prince was borne | They kept not back their tears. |
| to his grave. | And in sorrow the folk often |
| Heavy then was the burden | Thought of their king. |
| Of those to whom he gave gold. | |

29. After these tidings King Harald held a thing with his men and told them his plan of going with his army to the Vebjorg thing[3] and of having himself taken as King of Denmark and then winning the land. He reckoned it as his inheritance from Magnus his kinsman, just as he did Norway. He asked his men to help him and thought that the Norsemen would then always be the rulers of the Danes.[4] Then Einar Tambarskelver answered and said that he was more bound to bear his foster-son, King Magnus, to his grave and bring him to his father, King Olav, than to fight abroad or to long for another king's lands and possessions. He so ended his speech that it seemed to him better to follow King Magnus dead than any other king alive.[5] He had the body taken and laid out with honour, so that it could be seen when placed upon the king's ship. Then all

---

1 *Sudertorp* is in *Sönder Jylland* (or Southern Jutland). 2 *Tore* was Magnus' half-brother. He was Alvhild's (Magnus mother's) son, in second marriage. Snorre Sturlason makes no distinction between brothers and half-brothers. This was apparently not customary, even with children of a different father. 3 *Vebjorg*, now Viborg in Jutland, was in olden times used for important thing meetings, such as elections of kings. Cf. 'History of Magnus the Good', chapter 21. 4 This is characteristic of Harald Hardrade's ambition and strong belief in his own and his countrymen's power. 5 Einar Tambarskelver wielded a similar power in North Norway to that of Erling Skjalgson in the south.

the Tronds and Norsemen made themselves ready for the journey home with King Magnus' body, and the levy broke up. Then King Harald saw that it was best for him to choose to go back to Norway and first possess himself of the kingdom and thereby increase his might. Harald now went back to Norway with the whole host. And as soon as he came to Norway he held a thing with the men of the land and had himself taken as king thereof. Then he went from the east, right from the Vik, and was taken as king in every folk district in Norway.

30. Einar Tambarskelver went with King Magnus' body and with him there went all the Tronds' army; they brought the body to Nidaros and it was buried in St Clement's Church, where also rested St Olav's shrine. King Magnus was of middling height with straight fair countenance, fair-haired, a good speaker and a quick thinker, strong-minded, generous with his wealth, a great warrior and very bold with weapons. He was the best befriended of all kings. Friend and foe praised him alike.

31. That autumn Swein Ulfson was in Scania and would go east to Sweden; he was thinking of giving up the name of king which he had taken in Denmark. As he was mounting his horse, some men rode up to him and told him tidings: first that King Magnus Olavson was dead, and next that all the Norsemen had gone away from Denmark. Swein answered quickly and said: "I call God to witness that never again shall I flee from Denmark, as long as I live". Thereupon he stepped on to his horse and rode southwards in Scania; straightway many folk drew to him. That winter he subdued all Denmark and all the Danes took him as their king. Tore, King Magnus' brother, came to Swein with King Magnus' messages, such as were written about before (chapter 28). Swein greeted him well and Tore was with him for a long time in good cheer.

32. King Harald Sigurdson took the kingdom of all Norway after King Magnus Olavson's death. And when he had ruled one year in Norway, and spring came, he called out a levy from the whole land, half in men and half in ships, and he sailed south to Jutland, where he harried and burned far and wide in the summer; he then came into Godnarfjord.[1] Then King Harald composed this:

> Whilst the linen-white woman  
> Sang her song to her man,  
> We let our anchors hold  
> The oaken ships in Godnarfjord.

---

1 The present Gudena or Guden River flows into the Godnarfjord, now called Randersfjord (Jutland).

He then spoke to Tjodolv the Scald and bade him compose something; Tjodolv quoth:

| | |
|---|---|
| I tell a forecast: next summer | The ship farther south; |
| The anchor will hold with its hooks | We shall cast the anchor deeper. |

About this Bolverk tells in his drapa that the summer after King Magnus' death King Harald went to Denmark:

| | |
|---|---|
| The next year thou didst ask | On the dark billows the dear |
| For a fair levy from the land; | Dragons lay, laden |
| Thou then didst cut through the sea | With warriors ready to fight; |
| With the richly dight sea steeds. | The Danes were ill in mind. |

Then they burned Thorkel Göisa's garth; Thorkel was a great chieftain. His daughters were brought bound to the ships, for the winter before they had made much mockery of King Harald's wish to go to Denmark with his warships; they cut anchors out of cheese and said that such would hold the King of Norway's ships well enough. Then was this said:

| | |
|---|---|
| The maids of the Danes cut | Now in the morning I see |
| Rings of anchors | Many maids going to the king's |
| From the spoilt cheese; such deeds | Ships in great chains. |
| Made the king wrathful. | Fewer of them laugh now. |

It is said that the watchman who had seen King Harald's fleet had said to Thorkel Göisa's daughters: "Daughters of Göisa, ye said that Harald would not come to Denmark", and Dotta answered: "That was yesterday!" Thorkel freed his daughters with great wealth. Thus sayeth Grani:

| | |
|---|---|
| Never did the witless | The lord of the Filers[1] drove |
| Women have | The fleeing foes to the shore; |
| Their eyes dry of tears | Dotta's father must |
| In the thick Hornskog. | Give much wealth. |

All this summer King Harald harried in Denmark and got much booty. But he did not then possess himself of Denmark. In the autumn he went back to Norway and was there during the winter.

33. The winter after the death of King Magnus the Good, King Harald wedded Thora, the daughter of Torberg Arneson. They had two sons, the elder Magnus, the second Olav. King Harald and Queen Ellisiv had two daughters; one was called Maria, the other Ingegerd. The next spring after the journey which has just been

---

1  *Filers*, i.e. the inhabitants of Fjalir. Cf. 'History of Harald Hairfair', p. 51.

described (chapter 32) King Harald called out the army and in the summer he went to Denmark and harried, and so he did one summer after another. Thus quoth Stuf the Scald:

Falster was wasted, and ill-luck
The folk had, as I heard.

The raven was fed, and each year
The Danes were afraid.

34. King Swein ruled over all Denmark after King Magnus died; he sat in peace in the winters but went out in the summers with his army and threatened to go north with the Danish host and do no less evil there than King Harald had done in Denmark. In the winter King Swein bade King Harald meet him in the summer on the Elv and fight with him there to the end or else make peace. Then all the winter they were busy fitting out their ships in order to have half the common folk out the following summer. That summer Torleik the Handsome came from Iceland and began to compose a flokk about King Swein Ulfson; he heard when he came to Norway that King Harald had gone south to the Elv against King Swein. Then Torleik quoth this:

It is expected that in the spear fight
The Inner Tronds' bold men
Will meet the bold king
On the sea king's path.

Yet can God bring it about
That one will there take
The other's life or land;
Swein thinks little of peace.

And further he quoth this:

The wrathful Harald who oft
Bears the bloody shield from the land
Brings the broad longships
From the north on Budli's ways.[1]

And from the south o'er the sea
There came the warlike Swein's
Gold-mouthed, high-masted beasts,
All painted in fair hues.

King Harald came to the meeting-place with his army, and then he heard that King Swein lay in the south off Zealand with his fleet. King Harald then divided his army; most of the bonders' levy he bade go back, and he went with his bodyguard and friends and the landed men and all the host of bonders who dwelt nearest the Danes. They went south to Jutland south of Vendilskagi,[2] then south past Tjoda,[3] and everywhere they went with the shield of war. Thus sayeth Stuf the Scald:

The folk in Tjoda fled
From meeting the king.

Great plans had the proud-hearted man.
(Harald's soul in Heaven.)

1 *Budli*, i.e. sea king. *Budli's ways* = the ocean.   2 The Scaw.   3 *Tjoda*, now Tyland, on the north-west coast of Jutland.

They went right south to Hedeby,[1] where they took and burned the market town. Then King Harald's men composed this:

| | |
|---|---|
| All Hedeby was burned | I hope our work raised |
| From end to end. | Sorrow for Swein. In the night |
| A strong deed, I think, | Before dawn I was in the town; |
| It can be called. | Fire rose up from the houses. |

About this Torleik also speaks in his flokk, when he had learned that there had been no battle on the Elv:

| | |
|---|---|
| Every man who knows it not | When Harald sped west |
| Asks the king's followers | With ships to the king's town |
| Why the avenging prince | So needlessly early, |
| Has gone to Hedeby; | This he should have avoided. |

35. After this Harald went north with sixty ships, most of which were great and laden with booty he had taken in the summer. And when they came north past Tjoda, King Swein came down from the land with a great host and he bade King Harald go on land and fight. King Harald had less than half as many men, but all the same he bade King Swein fight with him on ships. Thus sayeth Torleik the Handsome:

| | |
|---|---|
| Swein who was born | But the eager Harald |
| To the best luck on earth | Would rather, he said, |
| Bade the mighty king | Fight on ships, if the bold |
| Come to bloody fight on land. | King would keep the land. |

After that Harald sailed north past Vendilskagi. The wind turned against them and they lay in under Lesö[2] for the night. Then a thick mist came over the sea. And when morning came and the sun rose, they saw that on the other side of the sea it was as if fires were burning. This was told to King Harald, and when he saw it he straightway said: "Throw off the awnings from the ships, and begin to row. The Danish army is indeed coming after us. The darkness will have cleared there where they are, for the sun is shining on their dragon heads which are overlaid with gold". So it was as Harald had said; Swein, the Danish king, was coming with a mighty host. Both armies now rowed their utmost. The Danish ships floated more lightly under the oars, and the Norse ships were both water-logged and heavily laden. They drew nearer to each other and then Harald saw that they could not go on in this wise. He said that they should throw planks overboard and put clothes and other good things thereon. The sea was so calm that the planks were driven by the

---

1 *Hedeby*, the present town of Sleswick.  2 An island in the Kattegat.

current. And when the Danes saw their own goods floating about on the sea, they who were foremost turned away towards these things, for it seemed to them easier to take what was floating loose than to go alongside the Norsemen; then the pursuit was delayed. And when King Swein came after them with his ships, he egged them on and said it was a great shame if with so great an army they should not be able to take the Norsemen, since they had so few men, and get them in their power. Then the Danes began to row more strongly a second time. And when King Harald saw that the Danish ships were going faster, he bade his men lighten the ships and throw malt and wheat

When the sun rose they saw the Danish ships

and bacon overboard, and cast out their drink; this helped for a time. King Harald then bade them take part of the loose railing-boards and vats and empty casks and throw them overboard, and with them the war prisoners also. And when they were floating on the sea, King Swein bade them help the men, and this was done. Whilst they were doing this, the distance between the two armies grew greater and the Danes turned about but the Norsemen went their way. Thus sayeth Torleik the Handsome:

I have heard tell how
Swein chased the Eastmen
On the sea, and how the swift-
Minded king got away.

The whole booty of the Tronds'
Leader was floating out
On the waves of the Jutland sea;
Many ships he lightened.

King Swein turned back with his fleet under Lesö; there they found seven of the Norsemen's ships—they were levied men and bonders only. When King Swein came to them they asked quarter and offered goods for themselves. Thus sayeth Torleik the Handsome:

| | |
|---|---|
| Harald's stout-hearted friends | And the sharp-minded bonders |
| Asked the king for quarter; | Afterwards refused to fight |
| They who had fewer men | When they could talk; these men |
| Laid down their weapons. | Wanted to keep their lives. |

36. King Harald was a mighty man and a strong ruler in the land; he was a very understanding man, so that it is commonly said that there never has been a ruler in Norway who was so deep-thinking or of such good counsel as Harald. He was a great warrior and very bold with weapons; he was stronger and sharper with weapons than any other man as is written above (chapter 9). But many more of his famous deeds have not been written about, and this comes in part from our lack of knowledge and in part from the fact that we do not wish to set in this book tales for which there is no witness. Even though we have heard such things said or spoken of, it seems to us better that some things might be put in hereafter than that it should be needful to take them out. Many tales about King Harald are found in poems which Icelanders recited to him or his sons; for this reason he was also a great friend to such men. He was also a great friend of all the men of our land; when there was great dearth in Iceland, King Harald gave four ships leave to take meal to Iceland and decided that the ship pound should be no dearer than a hundred ells of homespun; he allowed all poor folk to go to Norway, if they could obtain a passage across the sea. Thus this land just survived and then the season improved. King Harald sent out here a bell for the church for which St Olav had sent wood and which was erected at the Althing.[1] Such memories have men here of King Harald and of the many other great gifts which he granted the men who went to him. Haldor Snorrason and Ulf Ospakson, who have been mentioned before (chapter 9), came to Norway with King Harald. They were very unlike in many ways. Haldor was very big, strong and fair. King Harald bore this witness about him, that among all his men Haldor was the one who was least alarmed at unexpected happenings, whether it was of risk of life or of joyful tidings or whatever perils befell; he was always unperturbed and no more and no less glad. He never slept longer or took food and drink other-

---

1 *Althing* in Iceland was the legislative assembly and supreme court of judicature for the whole country. It was held at Thingvold (in O.N. *þingvellir* or *Thingvellir*) some thirty miles east of Reykjavik the capital of Iceland. It dates its origin from A.D. 930 and is therefore the oldest parliament in North Europe.

wise than was his wont. Haldor was a man of few words and stubborn, straight-speaking, bad-tempered and haughty. This seemed ill to the king, as he had enough noble and service-willing men. Haldor stayed a short time with the king. He went to Iceland and set up his houses in Hjardarholt,[1] where he lived for the rest of his life and became an old man.

37. Ulf Ospakson was with King Harald in great favour. He was a very wise man, well-spoken, strong, great-minded and upright. King Harald made Ulf his marshal and married him to Jorunn, Torberg's daughter, the sister of Thora, whom King Harald had wed. The children of Ulf and Jorunn were John the Strong of Rasvold,[2] and Brigida, the mother of Sauda-Ulf, the father of Peter Burthenswain,[3] the father of Ulf the Fly and his brothers and sisters. John the Strong's son was Erlend Himaldi, the father of Archbishop Eystein[4] and his brothers. King Harald gave Ulf the Marshal the rights of a landed man and twelve marks land rent, besides half a folk district in Trondheim; Stein Herdisarson tells this in Ulf's flokk.

38. King Magnus Olavson had St Olav's Church built in Kaupang;[5] on that site the king's body had been placed through one night and it was above the town.[6] He also built there a king's residence. The church was not fully ready when the king died, but King Harald had that finished which was not complete, and he also had a stone hall built by the king's residence, but it was not finished before he began to build St Mary's Church up on the sandhill near the place where the king's holy remains had lain in the earth the first year after his death. It was a great minster and was built so strongly with cement that it could scarcely be broken up when Archbishop Eystein had it taken down.[7] King Olav's relics were kept in St Olav's Church whilst St Mary's Church was building. King Harald had the king's residence built below St Mary's Church, near the river, where it is now. But the hall he had previously built he now had hallowed as St Gregory's Church.

39. There was a man called Ivor the White[8] who was a noble landed man. He had his seat in the Uplands and was the son of the

1 In Laxardal, in Dala district, West Iceland. 2 Now Rosvold in Værdale (in North Trondheim folk district). 3 About him cf. 'History of Sigurd, Inge and Eystein', chapter 9. 4 *Eystein* was Archbishop from 1161 to 1188. 5 I.e. Trondheim. 6 The foundations of the old St Olav's Church are under the present Town Hall in Kongen's Gate. 7 Archbishop Eystein moved St Mary's Church to Elgesæter in Trondheim about 1178, where it was the church for the cloister. 8 The Scandinavian Christian name Ivar has in English become Ivor.

daughter of the mighty Hacon the Jarl. Ivor was the fairest of men to look upon. His son was called Hacon, about whom it is said that he was far above all men in Norway in courage and strength and doughtiness; he went even in his youth on raids and thereby shaped his own success; he became a very famous man.

40. Einar Tambarskelver was the mightiest of the landed men in Trondheim, but there was little friendship between him and King Harald. Einar, however, had the land rents he had had as long as King Magnus lived. Einar was a very rich man and he had married Bergliot, the daughter of Hacon the Jarl, as was before written of ('History of St Olav', chapter 21). Eindridi, their son, was now full-grown and he had married Sigrid, the daughter of Ketel Kalv and Gunhild, King Harald's sister. Eindridi had inherited his good looks from his mother's father Hacon the Jarl and his sons, but from his father Einar he had big stature and strength and all the doughtiness which Einar had above all men. He was a well-befriended man.

41. At that time Orm was a jarl in the Uplands; his mother was Ragnhild, daughter of Jarl Hacon the Mighty. Orm was a very outstanding man. At that time Aslak Erlingson lived at Sola in Jæderen and he had married Sigrid, the daughter of Jarl Swein Haconson. Gunhild, another daughter of Swein the Jarl, was married to the Danish king, Swein Ulfson; these were Hacon the Jarl's offspring in Norway, besides many other noble men; the whole family was much more handsome than other folk and most of them were very doughty men, and all were noble-minded.

42. King Harald was an eager man for power and his lust grew as he fixed himself more firmly in the land; it went so far that it little availed most men to speak against him and put forward other matters than those he would have. Thus sayeth Tjodolv the Scald:

The war-making chiefs;      Before this feeder of ravens
Loyal men shall always       Many men bow; few men there are
Sit and stand there where    Who will not do anything
The dear king wishes.        But what the king bids.

43. Einar Tambarskelver was the greatest leader of the bonders throughout all Trondheim. He answered for them at the things when the king's men took action against them. Einar knew the laws well and he was not short of courage to bring his case before the things, even if the king were present; all the bonders supported him. The king was very wroth at that and at last matters went so far that they bandied words of strife. Einar said that the bonders would not

suffer injustice from him if he broke their land rights, and this happened between them many times. Einar then began to have a troop of men about him at home and still many more when he came to the town and the king was there. Once he went into the town with many men; he had eight or nine longships and nigh on five hundred (six hundred) men. And when he came to the town, he went ashore with this troop. King Harald was then in residence in the town; he was standing outside on the balcony and saw that Einar's men were going up from the ships; it is said that Harald then quoth:

Here I see the noble-born
Einar Tambarskelver,
Who can cut through the sea,
Hastening with a great following.

This strong man wishes well enough
To fill the king's seat;

Often fewer huscarls follow
At the heels of a jarl.

He who makes the sword bloody
Will drive us away from the land,
Unless Einar doth kiss
The thin mouth of the axe.

Einar stayed some days in the town.

44. One day a mote[1] was held and the king himself was there. A thief had been taken in the town and he was being brought forward at the mote; this fellow had before been with Einar, who had liked him well. This was told to Einar, who knew that the king would not let the man slip away, because of Einar's laying weight on it. Einar then bade his men arm themselves and go to the mote. Einar took the man from the mote by force. After this the friends of both went bearing peace terms between Einar and the king. And it went so far that a conference was arranged and they both went to the meeting. There was a speech room in the king's residence down by the river, and into this room the king went with few men, though his other men stood outside in the yard. The king had a board put over the smoke hole (luffer) and the opening was small. Einar then came into the king's residence with his men; he said to his son Eindridi: "Stay thou outside with the men; then there will be no risk for me". Eindridi stood outside near the door. And when Einar came into the room he said: "Dark it is in the king's speech room". At the same moment men rushed on him, some thrusting, others striking. And when Eindridi heard that, he drew his sword and rushed into the room. He was at once felled with his father. The king's men rushed to the room and stood before the door, but the bonders dropped their hands, for they had now no leader; each egged the

1 The O.N. text reads *mot*, the same as the English *mote*, i.e., 'meeting' or 'thing meeting' in a town.

other on and said it was a shame if they should not avenge their chief, but it did not come about that they went forth to fight. The king went out to his men, drew up a battle line, and set up his standard, but the bonders did not attack. The king and all his men then went on board his ships; they rowed out along the river and so out into the fjord. Bergliot, Einar's wife, learned of Einar's fall; she was then in the house which she and Einar had taken in the town. She went up to the king's residence where the bonders' troop was and egged them on to battle, and at the same moment the king was rowing out along the river. Then said Bergliot: "We now lack my kinsman, Hacon Ivorson; the slayer of Eindridi would not be rowing out along the river if Hacon stood on the river bank". Afterwards Bergliot had the bodies of Einar and Eindridi laid out. They were buried in St Olav's Church near King Magnus Olavson's tomb.[1] After the fall of Einar, King Harald was so much hated for that deed that the only reason the landed men and bonders did not go to battle with him was that there was no leader to raise the standard in the bonders' army.

45. Finn Arneson dwelt at Austratt in Yrjar; he was at this time one of King Harald's landed men. Finn was married to Bergliot, daughter of Halvdan, the son of Sigurd Syr; Halvdan was the brother of St Olav and King Harald. Thora, King Harald's wife, was Finn Arneson's brother's daughter; Finn and his brothers were friends of the king. Finn had been some summers on western viking raids and he and Guthorm Gunhildson[2] and Hacon Ivorson had been together in the raids. King Harald went out along the Trondheimsfjord to Austratt, where he was well received. Then the king and Finn talked together and spoke between themselves about these things which had lately befallen, the slaying of Einar and his son and the unrest and uproar which the Tronds made against the king. Finn said quickly: "Everything goes amiss with thee, whatever thou doest is ill, and then thou art so afraid that thou knowest not what to do with thyself". The king answered laughing: "I will now send thee to the town and I wish thee to make peace between the bonders and me; if

1 It appears that both St Olav and Magnus were buried in St Clement's Church, and were afterwards temporarily removed to St Olav's Church, built by King Magnus, whilst Harald Hardrade built St Mary's Church. It is not stated whether they were ever removed to St Mary's Church; but in the 'History of Olav Kyrre' it is mentioned that St Olav's body had been taken to Christ Church, which Olav Kyrre had built and where he himself was buried (cf. 'History of Olav Kyrre', chapter 6). St Mary's Church was removed to Elgesæter about 1178, as written in chapter 38, n. 7.   2 Son of Ketel Kalv and Gunhild; cf. chapter 40.

that does not succeed I want thee to go to the Uplands and settle matters with Hacon Ivorson so that he does not decide to withstand me". Finn answered: "What wilt thou grant me if I go on this dangerous errand, for both the Tronds and the Uplanders are such great foes to thee that none of thy messengers can go there unless he has sufficient confidence?" The king answered: "Go thou on this errand, kinsman; for I know that if anyone can bring us peace, thou wilt do it; ask what thou wilt of us". Finn said: "Keep thy word then, and I will choose my boon. I choose peace and right to live in the land for my brother Kalv and all his possessions, and likewise that he shall have such rank and power as he had before he went from the land". The king said 'yes' to all that Finn said; to all this they had witnesses and hand-shaking. Then Finn said: "What shall I bid Hacon in order that he shall promise thee peace? He rules most over his kinsmen now". The king said: "Thou shalt first hear what Hacon will demand on his side in order to come to terms. Then thou mayest further my case as best thou canst and in the end thou shalt refuse him nothing except the kingship alone". King Harald then went south to Möre and he drew men to him and soon had a great strength of men.

46. Finn Arneson went into the town and he had with him his huscarls, nigh on eighty men. And when he came to the town he had a thing with the townsmen. At the thing he spoke long and wisely; he bade the townsmen and the bonders take any counsel but that of creating hatred against their king or driving him away, and reminded them how badly things had gone with them when they had done so before against St Olav. He also said that the king would atone for these murders as the best and wisest man would deem. Finn so ended his speech that the men promised to let the matter stand quietly until the messengers whom Bergliot had sent to the Uplands to Hacon Ivorson came back. Finn then went out to Orkedale with those men who had followed him to the town; then he went up to the Dovre-fell and so east over the fell. He went first to his kinsman Orm the Jarl—the jarl was married to Finn's daughter, Sigrid—and told him about his errand.

47. They then arranged a meeting with Hacon Ivorson. And when they met, Finn brought before Hacon the business which King Harald bade him further. It was soon found from Hacon's talk that he thought he was strongly bound to avenge his kinsman Eindridi; he said that such words had come to him from Trondheim that he would get there strength enough to make a rising against the king.

Finn then explained to Hacon how much better it would be for him to take from the king such great honours as he himself might demand than to risk raising strife against the king to whom he was already bound in service; he said that he could not get the victory: "and then thou wilt lose both wealth and peace; but if thou winnest the victory over the king, then thou wilt be called traitor to thy lord". Orm the Jarl also supported this speech of Finn's. And when Hacon had thought over this for himself, he laid bare what was in his mind and said: "I will make terms with King Harald if he will wed me to his kinswoman Ragnhild, Magnus Olavson's daughter, with such a dowry as beseems her and is to her liking". Finn said that he would promise this on the king's behalf; they then settled the matter between them. Afterwards Finn went back north to Trondheim. Thereafter this unrest and disquiet ceased so that the king still held his kingdom in peace within the land, for now all those alliances were put aside which Eindridi's kinsmen had made to withstand King Harald.

48. And when the time came that Hacon was to demand the

Hacon Ivorson woos Ragnhild

fulfilment of this agreement, he went to King Harald, and when they began talking together the king said that on his side he would keep all that stood in the agreement between Harald and Finn; "Thou, Hacon", said the king, "shalt speak about this matter to Ragnhild to see if she will assent to this plan, but it is not advisable for thee or any other man to get Ragnhild in such a way that she does not assent to it". Hacon then went to Ragnhild and wooed her. She answered thus: "Often do I remember that my father King Magnus is dead if I shall be married to a bonder, even though thou art a handsome man and skilled in all sports and accomplishments. If King Magnus were alive he would not wed me to any man less than a king. Now it is not to be expected that I wish to be married to a commoner". Hacon then went to King Harald and told him about the conversation between Ragnhild and himself, and reminded him of the agreement between himself and Finn. Then also there were present Finn and many men who had been at the talk between Hacon and Finn. Hacon claimed the witness of all these men that it was settled that the king should give Ragnhild such a dowry as was to her liking: "Now she will not have a commoner; thou canst give me the name of jarl. I am of such stock and have such possessions, that I can be called jarl, according to what folks say". The king answered: "When King Olav, my brother, and King Magnus his son ruled the kingdom, they bade that there should be only one jarl at a time in the land. So also have I done since I became king. I will not take from Orm the Jarl the rank which I have already given him". Hacon then saw that his case would have no success and it pleased him ill; Finn also was very wroth. They said that the king did not keep his word and thereafter they parted. Hacon then went straightway from the land with a well-manned longship; he came south into Denmark and went at once to his kinsman, King Swein. The king greeted him with gladness and gave him great land rents there. Hacon became King Swein's land-ward against vikings who often harried in Denmark—Vends and Kurlanders and other men from the easterway. He was out on his ship winter and summer.

49.   There was a man called Asmund[1] who, it is said, was King Swein's sister's son and foster-son; he was a very bold man and the king loved him much. And when Asmund grew up he soon became an unruly fellow and a great slayer. The king liked that ill; he sent him away, giving him a good grant of land whereby he could well keep himself and a troop of men. And as soon as Asmund had got the king's grants he gathered many men to himself. But when the grants which the king had given him did not cover his expenses he took more property which was the king's. When the king heard that he called Asmund to him and, when they met, the king said that Asmund should be in his bodyguard and should keep no troop of men. It had to be as the king wished. But when Asmund had been some time with the king he did not like it there, and one night he ran away and went back to his men and then did still more harm than before. And when the king was riding about in the land and came near the place where Asmund was, he sent his men out to take Asmund by force. The king had him placed in irons and thus held him for a time, thinking that he would become meeker. But when Asmund was out of irons he straightway ran away and got himself

1 I.e. Osmond.

men and warships. He then began to harry both without and within the land, and made the greatest havoc, slaying many folk and robbing far and wide. The men who fell foul of this unrest came to the king and complained to him of the harm. He answered: "Why do ye say this to me? Why do ye not go to Hacon Ivorson? He is my landward and makes peace for you bonders and keeps the vikings away. It was told me that Hacon was a bold, brave man, but now it seems to me that he has no wish to be in any place where he thinks there is risk of life". These words of the king came to Hacon with many others added. Afterwards Hacon went with his men and followed Asmund. They met at sea and Hacon at once went to battle. There was a hard, great fight. Hacon went up on Asmund's ship and cleared it, and then it came about that he and Asmund exchanged blows. Asmund fell; Hacon struck his head off. Thereafter Hacon went speedily to King Swein and came to him as he sat at table. Hacon went up to the table and on it he laid the head before the king, and asked him if he knew it. The king answered nothing and went as red as blood looking at it. Then Hacon went away. A little later the king sent men to him and bade him leave his service; he said: "I will not do him any harm, but I cannot take care of all our kinsmen".

50. After this Hacon went away from Denmark and went north to Norway to his possessions. His kinsman Orm the Jarl was then dead. Hacon's kinsmen and friends were very glad at his coming and many noble men began to work for peace between him and King Harald. It came about that they made peace in this way: Hacon got Ragnhild, the king's daughter, and King Harald gave Hacon the jarldom and such power as Orm the Jarl had had. Hacon swore fealty to King Harald in the service to which he was bound.

51. Kalv Arneson had been on a western viking raid since he had left Norway, and in the winters he was often in the Orkneys with his kinsman, Torfinn[1] the Jarl. Finn Arneson, his brother, sent word to Kalv to tell him of the arrangements which he and King Harald

---

[1] This *Torfinn* was the great Earl of Orkney. He married Ingebjörg, the daughter of Finn Arneson. His father was Sigurd the Stout, who fell at Clontarf in 1014, and his mother a daughter of Malcolm II of Scotland. Torfinn's rule included, besides the Western Isles, Caithness and Sutherland. The Orkneyinga Saga states that he had eleven earls in Scotland subject to him, and his dominions extended as far as to Galloway. This is not confirmed by Scottish history books. Earl Torfinn died in his bed in 1064 and was buried in Christ Church (or Kirk) at Birsay (on Mainland, Orkneys) after he had been Earl of Orkney for seventy winters. For his relationship to William the Conqueror cf. 'History of Hacon the Good', p. 81, n. 1.

had made with each other, that Kalv was to have the right to live in Norway and to have his possessions and such land rents as he had had of King Magnus. And when the message came to Kalv, he straightway made himself ready for the journey. He went east to Norway and came first to his brother Finn. Finn made a truce for Kalv, and the king and Kalv met and made their terms according to what the king and Finn arranged. Kalv submitted to the king, and gave all the assurances he had before given to King Magnus, namely, that Kalv was bound to do all the deeds which King Harald wished and which he thought would strengthen his kingdom. Kalv then took all the possessions and land rents which he had had before.

52. The next summer King Harald had a levy out; he went south to Denmark, where he harried in the summer. But when he came south to Fyn, there was a great host against him. The king then bade his men go from the ships and make themselves ready for going on land. He divided his army and put Kalv Arneson over a troop, bidding them first go ashore, and told them where they should go; he said that he would come up afterwards and bring them help. Kalv and his men went on land and soon a troop came against them. Kalv went straightway to battle, but the fight was not long, for Kalv was overpowered by numbers and fled with his men, but the Danes followed them. Many of the Norsemen fell there and so did Kalv Arneson. King Harald went up on land with his troops, and on their way they happened to see the fallen lying before them and they found Kalv's body and bore it down to the ships. The king went up into the land and harried and slew many men. Thus sayeth Arnor:

The sharp edge on Fyn        Went through the houses; there were
He dyed red; and fire        Fewer dwellers in Fyn after this.

53. After this, Finn Arneson showed enmity against the king for his brother Kalv's death; he said that the king had planned Kalv's fall and that it was but treason against Finn himself when the king had called his brother Kalv from the west across the sea into his power. And when that talk came out, many men said that it had seemed foolish of Finn to have believed that Kalv would gain King Harald's trust; the king seemed to them to wreak vengeance for smaller things than those which Kalv had done against King Harald. The king let the men say what they would about it; he neither said it was true nor yet denied it. This alone did they find in his words—

that the king thought well of what had befallen. King Harald then said this song:

| | |
|---|---|
| Now have I planned the death | The mind, which works in treason, |
| Of two men and eleven in all. | Seeks to bridle men with evil; |
| We egg on to battle; I still | They say that with little |
| Remember so many murders. | Can the balance of powers be swayed. |

Finn Arneson so took this matter to heart that he went away from the land and came south into Denmark, where he went to King Swein and was well received. They talked for a long time in a private room and at length it came to this, that Finn submitted to King Swein and became his man. Swein gave him a jarldom with the rule of Halland, and Finn was there as land-ward against the Norsemen.

54. Guthorm of Ringanes was the name of a son of Ketel Kalv and Gunhild, and he was the sister's son of King Olav and King Harald. Guthorm was a doughty man and full-grown at an early age. Guthorm was often with King Harald and was in great friendship and influence with the king, for he was a wise man, and well befriended. Guthorm was often on raids and harried much in the western lands; he had many men. He had peace land[1] and a winter seat at Dublin in Ireland, and he was in great friendship with King Margad.[2]

55. The following summer King Margad and Guthorm went together and harried in Wales, where they got much goods. Afterwards they came into the Menai Straits,[3] where they were to share the booty. But when the heap of silver was brought forth and the king saw it, he wished to have all that wealth for himself and gave little heed to his friendship with Guthorm. Guthorm was ill pleased that he and his men should be robbed of their share. The king said that Guthorm should have two things to choose between; "one is to fall in with what we wish to have; the other is to hold battle with us and let him have the goods who wins; likewise thou shalt go from thy ships and I shall have them". Guthorm thought there were great difficulties either way; it did not seem to him that he could fittingly give up his ships and his goods without the least guilt, but it was also disastrous to fight against the king and the great host which followed him. There was so great a difference in their numbers that the king had sixteen longships and Guthorm five. Guthorm then asked the

1 *Peace land*, in O.N. *fridland* (cf. 'History of St Olav', chapter 20).    2 *King Margad Ragnvaldson* (in Irish *Eachmargach*) was king in Dublin from 1035 to 1038 and from 1046 to 1052.    3 Menai Straits, the sound between Anglesey and Wales.

king for three nights' delay, so that he could take counsel with his men about this matter; he thought that he could make the king meeker in this time and also that by the entreaties of his men he could put his case on a better footing with the king. But he did not get what he asked for. This was the eve of Olav-Mass.[1] Guthorm now chose to die like a man or win the victory, rather than suffer shame and dishonour and mockery at having lost so much. He then called on God and the holy King Olav, his kinsman, and prayed for their help and support and vowed to give to the house of the saint a tenth of all the booty they would get if they won the victory. He then fitted out his army and drew it up in lines against the great host, rushed forth and fought against them. And by the help of God and King Olav, Guthorm got the victory; King Margad fell and so did every man who followed him, young and old. And after this victory Guthorm turned gladly home with all the goods he had got in the fight. From all the silver he had won they took every tenth penny such as had been vowed to St Olav: there was a countless quantity of money, so that from this silver Guthorm had a rood[2] made as high as himself or the leader of his forecastle men, and that was seven feet. This rood Guthorm gave to St Olav's Church and it has since been there as a memorial of Guthorm's victory and of the miracle of St Olav.

56. In Denmark there was a count, evil and full of envy. He had a Norse serving-maid whose family came from Trondlaw. She worshipped St Olav and strongly believed in his sanctity. But the count, whom I have mentioned, mistrusted everything that was told him about the miracles of this holy man. He said that it was nothing but hearsay and idle talk, and he made mockery and sport of all the praise and worship which all the folk of the land granted the good king. But now the festival was coming whereon the mild king lost his life and which all Norsemen keep. The witless count would not keep it holy and bade his serving-woman bake and fire the oven for bread that day. She thought she knew the count's mood, that he would soon take vengeance on her if she did not obey what he bade her. She went of necessity and put fire under the oven and wailed much whilst she was working, and called on King Olav, saying that she would never again believe in him if he did not avenge this unseemly thing by one miracle or another. Now you shall hear of a fitting punishment and a true miracle: forthwith and in that same hour it befell that the count became blind in both eyes, and that the

---

1 28th of July, 1052.    2 I.e. a cross generally bearing the figure of Christ.

bread she had put in the oven became stone. Some of the stones have come to the church of St Olav and to many other places. Since then Olav-Mass has always been kept holy in Denmark.

57. In the west in Valland[1] there was a man so lame that he was a cripple and went on his knees and knuckles. One day he was out on the road and was asleep: he dreamt that a noble man came to him

and asked where he would go, and he mentioned some town. And the noble man said to him: "Go thou to St Olav's Church which is in London and there thou wilt be healed". Then he awoke and straightway went to find St Olav's Church. At length he came to London Bridge and there he asked the townsmen if they could tell him where St Olav's Church was. But they answered and said that there were too many churches there for them to know to what man each of them was hallowed. But

Afterwards they went over London Bridge

a little later a man came up to him and asked where he might be going; he told him and the man then said: "We two shall both go to St Olav's Church; I know the way there". Then they went over the bridge and on the street which brought them to St Olav's Church. And when they came to the churchyard gate the man stepped over the threshold of the gate, but the cripple rolled in across the threshold and forthwith rose up healed. But when he looked about him, his companion had gone.

58. King Harald had a market town built in the east in Oslo, and he often stayed there, for it was easy to get supplies there and it had great stretches of land round it. There he was in a good position for guarding the land against the Danes, as also for making raids on Denmark, as he was often wont to do even if he had no great army out. One summer King Harald went with some light ships, and with no great army. He sailed south from the Vik, and when he got a fair wind he sailed over the sea to Jutland and began to harry; but the landsmen gathered together and guarded their land. King

1 North of France.

Harald then sailed to the Limfjord and came into the fjord. The Limfjord is such that one enters it as through a narrow river, but when one gets into the fjord it is like a great sea. Harald harried on both sides, but everywhere the Danes were gathering men. King Harald then brought his ships near an island which was small and uninhabited. But when they looked for water, they found none and told the king. He bade them look whether any lingworm was to be found on the island, and when one was found they brought it to the king. He bade them put the worm near the fire and warm it and exhaust it so that it should be as thirsty as possible. Then a thread was tied round its tail and the worm let loose. It hastened away and the thread unwound from the ball. They went after the worm until it thrust itself down into the earth. The king bade them dig there for water; this was done and they found there so much water that they were not short. King Harald learned tidings from his spies that King Swein had come with a great fleet outside the mouth of the fjord, but he could go but slowly because not more than one ship could go through at a time. King Harald sailed with his ships farther up the fjord to where it is broadest, at the place called Lusbreid. There is in the creek a narrow neck of land in the west towards the sea; thither Harald's men rowed in the evening. And in the night when it was dark, they unloaded the ships and dragged them over the neck of land. They had done it all before day and made the ships ready a second time. They sailed north past Jutland. Then they said:

> From the Dane's hands
> Harald glided.

Then the king said that another time he would come to Denmark in such a way that he would have more men and greater ships. Thereafter the king went north to Trondheim.

59. In the winter King Harald stayed in Nidaros, and that same winter he had a ship built out at Öre; it was a broad warship. The ship was built after the size of the *Long Serpent* and made as carefully as possible in all ways. At the bow there was a dragon's head and in the stern a dragon's tail, and both sides of the neck were all overlaid with gold. It had thirty-five rooms between the benches and was spacious as well and very handsome. The king had all the fittings of the ship chosen carefully, both sails and rigging, anchors and hawsers. In the winter King Harald sent word south to Denmark to King Swein that the following spring he should come from the south to the Elv to meet him, and then they should both fight in such a way

as to share their lands, and that one of them should have both kingdoms.

60. That winter King Harald called out a full levy from Norway; and when spring came, a great host gathered. Then King Harald had the great ship launched on the River Nid and afterwards he had the dragon's head set up. Then quoth Tjodolv the Scald:

Fair maid! The noble ship was
Borne forth from the river to the sea.
Mark where the long body of the
    dragon
Lies off the land.

The dragon's gold-green mane
Shines o'er the deck; the neck
Bore burnt gold. Then
It glided from its moorings.

The womenfolk watch the ship rowed by seventy oars

Then King Harald fitted out the ship and made himself ready for the journey. And when he was ready he sailed the ship out of the river; the men rowed very skilfully. Thus sayeth Tjodolv:

On Saturday the prince cast off
The long land-tent,
Where the proud women
Saw the *Serpent* glide from the town.
Westward from the Nid
The king sailed the new ship,
And down into the deep sea
The boatmen's oars were falling.

The king's warriors can move
The straight oars in the sea.
The woman stands and wonders
At the sharp strokes of oars.

The maid is ill at heart
If the swarthy sea-hunter
Should go asunder, yet she
Gives her leave for peace.

The ship's side suffers ill
When seventy oars bring it
Into the sea, before the host
Slip their oars in the ocean.
The Norsemen row the *Serpent*,
All nailed, out to the icy
Billows. There it was
As if one saw an eagle's wings.

King Harald sailed with his army south along the coast with all his levy of men and ships. And when they came east into the Vik a strong wind rose against them and the host lay far about in the

havens, both near the outer isles and within the fjords. Thus quoth
Tjodolv:

| | |
|---|---|
| The smooth stems of the vessels | The troops lie within |
| Have cover under the woods. | The skerries in the creeks; |
| The king's levy turns | The high brynied cutters |
| To land with the stems. | Hide under the land. |

And in that great storm which came over them, the big ship
needed good anchorage. Thus sayeth Tjodolv:

| | |
|---|---|
| The prince split the sea's | The wind is unfriendly |
| High fence with his stem. | To the bent anchor-iron. |
| The king strained the cutter's | Gravel and strong winds |
| Cables to the utmost. | Gnaw at the anchor hook. |

And when they got a good wind King Harald brought the army
east to the Elv, where they came one evening. Thus sayeth Tjodolv:

| | |
|---|---|
| Harald now brought his ships | The king now held a thing |
| Boldly to the Elv. | At Tumla.[2] There Swein shall |
| The lord of Norway in the night | Meet strife, if the Danes |
| Was near Land's End.[1] | Keep not away. |

61. But when the Danes heard that the Norsemen's host was
come, all fled who could. The Norsemen heard that the Danish king
too had his army out and was lying to the south near Fyn and the
Smalands.[3] But when King Harald learned that King Swein would
hold neither meeting nor battle with him as was arranged, he again
took the same plan as before, letting the bonders' host go back and
putting his men on to one hundred and fifty (one hundred and eighty)
ships. With this army he then sailed along Halland and harried far
and wide. He brought the army into Lovefjord[4] and harried there
up in the land. A little later, King Swein came against them there
with the Danish army; he had three hundred (three hundred and
sixty) ships. And when the Norsemen saw this host, King Harald
had his army called together, and many said that they should flee and
that it was impossible to fight. The king answered thus: "Everyone
of us shall fall, one on top of the other, rather than flee". Stein
Herdisarson quoth:

| | |
|---|---|
| The great-minded leader said | The king shouted that rather |
| What he now expected. | Should each fall, one |
| Here said the king, he had | Over the other, than yield. |
| Lost hope of peace. | All the men took their weapons. |

1 I.e. the frontier between Norway and Sweden by the Göta River.   2 *Tumla*, now
Tumlahed, the south-western point of the island of Hising, outside Gothenburg.
3 I.e. the small islands south of Fyn and Zealand.   4 In Halland (Sweden) north
of Scania.

After this King Harald drew up his ships to go against the foe, and he placed his great dragon ship forward in the middle of the fleet. Thus says Tjodolv:

The giver of friendly gifts,                Had his dragon brought forth
Who gladly fed the wolves,                Foremost in the midst of the fleet.

This ship was well fitted out and had a great crew. Tjodolv quoth:

The peace-eager king bade his men          The doer of manly deeds
Bind fast their shields                     Locked the strong dragon
On the bulwarks. The prince's friends       With shields outside Nissa.
Appeared to stand in good order.            One overlapped the other.

Ulf the Marshal put his ship on one side of the king's ship. He said to his men that they should put the ship well forward. Stein Herdisarson was on Ulf's ship and he quoth:

Ulf the king's marshal                      The strong friend of the wise king
Fired us all,                               Well bade his men
When the ships were to row                  Bring forth his ship alongside
To battle. The spears trembled.             The prince's; the men did so.

Hacon Ivorson lay right outside on one wing; many ships followed him and his men were well armed. And right outside on the other wing lay the Trond chiefs, also with a great and fair host.

62. King Swein also lined up his fleet. He placed his ship opposite King Harald's in the midst of his host, and next to him Finn the Jarl brought up his ship, and nearest him the Danes placed the men which were boldest and best arrayed. Then both sides roped their ships together in the midmost parts of their fleets. But because the armies were so big there was a great number of ships which went loose, and each one put his ship as far forward as he dared; thus there was much unevenness. But although the difference of men was great, both sides had a mighty host. In his army King Swein had six jarls. Thus said Stein Herdisarson:

The hersers' mind-strong                    Then it was that the dear
Lord risked himself.                        Lord who dwelt in Leidra[1]
With a hundred and fifty ships              Cut thither through the sea
He waited for the Danes.                    With three hundred warships.

63. King Harald had the war blast blown as soon as he had made his ship ready, and then bade his men row forward. Thus sayeth Stein Herdisarson:

Before the mouth of the river              He was hard withstood,
Harald did Swein harm.                      For Harald gave him no peace.

1 *Leidra*, later called Leire, near Roskilde.

A PHOTO OF A MODEL OF THE GOKSTAD SHIP

## STERN VIEW OF THE OSEBERG SHIP

Found in 1903 at Oseberg in Vestfold and exhibited at the Sjöfartsmuseum at Oslo. Peat and clay had preserved the ship from destruction. She is built of oak and dates from the ninth century. As remains of two women were found in the burial chamber, it is assumed that the vessel belonged to a queen, buried together with her serving-maid, who wished to follow her mistress to the grave. Numerous objects were found in the ship, including a well-preserved chariot, also skeletons of fifteen horses, four dogs and an ox, buried inside and outside the ship. Her dimensions are 70 ft. long over all and about 16 ft. beam. The vessel is lower built than the Gokstad ship and gives every appearance of having been a pleasure ship, not intended for long and perilous voyages. This may also account for the many beautifully carved objects found in the ship. Both stem and stern show exquisite carving.

The sword-swinging men
Of the king rode forth
Outside Halland; into the sea
Blood poured from their wounds.

Then the battle began and it was very sharp. Both kings egged on their men. Thus quoth Stein Herdisarson:

Both the good strife-eager
Skjoldungs[1] bade
Their men shoot and strike.
The hosts were near each other.
Both stones and arrows
Poured down when the sword
Shook off the bright blood,
When it took the men's lives.

It was late in the day when the fighting men came together, and they kept fighting all night. For a long time King Harald shot with a bow. Thus sayeth Tjodolv:

The Upland king drew
His bow all the night.
The wise land-ruler sent
Arrows against the white shields.
The bloody point wounded
The bonders, whilst the king's
Arrows stood fast in the shields.
The shooting of spears increased.

Hacon the Jarl and the men who followed him did not rope their ships, but rowed against the Danish ships which went loose, and he cleared every ship that he could grapple. And when the Danes noticed that, each of them took his ship from where the jarl was going, but Hacon went after the Danes whenever they turned away, and they were then near turning in flight. A cutter then rowed to the jarl's ship and someone shouted to him and said that King Harald's second wing had turned back and that many of the men had fallen. The jarl then rowed there and went so hard upon them that the Danes again let their ships give way. Thus the jarl went all the night, going forth where it was needed, and wherever he came nothing could withstand him. Hacon rowed on the edge of the battle. In the latter part of the night there was a general flight amongst the Danes, for King Harald with his men had gone up on King Swein's ship and it was so thoroughly cleared that every man fell except those who leaped into the sea. Thus sayeth Arnor Jarlascald:

The bold Swein went not
Without cause from his ship.
That is my thought. Heavy
Was the strife about the helmets.
The sea craft did float empty,
Before the Jutes' flattering friend
Fled from his fallen bodyguard.

And when King Swein's standard fell and his ship lay empty, all his men fled and some fell. And from the ships which were roped together, the men leaped into the sea or got on to other ships which were loose; and all King Swein's men who could then rowed away. The loss of men was great. And there where the kings themselves

1 *Skjoldung* is here used for king.

had fought and most ships were tied together, more than seventy of King Swein's ships were left empty. Tjodolv quoth:

| The bold king of the Sogn men | Seventy ships together |
|---|---|
| (They say) cleared at least | Of Swein's fleet in the fight. |

King Harald rowed after the Danes and pursued them, but it was not easy, for the fjord was so thronged with ships floating about that they could scarcely get forward. Finn the Jarl did not wish to flee and he was taken prisoner, for he could see but little. Thus sayeth Tjodolv:

| Swein, thou hadst no victory | The battle-bold Finn Arneson |
|---|---|
| Though six Danish jarls | Was with manly heart |
| Fought for thee— | Seized in the midst of the lines. |
| They increased the heat of battle. | He would not flee. |

64. Hacon the Jarl stayed behind with his ship when the king and the others were following the fleeing Danes, for the jarl's ship could not get forward because of the ships which lay in the way. A man rowed up in a boat to the jarl's ship and came up by the stern; he was a big man and had a wide hat. He shouted up to the ship, "Where is the jarl?" He was in the forehold staunching the flow of blood for some man. The jarl looked at the man with the hat and asked him his name. He answered: "Vandrad[1] is here; speak thou with me, jarl". The jarl looked out over the railings at him. Then said the boatman: "I will receive peace if thou wilt give it me". The jarl got up and called two of his men who were both dear to him and spoke thus: "Step ye into the boat and take Vandrad ashore. Follow him to my friend Karl the Bonder and tell him by the way of token that he shall let Vandrad have the horse which I gave him two days ago, and he shall give him his own saddle and his son as a follower". They then stepped into the boat and took up the oars whilst Vandrad steered. This was just at dawn when the movement of ships was at its height; some ships were rowing to land, others out to sea, small ships and great ships alike. Vandrad steered where there seemed most room between the ships. And when the ships of Norsemen rowed near, then the jarl's men told who they were, and they all let them go where they would. Vandrad steered on along the shore and he came not to land until they got beyond where ships were moving. They then went up to Karl's garth and the day began to brighten. They went into a room and there was Karl, just clad. The jarl's men told him their business. Karl said that they should first have food,

---

1 *Vandrad* is a general name for a man who does not know what to do when he is in difficulties. The man in question turned out later to be King Swein (cf. chapter 67).

and he had the table laid before them and got them water to wash themselves. Then the housewife came into the room and said at once: "Very strange it is that we got no sleep or rest in the night for shrieking and howling". Karl answered: "Didst thou not know that the kings have fought in the night?" She asked: "Who won?" Karl answered: "The Norsemen have got the victory". "Then I suppose our king has fled again", she said. Karl answered: "It is not known whether he has fled or is fallen". She answered: "Luckless we are with our king. He is both halt and afraid". Then said Vandrad: "The king is not afraid, but he is not victorious". Vandrad washed himself last, and when he took the towel he dried himself with the middle of it. The housewife took the towel and pulled it from him, saying: "Thou knowest no manners; it is the way of simple folk to wet the whole cloth at once". Vandrad answered: "I shall soon again be able to dry myself with the middle of the towel". Karl then put the table before them and Vandrad sat in the middle. They then ate for a time and afterwards they went out, and the horse stood ready and Karl's son was to follow him on another horse. They rode away to. the wood, and the jarl's men went to their boat and rowed out to the jarl's ship.

65. King Harald and his men followed the fleeing men but a short way and then they rowed back to the ships which lay empty. They robbed the fallen, and on the king's ship a great number of dead men were found, but King Swein's body was not found; they thought they knew, however, that he was dead. King Harald had the bodies of his own men laid out and the wounds of those who needed it were bound up. He had the bodies of Swein's men taken ashore and he sent word to the bonders to bury these bodies. He had the booty shared out, and he stayed there for a time. He then learned the tidings that King Swein had come to Zealand, also that there were come to him all his army which had fled in the battle, besides many other men, and that he had now got a very great host of men.

66. Finn Arneson the Jarl had been taken prisoner in the battle, as is written above (chapter 63); he was now led forth to the king. King Harald was then very happy and said: "Here we two now meet, Finn, but the last time was in Norway. The Danish bodyguard did not stand fast enough about thee, and the Norsemen have an awkward job to drag thee, a blind man, after them, and keep thee alive". Then the jarl answered: "Much ill can the Norsemen now do, but worst of all is that which thou biddest". Then said King Harald: "Wilt thou now have peace, although thou dost

not deserve it?" The jarl answered: "Not from thee, thou hound". The king said: "Wilt thou then that thy kinsman, Magnus, give thee peace?" Magnus, King Harald's son, was then steering a ship. The jarl said: "How can that whelp decide the giving of peace?" Then the king laughed, and he thought it a joke to tease him, and he said: "Wilt thou take peace of Thora, thy kinswoman?" Then said the jarl: "Is she here?" "She is here", said the king. Then Finn spoke those scurvy words which were long afterwards remembered in evidence as to how wroth he was when he could not control himself: "It is not strange that thou hast bitten well when thy mare follows thee". Finn the Jarl got peace, and King Harald had him with him for a time. Finn was rather unhappy and outspoken. King Harald then said: "I see, Finn, that thou wilt not be friends with me or thy kinsmen. I will now give thee leave to go to Swein thy king". The jarl answered: "I will take it, and so much the more thankfully the sooner I get away". Then the king had Finn taken ashore and the men of Halland greeted him well. King Harald then sailed north with his army to Norway. He went first to Oslo and thereupon he gave all his men who wished it leave to go home.

67. It is said that King Swein stayed that winter in Denmark and held his kingdom as before. In the winter he sent men north to Halland for Karl the Bonder and his wife; and when they came to the king, he called Karl to him. Then the king asked whether Karl recognised him, or thought he had seen him before. Karl answered: "I know thee now, king, and I knew thee before as soon as I saw thee, and I may thank God that the little help I gave thee was of use". The king answered: "All the days that I live since then I have to reward thee for. Now the first thing shall be that I will give thee that garth in Zealand which thou wilt choose for thyself, and thereto I shall make thee a great man if thou canst keep it up". Karl thanked the king well for his words and said that there was still one boon which he would crave. The king asked what it might be. Karl said: "I will ask, king, that thou wilt let me have my wife with me". The king answered thus: "That will I not grant thee, for I shall get thee a much better and wiser wife, and thy wife can go on with the small garth which thou hast had before. She can support herself by it". The king gave Karl a great and noble garth and got him a good match, and after that he became a man of much worth. This was known and heard of far and wide, and the news came north to Norway.

68. The winter after the battle of Nissa[1] King Harald stayed in

1 The battle was fought outside the mouth of the River *Nissa* (in Halland); cf. chapter 61.

Oslo. In the autumn when the army had come from the south there was much talk and many tales about the battle which had taken place in the autumn outside Nissa. And every man who had been there thought he could say something about it. Once some men were sitting in a little room drinking and they were very talkative. They spoke about the battle of Nissa and as to who had the greatest fame therefrom. They all agreed about one thing, that there had been no other man like Hacon the Jarl; "he was the boldest of men with weapons, he was the doughtiest and the most fortunate; what he had done was of the greatest help and he won the victory". Harald was outside in the yard talking with some men. He then went to the door of the room and said: "Every man here would like to be called Hacon", and so he went his way.

69. In the autumn Hacon the Jarl went to the Uplands and was in his district in the winter; he was well beloved by the Uplanders. Once when spring was passing certain men were sitting at their drink, and the talk was again about the battle of Nissa; the men praised Hacon the Jarl much, but some praised others no less. And when they had been talking about it for a while, a man answered: "It may be that others have fought more boldly at Nissa, but there cannot have been any man there, who, I believe, had such good luck for himself as Hacon". They said that it was surely his greatest luck that he had driven many of the Danes into flight. The same man answered: "Greater luck it was that he gave King Swein his life". Another man answered him: "Thou knowest not of what thou sayest". He answered: "This I know very clearly, for the man who took the king ashore told me himself". But then it was, as is often said, that "many are the king's ears". This was told the king and forthwith he got many horses and rode away in the night with two hundred (two hundred and forty) men; he rode all night and the following day. Then certain men were riding towards them, who were coming into the town with meat and malt. There was a man called Gamal who was on this journey with the king; he rode up to one of the bonders who was his acquaintance and he spoke in private with him. Gamal said: "I will give thee money to ride as fast as thou canst on the lone ways which thou knowest to be the shortest and to go to Hacon the Jarl; tell him that the king will slay him, for he knows now that the jarl helped King Swein to get ashore at Nissa". They arranged this together, and then the bonder rode and came to the jarl, who was sitting drinking and had not gone to bed. And when the bonder had told him his message, the jarl and all his folk straightway

stood up. The jarl had all his wealth moved away from the garth out to the wood, and all the jarl's men had left the garth when the king came. He stayed there during the night, and Hacon the Jarl rode on his way and came forth in the east to Sweden to King Steinkel,[1] with whom he stayed during the summer. King Harald afterwards turned back to the town, and in the summer he went north to Trondheim and stayed there, but in the autumn he went back east to the Vik.

70. In the summer Hacon the Jarl went back to the Uplands, as soon as he heard that the king had gone north. There he stayed till the king came south. Then the jarl went east into Värmland and stayed there for a long time during the winter; King Steinkel gave the rule of that district to the jarl. When winter was passing, the jarl went west into Raumarik; and he had many men whom the Gauts and Värmlanders had given him. He took the land dues and taxes which he had to take from the Uplanders. Then he went back east to Gautland and stayed there during the spring. King Harald stayed in Oslo during the winter, and he sent men to the Uplands to demand the taxes and land dues and the king's fines. But the Uplanders said that they would pay all the dues they had to pay, and that they would hand them over to Hacon the Jarl as long as he was alive and had not forfeited his life or his jarldom; and so the king got no land dues from the Uplands that winter.

71. That winter word and messengers went between Norway and Denmark, and it was agreed that both Norsemen and Danes should make peace and terms between themselves, and they bade the kings do this. The messengers seemed anxious to conclude peace, and the end of it was that a peace meeting was arranged by the Elv between King Harald and King Swein. And when spring came, both kings gathered many ships and men for the journey. And in a flokk some scald says this about the journey:

The grim man who guards the land
Locks up his realm with longships
From the Sound to the north.
He went to the haven,
The stems gleaming with gold.
They cut through the sea
Eagerly west of Halland;
The spray boards quivered.

Oath-fast Harald! Thou oft
Didst gird the land with ships.
Swein, too, through the sounds
Didst sail to meet the king.
The high-praised raven-feeder
Who locked up every inlet with stems
Had out a mighty host
Of all the Danes from the south.

Here it should be said that these kings kept the arrangement to

1 *Steinkel* was king in Sweden from about 1056 to 1066.

meet which was made between them and they both came to Land's
End, even as it is said:

Kind leader, thou didst sail
South again to the meeting,
Which all the Danes wished;
The matter was important.

Swein now went north
Near to Land's End
To meet Harald. Hard
It was to sail along the coast.

And when the kings met, men began to talk about the terms between the kings. And as soon as they fell to talk, many complained
over the scathe they had got from warring, robbery and loss of life.
They kept on for a long time, even as it is said here:

The brisk bonders said
Such words loudly
Even such as, when men meet,
Most anger the others.
Men who quarrelled about every-
    thing
Did not seem to want
To seek an early peace.
The wrath of the princes grew.

The wrath of the princes would be
    perilous
If peace was in sight.
The men who made peace
Had to weigh all in the scales.
It suited the kings to say
All such as the armies like.
Ill would result if the bonders
Were left in a worse position.

After this the best and wisest men came together and a peace was
made between the kings in this wise; King Harald was to have Norway, and Swein Denmark up to the landmarks which had been between Norway and Denmark from former times; neither of them was
to pay fines to the other; where it had been harried they should take
it as they found it, and he who had got the booty should keep it. This
peace was to hold as long as they were kings. The treaty was bound
with oaths, and then the kings gave each other hostages, as is told here:

I have heard that gladly
Did both Harald and Swein
Give hostages one to the other;
God brought it about.

May they keep their oaths
And fully hold their peace.
Nobody can break the treaty;
It was sealed by witnesses.

King Harald sailed north to Norway with his men and King Swein
went south to Denmark.

72. King Harald was in the Vik in the summer and he sent his
men to the Uplands for the dues and taxes which he had there. The
bonders made no payment, but said that they would let everything
wait for Hacon the Jarl if he came to them. Hacon the Jarl was then
up in Gautland with a great army. When summer was passing, King
Harald sailed south to Konungahella. He then took all the light
ships he could get hold of and sailed up along the Elv. He had them
drawn off the water near the waterfalls and so he brought his ships

up into Lake Väner. He then rowed east across the lake to where he had heard Hacon the Jarl was. And when the jarl got news of the king's journey, he came down from the land and would not that the king should harry there. Hacon the Jarl had a great army which the Gauts had given him. King Harald brought his ships into a river mouth; he then made a landing but left some of his men behind to watch the ships. The king himself and some of his men rode, but many others went on foot. They had to go through a wood and thereafter they had before them certain marshes overgrown with brushwood, and then a holt. When they came up to the holt they saw the jarl's army, but there was still a marsh between them. Both armies then drew up their lines. King Harald said that his men should first sit up on the bank: "Let us first try and see if they will fall on us; Hacon has no wish to wait", he said. It was frosty weather and some drifting of snow, and so Harald's men sat under their shields; but the Gauts were not clad so well and it was cold for them. The jarl bade them wait until the king went against them and they might all stand on high ground. Hacon the Jarl had the standard which King Magnus Olavson had owned. The Gaut's lawman was called Torvid and he was sitting on a horse, whose reins were fastened to a stoop which stood in the marsh. He spoke and said: "God knows that we have here a great host and very brave men. Let not King Steinkel learn that we did not help the good jarl well. I know that if the Norsemen fall on us we shall stand up to them, but if the young men falter and will not wait, let us not run nearer than this beck; and if the young folk still waver, as I do not know will happen, let us go no nearer than to that howe". At the same moment the Norse army rushed up, shouting their war cry and striking on their shields. The Gauts' army also began to shout and the lawman's horse tugged so strongly at his reins when he was frightened by the shouting that the stoop came up and flew past the lawman's head; he shouted: "An unlucky shot, thou Norseman!" The lawman then rode away. King Harald had beforehand said this to his men: "Even though we make a din and shout, let us not go down the bank ere they come to us here", and so they did. But as soon as the war cry arose, the jarl had his standard borne forth, and when they came under the bank, the king's men fell upon them and some of the jarl's men straightway fell, whilst others fled. The Norsemen did not drive the fleeing men far, for it was late in the day. They took Hacon the Jarl's standard and as many weapons and clothes as they could get hold of. The king had both standards borne before him when he went down. They talked amongst themselves as to whether the jarl was fallen, but when they rode through the wood, they could only ride forth one at a time. A man rode across the path and thrust a spear through him who bore the jarl's standard; he grabbed the pole and rode another way through the wood with the standard. And when this was told the king, he shouted: "The jarl is alive! Give me my brynie!" In the night the king rode to his ships and many said that the jarl had avenged himself. Then Tjodolv quoth:

Steinkel's men, who should have
Strengthened the war-glad jarl,
Have certainly gone to Hel.[1]
The strong king brought this about.

He who will have a better case
Says that Hacon had
To flee hastily, for help
From there was hopeless.

King Harald was on his ships during that part of the night which was left. But in the morning when it was light, there was ice all about so thick that one could walk round the ships. The king then bade his men break up the ice from the ships to the open water. The men went and fell to striking the ice. King Harald's son Magnus steered the ship which was in the lower part of the river, nearest the lake. And when the men had almost broken up the ice, a man ran out along the ice to the spot where they were to break it up, and he then began to strike the ice as if he were mad and frantic. Then a man said: "Once again it is as often before that no one is of such help in whatever he undertakes as Hall Kodransbane; see now how he is striking the ice". And there was on Magnus' ship a man called Tormod Eindridason; and when he heard Kodransbane mentioned, he ran up to Hall and struck him a death blow. Kodran was the son of Gudmund Eyolfson,[2] and Gudmund's sister Valgerd was the mother of Jorunn, Tormod's mother. Tormod was one year old when Kodran was slain and he had never seen Hall Otryggson before this. The ice was then broken up to the open water and Magnus took his ship into the lake, got straightway under sail and sailed west over the lake. But the king's ship lay innermost in the creek and he was the last to come out. Hall had been in the king's following and was very dear to him; the king was very wroth. He was late coming to the haven, and by that time Magnus had helped the murderer to the woods and offered fines for him. But the king was very nearly attacking Magnus and his men, until the friends of both came and made terms between them.

73. This winter King Harald went up into Raumarik and he had a great army. He brought these matters before the bonders, that they had withheld from him his dues and taxes and had strengthened

1 I.e. the goddess of death.   2 Cf. 'History of St Olav', p. 294, n. 2.

his foes in their enmity to him; he had the bonders taken, some maimed, some slain and many robbed of all their goods. Those who could fled. He had the districts burned far and wide and laid them waste. Thus quoth Tjodolv:

The destroyer of the isle-dwellers laid
Heavy bonds on the Raumalanders.
Harald's war lines went forth
Quickly there, as I believe.

Fire was given in return;
The grim man planned it,
The high fires must lead
The poor bonders to lealty.

After this King Harald went up to Hedemark and burned there and made no less havoc than in the other places. From there he went to Hadeland and so out to Ringerik where he burned and went forth with the shield of war. Tjodolv said:

The warriors' homesteads burned;
The glow shone up from the thatch.
The lord of the chieftains struck
The Hadelanders with evil stones.

The sufferers craved their lives;
The flame brought the Ringers
Hard scathe ere
The fire could be stopped.

The bonders then put the whole of their case in the hands of the king.

74. After King Magnus died, fifteen years had passed since the battle of Nissa was fought and after that two more years elapsed before Harald and Swein made peace. Tjodolv quoth:

The prince of the Horders brought
Strife to an end; peace was made

The third year; on the strand,
The steel swords bit the shields.

After this peace was made, the king's trouble with the Uplanders lasted three half-years. Thus sayeth Tjodolv:

Hard it is to speak
Fittingly of the king's deed,
When he taught the Uplanders
To own an idle plough.

The wise leader has
Won honour so great,
In these three half-years,
That it will always be remembered.

75. Edward Ethelredson was King of England after his brother Hardicanute; he was called Edward the Good, and so he was too. King Edward's mother was Queen Emma, daughter of Richard, Jarl of Rouen; her brother (nephew) was Robert the Jarl, father of William the Bastard, who was then Duke of Rouen in Normandy. King Edward was married to Queen Gyda, daughter of Jarl Godwin Ulvnaderson.[1] Gyda's brothers were Jarl Tosti the eldest, Jarl Morcar the second, Jarl Waltheof the third, Jarl Swein the fourth

---

1 *Ulvnaderson* was the surname in O.N. for Godwin Wulnothson, the famous Earl of Wessex. Goodwin sands, the dangerous sandbanks off Dover, the scene of so many wrecks, take their name from him.

and Harold the fifth;[1] Harold was the youngest[2] and was brought up at King Edward's court. He was King Edward's foster-son, and the king loved him much and took him for his son, for he had no children.

76. One summer Harold Godwinson had to go to Bretland,[3] and he went on a ship. And when they were on the water the wind turned against them and they were driven out to sea. They got near land in the west of Normandy and they had a perilous storm. They proceeded to Rouen and there they found William the Jarl, who gladly greeted Harold and his followers. Harold stayed there in good cheer for a long time in the autumn, for the storms continued and it was not sailing weather out on the sea. And when it drew nigh to winter, the jarl and Harold spoke about Harold staying through the winter. Harold sat in a high-seat on one side of the jarl and on the other side sat the jarl's wife, who was fairer than any other woman whom men had seen. They often had lively talks together at their drink. Most often the jarl went to bed early, but in the evenings Harold sat long talking with the jarl's wife. Thus it went on for a long time during the winter. Once when they were talking together, she said: "The jarl has spoken with me about this and asks what we two talk about so steadfastly, and now is he wroth". Harold answered: "We shall at once let him know all our talk". Next day Harold called the jarl to talk with him and they went into the council room; there, too, were the jarl's wife and their counsellors. Harold then began: "I must tell you, jarl, that there is more in my coming here than what I have put before you. I wish to ask for thy daughter

1 Harold had five brothers—not four as Snorre states—and two of them are given wrong names. Instead of Morcar (who was Harold's brother-in-law) and Waltheof, their names were Leofwin and Wulnoth. His other brothers were Swein (the eldest), Tosti and Gyrth. Wulnoth (the youngest) was kept a prisoner by William the Conqueror and later by William Rufus. Leofwin and Gyrth fell at Hastings. 2 *Harold* was the second or third son of Godwin. Swein was outlawed in consequence of an offence committed against an abbess and died in 1052. Tosti declared (according to Ordericus Vitalis) that he was older than Harold. Harold succeeded to the Earldom of Wessex on the death of Godwin, which should indicate that he was older than Tosti. The choice of names of this family witnesses to the influence of Harold's mother Gyda (or Githa), the sister of the Danish Earl Ulf, brother-in-law of King Canute. Ulf was father of the later Danish king Swein Ulfson. Harold's sisters were Gyda (usually called Eadgytha) who married Edward the Confessor, Gunhild and Algivu (Algiva). Harold's marriages are somewhat obscure. With his first wife (or concubine) he is supposed to have had three sons, viz. Godwin, Edmund and Magnus, besides two daughters Githa and Gunhild. With his second wife Edith (often called in Anglo-Danish Edith Swanne Hals, i.e. Swan's neck) he had two sons, viz. Harold and Ulf (who must have been twins and born after his death). These particulars of Harold's children are taken from the *Encyclopædia Britannica* (published 1903). 3 *Bretland*, O.N. for Wales.

as my wife. I have often spoken about this with her mother who has promised to help me in this matter with you". And as soon as Harold had made this known, all who were there took it well and furthered the matter with the jarl; the end of it was that the maiden was betrothed to Harold. But as she was young, a delay of some years was settled upon before the marriage.

77. And when spring came, Harold fitted out his ship and went away; he and the jarl parted with the greatest of friendship. Harold then went out to England to King Edward and never afterwards went to Valland to seek his bride. King Edward ruled over England for twenty-four years and he died in his bed in London *Nonæ Januarii* (5th of January); he was buried in St Paul's[1] and the English called him holy. Godwin the Jarl's sons were then the mightiest men in England. Tosti was made leader of the English king's army and he was the land-ward, when the king grew old; he was set above all other jarls.[2] His brother Harold was always at the court and was the next man in all service, and he had to watch over all the king's wealth. It is the saying of men that when the king's death drew nigh, Harold and a few others only were near. Harold then bent over the king and said: "I claim you all as witnesses that the king has now given me the kingship and all the realm of England". Thereupon the king was carried out dead from his bed. The same day there was a meeting of the leaders, and then they talked about taking a king; Harold had his witnesses brought in to show that King Edward had given him the kingdom on the day of his death. The meeting ended with Harold being taken as king, and crowned on the thirteenth day in St Paul's.[3] All the leaders and all the folk submitted to him. But when his brother Tosti the Jarl learned this, he liked it ill; he thought that he was as fit to be made king. "I will", he said, "that the land-chiefs choose him as king whom they think best fitted." Such words then passed between the brothers. King Harold said that he would not give

---

1 Should be St Peter's Church, the old name for Westminster Abbey. Edward, the son of Edmund Ironside, was brought over from Hungary by Edward the Confessor and died soon after his arrival in England. He was buried in St Paul's (1057).
2 Snorre Sturlason's account of Earl Tosti is probably right, in as far as it relates to events up to 1065. He became Earl of Northumberland in 1055, which promotion would probably make him *land-ward* of the whole east coast of England, and Northumberland was more exposed to viking raids than the remainder of the country. In 1065 he was deposed by the Northumbrians and went to Flanders.    3 The thirteenth day of Christmas or 6th of January. Harold was crowned by Aldred, Archbishop of York, on the same day as Edward was buried (6th of January) (Simeon of Durham, Florence of Worcester and Roger of Wendover). These chroniclers do not state where Harold was crowned and the probability is that he was crowned at St Peter's (or Westminster Abbey) and not St Paul's.

up the kingdom, for he was now enthroned in the seat which the king had, and had since been elected and consecrated king. The whole people also held to him, and he had also all the king's crown property.

78. And when King Harold was aware that his brother Tosti wished to take the kingship from him, he believed him to be wicked, for Tosti was a very wise man, a great warrior and in good friendship with the land's chiefs. Harold then took from Tosti the leadership of the army and all that power which he had had over and above the other jarls in the land. Tosti would by no means suffer being his own brother's servant; he then went away with his men southwards across the sea to Flanders, where he stayed a while; then he went to Frisia and so to Denmark to his kinsman King Swein. King Swein's father Ulf the Jarl and Tosti the jarl's mother Gyda (Githa) were brother and sister. The jarl asked King Swein for support and help in men. King Swein bade him stay there with him and said that he should have a jarldom in Denmark so that he could be a worthy chief there. The jarl answered thus: "My wish is to go back to England, to my *odal* lands; but if I cannot get help from thee, I would rather set this before thee: to grant thee all the strength I can get in England if thou wilt go with the Danish army to England to win the land, as thy uncle Canute did". The king answered: "I am so much less mighty than my kinsman King Canute, that I find it hard to hold Denmark against the Norsemen. Canute the Old got the inheritance of Denmark and won England by war and strife; yet for a time it was not unlikely that he would lose his life; Norway he got without battle. Now I can hold myself in greater moderation to arrange things more according to my own small matters than according to my kinsman Canute's success". Then said Tosti: "My errand here is less important than I thought, when thou, so noble a man, wouldst leave me in such difficulty. It may be now that I shall seek friendship where it can be less expected; but I may find a chief who is less afraid of taking up great plans than thee". The king and the jarl then parted, but they were not very friendly.

79. Tosti the Jarl now turned another way; he arrived in Norway and went to King Harald, who was then in the Vik.[1] And when they met, the jarl brought forward his business; he told him all about his journey since he had left England, and asked the king to give him

---

[1] Ordericus Vitalis states that Tosti went to Normandy and afterwards (through stress of weather) landed in Norway. Ordericus relates his conversation with King Harald. Tosti was William the Conqueror's brother-in-law. The other chroniclers refer to an arrangement between Harald and Tosti, but do not say where it was made.

help to get his realm in England. The king said that the Norsemen had no wish to go to England and make war there when they had an English chief over them; "Folk say", he said, "that the English are not altogether to be relied on". The jarl answered: "Is it true, as I have heard men say in England, that thy kinsman, King Magnus, sent men to King Edward and it was said in his message that King Magnus owned England with the same right as Denmark, taken by inheritance after Hardicanute, even as their oaths stood?" The king answered: "Why did he not have it if he owned it?" The jarl answered: "Why didst thou not have Denmark, just as King Magnus had it before thee?" The king said: "The Danes have no need to boast against us Norsemen; many a hole have we burned there among thy kinsmen". Then said the jarl: "If thou wilt not tell me, I will tell thee; King Magnus took Denmark into his possession because all the chiefs of the land helped him, but thou didst not get it because all the country was against thee. King Magnus did not fight to win England because all the folk would have Edward as their king. If thou wilt win England, then I can make it so that most of the chiefs in England will be thy friends and helpers. Against my brother Harold I am short of nothing but the name of king. All men know that there never was such a warrior born in the Northlands as thou, and it seems strange to me that thou wilt fight fifteen years to get Denmark but thou wilt not have England, which is now lying free for thee". King Harald thought carefully on what the jarl had said; he perceived that there was truth in much of it and at the same time he had a wish to win that kingdom. After this the king and the jarl talked long and often together, and they took up the plan of going to England in the summer and winning the land. King Harald sent bidding through all Norway and called out a levy on half the people. This was much talked about, and there were many guesses as to how it would go on the journey; some related and reckoned up all King Harald's great deeds and said that nothing would be impossible for him; but some said that England would be hard to win, for the folk were more numerous and the warriors who were called the thingmen troop[1] were so bold that one of them was better than two of Harald's best men. Then Ulf the Marshal answered:

| | |
|---|---|
| I always won riches | If, noble woman, two of us |
| Without force. No need | Should ever turn away |
| There is for the king's marshals | Before one of the thingmen; |
| To step in the king's ships, | In my youth I learned otherwise. |

1 Cf. 'History of St Olav', p. 226, n. 1.

Ulf the Marshal died that spring. King Harald stood by his grave, and before he went away he said: "There lies one now who was most trusty and faithful to his lord". In the spring Tosti the Jarl sailed to Flanders to meet the men who had followed him from England and also the others who had there gathered to him from England and Flanders.

80. King Harald's army gathered in Solunder;[1] and when King Harald was ready to go out from Nidaros, he went first to King Olav's shrine, unlocked it, cut King Olav's hair and nails, and then locked up the shrine and threw the key out into the Nid. But some say he threw the key into the sea outside Agdenes. Since then St Olav's shrine has not been unlocked.[2] It was then thirty-five winters after his death and he had lived thirty-five winters in this world.

King Harald then sailed south with his followers to meet his army. There so great a force of men gathered together that it is the tale of men that King Harald had nearly two hundred (two hundred and forty) ships, besides supply ships and small ships. When they were lying in Solunder, a man called Gyrd, who was on the king's ship, had a dream. He thought he was there on the king's ship and he looked upon an island where a great troll woman was standing with a sword in one hand and a trough in the other; he also thought he looked out over all their ships and saw a bird on every ship stem; they were all eagles and ravens. The troll woman quoth:

Certain it is that the king
Eggs them on to hold battle
Against many warriors westward.
It is all to my gladness.

There may the raven find
Food for himself on the ships;
He knows there will be enough to eat;
Always shall I follow thee.

81. There was a man called Tord who was on the ship which lay nearest to the king's ship. One night he dreamed that he saw King Harald's fleet going towards land which he seemed to know was England. On the land he saw a great battle line and it looked as if both armies were getting ready for battle and had many standards. But in front of the host of men of that land there rode a great troll woman; she was sitting on a wolf and the wolf had a man's body in its mouth, and blood was flowing out of the corners of its mouth. And when it had eaten the man, the troll woman threw

1 The Solunder Islands, outside the Sognefjord.    2 I.e. up to the time when Snorre wrote his Sagas, about 1230. The shrine was again opened during Magnus Haconson's reign by Archbishop John, between 1258 and 1280.

another into its mouth, and so one after another; and it finished them all. She quoth:

| | |
|---|---|
| The troll lets the red shield | The woman flings to the jaw |
| Shine, when battle nears. | The flesh of the fallen men; |
| The giant's bride foresees | Madly she dyes inside |
| An unlucky journey for the king. | The wolf's mouth with the blood. |

82. Moreover King Harald dreamed one night that he was in Nidaros, and that he met his brother, King Olav, who quoth a verse to him:

| | |
|---|---|
| In many a battle the Digre | I still fear that death |
| King fought with honour: | Is near thee, my king. |
| I got a holy fall to the earth, | Thou wilt feed the greedy wolves; |
| For I sat at home. | God doth not bring this about. |

Many other dreams and other kinds of forebodings were told of, and most of them were sad. Before King Harald went from Trondheim he had his son Magnus taken as king and set over the realm of Norway whilst he himself was away. Thora, Torberg's daughter, was also left behind, but Queen Ellisiv went with him, as did her daughters Maria and Ingegerd. Olav, son of King Harald, also went with his father from the land.

83. And when King Harald was ready and had a fair wind he sailed out to sea and came to land near the Shetlands, though some of his ships got to the Orkneys. King Harald stayed there a short while before he sailed to the Orkneys; from there he got many men and the Jarls Paul and Erlend, sons of Torfinn the Jarl. He left Queen Ellisiv and his daughters Maria and Ingegerd there. Thence he sailed southwards off Scotland and so along the coast of England; he came to land at the place called Cleveland.[1] There he went ashore and straightway harried and subdued the district; he was not withstood. After this King Harald went to Scarborough[2] and fought with the townsmen. He went up on the hill[3] which is there and had a great pile built and set alight. And when the fire was blazing they took great forks and shot the burning wood into the town; then one house after another caught fire, and the whole town surrendered. The Norsemen slew many men and took all the goods they could lay

1 *Cleveland,* the hilly country in the north-east of Yorkshire.   2 *Scarborough* was founded by the Norsemen Torgils and Kormak in 966 or 967. The name is derived from O.N. *skarði* (the hare lip) and *borg* (stronghold). Torgils was known to have a hare lip, as his brother Kormak uses the nickname *Skarði* in two poems. Cf. Dr A. H. Smith's *Place-names of North Riding,* pp. 105–6.   3 Castle Hill, the prominent lofty headland in Scarborough, on which the castle ruins now stand.

hands on. The Englishmen had then no other choice, if they wished to keep alive, than to submit to King Harald. He subdued the land wherever he went. After this King Harald went south along the coast with all his host and came to Holderness,[1] where a troop of men came against them and where King Harald held battle and got the victory.

84. After this King Harald went to the Humber, then up along the river and there came to land.[2] Morcar the Jarl and his brother Waltheof the Jarl[3] were then up in York with a powerful army. King Harald was in the Ouse when the jarls' army came down against him. King Harald then went ashore and began to draw up his lines; one wing stood forth on the river bank, whilst the other went farther inland towards a dike, where there was a deep wide marsh full of water. The jarls had their lines placed with the whole crowd of men down along the river. The king's standard was near the river, where the line was thick; towards the dike it was thinnest and the men there the least reliable. The jarls then came down along the dike and the wing of the Norsemen, which was towards the dike, fell back and the Englishmen went after them, thinking that the Norsemen would flee. Morcar's standard it was that went forth there.

85. And when King Harald saw that the Englishmen's wing was coming down upon them alongside the dike, he had the war blast blown and egged on his army eagerly; he had his standard, the Land-Waster, borne forth. Then the onset was so hard that everything

1 _Holderness,_ the south-east part of East Riding, culminating in Spurn Head.
2 Near Riccall (River Ouse) about five miles north of Selby and ten miles south of York. 3 The English chroniclers give the names of Earl Morcar and Edwin Earl of Chester as the leaders of the English army. Earl Waltheof was son of the celebrated Scandinavian Earl Siward (which is a corruption for Sigurd). Siward was Earl of Northumberland; he fought against Macbeth in 1054 and put Malcolm on the Scottish throne. Shakespeare gives him a prominent place in his tragedy of _Macbeth._ He was nicknamed _Digre,_ the same as St Olav. Earl Waltheof was a great fighter, muscular of arm, brawny in the chest, tall and robust in his whole body. He was of tender years when his father Siward died in 1055 and Earl Tosti then succeeded to the earldom of Northumberland, until he was expelled in 1065. Earl Waltheof is mentioned in English history as having been elected Governor of the city of York in 1069, when the Northumbrians revolted against William the Conqueror and killed the Norman garrison at York. The English were aided in this revolt by King Swein of Denmark, who sent an army across under the command of Osborn (Asbiorn). Snorre was no doubt aware of the great position which Earl Waltheof held in the north of England, and that this valiant man was also one of the leaders at the battle of Fulford is more than probable. Earl Waltheof made peace with William the Conqueror in 1070, but William did not trust him and he was beheaded at Winchester in 1075 and buried afterwards with great pomp in the church at Croyland (Crowland), about eight miles north-east of Peterborough (Roger de Hoveden).

gave way before them and there was a great loss of men in the jarls' army. The army quickly turned in flight, some fleeing up the river, others down, though most of the men leaped into the dike, where the fallen lay so thickly that the Norsemen could go dry-foot across the marsh.[1] Morcar the Jarl fell there.[2] Thus sayeth Stein Herdisarson:

Many sank in the river,
And the sinking men drowned.
Soon it happened that many a dreng
Lay about the young Morcar.

The chief put them to flight;
The army began speedily
To run before the noble king.[3]

This drapa was composed by Stein Herdisarson about King Harald's son Olav, and here it is mentioned that Olav was in the battle with his father, King Harald. This is also spoken of in "Harald's stick":

Waltheof's fighters,
Bitten with weapons,
There lay dead
Deep in the marshes,

So that the war-keen
Norsemen could
Cross over there
On corpses only.

Waltheof the Jarl and those men who could get away fled up to the town of York, and there was the greatest fall of men. This battle was on the Wednesday before the Feast of St Matthew.[4]

86. Tosti the Jarl came westward from Flanders to King Harald as soon as the latter was come to England, and the jarl was with him in all these battles. It now befell even as Tosti had told Harald when they met before, that a great number of men would come to them in England. They were Tosti's kinsmen and friends, and the troop was a great strength to the king. After the battle, which has just now been spoken of, all the folk in the nearest districts submitted to King Harald, but some fled. King Harald then went on his way to win the town (of York) and he brought his host to Stamford Bridge.[5] But because the king had won so great a victory over great chiefs and a mighty army, all the folk were afraid and had no hope of withstanding him. Then the townsmen made this plan, that they should send word to the king and put themselves, and likewise the town, into his power. This was all so ordered that on the Sunday[6] King Harald went with all his army to the town and they sat at a

---

1 The battle was fought at Fulford (a mile south-east of York) on the 20th of September, 1066.    2 Snorre was misinformed about Morcar's death, because he escaped after the battle and joined forces with King Harold Godwinson at Hastings.
3 The refrain to this song is "Olav the Mighty is the best prince born under the sun".
4 I.e. 20th of September, 1066.    5 About seven miles east of York.    6 24th of September, 1066.

thing outside the town and the townsmen came out to it. All the folk promised obedience to King Harald and as hostages they gave him the sons of the foremost men, according to Tosti the Jarl's knowledge of all the men in the town.[1] In the evening the king went to his ships after this easy victory and was very happy. Early on Monday a thing was held in the town and then King Harald was to set rulers in the city and give fiefs and rights. The same evening after sunset, King Harold Godwinson came from the south to the town with a mighty army; he rode into the town by the wish and consent of all the townsmen. Then men were set at all the town gates and on all the highways so that news thereof should not come to the Norsemen; this army was in the town during the night.

87. On Monday[2] when Harald Sigurdson had had his breakfast he had the landing signal blown. He got his army ready and separated the men who were to go from those who were to stay behind. In each party two men were to go up and one stay behind. Tosti the Jarl made himself ready to go up with his troop, and the men left behind to watch the ships were Olav the king's son, Paul and Erlend, jarls of the Orkneys, and Eystein Orre, son of Torberg Arneson, who was then the most renowned of all the landed men and dearest to the king: King Harald had promised him his daughter Maria. At this time there was very good weather and the sun was hot. The men left their brynies behind and went up with their shields, helmets and spears and with swords girded; many had bows and arrows also, and they were very merry. But when they came near the town, a great army rode out against them; they saw the smoke from the horses, and fair shields and white brynies. The king stopped his army, called Tosti the Jarl to him and asked him what army that might be. The jarl answered and said that he thought that there might be trouble, but it might also be that they were some of his kinsmen seeking mercy and friendship and vowing the king help and trustiness in return. The king then said that they should first stop and get to know more about this army. They did so, and the army grew greater the nearer it came, and it all looked like a sheet of ice when the weapons glistened.

88. King Harald Sigurdson then said: "Let us now decide upon a

---

[1] Florence of Worcester states: "The Norsemen remained in possession of the field and having taken one hundred and fifty hostages from York and leaving there one hundred and fifty hostages of their own, returned to their ships". Simeon of Durham mentions that they took five hundred hostages and left one hundred and fifty of their own men.    [2] 25th of September, 1066.

wise plan, for it cannot be hidden that there is trouble and that the king himself is there". The jarl answered: "The first thing to do is that we turn about as quickly as we can to our ships for our other men and weapons, and then withstand them according to our might, or else let the ships protect us and then their riders will have no power over us". Then said King Harald: "I will choose another plan: to set three bold men on the swiftest horses and bid them ride as fast as they can and tell this to our men; then they will come quickly to our help, for the Englishmen shall have a sharp fight ere we bow down". Then the jarl said the king should decide in this as in everything else; nor had he himself any wish to flee. King Harald then had his standard, the Land-Waster, set up, and the man who bore it was called Fridrek.[1]

89. King Harald then drew up his army; his line was long and not thick: both wings he bent back so that they came together and there was a wide ring, thick and even on all sides, shield to shield, and likewise behind. The king's troop was outside the ring; his standard was there and they were well-chosen men. In another place there was Tosti the Jarl with his troop; he too had a standard. The line was drawn up in this way because the king knew that the riders were wont to ride on in troops and straightway turn back. The king said that his troop and the jarl's troop should go where it was most needful and "the bowmen shall also be there with them and they who stand foremost shall set their spear shafts in the earth and turn the points towards the riders' breasts, in case they ride on us; and they who stand in the second rank shall set their spear points towards the horses' breasts".

90. King Harold Godwinson was come there with a mighty host of cavalry[2] and infantry. King Harald Sigurdson then rode through his lines and saw how the lines were; he sat on a black blazed horse; the steed fell under him and the king fell forward; he stood up quickly and said: "A fall is good luck on a journey". Then said

1 The English chroniclers relate that a Norseman showed the utmost bravery at the beginning of the battle. Although almost incredible, they state that the Norse giant defended the bridge at Stamford alone for some time, and prevented the whole English army from crossing the river, and killed more than forty men with his battle-axe. In the end one of the king's huscarls came under the bridge and treacherously thrust a spear into him, through the chinks of the flooring (Henry of Huntingdon; Roger of Wendover).
2 English historians agree that Harold Godwinson had a certain amount of cavalry, although not so highly developed as that of the Normans. In the battle against the Welsh in 1055 at Hereford, the English fought on horseback, although contrary to their custom (Simeon of Durham).

Harold, King of the Englishmen, to the Norsemen that were with him: "Do ye know the big man who fell off the horse there, the man with the blue kirtle and the fine helmet?" "It is the king himself", they said. The English king then said: "A big man he is and powerful to look upon, but now it is likely that he will be without good luck".

91. Twenty riders rode forth from the thingmen troop in front of the Norse lines; they were all brynied and so were their steeds. Then said a rider: "Is Tosti the Jarl in the army?" He answered: "That cannot be hidden, thou canst find him here". Then said a rider: "Harold thy brother sends thee greeting and likewise word that thou shalt have peace and all Northumbria, and rather than thou shouldst refuse this offer, he will give thee a third of all his kingdom". Then the jarl answered: "This is somewhat different from the trouble and shame of last winter. If this behest had come then, many a man who is now dead would have been alive and the kingdom of England would have stood better. Now if I take this choice, what will he offer King Harald Sigurdson for his work?" Then said the rider: "He has said something about what he will grant him in England: seven feet of ground or as much more as he is taller than other men". Then said the jarl: "Go now and tell King Harold to make ready for battle. It shall not be said with truth amongst the Norsemen that Tosti the Jarl left King Harald Sigurdson and went to his enemies' troops when he had to fight in the west in England. Rather shall we all take one counsel—to die with honour or win England by victory". The riders then rode back. King Harald Sigurdson then said to the jarl: "Who was that well-spoken man?" Then the jarl said: "That was King Harold Godwinson". King Harald Sigurdson then said: "Too long was this hidden from us. They were come so near our army that this Harold might never have told about the death of our men". Then said the jarl: "True it is, lord; he went unwarily for such a chief and it might have been as you say. I saw that he would offer me peace and great rule and that I might have been his slayer if I had told who he was, but I would rather that he were my slayer than I his". Then said King Harald Sigurdson: "A little man he was, but he stood fast in his stirrup".[1] So it is said that King Harald Sigurdson quoth this verse:

| Forth we go | The helmets shine; |
| In our lines | I have no brynie. |
| Without our brynies | Our shrouds now lie |
| Against blue edges. | Down on those ships. |

1  In O.S. *stigreip*.

His brynie was called Emma; it was so long that it stretched half-way down his legs and so strong that a weapon had never fastened on to it. Then said King Harald Sigurdson: "That was ill-composed; I must make a better verse than that". Then he quoth this:

In battle we creep not
Behind our shields
Through fear of the weapon-crash;
Thus bade the faithful woman.

Once the necklet-wearer
Bade me bear my head
High in battle where the sword
And the skulls met.

Then Tjodolv also quoth:

If the prince himself falls
To the earth, I shall not
Flee from the grim king's heirs;
It will go as God wills.

The sun shines on no better
King's sons than these two.
The swift-thinking Harald's avengers
Are full-grown hawks.

92. The battle[1] began and the Englishmen rode forth against the Norsemen. The opposition was hard and it was not easy for the Englishmen to ride on to the Norsemen because of the archers, and so they rode in a ring around them. At first it was not a severe battle so long as the Norsemen kept their lines; but the Englishmen rode hard upon them and when they could do nothing retreated from them. And when the Norsemen saw that they seemed to ride upon them without strength they went against them and wished to pursue the fleeing men. And when they had broken the shield line, the Englishmen rode upon them from all sides and threw spears and shot at them. And when King Harald Sigurdson saw that, he went forth into the strife where the weapon fighting was greatest. It was then the hardest of battles and many men fell in both armies. Then King Harald Sigurdson grew so heated that he rushed forth right out of the line and struck with both hands; then neither helm nor brynie could stand against him. All who were nearest turned away. Then

---

1 It is not quite clear from Snorre's narrative why the battle took place at Stamford Bridge. English sources state that the Norsemen entrenched themselves there in such an extraordinary manner that it seemed almost impossible to dislodge them. On their right hand they had the River Derwent, which was not fordable and could only be crossed by means of a small wooden bridge, and their left was flanked by the River Ouse. However this may be, it seems reasonable to assume that Harald Hardrade must have fallen back to Stamford Bridge when he saw the English army proceeding towards him from York, and that he chose this position only on account of its strong strategical situation. Some Norwegian historians state that the battle took place at this spot because he had arranged a thing meeting there with the principal citizens of York and that hostages should at the same time be exchanged; but why this meeting should be held at such an out-of-the-way place—seven miles from York and some fifteen miles from Riccall, where the fleet was— is difficult to explain; besides, the English chroniclers are in agreement with Snorre Sturlason that hostages had already been exchanged.

were the Englishmen near fleeing. Thus quoth Arnor Jarlascald:

| | |
|---|---|
| The fight-sharp leader's heart | Where near the hersers' leader |
| Wavered not. The strong king | The host could see |
| Showed before him the greatest | That his bloody sword |
| Courage in the thunder of the helms, | Wounded men to death. |

King Harald Sigurdson was wounded in the throat by an arrow. This was a fatal wound. He then fell and so did all the troop which went forth with him except those who turned back, and they held fast to the standard. Tosti the Jarl then went under the king's standard. Both armies then began to draw up their lines a second time and there was a very long pause in the battle. Tjodolv says:

| | |
|---|---|
| Great ill-luck has come to us. | The wise prince's life |
| The host is now in peril. | Has so ended that we are now |
| Without cause did Harald bid | In peril of death. The high-praised |
| Us on this westward journey. | King got a fatal stab. |

But before the fighters came together again Harold Godwinson offered peace to his brother Tosti the Jarl and to the other men who were left in the Norse army. But the Norsemen shouted all at once that every man would fall, one over the other, before they would take quarter from the Englishmen; they shouted their war cry and then the battle began again. Thus sayeth Arnor Jarlascald:

| | |
|---|---|
| In a moment of ill-luck | The mild king's friends |
| The strong king fell dead. | All chose to fall |
| The gold-mounted arrows | Around their war-wont leader |
| Spared not the foe of thieves. | Rather than ask for peace. |

93. Eystein Orre[1] came up at the same moment from the ships with the men who were following him; they were all in full armour. Eystein then got King Harald's standard, the Land-Waster. The strife now began a third time and it was very hard; many Englishmen fell and they were near fleeing. This battle was called "the Orre attack". Eystein's men had gone so heatedly from the ships that from the beginning they were so tired that they were almost unfit for battle when they came into it. But they were so mad that they did not protect themselves so long as they could stand up. They threw off their ring-brynies and then it was easy for the Englishmen to find places to strike them. Some of them collapsed through exhaustion and died unwounded. Almost all the great men amongst the Norsemen had then fallen. It was late in the day. As was to be expected, it happened that their fortunes were not alike; many fled and many

1 Orre or Orr is a family name often met with in England. A farm in Jæderen (near Stavanger) is called Arre or Orre.

of those who thus got away had various turns of good luck. It also grew dark in the evening before all the man-slaying was at an end.

94. Styrkar, Marshal of King Harald Sigurdson, and an outstanding man, escaped. He got hold of a horse and rode away. In the evening a wind arose and it was somewhat cold, whilst Styrkar had no clothes except a shirt. He had, however, a helmet on his head and a naked sword in his hand. He felt very cold when his weariness left him. Then a carl came driving towards him, a carl who had a lined jacket on. Then Styrkar said: "Wilt thou sell thy jacket, bonder?" "Not to thee", he said, "thou art a Norseman, I recognise thy speech."[1] Then said Styrkar: "If I be a Norseman, what wilt thou do then?" The bonder answered: "I would slay thee; but unfortunately I have no weapon that would do". Then said Styrkar: "If thou canst not slay me, bonder, then I shall try to slay thee". He lifted his sword and brought it down on the bonder's neck so that his head fell off; he took the fur-lined coat, leaped on his horse and went down to the shore.[2]

95. William the Bastard, Jarl of Rouen, heard of the death of his kinsman King Edward and likewise that Harold Godwinson had been taken as king in England and had been crowned. But William thought he had a better right to the kingdom of England than Harold by reason of the kinship[3] between him and King Edward; and moreover he thought he had to pay Harold back for his unfaithfulness in breaking his betrothal to William's daughter. For these reasons William gathered an army in Normandy; he had a great number of men and a fair number of ships. The day he rode from the castle to his ships and had mounted his horse, his wife went to him and would speak with him. And when he saw that, he struck her with his heel and thrust his spur into her breast so that it sank deep in. She fell and died straightway.[4] The Jarl rode to his ship and went out with his army to England. His brother, Bishop Odo, was with him at that time. And when the jarl came to England he harried and subdued the land wherever he went. Jarl William was

---

1 An instance showing how similar the languages were.　2 Ordericus Vitalis in his chronicle makes the following statement about Stamford Bridge: "The field of battle may be easily discovered by travellers, as great heaps of the bones of the slain lie there *to this day*, memorials of the prodigious numbers which fell on both sides". Ordericus lived from 1075 to about 1142 and wrote his chronicle in the latter part of his life. Most of the English chroniclers agree that the battle was one of the fiercest ever fought in England.　3 William's father and Edward the Confessor were first cousins. 4 Snorre must have been misinformed about this event. Mathilde, William's queen, died in 1083. William of Malmesbury states: "Mathilde was scourged to death with a bridle"; but adds: "I esteem it folly to believe this of so great a king".

bigger and stronger than other men, a good rider, the greatest of warriors and rather hard, a very wise man, but said to be untrustworthy.

96. King Harold Godwinson gave Olav, son of King Harald Sigurdson, leave to go away and likewise those men of the army who were with Olav and had not been slain in the battle. King Harold then turned southward through England with his army, for he had heard that William the Bastard was going northward through England and subduing the land. There were then with King Harold his brothers Swein, Gyrth and Waltheof. King Harold and Jarl William met in the south of England near the port of Helsingja,[1] where there was a great battle. King Harold fell there, and so did his brother Gyrth the Jarl[2] and a great part of their army. This was nineteen days after the fall of King Harald Sigurdson. Harold's brother Waltheof[3] escaped in flight, and late that evening he met a troop of William's men; and when they saw Waltheof the Jarl's men, they fled to an oak wood; they were one hundred men. Waltheof the Jarl had the wood set on fire and all were burnt. Thus quoth Thorkel Skallason in Waltheof's flokk:

| | |
|---|---|
| The warriors had a hundred | It was heard that these men had |
| Of the king's bodyguard burnt | To lie under the wolf's claws. |
| In the hot fire. The evening | The swords gave food |
| Was hot for these men. | To the troll woman's grey steeds. |

William had himself elected king of England. He sent word to Waltheof the Jarl[4] that they should make peace and that he would give him quarter for a meeting. The jarl went with a few men; and when he came on to the heath north of Castle Bridge,[5] two stewards came towards him with a troop of men, seized him, and set him in chains; and after this he was beheaded. Englishmen called him 'holy'. Thus sayeth Thorkel:

| | |
|---|---|
| Certain it is that the manly Waltheof | True it is that man-slaying in England |
| Was betrayed in his trust | Will be a long time ending. |
| By William, who from the south | Doughty and swift was my lord, |
| Had crossed over the icy sea. | Braver prince does not live. |

1 The O.N. text reads *Helsingja-port*. It is evident that Snorre has read *ls* instead of *st* from the English reports which he had about the battle. Hastings was in olden times called *Haestingas* or *Haestinga-port*.    2 Also their brother Leofwin. Swein had died on a journey home from Jerusalem in 1052; but his son Hacon fell with Harold at Hastings.    3 Harold had no brother called Waltheof. Tales have been written about Harold's brother Gyrth having escaped; in fact Harold himself is supposed to have fled from the battle and lived in obscurity for the remainder of his life; but no credence can be attached to these stories.    4 Cf. chapter 84, note 3 about Earl Waltheof.    5 The O.N. text reads *Kastala-bryggja* and may refer to Castleford in Yorkshire.

William was afterwards king in England for twenty-one years;[1] his offspring have always been kings in England since then.[2] William died in his bed in Normandy[3] and after him his son William

1 Roger de Hoveden (Bohn's edition, vol. 1, p. 556) writes about William under the following heading:

> For What Reason King William abolished the Laws of the English and retained those of the Danes.

"The Law of the Norsemen and Danes prevailed in Norfolk, Suffolk and Cambridgeshire. As regards payment of penalties (by hundreds) for offences committed, when these counties had eighteen hundreds, the former ones had only ten and a half, which arose from their being in the vicinity of the Saxons, the whole sum of contribution in cases of the largest penalty among the Saxons in those times being eighty-four pounds. But in all other matter for trial and penalties they had the same law with the (Danes and) Norsemen above named. When William heard of this, together with the other laws of his kingdom, he greatly approved thereof, and gave orders that it should be observed throughout his kingdom. *For he stated that his ancestors, and those of nearly all the barons of Normandy, had been Norsemen, and had formerly come from Norway.* And for this reason he asserted that he ought to follow and observe their laws before the other laws of his kingdom, as being more profound and more consistent with what was right: whereas the laws of other nations, Britons, Angles, Picts and Scots, were prevailing in every quarter." He goes on to say that the whole of the English people entreated William to allow them to retain the laws of Edward the Confessor, and after due consideration and at the earnest request of his barons, he at length acceded to their entreaties. Henry of Huntingdon, Robert Wace, and Geoffrey Gaimar (in his Norman-French metrical history), attribute to William the Conqueror the following exclamation in his speech to his army before the battle of Hastings: "Ah! let anyone, whom our predecessors, both Danes and Norsemen, have defeated in a hundred battles, come forth and show that the race of Rolf ever suffered a defeat from his time until now, and I will submit and retreat". The above-mentioned passages are cited in order to exemplify the pride William the Conqueror and his barons took in their Norse ancestry. The Norse language was spoken at Bayeux (Normandy) until about 1030 and the children of the Norman dukes were sent to Bayeux to be instructed in it.   2 After this chapter a genealogy has been inserted relating to various royal and other families. P. A. Munch states that this genealogy has principally been taken from *Fagrskinna* or *Ættartal*, and was probably not written in Snorre's original manuscript, although it might have been added to a copy of it. The chapter is not included in this edition, but can be found in P. A. Munch's Norwegian translation (printed 1881), p. 423, n. 2; also in Samuel Laing's translation.   3 William proceeded to Normandy in the summer of 1087 to allay some disturbances caused by the French on the banks of the Eure. William appeared before Mantes at the end of July and burnt part of the town. It was here that his illness commenced. His horse leaped a ditch and William, who was very corpulent, was seriously injured in the bowels by the pommel of the saddle. He was taken to Rouen; but the noise of the town became insupportable to the suffering king and he gave orders that he should be conveyed out of the city to the priory of the church of St Gervase, standing on a hill to the west. Here he died on the 9th of September, 1087. Ordericus Vitalis (in his *Ecclesiastical History* of England and Normandy) gives lengthy details of William's last expedition to Normandy, his illness, death and funeral. He states: "*His death was worthy of his life.* To the very last, through all his illness, his intellect was clear and his conversation lively". He held a long discourse on his death-bed, reviewing his whole life and making dispositions about the future. This discourse is probably the finest effort ever made by a

Rufus was king for fourteen years.[1] Then Henry, his brother, took the kingdom. He was a son of William the First.[2]

98. Olav, son of King Harald Sigurdson, sailed away from England with his men. They sailed out from Ravenser[3] and in the autumn they came to the Orkneys and there they heard the tidings that Maria, daughter of King Harald Sigurdson, had died suddenly on the same day and at the same time as her father King Harald fell. Olav stayed

dying monarch, and Ordericus cites it word for word. But, strange to say, as soon as William had breathed his last, everyone present mounted his horse and hastened away to secure his property, only some inferior attendants remaining with the body. These, when they saw that their masters had disappeared, laid hands on the arms, plate, robes and royal furniture, and, after leaving the body almost naked on the floor, hastened away. When the clergy and monks finally recovered their courage and the use of their senses, they went in procession to St Gervase to attend to the body. Archbishop William ordered the body to be removed to Caen, but none of the Conqueror's relations were there to undertake this removal. Finally a country knight called Herluin was induced to take charge of the funeral. He procured at his own expense persons to embalm the body, hired a hearse to convey it to the Seine and, embarking on a vessel, conducted it by water and land to the abbey of St Stephen at Caen. There all the bishops and abbots of Normandy assembled to perform the obsequies of the illustrious king. But another strange occurrence took place. When Mass ended, and the coffin was already lowered into the grave, the great Gilbert, Bishop of Evreux, delivered a funeral oration. Then Ascelin, son of Arthur, came forward among the crowd and forbade that the king's body should be covered with earth which was on his property and be buried in his inheritance. Ascelin claimed that the Conqueror had unlawfully possessed himself of the land upon which he built the abbey of St Stephen. The bishops and other great men, in order to appease Ascelin, agreed to pay him sixty shillings for the small space in which the grave was made and promised a proportionate price for the rest of the land. *Sic transit gloria mundi.* This narrative, which is taken from Ordericus Vitalis (1075–1142), agrees with that of the Norman chronicler Robert Wace. William of Malmesbury states that the Conqueror's son Henry (afterwards Henry I) was present at the funeral and that he paid to Ascelin, who was called a knight and a brawler, a hundred pounds of silver in order to quiet his audacious claim. In St Stephen's at Caen the spot is shown where William the Conqueror was buried, but nothing remains of his tomb.    1 *William Rufus* reigned from 1087 to 1100.    2 It might seem superfluous for Snorre to mention that Henry, the brother of Rufus, was son of William the First; but it must be remembered that half-brothers and half-sisters were all called brothers and sisters. Snorre apparently wanted to emphasise that Henry was William the Conqueror's son, so that Rufus and Henry were brothers, and not half-brothers like St Olav and Harald Hardrade, who had the same mother but different fathers. Bishop Odo is called William the Conqueror's brother by the chroniclers. They had also the same mother but different fathers. William the Conqueror was illegitimate. It is not generally known that he had any illegitimate children; but Ordericus Vitalis mentions that the Conqueror built a castle at Nottingham for his illegitimate son William Peverel. About the same time he built a castle at Warwick for Henry (son of Roger de Beaumont) who was created Earl of Warwick. Roger de Beaumont's father was Humphrey de Vieilles, the son of Thorold. Humphrey appears to be the same as Umfrid, also mentioned by Ordericus. A Welsh chief of Scand. extraction was called by a similar name 'Amfrid'.    3 *Ravenser*, later Ravenspur, the landing place of Henry, Duke of Hereford, afterwards Henry IV, was situated at the south point of Holderness (in Yorkshire), but it has since been swallowed up by the sea.

there during the winter and the following summer he went east to Norway; there he was taken as king with his brother Magnus. Queen Ellisiv went east with her step-son Olav and so did her daughter Ingegerd. Skuli, Tosti the Jarl's son who was afterwards called the king's foster-father, and his brother Ketel the Crook also went east over the sea with Olav. They were both noble men of great family in England and both were very wise; they were both dear friends of the king. Ketel the Crook[1] went north to Halogaland; there King Olav arranged a good match for him and from him many great men are come. Skuli the king's foster-father was a wise and skilful man, the most handsome of all to look upon; he was the leader of King Olav's bodyguard; he spoke at the things and with the king he decided about the rule of the land.[2] King Olav wished to give Skuli a folk district in Norway which he thought best, with all the rents and dues which the king had. Skuli thanked him for the offer, but said he would rather ask other things of the king, for if there were a change of kings it might be that the gift would be taken back; "I will take", he said, "certain possessions which lie near the market towns where you, my lord, are wont to sit and hold Yule feasts". The king promised him this and granted him lands east near Konungahella, near Oslo, near Tunsberg, near Borg, near Björgyn[3] and north near Nidaros. They were almost the best possessions in each of these places and since then they have always belonged to the men who are of Skuli's stock. King Olav married him to his kinswoman Gudrun Nevstein's daughter; her mother was Ingerid, daughter of King Sigurd Syr and Asta; she was sister of St Olav and King Harald. The son of Skuli and Gudrun was Asolv of Rein;[4] he was married to Thora, daughter of Skofti Agmundson, and this Skofti was grandson of Torberg Arneson. Skuli's and Gudrun's daughter was Ragnhild, who married Orm Kyrping, his daughter was Asa, the mother of Björn Buck. The son of Asolv and Thora was Guthorm of Rein, the father of Bard, who was father of King Inge and Duke Skuli.[5]

---

1 In O.N. *Krokr* means probably that he had a crooked back.      2 This is another instance that the languages spoken in England and in the northern countries before the Conquest resembled each other much more than they do now.      3 *Björgyn* or *Björgvin* was the old name for Bergen.      4 *Rein* is a well-known estate in Nordmöre in South Trondheim folk district or county.      5 After this chapter another important genealogy is written, which P. A. Munch also considers belonged to *Ættartal* or *Fagrskinna* (cf. p. 570, n. 2). This genealogy has also been left out of this edition, but can be found in Samuel Laing's translation (vol. III (1844), p. 99) and in P. A. Munch's Norwegian translation (1881), p. 425, n. 1.

99. One year after King Harald's fall his body was moved eastward from England and north to Nidaros, and it was buried in St Mary's Church, which he had had built. It was the talk of all men that King Harald had been above other men in wisdom and in counsel, whether he was to work a plan quickly or nurse it for a long time for himself or others. He was the boldest of all men with weapons and he was also victorious, even as it has just now been written about. Thus says Tjodolv:

| | |
|---|---|
| The destroyer of the Zealand-dwellers | The heart is half the victory; |
| Never lacked courage. | Harald showed it to be true. |

King Harald was a handsome man and dignified; he had fair hair and a fair beard, with a long moustache. Of his eyebrows one was somewhat higher than the other. He had large hands and feet, but both well-proportioned; his height was five ells; he was grim to his foes and punished all opposition. Thus sayeth Tjodolv:

| | |
|---|---|
| The wise Harald punished | Such burdens they bore |
| Over-boldness in his underlings. | As they made for themselves; each |
| I believe that the king's men | Enjoyed right against the other; |
| Were punished for what they did. | Harald thus shared his vengeance. |

King Harald was very eager for power and all worldly gain. He was very generous to his friends whom he liked well. Tjodolv quoth:

| | |
|---|---|
| The rouser of the sea fight | He honours with his favour |
| Gave me a mark for my work. | Each who shows himself worthy. |

King Harald was fifty years old when he fell. We have no outstanding tales about his youth until he was fifteen winters old, when he was at the battle of Stiklastader with his brother King Olav. He lived thirty-five years after that and in all that time he always had trouble and unrest. King Harald never fled from any battle, but he often sought clever ways by which to escape when he had to do with great odds. All men who followed him in battle or in warfare said that when he was placed in great peril and when a quick decision depended on him, he always chose that plan which all men afterwards saw was the most likely to succeed.

100. Haldor, son of Brynjulv Ulvaldi the Old,[1] was a wise man and a great leader. When he heard men's talk about the difference in character between the brothers St Olav and King Harald, he spoke thus. He said: "I was in great favour with both the brothers and I knew both their minds. I never found two men so like each other;

---

1 Cf. 'History of St Olav', chapter 61.

they were both very wise and weapon-bold men, eager for wealth and power, imperious and not condescending, domineering and swift to punish. King Olav forced the land folk to adopt Christianity and the right faith and grimly punished those who made themselves deaf to it. The chief men of the land would not suffer his righteousness and fair judgments; they raised an army against him and felled him down in his own land; for that he has become holy. But King Harald harried to win fame and power, he broke down all the folk he could and he fell in another king's land. They were both in everyday life men of good morals and they took care of their honour; they journeyed abroad far and wide and were enterprising men; through all this they became outstanding and renowned".

101. King Magnus Haraldson ruled over Norway for the first year after King Harald's death, and after that he ruled the land for two years with his brother King Olav. They were then kings together, and Magnus had the northern part of the land and Olav the eastern. King Magnus had a son who was called Hacon; Steigar-Tore fostered him and he was a promising youth. After King Harald Sigurdson's death, Swein the Danish king asserted that the peace between Norsemen and Danes was at an end. It had not been arranged for a longer time than the lives of Harald and Swein. Then there was a levy of troops in both kingdoms; the sons of Harald called a levy of troops and ships from Norway, and King Swein went from the south with the Danish army. Messengers then went between them with offers of peace. The Norsemen said that they would either keep the same peace as was made before or else fight. This was therefore uttered:

> With threats and words of peace    So that no king
> Olav guarded the land              Could claim it.

Thus sayeth Stein Herdisarson in Olav's drapa:

> The strife-eager king will guard   King Olav must grant
> His heritage against Swein         All Norway to his kin.
> In Kaupang where the holy warrior   Therefore Ulf's heir cannot
> Who is mighty rests.                Lay claim to it.

At this meeting terms were made between the kings and peace between the lands. The agreement was confirmed by Olav taking in marriage Ingerid, King Swein's daughter, and this peace lasted for a long time. Never before had there been such peaceful times in Norway. King Magnus fell sick with the ringworm plague and lay thus for a while. He died in Nidaros and was buried there. He was a king well beloved by all the folk.

## CHRONOLOGY

### HARALD HARDRADE. BORN 1015. KING OF NORWAY 1047–66

1048. Harald harries in Denmark.
1050. Harald brings an army to Denmark.
1062. Battle of Nissa (River Nissa) in Sweden, against Swein Ulfson, who contests Harald's right to the crown of Denmark.
1064. Peace concluded between Harald and Swein.
1066. Death of Edward the Confessor. Harold Godwinson becomes King of England.
Harald goes with an army to England at the instigation of Earl Tosti.
Battle of Fulford (outside York) where Harald defeats Earl Morcar and Earl Edwin and conquers York.
Harold Godwinson comes north and fights the Norsemen at Stamford Bridge. After a fierce contest lasting from morning till night Harold Godwinson is victorious and Harald Hardrade and Earl Tosti are both slain.
William, Duke of Normandy, lands at Pevensey and defeats Harold Godwinson at Hastings, where Harold is killed.
William becomes King of England and is consecrated by Aldred, Archbishop of York, the following year.
Death of King Steinkel of Sweden.
1067. Harald Hardrade's body taken from Stamford Bridge to Norway and buried in St Mary's Church at Nidaros.

# XI

# THE HISTORY OF OLAV KYRRE (OR THE PEACEFUL) (1067–93: sole king from 1069)

1. Olav was king alone over Norway after the death of his brother Magnus. He was a big well-grown man, and it was the talk of all men that no one had seen a fairer or more dignified man; he had silky golden hair which was very becoming; he had a light skin, beautiful eyes and well-shaped limbs; most often he was a man of few words and said but little at the things; he was merry at his ale, a great drinker in company, fond of conversation, happy and peaceful so long as his rule lasted. About this Stein Herdisarson says:

The edge-bold prince of the Tronds
Thought to lay all
Lands in peace by wisdom;
The bonders liked it well.

The folk were glad that the foe
Of England eagerly wished
To accustom his folk to peace.
(Born under the sun.)[1]

2. It was an old custom in Norway that the king's high-seat was in the middle of the long bench, and the ale was borne round the fire. But King Olav was the first to have his high-seat on the long bench which went across the hall; he, too, was the first to have rooms built with stoves[2] and the floor strewed[3] in winter as in summer. In King Olav's days market towns grew much in Norway and some were founded then. King Olav set up a market town in Bergen; many rich men soon settled there and thither sailed merchants from other lands; there he laid the foundation of Christ Church[4]—the great stone church—but little of it was done; he had the wooden church[5] finished. King Olav founded the Great Guild[6] in Nidaros and many

1 Cf. 'History of Harald Hardrade', p. 562, n. 3, about the refrain "Olav the Mighty is the best prince born under the sun". 2 I.e. stone ovens. In O.N. 'stove' is called *ofn-stofa*, lit. 'oven stove', but *stofa* means also 'room' or 'hall'. 3 Strewing the floors with fresh juniper tops is still a custom in certain country districts in Norway. 4 The great Christ Church (later Bergenhus) at Holmen was finished in 1160. 5 I.e. the little Christ Church, which was in use until the stone church was ready. 6 *Great Guild*, in O.N. *Mikla Gildi*. Although the guilds in England existed before Edward III's reign (1327–77) they then came into prominence in London and obtained a certain power in the government of the city; but traces of guilds have been found in England much earlier. King Alfred organised the common responsibility of the members of the *frith gild* and King Athelstan accepted *frith gilds* (= peace clubs) as a constituent element of borough life in London (John Richard Green). The tendency

other guilds in the market towns, whereas formerly there had only been drinking parties; in Nidaros the bell called Town-boon was the great guild bell. The guild brothers there had a stone church, St Margaret's, built. In King Olav's days guildhalls and burial feasts became common in the market towns and men then took up new fashions in clothes; they had fine hose laced to the leg, and some wore gold rings on their legs; men then wore long kirtles with cords on the side and with sleeves five ells long and so tight that they had to pull them on with hand cords and tie them tight up to the shoulders; they wore high shoes, all of which were silk-sewn and some overlaid with gold.[1] There were also many other fashions in dress then.

3. King Olav had these foreign customs at his court; he bade the attendants stand before his table and they were to pour out the drinks into bowls for himself and all princely men who sat at his table. He had taper lads who held the candles at his table, and there were as many of them as there were princely men sitting at his table. The marshal's bench was by the sideboard and there the marshals and other leaders sat with their faces turned towards the high-seat. King Harald and other kings before him had been wont to drink out of horns and had had the ale borne from the high-seat round the fire, and they had drunk healths (*skål*) with whomsoever they wished. Thus sayeth Stuf the Scald:

> The victorious fight-rouser
> (As I knew well) greeted me
> Welcome with friendly heart;
> He was good to know.
>
> Once this feeder of ravens,
> This foe of the rings, himself
> Went to Haug to meet me
> To drink from the golden horn.

4. King Olav had a bodyguard of one hundred (one hundred and twenty) men besides sixty guests and sixty huscarls, all of whom were to move to the king's garth those things which were needed or deal with other things which the king wished. And when the bonders asked the king why he had more men than the law allowed and than former kings had had when he went to the feasts which the bonders made for him, he answered: "I may not rule the realm better than my father, nor is there more fear of me than of my father, even though

---

to unite in guilds originated on the continent, and they were known in ancient Greece and Rome. King Canute established a *frith gild* at Roskilde (Denmark) to protect the country against the vikings. The Guildhall in London was originally built in 1411. *Gildi* in O.N. meant 'payment', or 'compensation'; later it became 'banquet', or 'entertainment'. In M.S. *gilde* still means 'banquet' or 'guest gathering' (*Gjæstebud*).
1 The livery or dress of the City of London companies was first formally adopted in the reign of Edward III and was ultimately worn only by the higher grade members called liverymen.

I have double as many men as he had; but I will not use any constraint against you or make your lot harder".

5. King Swein Ulfson died in his bed ten winters after the death of both the Haralds.[1] After him his son Harald Hein was king in Denmark for three winters; then Swein's son Canute was king for seven winters[2] and he is a holy saint; then Olav, the third son of Swein, was king for eight winters.[3] After him Eric the Good,[4] the fourth son of Swein, was king for eight winters. Olav, King of Norway, married Ingerid, daughter of Swein the Danish king, and the Danish King Olav Sweinson took Ingegerd, daughter of King Harald and sister of Olav, King of Norway. Olav Haraldson, whom some call Olav the Peaceful, but many Olav the Bonder, because he had no strife in or without the land, and gave nobody any cause for harrying his country, got a son by Thora, John's daughter, and he was called Magnus. He was a fine boy and gave great promise; he grew up at the king's court.

6. King Olav had a stone minster built in Nidaros on the place where King Olav's body was first buried, and the altar was set over the spot where the king's grave had been. The minster was hallowed as Christ Church and thither King Olav's shrine was moved and set over the altar; many miracles straightway befell. And the following summer, on the first anniversary of the consecration of the church (27th of July), a great crowd of folk was there. On the evening before the Feast of St Olav (28th of July), a blind man got his sight there. And on the feast day itself (29th of July), when the shrine and holy relics were carried out and the shrine set down in the church-yard as was wont, a man who had been dumb for a long time got his speech and he then sang praises to God and St Olav with a weak voice. The third was a woman who had come there from the east from Sweden and who had suffered much need on her journey because of her blindness. But she trusted in God's mercy and came there on the feast day. She was led blind into the minster to the day's Mass, but before the service was at an end she saw with both eyes and was sharp-sighted and clear-eyed, though she had been blind for fourteen years before; she went thence gladly exulting.

7. It befell in Nidaros when King Olav's shrine was being borne through the street that the shrine grew so heavy that the men could not carry it any longer. The shrine was then set down and the street broken up; they sought to find out what was underneath

1 Harald Hardrade and Harold Godwinson.    2 From 1080 to 1086.    3 From 1086 to 1095.    4 Eric Eiegod (the Good) from 1095 to 1103.

and they found the body of a child that had been murdered and hidden there. The body was taken away and the street put right again just as it had been; the shrine was then carried as before.

8. King Olav Kyrre was a great friend of his kinsman, St Canute, King of Denmark. A meeting was arranged, and they met at the Göta River, at Konungahella, where it was customary for kings to have their meetings. Then King Canute suggested that an army should be sent westward to England, where they had suffered great scathe which ought to be avenged; and both King Olav and the Danish king had good reason for seeking revenge.

"Do one of two things," said Canute; "either be thou the leader of sixty ships which I will give thee, or I will be leader of sixty ships which thou wilt give me." Then replied King Olav: "Thy speech is agreeable to me, but the great difference between us is that thy family has had much success in conquering England, especially Canute the Great, and it may hap that this good luck will continue for thee. Whereas, when my father, King Harald, went westward to England he met his death there. Then Norway lost the best and noblest of her men, and never since have there been such fine men in the country, nor so brave and wise a leader as was King Harald. For that expedition there was the best possible equipment, yet the result was as thou knowest.

"Now I see well enough how little I am fitted to be the leader; so it were better if thou shouldst go, and that I should provide thee with ships".[1]

Canute received from King Olav sixty fine ships, well fitted out and with brave men, and all agreed that this was a great and noble army. It is said in St Canute's History that it was the Norsemen who did not try to break up the levy when the whole fleet came together. They were all loyal to King Canute. But the Danes would not wait for the king's arrival.

Afterwards the Norsemen returned to Norway, but only after the Danish king had given them permission. King Canute appreciated the loyal attitude of the Norsemen, and when they left he allowed

---

[1] Olav Kyrre declined to avenge in person his father Harald Hardrade's death at Stamford Bridge in 1066; but Olav's son Magnus Barefoot (cf. his 'History') was possessed of the same revengeful and ambitious spirit as his grandfather Harald Hardrade and attacked England from the west and by way of Ireland. He also failed, and it may be inferred that if Harald Hardrade paved the way for William the Conqueror, Magnus Barefoot's attacks on England and Ireland had the effect of establishing the Normans even more firmly on the English throne. Henry the First rejoiced when he heard of Magnus Barefoot's death. Cf. 'History of Magnus Barefoot', p. 605, n. 1.

them to trade where they pleased in his lands and through his sounds. He also sent the Norse king valuable presents for his help. But he was wroth with the Danes and he put heavy taxes on them, when he came home to Denmark. The trouble ended in this way that they would not endure St Canute's just treatment, and the Danes killed their own king.

9. It happened, one summer, when King Olav's men had returned from a journey collecting scot, that the king wished to know in what parts of the country they had received the warmest welcome. They said it was in the house of a bonder in Lister. They said that this wise old bonder could foretell many things, and that he could reply to all questions they asked him, because he knew about everything, and, "we believe that he even understands the language of birds". The king answered: "Why have ye faith in such taunt? It is mockery and nonsense to believe it".

It came to pass that, soon afterwards, the king was sailing along the coast, and when passing up one of the sounds he asked: "What is that district up in the land?" His men replied that it was the district in which they had told him already that they had received the warmest welcome. Then said the king: "Whose house is that up yonder not far from the sound?" "That is the house", they replied, "which belongs to the wise old bonder about whom we have spoken." They saw a horse standing near the house, and the king bade them take the horse and kill it. The king's men replied that they were loath to do the old man such grievous wrong. Whereupon the king was wroth, and commanded again that it should be done, and that the horse's head should be so cut off that not one drop of blood should fall to the ground. This being done the body should be borne to the ship. "Afterwards ye shall fetch the old bonder himself, but no word of the dead horse must reach his ears." They did as they were told and brought the old bonder to the king. When he came before the king, the king asked him: "Who owns the house in which thou art living?"

He replied: "My lord, you own it, and take rent for it".

The king said: "Thou must know these parts; show us the way round the ness".

The bonder got into his own boat, and rowed before the king's ship, but before he had rowed very far a crow came flying over the ship and croaked and screeched. The king said: "Dost thou think, bonder, that betokens any ill?" "I am sure, my lord", said he. Then a second, and a third crow flew over the ship and screeched terribly.

By this time the bonder was so perturbed that he forgot to row, and the oars nearly fell out of his hands. The king said: "Thou art too much disturbed about these crows and their croaking". The bonder said: "My lord, I now almost believe what they say". "Go on", said the king. The the bonder replied in a song:

The year-old bird speaks,　　　What seems unthinkable;
But she knows little—　　　　She says I am rowing
The two-year-old chats,　　　Over a mare's head
But I trow her not.　　　　　And that you, O king,
The three-year-old says　　　Hast stolen my property.

"The three-year crow says that you bid me row here on the ship and you have taken my goods." Then the king said: "Bonder! Wilt thou call me a thief?" "My lord," replied the bonder, "it would ill become me to do so, neither do I believe this thing, yet the crow avowed my horse is on your ship. It is some joke that you are playing on me."

After some talk with the bonder, the king gave him presents, freed him from paying scot on his farm, which ever afterwards became the bonder's tax-free property; he gave him other valuable gifts besides.

The king was always generous to his men and gave them all kinds of costly presents.

Stuf the Scald quoth:

The pillar of kingly grace　　　Readily pours out his riches
In bountiness is shown;　　　　To the people of the land.
What other king took pride
In giving his wealth to all?　　The high-born prince
　　　　　　　　　　　　　　Rewards his servants with helmets
To one he gives a warship　　　And brynie coats, or axe and sword and
With brynied sides;　　　　　　Heavy armour for the battle plains.
To another, a trading ship
With painted walls.　　　　　　Olav, the ruler of jarls,
　　　　　　　　　　　　　　Rewards them with gold;
Golden rings his warriors get,　So for his kindness
They boast of royal presents;　　All ill feeling must vanish.
His table guests with gifts
Are favoured from Olav's hand.　The generous prince,
　　　　　　　　　　　　　　Born under a clear sky,
King Olav, Norway's royal son,　Is the uppermost of princes;
Who won glory from the English,　Who could equal him?

10. King Olav was often in the country at the big estates he had. And when he was east in Ranrik at his estate at Haukbo[1] he fell sick,

---

[1] Now Hakeby in Tanum district (Bohuslän, Sweden).

and this brought him to his death. He had been king in Norway for twenty-six winters, and had been taken as king one year after the death of King Harald. King Olav's body was moved north to Nidaros and buried in Christ Church which he himself had built. He was the most beloved of kings, and under his rule Norway grew much in wealth and power.

# XII

# THE HISTORY OF MAGNUS BAREFOOT
## (1093–1103)

1. Magnus, son of King Olav, was, after King Olav's death, straightway taken as king in the Vik over the whole of Norway. But when the Uplanders learned of King Olav's death they took Hacon, Tore's foster-son, Magnus' cousin, as king. Hacon and Tore then went north to Trondheim; and when they came to Nidaros, Hacon summoned the Örething, at which he claimed the name of king; the bonders granted that he should be king over that half of the land which his father King Magnus had had. Hacon relieved the Tronds of the land duty[1] and gave them many other rights; he relieved them of the Yule gifts. Then all the Tronds turned in friendship to King Hacon. Hacon now took his bodyguard and went back to the Uplands and he gave the Uplanders the same rights as the Tronds; they too were his good friends. This was then quoted in Trondheim:

Hither came Hacon the Young;  
He is the best of men.  
This renowned prince  
Came with Steigar-Tore.  

To the generous son of Olav  
He offered half of Norway;  
But the well-spoken Magnus  
Would have it all.

2. In the autumn King Magnus went north to Kaupang, and when he came there he went to live at the king's residence; there he stayed in the beginning of the winter. He kept seven longships afloat in the Nid River in front of the king's residence. And when King Hacon heard that King Magnus was come to Trondheim, he went from the east over the Dovre-fell to Trondheim and so to Kaupang, where he went to live at Skulagarth, below St Clement's Church; it was the old king's residence. King Magnus liked it ill that King Hacon had given the bonders great gifts to win their friendship; it seemed to Magnus that his possessions had been given away in a heedless way, and his mind was much troubled over it; he thought he had been ill-used by his kinsman, in that he would get so much less income than his father and

1 These were harbour dues payable when Icelanders landed in Trondheim. Cf. 'History of St Olav', p. 248, n. 1.

forefathers; he gave Tore the blame. King Hacon and Tore noticed this and they had misgivings as to what Magnus would take upon himself to do. It seemed to them very suspicious that Magnus had longships afloat, covered with awnings and fitted out. In the spring near Candlemas[1] King Magnus put out one dark night and proceeded, with awnings up and lights under the awnings, out to Hevring.[2] They stopped there for the night and made great fires up on land. King Hacon and the warriors who were in the town thought that treason was being done; the king then

The Uplanders go to a thing meeting

had his army called out, and all the Kaupang men came up and gathered in the night. And in the morning when it began to grow light and King Magnus saw an army on Öre, he sailed out of the fjord and thereafter south to the Gulathing. King Hacon made himself ready for his journey and intended going east to the Vik; beforehand he held a mote in the town, where he spoke and asked for their friendship, promising them his. He said he was uncertain what his kinsman, King Magnus, would do. King Hacon sat on horseback ready for his journey. All men willingly promised him their friendship and a following if it were needed, and a whole crowd followed

1 *Candlemas*, i.e. the 2nd of February.    2 *Hevring*, now Hövringen outside Ilsviken, west of Trondheim.

him as far as to Steinbjörg.[1] King Hacon went up to the Dovre-fell, and when he was going over the fell he rode one day after a ptarmigan, which flew away from him. He then fell ill and got a fatal illness; he died there on the fell. His body was taken north, and it came to Kaupang a fortnight after he had gone away. All the townsfolk went to meet the king's body, most of them weeping, for they all loved him greatly. King Hacon's body was placed in Christ Church. King Hacon was little more than five and twenty years old; he was one of the chiefs most beloved by the common folk. He had been north to Bjarmaland[2] where he had held battle and won the victory.

3. King Magnus sailed east in the winter to the Vik, and when spring came he went south to Halland and harried far about there. He burned in Viskardale[3] and in other lordships; there he got much booty, and then he went back to his kingdom. Thus quoth Björn Cripplehand in Magnus' drapa:

The lord of the Vossings[4] went forth
Far and wide with sword through
  Halland;
The king of the Horders[5] burned the
  houses.
Hotly they followed the fleeing men.

Afterwards the prince of the Tronds
Burned many lordships;
The Viskardale widows watched;
The fires flamed in the wind.

Here it is mentioned that King Magnus made great havoc in Halland.[6]

4. There was a man called Swein, son of Harald Fletti, a Danish man by birth. He was the foremost of vikings and a great warrior, very skilful, and of good family in his country. He had been for some time with King Hacon, and was very dear to him. After Hacon's death, Steigar-Tore did not think he could make terms or friendship with King Magnus if he got power over the whole land, because of his actions and the opposition that Tore had made beforehand against King Magnus. Thereafter Tore and Swein adopted this plan which afterwards came about, that they should raise a troop with the help of Tore and his dependents. And as Tore was now an old and slow-moving man, Swein took command of the troop and got the name of chief. In that counsel there were many other chiefs; the foremost of

1 *Steinbjörg*, now Stenbjerget, where the road leads towards Nidaros on the western side.    2 The country round the White Sea.    3 *Viskardale*, i.e. Viskadale by the River Visk (Sweden).    4 *Vossings*, i.e. men from Voss, near Bergen.    5 *Horders*, i.e. men from Hordaland, round the Bergen district.    6 I.e. South-west Sweden (north of Scania).

them was Egil, son of Aslak of Forland.¹ Egil was a landed man; he was married to Ingebjörg, daughter of Agmund Torbergson—sister of Skofti of Giske. Skjalg Erlingson from Jadar² was the name of a rich and powerful man who also came into that troop. About this Thorkel Hammerscald says in Magnus' drapa:

| | |
|---|---|
| The great-minded Tore | I heard that Skjalg's friends |
| Drew his troops together | Got hard hurt therefrom |
| Along with Egil; the bonders | When the landed men too mightily |
| Found not this plan lucky. | Cast stones against the king. |

Tore and Swein raised a troop in the Uplands and came down into Raumsdale and South Möre and there got themselves ships. Then they sailed north to Trondheim.

5. There was a landed man called Sigurd Woolstring, the son of Lodin of Vigg; Sigurd gathered an army by cutting up the war arrow as soon as he heard about Tore's troop, and after gathering all the men he could get he went to Vigg. Swein and Tore went there with their army, they fought with Sigurd's troop, got the victory and brought about a great fall of men; Sigurd fled and went to King Magnus. Tore and his army went to Kaupang and stayed there for a time in the fjord, where many men came to them. King Magnus learned these tidings and straightway called an army together; he afterwards sailed north to Trondheim. And when he came into the fjord and Tore's men learned this—they were lying off Hevring and were ready to sail out of the fjord—they rowed to Vagnvika-strand³ where they left their ships and went north to Teksdale to Seljuhverfi,⁴ and Tore was carried in a litter over the fell. There they got ships and went north to Halogaland. And as soon as King Magnus was ready in Trondheim he went after them. Tore and his men went right north to Bjarköy, and John and his son Vidkunn fled away. Tore stole all the valuables there and burned the garth and a good longship which Vidkunn owned. As the cutter was burning and heeled over, Tore said: "More to starboard, Vidkunn!" Then was this composed:

| | |
|---|---|
| In the midst of Bjarköy the noblest | John will not be glad |
| Dwelling I know was burnt, | Of fire and robbery when evening comes. |
| The fire roared. Evil | The bright flames round the garth |
| Enough comes from Tore. | Played; the smoke goes skyward. |

---

1 *Forland*, now Folland, an important farm at the Averöy in North Möre.   2 *Skjalg Erlingson from Jadar*, a descendant of the famous Erling Skjalgson.   3 The strand by Vagnvik.   4 Now in Jössund district (South Trondheim folk district).

6. John and Vidkunn went day and night until they found King Magnus. Swein and Tore also sailed south with their army and robbed far and wide in Halogaland. And when they were lying in the fjord which is called Harm[1] they saw King Magnus' sail, and Tore and his troop thought they had no strength to fight, and rowed away and fled. Tore and Egil rowed to Hesjutun,[2] but Swein rowed out to sea; some of their troop rowed into the fjord. King Magnus sailed after Tore and Egil. And when the ships ran against each other at the landing-place, Tore was in the forehold of his ship. Then Sigurd Woolstring shouted to him: "Art thou well, Tore?" Tore answered: "Well of hand, but frail of foot". Tore's troop then fled right up on land, but Tore was taken. Egil was also taken, for he would not run from his wife. King Magnus had them both moved to Vambarholm.[3] And when Tore was led up, he tottered on his feet and Vidkunn said: "More to port, Tore!" Tore was afterwards led to the gallows, and then he said:

> Four fellows we were
> Once, with one at the helm.

And when he went to the gallows he said: "Evil are evil counsels". He was then hanged. And when the gallows tree was swung up, Tore was so heavy that his neck was slit and his body fell to the ground. Tore was a very big man, both tall and broad. Egil was also led to the gallows; and when the king's thralls were about to hang him, he said: "You should not hang me, because each of you indeed has deserved well enough to be hanged". Even so it was said:

> Thou fair woman, I have          Each of them better deserves
> Heard that Egil gave tongue      To hang higher (he quoth)
> To these true words              Than himself; the sword warrior
> To the sea king's faithless thralls:   Sadly was stricken by fate.

King Magnus sat near whilst they were being hanged and was so wroth that none of his men were bold enough to ask peace for them. When Egil was hanging on the gallows, the king said: "Badly do thy good kinsmen come to thy help". Thereby they saw that the king wished that they should have asked him to let Egil live. Björn Cripplehand says:

> The sharp lord of the Sogn men    Thou didst hear how the king
> Dyed his sword in *Harm*          Checked high treason.
> With the blood of the robbers;    Straight was the war king's journey;
> The wolf got warm food enough.    So it went that Tore was hanged.

1 This fjord is now called Velfjord in Southern Halogaland. In O.N. *harmr* means 'sorrow', 'grief' or 'pain'.    2 *Hesjutun*, now Hestun, north of the mouth of the Velfjord.    3 Now Vomba (or Vomma) off Hamnöy.

7. King Magnus then sailed south to Trondheim and laid great punishment on those men who had openly planned against him; he slew some and burned the goods of others. Thus sayeth Björn Cripplehand:

| | |
|---|---|
| The feeder of ravens made | I know that the king in one blow |
| The Tronds' troops afraid | Ended the lives of two hersers. |
| When they noticed the flame | The wolf was fortunate again; |
| Was wasting their districts. | The eagle flew to the gallows-tree. |

Swein, Harald Fletti's son, first fled out to sea and thereafter southwards to Denmark, where he stayed until he came to terms with King Eystein Magnusson. He took Swein into his favour and made him his dish-bearer[1] and held him in friendship and honour. King Magnus now had the kingdom alone. He kept his land in peace and destroyed all vikings and waylayers. He was a brisk man, eager for war and active, and in character he was in everything more like his grandfather, King Harald,[2] than his father.

8. Sveinki Steinarson was the name of a man who lived in the Vik near the Göta River and was very rich. He had fostered Hacon Magnusson before Hacon came to Tore of Steig. Sveinki had not yet submitted to King Magnus. King Magnus let Sigurd Woolstring be fetched, and told him to go to Sveinki and bid him leave the country, "for he has not yet helped us, or shown us any honour", adding that his landed men east in the Vik, namely Swein Bridgefoot, Dag Eilivson, and Kolbjörn Klakka, could enforce this matter. Then Sigurd said: "I did not know that there was a man in Norway against whom three landed men besides my own power and strength were needful". The king replied: "Don't use this help, unless it should be needed". Then Sigurd made himself ready for the journey, sailed east to the Vik, and summoned the landed men. A crowd of people who lived on the east side came to the thing meeting, others were summoned, and it was a big gathering. When the thing was assembled they waited for Sveinki. Soon afterwards they saw a troop of men approaching, so well armed that they looked at a distance like shining ice. This was Sveinki and his men, who came to the thing, and sat down in a circle. They were all clad in iron, with shining arms, and numbered five hundred. Sigurd stood up and spoke. "My master, King Magnus, sends God's greetings and his own to all friends, landed men, and to the rich bonders, as well as common folk, with kind words and offers of friendship; and to all who will

1 *Dish-bearer*, in O.S. *skutil-svein*, was an office of dignity with royalty.    2 Harald Hardrade.

obey him he offers his friendship and good will. And the king will be a kind and generous master to all who will be ruled by him. He also undertakes to be the protector and defender of all Norsemen; and it will be to your advantage to accept the king's friendly offer."

Then a man got up in the troop of the dwellers by the river who was of great height and grim to look at. He was clad in a rugged cloak, had an iron-fastened spear on his shoulder, and a great steel hat on his head. He looked wroth and said: "'There is no need of rollers', said the fox, when he drew the harp over the ice!" He said nothing more, and sat down.

A little while after, Sigurd Woolstring got up, and spoke thus: "Little help and good will have we from you river men, and very little friendship; yet in this way every man shows where he stands, and now I shall speak more clearly to you of the king's errand". He then demanded from the bonders land taxes and levy dues, together with all other rights of the king. He bade everybody remember how they had behaved in these matters; and asked them to act in an honourable way, and to do the king justice, if they hitherto had not done so. He then sat down.

The same man of the troop of dwellers by the river who had spoken before then got up, raised his hat a little, and said hastily: "'It looks like snow', said the Laplanders, who had skis to sell". Then he sat down again.

Soon afterwards, Sigurd got up again after speaking with the landed men, and said that the king's message ought not to be coldly treated. He was now somewhat wroth and said that it did not become them well to scorn the king's message and errand, for it was not honourable. Sigurd was clad in a scarlet kirtle, and had a blue cape over it. He cast off his cape, and said: "Now it is come so far that everybody must be careful, and not jest with others; for thereby every man shows what he is. It is not necessary to tell us; for now we can see for ourselves how little we are considered. But worse it is, that ye reply so scornfully to the king's message. Thereby every one shows his overmight. One man is called Sveinki Steinarson, who lives east by the river; and from him the king will have scot and dues of his own land or he will outlaw him. It is of no use to hang your heads or to reply with sharp words; for men are to be found who are as powerful as Sveinki, although he now scorns our speech. It is therefore much better to give in at once, and with honour, than get into disgrace on account of obstinacy". He then sat down.

Sveinki then rose, threw back his steel hat, and gave Sigurd many bitter words, and said: "Tut! tut! It is a shame for the hounds, that the foxes have made water in the bonders' well.[1] This is indeed funny, thou useless man; with a cape without arms, and a coat without shirt, wilt thou outlaw me? Some folk were already sent on this errand of thine; one was called Gilli the Backthief, and one had a worse name still. Darest thou send me out of the country? Formerly thou wast not so mighty, and thou wast not so conceited when King Hacon, my foster-son, was alive. Then, when he met thee on his way, thou fearest him as much as a mouse is frightened when caught in a trap, and hiddest thyself under a lot of clothes, like a dog on a ship. Thou wast thrust into a sack like corn, and driven from thy *odal* lands like a year-old gelding from the stud-farm; thou couldst hardly breathe in the sack like the otter in its trap. Darest thou still drive me from the land? Thou shouldst rather consider thyself lucky to escape with thy life. Let us stand up and fight them".

All his men got up, and made a great clash with their weapons. Then Swein Bridgefoot and the other landed men saw no other chance for Sigurd to escape than to get him a horse, and he rode off through the woods. The end was that Sveinki returned to his garth, and Sigurd Woolstring travelled, very down-hearted, by land north to Trondheim to King Magnus, and told the outcome of his errand. The king said: "Didst thou not need the help of my landed men?" Sigurd was ill pleased and said that it should be avenged, cost what it might; and egged on the king much. The king ordered five ships to be made ready, put a crew on board and sailed south along the land, and east to the Vik, where his landed men gave great feasts in his honour. The king told them he wanted to find Sveinki; "for I have some thought that he wants to become King of Norway". They said that Sveinki was both a mighty and a stubborn man. The king then proceeded from the Vik and arrived at Sveinki's garth. The landed men now proposed that they should go ashore and find out about things; and when they got ashore they saw Sveinki coming down from the garth, with a troop of well-armed men. The landed men held up a white shield, as a sign of peace; and when Sveinki saw it he bade his men halt, and they now met. Then said Kolbjörn Klakka: "King Magnus sends thee God's greetings and his own, and bids thee think of thine own and his honour, and not go to battle against him". Kolbjörn offered to make peace between them, and told him to keep his men back.

---

[1] This remark indicates that the old Scandinavians kept hounds for killing the foxes. In O.S. 'hound' is *hundr*.

Sveinki promised to wait. "We came to meet ye", he said, "that ye should not tread down our corn."

The landed men went back to the king, and told him that Sveinki would lay everything in the king's hands.

The king said: "My judgment is soon given. He shall leave the country, and never come back to Norway as long as I rule the land; and all his possessions he shall forfeit".

"Would it not give thee greater honour", said Kolbjörn, "and a higher esteem among other kings, if, in outlawing him, thou shouldst let him keep his possessions, so that he will have means to live abroad among mighty people? But we shall see to it that he never comes back while we look after his estate. This would be a noble act and worthy of a great king. Consider this and disdain not our counsel."

The king replied: "He must leave immediately".

They then went back to Sveinki, and told him the king's blithe words; and also that the king bade him leave the country, and that he must obey him, as he had acted wrongly.

Then Sveinki said: "The king must have altered his mind if he speaks blithe words; but why should I flee from my goods and possessions? Look here what I will say. It seems better to die here than to leave my *odal* lands. Tell the king that I will not flee even an arrow flight".

Kolbjörn replied: "This is hardly wise. It is quite honourable to give way to the greatest chief, and thereby avoid serious difficulties. A brave man will get on anywhere; and thou wilt be esteemed wherever thou art, because thou hast made a bold stand against so mighty a king. Listen to our promises, and think the matter over well. We undertake to look after thy garths, and take good care of them, and also never to pay scot until thou returnest; and we will pledge our lives and goods on this. Do not throw away good advice whereby other doughty men might suffer scathe".

Sveinki was silent for a while and then said: "Thy advice is sound; but I have an idea that thou art altering somewhat the king's message. However, on account of the good that thou hast shown me, I will take thy advice and leave the country for a winter, if I can then get my estates back in peace. Tell the king this and that I do it for thy sake, not for his".

Then they went back to the king, and said that Sveinki left all in his hands, "but begs you uphold his honour. He remains away for three years, and will then come back, with the king's permission. Agree to this; and do it all for your royal dignity, and at our request.

The matter is now all in your power, and we shall do all we can to stop him coming back unless with your consent".

The king replied: "Ye have acted like men, and everything shall be as ye wish. Let him know this".

They thanked the king with fair words. Afterwards they went to Sveinki and told him what the king had been kind enough to say. "We shall be glad", they said, "if ye two can make peace. The king demands that thou shalt be away for three years; but if we are not mistaken, we should think he will want thee back before that time has passed, because he cannot be without thee in this part of the land. It is therefore to thine own honour and advantage that thou sayest not 'nay' to this." Sveinki said: "Why then should I not do it? Go and tell the king that I shall not annoy him with my presence here any longer, and look well after my garths and goods". He then went home with his men and started off at once, as he had made everything ready beforehand. Kolbjörn stayed behind and prepared a feast for King Magnus, for which preparations had also been done before Sveinki left. Now Sveinki rode up to Gautland with as many men as he thought would be necessary. When the king had finished feasting at his garths he went back to the Vik, and the garths which had belonged to Sveinki were then called the king's property, and Kolbjörn looked after them. The king went to feasts in the Vik and afterwards he travelled north in the land and everything was peaceful for a while. It then happened that a troop of adventurers and robbers attacked the folk living by the river,[1] and the king was afraid that this eastern part of his land would soon be laid waste. He therefore thought it best to give the honour to Sveinki to defend the land against these attacks. Twice the king sent messengers to Sveinki; but he did not come till King Magnus himself went south to Denmark, where they met and became reconciled. Sveinki now returned to his garths and remained from that time King Magnus' best and most trusted friend. He guarded his kingdom east in the land and their friendship lasted as long as they lived.

9. King Magnus went on a journey from the land; he had with him a big fine army and good ships. With this army he sailed west over the seas and came first to the Orkneys. He took the jarls Paul and Erlend prisoner, and sent them both east to Norway; he set his son Sigurd[2] as lord of the isles and gave him counsellors. King Magnus then sailed south with his army to the Hebrides, and when he came thither he straightway began to harry and burn the settle-

1 I.e. Göta River.    2 The later King Sigurd, the Crusader.

THE OSEBERG SHIP IN ITS BURIAL-PLACE AT OSEBERG IN VESTFOLD

THE OSEBERG SHIP IN THE MOUND

Showing the beautiful carvings on stem and railing

ments; he slew the men wherever he went. The land folk fled far and wide, some into the fjords of Scotland, some south to Cantire[1] or out to Ireland. Some got quarter and submitted to him. Björn Cripplehand quoth:

| | |
|---|---|
| The fire over Lewis[2] | He sated the eagles' hunger |
| Played high in the heaven; | And harried far about Skye.[4] |
| Far fled the folk; | The glad wolf battened his teeth |
| The flame rose from the houses. | In blood, on Tirey.[5] |
| | |
| The prince went through Uist[3] | The maidens south in the isles |
| With fire; and the bonders lost | Got sorrow from the lord of Grenland. |
| Wealth and life; the king | The foe of the Scots harried, |
| Dyed his sword red in blood. | The folk in Mull[6] fled. |

10. King Magnus came with his army to the holy isle[7] and there gave quarter and peace to all men and their goods. It is said that he wished to open Colomba Church the Little, but the king went not within and straightway locked the door with a lock, saying that no one should afterwards be so bold as to go into the church, and thus it has been since. King Magnus then went with his army south to Il,[8] where he harried and burned. And when he had won the land he went farther on his journey southwards past Cantire, and harried on both sides (of the sea), both in Ireland and in Scotland; he went everywhere with the shield of war south to the Isle of Man, and he harried there as in other places. Thus sayeth Björn Cripplehand:

| | |
|---|---|
| To the level Sandey[9] the sharp | South of Cantire the folk |
| King brought the shield of war. | Sank down beneath the swords; |
| There was smoke over Isla, where the men | The wise lord of victory |
| Of Magnus increased the burning. | Then felled the dwellers of Man. |

Lagman was the name of the son of Gudröd, King of the Hebrides; Lagman was set as land-warder in the northern isles.[10] But when King Magnus came to the Hebrides with his army Lagman fled before the army; but at last King Magnus' men took him prisoner with his crew, when he wished to flee to Ireland; the king had him set in irons and kept under watch. Björn Cripplehand composed the following:

| | |
|---|---|
| No hiding-place could | Outside the nesses the Agder men's |
| Gudröd's son find. | Young king, the gold-spender, |
| The Tronds' king did | At last seized him there |
| Drive Lagman from the land. | Where the sword was swung. |

1 In O.N. *Satiri* or *Santiri*.   2 *Ljodhus* in O.N.   3 *Vist* in O.N.   4 *Skid* in O.N.
5 *Tyrvist* in O.N.   6 *Myl* in O.N.   7 I.e. Iona.   8 *Il*, now Isla.   9 The island of
Sandey, south of Cantire, now usually called Kintyre.   10 The northern Hebrides.

11. Afterwards King Magnus sailed with his army to Wales, and when he came to the Menai Straits an army came against him from Wales; two jarls, Hugh the Proud[1] and Hugh the Stocky,[2] were in command of it and they straightway came to battle. It was a hard fight. King Magnus shot with a bow, but Hugh the Proud was clad in a brynie so that nothing of him was bare except his eyes alone. King Magnus and a man from Halogaland standing near the king both shot arrows at Hugh; they both shot at the same time. One arrow fell on the nose-guard of the helm and it was pushed out to the side by it, but the other shot fell on the jarl's eye and flew crosswise through his head; this shot is ascribed to the king. Hugh the Jarl fell there, and afterwards the Welshmen fled; they had lost many men. Björn Cripplehand quoth:

In Menai Straits where the spears      The leader brought about
Sang and the arrows flew,                    A death shot for Hugh the Proud.

And furthermore this was also said:

The arrows broke on the brynies;      The foes fell and like hailstones
The prince shot with strength.            The arrows flew against the brynie rings;
The Agder men's king stretched         And the king of the Hordalanders felled
His bow; blood flowed on the helmets.   The jarl in the hard onset.

King Magnus got the victory in this battle and he then possessed himself of Anglesey, which was the farthest south the Norse kings had ever extended their rule. Anglesey is a third part of Wales. After this fight King Magnus turned back with his army and sailed first to Scotland. Men then passed between him and Malcolm, the Scottish king,[3] and they made these terms between themselves: King Magnus was to own all the islands which lay to the west of Scotland, i.e. all those islands between which and the mainland a ship could pass with her rudder shipped. And when King Magnus came north to Cantire he had a cutter dragged over the neck of Cantire[4] and he had the rudder shipped; the king himself sat on the quarterdeck and held the tiller; in this way he possessed himself of the land which lay to larboard. Cantire is a large land and better than the best island in the Hebrides, but not better than the Isle of Man. There is a narrow neck of land between it and the mainland of Scotland and over this neck dragon ships were often dragged.

12. King Magnus was in the Hebrides during the winter, and

1 I.e. Hugh of Montgomery, Earl of Shrewsbury.    2 I.e. Hugh, Earl of Chester.
3 Scottish authorities contend that this peace was probably concluded after Malcolm III was dead, by his brother Donald Bane. See further, p. 595, n. 2.    4 Between East and West Loch Tarbert.

then his men went through all the fjords of Scotland on the inside of all the islands, both settled and unsettled, and thus secured possession of all the islands for the King of Norway. Magnus got his son Sigurd a wife called Bjadmynja, daughter of King Myriartak Tjalfi,[1] the Irish king who ruled over Connaught. The following summer King Magnus went east with his army to Norway.[2] Erlend the Jarl died in his bed in Nidaros and was buried there, but Paul died in Bergen. Skofti, the son of Agmund Torbergson, was a renowned landed man; he dwelt at Giske in South Möre, and was married to Gudrun, the daughter of Tord Folason. Their children were Agmund, Finn, Tord, and Thora who was married to Asolv Skulason. Skofti's sons gave great promise in their youth.

13. Steinkel, the Swedish king, died about the time of the death of the two Haralds. The King of Sweden who followed Steinkel was called Hacon. After him Steinkel's son Inge was king, and he was a good and mighty king and very big and strong; he was king in Sweden when Magnus was in Norway. King Magnus said there had been a land boundary from former times: the Göta River and then Lake Väner as far as Värmland, had divided the realms of the Swedish and Norse kings. Magnus said that he owned all the inhabited land which was west of Väner, that is, Sunndale and Nord-

---

1 *Myriartak Tjalfi*, i.e. Muirkertach, King of Munster, son of Tirdelvagh, son of Brian, who fell at Clontarf in 1014, where the Norsemen were defeated. The Norsemen's rule in Ireland gradually diminished after this battle, and the Norse element became merged into the Irish nation. A somewhat similar evolution took place in England and Scotland and other countries where the Scandinavians settled. But the Nordic type of man and woman still lives in these countries, as it does in Normandy, which is probably the most striking example. Although living side by side with a Latin people for over 1000 years the Scandinavian type is still prevalent in the north of France.    2 It is somewhat difficult to estimate when the first expedition to the west actually took place. Judging from Snorre Sturlason's narrative it must have happened four or five years after Magnus Barefoot ascended the throne, or about 1098. The *Anglo-Saxon Chronicle* does not mention Magnus, but states that some pirates in 1098 slew Earl Hugh in Anglesey. Simeon of Durham is more explicit and states: "At the same time (1098) Hugh Earl of Shrewsbury and Hugh Earl of Chester went with an army to the island of Menavia commonly called Anglesey and took many of the Welsh prisoners, killed some and blinded some, cutting off their hands and feet and emasculating them. They dragged from the church a certain priest of advanced age, named Cenred, from whom the Welsh received advice in their proceedings, and having emasculated him and put out one of his eyes, they cut out his tongue; but by the mercy of God, speech was restored to him on the third day. At that time Magnus, King of the Norsemen, son of King Olav, son of King Harald, having added to his empire the Orkney and Menavian Islands, came thither in a few vessels. And when he brought his ships to land, Hugh Earl of Shrewsbury with many armed soldiers met him on the very shore, and as it is said, soon was speedily stricken with an arrow, shot by the king himself, on the seventh day after he had practised this

THE HISTORY OF MAGNUS BAREFOOT

dale, Vear[1] and Vardynjar[2] and all Mark districts pertaining thereto.[3] But it had for a long time then been under the Swedish king's dominion and had belonged to Gautland for dues. But the men of the Marks wished to be under the Swedish king's rule as before. King Magnus rode from the Vik up into Gautland with a great and fine army. And when he came to the Mark districts he harried and burned and in this way went through all the settlements; the folk submitted to him and swore their lands over to him. And when he came up to Lake Väner, autumn was passing. They then went to Kvaldinsey[4] and there made a stronghold of turf and wood, and dug a ditch around it. And when the stronghold was made, food and other goods which were needed were moved there. The king set three hundred (three hundred and sixty) men therein, and the leaders were Finn Skoftason and Sigurd Woolstring; they had chosen men. The king then turned about and went back to the Vik.

14. And when the Swedish king learned this, he called his men together and word went about that he would ride down, but there was some delay. Then the Norsemen quoth this:

> Long doth Inge Broad-thigh
> Tarry, before he rides.

And when the ice lay on Lake Väner, King Inge rode down with nearly thirty hundred (thirty-six hundred) men. He sent word to the Norsemen who sat in the stronghold and bade them go away back to Norway with the booty they had. And when the messengers brought forth the king's words, Sigurd Woolstring answered and

---

cruelty on the aforesaid priest". The chronicler who has collected most information about Magnus Barefoot is Ordericus Vitalis. His book was written some twenty or thirty years after Magnus' death. Ordericus states that Magnus, as early as 1090, prepared to attack the Irish with a naval expedition of sixty ships and sailed across to the Orkney Islands in the fifth year of William Rufus' reign (i.e. 1092) but did not then attack Ireland. The fight with the earls is mentioned with many details. It is difficult to reconcile Ordericus' dates with Snorre's, and as both Simeon of Durham and the *Anglo-Saxon Chronicle* agree with Snorre, we must assume that 1098 is the right year for Magnus' first expedition to the west. Some historians consider that Magnus undertook three or even four expeditions to the west, but Snorre, Ordericus Vitalis and the Orkneyinga Saga only mention two voyages to the Western Isles and Ireland. Ordericus gives some details of Magnus' fall in Ireland. He writes about Magnus' person as follows: "He was strong and handsome in person, of a bold and liberal disposition, brave and active and endowed with many virtues. His power extended over the islands in the Ocean, and he was possessed of great wealth and abundant resources of all kinds". Later on he states: "Norway is enriched by the commercial enterprise of the Norsemen, whose ships sail to every part of the world".
1 Now Vedbo district.    2 Now Valbo district.    3 I.e. Nordmark district, now in Värmland (Sweden).    4 Now Kallandsö, on the south side of Lake Väner.

said that King Inge could well enough think of another plan than to show them out like a herd into a field, and that he could quite well come nearer first. The messengers brought these words back to the king. Afterwards King Inge went out to the isle with all his army. And he then sent men a second time to the Norsemen and bade them go away and take their weapons, clothes and horses, but leave behind all the goods they had robbed. They refused, and after this they fell upon each other and shot at each other. The king had stones and trees brought up and filled the ditch. He then bade his men take an anchor, fasten it to long beams and lift it up to the timber wall; many men then went up and dragged the wall down. Then great fires were made and they shot burning brands at the Norsemen, who asked for quarter; and the king bade them go out without weapons or cloaks, and as they came out each of them got a stroke from a stick. After such handling they went away back to Norway. All the men of the forests again turned to King Inge. Sigurd and Finn and their men sought King Magnus and told him of their ill-luck.

15. Straightway in spring, when the ice thawed, King Magnus went with a great army eastward to the Elv; he sailed up the south-eastern arm and harried everywhere in the Swedish king's realm. And when he came up to Foxerni,[1] he went up on land from the ships, and after crossing a small river which runs there the Gauts' army came against them and there was a battle. The Norsemen were outnumbered and fled, and many were slain near a waterfall.[2] King Magnus fled, but the Gauts followed and slew as many as they could. King Magnus was easily recognised, as he was the biggest of men; he had a red jacket over his brynie and fair silky hair which fell down over his shoulders. Agmund Skoftason rode by the side of the king and he, too, was big and fair; he said: "Give me thy jacket, king!" The king said: "What wilt thou do with the jacket?" "I will have it," he said; "thou hast given me greater gifts." The land there consisted of level fields far about and the Gauts and Norsemen then saw each other continuously; but soon they came through hilly slopes and woods and then they got out of sight. The king gave Agmund the jacket and the latter put it on. They then rode forth through the fields and Agmund and his men turned away on a cross-way. And when the Gauts saw that, they thought it was the king and they all rode after them. The king rode on his way to the ships, but Agmund narrowly escaped; he came unscathed, however,

---

1 Now Fuxerna, on the east side of the Göta River.    2 The battle is presumed to have taken place near Fors Church (Ranrik in Sweden).

to the ships. King Magnus then sailed south down the Elv and thereafter northwards to the Vik.

16. A man came to King Magnus, when he was east in the Vik. His name was Gifford and he was a Welshman and said he was a great fighter. He offered the king his services, for he had heard that the king ruled a troublesome country. The king received him well. King Magnus then made himself ready to go to Gautland, for he had certain interests in that country and he said he would pay back to the Gauts the scathe and shame he had suffered in the spring, when he had to flee. He had a great army and the West Gauts in the northern parts submitted to him. He put up his tents along the frontiers and planned to make an onslaught. When King Inge heard this he gathered folk and went to meet King Magnus, and when King Magnus got to know of this, many of his chiefs advised him to turn back; but the king would not listen to that and went against the Swedish king and came upon him unexpectedly in the night. They met at a place called Foxerni. When the king was lining up his men for battle he asked for Gifford; but he could not be found anywhere. Then quoth the king:

> Will not the Welsh knight fight,
> Or has this warrior of the Welshmen hidden himself?

A scald in the king's following replied:

> The king asked where Gifford was,
> Whilst the folk battled—
> We dyed our swords in blood,
> And he had not come forward.
>
> The dastard on the red horse
> Was loath to join in battle,
> This false knight of the Welshmen
> Would not fill our ranks.

There was much slaughter and the field was covered with the Swedish slain. King Inge got away by flight. King Magnus won a great victory. Then came Gifford riding down from the country, and he was much scolded for not having been in the fight. He afterwards went away and sailed west to England. They had a stormy voyage, and Gifford was always in bed. An Iceland man by name of Elldjarn went to bale out the water, and when he saw that Gifford was laid up, he quoth this:

> Does it beseem a courtier bold
> To doze in such a way?
> Rise up, you fair-haired knight,
> Don't wallow in the keel.
>
> Help, Gifford, to bale the ship,
> And lift this bucket full.
> The water stands high
> In the big-bellied sea steed.

When they came west to England, Gifford said the Norsemen had insulted him. A mote was called and a count came to it; and when the dispute was placed before him he said that he had not much knowledge of the law, as he was young and had only held office for a short time. He also said that what he least understood was scaldcraft. "But all the same, let us hear what it is."

Then Elldjarn quoth:

I have heard thou
Didst chase the enemy,
Whilst others fell.
I have heard of
A sharp fight at Foxerni.

The attack of the warriors
Was never fiercer than
When thou, Gifford, wast present
And didst fell the Gautland men.

Then the count said: "Although I do not understand much about scaldcraft, still I can hear that this is not an insult but rather praise and honour". Gifford had nothing to say against that; but he felt that they made fun of him.

17. The next summer a meeting was arranged at Konungahella on the Elv[1] and thither came Magnus, King of Norway, Inge the Swedish king, and Eric Sweinson, the Danish king, and the meeting was bound with a truce. When the thing was assembled the kings went forth on the field away from the other men and spoke for a short time. They came back to the army and the agreement was made that they should each have the kingdoms their fathers had formerly had, and that each of the kings should punish his own men for robbery and hurt, and each should afterwards make it even with the others. King Magnus was to have Margaret, King Inge's daughter; she was afterwards called the Peace Maiden. It was the tale of men that more lord-like men had never been seen. King Inge was the biggest and most skilful and he seemed most venerable; Magnus seemed boldest and most active, but King Eric was most handsome of them all. But they were all handsome and big men, of noble looks and well-spoken—and they parted after the settlement was made.

18. King Magnus took Margaret as his queen; she was sent from the east from Sweden to Norway and she was given a noble following. But King Magnus had before had several children whose names are these: Eystein was the name of his eldest son, and his mother was of low kin. The second was called Sigurd and he was a year younger; his mother hight Thora. Olav was the name of the third and he was much younger; his mother was called Sigrid and she was the daughter of Saxi of Vik,[2] a noble man of Trondheim; she was the king's concubine. So men say that when King Magnus came from his western viking expedition he and many of his men had

1 I.e. the Göta River.     2 Now Saxvik at Strinden, east of Trondheim.

the customs and fashions which were common in the western lands; they went about with bare legs and had short kirtles (kilts) and over-capes. Men then called him Magnus "Barefoot"[1] or "Bareleg"; some called him Magnus "the High" and some "Warlike" Magnus. He was very tall. A mark was made for his height in St Mary's Church at Kaupang,[2] the church which King Harald[3] had had built. Near the north door of the church three crosses were cut on the stone walls; one showed Harald's height, the second Olav's and the third Magnus' height: and it was marked where it was easiest for them to kiss; Harald's cross was highest, Magnus' lowest, and Olav's mark equally near both.

19. It is told that Magnus made these verses about the emperor's daughter:

There is only one Mathilda
Who in the South
Fills me with joy and pleasure,
And wakens my war spirit,
For the blood birds to drink.

The fair-haired lady,
Who defends her hand with weapons
And brynied hosts,
Gives me little sleep.

He also quoth:

What is better in this world
To comfort scalds in slow times
Than the fair maids?

Heavy I leave the thingstead,
As never henceforth shall my maiden I see
Full dressed for a joyous meeting.

King Magnus then heard that the emperor's daughter[4] had said some kind words about him, and she had also said that such a man as King Magnus seemed to her to be a fine man. Magnus then sang:

From the maiden's bower I hear
Secret sighs, these
Shall not be wasted.
I love her words,

Though I cannot see her;
Let everybody know
How highly I praise her friendship.

20. Skofti Agmundson disagreed with King Magnus and they quarrelled about a heritage. Skofti held fast to it, but the king claimed it so strongly that they nearly came to fighting. Many meetings were held; Skofti made this decision, that he and his sons should never all be in the king's power at the same time, and he said that it would be safest thus. When Skofti was with the king he

---

1 'Bareleg' would have been a more appropriate name than 'Barefoot'.    2 Trond-heim.    3 Hardrade.    4 Mathilda is considered by Torfæus to have been a daughter of the Emperor Henry IV. King Magnus Barefoot had inherited his grandfather Harald Hardrade's love for poetry (scaldcraft).

gave it out that there was near kinship between himself and the king, and likewise that he had always been a dear friend of the king and of the king's father and that their friendship had never been broken; he said further that folk could see that he was so understanding that "I should not have quarrelled about this matter with thee, king, if I was not right. But therein I follow my forefathers that I hold my right against any man, and in this I make no distinction between men". The king was the same, and his mind was not meeker by such talk. Skofti went home.

21. After this Finn went to the king and spoke with him; he bade the king let him and his father have their rights in this matter. The king answered shortly and wrathfully. Then said Finn: "Other things did I expect of you, my lord, than that you would rob me of law and right, when I stayed in Kvaldinsey and few others of your friends would do it. And they said, as was true, that they who stayed there were sold and doomed to death, if King Inge had not shown us a greater mind than you have shown us; many will, however, think that we brought shame away with us if that is of any weight". The king did not let himself be turned by such talk, and Finn then went home.

22. Agmund Skoftason then went to the king. And when he came before the king he brought forth his business and bade the king do right to them and their father. The king answered that what he said was right and that they were bold beyond telling. Then said Agmund: "Thou wilt get thy wish, king, by doing us injustice with thy might. It will be true here, as is said, that most men do not reward except with evil when someone gives them his life. These words of mine shall follow, that never again shall I come into thy service; nor shall my father or my brothers, if I can decide it". Agmund then went home, and they and King Magnus never saw each other again.

23. In the spring Skofti Agmundson made himself ready to go away from the land; he had five longships, all well fitted out. His sons, Agmund, Finn and Tord, joined their father on this journey. They were ready somewhat late; but in the autumn they sailed to Flanders and were there in the winter. Early in spring they sailed west to Valland and in the summer they sailed out through the Straits of Gibraltar, and in the autumn to Rome. Skofti died there; all his sons, too, died on this journey. Tord lived longest of them all and he died in Sicily. It is the saying of men that Skofti was the first Norseman to sail through the Straits of Gibraltar. This journey became very well known.

24. It befell in Kaupang where King Olav reposed that fire broke out in a house in the town and the burning spread. King Olav's shrine was borne out of the church and set against the fire. Then a reckless and witless man ran up and beat the shrine and threatened the saint; he said that now everything would burn up, both the church and the other houses, unless he helped them with his prayers. Almighty God staved off the burning of the church, and the night after He sent eye pains to the witless man; there he lay until the holy King Olav begged mercy for him from Almighty God and he was healed in that same church.

25. It happened also in Kaupang that a woman was brought to the church where King Olav rests. She was very unhappy because she was much crippled; both her feet lay crooked up against her thighs. And as she lay always at her prayers and weeping she had called on St Olav, and he healed the great disfigurement so that her feet and legs and other limbs straightened out their bends, and every joint and limb then got into its right position. Beforehand she could not creep thither, but she went home from there healed and happy.

26. King Magnus fitted himself out for a journey from the land and he had a great army. He had then been king in Norway for nine years. He went west over the sea and he had the fairest warriors who were in Norway. He was followed by all the great men who were in the land—Sigurd Ranason, Vidkunn Johnson, Dag Eilivson, Serk of Sogn, Eyvind Elbow, the king's marshal, Ulf Ranason, Sigurd's brother, and many others. With all this host the king went west to the Orkneys and from there he took with him Magnus and Erling, sons of Erlend the Jarl. Thereupon he sailed to the Hebrides one night, and when he lay off Scotland Magnus Erlendson[1] leaped off the king's ship, swam to land and then went up into the wood and came forth to the Scottish king's bodyguard. King Magnus sailed with his army to Ireland and harried there. King Myriartak then joined him with an army and they won Dublin and County Dublin. In the winter King Magnus was up in Connaught with King Myriartak, but he set his men to rule the land he had won. And when spring came, the kings went west with their army to Ulster,[2] where they fought many battles and won the land. After winning the greater part of Ulster, Myriartak went home to Connaught.

1 *Magnus Erlendson* was the later St Magnus, to whom the cathedral of Kirkwall (Orkneys) is dedicated, and where many miracles took place. He was Earl of Orkney.
2 *Ulster*, in O.N. *Uladstir* or *Uladstadr*. (Cf. 'History of St Olav', p. 283, n. 1.)

27. King Magnus made his ships ready and would go east to Norway. He set his men to rule the land in Dublin.[1] He lay off Ulster with all his army and they were ready to sail. They thought they needed a shore-killing of cattle, and King Magnus sent his men to King Myriartak with word that he should send him a shore-killing, and mentioned the day before the Feast of St Bartholomew— if his messenger got there safely. But on the eve of the feast day the cattle had not come. On the feast day itself when the sun rose, King Magnus went up on land with the greater part of his army and left the ships. He would look for his men and the shore-killing. The weather was calm and the sun was shining; their way led over marshes and mosses, and plank bridges were laid thereover; there were copses on both sides. As they proceeded they came to a very high hill, and from there they looked far and wide and saw a great cloud of dust

At sunrise Magnus and his men went ashore

up in the land. They talked amongst themselves as to whether it might be the Irish army, but some said that it might well be their own men with the shore-killing. They stopped there. Then said Eyvind Elbow: "King! What thinkest thou of this journey? Thou art thought to go unwarily. Thou knowest that the Irish are treacherous. Think now of a good plan for thy army". Then said the king: "Let us draw up our lines and be ready if it is treachery". The lines were then drawn up and the king and Eyvind went forth before the lines. King Magnus had his helm on his head and a red shield whereon a lion was laid in gold; he was girded with a sword called Leg-biter,[2] the best of weapons; its hilt was of walrus tooth and the handle was covered with gold. He had a spear in his hand, and over his shirt he wore a red silk jacket, whereon a lion was sewn with gold silk both in front and behind; it was the talk of men that no one had seen a manlier or bolder man. Eyvind also had a red silk

1 In O.N. *Dyflin*.          2 In O.N. *Legg-bitr*.

jacket, rather like the king's; he, too, was a big, handsome man and of very warlike appearance.

28. And when the cloud of dust came nearer they recognised their own men, and they came with the shore-killing which the Irish king had sent them; he had kept all his promises to King Magnus. They then turned back to their ships and that was towards midday. And when they came out on the marshes, they were slow going past the mosses. Then the Irish army broke out from every corner of the wood and straightway fell to battle; but the Norsemen were marching separately and many soon fell. Then said Eyvind: "King, it goes unluckily with our men; let us quickly choose a good plan". The king said: "Call the whole army round the standard with the war blast; and the men who are here shall make a shield wall. Thereafter we shall draw away over the marshes. There will be no risk when we are on the level land". The Irish shot boldly and they fell thickly; but there always came other men in their places. And when the king came to the next dike it was hard to go forward and there were only a few places to cross over. Many Norsemen fell there. Then the king shouted to Torgrim Skinhood, his landed man (he was an Uplander), and bade him go over the dike with his troop: "We shall guard it meanwhile", he said, "so that there shall be no harm for you. Then go to the holme which lies there and shoot at them whilst we go over the dike; thy men are good bowmen". But when Torgrim and his men came over the dike they threw their shields over their backs and ran down to the ships. And when the king saw that, he said: "Unmanly dost thou leave thy king. Unwise I was when I made thee a landed man and outlawed Sigurd the Hound;[1] he would never have gone in such a way!" The king was wounded; he was stabbed with a spear through both thighs above the knee. He grabbed the spear between his feet, broke it off and said: "Thus break we every spear shaft, my lads!" Thereafter King Magnus got a blow on the neck from an axe, and that was his death wound. They who were left then fled. Vidkunn Johnson carried the sword Leg-biter and the king's standard to the ships; he and Sigurd Ranason and Dag Eilivson were the last to flee. There fell with King Magnus, Eyvind Elbow, Ulf Ranason, and many other great men; many Norsemen fell, but many more of the Irish. The Norsemen who escaped sailed away at once in the autumn. Erling, son of Erlend the Jarl, fell in

[1] *Sigurd the Hound* was elder brother of Vidkunn Johnson of Bjarköy. The surname 'Hound' he inherited from his great-grandfather (on the mother's side), Tore the Hound. Cf. 'History of Magnus the Good', chapter 11.

Ireland with King Magnus. And when the men who had fled from Ireland came to the Orkneys and Sigurd learned of the death of his father, King Magnus, he forthwith joined company with them and in the autumn went back to Norway.[1]

29. King Magnus had been King of Norway for ten winters and in his days there was good peace in the land, but folk had great toil and expense through his levies. King Magnus was very much beloved by his men, but the bonders thought he was hard. Men tell of the words he said when his friends told him he often went unwarily when harrying abroad: his words were: "A king shall stand for his country's honour and glory, but not for a long life". King Magnus was barely thirty years old when he fell. In the battle Vidkunn had slain the man who had slain King Magnus; Vidkunn had then fled with three wounds. For that reason King Magnus' sons showed him great love.

[1] This last expedition of Magnus Barefoot to the west took place in 1103. Ordericus Vitalis gives some additional details, of which the following are extracts: "At that time Magnus, the powerful King of Norway, sailed round the British Isles, and landing on the islands as far as Ireland prudently founded colonies in them, and commanded towns and villages to be constructed as in other countries. In consequence the Irish were extremely hostile to him and did all in their power to oppose him, using every device to crush their enemy, either by force or fraud. Thereupon the valiant king undertook an expedition against them, appearing with his fleet off the coast of Ireland. The Irish, struck with terror at the king's power, called on the Normans and Arnulph de Montgomery (being at this time Keeper of Pembroke Castle in Milford Haven), and his auxiliaries hastened to bring them succour. But the united forces were awed by the presence of the formidable Magnus, and not daring to give him battle, consulted how they might best manage to lead him into a snare by base treachery". The narrative goes on to tell of Magnus' death, but the story is not complete. Ordericus continues as follows: "A rich citizen of Lincoln kept the treasure of King Magnus and supplied him with ornaments, plate, arms, furniture and whatever else the royal service required. This man having learnt of the king's death, hastened home, and trafficking with the king's treasure, speedily amassed vast wealth. Meanwhile the King of England received the intelligence that Magnus was slain, with great satisfaction, feeling himself relieved from a great burden, and some time afterwards required the citizen of Lincoln to give up the late king's treasure. The merchant at first denied that he had any such deposit; but the king, having convicted him of the falsehood, suddenly arrested him and extorted from him, as it is said, more than twenty thousand pounds of silver". The king referred to by Ordericus was Henry I, the son of the Conqueror. The translator of Ordericus Vitalis, Thomas Forester, adds the following footnote to the above: "Our author supplies us in this paragraph with a short notice of the mercantile connection which subsisted at that period between England and Norway. The Norsemen had long been the greatest maritime power in Europe, and besides their trade by sea, had commercial relations with the east. Their merchants were settled in many of the great towns in England and particularly in the *Five Boroughs*, of which Lincoln, where this agent of Magnus Barefoot is stated to have lived, was one. He was doubtless of Anglo-Norse origin, as almost all the free people of the north and east of England were".

# XIII

## THE HISTORY OF SIGURD THE CRU-
## SADER AND HIS BROTHERS
## EYSTEIN AND OLAV

1. After the fall of King Magnus, the kingship of Norway was taken by his sons Eystein, Sigurd and Olav. Eystein had the northern part of the land and Sigurd the southern. King Olav was then four or five winters old, and the third part of the land which he owned the other two both ruled. Sigurd was taken as king when he was thirteen or fourteen winters old; Eystein was one year older. King Sigurd left the Irish king's daughter west across the sea.

When the sons of Magnus were taken as kings, men who had gone out with Skofti Agmundson came back from Palestine and Miklegarth;[1] they were very renowned and could tell many kinds of tidings. And through this news a crowd of men in Norway got a wish to go on this journey. It was said that in Miklegarth Norsemen who would go into paid service would get plenty of goods. The king's men then bade that one of the kings, either Eystein or Sigurd, should go and be leader of the men who wished to go on this journey abroad. And the kings agreed to it and fitted out the journey at the expense of them both. Many great men, both landed men and mighty bonders, took part in that journey. And when they were ready, it was decided that Sigurd should go, and that Eystein should rule the land on behalf of both of them.

2. A year or two after the fall of Magnus Barefoot, Hacon, son of Paul the Jarl, came east from the Orkneys. The kings gave him the jarldom and rule of the Orkneys, such as the jarls, Paul his father and Erlend his father's brother, had had before him. Hacon then went west to the Orkneys.

3. Four winters after the fall of King Magnus, King Sigurd went with his army from Norway; he had sixty ships.[2] Thus sayeth Toraren Stuttfeld:

> So many were
> The mighty men
> Who came together
> Loyal to the king,
>
> That sixty ships,
> All well found,
> Glided out hence
> By the will of God.

1 I.e. Constantinople.    2 Cf. also William of Malmesbury's report of Sigurd's voyage, below, p. 643.

King Sigurd sailed in the autumn to England, where Henry, son of William the Bastard, was king. King Sigurd was there during the winter. Thus sayeth Einar Skulason:

The sea-farer sailed
With a great following west;
Ægir's[1] steed sped
'Neath the king, to England.

The fight-happy leader rested
His ships, and through the winter
He was there; never a better warrior
Stepped on a warship.

4. King Sigurd went south the following spring with his army to Valland, and in the autumn he came forth to Galizuland,[2] where he stayed the next winter. Einar Skulason quoth:

And the folk king who ruled
Over the best realm 'neath
The sun's path, lived in the land
Of Jacob[3] the next winter.

The war king there punished
(I heard) the bold jarl
For breaking of vows; the grim man
Gave the war ravens food.

This is what happened: the jarl who ruled the land made a bargain with Sigurd; the jarl was to have a food market held for King Sigurd during the whole winter, but the jarl kept his promise no longer than Yule and it was then hard to get food, for the land is barren and a bad land for food. King Sigurd then went with a great army to the castle which the jarl owned. The jarl fled away, for he had few men. King Sigurd then took many foodstuffs and much other war booty and he had it shifted to his ships. Afterwards he made himself ready to go away, and he went west along the Spanish coast. When King Sigurd was sailing along the Spanish coast it happened that some vikings who were going after booty came against him with a host of galleys. King Sigurd took to battle with them and it was his first fight against heathen men; he won eight galleys from them. Thus sayeth Haldor the Chatterer:

And the wicked vikings
Hied forth against the mighty
Leader of battle; the king
Slew warriors in the fight.

His army speedily managed
To clear eight galleys;
Most of the men were slain;
The prince got mighty booty.

King Sigurd then sailed to the castle which is called Cintra,[4] where he fought the second battle. In Spain heathen men were settled and they harried the Christian men. He won the castle and slew all the

1 *Ægir* was the god of the ocean. *Ægir's steed* = the ship.   2 I.e. Galicia, north-west part of Spain.   3 *The land of Jacob*, i.e. Galicia, which the Apostle James or Jacob visited. The town Santiago is named after the Apostle.   4 *Cintra*, the celebrated castle near Lisbon. King Sigurd helped Count Henry of Portugal in 1110 to drive the Moors from the town. They had conquered Cintra in 1009, on the death of King Alfonso.

folk there, for they would not let themselves be christened; there he took many goods. Haldor the Chatterer quoth:

Now I shall mention the king's
Great work which he did
In Spain; towards Cintra
The king went boldly.

The warriors who would not
Take their faith as he bade them
Got great scathe
From the hard chieftain.

5. After this King Sigurd sailed with his host to Lisbon which is a great town in Spain, half Christian and half heathen. It separates Christian Spain and heathen Spain, and the heathen part includes all those lordships which lie to the south. There King Sigurd had his third battle with the heathen men and he won the victory; there he got great wealth.[1] Thus sayeth Haldor the Chatterer:

In the south thy third victory,
O wise prince,

Thou didst win where ye landed;
Lisbon is the town called.

Thereupon King Sigurd sailed south with his army past heathen Spain and came to a town which is called Alcasse,[2] and there he had his fourth battle with the heathen men and won the town. There he slew so many folk that he laid the town waste. He got untold wealth. Haldor the Chatterer composed the following:

Outside Alcasse
Thou didst wish (I heard),

O war king, a fourth time
To win the keen strife.

And further he says this:

In the wasted town thou didst win
The victory (I heard) to the sorrow

Of the heathen women; to flight
Thy army drove these men.

6. Thereafter King Sigurd continued his journey and sailed to Norvasund,[3] but in the sound he met a great viking host; the king went to battle with them, and there he had his fifth battle and won the victory. Thus quoth Haldor the Chatterer:

Thou didst wish to dye
Thy sword edge in the east

Of Norvasund; God helped thee;
The eagle got food afresh.

After this King Sigurd sailed with his host on the south side along the coast of Serkland,[4] and came to an island which is called Formentera.[5] There a great army of heathen blackamoors had set themselves down in a cavern and they had set a great stone wall before the opening of the cavern; they harried far about the land and brought all their booty to the cave. King Sigurd made an onslaught

[1] King Sigurd helped Count Henry to attack Lisbon; but some historians say without success.    [2] Probably Alcacer do Sal near Setubal.    [3] I.e. the Straits of Gibraltar.    [4] *Serkland* was Africa.    [5] The most south-westerly of the Balearic Islands.

on the island, and he went to the cavern which was in a hill side; it was steep to go up to the stone wall by the cave, for the hill side overhung the stone wall. The heathens guarded the stone wall and were not afraid of the Norsemen's weapons, for they could hurl stones and shoot down at the Norsemen under their feet. The men did not like making an onset under these conditions. Then the heathens took pall cloth and other costly things, bore them out on to the wall and swung them before the Norsemen, shouting to them, egging them on and calling them craven. King Sigurd then tried to find a plan. He bade his men take two ship boats, which are called barks, and he had them drawn up on to the hill side over the cave opening. He had thick cords bound round the bulwarks and the stems. Then as many men went in as there was room for and they let the ships down over the cavern with ropes. They who were in the boats shot and hurled stones so that the heathens turned away from the stone wall. King Sigurd then went up the hill with his army under the stone wall. They broke the wall and thus got into the cave. But the heathens fled in past a stone wall which was set across the cave. The king then had great trees shifted into the cave and built up a great fire-heap in the cave opening and set light to it; and when the fire and smoke got to the heathens, some lost their lives, others went against the Norsemen's weapons and all the folk were either slain or burnt. There the Norsemen got the greatest booty that they had taken on this journey. Haldor the Chatterer quoth:

| | |
|---|---|
| The strife-eager | Ere they got their bane |
| Peace-waster | The blackamoors' army |
| Thus sailed | Had to endure |
| To Formentera. | Both sword and fire. |

And this too:

| | |
|---|---|
| War king, thou didst let | And up against the wall, |
| The barks down the hill side; | O manly prince, |
| This prince's deed against the serks[1] | Against the folk-filled cavern |
| Is now well known. | Thou wentest with thy following. |

Further Toraren Stuttfeld sayeth:

| | |
|---|---|
| The king bade his men | So that on ropes |
| Drag two | They were let down |
| Blue-black boats | Full of warriors |
| Up the hill, | Before the cave door. |

7. King Sigurd then went forth on his journey and came to the island which is called Iviza where he had a battle and won

---

[1] I.e. Saracens.

the victory. That was the seventh battle. Haldor the Chatterer says:

| | |
|---|---|
| The well-known shield-bearer | To Iviza; the prince wished |
| Came with his fleet of ships | To rouse up the breaking of peace. |

After this Sigurd came to the island which is called Minorca and there he held his eighth battle with the heathen men and won the victory. Thus sayeth Haldor the Chatterer:

| | |
|---|---|
| The eighth battle | On the green Minorca; |
| Was afterwards fought | The men shot with arrows. |

8. In the spring King Sigurd came to Sicily, where he stayed a long time. Roger was then duke there and he greeted the king well and bade him come to a feast. King Sigurd went and many men were with him. It was a noble welcome, and each day of the feast Duke Roger stood and did service at King Sigurd's table. On the seventh day of the feast when the men had taken their baths, King Sigurd took the duke by the hand, led him up to the high-seat and gave him the name of 'king' and the right of being king over the realm of Sicily; before, there had been jarls over that realm.[1]

It is written in the chronicles[2] that Earl Roger let himself first be called King of Sicily in 1102, having previously been contented with the title of 'earl', although he was Duke of Calabria and Apulia, and was called Roger the Great; and when he afterwards made the King of Tunis tributary to him, he had these words engraved on his sword:

*Apulus et Calaber, Siculus mihi servit et Afer.*

9. Roger, King of Sicily, was the mightiest of kings; he won all Apulia and likewise subdued many great islands in the sea of Greece. He was called Roger the Mighty. His son was King William[3] who

---

1 The Normans in Sicily looked upon the Norsemen as their kinsmen, the same as they did in Normandy. According to the feudal idea of the times the kingly title could only be conferred by a king or an emperor. The title was confirmed by the Church much later, first by Petrus Anacletus in 1130 and finally by Pope Innocent II in 1139. Roger was the first King of Sicily.    2 This remark makes it clear that Snorre had also access to foreign chronicles, when he compiled his book.    3 Roger's father died in 1101 and his mother, the famous Adelaide, chose Robert, son of Robert I, Duke of Burgundy, to rule Sicily during Roger's minority (Ordericus Vitalis). Robert and Adelaide were no doubt the instigators of the change of title. Constantia was a posthumous child of Roger (who died in 1154), and Snorre has been misled about her being the daughter of William I (1151–66) owing to the great difference of age that existed between her and Henry VI, who married her at Milan in 1186. Probably also, because William II (1166–89) gave her in marriage to Henry. William II is generally considered to have been the son of William I. Henry VI (1165–97) was son of Frederic I, surnamed Barbarossa (1123–90), and Henry's son by Constantia was Frederic II, Hohenstaufen (1194–1250). The O.N. name for Roger is *Rodgeir*.

for a long time had had great trouble with the emperor in Mikle-garth. King William had three daughters but no son; one of his daughters he married to the Emperor Henry, son of the Emperor Frederic, and their son was Frederic who is now emperor in Rome. A second daughter of King William married the Duke of Cyprus.[1] The third was married to Margrit,[2] the leader of the corsairs; both these the Emperor Henry slew. The Emperor Manuel in Mikle-garth married a daughter of Roger, King of Sicily;[3] their son was the Emperor Kyrialax.[4]

10. In the summer King Sigurd sailed out through the sea of Greece to Palestine. He landed at Acre, and then went overland to Jerusalem. When the tidings of King Sigurd's visit came to Bald-win, King of Palestine, he ordered costly clothes to be spread on the roads, and the most costly to be placed near the town. Then he said: "I suppose you know that a great king from the north is coming to visit us. Many wonderful tales are told about his prowess and brave deeds, so we shall give him a royal welcome. Should he approach Jerusalem giving little heed to our preparations, I shall understand that he is well used to such grandeur. If, however, he rides on the side of the road wishing not to harm the clothes, then I shall think his dignity at home is of little worth".

Now King Sigurd rode onward with great pomp, right over the clothes, and ordered his men to do likewise. King Baldwin received King Sigurd extremely well and they rode together to the River Jordan and then back to Jerusalem.

Thus sayeth Einar Skulason:

The chieftain let his sea-cold
Ship's hull glide
Forth through the sea of Greece;
I offer praise to the prince.

He went till he cast anchor
Near the wide town of Acre.
All welcomed the king gladly
Early that morning.

I know that the battle-glad king
Came to the town of Jerusalem;
Nowhere under the heavens
Is a more noble prince known.

And the swift foe of the gold
Could bathe himself in Jordan's
Clear stream. This deed
Must be praised by all.

King Sigurd stayed a long time in Palestine in the autumn and the beginning of winter.

1 Isaac Komnenos (1184–95). In 1195 Richard I, Cœur de Lion, King of England, conquered Cyprus.   2 Admiral Margarito whom William II set to rule over Corfu, Durazzo, Cephalonia and Zante.   3 In Ordericus Vitalis reference is made in the translator's footnotes to a contemplated marriage between Manuel and a daughter of Roger of the Principality, i.e. Antioch, but nothing came of the marriage.   4 Alexios II (1180–83). His mother was daughter of Raymond of Antioch.

11. King Baldwin made a fair banquet for King Sigurd and many of his men, and then King Baldwin gave Sigurd many holy relics; a chip was taken from the holy cross by the counsel of King Baldwin and the patriarch, both of whom swore on the holy relic that the wood was of the holy cross whereon God himself had suffered. Afterwards the relic was given to King Sigurd on condition that he and twelve of his men first swore that he would further Christianity with all his might and take an archbishop's see into his land if he could; also that the cross should be there where St Olav rests, and that he would further the paying of tithes and pay them himself. King Sigurd then went to his ships at Acre; King Baldwin also fitted out his army to go to Syria to the town which is called Sætt, which some think was Sidon;[1] the town was heathen, and he wished to conquer it for the Christians. King Sigurd accompanied him on that journey with all his men and sixty ships. And when the kings had sat a short time round the town, the heathen men gave themselves up and the kings won the town and enormous goods; the men got other booty. King Sigurd gave Baldwin his part of the town.[2] Haldor the Chatterer indited the following:

| The heathen town thou didst win | Generous feeder of the wolves! |
| By might, but thou gavest it away. | Thou dost always win in battle. |

Thereof Einar Skulason also says:

| The lord of the Dalesmen[3] took Sætt; | There the strong war-man |
| The men will remember it; | Could break the great walls; |
| The death-weapons quickly began | The fair swords were dyed, |
| To swing in the strife. | And the prince could greet victory. |

After that King Sigurd went to his ships and left Palestine. They sailed north to the island which is called Cyprus, and King Sigurd stayed there for some time. Afterwards he went to Greece and brought all his ships near Engilsnes[4] where he stayed for a fortnight; each day there was a strong wind blowing for sailing north over the sea, but he waited for a wind that would blow sideways and they could stretch their sails fore and aft in the ships, for all his sails were covered with pall cloth, on both sides; this was because no one, either the forehold-men or those who were aft, would look on the plain side.

1 *Sidon* is also called *Seida* or *Saida*.    2 Sidon was conquered by King Baldwin, 19th of December, 1110.    3 The men from Gudbrandsdale.    4 *Engilsnes* is supposed to be the ness at the mouth of the River Aegos (called Aegisness in the Orkneyinga Saga), a short distance south of Gallipoli. It is inside the Dardanelles. Others consider it to be Cape St Angelo or Malia (in South-east Greece), but as Sigurd was bound for Constantinople it is most improbable that he would remain at Cape Malia for a fortnight, waiting for a side wind.

12. When King Sigurd and his men sailed into Miklegarth,[1] he sailed near the land. Everywhere upon the land there were strongholds and castles and small villages, one after another without interval. Then the folk saw from the shore all the sails spread and no opening between, just as if they formed an enclosure. All the folk stood on the shore to see King Sigurd sailing by. The Emperor Kyrialax[2] had also learned of King Sigurd's journey and he had bidden his men unlock the town gate in Miklegarth which is called the Golden Porte. Through that gate shall the emperor ride when he has been away for a long time and has won a great victory. The emperor then had pall cloths spread over all the streets of the town from the Golden Porte to Laktjarnar,[3] where are the emperor's noblest halls. King Sigurd told his men to ride proudly into the town and show little wonder at the new and unusual things they saw—and they did so.

The emperor sent singers and musicians to meet them, and King Sigurd rode with great pomp into Miklegarth. It is said that King Sigurd's horse wore shoes of gold, and that it was arranged for one of the shoes to fall off in the street, but that none were to pay attention to it. When King Sigurd entered the hall, he found everything splendidly arranged. And when they were all seated and about to drink, the emperor's messengers came offering purses of gold and silver sent by the emperor. Sigurd did not look at them, but ordered his men to share them among themselves. When the messengers took word of this to the emperor, he said: "This king must be a very rich and powerful man not to be impressed by the gifts I sent to him, or even to send thanks for them!" Whereupon he next sent great coffers filled with gold which the messengers said the emperor sent him. King Sigurd replied that this was a great and noble gift, and turning to his men told them to share it among themselves. The messengers reported this to their emperor, who remarked: "Either this king is far more wealthy and more powerful than other kings are, or else he is not so wise and understanding as a king ought to be".

Yet a third time the emperor sent to King Sigurd, and now they bore with them a garment of costly purple and chests full of gold in which he laid two rings. This time Sigurd stood up, placed the rings on his hand, and made a fine speech in Greek, in which he thanked

[1] The Norsemen's name for Constantinople.  [2] *Kyrialax* was the Emperor Alexios Komnenos I (1081–1118).  [3] I.e. the palace Blachernæ, on the north side of Constantinople.

the emperor for the magnificence with which he had been received, and then divided the rare gifts among his followers. King Sigurd stayed there for some time, and on one occasion the Emperor Kyrialax sent word to ask him whether he would prefer six ship-pounds in weight of gold, or whether he would rather that the emperor should order all his favourite games to be played at the Padreimr.[1] King Sigurd chose the games, and the messengers told how this entertainment would be just as costly as the gold which had been offered.

The games were then held according to custom; but on this particular day, everything went better for the king than for the queen. The queen always backed half the players in the games, so that either side did their best to win. It was thought, therefore, by the Greeks, that as the king won most games he would also win the victory when he went to war.

Those who have been to Miklegarth say that the Padreimr consists of a flat plain, surrounded by a high wall. On this wall are earthen banks on which the spectators sit, and the games are held in the plain. Events concerning the Asers, the Volsungs, and the Giukungs are shown, and the figures are made of copper or other metal, and are so cleverly done that they might be alive, and they seem at times to be riding in the air. Besides, there is shooting fire, all kinds of string music with singing and harp-playing.

It is told that King Sigurd once invited the emperor to a feast. He ordered his men to spare no pains or expense in providing all that was necessary for this feast. And when they had procured everything for feasting such a mighty emperor, King Sigurd sent his men forth in the streets to obtain firewood, of which a great lot was required. And when they tried to buy it the men found that it had all been sold, and brought word to the king. He replied: "Try and get walnuts instead, for they will serve the same purpose". They went and bought all the walnuts that were wanted. And then came the emperor with his queen and the court and were splendidly feasted. When the emperor and the queen saw that nothing was lacking, the queen sent to enquire what kind of firewood was used.

The answer was that walnuts had been used. The queen replied: "Surely this king is high-minded. He does not care to what expense he goes, where his honour is concerned. No wood burns better than walnuts".

It was the queen who had caused that no wood could be bought, as she wanted to see what King Sigurd would do.

[1] The hippodrome, where all the great spectacles were shown.

13. After this King Sigurd made himself ready for his journey home. He gave the emperor all his ships and there were gold-decked heads on the ship whereon the king sailed; they were put in St Peter's Church.[1] The Emperor Kyrialax gave King Sigurd many horses and let him have guides through all his kingdom, and appointed markets for him through all his dominions, where he could buy food. King Sigurd then went away from Miklegarth, but a great number of his men stayed behind and went into service. King Sigurd first went into Bulgaria[2] and from there through Hungary,[3] Pannonia,[4] Bavaria and Swabia. There he found the Emperor Lotharius[5] of Rome, who greeted him well, gave him guides through all his kingdom and caused markets to be held for him for such kinds of goods as he needed. And when King Sigurd came to Sleswick in Denmark, Eiliv the Jarl made a sumptuous feast for him; that was near midsummer. In Hedeby[6] he found the Danish king Nicholas[7] who greeted him well, and who himself followed Sigurd north to Jutland and gave him a fully manned ship on which he sailed to Norway. King Sigurd then went home to his kingdom and was joy-fully welcomed; it was the talk of men that no one had gone from Norway on a journey of greater honour than this; he was then twenty years old and he had been three years on the journey. His brother Olav was then twelve years old.

14. King Eystein had done much that was useful in the land whilst King Sigurd was on his journey. He founded a monastery at Nordnes in Bergen and gave much wealth to it; there he had St Michael's Church[8] built, the most noble of stone minsters, and in the king's residence he had the Apostles' Church built of wood. There he had also a great hall[9] built—the noblest wooden house which has been built in Norway. He also had a church built at Agdenes with a pier and a harbour where before there had been none. In the king's residence at Nidaros he also built St Nicholas' Church, and this building was very carefully finished with carvings and all kinds of work. He also had a church built at Vagar[10] in Halogaland, and added a prebend thereto.

1 *St Peter's Church* was situated between St Sophia's Church and the Great Palace (east side of the town). 2 At that time a province of the Greek Empire. 3 *Hungary* bordered at that time on the western part of Bulgaria (by the River Danube). 4 *Pannonia* is the Latin name for West Hungary. 5 I.e. Duke Lothair of Saxony, who afterwards in 1133 became Roman Emperor after Henry V (1106–25). 6 *Hedeby* is the present town of Sleswick. 7 Danish king from 1103 to 1134. 8 *St Michael's Church* was the monastery church. 9 The oldest king's hall in Bergen was situated where the military head-quarters are at present (Bergenhus). 10 Now Vaagen in Lofoten (North Norway).

15. King Eystein sent word to Jämtland to the wisest and mightiest men bidding them come to him, and all who came he greeted with much gladness; and he sent them away with friendly gifts and thus secured their friendship. And when many of them grew accustomed to going to him and receiving his gifts, and whereas he sent gifts to some who did not come there, he got into full friendship with all the men who ruled that land. He afterwards spoke to them and said that the Jämtlanders had done ill when they turned away from the kings of Norway in loyalty and dues. He told how the Jämtlanders had gone under the rule of King Hacon, Athelstan's foster-son, and had for a long time since then been under the kings of Norway. He also mentioned how many necessary things[1] they could get from Norway and how much trouble it would be for them to get what they needed from the Swedish king. And he went so far with his talking that the Jämtlanders themselves offered to show fealty to King Eystein and they called it their need and want.

They bound themselves in this way so that the Jämtlanders gave over all their land to the rule of King Eystein. The mighty men first took oaths of trustiness from all the folk in this matter; then they went to King Eystein and swore the land to him, and it has always been kept since. Thus King Eystein won Jämtland by wisdom and not by onset as some of his forefathers had done.

16. King Eystein was the most handsome of men to look upon; he had rather big blue eyes and fair curly hair; he was of middle height, wise and understanding, clever in everything concerning law and history, and in the knowledge of men; swift of counsel, wise of word and eloquent; very merry, yet modest, pleasing to and wellbeloved by the whole folk. He was married to Ingebjörg, daughter of Guthorm, son of Steigar-Tore; their daughter was called Maria and Gudbrand Skavhoggson afterwards took her to wife.

17. King Eystein had bettered the laws and rights of the people and abided himself by the laws. He studied the laws of Norway and showed tolerance and understanding in all things. Thus it could be seen how splendid a man King Eystein was, and how true he was to all his friends and what care he took to know what scathe they might suffer.

There was a man in the king's household named Ivor Ingemundson. He was an Icelander of good family, was witty and wrote poetry, and the king loved him much. One day Ivor was lowspirited; and when the king perceived it, he called Ivor to him and

1 Dried fish was a necessary article of food, which could be most easily obtained from Norway.

asked him why he was so sad, saying: "Last time thou wast with us thou wast amusing in thy talk; art thou dissatisfied with us?"

Ivor replied that he was well content with everything. The king said: "I know thee to be a man of good sense, so tell me if I have done anything against thy wish and let me know what it is". The other replied: "I cannot tell thee, my lord, what it is". Then said King Eystein: "I will guess what ails thee. Is there any man who causes thee uneasiness?" To this he replied "nay". "Dost thou think I hold thee too lightly in my regard for thee?"

He replied that it was not the case. "Hast thou seen anything which makes thee sad, which thou might miss, and cannot be without?" Still he replied that it was not so.

The king said: "Wouldst thou like to go travelling and visit other princes?" For this he said he had no wish. Then the king said: "I cannot guess much longer". "Is there perhaps some maid either here or elsewhere of whom thou art fond?" To this Ivor replied that it was so.

Then said the king: "Be not sad about this; as soon as spring comes, go to Iceland and I shall give thee money, gifts and letters to those who have most say in the land, and there is not a man in Iceland who will dare to disobey my wishes".

Ivor replied: "Things are worse with me than you think, my lord; for my own brother hath this maid".

The king replied: "Think no more of it; I shall shortly travel with much feasting and thou shalt come with me. Then wilt thou see many lovely maidens, and, so long as she be not of royal blood, I will get for thee the one thou choosest, in marriage".

But Ivor replied: "My lord, it is still worse with me, for the more I see other lovely maidens, the more do I think of this one maid, and my misery is greater".

Then said the king: "I had better give thee property and estates to manage for thy pleasure".

Ivor replied that for this he had no wish. The king said: "Then I can only give thee some goods and money so that thou canst travel far and wide, wherever thou wishest". But this he said he did not care to do.

Then said the king: "I have suggested everything that comes to my mind. There is but one thing else that might help thee, although it is little compared to what I have offered thee. Every day when I am not taken up with important matters, thou shalt come to me and we will talk over this matter about the maid, for it often happens that sorrow shared is sorrow lessened, and every time I shall give thee something before thou goest away".

He replied: "That I will do, my lord", and he thanked the king for his great kindness. This he afterwards did, and as often as the king was not engaged on important matters, he spoke with Ivor. He was thereby consoled in his sorrow and he became glad again.

18. King Sigurd was of big build and brown of hair; he was great-minded; he was not good-looking, but he was well-grown and manly; of few words, and most often not friendly; good to friends and trust-worthy, moral and dignified, but not very eager to talk. King Sigurd was jealous of his power and stern in punishing; he kept the laws well, was generous with his goods, mighty and much honoured. King Olav was tall and thin, fair to look upon, happy, modest and well befriended. When these brothers were kings in Norway they took off many of the burdens which the Danes had laid on the people when Swein Algivason ruled the land, and for that they were much beloved by the common people and also by the great men.

19. King Sigurd once had a fit of depression and it was almost impossible to get him to talk. He did not remain long drinking (after dinner), and his friends, advisers and courtiers were much troubled over it. They asked King Eystein how it was that when people came to King Sigurd to lay weighty matters before him, they could get no answer. King Eystein replied: "Difficult is it to rede and to talk with the king about these matters"; but at the request of many King Eystein finally agreed to do so.

Thus, one day, when they were both together, King Eystein asked his brother why he was so depressed. "It is, my lord, a great grief to many people that thou art so low-spirited and heavy-minded, and we would like to know the cause of it. Hast thou heard some news which weighs heavily on thee?"

King Sigurd answered that it was not the case. "Perhaps the reason is", King Eystein said, "that thou wishest to leave the country and increase thy kingdom, which our father did?"

He replied "nay" to that.

"Is there anybody in the land who has offended thee?" The king said it was not so.

"Then I wish to know if thou hast had a bad dream which is causing thee trouble." The king replied that he had had a bad dream lately. "Let me then, brother, know thy dream", said Eystein.

King Sigurd replied: "Thou wilt not hear my dream, unless thou canst promise to interpret it correctly. I shall soon know if thou explainest it right or not". King Eystein answered: "This is indeed a difficult matter, for on the one hand I am risking to displease thee, if I tell something wrong, and besides I shall anger the people, if I cannot interpret it. Therefore I will leave myself entirely in thy hands, if thou shouldst not agree to my explanation".

King Sigurd replied: "The dream was as follows. I thought we brothers were seated on a bench outside Christ Church in Trondheim, and it seemed to me that St Olav, our kinsman, came out of the church arrayed in his royal robes, brilliant and dazzling with the mildest and most lovely countenance. He went to our brother Olav, took him by the hand and spoke to him kindly words. 'Come with me, my kinsman', he said. It seemed to me that he got up and went with him into the church. After a short time St Olav came out of the church but not so blithe and lovable as before. He went to thee, brother, and said that thou shouldst follow him. Then he took thee by the hand and ye both went into the church. I thought that he would now come for me and I waited for him for some time, but he came not. Great sorrow and anxiety now came over me and I fainted and lost all my strength, and with that I awoke".

King Eystein replied: "My lord, thus I explain thy dream. The bench is the kingdom we brothers share between us, and when St Olav came first to our brother Olav that means that he will die first and will have his reward in heaven, for he is young and well befriended and has fallen in few excesses, so that St Olav will help him. Then he came to me with a stern countenance, because I shall live a few years longer and not get old. But I hope that he will still hold his hand over me. He came to me with less friendliness than he did to our brother Olav, because I have sinned more against God. That he did not come to thee, no doubt means that thou shalt live longest of us three brothers, and it may be that some ill will befall thee, as some dreadful fear came over thee; but thou shalt be the eldest of us and rule the land longest".

Then said King Sigurd: "This is well and truthfully explained, and probably things will happen thus".

Afterwards the king was glad and well again.

20. King Sigurd's spouse was Malmfrid, King Harald Valdemarson's daughter, east from Holmgard. Valdemar was son of Jarisleiv the Old and Ingegerd, daughter of the Swedish King Olav.

King Harald Valdemarson's mother was Queen Githa the Old, daughter of Harold Godwinson, King of England.

Queen Malmfrid's mother was Queen Christina, daughter of Inge Steinkelson, King of Sweden.

Harald Valdemarson's second daughter, sister of Malmfrid, was called Ingebjörg, whom Knut Lavard married. Knut was a son of Eric the Good, the Danish king, who again was son of Swein Ulfson. Knut's and Ingebjörg's children were Valdemar, who ruled in Denmark after Swein Ericson; and Margaret, Kristin and Catherine. This Margaret was Stig Whiteleather's wife and their daughter was Christina, who married the Swedish King Karl Sorkvison. Their son was King Sorkvir, the father of King John.

The daughter of King Sigurd and Malmfrid was Kristin, the wife of Jarl Erling Skakki.

21. Sigurd Ranason, the king's brother-in-law, had a quarrel with King Sigurd. He had married Skjaldvor, King Magnus Barefoot's sister on his mother's side. He had the Finnish trade on the kings' behalf, because of their kinship and long friendship and on account of many other services which Sigurd Ranason had rendered the kings, for he was an outstanding and well-befriended man. But things happened as they often do, that some people were more evil-minded and jealous than truthful, and they spoke badly of him to the king and whispered into his ears that Sigurd Ranason had a bigger share of the Finnish trade than was due to him. They spoke so long about this, that the king got angry and hated him and sent messengers after him. And when he came to the king he accused Sigurd of what was said about him. "I least thought that thou shouldst reward me for the honour and great office I have granted thee, by defrauding me and taking more of my income than thou hast been promised."

Then Sigurd Ranason replied: "What people have told thee is untrue. I only obtain so much from the Finnish scot as thou hast allowed me". King Sigurd said: "Thou shalt not get away with this excuse, for this matter shall be taken seriously in hand, before it is settled". Afterwards they parted. Shortly thereafter King Sigurd was advised by his friends to summon Sigurd Ranason to a thing meeting at Bergen where he intended to outlaw him. And when it appeared that there was danger ahead Sigurd Ranason went to see King Eystein and told him how seriously King Sigurd regarded this matter and asked the king to help him. King Eystein replied: "It is a difficult business for me to go against my brother, but there is a great difference between helping thee and giving thee good advice, as compared with taking up your case at the thing". He added: "This

Finnish trade concerns me as much as my brother Sigurd, so I will try and put in a good word for thee on account of our kinship".

Some time afterwards King Eystein had a talk with King Sigurd and reminded him of their close kinship to Sigurd Ranason, who had taken for wife their father's sister Skjaldvor. He said further that he would be willing to pay any fines which the king might impose, although he would not admit that he was guilty of any offence. Eystein also asked the king to remember that they had long been good friends. King Sigurd replied that it was good government to punish such wrongdoing. King Eystein replied: "If thou, my brother, wilt pursue this case and punish according to the law of the land, then it would only be just that witnesses are brought forward, for this case must be judged at a law-thing and not at a town meeting. The Finnish trade comes under the district law, and not under the Bjarköy law".

Then King Sigurd said: "It may be, King Eystein, as thou sayest, that the case comes under the district law; and if it be illegal to bring the case before a town meeting, then I shall call a thing". Afterwards the kings parted and they were both dissatisfied.

Thereafter King Sigurd brought the case before the thing at Arnarnes, where he intended to plead. King Eystein went there and came to the thing whilst the case was being heard and before judgment had been delivered. King Sigurd then asked the lawmen to give their verdict, but King Eystein stood up and said: "I doubt not that here are present many wise and able men well acquainted with the Norse law; but who also know that a landed man cannot be judged an outlaw at this thing". And he continued to explain the law so that all could understand that it was true what he said.

Then King Sigurd replied: "Thou, King Eystein, takest great pains over this Finnish trade, and perhaps we shall have to take more trouble over this case than we thought first was necessary. But all the same I intend to pursue it, and perhaps it is best that the case be transferred for judgment to his own district".

King Eystein replied: "There is not much that does not succeed for thee, if thou wilt persist in following things up, and this is not to be wondered at, because thou hast accomplished so many great deeds; and here it seems that only a few small men are against thee". Therewith they parted and nothing was decided. King Sigurd now summoned the Gulathing, went there himself and called many great chiefs. King Eystein also came with his followers, and now many conferences were held by wise men and the law was thoroughly discussed by the lawmen. King Eystein said that any actions brought there must be against people living in that thing district, and those concerned in the present case must be sued in Halogaland. The thing now ended and nothing was done, as King Eystein had made the summons illegal. Thereafter the kings parted and they were very wroth. King Eystein went north to Trondheim. King Sigurd however summoned all the landed men and their huscarls and named from each folk district a crowd of bonders right south from the land, so that a great army gathered. With this army he sailed along the coast and north to Halogaland and set his mind to proceed with the case, so as to make Sigurd Ranason an outlaw among his own kinsmen. He summoned the Haleygers and Naumadale men to a thing at Rafnista. King Eystein proceeded from Kaupang with a great army and came to the thing where he, before witnesses and by hand-shake, took charge of defending Sigurd Ranason's case. At this thing each of the kings pleaded his case personally.

Then King Eystein asked the lawmen whether the law of Norway gave the bonders the right to judge between the kings of the land, when they both pleaded in person. "I can here", he said, "prove by witnesses that King Sigurd sues me in this case. King Sigurd has therefore to do with me, but not with Sigurd Ranason." The lawmen said that disputes between kings could only come before the Örething at Nidaros. King Eystein replied: "I also thought that this was the case and that the summons must be transferred to this thing. There we shall receive a just verdict for Sigurd Ranason".

Then King Sigurd said: "The more thou triest to make this case difficult for me, the more I shall persevere with it", and therewith they parted.

Both parties now went south to Kaupang and summoned a thing from eight folk districts. King Eystein remained meantime in the town and had many men with him, but King Sigurd stayed on the ship.

Before they went to the thing a truce was proclaimed. When the thing was set and all people gathered, Bergthor Buck, son of Swein Bridgefoot, got up and gave evidence that Sigurd Ranason had stolen a part of the Finnish trading scot. Now King Eystein stood up and said: "Even if this accusation which thou bringest forward be true, and although I do not know whether thou hast good reason for it or whether thou canst prove it, I now contend that this case has already been dismissed at three things, and a fourth time at a town meeting. I therefore demand that the lawmen shall declare

Sigurd 'not guilty' according to the law of the land". And this was done.

Then King Sigurd said: "I see well enough, King Eystein, that thou hast used some law tricks, which I do not understand; but there still remains a way by which I can further my right and to which I am more used than thou, King Eystein, and I am now going to avail myself of this right". Afterwards he returned to his ships, took down the awnings and sailed his whole fleet out to Holm. He then held a thing and told his men that early next morning they should land at the Ilevolds and go to battle against King Eystein.

But in the evening, when King Sigurd was having his meal, a man suddenly threw himself down on the floors in the forehold at the king's feet, before the king was aware of his presence. It was Sigurd Ranason, who asked the king to decide everything for him as the king might wish, for he said that he would not that the brothers should fight for his sake. Then came Bishop Magne, Queen Malmfrid and many other great people and asked for peace for Sigurd Ranason, and at their entreaties King Sigurd raised him from the floor, shook him by the hand and placed him amongst his men, and they sailed to the south of the land. In the harvest, King Sigurd gave him leave to go home to his garths north in the land, and he received some kingly appointment at the same time. But after this the kings did not see much of each other and there was no friendliness between the brothers.

22. In the thirteenth year of the rule of the brothers, King Olav got an illness which brought him to his death; he was buried in Christ Church in Nidaros and they sorrowed much over him. After this the other two brothers, Eystein and Sigurd, ruled the land, but previously these three brothers had been kings together for twelve years, five since Sigurd had come back to the land, and seven before that. King Olav was seventeen winters old when he died and that was on *XI kalendas Januarii* (22nd of December), when King Eystein had been one winter in the east of the land and Sigurd in the north. King Eystein sat a long time during the winter in Sarpsborg.

23. Olav of Dale was a mighty bonder and a wealthy man; he lived in Mikledale[1] in Amord.[2] He had two children. His son was called Hacon Fauk and his daughter Borghild; she was the most beautiful of women, wise and well informed about many things. Olav and his children were in the winter at Borg,[3] and Borghild was

---

1 Now Store Dal or Great Dale.    2 *Amord*, now Borge district (Smalenene).
3 I.e. Sarpsborg.

always talking to the king and folk spoke very differently about their friendship. But the next summer King Eystein went north in the land and Sigurd went east. And the following winter King Sigurd was in the east. He stayed for long periods in Konungahella and strengthened the market town much. There he made a great castle and had a big ditch dug around it; the castle was made of turf[1] and stone. The king had houses built within the castle grounds and also a church. The holy cross he had in Konungahella, and in this matter he did not keep the oaths which he swore in Palestine, but he furthered the paying of tithes and most other things which he had sworn. But in setting the cross in the east near Land's End he believed that it would be as a protection for everything, but it was the worst of plans to set the holy relic almost under the heathen men's power, as it afterwards proved. Borghild, Olav's daughter, heard the rumour that folk were speaking ill of her and King Eystein about their talks and friendship. She then went to Borg and fasted and underwent the ordeal of hot irons for this matter and was well cleared. And when King Sigurd heard this, he rode two long days' journeys in one day and came forth into Dale to Olav. He was there during the night. He then had Borghild as his concubine and took her away with him. Their son was Magnus; he was soon sent away to be fostered in the north in Halogaland with Vidkunn Johnson of Bjarköy, where he was brought up. Magnus was a fine boy, and made quick progress in growth and strength.

24. King Eystein and King Sigurd were both at guest quarters one winter in the Uplands, and each had his own residence; but as there was but a short distance between the garths where the kings should hold their feasts, the men counselled that they should both be together in their feasting alternately at each other's garth. They were first both together at the garth which King Eystein owned. And in the evening when the men began to drink, the ale was not good and the men were silent. Then said King Eystein: "The men are so silent; it is indeed a better ale custom that they make themselves merry. Let us get some amusement with the ale; then there will yet be some jollity amongst the men, for surely, brother Sigurd, they will all think it most fitting if we two start some bantering talk". King Sigurd answered somewhat shortly: "Be thou as talkative as thou wilt, but let me be allowed to be silent". Then said King Eystein: "It has often been an ale custom to match men one against another, and so I will let it be now". King Sigurd remained silent.

1 I.e. peat.

"I see", said King Eystein, "that I must first start this game; I will take thee, my brother, as a match for me. I do this because we have both an equal name and like possessions and I can make no difference between our kindred and breeding." Then answered King Sigurd: "Dost thou not remember that I used to throw thee on thy back when I would and thou wast a year older too?" Then said King Eystein: "I remember no less that thou didst not win a game which demanded cleverness". Then said King Sigurd: "Dost thou remember how it went with us when we swam? I could duck thee when I wanted". King Eystein said: "I swam as far as thou and I could dive and swim under the water as well as thou; I could also go on ice skates and I knew no one who could beat me therein; thou couldst do it no better than an ox". King Sigurd said: "There does not seem to be a more lordly and useful sport than to shoot well with a bow; I think that thou canst not stretch my bow, even if thou didst try it with thy feet". Eystein answered: "I am not so strong with a bow as thou, but there is less difference in our ability to shoot at a mark; but I can go much better on skis, and this too has been called a good sport before now". King Sigurd said: "This, I think, is much more lordly; that he who is leader shall be a great man in the army, strong and more skilful with weapons than other men and easy to see and recognise when many are together". King Eystein said: "It is no less outstanding for a man to be handsome, for he is easily recognised in a crowd. It also seems lordly to me, for the best ornament is allied to beauty; I can also make better laws than thou; likewise in whatsoever we talk of, I am much better spoken". King Sigurd said: "It may be that thou hast learnt more law tricks, for I have had much else to do, and no one denies that thou hast a smooth tongue; but many say that thou dost not keep thy word, that thou layest little weight on what thou dost promise and that thou speakest in order to please those who are with thee, and that is not kingly". King Eystein said: "This happens when men bring their matters before me and I have to give the best advice to each man's case; thereafter another comes who has a case against the first and then it is necessary to even out differences so that both shall be at peace. It may happen that I then promise what I am asked for, because I wish all men to go happily from their meeting with me. It would be an easy matter for me to do as thou dost, to promise all men evil. I hear no man complaining that thou hast not fulfilled thy promises". King Sigurd said: "It has been the talk of many men that the journey which I made from this land was very lordly but thou, meanwhile, didst sit at home like thy father's daughter". King Eystein answered: "Now thou hast touched the boil! I would not have started this talk if I could not have answered thee about this; it seems as if I sent thee from home like my sister when thou wast ready for the journey". King Sigurd said: "Thou must have heard that I held many battles in Serkland, and in them all I got the victory and many kinds of costly booty, the like of which has never come to this land. I was thought most worthy there where I found the noblest men, but I believe that thou still lovest the home fires best".

"I went to Palestine," King Sigurd said, "and visited Apulia on the way, but did not see thee there, my brother. I gave Jarl Roger the Mighty the title of 'king' and had the victory in eight battles, and thou wast not present in any of them. Afterwards I travelled to our Lord's grave, and did not see thee there. On this voyage I came as far as the Jordan, where our Lord was baptised, and swam across the river; there I did not see thee either. On the other side of the river are some willow bushes. I tied a few of them into a knot and vowed that thou shouldst untie it. It is still waiting for thee down there and thou art called upon to fulfil this vow of mine."

Then King Eystein said: "There is not much that I can speak of compared to what thou hast achieved. I have heard that thou hast won many battles in foreign lands, but it might have been more useful for the land what I meantime did at home. North at Vagar I built booths for the fishing folks, so that poor people could get help, and earn their living. There I founded a priest's garth and endowed the church. Before this the place was almost heathen. These men will remember that Eystein was King of Norway. The road from Trondheim went once over Dovre-fell, where people were lost in bad weather or had to sleep out of doors and suffer hardships. There I built a mountain inn and gave it an income; those people will know that Eystein has been King of Norway. At Agdenes there is a dangerous rocky coast and no harbour; and many ships were lost every year. There is now a harbour and a landing place for wintering ships, also a church. Afterwards I raised beacons on the high fells and this I hope will be useful for the country. I built at Bergen a king's hall and the church of the Apostles, with an underground passage between the two. The kings that come after me will remember my name for that.

"I built St Michael's Church and a monastery besides. I have also, my brother, shaped the laws so that the people can now obtain justice, and when the laws are kept the country will be better ruled. I have set a warping pole with iron rings in Sinholm sound.[1] The Jämtland people are again under the Norse king's rule, and this was brought about by blithe words and wise persuasion and not by force or fighting. Now these matters are of small importance, still I do not know, if the people in the land are not better served by them, than if thou hast killed black men in Serkland and sent them to hell. When thou praisest thyself for good deeds, I think these places I have built for chaste[2] people will sooner give peace to my soul. The knot thou hast tied for me, I will not untie; but if I had wished it I could have tied such a knot for thee that thou wouldst never have become King of Norway. That could have been done when thou camest back to Norway with only one ship and camest alongside my powerful fleet. Let now wise men say in what way thou art above me, and ye braggarts shall know that there are still people in Norway who are thine equals".

After this the kings were both silent, but they were very wroth. Other matters cropped up between the brothers and each of them would have his own way; yet, peace was kept between them as long as they lived. It is told that once when King Sigurd had seated himself and King Eystein had not arrived, Ingebjörg, Guthorm's daughter, the wife of King Eystein, said to Sigurd: "The many brave deeds which thou, King Sigurd, hast done in foreign lands will long be remembered". He replied with this song:

| The white shields | There in Serkland |
|---|---|
| I carried in battle | I gave strong blows. |
| Became red when | Woman, thy husband |
| The fighting ceased. | Could thus not have fought; |
| | God gave me victory. |

25. King Sigurd was in the Uplands at a feast and there a bath was made for him. And when the king was in the bath and the tub was covered over he thought that there was a fish in the bath with him; and he fell to laughing so much that on account of it his mind wandered and this very often came upon him.

Ragnhild, King Magnus Barefoot's daughter, was married by her brothers to Harald Kesja; he was the son of the Danish king, Eric the Good. Their sons were Magnus, Olav, Knut and Harald.

26. King Eystein had a big ship built in Nidaros. In size and appearance it was built like the *Long Serpent*, the ship which Olav

---

1 The sound between Senholmen and the mainland; in North Bergenhus folk district.
2 In O.N. *hrein-lifi*, i.e. 'clean living', referring to monks and nuns.

Trygvason had built; there was also a dragon head fore and a crooked tail abaft, and both were gilded. The ship was built high, but stem and stern seemed to be somewhat too small to make the ship look smart. There in Nidaros he also had boathouses built, and so big that everybody talked of them. They were made of the best materials and nobly built. Six years after King Olav's death it happened that King Eystein was at a feast at Stim[1] in Hustader, where he got a sudden illness which brought him to his death. He died *IV kalendas Septembris* (29th of August), and his body was moved north to Kaupang where he was buried in Christ Church. It is the talk of men that never have so many men in Norway stood sorrowing over any man's body since King Magnus, St Olav's son, died. Eystein had been king in Norway for twenty winters, and after his death Sigurd was sole king in the land as long as he lived.

27. The Danish King Nicholas, son of Swein Ulfson, afterwards married Margaret, Inge's daughter, whom King Magnus Barefoot had had before; her son by Nicholas was called Magnus the Strong. King Nicholas sent word to King Sigurd the Crusader bidding him give him men and help from his kingdom and go east with him along the coast of Sweden to Smaland and baptise the folk there, for they who dwelt there held not to Christianity even though some had taken the Christian faith. At that time there were far about in Sweden many heathen folk and many who were scarcely Christian, for there were certain kings who had cast aside Christianity and upheld the blood sacrifices, just as Blotsvein and afterwards Eric the Victorious did. King Sigurd promised to go and the kings arranged to hold a meeting in the Sound. King Sigurd called out a levy of men and ships in Norway, and when they were come together, he had fully three hundred (three hundred and sixty) ships. King Nicholas came much too soon to the meeting place and waited there a long time; the Danes murmured much and said that the Norsemen would not come. They then broke up the levy; and the king and all his army went away. King Sigurd afterwards came there and he liked it ill; they sailed east to Svimraros[2] and there held a husthing; King Sigurd spoke of King Nicholas' loose words and they agreed to make havoc in his land because of this. They took the village which is called Tumatorp[3] and which lies not far from Lund; they then moved eastward to the market town which is called Kalmar and harried

---

1 The peninsula between Raumsdale and Sundale's fjord, where the mountain Stemshesten is situated. The king had an estate at this place called *Husstadr*, now Hustad.
2 Now Simrishamn (in Scania).    3 Now Tomarp, south of Simrishamn (in Scania).

there as well as in Smaland;[1] they forced Smaland to feed the army with fifteen hundred (eighteen hundred) cattle, and the Smalanders took up Christianity. King Sigurd then turned back with his army and came to his own realm with many great and costly things and much booty which he had won on the journey; the levy was called 'the Kalmar levy'. That was the summer before the great darkness.[2] It was the only levy King Sigurd made while he was king.

28. It happened once when King Sigurd went from the drinking table to Vespers that his men were very drunk and jolly. Some of them sat outside the church and sang Evensong but their song was somewhat broken. Then the king said: "Who is that carl, whom I see standing by the church, wearing a fur coat?" They answered that he was not known to them. Then the king quoth:

> The carl with the fur coat
> Is causing us trouble.

Then the carl stepped forward and said:

| | |
|---|---|
| I think you know, who wears | O king, you would be generous |
| The short fur coat | If you would give me a better coat; |
| Which must me satisfy. | Used I was to better clothes than these rags. |

Then said the king: "Come to me to-morrow, when I am having my drink".

The following morning the Icelander, whose later name was Toraren Stuttfeld, came to the drinking room. There was a man outside the door with a horn in his hands. He said: "Thou Icelander, the king hath said, 'if thou wilt have a gift from me thou shalt, before thou goest inside, make a poem about a man called Hacon Serkson, whose name is also Morstrutt, and mention about this in the poem'".

The man to whom he spoke was called Arne Fioruskeif.

Afterwards they entered the room, and when Toraren came before the king he quoth the following:

| | |
|---|---|
| Valiant king, you gave me | O generous king, |
| Hope of some present, | You let me know |
| When I came to you and made | (I well remember) |
| A poem about Serk's kinsman. | That his name |
| | Was Hacon Morstrutt. |

Then the king replied: "I have never said anything of the kind; somebody must have had a joke with thee. It is best that Hacon him-

---

1 In Swedish *Smaland* means lit. 'small land'. It is a well-known folk district in the south-east of Sweden. 2 I.e. the eclipse of the sun, which took place on the 11th of August, 1124.

self decides about thy punishment, and thou hadst better go and sit
with him". Hacon said: "He shall be welcome with me, for I can
see whence the mockery has come". He let the Icelander sit next
to him and they were very merry. As the day came to an end, and
the drink went to their heads, Hacon said: "Dost thou not think,
Icelander, that thou owest me some compensation? And thinkest
thou not that somebody hath made fun of thee?" Toraren answered:
"Of course I am indebted to you". Hacon said: "We shall both be
friends, if thou makest another poem about Arne". He was willing
to do this. Then they went to where Arne was sitting and Toraren
quoth:

| | |
|---|---|
| Fioruskeif, thou hast often | Scolding man, thou hardly |
| Made mocking poems | Didst dare feed a crow |
| And verses full of spite. | In Serkland; thou always wouldst walk |
| True scaldcraft is made of sterner stuff. | With weapons warily. |

Arne sprang up and drew his sword and wanted to fall on him.
Hacon bade him leave it alone and keep quiet and asked him to
mind that if they were to fight, he would surely come off worse.
Toraren afterwards went to the king and said that he had made a
drapa about him and asked him to listen to it, whilst he recited it.
The king was willing to listen to it. This poem was called "Stuttfeld's
drapa". The king asked Toraren what he wished to do. He answered
that his greatest wish was to go to Rome. Then the king gave him
much money and asked him to come and see him when he returned.
The king then promised to support him, but it is not known whether
they ever met afterwards.

29. It is the common saying among men that never was there a
stronger or more able king in Norway than King Sigurd. But in
later life he had not always the power to control himself and his mind
wandered. He was at times visited by a serious illness; but all the
same he was always held to be a great and beloved king on account
of his famous voyage abroad. It is told that once at Whitsuntide the
king sat at table with many people and many of his friends, and when
he had sat himself in the high-seat, he looked very tired and had a
worried countenance. The men had some misgiving about him and
did not know what was going to happen. The king looked fiercely
at the men sitting round the tables and nobody dared speak to him.
He then took hold of the Bible which he had brought home from
abroad. It was written in golden letters, and no more precious book
had ever come to Norway. The queen sat next to him. Then said
King Sigurd: "Many changes take place in a man's lifetime. When

I came home to Norway, I had two possessions which I valued above anything else. One was this book and the other was my queen, but they are now both loathsome to me and I think they are the worst and most detestable things which I own. The queen does not herself know how ugly she is, for she seems to have a goat's horn in her head and the better I thought of her in former days the worse I think of her now in looks and everything. And this book is of no use". Thereupon he threw the book on the fire, which burned on the floor in the king's hall, and gave the queen a blow near her eyes. The queen wept, more on account of the king's illness than of the blow she had received, or the insult offered to her.

Then a man stood up before the king. He was one of the king's torch-bearers, called Ottar Birting, a son of a bonder, but he had all the same become the king's torch-bearer and it was his day for service. He was of small build, but good-looking and kind, brave and amusing. He had black hair and dark skin; therefore it was an unjust nickname that had been given to him, as Birting means "fair". He rushed forward and rescued the book from the fire, held it up before the king and said: "This day is unlike the day, my lord, when you sailed in great state to Norway and came ashore with great fame and honour. Then all your friends met you with gladness and rejoiced at your home-coming. All would have you for their king and ruler, and showed you the greatest esteem and honour. But now we live in sad times, because on this holy festival many of your friends have come to you, and cannot be glad on account of your heavy mind and ill health. I wish, my lord, that you could be glad with them, and be so good, my lord, to receive this well-meant advice. Firstly, make peace with the queen, whom you have much offended, and speak kind words to her and afterwards be kind to all your chiefs, friends and servants; that is my advice".

Then King Sigurd replied: "Thou art the right person to give me advice, thou dirty village boy and foul bonder's urchin. Thou art born of a poor and contemptible family". The king got up, drew his sword, lifted it up with both hands as if he would cut Ottar down. But Ottar stood still and raised up his head and did not move. He did not seem to care what happened and showed not the slightest sign of fear. Then the king turned the blade and let the sword fall gently on Ottar's shoulders. Afterwards he sat quietly down in his high-seat and everybody in the king's hall was silent and none of the king's men dared say a word. The king now looked upon the tables and had a milder and more friendly expression. He said: "It takes a long time before one knows one's own men. Here are now present my landed men, marshals, dish-bearers and all the best men in the land. Still none of ye did me such a great service as this young man, whom ye think is of such little worth. I came here as a madman and would destroy my costly possession, but he prevented it and did not fear even death in doing so. Afterwards he made a clever speech and worded it in such a way that it increased my fame and honour and never did he mention anything that could have given me offence or sorrow. His speech was so fine and stately that the wisest of ye who are present here could not have spoken with more eloquence. Then I sprang up furiously, and pretended that I would kill him, but he showed such wonderful bravery as if he had nothing to fear. And when I saw that, I let go my purpose, for he had done nothing wrong. Now ye shall know, my friends, how I will reward him, who was previously only a torch-bearer. He shall now be my landed man and more shall follow. He shall soon become the most powerful of my landed men". Thereupon the king thanked the bonder's son in the presence of everybody, for having spoken sensible words and shown manliness, and for having done what his other landed men did not dare to do. Later on the king made him his greatest landed man.

King Sigurd thus often became ill of mind, and strange humours came over him, but on these occasions he would listen most to the advice of his inferior servants and obey them, and he gave them properties and garths. Ottar was later one of the greatest men in Norway on account of many good and praiseworthy deeds.

30. King Sigurd was once at one of his garths, and in the morning when he was clad, he said little and was not himself; his friends were afraid that his mind was again beginning to wander. But the steward was a wise and bold man, and he spoke to the king and asked him if he had heard any tidings which were so weighty that they made him unhappy, or if it might be that he was ill-pleased with the banquet, or if there were other things which might be mended. King Sigurd said that it was not through such things as he spoke of, "it comes rather from thoughts of a dream which I had in the night". "My lord," he said, "would that it were a good dream; but we should like to hear it." The king said: "I thought I was standing out here at Jadar[1] and I looked out on the sea and saw a deep darkness moving with great speed and it came near me; thereafter it seemed to me as if it were a great tree, and the branches stretched up, but the roots went down into the sea. And when the tree came

_____
1 I.e. Jæderen, the flat coast land south of Stavanger.

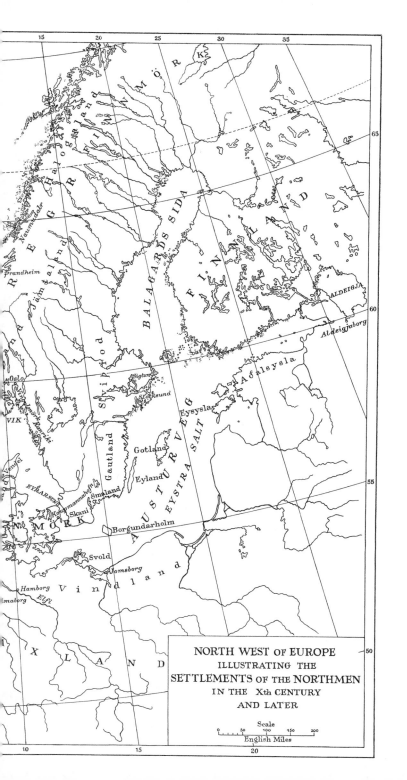

NORTH WEST OF EUROPE
ILLUSTRATING THE
SETTLEMENTS OF THE NORTHMEN
IN THE Xth CENTURY
AND LATER

Scale
0    50    100    150    200
English Miles

to land it broke up and pieces of the tree were driven far about the land, both on to the mainland and the outer isles, the skerries and the strands; and then I had a vision that I thought I saw the whole coast of Norway, and I saw that pieces of the tree were driven into every creek; most of them were small, but some of them were bigger". Then the steward said that it was most likely, "that you yourself will best understand it, and we should like to hear what you counsel thereon". Then the king said: "It seems most likely to me that it betokens the coming of some man to this land, and that he will settle himself firmly here and his offspring will spread far and wide about the land; but they will be of uneven greatness, as the dream shows".

31. Once it happened that King Sigurd sat with many great men and felt very depressed. It was Friday evening, and the steward asked what kind of food should be cooked. The king answered: "What should be cooked except meat?" And his words were spoken so sternly that nobody dared to contradict him and everybody felt uncomfortable. Afterwards they went to dinner and hot meat was served; but all were silent and sorry on account of the king's illness. Before grace was said a man called Aslak Hani began speaking. He had long been with King Sigurd on his travels abroad. He did not come from great kin, and was a little man, but quick and spirited. When he noticed how things had come to pass and that nobody dared to speak to the king, he asked: "What reeks in the dishes in front of you, my lord?"

The king replied: "What wilt thou it should be, Aslak Hani, or what dost thou think it is?" The other answered: "I think, my lord, it is meat, which I would rather not see on the table to-day". The king said: "What then if it be so, Aslak Hani?" He answered: "It is sad to know that a great and noble king who has won so much glory in the world on account of his travels and otherwise, should forget himself in this way. When you rose from the Jordan after bathing in the same water as God himself, with a palm-branch in your hand and a cross on your breast, then, my lord, you promised something else than to eat meat on a Friday! If men of low standing did that, they would deserve punishment. There are in this kingly hall to-day not many fearless men present if it is left to me, a mean man, to take exception to such an act". The king said nothing and did not begin to eat; and when meal-time was nearly over, the king asked them to take away the meat dishes. Other food was then brought in, which could be eaten. When they had eaten for a while, the king was more cheerful and began to drink. Men advised Aslak to flee; but he refused and said that it would not help him—"And surely it would be better for me to die now after I have prevented the king from doing a misdeed. He can kill me if he wishes".

In the evening the king called Aslak and said: "Who did egg thee, Aslak Hani, to speak so openly to me in front of everybody?" He replied: "Nobody, my lord, except myself". The king said: "Then thou wouldst no doubt wish to know what thou shalt have for thy daring and what reward thou art worth?" He answered: "If you, my lord, will reward me, I shall be glad, but if you wish to treat me otherwise, then I leave myself entirely in your hands". The king replied: "Thy reward will not be enough compared to what thou hast deserved. I will give thee three garths. I never expected that thou shouldst have spared me from a great misfortune and not my landed men, who owe me so much". Therewith the talk ended.

32. It happened one Yule-eve, when the king sat in his hall and the tables were set forth, that the king said: "Give me meat". "My lord," they answered, "it is not the custom in Norway to eat meat on Yule-eve." The king answered: "If it is not the custom, I will make it a custom". They went away and brought the king a porpoise. The king cut the meat with his knife, but did not eat it. Then he said: "Bring me a woman here into the hall". They brought him a girl whose forehead was partly covered by her head-dress. The king took her head in his hands, looked at her and said: "Thou hast an ugly face, but perhaps not so ugly that one could not put up with thee". Then he looked at her hands and said: "Ugly hands and badly shaped, but all the same they might be endured". He now asked her to put forward her foot; and when she did this he looked at it and said: "A hideous and large foot, but not much heed need be given to that and it also could be endured". Then he asked her to lift up her skirt; and when he saw her leg he said: "Dreadful is thy leg, it is both thick and blue and a mere harlot must thou be". And he bade them take her out, "For I will not have her".

33. Halkel Huk, the son of John Smorbalta, was a landed man in Möre;[1] he went west over the sea right to the Hebrides. Thither there came from Ireland to meet him a man who was called Gilchrist,[2] and who said he was the son of King Magnus Barefoot; his mother followed him and said that by another name he was called

---

[1] This family lived at Blindheim (in South Möre).    [2] *Gilchrist* means 'the servant of Christ'. *Gil* is a Gaelic word which was sometimes applied to Scandinavian names such as Torgil—'the servant of Thor', Gillibert, Gillibrand, etc. Gilchrist became later King Harald Gilli.

Harald. Halkel welcomed these two and took them with him to Norway, and he went straightway to King Sigurd with Harald and his mother. They put their business before the king. King Sigurd spoke about the matter with his chiefs and said that each should give counsel thereon according to his mind; but they all bade him take his own counsel in the matter. King Sigurd then had Harald called to him and told him he would not refuse Harald to prove by the hot-iron ordeal who his father was; but it was on condition that Harald would let it be settled that even if he made good his claim to such a father, he would not claim the kingship whilst King Sigurd or Magnus the king's son was alive; this arrangement was bound with oaths. King Sigurd said that Harald should tread on hot irons to show his parentage, but this ordeal seemed by many to be very hard, for he would undergo the ordeal to prove his fatherhood, and not to win the kingship, which he had already foresworn. But Harald went on with it and now the greatest ordeal that has been seen in Norway was made; nine glowing ploughshares were laid down and Harald walked over them with bare feet, two bishops leading him, Harald invoking the holy St Colomba. His bed was ready on the spot. Then said Magnus, Sigurd's son: "He does not tread on the irons in a manly way". The king replied: "Evil and wicked is thy speech". Thereupon Harald was laid in bed and three days later the ordeal was proved, for his feet were then unhurt. After that King Sigurd took well to his kinship with Harald, but his son Magnus was very unfriendly towards him, and many chiefs followed him in this. King Sigurd put trust in his friendship with all his people, and claimed that all should swear that Magnus, his son, should be king after him; and this oath he then got from everybody.

34. Harald Gilli was a tall, slim man with a long neck and a somewhat long face, black-eyed, dark-haired, and he was sharp and swift; most often he wore Irish dress of short and light clothes. He had difficulty in speaking Norse and fumbled much in finding words; many a man made much fun at him for that, but King Sigurd did not permit this when he was present. Harald used to attend the king to bed in the evening; but it once happened that Magnus and his people detained him, and they sat late drinking. Harald talked to a man and told him something from the west, from Ireland; it was in his tale that there were men in Ireland who were so fleet of foot that no steed could overtake them in a race.[1] Magnus, the king's son, heard this and

---

1 The O.N. word for 'race' is *skeid*. The old Scandinavians were fond of horse races. *Skeid* is also used for the swiftest ships.

said: "He is now lying again as he is wont to do". Harald answered: "It is true that such men may be found in Ireland, that no horse in Norway can run past them". They had words over this; both were drunk. Then said Magnus: "Thou shalt wager thy head that thou canst not run as fast as I ride with my horse; I will lay my gold ring against it". Harald answered: "I do not say that I can run as fast; but I can find men in Ireland who can and I will bet on it". Magnus, the king's son, answered: "I will not go to Ireland; we two shall bet here, and not there". Harald then went to sleep and would have no more talk with him. This happened in Oslo. Next morning after Mass, Magnus rode up in the street; he sent word to Harald to come there. And when he came he was clad in this way; he had on a shirt and breeches with straps, a short cape, an Irish hat on his head, and a spear shaft in his hand. Magnus set up a mark for the race. Harald said: "Thou makest the run too long". Magnus straightway made it much longer and said that it was even then all too short. Many men were present. They then began the race, and Harald always kept pace with the horse. And when they came to the end, Magnus said: "Thou didst hold to the saddle strap and the horse pulled thee". Magnus had a very fast horse from Gautland. They now ran the race again and Harald ran all the time in front of the horse. And when they came to the end of the race, Harald asked: "Did I hold on to the saddle strap then?" Magnus said: "Thou wast first off". Then Magnus let his horse breathe a while; and when he was ready, he smote the horse with his spurs and straightway came to a gallop. Harald then stood still, and Magnus looked round and shouted: "Run now", he said. Then Harald ran and at once came forth past the horse and much farther in front and so to the end of the race; he was so much to the fore that he lay down and sprang up and greeted Magnus when he came. Afterwards they went back to the town, and King Sigurd had meanwhile been at Mass; he knew nothing of this until after the meal that day. Then he said wrathfully to Magnus: "Thou callest Harald witless, but methinks thou art the fool;[1] thou didst not know before that foreign men train themselves to other sports than pouring drink into themselves or making themselves dazed and good for naught so that they have neither wit nor sense; give Harald his ring and mock him no more whilst my head is above the ground".

35. Once when King Sigurd was on board his ship he was lying in a harbour and a merchant ship, an Iceland boat, lay alongside them.

[1] The O.N. word is *fol*.

Harald Gilli was in the forehold of the king's ship, but next to him in front lay Swein Rimhildson; he was the son of Knut Sweinson[1] from Jadar. There was also Sigurd Sigurdson, a renowned landed man, and he commanded a ship. The weather was good and the sun shone brightly and many men went swimming from the longships and the merchant ships. An Icelander who was out swimming found sport in ducking the men who did not swim well, and they laughed at it. King Sigurd saw and heard it; he then threw off his clothes, jumped into the water and swam to the Icelander; he grabbed him, pulled him under the water and held him down. And straightway after, when the Icelander came up, the king pulled him down again, and so on time after time. Then said Sigurd Sigurdson: "Shall we let the king kill the man?" A man said that no one had any great wish to interfere. But Sigurd said: "There would indeed be a man to do it, if Dag Eilivson were here". Sigurd then leaped overboard, swam to the king, took hold of him and said: "My lord, do not kill the man. We all see now that thou swimmest much better". The king answered: "Let me loose, Sigurd; I shall kill him; he will drown our men". Sigurd answered: "We two shall play first; and thou, Icelander, get thee to land". He did so, but the king let Sigurd loose and swam to his ship; so too did Sigurd. But the king spoke and bade Sigurd never be so bold as to come into his sight. This was told to Sigurd, who then went up on land.

36. In the evening when the men went to sleep some men were playing up on land. Harald took part in the game and he bade his foot-boy go out to the ship and make his bed ready and wait for him. The boy did so. The king had gone to rest. And when the boy thought that he was a long time, he lay down in Harald's berth. Swein Rimhildson said: "It is a great shame for doughty men to have to leave their garths and that serving-lads are dragged up as high as themselves". The boy answered that Harald had allowed him to use his berth. Swein Rimhildson said: "It is not very seemly for Harald to lie here, and still less so, when he drags with him thralls and staff-carls". Then he snatched a stick and struck the fellow on the head so that blood poured over him. The foot-boy straightway leaped on to the shore and told Harald what had befallen. Harald at once went on board the ship and into the forehold; he struck at Swein with a hand-axe and gave him a great wound in the arm. Harald then at once went ashore. Swein ran after him on to the

1 *Knut Sweinson* of Sola was grandson of Aslak Erlingson. Cf. 'History of St Olav', chapter 31.

shore; and thereafter Swein's kinsmen drew up, took Harald prisoner and wished to hang him. But when they were proceeding with this Sigurd Sigurdson went on board King Sigurd's ship and awakened him. And when the king opened his eyes and recognised Sigurd, he said: "For this same thing thou shalt die, for coming into my sight; I forbade thee to do so"—and he leaped up. Sigurd said: "Thou canst do it, king, when thou wilt, but other business is first more needful now. Go at once as fast as thou canst ashore and help Harald, thy brother. The Rygers[1] will hang him". The king said: "God help us now! Sigurd, call the horn-blower; let the men be called up after me". The king straightway leaped ashore, and all who recognised him followed him to where the gallows was raised; he forthwith freed Harald, and as soon as the horn had sounded all the men gathered fully armed to the king. Then the king said that Swein and all his fellows should be outlawed. But at the request of all the men the king promised that they should have the right to live in the land and keep their possessions, but that there should be no fines paid for the wound. Then Sigurd Sigurdson asked if the king wished him to leave the country. "That I wish not", said the king, "for I can never be without thee."

37. Kolbein was the name of a poor young man. Thora, the mother of King Sigurd the Crusader, had his tongue cut out for no greater reason than that he had eaten half a morsel out of the king's mother's dish and had said that the cook had given it to him, but the cook dared not admit this. This man afterwards went speechless for a long time; about this Einar Skulason says in Olav's drapa:[2]

| | |
|---|---|
| For a very small matter | This man I saw |
| The mighty woman had | Truly bereft of speech, |
| The tongue cut out | A few weeks later, |
| From the poor young man's head. | When I came to Lid.[3] |

He afterwards went to Trondheim and to Nidaros and prayed in Christ Church. But at Matins on the second vigil of St Olav, he slept and seemed to see St Olav come to him, and take the stump of his tongue in his hand and draw it towards himself. And when he awoke he was healed and thanked joyfully our Lord and St Olav for having healed him and shown him mercy. He had gone there speechless and had sought the holy shrine, but he went from there healed and with fluent speech.

1 The men from Rogaland, the county round Stavanger.    2 I.e. *Geisli*; cf. p. 708, n. 2.    3 *Lid* was a farm in South Trondheim folk district, now called Lien.

38. A young man, Danish by birth, was caught by heathen men and taken to Vendland, and in that band with him were other prisoners of war. Now in the daytime he was alone in irons and without guard, but at night a bonder's son was in chains with him so that the young man should not run from him. But the unlucky man never got sleep or rest because of his harm and sorrows. He was always thinking of what there might be to help him, and he sorrowed much over his need and lived in fear of both hunger and torment; he expected no ransom from his kinsmen, for they had twice freed him from heathen lands and he therefore seemed to know that it would be both hard and costly for them to take it upon themselves a third time. Fortunate is that man who does not suffer such ill-luck in this world as this man! Now no other way was open to him than to run away and escape if he were lucky. He tried this at night and slew the bonder's son, struck off his foot and made his way to the wood with the chains round his foot. But next morning when it was light they were aware of what had happened, and went after him with two hounds which were used for seeking those who escaped; they found him in the wood where he lay hidden. They now took him prisoner, beat him and struck him and ill-used him in all ways. After this they dragged him home and left him in dire straits and hardly alive and showed him no mercy; they dragged him to a place to be tortured and set him in a dark chamber where there were already sixteen Christian men, and they bound him in irons and other bonds as tightly as they could. Now he thought of his former ill-luck and tortures as but a shadow of all the evil he had now. He saw no man in this prison who begged mercy for him; no man pitied the unlucky man except the Christian men who lay bound there with him; they sorrowed and wept over his hurt and their own need and ill-fortune. And one day they gave him counsel and bade him vow himself to St Olav and offer himself as a serving-man in St Olav's holy house, if by God's mercy and his prayers he could escape from that prison. He promised this gladly and forthwith gave himself to the church which they bade him do. The night after he seemed in his sleep to see a man, not tall, standing rather near to him and speaking in this wise: "Hearken, thou wretched man," he said, "why dost thou not stand up?" He said: "My lord, what man art thou?" "I am King Olav, whom thou didst call upon." "Ah, my good lord," he said, "I would gladly stand up if I could, but I now lie bound in irons as well as in chains with these men who are sitting here bound." St Olav then called on him and spoke to him thus: "Stand up quickly

and fear not; certainly thou art free now!" He next awakened and
told his fellows what he had dreamed. They then bade him stand up
and see if it were true. He stood up and noticed that he was free.
But then his fellows said that it would not be of use to him, as the door
was locked within and without. An old man who was sitting there in
hard bondage uttered words and bade him not mistrust the mercy of
the holy man who had freed him; he likewise said: "He hath indeed
given thee this token that thou shouldst enjoy his mercy and be free
from this, and not that thou shouldst get greater ill-fortune and torture.
Be quick now", he said, "and seek the door, and if thou canst get out
thou art helped by him". He did so and forthwith found the door
open; he ran out at once away to the wood. As soon as they were
aware of this, they slipped their hounds and went after him as quickly
as they could, but the poor man was lying hiding, and he saw clearly
where they were going after him. Now the hounds lost the scent at
once when they came near him and the sight of all grew bewildered
so that no one could find him, though he lay there before their feet.
They then turned home again and complained, and were vexed at
not being able to find him. King Olav let him come to no harm
when he came to the wood but gave him hearing and full health, for
they had before struck and beaten him over the head until he was
deaf. Thereafter he came to a boat with two Christian men who had
long been tormented, and they all used that boat together as best
they could and in this craft they got far away. He afterwards sought
the saint's house and by then he was healed and strong. He then
rued his vows and broke his word to the merciful king; he ran away
one day and towards evening he came upon a bonder who gave him
shelter for the sake of God. Later in the night when he lay asleep
he saw three maidens coming to him, beautiful and finely clad, and
they straightway spoke to him and cast hard words at him because
he had been so bold as to run from the good king who had shown
him so great mercy that he had freed him first from irons and then
from prison, and because he had betaken himself from the dear lord
into whose service he had gone. After this he woke, full of fear; he
got up early in the morning and told his dream to the bonder; and
the good bonder gave him leave and begged him to turn back to the
holy place. The man who first wrote about this miracle was one who
had himself seen the man and the marks left on him by the irons.

39. When King Sigurd got on in years the unusual happening
was talked about, that he wanted to divorce his queen and take for
his wife Cecilia, who was daughter of a rich man. He arranged for

a big feast to be prepared and wished to hold his wedding with her at Bergen. When Bishop Magne heard of this, he was very upset. He went one day to the king's hall together with a priest called Sigurd, who later became Bishop of Bergen. When they came to the king's hall the bishop asked to see the king and requested him to come out to him. The king did this, and came out with drawn sword; but he greeted the bishop in a friendly way and asked him to come in and drink with him. The bishop replied: "Another errand have I now; is it true, my lord, what I have heard, that you intend to hold a wedding and leave your own queen and marry another woman?" The king replied: "That is quite true". Then the bishop got purple red in his face and replied in great anger: "How could you, my lord, think of doing such a thing in my bishopric and thereby scorn God's laws and commandments and the holy Church? I am astonished that you, my lord, intend to treat our episcopal office as well as your own royal dignity with such great contempt. And I will now do my duty and forbid this wrong act in the name of God, St Olav, the apostle St Peter and all the Saints".

Whilst he thus spoke, he stood upright and stretched out his neck so as to make it easy for the king to let his sword fall, if he should choose. Sigurd, the priest, who later became bishop, said that the heavens appeared to him as small as a calf-skin for fear of the king's wrathful face. Afterwards the king went to his rooms and replied nothing and the bishop returned to his home so blithe and satisfied that he greeted every child he met and played with his fingers. Then Sigurd, the priest, asked how it was that he was so happy. "Don't you think that the king is wroth with you and might it not be best that you get away?" The bishop replied: "I have no misgivings about that, but I would like to ask you what death could be better and more wishful than to lose your life for the glory of God, or to die for the holy faith and your own sacred office, because you have tried to prevent something which is not right. I am so happy because I have done my duty". Soon after this the town suddenly got busy, for the king prepared to leave, carrying with him much corn, malt and honey. He went south to Stavanger and arranged a wedding feast for marrying Cecilia.

When the bishop[1] who was there heard the news, he had a talk with the king and asked him if it were true that he wished to take another wife whilst the queen was still alive. The king admitted it was true. The bishop replied: "If that is true, my lord, then I ask you

1 Bishop Reinald or Reginald. Cf. p. 650.

to consider how sternly this is forbidden to your humble subjects, whilst it seems to be permissible to you, because you have more power and think that everything is right that you do, although it is much against all the land rights. I do not know why you will do this in our bishopric and thereby disdain God's commandments, the holy Church and our episcopal authority. It now occurs to me that it would be fitting that you, my lord, should bestow some gifts and goods upon this town, and thereby make amends to God and to us". The king answered: "Take what thou likest of our goods; thou art unlike Bishop Magne".

Afterwards the king went away and was not more satisfied with this bishop than with the one who had banned his marriage. Thereafter the king married Cecilia and loved her dearly.

40. King Sigurd had so strengthened the market town in Konungahella[1] that there was not at that time any mightier town in Norway, and he stayed there for long periods to ward his land. He had a king's residence built in the castle. He imposed on all the neighbouring lordships and likewise on the townsmen that each year every male nine years old and over should bring to the castle five weapon stones or five beams, which should be made sharp at one end and five ells long. There within the castle King Sigurd built the Church of the Cross; it was a wooden church and carefully built both in materials and finish. The Church of the Cross was hallowed when Sigurd had been king for four and twenty years. The king let the holy cross and many other holy relics be there. The church was usually called the Castle Church. Before the altar he set up the table he had had made in Greece; it was made of brass and silver and finely gilded, and it was set with enamel and gems. There was also a shrine which the Danish King Eric Eimune[2] had sent to King Sigurd as well as a *plenarium*,[3] written with letters of gold, which the Patriarch[4] had given to him.

41. Three years after the hallowing of the Church of the Cross, King Sigurd fell sick when he was in the Vik. Then his friends begged him to separate from his wife (Cecilia), which she also desired, and she begged the king that she might be allowed to go away, which would be best for both of them. The king said: "Little did I think that thou wouldst leave me like the others", and turned from her and got red as blood in the face. She went away nevertheless.

---

1 *Konungahella* is Kungälf on the north side of the Göta River.    2 King of Denmark from 1134 to 1137.    3 *Plenarium* is a complete altar-book.    4 The *Patriarch* in Constantinople.

His illness got worse and he died of it, and his body was removed for burial to Oslo. He died the night after the Feast of St Mary[1] in Lent and was buried in Halvard's Church, being laid in the stone wall by the choir on the south side. Magnus, King Sigurd's son, was then in the town; as soon as King Sigurd died, he took over all the king's wealth. Sigurd had been King of Norway for seven and twenty winters, from the death of his father Magnus Barefoot; he was forty years old and the land was prosperous during his rule, for there were both good seasons and peace.

1  26th of March, 1130.

## CHRONOLOGY

SIGURD THE CRUSADER. BORN 1090. KING 1103–30
EYSTEIN. BORN 1089. KING 1103. DIED 1123
OLAV. BORN 1098. KING 1103. DIED 1115

1107. Sigurd the Crusader starts on his voyage to the Holy Land, and returns to Norway overland in 1110.

William of Malmesbury writes as follows about Sigurd the Crusader's voyage to Palestine:

"Foreigners willingly resorted thither (to England), as the only haven of secure tranquility. Siward, king of Norway, in his early years comparable to the bravest heroes, having entered on a voyage to Jerusalem, and asking the king's permission, wintered in England. After expending vast sums upon the churches, as soon as the western breeze opened the gates of spring to soothe the ocean, he regained his vessels, and proceeding to sea, terrified the Balearic Isles, which are called Majorca and Minorca, by his arms, leaving them an easier conquest to the afore-mentioned William of Montpelier. He thence proceeded to Jerusalem with all his ships in safety except one; she, while delaying to loose her cable from shore, was sucked into a tremendous whirlpool, which Paul the historian of Lombardi describes as lying between the coasts of the Seine and Aquitaine, with such a force of water that its dashing might be heard at thirty miles' distance. Arriving at Jerusalem he, for the advancement of the Christian cause, laid siege to, battered, and subdued the maritime cities of Tyre and Sidon. Changing his route and entering Constantinople, he fixed a ship, beaked with golden dragons, as a trophy, on the church of Sancta Sophia. His men dying in numbers in this city, he discovered a remedy for the disorder, by making the survivors drink wine more sparingly, and diluted with water; and this with singular sagacity; for pouring wine on the liver of a hog, and finding that it presently dissolved by the acridity of the liquor, he immediately conjectured that the same effect took place in men, and afterwards dissecting a dead body, he had ocular proof of it. Wherefore the emperor contemplating his sagacity and courage, which promised something great, was inclined to detain him. But he adroitly deluded the expectation in which he was already devouring the Norwegian gold; for, obtaining permission to go to a neighbouring city, he deposited with him the chests of his treasures, filled with lead and sealed up, as pledges of a very speedy return; by which contrivance the emperor was deceived, and the other returned home by land."

# XIV

# THE HISTORY OF MAGNUS THE BLIND
# AND HARALD GILLI (GILCHRIST) 1130–36

1. King Sigurd's son Magnus was taken as king, in Oslo, over all the land, such as the common folk had sworn to King Sigurd. Many straightway submitted to him and many became landed men. Magnus was more handsome than any other man who was then in Norway; he was arrogant and cruel, but doughty in all sports and accomplishments. It was their friendship for his father that mostly got him the friendship of the common folk; he was good at drinking, eager for money, unfriendly and ill to deal with. But Harald Gilli was friendly, merry, frolicsome, humble and generous, so that he gave to his friends all they wanted. He was accommodating and let others counsel with him in everything. All such things got him friendship and good praise, and many great men became his friends, and he had as many friends as King Magnus. Harald was in Tunsberg when he heard of the death of his brother Sigurd. He met his friends forthwith and they agreed to hold the Haugathing[1] in the town there. At that thing Harald was taken as king over half the land; the oaths by which he had sworn away half his father's heritage were then called forced oaths. Harald then took himself a bodyguard and made landed men, and soon there drew folk to him no less than to King Magnus. Men then went between them and thus it stood for a week. But as Magnus got far fewer folk he saw no other choice for himself than to share the land with Harald. It was then shared so that each of them had half the kingdom with the other, just as King Sigurd had had, but Magnus got the ships and table service and costly things and all the personal property that King Sigurd had had; and still was he less pleased with his lot. They ruled the land in peace, however, for some time, but they were very little together. King Harald got a son called Sigurd by Thora, Guthorm Greybeard's daughter. King Harald married Ingerid, daughter of Ragnvald, who was the son of King Inge Steinkelson. King Magnus married Kristin, daughter of Knut Lavard[2] and sister

---

1 *Haugathing* was held at Haugar, now Möllebakken in Tönsberg. Cf. 'History of Harald Hairfair', p. 75, n. 2.   2 *Knut Lavard* was son of Eric Eiegod and was Duke of Sönder Jylland (Southern Jutland).

of Valdemar, the Danish king. King Magnus could not love her and sent her back south to Denmark; after this everything went more heavily with him and he got much enmity from her kinsmen.

2. When King Magnus and King Harald had been kings for three years, they both stayed the fourth winter at Kaupang, and each made a feast for the other, but their men, however, were almost near coming to battle. And in the spring King Magnus went south with a fleet along the coast and drew to him all the men he could get. He then sought to ask his friends if they would grant him help to take the kingship from Harald and to give him only as much rule as he (Magnus) thought fit; he mentioned to them that Harald had once forsworn the kingdom. To that Magnus got the assent of many great men. Harald went to the Uplands and by road east to the Vik; he, too, drew folk to him when he heard about King Magnus; and wherever they went they both struck down each other's cattle and likewise slew each other's men. King Magnus had a much greater strength of men, for he could gather men from the whole land. Harald was then in the Vik on the east of the fjord and he gathered men, and each took both men and goods from the other. With Harald was Kriströd, his brother on his mother's side, besides many landed men; but King Magnus had many more. King Harald was with his host at a place which is called Fors[1] in Ranrik, and he went out from there towards the sea. On the eve of the Feast of St Lawrence[2] they got food for their night meal at the garth which is called Fyrileiv, but the guardsmen were on horseback and kept a horse watch on all the ways from the garth. And then the guardsmen became aware that King Magnus' army was coming towards the garth. Magnus had sixty hundred (seventy-two hundred) men, but Harald had only fifteen hundred (eighteen hundred). The watchmen then came and brought tidings to King Harald, saying that King Magnus' army was come near the garth. Harald answered: "What does King Magnus, my kinsman, wish? It cannot be that he will fight with us?" Then said Tjosdolv Alason: "My lord, as truly as you will have to counsel now for yourself and your army, has King Magnus been gathering an army during the whole summer to fight with you as soon as he finds you". Then the king stood up and spoke to his men, bidding them take their weapons; "if Magnus will fight, then we, too, shall fight". Next the war blast was sounded and the whole of King Harald's army went out of the garth to a field where they set up their standards. King Harald had two ring-brynies, but his

1 Now Foss in Tunge district (Bohuslän). 2 9th of August.

brother Kriströd had none; he was called the boldest of men. When King Magnus and his men saw Harald's army, they drew up their own host and made a line as long as to go right round King Harald's army. Thus quoth Haldor the Chatterer:

| Magnus had much | Many men were in his following; |
| Longer army wings; | Folk fell there in crowds. |

3. King Magnus had the holy cross borne before him into battle; there was a great and hard fight. Kriströd, the king's brother, had gone with his following into the midst of King Magnus' line and he struck on both sides; the men turned from him everywhere. But a mighty bonder who was in King Harald's army stood behind Kriströd; he swung his spear up with both hands and thrust it through Kriströd's shoulders so that it came out of his chest; Kriströd fell. Then many who stood near asked why he had done that evil deed. He said: "Now he hath been rewarded, because they struck down my livestock in the summer and took all which was at home, and forced me into the army with them; such have I intended for him before, if I could have got at him". After this, flight fell on King Harald's army. There, Ingemar Sweinson of Ask,[1] one of King Harald's landed men, got his death wound, and he sang these verses while dying:

| The evil witches | The arrows bit me |
| To Fyrileiv lured me, | From the elm-tree's bow, |
| Against this strife | Never to behold |
| Always I was. | Ask again. |

There fell nigh on sixty of the bodyguard, and King Harald then fled east to the Vik to his ships and then went to Denmark to King Eric Eimune and sought help from him. Thus says Haldor the Chatterer:

| Thou, who sharpenest | The Jutlanders' quick-tongued king, |
| The hard strife, | The fear of all Holsten, |
| Launched ships on the sea, | Gave thee bold men's following. |
| To visit King Eric. | |

And thus says Einar Skulason:

| Over the fishes' flat fields | Thou, noble and swift warrior, |
| Thou, gold-giver, wentest | Who gavest food to the wolves, |
| To Scania's land. | Found the king of the Danes. |

They met in Smaland[2] and King Eric greeted him well, mostly because they had sworn brotherhood to each other. He let Harald

---

1 *Ask* is a big farm in Norderhov district, Ringerik.    2 The O.N. text is *Smaland* = Smaland, bordering on Scania.

have Halland to support him and to rule and he gave him eight long-ships without tackle. After that Harald went north through Halland, and then many Norsemen came to him. After this battle King Magnus took to himself the whole land; he gave quarter to the men who were wounded and he let them be healed like his own men. He now claimed all the land for himself and he had the pick of the men who were in the land. And when they took counsel, Sigurd Sigurdson and Tore Ingeridson and all the wisest men wished to keep a troop in the Vik and there wait for Harald to come north. But King Magnus through his wilfulness chose to go north to Björgyn,[1] and he stayed there during the winter; but he let the army go from him and he bade the landed men go to their garths.

4. King Harald came to Konungahella with the army which had followed him from Denmark. The landed men and townsmen had a gathering against him and drew up a line of men from the town, but King Harald went up from his ships and sent men to the bonders' army demanding of them that they should not hinder him with weapons from going to his own land; he said he would demand no more than what was his by right; and men now went between them. At length the bonders broke up their gathering and submitted to King Harald, and to win helpers Harald gave fiefs and land rents to the landed men who were in his army and made good the bonders' losses. Thereafter many folk gathered to King Harald; he went west over the Vik and gave all men good peace, except King Magnus' men who, he bade, should be robbed or slain wherever he came upon them. And when he came north-west to Sarpsborg, he took there two of King Magnus' landed men, Asbiorn and his brother Nereid, and offered them the choice, that one should be hanged and the other cast into the Sarp-falls,[2] and he bade them choose for themselves. Asbiorn chose to go into the Sarp-falls, for he was the elder and this death seemed the hardest; so it was done. About this Haldor the Chatterer says:

| | |
|---|---|
| Asbiorn, who ill kept | The king bade Nereid hang |
| His word with the king, must | On Hagbard's grim death-tree; |
| Step into Sarp; the prince | The gold-spender had to suffer |
| Gives food to the ravens. | For loose speech at the husthing. |

After this King Harald went north to Tunsberg where he was welcomed and where a great army also gathered to him.

1 Bergen.    2 *Sarp-falls* or *fos* is the well-known waterfall near Sarpsborg (East Norway).

5. King Magnus sat in Björgyn and heard these tidings. He then called the chiefs who were in the town to a talk with him and asked their counsel as to what they should do. Then Sigurd Sigurdson answered: "I can give a good counsel. Have a ship manned with good men and set me or some other landed man to command it and send it to thy kinsman, King Harald; offer him terms according as right-minded men here in the land made between you, that is, that he shall have half the kingdom with thee. It seems likely to me that with the help of good men Harald will accept this offer so that there may be peace in the land". Then King Magnus answered: "I will not have this choice; of what use is it that this autumn we have won the whole kingdom, if we now divide it in two? Give some other counsel thereon". Then Sigurd Sigurdson answered: "It seems to me, my lord, as if thy landed men, to whom thou didst this autumn grant leave to go home, are now there and will not come to thee; thou didst much against my counsel when thou didst thus scatter the host of men we then had—for I thought I knew that King Harald and his men would come back to the Vik as soon as they heard that there was no leader there. Now here is another plan and it is bad, but it may be that it will do: take thy guests and other men with them and let them go home to the landed men who will not help thee when need arises, and bid them slay them; then give their goods to some of them who are true to thee even though they have not been so highly placed hitherto. Bid them drive the folk together and take evil men no less than good; then go east against Harald with the army which thou gettest and fight with him". The king answered: "I shall be without friends if I have many great men slain, and raise up the little folk; such men have often been so treacherous and ruled the land worse. I will yet hear more counsels of thee". Sigurd answered: "It is hard to give counsel since thou wilt not make peace and wilt not fight. Let us go north to Trondheim, where the strength of the land is greatest, and let us take away all the folk we can get. It may be that the Elvgrims[1] will weary of following us". The king answered: "I will not flee before those whom we put to flight this summer; give me a better plan". Sigurd then stood up, made himself ready to leave and said: "I will, then, give thee the counsel which I see thou wilt have, and which will be furthered. Stay here in Björgyn till Harald comes with a great army and then thou wilt have to suffer either death or shame". Sigurd did not join in this talk any longer.

6. King Harald went west along the coast and he had a great army.

---

1 I.e. the inhabitants by the Elv (Göta River).

This winter was called on that account "the crowd winter". On the eve of Yule King Harald came to Björgyn and brought his ships into Floruvagar.[1] He would not fight during Yule because of its holiness. But King Magnus got ready for him in the town. He had a sling[2] raised out on Holm[3] and he had chains made of iron and partly of tree stocks; he had these laid across the Vag[4] from the king's residence. He had foot-traps forged and cast over Jonsvolds,[5] and Yule was kept holy for only three days, when no work was done. But on the last day of Yule King Harald gave the signal for his army to come out of the haven; nine hundred (ten hundred and eighty) men had gathered to King Harald during Yuletide.

7. In order to get the victory King Harald made a vow to St Olav to have a church built to St Olav at his own cost.[6] King Magnus drew up his lines out in Christ Churchyard, whilst King Harald rowed first towards Nordnes. And when King Magnus and his men saw that, they turned into the town and to the bottom of the Vag. But when they were going into the street,[7] many townsmen ran to the garths and to their homes, and they who walked over the Volds[8] went on the foot-traps. Then King Magnus and his men saw that King Harald had rowed with all his army over to Hegravik[9] and were going up the hill above the town. King Magnus then turned back along the streets and his men fled from him, some up to the fell,[10] some up past Nonneseter, some into the churches, or they hid themselves in other places. King Magnus went to his ships, but they could not get away because the iron chains stopped them. There were also few men who followed the king; they could therefore do nothing. Thus sayeth Einar Skulason in Harald's drapa:]

They locked the Björgyn water
For a week; and there they

Could not get the lofty steeds
Of the sea away from the town.

A little later King Harald's men came out on the ships and King Magnus was taken prisoner. He sat aft in the forehold on the high-seat chest and with him sat his mother's brother Hacon Fauk; he was a handsome man but was not reckoned to be very wise. There, too, were Ivor Assurson and many others of his friends taken prisoner, but some were slain forthwith.

1 Now Florevaag on Asköy, west of Bergen.  2 This was a machine for throwing stones on the enemy.  3 Now Bergenhus (in Bergen).  4 Vaagen.  5 Now Engen. The Jonsvolds took their name from the adjacent John's Church or Augustine monastery.  6 The later St Olav's Church on the Hills.  7 Probably Övregaten above Tyskebryggen.  8 I.e. Jonsvolds.  9 Now Sandviken.  10 I.e. Flöifjeldet.

8.  King Harald then held a meeting with his advisers and bade them counsel: at the end of this meeting it was agreed that Magnus should lose his kingdom in such a way that he could never afterwards be called 'king'. He was then handed over to the king's thralls; they maimed him, thrust out his eyes, struck off one of his feet and at last he was gelded. Ivor Assurson was blinded and Hacon Fauk slain. After this the whole land submitted to King Harald's rule. Then there was much seeking after those who had been King Magnus' best friends or who might know most about his wealth and treasures. King Magnus had had the holy cross with him since the battle of Fyrileiv and he would not say what had become of it. Bishop Reinald in Stavanger was English,[1] and was reckoned to be very eager for wealth; he was a dear friend of King Magnus and it seemed likely to many that both goods and costly things had been given into his care. Men were sent for him and he came to Björgyn. These misgivings were now put to him, but he denied it and offered to undergo the ordeal. King Harald did not wish that; he imposed on the bishop a fine of 15 marks in gold. The bishop said that he would not thus impoverish his bishopric; he would rather risk his life. They then hanged Bishop Reinald out at Holm on the sling.[2] But when he was going to the gallows he shook his shoe off his foot and said with an oath: "I know no more of King Magnus' wealth than what there is in that shoe". There was a gold ring in it. Bishop Reinald was buried at Nordnes in St Michael's Church, and that evil deed was much blamed. Afterwards King Harald was sole King of Norway as long as he lived.

9.  Five years after the death of King Sigurd great things befell in Konungahella. At that time the sheriffs there were Guthorm, son of Harald Fletti, and Sæmund Husfröya, who was married to Ingebjörg, daughter of Andreas Brunson the Priest; their sons were called Paul Flip and Gunni Fis. Asmund was the name of Sæmund's bastard son. Andreas Brunson was a very noteworthy man: he was a priest at the Church of the Cross. Solveig was the name of his wife. With them John Loftson[3] was fostered and brought up, and he was then eleven years old. Loft Sæmundson the Priest, John's father, was also there. One daughter of Andreas the Priest and Solveig was called Helga and she was married to Einar. On the night of the first Sunday after Easter week[4] it happened in Konungahella that a great din was heard

---

1 The O.N. text reads *Reinhalldr Biskop i Stafangri var Enskr.*    2 Bishop Reinald died on the 18th of January, 1135.    3 *John Loftson* of Odda (Iceland), born 1124, died 1197, was Snorre Sturlason's foster-father.    4 The night of the 14th of April.

out in the streets all over the town, as if the king was going with all his bodyguard; and the hounds were so furious that no man could hold them in, and they broke loose. And all those that could get loose went mad and bit everything they met on their way, men and cattle alike. And everything which was bitten and bled became mad, and those that bore young lost their young and became frantic. Such things happened almost every night from Easter to Ascension Day. The men were much afraid at these happenings; many made themselves ready to move away, sold their garths and went up into the land or to other towns, and the wisest men found it remarkable and were afraid that, as it turned out, these things foretold great events which had not yet come to pass. But on Whitsunday Andreas the Priest spoke long and well, and at the end of his sermon he turned to speak about the townsmen's trouble and bade them harden their hearts and not leave this great town empty, but rather watch everything that might arise such as fire and unrest and find some plan for prevention, and pray to God for mercy for themselves.

10. Thirteen ships of burden[1] were sailing from the town to go to Björgyn; eleven of them sank with men and goods and everything that was on board; the twelfth broke up, too, but the men were saved though the goods were lost. Loft the Priest then went north to Björgyn with all that was his and he escaped unscathed. It was on the feast of St Lawrence[2] that the ships of burden sank. Eric Eimune, the Danish king, and Assur the Archbishop[3] both sent word to Konungahella bidding them take care of their town; they said that the Vends had a great army out and were harrying the Christians far and wide, and always won the victory. The townsmen laid all too little weight on this matter, and became more and more careless and did not bother what would happen next. But on the Feast of St Lawrence, when High Mass was being said, Rettibur,[4] the King of the Vends, came to Konungahella and he had two and a half hundred (three hundred) ships, and on each ship there were four and forty men and two horses. Dunimiz was the name of the king's sister's son and Unibur was the name of a chieftain who commanded a great strength of men. These two leaders rowed up with a part of the army by the eastern arm round Hising[5] and thence

---

1 *Ships of burden* were in O.N. called *byrdingar*.    2 10th of August.    3 *Assur, Archbishop* of Lund (died 1137).    4 Duke Ratibor of Pommern (now part of Prussia). He died a Christian. Some of the Vends (i.e. East Germans) became Christians long after the Scandinavians.    5 I.e. Hisingen, the island outside Gothenburg.

they came down upon the town; with a second part they came up by the western arm to the town. They came to land out by the piles; there they brought up their horses and then rode over Brattsas and up round the town. Einar, Andreas' son-in-law, bore these tidings up to the castle church, for the townsfolk were there, having gone to High Mass. And Einar came whilst Andreas the Priest was speaking. Einar told the men that an army had come against the town with a great number of ships, and some of the army were riding down over Brattsas. Many then said that it might be Eric the Danish king, and they expected quarter from him. All the folk rushed down to the town for their goods, and they armed themselves and went down to the jetties. But then they saw at once that it was a hostile and mighty army. Nine east-going ships[1] which merchants owned were afloat in the river by the jetties. The Vends came there first and fought with the merchants, who armed themselves and fought long and boldly; it was a hard fight until the merchants were overpowered. In that fight the Vends lost one and a half hundred (a hundred and eighty) ships. When the fight was at its fiercest the townsmen stood on the jetties and shot at the heathens. But when the strife slackened, the townsmen fled up into the town and then they all rushed to the castle; the men had with them their treasures and all the goods they could bring. Solveig and her daughter and two other women went up into the land. When the Vends had won the merchant ships, they went on shore and mustered their army; then the scathe they had suffered was seen. Some of them ran into the town, but some went out on to the merchant ships and took all the goods they would have with them. Next they set fire to the town and burned it down and likewise the ships. After that they went with all their host against the castle, and drew up their array to attack it.

11. King Rettibur bade those who were in the castle come out with weapons, clothes and gold, and get quarter. But they all shouted against it and went out on the fortifications; some shot, and some cast stoops, and there was a hard fight; folk fell on both sides, but most among the Vends. Solveig went up to Solbjargir and told these tidings. The war arrow was cut and sent on to Skurhagi, where there was an ale feast and many men were present. There was a bonder called Ölvir Micklemouth; he leaped up at once, took his shield and his helmet and a great axe in his hand and shouted: "Let us stand up, good fellows, and take our weapons, and let us go and

1 I.e. ships that went to the Baltic, principally to the island of Gotland and Russia.

help the townsmen, for it will seem a shame to every man who hears that we are sitting here swilling ale into ourselves, whilst those good fellows are sitting in peril of their lives in the town for our sake". Many answered and spoke against it; they said they would only be killed and bring the townsmen no help. Then Ölvir leaped up and said: "Even if all the others stay behind, I will yet go alone, and one or two of the heathens shall die for me ere I fall". He rushed down to the town. The folk followed him to see him go and likewise to see if they could help him in anything. And when he came so near the castle that the heathens could see him, eight fully armed men rushed against him. And when they met, the heathens ran round him. Ölvir swung his axe and with the front edge thereof he caught the man who stood behind him under the chin so that it cut asunder his jaw and his throat, and the man fell down on his back. Ölvir then swung the axe forward and struck another on the head and split it down to the brains. Then they shot at each other and he then slew two more, but he himself was much wounded. But the four who were left now fled. Ölvir ran after them and they came to a ditch; two of the heathens leaped in and Ölvir slew both of them, but he, too, then stood fast in the ditch. Two heathens only escaped out of the eight. The men who had followed Ölvir lifted him up and bore him back to Skurhagi and he was soon quite healed. It is the talk of men that no man ever went on a more manly journey. Two landed men, Sigurd Gyrdson, the brother of Philip, and Sigurd came with six hundred (seven hundred and twenty) men to Skurhagi, but Sigurd turned back with four hundred (four hundred and eighty) men; he was afterwards thought of little worth and he lived but a short while. Sigurd went with two hundred (two hundred and forty) men to the town and fought against the heathens, and he fell there with his army. The Vends then turned to the castle, but the king and the steersmen kept out of the fighting. In one place where the Vends were, there was a man shooting with a bow and he shot a man dead with each arrow; two men stood before him with shields.[1] Sæmund then told his son Asmund that they should both shoot together at him: "but I will shoot at one of those who bears the shield". He did so, but the man thrust the shield in front of him. Asmund then shot between the shields and the arrow hit the shooter's forehead so that it came out of his neck and he fell back dead. And when the Vends saw that, they all howled like hounds or wolves. King Rettibur shouted to the Christian men, and offered them

[1] *Shield* was in O.N. *skjöldr*. The dative form was *skildi* sing., *skildir* nom. plur.

quarter, but they refused. The heathens then turned hardily against them, and one of them went so near that he went right up to the castle gate and thrust with his sword at the man who stood within the gate, but the men dropped shot and stones on him; he was without shield but he was so troll-wise that no weapon could touch him. Andreas the Priest then took hallowed fire and made the sign of the cross over it; he then took tinder and set fire to it; he set it on an arrow point and gave it to Asmund. Asmund shot this arrow at the troll-wise man, and the shot hit so well that he got his bane and fell dead on the ground. Then again the heathens bore themselves as badly as before, and they howled and whined. All the folk then went to the king, and the Christian men thought that there might be some plan about turning away. Then the interpreter who knew Vendish understood what Unibur, the chieftain, was saying; he spoke thus: "These men are grim and evil to have to deal with, and even if we take all the goods that are in the town, we might have given as much wealth not to have come here, so many men and leaders have we lost. But to-day when we first began to fight against the castle, they had shot and spears for their protection; then they fought us with stones and now they beat us with sticks like dogs. I see by that that the weapons they have for their protection are diminishing, so we shall once more go hardily forward and try to defeat them". And it was as he had said that they now shot beams, whereas in the first fight they had heedlessly cast shooting-weapons and stones. And when the Christian men saw that the stock of beams was lessening they cut each beam in two. But the heathens came against them and roused up a hard fight; they rested in between. Both armies were now tired and wounded. And during the rest the king again offered them quarter, that they should have their weapons and clothes and what they could themselves carry out of the castle. Sæmund Husfröya was then fallen, and it was the counsel of the men who were still alive, to give up the castle and themselves into the power of the heathens. That was the unwisest of plans, for the heathens did not keep their word; they took them all prisoner, men and women and children, and slew all who were wounded and young and who did not seem fit to be taken with them; they took all the goods that were in the castle and they went into the castle church and robbed it of all its hangings. Andreas the Priest gave King Rettibur a silver-mounted pike-axe and Rettibur's sister's son Dunimiz a gold ring; they therefore thought that he must have some say in the town, and they honoured him more than the other men. They took the holy cross and bore it away; they also took the table which stood before the altar and which King Sigurd had had made in Greece and brought to the land, and they laid it down on the steps before the altar. Thereafter they went out of the church. The king said: "This house has been fitted out in great love for the God who owns it, and it seems as if they have watched but little the town and the house, for I see that the God is wroth with those who should defend it". To Andreas the Priest King Rettibur gave the church and the shrine, the holy cross, the plenarium and four clerks. But the heathen men set fire to the church and all the houses which were in the castle. The fire which they had lit in the church was slaked twice; they then struck the church down and it began to catch fire everywhere inside and burned like the other houses. The heathens then went to their ships with the booty and took stock of their army; and when they saw the scathe they had got they took all the folk for booty and shared them between the ships. Andreas the Priest and the clerks went to the king's ship with the holy cross; fear came over the heathens because there arose so great a heat in the ship that they all thought it was nigh on fire. The king bade the interpreter ask the priest why it was. He said that Almighty God in whom Christian men believed sent it to them as a sign of His wrath, for they who would not believe in their Creator were so bold as to take in their hands the token of His passion: "and there is so much strength in the cross that often before such signs as this, and some even still clearer, have befallen heathen men when they have had it in their hands". The king set the priests in the ship's boat and Andreas the Priest took the holy cross into his keeping. They brought the boat forth alongside the ship and pulled it round the bow and then aft along the other side of the ship; then they used boat-hooks and pushed the boat to the jetty. In the night Andreas the Priest went with the cross to Solbjargir, and there was both wind and rain. Andreas moved the cross to safe keeping.

12. King Rettibur and those of his army who were left went away back to Vendland, and many of the folk who were taken prisoner in Konungahella were for a long time after in Vendland in thraldom. But all those who were freed and came back to their inheritances in Norway were less thriving than before. The market town in Konungahella has never since risen to the importance it had before this event.

King Magnus, after he had been blinded, went to a monastery at Nidaros, and took monk's clothes; Great Hernes in Frosta was granted to the monastery for his upkeep. King Harald then ruled the land alone the year after and he gave peace to all men who would have it; he took many men into his bodyguard who had been in the bodyguard of King Magnus. Einar Skulason says that King Harald fought two battles in Denmark, one at Hvedn,[1] the other at Lesö.

| Manly feeder of the ravens, | Didst thou dye the thin swords |
| Boldly near high Hvedn | In the untrusty troops of thy foes. |

And furthermore he says this:

| Near the flat strands of Lesö | Warrior, where thy standard |
| Thou didst waken strife, hard | Wafted in the wind around the men. |

13. King Harald Gilli was the most generous of men. It is told that during his reign Magnus Einarson came from Iceland to be consecrated a bishop, and the king was very kind to him and held him in great honour. When the bishop was on the point of sailing back to Iceland and the ship was ready, he went to the hall, where the king was drinking with his friends, greeted him profusely and most politely, and the king received him with pleasure. The queen was also present.

The king said: "My lord bishop, are you now ready to leave?" He said that he was.

The king said: "You do not come to us at a convenient hour, for the tables have been taken away and we have nothing at hand to give you as a suitable present", and turning to his treasurer he said: "What can we give the bishop?"

He replied: "My lord, I know not better than that all the best gems have been given away". The king said: "This drinking mug still remains. Take that, bishop; it is of some worth". The bishop thanked him for this favour and gift. Then the queen said: "Farewell and live well, my lord bishop". The king then said to her: "When didst thou hear a high-born lady say 'farewell and live well, my lord bishop' and give him nothing?" She replied: "What can I give him?" The king answered: "Thou canst give him the cushion on which thou art sitting". Then that was taken; it was covered with pell and was a most costly thing. And when the bishop was going away the king took the cushion he was sitting on, gave it to the bishop, and said: "They have long been together".

Afterwards the bishop left and came to his bishopric in Iceland.

---

1 The island of Hven in the Sound.

It was then talked about what should be done with the drinking mug, which might please the king most. The bishop asked others to rede him, and many thought it should be sold and the proceeds given to poor people. Then the bishop said: "Another course will I take; I will make it into a communion cup for this place, and I am sure that the saints of whom there are relics in this holy church, will do some good act to the king every time Mass is sung over it".

Ever since, this communion cup has been with the bishop at Skalholt. And from the pell, with which the cushions were covered, and given by the king to the bishop, capes were made for the choir singers, and they are still at Skalholt. From this it can be gathered how high spirited and generous the king was, as also from other acts, although only a few have here been written about. King Harald took Thora, daughter of Guthorm Greybeard, for his mistress. She bore him a son called Sigurd. He had also a son with Queen Ingerid, who was called Inge. King Harald's daughters were called Birgitte[1] and Maria. His daughter Birgitte was first married to the Swedish king, Inge Hallsteinson, and afterwards to Magnus Heinrekson and last to Birger Brosa.

14. A man called Sigurd was brought up in Norway; he was called the son of Adalbrikt the Priest. Sigurd's mother was Thora, the daughter of Saxi of Vik[2] and sister of Sigrid, the mother of King Olav Magnusson and Kari King's Brother who was married to Borghild, Dag Eilivson's daughter; their sons were Sigurd of Austratt and Dag; Sigurd's sons were John of Austratt, Torstein and Andreas the Deaf; John was married to Sigrid, sister of King Inge and Duke Skuli. In his childhood Sigurd was set to books; he became a clerk and was consecrated a deacon. But when he was full grown in years and strength he became the doughtiest and strongest of men; he was big of build and in all kinds of sport he was before all men of his own age and almost before any men in Norway. At an early age he was very overbearing and violent; he was called Slembi-deacon. He was very handsome, but his hair was rather thin though beautiful. It then came to Sigurd's ears that his mother said King Magnus Barefoot was his father, and as soon as he came of age he laid aside the priestly occupations and went away from the land. He was a long time on journeys abroad. He also made a journey to Jerusalem and came to the Jordan; he sought the holy places which palmers are wont to seek. And when he came back,

1 In O.N. *Brigitt* similar to the Irish *Bridget*.    2 Cf. 'History of Magnus Barefoot', chapter 18.

he went on trade journeys. One winter he stayed some time in the Orkneys, and was with Harald the Jarl[1] on the death of Thorkel Fostri,[2] son of Sumarlide. Sigurd was also in Scotland with David, the Scottish king,[3] and there he was much honoured. Sigurd then went to Denmark and he and his men said that he had walked on irons to prove who his father was, and he bore it so well that it was proved he was King Magnus' son, and five bishops had been witnesses to it. Thus sayeth Ivor Ingemundson in Sigurd's balk:

| | |
|---|---|
| Five bishops | Thus it was shown |
| Who were thought the foremost | That the mighty king's |
| Were witnesses | Father was |
| To the prince's kinship. | The bounteous Magnus. |

King Harald's friends said that there had been treachery and lying on the part of the Danes.

It is told already of Sigurd Slembi, that he went for some years on trading voyages. He was one winter in Iceland and was a guest of Torgils Oddason of Stadarhol in Saurbær, and few knew where he was. It happened in the autumn, when the sheep were counted and driven to their fold, that one sheep leaped up at Sigurd. Sigurd thought the sheep wanted his help, stretched his hands to it and lifted it out of the fold and let it run up the fell and said: "Many do not want my help, so this sheep may as well get it". It also happened that winter that Torgils was wroth with a woman, who had stolen something, and wished to punish her, but she went to Sigurd for help and he let her sit next to him on a bench. Torgils asked him to give her up and told him what she had done, but Sigurd begged for her freedom, as she had sought his help, and entreated Torgils to forgive her. Torgils said that she should suffer for what she had done. When Sigurd saw that Torgils would not listen to him, he leaped up and drew his sword and told him to take her. Torgils then saw that he was prepared to fight in order to free the woman and he began thinking who this man with the strong face might really be. He thought it best to let the matter slide and leave the woman alone.

There were several foreign men living with Torgils, and Sigurd kept mostly in the background. One day Sigurd came into the room and saw an Eastman[4] playing chess with one of Torgil's huscarls.

1 *Harald* was son of Earl Hacon, and ruled the Orkneys from about 1122 to 1128. Cf. 'History of Sigurd the Crusader and his brothers Eystein and Olav', chapter 2. 2 *Fostri* means 'foster-father' or 'foster-son'.    3 David, King of Scotland (1124–53). 4 *Eastman*, i.e. Norseman. The Icelanders as well as the British and Irish often called the Norsemen 'Eastmen'.

The former was elegantly dressed and of good manners. The East-man asked Sigurd for advice regarding the play; and when Sigurd looked at it, he saw that the game was lost for him. The huscarl who played with the Eastman had a sore foot and a toe was bruised and showed a swollen wound. Sigurd sat himself on the bench, took a straw and drew it on the floor, so that some kittens ran after it. He drew the straw in front of the kittens until they came near the man's foot. He jumped up with a shout and threw the chess-board in disorder, and they afterwards quarrelled how the game stood. This is told in order to show how artful Sigurd could be. Nobody knew that he was a learned clerk until the Saturday before Easter when he consecrated the water, and the longer he stayed in Iceland the more he was esteemed. In the summer, when they parted, Sigurd said to Torgils that if he had anybody whom he wanted to help, he could recommend them to go and see Sigurd Slembi-deacon, who was his best friend. Torgils asked: "How art thou connected with him?" "I am Sigurd Slembi-deacon, a son of Magnus Barefoot." He afterwards went away from Iceland.

15. At that time Harald was sole king in Norway. It is said that he was not a wise king, but not so cruel as his kinsman, Magnus Sigurdson. When Harald Gilli had been king in Norway for six years, Sigurd came back to Norway and many advised him to go to King Harald and tell him about their kinship and see what he would say. Sigurd then went to his brother King Harald, and found him in Bergen. He at once went to see him, and placed himself in the king's hands, and told him about his parents and asked the king to recognise him as his brother. The king did not at once reply to his request, but put the matter before his trusted counsellors, whom he had called together. When the king's counsellors heard of it, they said that if Sigurd was given a share of the kingdom, he would soon become too big and important like his father Magnus Barefoot, and they said that everything was now peaceful and the landed men managed the whole government of the country.

The king then told them that he would charge Sigurd with some crime and kill him and find some good reason. During their talk the king decided to accuse Sigurd of having helped to kill Thorkel Fostri in the west. This Thorkel had accompanied King Harald to Norway, when he first came to the land, and had since all the time been King Harald's best friend. This matter was at once taken in hand, and Sigurd was condemned to death, and the landed men decided one evening to send some bodyguard-men after him. They took a ship and rowed Sigurd to Holdhella.¹ Sigurd sat aft on a chest and thought that this must be foul play. He was clad in blue trousers and over his shirt he had a cape which was tied together and served as a cloak. He looked down and held the cape-strings in his hands, and sometimes drew them over his head and then down over his neck. When they passed the ness near by the Melk River and the men were drunk and merry, but some rowed so eagerly that they took no notice of anything, Sigurd suddenly got up and went to the ship's railings and the two men who were to watch over him also got up. They followed him to the railings and held on to his cape, as was the custom when guard was kept on distinguished persons.

But as Sigurd was afraid that they might catch on to more of his clothes, he took hold of them both and leaped overboard with them. The ship had meantime gone some way and it took some time to turn back and pick up the two men. Sigurd swam under the water and got a good way from them and got ashore before they could swing the vessel round. Sigurd was very fleet of foot and ran up to the fell, and the king's men searched for him the whole night and did not find him. He lay down to rest in a cleft in the fells, and as he got very cold, he took off his trousers, cut a hole in the seat and put his head through it and his arms through the legs of them. His life was saved for that time. The king's men returned and could not hide their ill-luck.

16. Sigurd now thought that it would not help him to seek King Harald, and he was in hiding the whole of the autumn and the beginning of winter. He stayed secretly in the town of Bergen with a priest and spied out as to whether he could do treachery to King Harald; there were very many men with him in these counsels and some of them were King Harald's counsellors and room-mates: they had formerly been King Magnus' counsellors, and now they were in the greatest favour with King Harald, so that there were always one or two of them who sat at the king's table. On the night of the Feast of St Lucia² when the treason was proposed to be executed, two men who were sitting there talked together: one said to the king: "My lord, we now put the decision of our quarrel to your judgment; we have each wagered a basket of honey. I say that you will this night lie with Queen Ingerid, your wife, but he says that you will lie with Thora, Guthorm's daughter". The king answered with a laugh and did not suspect that this question was of such guile: "Thou wilt not

—————
1 Now Halle near Bergen.    2 13th of December.

win thy wager". From that they knew where they would find him that night; but the chief watch was kept outside the room wherein most men thought the king was and wherein the queen slept.

17. Sigurd Slembi-deacon and several men went to the room where the king was sleeping; they killed the watchman first, broke the door down and went in with drawn swords. Ivor Kolbeinson gave King Harald the first wound. The king had gone to bed drunk and slept fast; but he woke with folk wounding him and said, not knowing: "Hard thou dealest with me now, Thora!" She leaped up at that and said: "Sorely do they deal with thee, who wish thee worse than I!" There Harald lost his life. But Sigurd went away with his men. The men who went in with Sigurd to the king were Ogmund, a son of Trond Skagi, Kolbein Torljotson of Bataldr, and Erlend, an Icelander. Sigurd then had all the men called to him who had promised him their following if he could take King Harald's life. Sigurd and his men then went to a ship and the men sat at the oars and rowed out of the Vag in front of the king's residence; it then began to dawn. Sigurd stood up and spoke to those who stood on the king's jetty, proclaiming King Harald's death at his hands; and he bade them receive him and take him as king, as his birth befitted. Many men then drove down from the king's residence to the jetty, and all answered as if they spoke with one mouth saying that it should never befall them to show loyalty and service to a man who had murdered his brother; "and if he was not thy brother, then thou hast no claim to be king". They struck their weapons together and all deemed him outlawed and without peace. The king's horn was blown and all the landed men and counsellors came together. But Sigurd and his men found it most advisable to go away; Sigurd sailed to North Hordaland and there held a thing with the bonders who submitted to him and gave him the name of king. Thereafter he went to Sogn where he held a thing with the bonders and there, too, he was taken as king. After that he went north over the mountains and into the Fjords where he was well greeted. Thus quoth Ivor Ingemundson:

| | |
|---|---|
| The Horder and Sogn men | Many men at the things |
| There greeted Magnus' | There swore themselves |
| Generous son | To the prince's son |
| After Harald's fall. | Instead of his brother. |

King Harald Gilli was buried in old Christ Church.[1]

1 I.e. the little *Christ Church*. Cf. 'History of Olav Kyrre', p. 576, n. 5.

# XV

# THE HISTORY OF SIGURD, INGE, AND EYSTEIN, THE SONS OF HARALD GILLI (1136–57)

1. Queen Ingerid and the landed men and bodyguard which King Harald had had, agreed to man a swift cutter and send it north to Trondheim to announce the fall of King Harald and likewise to bid the Tronds take as king King Harald's son Sigurd who was then in the north and whom Sada-Gyrd Bardson was fostering. But Queen Ingerid went straight east to the Vik; Inge was the name of her son by King Harald and he was being fostered in the Vik by Amund the son of Gyrd Lag-Bersason. And when they came to the Vik, the Borgarthing[1] was called and Inge was taken as king; he was then in his second year. In that counsel there were Amund and Tjostolv Alason and many other great chiefs. And when tidings came north to Trondheim that King Harald had been deprived of his life, King Harald's son Sigurd was taken as king, and at the Örething there were Ottar Birting, Peter Sauda-Ulfson,[2] Guthorm Asolvson of Rein and his brother Ottar Balli and many other chiefs who supported this resolution. Next all the folk submitted to the two brothers and most of all because their father was reckoned as holy. And the land was sworn to them in this wise, that they should submit to no other so long as any of King Harald's sons were alive.

2. Sigurd Slembi-deacon went north past Stad; and when he came to North Möre, letters and tokens had already come from the great men who had turned their loyalty to King Harald's sons, and there he got no welcome or help. But as he had few men himself, they agreed to go to Trondheim, for he had already sent word there to his own friends and to the friends of King Magnus who had been blinded. And when he came to Kaupang, he rowed up the river Nid and fastened his landing ropes near the king's residence, but he had, however, to turn away, for all the folk withstood him. They then came to Holm[3] and took Magnus Sigurdson out of the mon-

---

1 *Borgarthing*, i.e. the thing by Borg (Sarpsborg).　2 About his family cf. 'History of Harald Hardrade', chapter 37.　3 I.e. Munkholmen.

astery against the monk's will, for he had already become a monk. It is the saying of several men that Magnus went willingly, though the opposite was said in order to better his case; Sigurd expected help by that and he got it also. And this happened immediately after Yule. Sigurd and his men went out along the fjord. They were followed by Björn Egilson, Gunnar of Gimsar,[1] Haldor Sigurdson, Aslak Haconson, the brothers Benedict and Eric, and the bodyguard which had formerly been with King Magnus, together with a crowd of other men. With this troop they went south past Möre right to the mouth of Raumsdale, where they divided their army; Sigurd Slembideacon went straightway in the winter west across the sea, but Magnus went to the Uplands and expected many men, whom he also got. In the winter and throughout the summer he was in the Uplands and he then had a great army. But King Inge went with his army against them and they met at a place called Mynni.[2] There was a great battle and King Magnus had the bigger army. It is said that Tjostolv Alason carried King Inge in his kirtle whilst the battle was on and he went under the standard. Tjostolv fell into great need and peril during the battle, and it is the tale of men that King Inge then got the ill-health which he afterwards had all his life; his back became crooked and one leg was shorter than the other, and it was so weak that he walked badly as long as he lived. The fall of men turned against King Magnus' men, and foremost in the lines fell these men: Haldor Sigurdson, Björn Egilson, and Gunnar of Gimsar; and a great number of Magnus' men fell ere he and his men would flee or ride away. Thus sayeth Kolli the Wise:

| | |
|---|---|
| Thou didst win a spear storm | With weapons thou warded |
| In the east: at Mynni, | Thy land, young king, |
| Thou hast gathered under thy helm, | And shields struck together. |
| With thy sword, food for ravens. | Thou denied thyself rest. |

And also this:

| | |
|---|---|
| Ere the ring-giving prince | Thou, fighter of the Tronds, |
| Would flee, there lay fallen | Split the shields asunder, |
| On the field the whole bodyguard, | And greater honour came to thee |
| O heavenly generous king. | Than Magnus earned. |

Magnus fled east to Gautland and from there to Denmark. At that time Jarl Karl Sonason was in Gautland; he was mighty and ambitious. Magnus the Blind and his men said when they came before him that Norway would be easy to take if some great chief

---

1 Now Gimsan in Melhus district in Guldale.　2 Now Minne by the south point of Lake Mjöse.

would go there when there was no king over the land and the landed men had the rule of the realm. They said also that the landed men who had first begun to rule were now disagreeing one with the other because of envy. And as Karl the Jarl was eager for power and listened to such talk thereon, he gathered his folk and rode from the east to the Vik, and through fear many people submitted to him. But when Tjostolv Alason and Amund heard that, they went against him with the men they could gather, and they took King Inge with them. They met Karl the Jarl and the Gautish army east of Krokaskog[1] and there they held a battle; King Inge got the victory. There fell Munan Agmundson, Karl the Jarl's mother's brother. Agmund, Munan's father, was a son of Jarl Orm Eilivson[2] and Sigrid, daughter of Jarl Finn Arneson; Astrid, Agmund's daughter, was Karl the Jarl's mother. Many others of the Gauts fell at Krokaskog, and the jarl fled east through the woods. King Inge drove them east right out of his kingdom, and their journey was a disgrace to them. Thus quoth Kolli:

I will tell, that the raven
Bent over the Gauts' wounds.
The eagle filled himself with food;
The sword was dyed in blood.

They who with the warriors
Had roused strife, were newly
Beaten at Krokaskog;
Now thy might is proven.

3. Magnus the Blind then went to Denmark to Eric Eimune and he was well greeted. He bade Eric follow him to Norway if Eric wished to subdue the land and go with the Danish army to Norway; he said that if he went with his army no man in Norway would dare shoot a spear at him. The king listened to his words and called a levy out. He went with two hundred (two hundred and forty) ships north to Norway, and Magnus the Blind and his men were with the Danish king on that journey. When they came to the Vik they went rather quietly and peacefully in the east of the fjord; but when they came with their army to Tunsberg, there was a great gathering of King Inge's landed men. Vatn-Orm Dagson, brother of Gregory, had the most say amongst them. There the Danes could not come to land nor could they get water, and many of their men were slain. They sailed in along the fjord to Oslo, and Tjostolv Alason was there. So it is said that some people would have St Halvard's shrine[3] borne out of the town in the evening when the fleet was first observed, and as many went to carry it as could grip under it; but it was so heavy

---

1 In Saurbö district, now Sörbygden (Bohuslän). 2 Cf. 'History of Harald Hardrade', p. 530. 3 *St Halvard* died on the 15th of May, 1044, and was buried in St Halvard's Church in Oslo.

that they could only move it a little way forward on the church floor. And in the morning they saw that the army was coming in by the Hovedöy and then four men bore the shrine up from the town; Tjostolv and all the townsfolk followed the shrine. It was carried to Fors in Raumarik and remained there for three months.

4. King Eric and his men went against the town and some went after Tjostolv and his men. Tjostolv threw a spear after a man called Askel—he was King Eric's stem man—and hit him in the neck so that the spear point stuck out of the nape. Tjostolv thought he had never made a better shot, for the man had nothing bare except where he was hit. Tiostolv went round about in Raumarik and gathered men in the night, and came down to the town in the morning. King Eric set fire to St Halvard's Church and to many other places in the town, and everything around was burnt. Then Tjostolv came down with a great army, but King Eric put off with his fleet and they could not then come to land anywhere on the northern side of the fjord because of the landed men's gathering, and wherever they sought to make a landing they left five or six or more behind. King Inge and his foster-father Amund Gyrdson were in Hornborasund[1] with a great host, where they fought King Eric and slew many of his men. And King Eric then fled and turned south to Denmark. King Inge followed them, and his men won from them what they could; it is the tale of men that no king ever made a worse journey with a great host into another king's realm; King Eric was ill pleased with it and thought that Magnus and his men had made a fool of him by bringing him on this journey; he said that thereafter he would not be so good a friend to them as before.

5. Now we shall tell about Harald's sons and Sigurd Slembi, according to what has been related by the wise and gifted man, Eric Oddson; and the narratives have come from Hacon Magi, the landed man, who told these tidings when they were first written down. Both he and his sons took part in all this fighting and strife, and could also tell of other fighting expeditions.[2]

Sigurd Slembi-deacon came that summer from the west to Norway, and heard about his kinsman Magnus' ill-luck, and then he thought that no welcome would await him in Norway. He then sailed by the outer lode and came south to Denmark, and stopped in the Sound. There by Skanör he met some Vendland

---

1 In Kville district in Bohuslän (now in Sweden).    2 These six lines have been taken from Schöning (Copenhagen, 1777). They are not in Peringskiold's translation (Stockholm, 1697).

ships[1] and went to battle with them and had the victory. He cleared seven ships and killed many men; but some were hanged. Sigurd remained south for some time, as he knew he could reckon upon no army to help him in Norway and least of all the Tronds and the men of Möre.

So says Ivor:

The Tronds and the Möre folk
Opposed the proud king
Who had come from the west.

The bonders turned against
The pious son of Magnus.

He also tells about the time when Sigurd went from Norway and came to Sweden:

The king's men tried
Themselves in bravery,
And hurled their ships
Into the thundering weather.

Some men stuck hard
To the wafting sails;

Others were baling water,
And the sea was lukewarm.

The towering billows and hard currents
Crashed on the ship in the hard weather.
The longship of the high-born king
(It is said) was moored at Kalmarnes.

When he came to the kingdom of the Danish king, he there made many friends among the mighty people; and the king himself was among the first, as told in the following:

The claws of the bloody eagle
Made his first friendship
With the king of the Jutes.[2]

He had also a fight off the island of Möen with men from Vendland and won the victory. Afterwards he went from the south and came to the Göta River by the eastern arm, where he captured three ships owned by Tore Hvinantorda and Olav, the son of Harald Kesja. Olav was Sigurd's sister's son, for Ragnhild, Olav's mother, was daughter of King Magnus Barefoot. Sigurd chased Olav up into the land districts.

Ivor quoth:

King Sigurd fought bravely
For his father's heritage.
He won the victory
Over the leaders at Göta-elv.

The arrows flew hotly
And the battle increased
With brave warriors
On both sides.

Tjostolv was then in Konungahella with many men in order to ward the land, and Sigurd came there with his ships. They shot at each other but he could not get ashore. Some men fell on each side and many

1 The *Vendland ships* came probably from the north-east coast of Germany. 2 The Danish king is often called "the king of the Jutes".

were wounded. There fell Ulfhedin Saxolfson, Sigurd's stem man. He was an Icelander from the Northland. Sigurd soon afterwards proceeded northwards to the Vik and harried far and wide. And when he lay in a haven called Portyria[1] by Lungard side and stopped and robbed the ships coming from, and going to, the Vik, then the Tunsberg men came with an army against him and attacked him unexpectedly when he and his men were ashore dividing their booty. Some came down from the land districts and others laid their ships across the haven outside of Sigurd's ships. Many of Sigurd's men fell there; amongst them Fider Geit and Askel Smithson, but Sigurd leaped to his ship and rowed towards the vessels lying outside. Vatn-Orm's ship was nearest to him, but Vatn-Orm had no wish to fight, so made off; and Sigurd rowed past him and got away with one ship, but he lost many of his men. This was said about Vatn-Orm:

> Vatn-Orm did not ward
> Well the land at Portyria.

6. Sigurd Slembi-deacon then sailed south to Denmark and a man called Kolbein Torljotson of Bataldr in Hadeland was drowned from his ship; Kolbein was in a small boat which was towed by the ship and they were sailing very fast. Sigurd wrecked his ship when they came south and he was during the winter at Alborg. But the summer after, he and Magnus went north with seven ships, and one day they came at night to Lister where they came to land with their ships. There they found Bentein Kolbeinson, of King Inge's bodyguard, a very bold man. Sigurd and his men ran ashore during the night and came upon them suddenly; they surrounded the house where Bentein was staying with his followers, and wished to set fire to the garth. But Bentein managed to get into a storehouse with his armour and he was well armed with weapons. He stood inside the door with his sword drawn; he had a shield before him and a helm on his head, and he was ready to protect himself; the door was rather low. Sigurd asked why they did not go in against Bentein—it would be a brave man's work. But no one seemed to be in any hurry.

Bentein, who heard what was said, replied: "Whoever of you comes inside shall find weapons against you".

It was dark in the house, and Bentein stood at the door with drawn sword. Sigurd stood a short distance from the house and noticed that nobody offered to go forward. He then tied a skin

1 Now Portör near Kragerö (South Norway).

round his hand, drew his sword and went up to the house. He had only a shirt on, and nothing on his head. He rushed into the house, as quick as a stick which is thrown in a game, and past Bentein. Bentein struck at him, but missed him. Sigurd at once turned against Bentein, and after they had exchanged a few blows, Sigurd gave him his bane and came out carrying Bentein's head in his hands. Sigurd was quick as lightning and very brave.

Ivor quoth:

The fair king kept his ships
Under Agder side by Lister[1]
East of Lidandisnes.
Sons of hersers fell;
The army of the king
Set garths on fire.

To the woods the king chased
The bonders from their burning garths;
The warriors struck with bloody swords.
Bentein gave many blows
Ere he fell down dead.

They took all the goods which were in the garth and then went back to their ships. But when King Inge and his men and Sigurd and Gyrd, the brothers of Bentein, heard of the killing of Bentein, the king sent men out against Sigurd and he himself went and took a ship from Hacon Pungelta, the son of Paul and the daughter of Aslak Erlingson of Sola, and the cousin of Hacon Magi. Inge drove Hacon up into the land and took all his belongings. Into the fjord there fled Sigurd Stork, the son of Eindridi of Gautdale,[2] Eric Hæl, his brother, and Andreas Kelduskiter the son of Grim of Vist.[3] But Sigurd Slembi and Magnus and Torleiv Skjappa sailed north with three ships in the outer lode to Halogaland. During the winter Magnus was in Bjarköy with Vidkunn Johnson. Sigurd cut the stems in his ship and made holes in her and sank her inside the Ægisfjord.[4] In the winter he stayed at Tjaldasund[5] in Kinn, in a fjord called Gljufrafjord. Within the fjord there is a hole in the fell and there Sigurd sat during the winter with more than twenty men; they hung a grey cloth in front of the hole so that it could not be seen from the shore. During the winter Sigurd was kept in supplies by Torleiv Skjappa and Einar, son of Agmund of Sand[6] and Gudrun the daughter of Einar Arason of Reykholar.[7] It is said that this winter Sigurd got the Finns to make him two cutters within the fjord, and they were bound with sinews and there was not a nail in them; they had withies for knees, and twelve men could row on either side. Sigurd was with the Finns whilst they

1 _Lister_ is the flat land on the south-west coast of Norway, where the town of Mandal is situated.    2 Now Guddal (Southern Bergenhus folk district).    3 Now Viste in Randabjerg district, near Stavanger.    4 Now Ögsfjord.    5 I.e. Tjældsund.    6 A farm on Tjældöy.    7 Cf. 'History of St Olav', p. 294, n. 3.

were building the cutters, and there the Finns had ale and they made a feast for him. Sigurd then quoth this:

Good it was in the game
Where gladly we drank,
And the bold man's glad son
Went between the benches.

Fun was not lacking
At that joyous drinking;
Each made the other
Happy as elsewhere.

The cutters were so fast that no ship could overtake them anywhere on the water. Even so it was said:

Few can follow
The fir boat of the Halogalanders.

Under the sail sweeps
The sinew-bound ship.

In the spring Sigurd and Magnus went south with the two cutters which the Finns had made. And when they came to Vagar,[1] they slew Swein the Priest and his two sons.

7. Sigurd then sailed south to Vikar[2] and there they took William the Skinner (who was a landed man of King Sigurd's) and Torald Kjeft and slew them both. Thereafter Sigurd went southwards along the coast, and south of Byrda[3] he met and slew Styrkar Glæsirofo who was then coming north from Kaupang. And when Sigurd came south to Valsnes[4] he met Swine-Grim whose right hand he struck off. Thereafter he went south to Möre outside Trondheim's Minne,[5] and there he took Hedin Hirdmagi and Kalv Kringle-eye; he let Hedin go away but Kalv was slain. King Sigurd and his foster-father Sada-Gyrd heard of King Sigurd Slembi-deacon's journey and of what he had taken upon himself to do, and then they sent men out to look for him and as leaders they gave them John Kauda, the son of Kalv the Wrong and brother of Ivor the Bishop,[6] and John Smyril the Priest. They put their men on the *Reindeer* which had two and twenty seats and was the fastest of ships. They went to look for Sigurd but found him not, and they went back with little honour, for folk said that they had seen them but had not dared to fight with them. Thereafter Sigurd went south along the coast and did much scathe everywhere. He came south to Hordaland, to Herdla[7] where Einar Laxa-Paulson had a garth; Einar had, however, gone into Hamarsfjord[8] to the Rogation Day thing.[9] They

---

1 Vaagen in Lofoten.    2 Vik in Brönnöy district (Halogaland).    3 Cf. 'History of Olav Trygvason', p. 126, n. 1.    4 *Valsnes* in Fosen (North Trondheim folk district). 5 *Trondheim's Minne.* Cf. 'History of St Olav', p. 373, n. 1.    6 *Ivor the Bishop* is mentioned later in chapter 10. He was bishop from about 1140 to 1150. 7 *Herdla,* now Herlöy outside Asköy (North Hordaland).    8 The outer part of Osterfjord, outside Hammar on the island of Oster (North Hordaland).    9 A thing held on the procession days of Ascension Week.

took all the goods that were in the garth and a longship of twenty-five seats that Einar owned, as well as his four-year-old son whom he had left with his workman; some of them wished to slay the boy, but others wished to take him away with them. The workman said: "Ye can have no joy in slaying this boy, and no use will it be to take him away; he is my son, not Einar's". And after these words they let the boy stay behind, but they themselves went away. And when Einar came home he gave the workman goods which were worth two ounces of gold and thanked him for his clever excuse and promised that he would always be his friend. Eric Oddson, who wrote this story first, says that he heard Einar Paulson tell about it in Bergen. Thereafter Sigurd went south along the coast and came right east to the Vik, and in Kvildir[1] he met Finn Sauda-Ulfson who collected King Inge's land dues; Sigurd had him hanged and after this went south to Denmark.

8. The men of the Vik and those of Bergen said that it was unfitting that King Sigurd and his friends should sit quietly in Kaupang in the north whilst his father's murderers were harrying everywhere outside the Trondheim's Minne and King Inge and his men were in peril in the east in the Vik, guarding the land and holding many battles. King Inge then sent a letter north to Kaupang and in it were these words: "King Inge, son of King Harald, sendeth the greetings of God and himself to his brother, King Sigurd, to Sada-Gyrd, Agmund Sviptir, Ottar Birting, to all the landed men, bodyguard, and huscarls, and to all the common people, rich and poor, young and old: All men know of the troubles we have, and of our youth, in that thou art five years old and I but three; we cannot do aught except we have the help of our friends and good men. It seems to me and my friends that we stand nearer the peril which affects both of us than thou and thy friends. Be so good as to come to me as speedily as possible and with as many men as thou canst get, and let us be both together for whatever befalls. Now he is our best friend who counsels that we be always united as much as possible and keep together in all things. But if thou wilt take thyself away and not come according to my message of need, even as thou hast done before, then must thou make thyself ready for my coming against thee with my army, and may God decide between us, for we can suffer it no longer that we sit here at so great cost and with such a strength of men as is needed because of the unrest, whilst thou hast taken half the

[1] Now Kville district in Bohuslän.

land dues and other incomes of Norway. Live in the peace of God".

9. Ottar Birting then answered; he stood up in the thing and spoke as follows hereafter: "This is King Sigurd's speech in answer to his brother King Inge: May God reward him for his good greeting and likewise for the toil and distress which he and his friends suffer in order to guard this realm for both of us. Even though there may seem some hardness in King Inge's words to his brother King Sigurd, he has, however, in many things great reason for it. Now I will make known my mind and hear the wish of King Sigurd and other great men, whether thou, King Sigurd, wilt fit out an army which shall follow thee to guard thy land, and go with as great a following as thou canst get, and as speedily as thou canst, to King Inge thy brother, so that ye shall strengthen each other in all things of gain, and may God Almighty strengthen ye both. Now we will hear thy words, O king". Peter Sauda-Ulfson, who afterwards got the name of Peter Burthenswain, carried King Sigurd into the thing. Then said King Sigurd: "All men shall know that, if I shall decide, I will go to my brother King Inge as soon as I can". And then each one spoke after the other and each began his speech in his own way, but all finished in the same way as Ottar Birting had done; it was then agreed to call an army together and go to the east of the land. King Sigurd afterwards went east to the Vik, and there he met his brother, King Inge.

10. The same autumn Sigurd Slembi-deacon and Magnus the Blind came from the south from Denmark with thirty ships and both Danes and Norsemen; it was near Winter's Night. And when the kings and their armies learned that, they went east against them. They met at Hvaler[1] near Holmengra;[2] that was the day after the Feast of St Martin and it was a Sunday. King Inge and King Sigurd had twenty ships, all big. There was a great battle, but after the first fight the Danes with eighteen ships fled home to the south. Then the ships of Sigurd and Magnus were cleared. And when King Magnus the Blind's ship was almost cleared—he lay in his bed—Reidar Grjotgardson who had long followed him and been his counsellor took Magnus in his arms and would leap on board another ship; Reidar then was shot by a spear through the shoulders. And it is said that King Magnus got his death from the same spear; Reidar

---

1 *Hvaler* is the name of the group of islands situated in the east of Norway, southwest of Fredrikstad.    2 *Holmengra* is the southernmost of the Hvaler Islands, now part of Bohuslän (Sweden).

fell back on the floors with Magnus on top of him. And every man says that he had followed his lord well and honourably: "Good it is for every man who can have such renown". On Magnus' ship there fell Lodin Saupproud of Linustader[1] and Bruce Tormodson, Slembi-deacon's forecastle man, and Ivor Kolbeinson and Halvard Fægir, his forehold men. This Ivor had been the first to attack King Harald and give him the first wound.[2] A great part of King Magnus' army fell there, for King Inge's men would let none get away whom they could get near, though only a few are mentioned here by name. On an island they slew more than forty men; there they slew two Icelanders, Sigurd the Priest, son of Bergthor Marson,[3] and Klemet, son of Ari Einarson.[4] Ivor Skrauthanki, Kalv the Wrong's son, who was afterwards Bishop of Trondheim,[5] was the father of Eric the Archbishop[6]; this Ivor had always followed King Magnus and escaped on board the ship of his brother, John Kauda, who was married to Cecilia, daughter of Gyrd Bardson, and they were both in King Inge's army. But Ivor came on board John's ship with two others, of whom one was Arnbjörn Ambi, who afterwards married the daughter of Torstein of Audsholt[7]; the other was Ivor Dynta Starrason, who was the brother of Helgi Starrason, but a Trond on his mother's side. He was the most handsome of men. When the levy men were aware that these men were there, they seized their weapons and went against John, but his folk set themselves to ward him and the troops nearly came to blows. But it was agreed between them that John should ransom his brothers Ivor and Arnbjörn and undertake to pay money for them; but the money was afterwards given back. But Ivor Dynta was led up on land and beheaded, for Sigurd and Gyrd, the sons of Kolbein, would not take money for him, for they blamed him for having been present at the murder of their brother Bentein. Bishop Ivor said that he thought that nothing worse had befallen him than when Ivor was led up on land under the axe and had first greeted them and wished that they should soon happily meet again. Gudrid, Birger's daughter, the sister of John the Archbishop,[8] told it to Eric Oddson and she said that she had heard Bishop Ivor speak of this.

1 Now Linnestad in Ramnes district, near Larvik.    2 Cf. 'History of Magnus the Blind', chapter 17.    3 Brother of the well-known leader Havlide Marson of Breida-bolstad in Vesterhop district (North Iceland).    4 Of Reykholar. Cf. 'History of St Olav', p. 294, n. 3.    5 Cf. p. 669, n. 6.    6 Archbishop of Trondheim from 1188 to 1205; died 1213.    7 Audsholt was a farm south of the bishop's seat Skalholt (in South Iceland).    8 Archbishop John (1152–57) had previously been bishop in Stavanger (after Reinald). He was the first archbishop in Norway.

11. Trond Gjaldkeri[1] was the name of a man who commanded a ship in King Inge's fleet. And it had come about that King Inge's men were rowing in small boats towards the men who were swimming and they slew every one they came near. Sigurd Slembi-deacon leaped into the sea from his ship when it was cleared; he threw off his brynie in the sea and then he swam with his shield over him. Some men from Trond's ship picked up a man from the water and would slay him; but he asked for freedom and said that he would tell them where Sigurd Slembi was, and they accepted. Shields and spears and dead men and clothes were then floating far and wide about the ships. "Ye can see", he said, "where a red shield is floating there; he is under that." They then rowed thither and took him and brought him to Trond's ship. And Trond sent word to Tjostolv and Ottar, Amund and Gyrd. Sigurd Slembi had a tinder-box with him and the tinder was inside a walnut-shell, covered over with wax. This is told because it was thought wise to carry it in this way so that it should not get wet. He had his shield over him when he was swimming so that no one could tell if it were his shield or that of anyone else when so many were floating about. They said that they would never have found him if they had not been told about him. And when Trond came to land with him, the levy men were told that he was taken; and the army broke out into a shout of glee. But when Sigurd heard it he said: "Many an evil man will be glad of my head to-day". Tjostolv Alason then went to where he was sitting, and struck a silk cap off his head. It was decked with a gold band. Then said Tjostolv: "Why wast thou so bold, thou son of a thrall, that thou daredst call thyself King Magnus' son?" He answered: "Thou hast no need to call my father a thrall, for thy father was of little worth by the side of my father". Hall, the son of Torgeir Steinson the Leech, was in King Inge's bodyguard and he was present at this; and he told it to Eric Oddson who wrote it down. Eric wrote the book which is called *Ryggjar Pieces*. In that book he tells of Harald Gilli and his two sons, and about Magnus the Blind and Sigurd Slembi right up to their deaths. Eric was a clever man, and at this time he was in Norway for long periods. Some stories he wrote according to the telling of Hacon Magi,[2] a landed man of Harald's sons. Hacon and his sons were present in all these strifes and happenings. Eric mentions even more men who told him of these events—wise and truthful men who

1 In O.N. *Gjaldkeri* means 'town sheriff', lit. the man who *cares* about people's debts.   2 *Magi* means 'maw'.

were present so that they heard or saw what befell. He also wrote of some events which he himself had seen and heard.

12. Hall said that the leaders would have Sigurd Slembi-deacon slain forthwith, but the men who were grimmest and who seemed to want to avenge his hurts upon them, advised the torture, and in that there are mentioned Bentein's brothers, Sigurd and Gyrd the sons of Kolbein, and Peter Burthenswain who would avenge his brother Finn.[1] But the leaders and most of the others went away. They broke his feet and arms off with axe-hammers; then they tore off his clothes and would flay him alive, and they ripped off his scalp: but they could not flay him because of the rush of blood. Thereupon they took whips of hide and beat him so long that his skin was almost off as if it had been flayed. Then they took a tree-stock and shot it at his back so that the spine broke. Thereafter they dragged him to a tree and hanged him; they struck off his head, and his body they dragged away and hid it in a stone cairn. It is the talk of all men, and of his friends and foes alike, that no man in Norway was doughtier in all things than Sigurd, in the memory of men who were then alive; but he was unlucky in one or two things. Hall said that he spoke little and answered with few words—under his torture—if a man spoke to him; but Hall says also, that he never moved when they tortured him and it was as if they struck a stock or a stone. He added that he who was hardy against pain could be reckoned a manly fellow if he could suffer tortures and yet hold his mouth and not give way; and he said that Sigurd never changed his voice and that he talked just as easily as if he had been sitting on an ale-bench; he spoke neither more loudly nor lower nor more falteringly than his custom was. He talked until he was dead and sang a third part of the Psalms: "he seemed", said Hall, "to be before all other men in courage and strength". But the priest who had the neighbouring church, had Sigurd's body brought there, for he was a friend of the sons of Harald. And when they learned that, they let their wrath fall on him; they had the body moved back to where it was before, and besides that, the priest had to pay fines for it. But Sigurd's friends afterwards came from the south from Denmark for the body, and they took it to Alborg and buried it there in the town in St Mary's Church.[2] Ketel the Priest, who had St Mary's as his parish church, told Eric that Sigurd was buried there. Tjostolv Alason had King Magnus' body brought to Oslo and buried there in

1 Cf. chapter 7.   2 *St Mary's Church* at Alborg (Denmark) was a church attached to a nunnery, situated on the site of the present Frue Church.

Halvard's Church near his father, King Sigurd; Lodin Saupproud they brought to Tunsberg. The others they buried near the place of battle.

13. Sigurd and Inge had now ruled six years over Norway. This spring Eystein came west from Scotland; he was the son of Harald Gilli. Arne Sturla and Torleiv Brynjulvson and Kolbein Ruga had gone west across the sea for Eystein; they had followed him into the land and sailed straightway north to Trondheim; the Tronds received him and he was taken as king at the Örething on Rogation Day, in such a way that he was to have a third part of Norway along with his brothers. Sigurd and Inge were then in the east of the land; men went between the kings and arranged that Eystein was to have a third part of the kingdom. No ordeal was made to prove Eystein's parentage, and they believed what King Harald had said about him. Bjadauk was the name of Eystein's mother and she came to Norway with him.

Magnus was the name of the fourth son of King Harald and he was fostered by Kyrpinga-Orm. He, too, was taken as king and had his share of the land. Magnus was weak in his legs; he lived but a short while and died in his bed. Einar Skulason mentions of him:

Eystein gives wealth;  
Sigurd increases the shield-din;  
Inge sets the swords swinging;  
Magnus makes peace.

In blood the dear king's  
Sons have dyed their shields;  
Never have four better  
Brothers been on this earth.

14. After the fall of King Harald Gilli, Queen Ingerid married Ottar Birting; he was a landed man, and a great chief, a Trond by birth; and he helped King Inge much whilst the latter was a child. King Sigurd was no great friend to him, for he thought he leaned altogether to his step-son, King Inge. Ottar Birting was slain in the north in Kaupang in a single fight one evening when he was going to Evensong. When he heard the whine of the blow he lifted up his hand and cape, for he thought that someone had thrown a snowball at him, as young boys often do. He fell with the blow. Alf Red, his son, then came walking into the churchyard; he saw his father's death and likewise that the man who had slain him ran east of the church. Alf ran after him and slew him near the corner of the choir; folk said he had avenged himself well and afterwards he was thought to be a greater man than before.

15. King Eystein Haraldson was in the neighbourhood of Trondheim when he heard of Ottar's death, and he called to him an army of bonders; he went out of the town with a great crowd of men. Ottar's kinsmen and other friends gave King Sigurd most blame for

the murder; he was then in Kaupang and the bonders were much incensed against him. But the king offered to undergo the ordeal and agreed to carry hot irons to prove his case; thereby peace was made. After this King Sigurd went south in the land and the ordeal was never performed.

16. Queen Ingerid got a son by Ivor Sneis: he was called Orm and afterwards he was called King's Brother; he was the most handsome of men to look upon and he became a great chief, as will be told hereafter. Queen Ingerid was afterwards married to Arne of Stodreim,[1] and he was afterwards called King's Kin. Their children were Inge, Nicholas,[2] Philip of Herdla[3] and Margaret, who was married to Björn Buck and afterwards to Simon Karason.

17. Erling was the name of the son of Kyrpinga-Orm and Ragnhild, the daughter of Sveinki Steinarson. Kyrpinga-Orm was the son of Swein, son of Swein, son of Erlend of Gerde.[4] Orm's mother was Ragna, daughter of Jarl Orm Eilivson and Sigrid, daughter of Finn Arneson the Jarl. Orm the Jarl's mother was Ragnhild, daughter of Jarl Hacon the Mighty. Erling was a wise man and a good friend of King Inge, and by his counsel Erling was married to Kristin, daughter of King Sigurd and Queen Malmfrid. Erling had a garth in Studla[5] in South Hordaland. He went from the land and with him there went Eindridi the Young and many other landed men; they had a fine army. They had made themselves ready for a journey to Jerusalem and went west over the sea to the Orkneys. From there Ragnvald the Jarl, who was called Kali, and Bishop William went; they had from the Orkneys fifteen longships in all and they sailed to the Hebrides and thence west to Valland, and then the way that King Sigurd the Crusader had taken to Norvasund; they harried far and wide in the heathen part of Spain. A little while after they had sailed through the Straits, Eindridi the Young and his followers with six ships left them, and each party now went its own way. But Ragnvald the Jarl and Erling Skakki came upon a *dromond*,[6] and they came up to it with nine ships and fought against it; and the cutters came alongside the dromond, and the heathen men then brought down on them both weapons and stones and pots full of boiling pitch and oil. Erling was nearest to them with his

---

1 *Stodreim*, now Staareim in Eid district (Northfjord).    2 *Nicholas* was the famous bishop in Oslo (1190–1225).    3 Cf. chapter 7. *Philip* fell in 1180 against King Sverre.    4 Now Gjerde. Cf. 'History of St Olav', chapter 94.    5 Cf. 'History of Olav Trygvason', chapter 195.    6 *Dromond* was the name of a large type of merchant vessel used in the Mediterranean in the Middle Ages. The name is of Greek origin.

ship and the weapons which the heathen men threw went clear of his ship. Erling's men then struck holes in the dromond, some down below the water-line, others up on the sides, so that they boarded the vessel through the holes. Thus sayeth Torbjörn Skakkascald in Erling's drapa:

Fearlessly the bold
Norsemen struck holes
In the hull of the new ship
On the deep with their axes.

The eagle-feeders noticed
Your cunning from the ship.
With iron weapons ye struck
Their defence down.

Audun Red was the name of a man; he was Erling's stem-man and he was the first to board the dromond; they won the dromond and slew a great number of men, took a large amount of wealth and won the victory. Ragnvald the Jarl and Erling Skakki continued their journey to Palestine and out to the River Jordan. Thereafter they turned back and came to Miklegarth[1] first of all; they left their ships here and went home by land; they had good luck and came home to Norway and their journey was much praised. Erling now seemed to be a greater man than before, both on account of his journey and because of his marriage; he was also a wise man, rich, of good family and well-spoken; and he leaned in friendship mostly to King Inge amongst the brothers.

18. King Sigurd rode out feasting east in the Vik with his body-guard; and he rode past a garth owned by a mighty man who was called Simon. And when the king rode through the garth, he was struck by a lovely voice coming from a house; he rode to the house and saw therein that a woman was standing by a handmill and it was she who sang so beautifully whilst she was milling. The king got off his horse and went in to the woman and lay with her. And when the king went away Simon the Bonder knew what business the king had had there. The woman hight Thora and was a serving-maid with Simon the Bonder. Simon then had her taken into his protection and thereafter she bore a son; he was given the name of Hacon and was called King Sigurd's son; Hacon was brought up there with Simon Torbergson and his wife Gunhild. There, too, were Anund and Andrew, the sons of Simon and Gunhild, also brought up, and they and Hacon thought so much of each other that nothing but death could part them.[2]

19. King Eystein Haraldson was once east in the Vik near Land's End and he disagreed with the men of Ranrik and Hising; they

1 Constantinople.    2 In the text it is mentioned "that nothing but *Hel* [= the goddess of death] could part them".

gathered folk against him and he held battle with them and won the victory. The place where they fought was called Leikberg.[1] He also burned far and wide in Hising. The bonders afterwards submitted to him and paid heavy fines, and the king took hostages of them. Thus sayeth Einar Skulason:

| | |
|---|---|
| The mild and generous king | The prince went forth |
| Made return against | And the men followed him |
| The Vik-dwellers' strife; | Near unto Leikberg |
| He had luck in battle. | And praise was heard there. |
| Most folk were afraid | The Ranrik men fled fast |
| Before they sought peace. | And paid out such |
| He took hostages | As the prince bade; |
| And fines of every man. | In their need the folk gave. |

20. A little later King Eystein started on a journey west across the sea and he sailed to Caithness.[2] There he learned that Jarl Harald Maddadson was in Torsa.[3] He went thither with three small cutters and came upon him suddenly. The jarl had one thirty-bench ship and in it were eighty men. But as they were not prepared, King Eystein and his men attacked the ship at once and they took the jarl prisoner and had him with them on their ships. He ransomed himself with three marks of gold, and therewith they parted. Thus sayeth Einar Skulason:

| | |
|---|---|
| There were with Maddad's son | With three cutters the sea king |
| Eighty men gathered together; | Took the jarl prisoner. |
| The mighty feeder of the birds | The warrior had to give |
| Of prey there got renown. | His head to the bold king. |

King Eystein then sailed south along the east of Scotland and he came to a market town in Scotland called Apardion,[4] and there he slew many men and robbed the town. Thus sayeth Einar Skulason:

| | |
|---|---|
| In Apardion there fell | The swords were broken; |
| All the folk, as I have heard; | Yonder the king plundered. |

A second battle he had farther south at Hiartapoll[5] with a company of knights; he put them to flight and cleared some ships. Thus sayeth Einar:

| | |
|---|---|
| The king's sword bit; | Gladly did the raven drink |
| Blood fell on the spear. | The warm blood there. |
| Loyally the bodyguard followed | He cleared the ships |
| Him near Hiartapoll. | Of the English, man for man. |

1 This place is unidentified. Lit. it means Play-mountain from O.S. *leika*, 'to play'. *Leika* is still used in the north of England.     2 In O.N. *Katanes*.     3 Thurso in Caithness.     4 Aberdeen.     5 West Hartlepool.

Thereafter he sailed farther south in England and he had his third battle near Hvitaby;[1] he got the victory and burned the town; thus sayeth Einar:

The king roused the strife
And there the sword whined;
The shield was struck
Near Hvitaby.

The hot fire of wood
Played high in the glow;
The wolf's tooth was reddened;
The men got harm.

After this he harried far and wide in England; Stephen was then king there. Next King Eystein had a fight with some knights near Skarpasker.[2] Thus sayeth Einar:

The king fought
Against the shield-host,

Near Skarpasker,
When the arrows fell down.

Next he fought near Pilavik[3] and got the victory. Thus sayeth Einar:

The prince dyed his sword
In blood; the wolves stood
And tore the port-dwellers'[4]
Bodies in Pilavik.

By the western ocean
He caused all Langatun[5]
To be burned;
The sword fell on the forehead

There they burned Langatun, a big town, and folk say that since then the town has not risen again. After that King Eystein went away from England and in the autumn he came back to Norway. Folk judged very differently about that journey.[6]

21. There was good peace in Norway at the beginning of the rule of King Harald's sons, their unity was fairly good whilst their old counsellors were alive. Inge and Sigurd were still children and they had one court together, but Eystein had one for himself when he was grown up. On the death of the foster-fathers of Inge and Sigurd, viz. Sada-Gyrd Bardson, Amund Gyrdson, Tjostolv Alason, Ottar Birting, Agmund Sviptir,[7] and Agmund Dengir, the brother of Erling Skakki (who was held of little worth whilst Agmund was alive), Inge and Sigurd parted their court and King Inge then got the support of Gregory, son of Dag Eilivson and Ragnhild, Skofti Agmundson's daughter. Gregory was rich and

---

1 Whitby.      2 *Skarpasker*, or 'the sharp skerries', is unidentified; probably a place on the coast of East Anglia.      3 Probably Pegwell Bay.      4 The O.N. text mentions the word *port*, which clearly refers to the Cinque Ports. Cf. also 'History of St Olav', p. 226, n. 4.      5 *Langatun* is Langton or Langston. This place is unidentified, but might refer to Langstone Harbour, near Portsmouth.      6 This remark of Snorre's evidently refers to the fact that harrying in foreign lands, especially among Christians, was going out of fashion among the Norsemen, and was beginning to be looked upon as dishonourable and lawless.      7 *Sviptir* means 'of quick movement', 'swift'.

he was the doughtiest of men. He became the leader in governing the land with King Inge, and the king allowed him to take as much as he would of his incomes.

22. King Sigurd became a very violent man and unpeaceful in all things as soon as he was grown up. And so was Eystein, though Eystein was rather more reasonable, but he was avaricious and miserly. King Sigurd was a big strong man, bold-looking, with brown hair and an ugly mouth, but otherwise good-looking in the face. He was the wisest and most able of men in speech. About him Einar Skulason says:

> Sigurd who dyed his sword
> In blood, surpassed
> All men in speech; God
> Has given him the gift.
>
> Thus when the Raumarik king
> Lifted his voice to speak,
> All other men were silent;
> The glad-spoken king got honour.

King Eystein was a swarthy, dark-haired man, a little over middle height, wise and discerning; but his power was lessened by his miserliness and avarice. He was married to Ragna, daughter of Nicholas Masi. King Inge had the fairest face; his hair was golden and somewhat thin, but very curly. He was small of build, and could scarcely walk alone, so weak was one of his feet; a twist he had on his shoulders and chest. He was gentle and friendly towards his friends, generous with his goods, and he let the chiefs have much say with him in the rule of the land and he was well liked by the common folk; through this there came to him much power and many men. King Harald Gilli's daughter hight Birgitte; she was married first to the Swedish king, Inge Hallsteinson, but afterwards to Jarl Karl Sonason, and thereafter to Magnus the Swedish king;[1] she and King Inge Haraldson had the same mother. Lastly, she was married to Jarl Birger Brosa[2] and they had four sons: Philip the Jarl,[3] Knut the Jarl, Folki and Magnus; their daughters were Ingegerd, married to Sorkvir the Swedish king[4] (their son was King John[5]), Kristin and Margaret. Maria was the name of Harald Gilli's second daughter and she was married to Simon Skalp, Halkel Huk's son, and Nicholas was the name of their son. Margaret was the name of Harald Gilli's third daughter and she was married to John Halkelson, Simon's brother. Now many things happened amongst these brothers which brought dissension. But I will only

---

1 King of Sweden (1160–1).    2 Jarl in Sweden from about 1170, died 1202.
3 *Philip* was Jarl in Norway in King Sverre's time and was slain in the year 1200.
4 King Sverker Karlson, King of Sweden (1195–1210).    5 *King John* of Sweden (1216–22).

mention that which seems to me to have been the cause of the greatest happenings.

23. Cardinal Nicholas of Rome came to Norway in the days of Harald's sons, and the Pope had sent him to Norway. The cardinal brought down his wrath upon Sigurd and Eystein and they had to

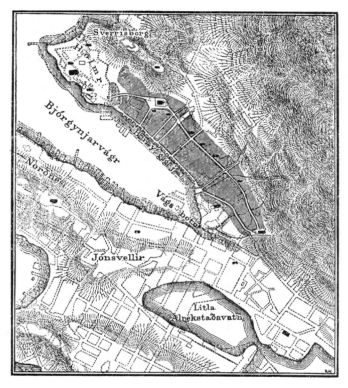

Björgyn (Bergen) in the time of Snorre

make terms with him; but he was exceedingly friendly to Inge and called him his son. And when they were all reconciled with him, he allowed them to consecrate John Birgerson as archbishop in Trondheim and gave him the vestment which is called a *pallium*, and said that there should be an archbishop's see at Nidaros in Christ Church, where St Olav rested; before that there had only been folk bishops[1] in Norway. The cardinal brought it about that no man

1 In O.N. *Lyd biskop* from O.E. *Leod bisceop.*

should carry weapons unpunished in the market towns except the twelve men who had to follow the king. He bettered men's customs in Norway in many ways whilst he was in the land. No foreigner has come to Norway whom all men set so high or who could rule the common folk so well as he did. He then went south with great gifts of friendship and promised that he would always be the Norsemen's best friend. And when he came south to Rome, he who had then been Pope suddenly died and all the folk of Rome would have Nicholas as Pope. He was then consecrated Pope with the name of Adrian.[1] So the men say who in his days went to Rome that never had he such weighty matters with other men but that he would always speak first with the Norsemen when they wanted to talk with him. He was not Pope for long; he was called 'holy'.

24. In the days of the sons of Harald Gilli it happened that a man called Haldor fell among the Vends,[2] who took him and maimed him, and cut open his throat; they drew out his tongue and cut it off at the roots. Afterwards he sought the help of St Olav, set his heart fast on the holy man, and weeping, begged King Olav to give him his speech and health. Thereupon he got his speech and he was shown mercy by the good king; he forthwith became his servant for the rest of his days and he was a lovable and true man. This miracle befell a fortnight before the Feast of St Olav on the day when Cardinal Nicholas came into the land.[3]

25. There were two brothers in the Uplands, Einar and Andres, sons of Guthorm Greybeard and uncles of King Sigurd Haraldson through their sister; they were men of good stock and wealthy, and they had in that part of the country their *odal* lands and goods. They had a sister, very fair to look upon, but not wary against the talk of evil men, as was afterwards shown. She showed much kindness to an English priest called Richard who was kept by her brothers, and she did much to please him and often she did much good for the sake of pleasing him. Then it went no better than that ugly words were said about her; afterwards it was on everybody's lips and then all men as well as her brothers blamed the priest. When they were aware of this, they said to the people that they laid the blame on the priest because of his great friendship with her. This became a great misfortune for them, as was to be expected, because they were planning secretly to revenge themselves, pre-

---

1 Cardinal Nicholas was Nicholas Breakspear. He was later Pope Adrian IV from 1154 to 1159, and being an Englishman it was a great distinction.    2 East Germans.
3 I.e. 20th July, 1152.

tending all the time that nothing had happened. One day they called the priest to them; he expected nothing but good from them. They took him from home and said that they had to go to some other lordship to do some business and bade him follow them; they had with them a man from home who knew their purpose. They went by boat along the water which is called Rand[1] and kept near the shore; they landed at a ness called Skiftasand. There they went up on land and played for some time. Next they went to a secret place and there they bade the workman strike the priest with an axe-hammer. He struck him so that he lay in a swoon. And when he came to himself he said: "Why do ye wish to handle me so hard?" They answered: "Even though no one tells thee thou shalt now find out what thou hast done". They then brought forth their complaints against him. He denied it and bade God and St Olav to settle between them. They then broke his foot; afterwards they dragged him between them to the wood and bound his hands behind his back. Then they put a cord round his head and a board under his shoulders and head; they put a stick in the cord and twisted it. Then Einar took a peg and set it over the priest's eye and his servant stood by and struck at it with his axe and struck the eye out, so that it fell down into his beard. Thereafter he put the peg over the other eye and said to the servant: "Strike less hard". He did so; the peg shot off the eyeball and tore off the eyelid. Einar then took the eyelid in his hand and held it up and saw that the eyeball was there. He then put the peg against his chin and the servant struck it, and the eyeball sprang out on to the cheek-bone where it was highest. They then opened his mouth, took his tongue, drew it out and cut it off, and at last they loosened his hands and head. As soon as he came to himself, it came about that he placed the eyeballs up in their place near the eyebrows and he held on to them with both hands as best he could. Thereafter they bore him to the ship and they went then to a garth called Sæheimrud[2] and landed there. They sent a man up to the garth to say that a priest was lying there on the shore near the ship. Whilst the man who had been sent up there was away they asked the priest if he could talk; and he wagged his tongue backwards and forwards and would try to speak. Then Einar said to his brother: "If he comes round and the tongue stump grows out, it is in my mind that he will again speak". Then with a pair of tongs they took the tongue stump, drew it out and cut twice into it, and the third time they cut into the tongue roots; they left him there half dead. Up

1 Randsfjord.    2 Unidentified.

in the garth there was a poor woman, and out she straightway came with her daughter and they bore him home in their cloaks to the house. They then went for a priest. And when he came, he bound up all his wounds and they sought to give him as much comfort as they could. The wounded priest then lay there in a pitiful plight, but he always trusted in God's mercy and never lost faith therein. Speechless he prayed to God in his thoughts and misery, and more trustfully than ever when he got worse. He turned his heart to the kind king, St Olav, the dear friend of God, and as he had heard much about his dear words he trusted so much more eagerly with all his heart in St Olav for help. But as he lay there lamed and robbed of all his strength he wept sorely and groaned, and prayed with sore heart for the dear King Olav to help him. And after midnight the wounded priest slept, and then he seemed to see a noble-looking man coming towards him and saying to him: "Badly hast thou been handled, friend Richard; I see that now thou hast no great strength". And he thought it true. Then the man said to him: "Thou art in need of mercy". The priest answered: "I am in need of the mercy of God Almighty and St Olav". He answered: "Thou shalt have it". Then he took the tongue stump and pulled it so hard that it hurt the priest. Next he stroked his hands over his eyes and his legs, as also over the other limbs which were wounded. The priest then asked who he was. He looked at him and said: "Here is Olav from the north from Trondheim". But then he disappeared and the priest awoke fully healed; and he straightway began to speak: "Blessed am I now; thanks be to God and St Olav; he has healed me". And grievously as he had been handled before, so speedily was he healed of all this misfortune, and he seemed as if he had been neither wounded nor ill; his tongue was whole, both his eyes were in their places; his broken limbs were healed, and all his other wounds were healed or free from pain, and he was in the best of health. But as a token that his eyes had been struck out he had a white scar on both eyelids, so that men could see the noble king's miracle on this man who had been so pitifully handled.[1]

26. Eystein and Sigurd were become foes because King Sigurd had slain one of King Eystein's bodyguard, Harald the Vik man, who owned a house in Bergen, and another, John Tabard the Priest,

[1] This gruesome tale shows how revengeful the Norsemen could be when something affected their honour, such as the shaming of a sister or a daughter. The story also gives a clear insight into the wonderful position which St Olav held in the imagination of the people.

son of Biarne Sigurdson. For that reason they arranged a meeting between themselves in the winter in the Uplands. They sat long in talk together. From their talk it came about that all the brothers were to meet the next summer at Bergen. In their talk they said that King Inge should have no more than two or three garths and so much other wealth that he could have thirty men about him; likewise they said that he did not seem to have good enough health to be king. Inge and Gregory learned these tidings and went to Bergen and they got many men. Sigurd came there a little later and he had much less folk. Inge and Sigurd had then been kings over Norway for nineteen winters. Eystein was longer coming from the east, from the Vik, than they were from the north. King Inge then had a thing called on the Holm,[1] and thither came the kings Sigurd and Inge with a great crowd of men. Gregory had two ships and nearly ninety men whom he kept; he kept his huscarls better than the other landed men did, for he never drank at guild feasts[2] unless all his huscarls drank with him. He donned a golden helmet as he went to the thing and his men also were helmeted. King Inge stood up and told the men what he had heard, how his brothers would treat him, and he begged their help. And all men cheered his speech well and said that they would follow him.

27. Then King Sigurd stood up and spoke. He said that what King Inge had accused them of was untrue and that Gregory had made it up; he said it would not be long, if he had his way, before Gregory should doff that golden helm; and he ended his speech by saying that Gregory and he would soon come to grips. Gregory answered and said that he hoped Sigurd had no need to wait; he said he was ready for him. A few days later one of Gregory's huscarls was slain out in the street, and one of King Sigurd's huscarls had slain him. Gregory then wished to go against Sigurd and his men. But

Queen Ingerid and Gregory counsel King Inge

1 Now Bergenhus.     2 Cf. 'History of Olav Kyrre', chapter 2.

King Inge and many others counselled him from it. And when Ingerid, King Inge's mother, went from Evensong, she came to a spot where Sigurd Skrudhyrna lay slain; he was one of King Inge's bodyguard; he was an old man and had served many kings. He had been slain by King Sigurd's men, Halvard Gunnarson and Sigurd son of Eystein Trafali, and men blamed King Sigurd for it. Ingerid then went straight to King Inge and told him of it; she said that long would he be a little king if he would not do something about it when his bodyguard were slain, one after the other, just like swine. The king was wroth at her taunting words, and whilst they were quarrelling with one another, Gregory came walking in, helmeted and brynied, and he bade the king not to be wroth and said that she spoke the truth: "I am now come to help thee, if thou wilt go against King Sigurd, and here, out in the garth, are more than a hundred men, my huscarls, helmeted and brynied, and we will attack them from the quarter the others think worst". Most of them counselled against it and said that Sigurd would be willing to atone for this misdeed. When Gregory saw that King Inge would let himself be counselled from it, he spoke to him as follows: "Thus they pluck from thee, blade by blade; but lately they slew my huscarl, and now it is thy bodyguard, and they would like to catch me or any other landed men whom they think thou wilt miss most. But they see that thou doest nothing about it, and thus they will take away thy kingship after thy friends are taken. Now whatever way the other landed men will take, I will not wait to be cut down like an ox, and this night shall Sigurd and I bargain over whatever business may befall. But thou art so ill-placed because of thy weakness and moreover I believe that thou hast little will to keep thy friends. Now I am fully ready to go to Sigurd from here, for my standard is without". King Inge then stood up and shouted for his weapons and bade everyone who would follow him make themselves ready; he said it could not avail to counsel him from it; he had long rowed away from Sigurd, but they must needs now try steel between them.

28. King Sigurd was drinking in Sigrid Sæta's garth; and he made himself ready, but thought there would be no battle. Then they went towards the garth, King Inge from above the Smidebodes[1] and Arne King's Kin from Sandbrygge,[2] Aslak Erlendson from his own garth and Gregory from the Street,[3] where it

---

1 The *Smidebodes* (or *Smithbooths*) are supposed to have been situated above Övregaten towards where the later Sverrisborg stood.    2 *Sandbrygge* (or *Sandbridge*) led from the king's grass-fields over the swampy land called Veisan, to Övregaten.    3 Övregaten.

seemed hardest. Sigurd's men shot much out of loft windows and broke up ovens and cast the stones down upon them. Gregory's men broke down the garth gate, and of King Sigurd's men Einar Laxa-Paulson fell there in the gateway and Halvard Gunnarson was shot in the loft, and over him no man sorrowed. They struck down the houses and King Sigurd's men left him and asked for quarter. King Sigurd then went up into a loft and would demand a hearing; he had a gilded shield and they recognised him but would not listen to him; and they shot at him so thickly that it looked like a snow-storm and he could not stay there. And when the men had left him and they had almost struck down the houses, he went out, and with him there went his bodyguardsman, Tord Husfröya, a Vik man; they wished to go to where King Inge was, and Sigurd called to his brother Inge to give him quarter. But they were both struck down and Tord Husfröya fell with great honour. Many of Sigurd's men fell there, even though I mention only a few, and so too did many of Inge's men, and four of Gregory's men, and likewise those who were not with any of these, but who had got in the way of the shoot-ing down on the jetties or out on the ships. They fought a fortnight before the Feast of St John the Baptist, and that was on a Friday.[1] King Sigurd was buried in the old Christ Church out on Holm.[2] King Inge gave Gregory the ship which King Sigurd had owned. Two or three nights later King Eystein came from the east with thirty ships and he had his brother's son Hacon with him on the journey; he did not go to Bergen but stayed in Floruvagar;[3] men went between them and would make terms. But Gregory wished to go out against them and said that later on it would be no better; he said that he ought to be leader this time: "and thou, king, shalt not go; there is now no shortage of men". But many men counselled against it and for that reason the journey was not made. King Eystein went east to the Vik and King Inge north to Trondheim; and they were then considered to be at peace, though they had not met.

29. Gregory Dagson[4] went east a little later than King Eystein and he was up in Havund[5] at his garth in Bratsberg.[6] King Eystein was in Oslo and he had his ships dragged up on the ice for more than two sea miles, for there was much ice in the Vik. He went up to

1 *Friday*, the 10th of June, 1155.      2 Bergenhus.      3 Now Florevaag on Asköy, west of Bergen.      4 *Dagson* is probably the same name as Dawson, in a similar way as *lag* means 'law' and *lagman* is 'lawman'. *Magi* = 'maw' and *felagi* = 'fellow'. A 'saw' is *sög* and 'roe' is *rogn* (sometimes spelt *hrogn*). Many other similarities exist between O.S. and English.      5 *Havund*, now Gjerpen district in Bratsberg.      6 East of the town of Skien.

Havund to kill Gregory; but Gregory was aware of it and went away up to Telemark with ninety men, and thereafter north over the fell and came down to Hardanger; he then went to Studla[1] in Etne, where Erling Skakki had his garth. Erling had gone north to Bergen but his wife, Kristin, King Sigurd's daughter, was at home and she bade Gregory take what he would from there; Gregory got a good welcome. He had from there a longship which Erling owned and all that he needed. Gregory thanked her well, and said that she had acted with a great mind, as he knew she would. They then went to Bergen and found Erling, who thought that she had done well.

30. Gregory Dagson then went north to Kaupang and came there before Yule. King Inge was very glad at his coming and bade him have such of his goods as he would have. King Eystein burned Gregory's garth and struck down the cattle. The boathouses which King Eystein the Elder had had laid down in Kaupang[2] and which were the noblest of buildings were burned in the winter, and with them were burned the food-ships which King Inge had. That was very ill-liked and King Eystein and Philip Gyrdson, King Sigurd's foster-brother, got the blame for that deed. The next summer Inge went south and he had a strong army; King Eystein came from the east and he, too, gathered folk to himself. They met in the Sel-isles[3] north of Lidandisnes, and King Inge had far more men; they were near coming to battle. But they came to terms and it was on the condition that King Eystein should undertake to pay five and forty marks of gold. Thirty marks of this was King Inge to have, because Eystein had counselled the burning of the ships and boat-houses, and besides, Philip was to be outlawed and so too were all those who had been at the fire when the ships were burned; those men also were to be outlawed who had taken part in the slaying of King Sigurd, for King Eystein blamed King Inge for upholding these men. Gregory was to have fifteen marks for what King Eystein had burned of his property. This was ill-pleasing to King Eystein and it seemed to him to be a forced peace. King Inge went east from the meeting to the Vik but Eystein went north to Trondheim. After this King Inge was in the Vik and King Eystein in the north and they did not meet; only such words went between them as did not bring peace, and likewise each of them caused the other's friends to be slain and there was no payment of money on Eystein's part; each

---

1 Now Stöle in Etne district (South Hordaland).    2 Cf. 'History of Sigurd the Crusader, and his brothers Eystein and Olav', chapter 26.    3 *Sel-isles* are situated on the north-west side of Lindesnes (The Naze).

of them blamed the other for not holding to what had been arranged. King Inge and Gregory drew many men away from King Eystein— Bard Standali, the son of Brynjulv, and Simon Skalp, Halkel Huk's son, and many other landed men, among them Haldor Brynjulvson and John Halkelson.

31. When two years had gone by since the fall of King Sigurd, the kings gathered their armies together—Inge from the east of the land with eighty ships, and King Eystein from the north with five and forty ships. He had the great dragon ship[1] which King Eystein Magnusson had had built after the *Long Serpent*, and he had a great and fine army. King Inge lay with his ships north of Moster[2] and King Eystein was a little farther north in Gröningasund.[3] King Eystein sent Aslak Johnson the Young and Arne Sturla, the son of Sæbjörn, south to King Inge, and they had one ship. And when Inge's men recognised them they came against them and slew many of their men, and they took the ship and all that was on board—every single thing. But Aslak and Arne and some men with them escaped on shore and they went to King Eystein and told him how King Inge had greeted them. King Eystein then called a husthing and told his men what trouble Inge and his men would make, and he bade his men follow him: "We have so good and strong an army, that I will flee nowhere if ye will follow me". But no cheer followed his words. Halkel Huk was there but both his sons Simon and John were with King Inge. Halkel answered so that many heard him: "Let thy gold chests now follow thee and let them guard thy land".

32. The night after they rowed secretly away with many ships, some to join King Inge, some to Bergen and some into the Fjords. But in the morning when it was light the king was left behind with only ten ships; he then left the great dragon behind, for it was heavy under the oars, besides several other ships, and they damaged much the dragon and likewise they emptied their ale-casks and destroyed all that they could not take with them. King Eystein went on board the ship belonging to Eindridi, John Mörnef's son, and they went north and into Sogn and from there they went east overland to the Vik. King Inge took the ships and went east in the outer lode[4] to the Vik. But King Eystein was there in the east of Fold[5] and he had nearly

---

1 Cf. 'History of Sigurd the Crusader and his brothers Eystein and Olav', chapter 26. A dragon ship in O.S. was called *dreki*, in M.S. *drake*.     2 *Moster*, now Mosteröy, an island situated in the most southern part of South Hordaland.     3 The sound situated between the Great and Little Sotraöy, by the entrance to Bergen.     4 *Lode*, or fairway. 5 The Oslofjord.

twelve hundred (fourteen hundred and forty) men. Then they saw King Inge's fleet and they thought they had not strength enough to meet them and they ran away to the woods. They all fled, every man his own way, so that the king was alone with one man. King Inge's men were aware of King Eystein's journey and they noticed likewise that he had few men; they went to look for him. Simon Skalp met him when he was coming out of a thicket towards them. Simon greeted him: "Hail, my lord!"[1] he said. The king said: "I do not know but what thou deemest thyself to be my lord". "It is now as it may happen", said Simon. The king bade him help him to escape and said that it beseemed him, "for there has been nothing but a long friendship between us two, even though it is otherwise now". Simon said that nothing could come of this now, and then the king asked if he might hear Mass first, and he was allowed that. He then lay down on his face in the grass and spread out his hands, bidding them strike him in the cross between the shoulders; he said they should prove now whether he could endure iron or not, as King Inge's friends had said. Simon spoke to the man who was chosen to kill the king and bade him go on with the deed; he said that this king had crept about in the ling long enough. He was then struck and he seemed to show himself manly thereat. His body was moved to Fors,[2] and during the night it was placed under the hill to the south of the church. King Eystein was buried in Fors Church and his body was laid in the middle of the church floor;[3] a carpet was spread over it and he was called 'holy'. There where he was struck and his blood fell on the earth a spring welled up and a second sprang up under the hill where his body had been placed in the night. From the waters of both these springs many men deem they have been healed. It is the saying of the Vikmen that many miracles happened at King Eystein's grave until his foes cast a broth made of dog-meat on the grave. Simon Skalp was much hated for this deed and many men gave him the blame. But some say that when King Eystein was taken prisoner, Simon sent a man to King Inge, and that the king bade that Eystein should not come into his sight. So has King Sverre had it written, but Einar Skulason says thus:

> Can the very evil Simon,    The king, in time to come
> Murderous man, who betrayed    Get favour for such deeds?

---

[1] The O.N. text reads: "*Heill, lavardr*". The word *lavardr* is from O.E. *hláford*, which later has become 'lord'.    [2] Probably Fors in Raumarik (mentioned in chapter 3), where St Halvard's shrine was deposited. The place is unidentified and some historians consider it to be Foss in Tunge district (Bohuslän).    [3] The O.N. word for 'floor' is *golf*.

# XVI

# THE HISTORY OF HACON BROAD-SHOULDER (1157–61)

1. Hacon, King Sigurd's son, was taken as leader of the army which before had followed King Eystein and the men gave him the name of 'king'; he was then ten winters old. There were with him then Sigurd, son of Howard Hauld of Röir[1] and Hacon's foster-brothers Andrew[2] and Anund, Simon's sons, and many other chiefs and friends of King Eystein and King Sigurd. They first went up in Gautland. King Inge then took as his own all that these men had in Norway and he made them outlaws. King Inge went north in the Vik and stayed there, but sometimes he was in the north of the land. Gregory was in Konungahella where the danger was greatest, and had with him a strong body of men, in order to guard the land.

2. The summer after, Hacon and his men came down from Gautland and went to Konungahella; they had a big, fine army. Gregory was there in the town and he called a numerous thing of bonders and townsmen and demanded their help. The folk seemed to him to show little willingness and he said that he trusted them little. He went away with two ships into the Vik and was very unhappy; he wished to meet King Inge, for he had learned that he had gone south through the Vik with a big host. But when Gregory had not gone far north, he met Simon Skalp and Haldor Brynjulvson and Gyrd Amundson, the foster-brother of King Inge. Gregory was very glad of their coming; he then turned back with them and they had eleven ships. But when they rowed up to Konungahella, Hacon and his men were holding a thing outside the town and they saw them coming. Then said Sigurd of Röir: "Now is Gregory a dead man, since he is coming into our hands with a small army". Gregory came to land just above the town and he would wait for King Inge—who was expected—but King Inge came not. King Hacon got ready in the town and he bade Torliot Skaufoskalli be leader of the men who were on the merchant ships that were lying by the town; Torliot was a viking and a robber.[3] But Hacon and

1 Now Rör in Ringsaker district (Hedemark).  2 The O.N. text in Peringskiold reads: *Andreas*, whilst in Schöning: *Andres*.  3 In O.N. *ransmaðr*, i.e. a man that harries in foreign lands.

Sigurd and the whole army were in the town and they mustered the men on the jetties. All the men there had submitted to Hacon.

3. Gregory's men rowed up along the river and let their ships drift down stream towards Torliot's ships. They shot at each other for a time until Torliot and his men leaped overboard; some were slain, but others swam ashore. Gregory's men then rowed towards the jetties and Gregory had the gangway laid from his ship close to where Hacon's men were stationed. There fell the man who bore his standard when he would go ashore. Gregory then bade Hall, son of Audun Hallson, take up the standard; he did so and bore it up on to the jetty, and Gregory walked immediately behind him and held forth a shield over his head. But as soon as Gregory came up on to the jetty and Hacon's men recognised him, they gave way and there was at once room on both sides. And when more of the host came up from the ships, Gregory and his men went forward. Hacon's men at once started retiring and then ran up into the town. But Gregory's men followed them and twice drove them out of the town, slaying many. According to what folks say, no fight was bolder than that which Gregory undertook, for Hacon had more than forty hundred (forty-eight hundred) men and Gregory had not quite four hundred (four hundred and eighty). After the battle Gregory said to Hall Audunson: "Many men seem to me doughtier in fighting than ye Icelanders, for ye have less training than we Norsemen; but no one seemed to me bolder with weapons than ye". Then King Inge came a little later and he had many men slain who had submitted to Hacon; but some he made pay fines, and for others he burned their garths, and some he drove from the land and did them much scathe. Hacon fled up to Gautland and in the winter he went north by land to Trondheim whither he came before Easter.[1] It is said that the Tronds took him as king, on condition that he should have his father's inheritance, and hold one-third of Norway, against King Inge. Inge and Gregory went into the Vik, and Gregory wished to go north against them, but many counselled against it and nothing came of it that winter.

4. In the spring Hacon went south and he had nearly thirty ships. The Vikmen in Hacon's host went beforehand with eight ships and they harried in North and South Möre. No man remembered that there had ever been any harrying before between the market towns (i.e. Bergen and Trondheim). John, son of Halkel Huk, gathered an army of bonders and went against them; he took Kolbein Odi[2] and

1 12th of April, 1159.    2 Odi, i.e. the Furious.

slew every man on his ship. He then looked for the others and found them on seven ships and fought with them. But his father Halkel did not come to meet him as they had arranged. There many good bonders fell and John himself was wounded. Hacon went south to Bergen with his army, and when they came to Stjorvelta[1] they learned that King Inge and Gregory had come a few nights before from the east to Bergen, and then they dared not stay there. They sailed outside the skerries south past Bergen and they found on three ships some of King Inge's men who were late in coming from the east. There were Gyrd Amundson, King Inge's foster-brother—he had married Gyrid, Gregory's sister—the second was the lawman Gyrd Gunhildson and the third was Howard Klining. Hacon had Gyrd Amundson and Howard Klining slain, and he took Gyrd the Lawman with him and went east to the Vik.

5. And when King Inge learned that, he went east after them and they met east by the Elv. King Inge went up the river by the north-western arm and sent spies to find out about Hacon's army. And King Inge lay to land outside by Hising and there waited for the spies. And when the spies came back they went to the king and said that they had seen King Hacon's army and all their strength: they lay up by the piles and had fastened their stems to the piles; they had two east-going trading ships and they had put these outside all the ships; on these ships there were *hun-kasteller*[2] in the stems of both. And when the king had learned what strength they had, he had the whole army called to a husthing. When the thing assembled, the king sought counsel with his men; he spoke to Gregory Dagson and to his kinsman Erling Skakki and the other landed men and the ship captains and told them of Hacon's army. Gregory answered first and made known his wishes; he said: "There have been some meetings between us and Hacon, and most often has he had more men, but he has always fallen short in his dealings with us. But now we have a much greater army and it will be thought fitting by the men who have lately lost their noble kinsmen that here will be an opportunity to take vengeance, for they have now for a long time been escaping us in the summer; we have often said that if they waited for us, even as it is now told us that they do, then we would risk a meeting with them. Now it may be said of my mind that I wish to come to battle with them, unless it is against the king's wish, for I still think that, as it happened before, they will

1 *Stjorvelta* or *Stjornvelta* is in Hordaland, north of Bergen.  2 *Hun-kasteller* or castles were built in the stem (or forecastle) where the men could throw stones and other missiles.

turn away if we go boldly forth. I will lay to where others think it is most perilous". Gregory's speech was loudly cheered and all said they were ready to go to battle with Hacon and his men. They then rowed with all their ships up along the river until both armies saw each other; King Inge's men then turned from the river stream out under the island. The king had a talk with all the leaders and he bade them keep themselves in readiness to go against the enemy; he spoke to Erling Skakki and said as was true that no man in the army was wiser or more skilled in war, even though some might be more aggressive. The king also turned in his speech to other landed men and mentioned some by name. He ended his speech by bidding each set forth the counsel which he thought of most gain, and after that all should act together.

6. Erling Skakki answered the king's speech: "I am bound, O king, to answer your speech, but if you will know what my counsel might be I will let you hear it. The plan which is now before us is against my mind, for I call it a bad plan for us to fight against them under these conditions, even though we have a big, fair army. If we go towards them and row up against the stream, where there are three men on each half-bench then must one row and the second shield him; that means that only a third of our army will go to battle. It seems to me that they will be badly off who sit at the oars and turn their backs to their foes. Give me time to take counsel and in return I promise to find such a plan ere three days are passed whereby we can come into battle with advantage". And they noted well in Erling's speech that he counselled against falling to; but no less did many others urge it, thinking that Hacon's men would leap up on land just as before; "and then we have none of them", they said; "now they have a small army and we have them altogether in our power". Gregory spoke but few words and objected that Erling's weightiest grounds for counselling against the onset were rather that he wished to make that plan useless that Gregory had brought forward, not that he had a better understanding of the position.

7. King Inge said then to Erling: "Brother-in-law, we will now follow thy counsel as to how we shall draw up for the attack; but since our counsellors rather wish it, we shall attack them to-day". Then said Erling: "All the cutters and light ships shall row outside round the island and up the eastern arm of the river and then down towards them; and they shall try if they can loosen them from the piles. Then we shall row the big ships up against them. But we shall not know—until it is proved—whether our leaders who are so eager

for fighting, will attack better than I ". All were well pleased with this counsel. A ness was between them and Hacon's army, and they could not see each other from the ships. But when the cutter fleet rowed up along the river Hacon's men saw them, and they had already been in talk and had held counsel; some thought that King Inge's men would attack, but many believed that they were not risking it when they seemed so slow in coming. They trusted much to their outfit and numbers. In their host there were many great men; there was Sigurd of Röir and the two sons of Simon, Andrew and Anund; there were also Nicholas Skjaldvorson and Eindridi, John Mörnef's son, who was then the most renowned and best befriended man in the Trondlaw; there were many other landed men and troop leaders. But when they saw Inge's men rowing out along the river with many ships, Hacon's men believed that Inge's army would flee; they struck the cables from the ships, seized their oars and rowed after them and would follow them. The ships went quickly down the stream, and when they came down the river past the ness which had been in front of them, they saw that Inge's main force was lying off the island of Hising. Inge's men then saw where Hacon's ships were going and they thought they would attack them. There was much ado and dashing of weapons and egging on, and they set up their war cry. But Hacon's men turned their ships towards the northern bank where there was a creek, and thus they got out of the stream. There they made themselves ready; they fastened the stern cables to the land, turning the prows outward; they bound all the ships together, and put the east-faring ships outside the other ships; one above, the other below, and they bound them fast to the longships. And in the middle of the fleet was the king's ship and next to it was Sigurd's ship, whilst on the other side was Nicholas and next to him was Eindridi Johnson. All the lesser ships lay farther out; they had almost filled all their ships with stones and weapons.

8. Sigurd of Röir spoke and said: "It is to be expected that it will now come about as we have been promised for a long time this summer that we shall meet King Inge; we too have for a long while been getting ready for them, and many of our men have said great things about them not wavering or fleeing before King Inge and Gregory, and it is good now to remember those words; but we who have been somewhat hurt in our dealings together can speak with less assurance; so it is, as everybody has heard, that we have very often done journeys of ill-hap on account of them. None the

less it is needful to make as manly an opposition as we can, and to stand as fast as we can, for the only escape we have is to win the victory. But even though we have somewhat fewer men than they, yet may fate, however, decide who shall win the victory and it is our best hope that God knows we have the most right. Inge has hitherto cut down two of his brothers; and every man can see what deserts he will grant King Hacon. He will strike him down like his other kinsmen, and it will be seen this day. Hacon in the beginning demanded no more than one-third which his father had and it was denied him. But according to my mind Hacon has a better right to take the inheritance after his uncle Eystein than Inge or Simon Skalp or the other men who took King Eystein's life. Many of those who would save their souls and had done such great wrongs as Inge would find it well not to dare before God to be called 'king'; I wonder that God suffers such boldness from him, and it is the will of God that we hurl him down. Let us fight boldly, for God will give us the victory. And if we fall, then He will give us manifold joys if He gives evil men the might to overrun us. Go forth now with set purpose and let us not lose courage when battle comes. Let each watch himself and his neighbours, and may God watch us all''. A great cheer was made at Sigurd's speech and all promised well to hold out. King Hacon went up into the east-faring ships and a wall of shields was set around him; but his standard was on the longship on which he had been before.

9. Now we must tell of Inge's men; when they saw that Hacon's men were making ready to fight—there was only the river between them—they sent a fast cutter out after that part of the army which had rowed away with word that they should turn back; the king and the whole army waited for them and they put their ranks in order to attack. The leaders then talked and told the army their intentions, first, which ships should be nearest and then where each ship should attack. Gregory said: "We have a big, fine army. Now it is my counsel, king, that you shall not be in the fight, for then everything is watched where you are and no one knows where a stray arrow may do injury. They have such an array that from the hun-kasteller on the merchant ships stones will be cast and shot down, and then there is little risk for those who stand farther off. They have no big army, and it is the wish of us landed men to hold battle with them. I will take my ship against the biggest of theirs, and I expect besides that it will be but a short trial to fight with them. So has it often happened at our meetings, even though the odds have been on the other side up

till now". All were well pleased with what Gregory said, that the king himself should not be in the battle. Then said Erling Skakki: "I will support the counsel, king, that you go not into battle. I see from their array that we shall need to watch ourselves well, if we are not to get a great loss of men. To me it seems 'best to bind up all our limbs'. Many spoke against the plan which we brought up before to-day and they said that I would not fight, but it seems to me that things have turned out lucky for us, since they are now away from the piles. It has gone so far that I will not any longer counsel against battle, for I see, as everybody knows, how necessary it is to drive off this evil troop which has overrun the land with rape and robbery, so that hereafter men can live in the land in peace and serve one king, and a king who is so good and righteous as King Inge is. Long has he had toil and trouble from the haughtiness and unrighteousness of his kinsmen; he has been a protection to the whole people and put himself into manifold perils to give peace to the land". Many wise things did Erling say, as did other chiefs, and they all ended in the same way, by egging them on to attack. They waited until all their army had come together. King Inge had the *Beykisudin*[1] and he submitted to the prayers of his friends that he should not go into battle but stay behind off the island.

10. Now when the armies were ready, they bade them row forward and both hosts set up their war cry. Inge's men did not lash their ships together and went not in a line, for they were rowing across the stream and the big ships were drifting down-stream. Erling Skakki went up to King Hacon's ship and struck his prow between it and Sigurd's ship. Then the battle began. Gregory's ship went aground and heeled over much, so that in the beginning it came not into the battle. And when Hacon's men saw that, they went up to them and fell to; but Gregory's ship stood fast. Then Ivor, son of Hacon Magi, came up and the sterns drifted towards each other. Ivor hooked a grapnel round Gregory and pulled at him, and Gregory tottered towards the railings but the grapnel slid past him; he had nearly hauled Gregory overboard. Gregory was little wounded, for he had on a plate-brynie. Ivor shouted to him and said that he had thick clothing on. Gregory answered that after this hard dealing he needed it, and he had not any too much on. Gregory and his men were almost forced overboard till Aslak the Young cast an anchor into their ship and dragged them off the ground.

1 This was the name of King Inge's ship. *Beyki* or *Bæki* is O.N. for 'beech', of which material the vessel was probably built.

Gregory then lay to by Ivor's ship and they now fought for a long while. Gregory's ship was bigger and had more men; many men now fell on Ivor's ship and some leaped overboard. Ivor was sorely wounded, so that he could not fight. But when his ship was cleared, Gregory let him get ashore, and helped him to escape. They were friends after that.

11. And when King Inge and his men saw that Gregory had run aground, the king called to his men to row to him. He said: "It was the unwisest counsel that we should stay behind here whilst our friends went to battle; we have the biggest and best-manned ship of the whole army. Now I see that Gregory needs help—the man whom I thought to reward most—and let us now go to battle as hard as we can. It is also most right that I should be in the fight, for I will have the victory for myself if it is won. But even if I knew before that our men would not get the victory, it was the only thing for us to be there where our other men are, for I shall be able to achieve nothing if I lose the men who are my protection and who are the boldest and have long been rulers for me and my kingdom". He then bade them set up his standard. This was done, and they rowed across the river. Then the fight was at its hottest and the king got no room for manœuvring, so close were the ships lying. They came up to the east-faring boats, and spears and poles and such big stones were thrown at them that no one could hold out and they could not stay there. And when the warriors saw that the king was come they made room for him and he then attacked Eindridi Johnson's ship. Hacon's men now went from the small ships up on to the east-faring ships, but some ran ashore. Erling Skakki and his men had a hard fight. Erling was in the forehold shouting to his stem men and bidding them board the king's ship. They answered that it was not easy, and that there were iron spikes on top of the railings. Erling then went forth into the stem and he had not been there long before they boarded the king's ship and cleared it. Then the whole army began to flee; thereafter many leaped into the sea, many fell, and a great crowd ran ashore. Thus sayeth Einar Skulason:

Many fell in the water
From the ships' stems,
There the wolf got food;
The bodies floated down-stream.
The icy cold river was dyed
In the hot blood;
The warm blood poured
With the water out to the sea.

In the strife floated many
Blood-stained ships; arrows
Were bent; and red swords
Were sent against the wet helmets.
Inside from the sea steeds
The chieftains' army fled
To land; Hacon's following
Grew few in number in the fight.

About Gregory Dagson, Einar composed the flokk which is called "Elv Verses".[1] King Inge gave Nicholas Skjaldvorson quarter when his ship was cleared and he then went to King Inge and was with him as long as he lived. Eindridi Johnson leaped up on to King Inge's ship when his ship was cleared and asked for quarter for himself. The king wished to give him quarter, but Howard Klining's son ran up and struck Eindridi a death blow, and that deed was much blamed. But he said that Eindridi had planned the slaying of his father, Howard. Eindridi was much mourned and most of all in Trondlaw. Many of Hacon's men had fallen there, but not many leaders; of Inge's men few had fallen but many were wounded. Hacon fled inland, and Inge went north with his army to the Vik; he and Gregory were in the Vik in the winter. When King Inge's men—Bergliot and his brothers, the sons of Ivor of Elda[2]—came to Bergen from the battle, they slew Nicholas Skegg who had been Hacon's sheriff and then went home to Trondheim. Hacon came north before Yule, but Sigurd was sometimes at home in Röir. Gregory had got quarter for him from King Inge so that he should have all his possessions, for Gregory and Sigurd were near kinsmen. King Hacon was in Kaupang through Yule, and one evening in Yuletide his men fought with each other in the guardsmen's quarters; eight were killed and many wounded. After the eighth day of Yule Alf Red, son of Ottar Birting, and nearly eighty of Hacon's men went into Elda and came there suddenly at the beginning of the night when the men were drunk, and set fire to the room. But they came out and defended themselves. There Bergliot Ivorson and his brother Agmund and many others fell. Nearly thirty men had been inside. In the winter in the north in Kaupang Andrew Simonson, King Hacon's foster-brother, died and he was much mourned. Erling Skakki and King Inge's men, who were in Bergen, once or twice let it seem as if they would go north and fight King Hacon, but nothing came of it. Gregory sent word from Konungahella in the east that, if he were as near to Hacon as were Erling and his men, he would not sit quietly in Bergen when Hacon was having King Inge's friends and their brother-counsellors slain in Trondheim.

12. King Inge and Gregory went west in the spring to Bergen. And as soon as Hacon and Sigurd learned that King Inge had left the Vik, they went east by the land-ways to the Vik. But when King

---

1 I.e. poems describing the battle at the Elv (= Göta River).  2 *Elda*, at the Nauma-daleseid (between Naumadale and Beitstadfjord).

Inge and his men came to Bergen, strife arose between Haldor
Brynjulvson and Björn Nicholson. Björn's[1] huscarl had asked
Haldor's huscarl one day when they met down on the jetties why
the other was so pale, and he said that he had been bled. "I would
not be so pale in the face as thou art through blood-letting."
"I think", said the other, "that thou wouldst take it much worse and
still less manfully." And there was no greater cause of the trouble
than that one word followed another until they quarrelled and

King Inge makes peace between Erling Skakki and Gregory

fought. It was then told Haldor Brynjulvson that his huscarl had
been wounded on the jetty; Haldor was drinking in the garth near
by and he then went down to the jetty. But Björn's huscarls had
already come and Haldor thought that they had managed the matter
unfairly, and his men pushed Björn's huscarls and struck them.
Then Björn Buck was told that the Vikmen were beating his
huscarls down on the jetty. Björn and his men then took their
weapons and went to avenge their men, and they now began
fighting. Then it was told Gregory that Haldor, his brother-in-law,
needed help and that his huscarls were being struck down out in the
street; Gregory and his men hurried into their brynies and went out.
Erling Skakki then heard that Björn, his sister's son, was fighting

1 Cf. p. 428, n. 1, about the name *Björn*.

with Haldor and Gregory on the jetty and needed help. Erling went and took many men with him and called every man to help them; "it is a shame on the folk here", he said, "if a Vikman shall overrun us here in the homes of our kinsmen; it would ever and always be brought up against us". Thirteen men fell there and nine of them died straight away; four died afterwards of their wounds, and many others were wounded. Word then came to King Inge that Gregory and Erling were fighting on the jetty and he went out to part them, but he could do nothing, for they were both so heated. Gregory then shouted to King Inge and bade him go away; he said he could do nothing under these circumstances, "it would be the greatest misfortune if he comes to harm, for somebody might commit an ill-deed and do him harm, if he got the chance". Then the king went away. And when the worst of the battle was over Gregory and his men went up to St Nicholas' Church, and Erling and his men went after them and they were shouting at each other. King Inge then came a second time and reconciled them; they both wished that he alone should decide between them. They then learned that Hacon was in the Vik, and King Inge and Gregory went east; they had many ships. And when they came to the east, Hacon and his men turned away and there was no battle. King Inge then went into Oslo and Gregory was in Konungahella.

13. Gregory heard a little later that King Hacon and his men were at a place called Saurbær,[1] up in the wood settlements. He went thither and came there in the night; he thought that Hacon and Sigurd might well be in the biggest garth and he set fire to the houses. Hacon and Sigurd were in the smallest garth; they came up to where they saw the fire and would help their men. There fell Munan, son of Ali Oskeins, and brother of Hacon's father, King Sigurd; Gregory's men slew him as soon as he would help those who were being burned inside the house; they came out and many men were slain. Asbiorn Jalda escaped from the garth; he was the worst of vikings and he was wounded. A bonder met him, and Asbiorn bade the bonder let him get away, saying that he would give him money for it. The bonder said that he would do that for which he had a greater desire, when he had often gone in fear of Asbiorn; he struck him his death blow. Hacon and Sigurd escaped but many of their men were slain. Thereafter Gregory went east to Konungahella. A little later Hacon and Sigurd went to Haldor Brynjulvson's

1 Now Sörbygden in North Bohuslän (Sweden).

garth in Vettaland[1] and set fire to the houses and burned them.
Haldor went out and was at once struck down, and so were his
huscarls; nearly twenty men in all were slain. Sigrid, his wife, was
Gregory's sister; they let her go away to the woods in her nightdress
only. They seized Amund, son of Gyrd Amundson and Gyrid
Dag's daughter, Gregory's sister's son, and took him with them; he
was then five years old.

14. Gregory heard of these happenings which he thought
serious and asked carefully where they had befallen. He then went
at the end of Yuletide with a great army and he came to Fors[2] on the
thirteenth day of Yule.[3] He was there during the night and on the
last day of Yule he went to Matins[4] and the gospel was afterwards
read to him; that was on a Saturday. And when Gregory and his
men saw Hacon's army it seemed much less than their own. There
was a river between them where they met and it was called the
Befja;[5] there was thin ice on the river, for the tide came up under
the ice from outside. Hacon's men had struck gaps in the ice and
had shovelled snow over so that the gaps could not be seen. When
Gregory came to the river he spoke and said that the ice seemed
poor and it was best for them to go to the bridge which was a little
farther up the river. The bonders answered and said that they did not
understand why he dared not attack them over the ice, no greater
host being against them; they thought that the ice was very good and
said that his luck might be out. Gregory answered and said that
seldom had they any need to blame him for fear, and no man should
do so either, hereafter. He bade them follow him closely and not
stand behind when he went out on the ice; it was their wish that
he should go out on thin ice and he did not want to do so; "but I
do not wish to hear your taunts", he said, and bade his standard
be borne forward. He then went out on the ice with his army, but
as soon as the bonders found that the ice was thin they turned back.
Gregory sank in the ice but not far. He bade his men take care of
themselves, but scarcely twenty men followed him; the others had
turned back. A man in Hacon's army shot an arrow at Gregory and it
struck him in the throat. Gregory fell and so did ten men with him,
and here ends the story of his life. And it is the talk of all men that he
had been the greatest chief amongst the landed men in Norway in the
days of those men who were then alive, and that he had been the best

---

1 Cf. 'History of St Olav', p. 263.    2 Now Fossum by the town of Uddevalla
(Sweden).    3 6th of January.    4 7th of January.    5 *Befja,* now Bäfeaan, at the
mouth of which Uddevalla is situated.

friend to us Icelanders since King Eystein the Elder died. Gregory's
body was brought up to Havund[1] and buried in Gimsöy[2] near the
nunnery there. Gregory's sister, Baugeid, was then the abbess.

15. Two stewards went to Oslo to tell King Inge these tidings;
and when they came there, they craved speech with the king. He
asked what tidings they brought. "The death of Gregory Dagson",
they said. "How did such ill befall?" asked the king. They told
him. The king answered: "Then they counselled who knew least".
It is said that he took it so badly that he wept like a child. But when
it passed off he said: "I would have gone to Gregory as soon as I
heard of the slaying of Haldor, for I think I know that Gregory
would not sit long without wishing to seek vengeance, but the folk
here went on as if nothing was so needful as this Yule drink and
as if it could not be interrupted; for I certainly know that if I had
been there things would have been done with better counsel or else
Gregory and I would have both gone to one banquet. The man is
fallen who has been the best friend to me and who has most helped
to keep the land in my hands. I did believe all the time that there
was only a short while between us. Now I shall promise this: I will
go to meet Hacon and his men, and one of two things shall happen: I
shall come to my death or else I will walk over Hacon and his men.
And even if they all come to harm, such a man as Gregory was could
not be fully avenged". A man answered and said that there would be
little need to seek them; "they intended to come against him".
Kristin, King Sigurd's daughter and King Inge's cousin, was there in
Oslo. The king learned that she would go away from the town and he
sent word to her asking why she would leave the town. She answered
that she thought it perilous and it was not meet for women to be here.
The king bade her not go away: "If we win the victory, as I think,
then thou wilt be well kept here; and if I fall my friends may not get
leave to lay out my body; thou shalt beg that leave be given thee to
lay out my body, and therewith mayest thou best reward me for
having been good to thee".

16. Towards evening on the Feast of St Blasius[3] word came to
King Inge that Hacon was being expected in the town. King Inge
then had the army summoned up from the town and drawn up in
lines and they were reckoned to be nigh on forty hundred (forty-
eight hundred) men. The king let the line be long and no more than
five deep. Then men told the king that he should not be in the battle

---

1 Cf. 'History of Sigurd, Inge, and Eystein', p. 687, n. 6.   2 *Gimsöy*, near the town
of Skien.   3 3rd of February, 1161.

and said that they laid great weight on his life; "let thy brother Orm be leader of the army". The king answered: "I believe that if Gregory were alive and were here now, and if I were fallen, he would avenge me; he would not lie in hiding but would himself be in the battle. Even though I am less doughty through my infirmity than he was, I shall show no less determination than he; it is not to be expected that I shall not be in the battle". Men say that Gunhild, whom Simon had to wife, King Hacon's foster-mother, had magic worked for Hacon's victory, and that the answer she got was that they should fight against King Inge in the night but never in the day-time, and then all would go well with them. Tordis Seggia was mentioned as the woman who, it is said, sat out working the magic,[1] but I know not if it is true. Simon Skalp had gone to the town and laid himself down to sleep; he woke up with the war cries. But as the night passed, word came to King Inge and he was told that Hacon and his men were then coming in over the ice,[2] and there was ice from the town right out to Hovedöy.[3]

17. King Inge went out with his army on the ice and drew up his lines outside the town. Simon Skalp was in the arm which stretched out towards Trælaberg,[4] and in the arm which was in front of Nonneseter[5] were Gudröd, Olav Bitling's[6] son, King of the Hebrides, and John, son of Swein, son of Bergthor Buck. And when Hacon's men came towards King Inge's line both armies shouted their war cry. Gudröd and John made signs to Hacon's men to let them know where they stood. Hacon's men then turned thither, and Gudröd's army straightway fled; there might have been

---

1 To 'sit out', in O.N. *sitia uti*, was the expression used for troll women or witches, who carried on their witchcraft outside in the night, in order to wake up the witches or trolls. 2 I.e. over Bundefjord and between the islands.   3 South of the town.   4 By Ekeberg and the present Grönlien.   5 *Nonneseter*, or cloister at Leiret, at present No. 73 in Oslo Gate.   6 *Olav Bitling* was a younger brother of Lagman; cf. 'History of Magnus Barefoot', chapter 10. Olav was King of the Hebrides from 1113 to 1153 and Gudröd from 1154 to 1187. Olav Bitling's daughter was married to Sumarlide or Sorle of Argyle, who became the founder of the dynasty known as Lord of the Isles. The chief seat of the Norse lords in the Hebrides was the island of Colonsay. The Norse King Hacon Haconson invaded Scotland in 1263 and fought the Scots at the battle of Largs. The battle was indecisive and Hacon retired to Kirkwall where he died the same winter. His son Magnus made peace with the Scots in 1266 and ceded the Hebrides and Isle of Man to the Scottish king Alexander, who agreed to pay the sum of 4000 marks in four yearly payments. The money was never paid. Magnus retained however the Orkneys and Shetland. The race of Sumarlide (Sorle of Argyle) continued to rule the Hebrides. From a younger son of Sumarlide sprang the first Lords of Lorne, who took the patronymic of Macdougall. John Macdonald of the Isle of Isla was the first to adopt the title of Lord of the Isles.

nearly fifteen hundred (eighteen hundred) men there. But John and a great troop with him ran over to Hacon's army and fought on their side. This was told King Inge, who answered: "A great difference is there between my friends; never would Gregory have done this whilst he was alive". They then bade the king that they should set him on horseback so that he could ride from the battle up into Raumarik; "there wilt thou get folk enough at once to-day". "I have no wish to do that", said the king; "often have I heard you say—and it seems to me true—that my brother King Eystein had little luck after he fled and he was well endowed with all that beseems a king. Now I can see how little luck I shall have, as I am infirm, if I do the same which was so unlucky for him, since there is so great a difference between our activity in health and strength of mind. I was in my second year when I was made king in Norway, but now I am over five and twenty. It seems to me that in my kingship I have had difficulties and perils rather than gladness and rest. I have had many battles, sometimes against more men, sometimes against fewer, and it has always been my good fortune that I have never yet fled; God may decide how long I shall live, but never shall I turn in flight".

18. Now as John and his men had broken the one arm of King Inge's line, many of those who had stood near by also fled. And then the whole line was broken and fell into disorder; but Hacon's men now came fast forward—it was drawing near dawn—and they made for King Inge's standard. In that strife King Inge fell but his brother Orm kept up the fight. Many men then fled up into the town. Orm went twice into the town after the king's fall and egged on the men, and both times he went out on to the ice and kept up the fight. Then Hacon's men went against the arm of the line which Simon Skalp commanded in that fight; there fell in Inge's army Gudbrand Skavhoggson, the king's kinsman. But Simon Skalp and Halvard Hikri went against each other and fought with their troops and they advanced past Trælaberg; in that strife both Simon and Halvard fell. Orm King's Brother got good praise there, and he fled last. The winter before, Orm had been betrothed to Ragna, daughter of Nicholas Masi, whom King Eystein Haraldson had had, and he was to hold his wedding the Sunday after;[1] the Feast of St Blasius was on a Friday. Orm fled east to Sweden to his brother Magnus,[2] who was then king there; Ragnvald,

---

1 *Sunday*, the 5th of February, 1161.  2 *Magnus* Heinrekson was King of Sweden from 1160 to 1161.

their brother, was a jarl there. They were the sons of Ingerid and Heinrek Halti;[1] he was the son of Swein, son of Swein the Danish king. Kristin King's Daughter attended to King Inge's body and it was laid in the stone wall of Halvard's Church outside the choir on the south side; he had then been king for twenty-five years. In that battle many men had fallen in both armies, but most of them in Inge's army. Arne Fridrekson fell in Inge's army. Hacon's men took all that was prepared for the wedding and much other booty.

19. King Hacon subdued the whole land and set his men in the shires and likewise over the market towns. King Hacon and his men held their meetings in Halvard's Church when they took counsel about the rule of the land. Kristin King's Daughter gave money to the priest, who had to take care of the church keys, to hide one of her men in the church so that he could overhear the talk of Hacon and his men. And when she became aware of what they had agreed upon she sent word to Bergen to her husband Erling Skakki, that he must never trust them.

20. It befell in Greece when King Kyrialax[2] ruled there that the king went on an expedition to Rumania. And when he came upon the fields of Pezina[3] a heathen king came against him with a mighty host. They had taken with them cavalry and very big waggons and on these were battlements. And when they made themselves ready for night quarters they drew the waggons up next to each other outside their war booths, and outside them they dug a great ditch. Altogether it was as great a protection as if it were a castle. The heathen king was blind. And when the Greek king came, the heathens drew up their lines on the fields in front of their waggon fortifications. The Greeks placed their line against them and they both rode towards each other and fought. It went badly and with ill-hap; the Greeks fled and had a great loss of men and the heathens got the victory. The king then drew up a line of Franks and Flemings, and afterwards they rode forth against the heathens and fought with them; it fared with them as before and many were slain and all who could escape fled. The Greek king was very wroth with his warriors, and they answered him and bade him take to the Værings,[4] his

1 *Heinrek* (died 1134) had been married to Ingerid before she married King Harald Gilli.    2 *Kyrialax* is the contracted pronunciation, which the Norsemen used for the Greek Kurios Alexios, the lord Alexios (Komnenos).    3 *Pezina* by the river Danube.
4 *Værings* were the Scandinavian warriors in the service of the Greek emperors. Cf. 'History of Harald Hardrade', chapters 3 and 4. They formed the emperor's bodyguard. Ordericus Vitalis writes in reference to the discontent, after the Conquest, of the Norse element in the north of England as follows: "Some, the very flower of

winebags. The king said that he would not spoil his best men in such a way as to lead so few men against so great a host, even though they were bold. Then Tore Helsing, who was leader of the Værings, answered the king's words: "Even if it were a flaming fire against us I and my men would straightway run into it if I knew that we could thereby get peace for thee hereafter, king". But the king answered: "Make vows to St Olav, your king, for help and victory". The Værings had four and a half hundred (five hundred and forty) men. They made a vow by hand-shaking to build a church in Mikle-garth[1] at their own cost and with the help of good men and to have the church hallowed to the honour and glory of St Olav. The Værings then rushed forth on the field. And when the heathens saw that, they said to their king that once again a troop of the Greek king's army was coming, "and it is but a handful of men", they said. Then the king answered: "Who is the noble-looking man who rides there on the white horse in front of their troop?" "We see him not", they said. The odds were so great that there were sixty heathens to one Christian, but none the less the Værings went boldly into battle. And as soon as the battle started fright and fear fell on the heathens' army so that they straightway began to flee and the Værings pursued them and soon slew a great number. And when the Greeks and Franks who had fled before the heathens saw that, they went forth and followed the fleeing heathens with the Værings. Then the Værings had come up to the waggon fortifications and there was the greatest fall of men. When the heathens fled the heathen king was taken prisoner and the Værings took him with them. The Christian men then took the heathen men's war booths and waggon fortifications.

21. It happened at the battle of Stiklastader which has been written about before ('History of St Olav', chapter 228), that King Olav had cast from him his sword *Hneitir*, when he got his wound. But a man, a Swede by birth, had broken his own sword and he then took up the sword Hneitir and fought with it. And the man escaped from the battle and went away with the others who fled; he came to Sweden and went home to his garth. He kept the sword all his life and after him his son, and so one after the other of his kinsmen took it, and with the possession of the sword it always followed that the one told the next the sword's name and likewise where it had come from.

English youth, made their way to distant regions and served valiantly in the armies of Alexios, Emperor of Constantinople". Greek writers state that finally the Værings became exclusively English.　1 I.e. Constantinople.

It happened a long time afterwards, when Kyrialax was emperor in Miklegarth, that there were great troops of Værings in the king's garth,[1] and one summer the emperor was out warring, and they lay in war booths. The Værings were keeping guard and watching over the king; they lay in the fields outside the war booths; they shared the night between them to watch and they who had already watched lay down thereafter and slept. They were all fully weaponed. It was their custom when they lay down to sleep that each of them had his helm on his head, his shield over him and his sword under his head and each was to keep his right hand on the sword handle. One of them, who had drawn the lot to keep guard the last part of the night, woke up at dawn, but his sword was gone; and when he looked for it he saw his sword lying in the field a long way from him. He stood up and took the sword; he believed that his comrades, who had kept watch, might well have done it to him as mockery, to steal the sword from him. They denied it. The same thing happened for three nights. Then he himself wondered much thereat, and so did the others who saw or heard it, and they asked what the reason for it was. He then said that the sword was called Hneitir and that St Olav had owned it and had himself borne it in the battle of Stiklastader; he also told what had afterwards become of the sword. This was then told to King Kyrialax. He had the man who went with the sword called to him and gave him three times as much gold as the sword was worth. And the king had the sword carried to St Olav's Church which the Værings kept, and it was afterwards there above the altar. Eindridi the Young was in Miklegarth when this happened; he told this story in Norway just as Einar Skulason bears witness in the drapa[2] which was composed about St Olav; there is this happening related.

1 I.e. the emperor's residence at Constantinople.    2 This refers to Einar Skulason's epic poem *Geisli*. Einar was born in Iceland about 1090 and descended from the great scald Egil Skallagrimson who lived at the time of King Harald Hairfair and King Athelstan. Egil fought with many Norsemen on the side of Athelstan at the battle of Brunanburgh in 938. Cf. further 'History of Hacon the Good', p. 80 in footnote. Einar Skulason solemnly recited *Geisli* in Trondheim Cathedral in the presence of three kings (Sigurd, Inge and Eystein) and of the first Archbishop of Norway, on the 29th of July (St Olav's Day) in 1153. This was a unique honour for the scald. *Geisli* can be found in O.N. and Danish in Schöning's translation of *Heimskringla* (Copenhagen, 1777).

# XVII

# THE HISTORY OF MAGNUS ERLINGSON

## (1161–77)[1]

1. Erling[2] had now got to know what counsel Hacon's men had taken, and he then sent word to all the chiefs whom he knew to have been true friends of King Inge and likewise to King Inge's bodyguard and sworn men who had escaped and to Gregory's huscarls, and he bade them come to a meeting. And when they met and held talk together they straightway agreed they should keep the troop together and they bound it between themselves. They then spoke as to whom they should take as king. Erling Skakki then spoke and asked if it was the counsel of the leaders and other great men that Simon Skalp's son, that is, Harald Gilli's daughter's son, be taken as king and that John Halkelson be leader of the army. John excused himself. They then asked Nicholas Skjaldvorson, King Magnus Barefoot's sister's son, if he would be leader of the army. He answered in this wise, that it was his counsel that they should take him as king who was of royal stock, and take him as leader of the army who could be expected to understand it; they would then be better off for getting help. Then they asked Arne King's Kin[3] if he would let them take as king one of his sons, King Inge's brothers. He answered that Kristin's son, King Sigurd the Crusader's daughter's son, had the best birth-right to be king in Norway; "there is", he said, "the man to rule for him who is bound to take the greatest care of him and the kingdom, namely, his father Erling, a wise and strong-minded man, well tried in battle and a good land ruler; he will not be short of success in this plan if good luck goes with it". Many were eager for this plan. Erling answered: "As far as I can see, most of those who have been asked will rather avoid taking upon themselves this difficult position. Now it seems to me likewise uncertain whether he who takes up this matter and puts

---

1 Snorre Sturlason's *Heimskringla* ends with the year 1177; but Magnus Erlingson reigned until 1184.    2 In the English chronicles the name Erling has sometimes become Irling. Urling or Yrling is still a surname in England. Arling and Arlington are possibly connected with the name. In the west of Norway Erling is often pronounced as Arling.    3 *Arne* of Stodreim married King Inge's mother Ingerid and was therefore Inge's step-father. In O.N. Arne is called *Konungs-magr*. Cf. further 'History of Sigurd, Inge and Eystein', chapter 16. *Magr* is a general term for father-in-law, brother-in-law, son-in-law, step-father, etc.

himself at the head of the army will have kingly power or if it will go the way that it has happened with many who have taken up such great plans, that they have lost all their possessions and their lives withal. But if this plan succeeds, it may be that there will be some who will then wish they had taken this offer. He who takes on himself this difficult task may need to keep a firm hand on these men, so that he will be strong against the opposition and enmity of those who now agree to this counsel". All promised to abide by this agreement. Erling said: "I may say of myself that I think it almost my death to serve Hacon, and although I think this plan is full of risk, yet I will rather let you decide; I will command the army if it is the counsel and wish of all of you, and you will all make it binding with oaths". All promised to do so, and at the meeting it was arranged that they should take Magnus Erlingson as king. They afterwards held a thing in the town and at that thing Magnus was taken as king over the whole land. He was then five years old. All the men who were there and who had been King Inge's liegemen submitted to him, and each of them had such rank as he had formerly had with King Inge.

2. Erling Skakki made himself ready for a journey and got himself ships; he took King Magnus with him and all the liegemen who were there. On that journey there were Arne King's Kin[1] and King Inge's mother Ingerid with her two sons, and John Kurteisa, Sigurd Stork's son, Erling's huscarls and likewise those who had been huscarls of Gregory; they had ten ships in all. They went south to Denmark to King Valdemar and Buris Heinrekson, King Inge's brother. King Valdemar was a near kinsman of King Magnus. Ingebjörg, King Valdemar's mother, and Malmfrid, mother of Kristin, King Magnus' mother, were sisters and daughters of King Harald from Gardar[2] in the east; he was the son of Valdemar, Jarisleiv's son. King Valdemar greeted them well and he and Erling were often at meetings and in counsel, and it came out of their talks that King Valdemar should grant King Magnus all the help of his kingdom as he should need to win Norway and keep it thereafter, and Valdemar was to have that kingdom in Norway that his former kinsmen, Harald Gormson and Swein Forkbeard, had had—all the Vik north-west to Rygjarbit.[3] That plan was bound

---

1 *Kin* in O.N. is *kyn*, meaning family, race, descent and used mostly for distant relatives, whilst *frændi* (pl. *frændr*) means nearer relatives.  2 Russia. Harald was also called Mstislav. His mother was Githa, daughter of Harold Godwinson, the last of the English kings before the Conquest.  3 The frontier between Nedenes and Bratsberg folk districts.

with oaths and terms. Erling and his following afterwards made themselves ready to go from Denmark, and they sailed out from Vendilskagi.[1]

3. In the spring after Easter[2] King Hacon went straightway north to Trondheim; he then had all the ships which King Inge had had. Hacon held a thing at Kaupang and there he was taken as king over the whole land. He then gave Sigurd of Röir a jarldom and Sigurd was taken as jarl. Hacon and Sigurd went back to the south and right east to the Vik; the king went to Tunsberg but he sent Sigurd the Jarl east to Konungahella with some of the army to guard the land if Erling came thither from the south. Erling and his men came to Agder and sailed straightway north to Bergen; there

Erling Skakki at Tunsberg

they slew Arne Brigidarskalli, King Hacon's sheriff, and from there they went back east to meet King Hacon. But Sigurd the Jarl was not aware that Erling had come from the south and he was still east on the Elv and King Hacon was in Tunsberg. Erling came up to Rossanes[3] and lay there some nights; Hacon got ready for him in the town. Erling drew near the town and his men took a ship of burden and loaded it with wood and straw and set fire to it; the wind was blowing up to the town and the ship drifted towards it. He had two cables carried out from the ship of burden and tied to two cutters, and he bade them row on behind as the merchant ship was drifting forward. And when the fire had almost reached the town they who

1 The Scaw.    2 16th of April, 1161.    3 The north point of the island of Nötteröy, outside Rambjerget.

were on the cutters held on to the cables so that the town should not catch fire. The smoke lay so thick over the town that they could see nothing from the jetties where the king's army stood. Erling then brought up the whole army upon the windward side of the fire and shot up at them. And when the townsmen saw that the fire was getting near their houses and that many were wounded by the shots, they held counsel and sent out Roald Longtalk the Priest to Erling to take quarter from Erling for himself and the town; when Roald told them that quarter was given them, they broke up the king's lines. And when the townsmen had gone away the host on the jetties was much thinned; some of Hacon's men urged them to make a stand, but Anund Simonson, who then had most say over the army, spoke thus: "I will not fight to win the kingdom for Sigurd the Jarl when he himself is not present". Anund then fled and thereafter the whole army with the king, and they went up into the land; a great many of Hacon's men fell there. Thus it was said:

| | |
|---|---|
| Anund sang that he would | Magnus' bold fighters |
| Not try battle, | Went in crowds up the street |
| Until there sailed from the south | Whilst Hacon's warriors |
| Sigurd the Jarl with his huscarls. | Hastened quickly away. |

Torbjörn Skakkascald said thus:

| | |
|---|---|
| I have heard, O lord, | The townsmen were afraid |
| That in wide Tunsberg thou didst win; | Of the bright point's flight; |
| Eager thou art to dye | They were afraid of the fire |
| The wolves' teeth in blood. | And of the bending elm bows. |

King Hacon then went north by the landway to Trondheim. And when Sigurd the Jarl learned that, he went northwards in the outer lode with all the ships he could get to meet King Hacon.

4. In Tunsberg Erling Skakki took all the ships which King Hacon had had. There he got *Beykisudin*[1] which King Inge had. Erling afterwards went and put all the Vik under Magnus and likewise the land to the north-west everywhere where he went, and he stayed the winter in Bergen. Then Erling had Ingebjörn Sipil, King Hacon's landed man, slain in the Fjords[2] in the north. During the winter King Hacon stayed in Trondheim, and next spring he called out a levy and made ready to go south against Erling. There were with him Sigurd the Jarl, John Sweinson, Eindridi the Young, Anund Simonson, Philip Peterson, Philip Gyrdson, Ragnvald

---

1 The *Beykisudin* was built by King Inge. Cf. 'History of Hacon Broad-Shoulder', p. 697, n. 1.    2 *The Fjords* were Nordfjord and Söndfjord.

Kunta, Sigurd Kapa, Sigurd Hjupa, Fridrek Köni, Asbiorn of Örland, Torbjörn, son of Gunnar Gjaldkeri, and Strad-Biarne.

5. Erling was in Bergen and had a great army. He took the plan of forbidding the movement of all merchant ships which intended going north to Kaupang,[1] for he believed that news would go too quickly to Hacon if ships sailed between them; but he gave as a reason that the men of Bergen should enjoy the good things which were on the ships (even the tradesmen had to sell them more cheaply than seemed right to them) rather than that they should be put in the hands of their foes and enemies to strengthen them. Ships now gathered to the town, for many came each day but none went away. Erling then had his lightest ships hauled ashore and let the report go round that he would wait there and would fight the enemy with the help of his friends and kinsmen. But one day Erling summoned a meeting of the ship captains and gave all the captains of the merchant ships leave to go wherever they would. And when the men who commanded the ships of burden, and who already lay (with their cargoes) quite ready to sail—some with merchandise, some on other business—got leave to go, there was good weather for sailing north along the coast; and before non[2] on that day all who lay ready had sailed. They who had the swiftest ships sought to go most eagerly, and all raced with each other. And when this fleet came north to Möre, they met King Hacon's men, and Hacon himself was still gathering men and fitting them out and calling to him the landed men and levies, but he had not for a long time heard any tidings from Bergen. But now they got news from all the ships sailing from the south that Erling Skakki had set up his ships in Bergen; they could find him there, and they said that he had a big army. From there Hacon sailed to Veöy[3] and he sent Sigurd the Jarl and Anund Simonson into Raumsdale to gather men and ships; he also sent men to North Möre and South Möre. And when King Hacon had stayed a few nights in the market town, he went away a little farther south, as he thought that they would then get on quicker and that folk would come to him without delay. Erling Skakki had let the ships of burden go away from Bergen on the Sunday; and on the Tuesday, when morning Mass was over, he had the king's horn blown, and summoned to him the warriors and townsmen, and he had the ships put out which had before been hauled ashore. Erling held a husthing with his army and the levied men;

1 I.e. Trondheim.    2 *Non*, i.e. nones in English, about 3 p.m.    3 A merchant town in Raumsdale, on an island bearing the same name, east of Sekken.

he told them his plan and named men as ship captains and he had the list read out of those who were to be on the king's ship. This thing ended by Erling bidding every man make himself ready in his place, wherever it might be; he said that everybody should lose either life or limbs who stayed behind in the town, when he put off in the *Beykisudin*. Orm King's Brother went off at once in the evening with his ship, and most of the other ships were already afloat.

6. On the Wednesday, before Mass was sung in the town, Erling went away with the whole army; they had twenty-one ships. There was a good wind for sailing northwards along the coast. Erling had with him his son, King Magnus; there were many landed men and they had the finest army. When Erling sailed north past the Fjords he sent a cutter in from the fairway to John Halkelson's garth and he bade them take Nicholas, son of Simon Skalp and Maria, Harald Gilli's daughter; they took him with them out to the army and he went on the king's ship. Early on Friday at dawn they sailed into Steinavag.[1] King Hacon was then in a haven near by and he had thirteen ships. Hacon and his men were up in the island playing games and his landed men were sitting on a howe, when they saw that a boat was rowing northwards to the island; two men were in it and they were bending right down to the floors, but all the same they took hasty strokes with their oars. And when they came to land, they did not fasten the boat, but ran off. The leaders saw this and said amongst themselves that these men would be able to tell them some tidings; they stood up and went towards them. And as soon as they met, Anund Simonson said: "Can ye tell us something of Erling Skakki, since ye come so quickly?" He who could first say a word in spite of his weariness answered: "Erling is sailing here against you from the south with twenty-one ships or thereabouts, and many are mighty big and you will soon see their sails". Then Eindridi the Young answered: "'Too near the nose', said the fellow when he was shot in the eye". They then went quickly to where the game was being played and the horn was blown for the whole army to go on board as quickly as they could, and it was the time of day when the food was being made ready. All the men ran to the ships and each leaped out into the ship which was nearest to him, and thereby the ships got an uneven number of men; they took to the oars, some set the mast and turned the ships northwards; they sailed to Veöy, for there they expected good help from the townsmen.

1 Between Hessöy and Aspöy, now the western part of the town of Alesund. Cf. further 'History of St Olav', p. 418, n. 2.

7. They then saw the sails of Erling's ships and both armies saw each other. Eindridi the Young had the ship called *Draglaun*, a great longship, but he had then got few men, for they who had been on it before had leaped aboard the other ships; it was to the rear of Hacon's ships. But when Eindridi was off the island of Sekk,[2] the *Beykisudin*, which Erling commanded, came behind them and these two ships were fastened together. Hacon had then almost come into Veöy, when they heard the horns sounding, and the ships which were nearest turned round and would help Eindridi. Both fleets now went to battle in such way as they could manage. Many sails fell down athwart the ships but no ships were lashed together; they lay board to board. The battle did not last long, before the position was broken; on Hacon's ship some fell and some leaped overboard. Hacon threw a grey cape over himself and leaped on to another ship, and when he had been there a short time he seemed to perceive that he had come amongst his foes. And when he looked about him, he could see none of his men or his ships near; he then went on board the *Beykisudin* forward in the stem and begged quarter for himself; the stem men received him and gave him quarter. In this strife there had been a great loss of men, mostly however amongst Hacon's men. Simon Skalp's son Nicholas had fallen on the *Beykisudin* and Erling's men themselves were blamed for his death. After this there was a lull in the battle and the ships parted from one another. Then Erling was told that King Hacon was there on the ship, and that his stem men had taken him and promised to guard him. Erling sent a man forward in the ship, and bade him tell the stem men that they were to watch Hacon so that he should not get away, and that he would not speak against Hacon getting quarter if it were the will of the great men and if they sought to obtain terms for him. The stem men all cheered and praised his word. Erling then had the horn loudly blown and bade the men make for the ships which were not cleared. He said that it would never be easier for them to avenge King Inge. They all shouted their war cry and each egged the other on and went forward. In that strife Hacon got his death wound. And after his fall when his men were aware of it, they fought desperately, cast away their shields and slashed with both hands, giving no heed to their own lives. This eagerness did them great harm, for Erling's men could now easily strike them down.

1 Now Sekken, meaning 'sack' or 'bag'. Islands were often named after their shape. For instance Flatholmen (in Norway) and Flatholme (in the Bristol Channel); another instance is Sark (in the Channel Islands), resembling a woman's sark (in O.N. *serkr*).

A great part of Hacon's army fell there and it was mostly because of the great odds against them and because Hacon's men spared themselves but little. But it was of no avail for Hacon's men to ask for quarter, except those whom the great men took under their protection and for whom they promised money. These men of Hacon's fell: Sigurd Kapa, Sigurd Hjupa, and Ragnvald Kunta. Some ships got away and rowed into the fjords and the men in them thus saved their lives. King Hacon's body was moved into Raumsdale and buried there. King Sverre, his brother, had King Hacon's body moved north to Kaupang and laid it in the stone wall of Christ Church on the south side of the choir.

8. Sigurd and Eindridi the Young, Anund Simonson, Fridrek Köni, and some other leaders kept their troops together; they left their ships behind in Raumsdale and then went to the Uplands. Erling Skakki and King Magnus went north with their army to Kaupang and subdued all the land wherever they went. Erling afterwards had the Örething called and there Magnus was taken as king over the whole land. Erling stayed there but a short time, for it seemed to him that the Tronds were not true to him and his son; Magnus was now called king of the whole land. King Hacon was a handsome man, and he was well-grown, tall and slim; he had broad shoulders and his warriors therefore called him Hacon 'Broadshoulder'. But because he was young in years other chiefs had ruled with him. He was happy and pleasant in his speech, fond of games and youthful in mind; he was well-befriended by the people.

9. Markus of Skog[1] was the name of an Uplander, a kinsman of Sigurd the Jarl. Markus had fostered King Sigurd's son, who was called Sigurd. The Uplanders then took Sigurd as king on the advice of Sigurd the Jarl and the other chiefs who had followed King Hacon; they had even then a great strength of men. The host often went in two parts; the king and Markus were less exposed to risk, but Sigurd the Jarl and the other leaders with their troops went more often into battle. With the host they went mostly through the Uplands, but sometimes they went down into the Vik. Erling Skakki always had his son Magnus with him and he had also the whole fleet and the whole guarding of the land. In the autumn he was for some time in Bergen and from there he went east to the Vik and sat in Tunsberg. There he made himself ready for winter quarters and gathered to himself in the Vik all the taxes and dues which the king should have; he had also a big, fine army. But inasmuch as

---

[1] Skog in Bröttum district, North Hedemark.

Sigurd the Jarl had little income from the land but many folk, he soon ran short of money; and when none of the leaders were there his men went after goods in an unlawful way, against some men by unfounded accusations, against others by open robbery.

10. At that time the realm of Norway was flourishing, the bonders were rich and powerful and unused to the constraint and unrest of the army. There was soon strong talk and angry words when robbery was done. The Vikmen were very friendly to King Magnus and Erling; the friendliness to King Inge Haraldson mostly brought this about, for the Vikmen had always served under his shield with their full strength. Erling had watch kept in the town every night by twelve men. Erling always held things with the bonders and the ill-doing of Sigurd's men was then often talked about. And after the proposal of Erling and the other warriors, the bonders gave a loud cheer to the speech that it would be a fortunate deed if they could get that troop destroyed. Arne King's Kin spoke long, and at the end he spoke hard about this matter. He bade all men who were at the thing, both warriors, bonders and townsmen, to condemn by wapentake[1] to the devil according to the law, Sigurd the Jarl and all his troop, both living and dead. In their eagerness and fierceness the crowd all agreed to it. This unusual act was approved and executed, as the law said, that they should judge at the things. Roald Longtalk the Priest spoke about this matter—he was a good speaker—and his speech dwelt mostly on the same things as had already been spoken of. Erling held a feast in Tunsberg at Yule, and he gave out the earnings at Candlemas.[2]

11. Sigurd the Jarl went about the Vik with the best part of his army, and many submitted to him because of his power and many paid him money; he thus went far up into the land and appeared in different places. There were some in his troop who secretly sought peace with Erling, and he always gave the answer that all men who asked for it should have quarter but only they should have the right to be in the land who had not grievously broken the law against him.

1 The O.N. text is *vapna-tak*. This old Scandinavian custom at thing meetings of beating their weapons against their shields to signify approval of a resolution was prevalent in Scandinavian England long before the Conquest. The word 'wapentake' was later used for a division or a district, and in Domesday Book the various wapentakes in England are mentioned. Nottinghamshire has still six wapentakes. Lincolnshire is primarily divided into three thrithings or ridings (in O.N. *þriðiung*) and Lindsey, which embodies over half Lincolnshire, contains seventeen wapentakes. The names North, West and East Riding in Yorkshire are also of Scandinavian origin. In Scotland the name 'wapenshaw' signifies a gathering for the exhibition of arms at certain times of the year
2 2nd of February, 1163.

And when the men in the troop heard that they were not to remain in the land, they held together, for there were many who knew themselves to be guilty of such offences for which Erling would deem that he could bring great charges against them. Philip Gyrdson came to terms with Erling, got back his possessions and went to his garths. A little later Sigurd's men came there and slew him. Much harm they did to each other by falling upon and slaying men, but here we only relate events when chiefs took part in them.

12. It was in the beginning of Lent[1] that word came to Erling that Sigurd the Jarl intended coming against him and they heard of Sigurd here and there, sometimes nearer, sometimes farther away. Erling then sent spies out so that he could get to hear of them wherever they appeared. Every evening he had the whole army called up from the town and at nights they lay gathered together; the whole army was divided into lines. Word then came to Erling that Sigurd the Jarl and his men were a short way from there up at Re.[2] Erling went away from the town and he had with him all the townsfolk who were bold in battle and fully weaponed, and likewise all the merchants except the twelve men who were left behind to watch the town. He went out of the town after non[3] on the Tuesday of the second week of Lent[4] and every man had with him two days' provisions; they went during the night and they were slow getting all their men out of the town. There were two men to every horse and shield. When the army was counted there were nigh on thirteen hundred (fifteen hundred and sixty) men. And when the spies came to meet them they were told that Sigurd the Jarl was at Re at the garth called Ramnes with five hundred (six hundred) men. Erling then had the army called together and told them the tidings he had heard; they all urged that they should hurry on and fall on them in the houses or fight at once in the night. Erling spoke thus: "It seems likely that we shall soon meet Sigurd the Jarl; in his troop there are many folk whose handiwork[5] we might deem worth remembering, in that they struck down King Inge and so many others of our friends that it would take long to reckon their numbers. They did the deed with the craft of the devil, witchcraft and cowardice, for it stands in our law and landright that men shall not slay each other at night and such offence is called cowardice and murder. This troop has sought its fortune according to the

1 *Lent* commenced on the 10th of February.   2 Now Ramnes district, north-west of Tönsberg.   3 Cf. p. 713, n. 2.   4 19th of February, 1163.   5 The O.N. text reads *handa-verk*.

counsel of troll-wise men, in that they were to fight by night but not by day; with such doings have they also won the victory, and stepped over the heads of such chiefs as they have laid on the ground. Now we have often said and shown how ill we have deemed their ways of planning battle at night. We shall therefore rather follow the ways of those chiefs whom we know to be better and whom it is better to imitate, of fighting in open day and in lines— rather than of stealing upon sleeping men during the night. We have good men against them, seeing their army is no bigger than it is. We shall wait for day and the light, and keep together in our line if they will fall upon us". After that the whole army settled down; some pulled down a few hayricks[1] and made themselves beds from them; some sat on their shields and waited for dawn. The weather was cold and there were drifts of snow.

13. Sigurd the Jarl had only lately got the news that the army was coming against them. His men stood up and armed themselves but they knew not clearly how great an army Erling had; some wished to flee but most of them would wait. Sigurd the Jarl was a wise and well-spoken man, but reckoned none too bold; he, too, had now more desire to flee and therefore got hard words from the warriors. And when it dawned, both sides began to draw up their armies. Sigurd the Jarl drew up his line on a hill above the bridge between the latter and the garth; a little river flowed there.[2] And Erling drew up his line on the other side of the river; at the back of his line were men on horseback and well-armed; they had the king between them. The jarl's men then saw that there would be great odds against them and found it advisable to make for the wood. The jarl said: "Ye say that I have no courage; but now it shall be proved and let each man watch himself lest he should flee or turn traitor before I do. We have a good position; we will let them cross the river, and when the standard comes over the bridge we shall rush down the hill upon them and then must no man flee from the others". Sigurd the Jarl had a brown-coloured kirtle and a red cape with the corners thereof turned back, and he wore hide shoes on his feet; he had a shield and a sword which was called Bastard. The jarl said: "God knows that rather than get much gold I would like to get one stroke in with Bastard at Erling Skakki".

14. Erling Skakki's army wished to go forth to the bridge; he spoke and bade them turn up along the river: "This river is little and

---

1 In O.N. *hey-hialmar*, i.e. hay helmets.   2 The small river below the farm at Ramnes, which flows into the Auli River.

not difficult to ford, for there are level lands along it". So it was done. The jarl's line went up along the hill opposite to them. And when the hill ended and it was flat and easy to cross the river, Erling said that his men should sing the *Pater Noster* and pray that he should get the victory who had the better cause. Then they all loudly sang the *Kyrial*[1] and all weapons they struck against their shields. But at that din three hundred (three hundred and sixty) of Erling's men turned and fled. Erling and his army went over the river and the jarl's men shouted their war cry. But there was no

Erling and his men crossed the river

rushing down the hill against Erling's line; the battle took place on the hill. The first spear was hurled and the battle began at once; the jarl's standard retired so that Erling and his men came up to the hill. There was a short fight until the jarl's army fled to the wood which was behind them. Then Sigurd the Jarl was told this and they bade him flee. He answered: "Let us go forward as long as we can". They then went very boldly forward and struck out on both sides. In that fight there fell Sigurd the Jarl and John Sweinson and nigh on sixty men. Erling's army lost few men and they drove the fleeing men into the wood. Erling had his army counted and then turned back. He came to where the king's thralls were on the point of tearing the clothes off Sigurd the Jarl. He was

1 I.e. the hymn *Kyrie eleison.*

not yet dead, but had lost consciousness. He had thrust his sword Bastard into its sheath and there it lay by his side. Erling picked it up and struck the thralls with it, bidding them get away. After that Erling turned back with his army and settled in Tunsberg. Seven nights after the jarl's fall Erling's men took Eindridi the Young and he was slain.

15. Markus of Skog and his foster-son Sigurd went down to the Vik in the spring and there got themselves ships. And when Erling heard that, he went eastward after them and they met at Konungahella. Markus and his men fled out to the island of Hising. The men of the island, the Hising-dwellers, came down and joined the lines of the men of Markus. Erling's men rowed to the island and Markus' men shot at them. Then said Erling: "Let us take their ships and not go up to fight with their land army; the Hising-dwellers are evil men to meet in their homes; they are hard and witless men. They will have this troop with them for but a short while, for Hising is a little land". So it was done, that they took the ships and moved them over to Konungahella. Markus and his army went up to Marker and intended making an onset there; and both troops then knew of each other. Erling had a large army and he called up the levy men from the lordships; and they made attacks on each other in turn.

16. Eystein, Erlend Himaldi's son, was chosen as archbishop after the death of John the Archbishop. Eystein was consecrated in the same year as King Inge fell. And when Archbishop Eystein came to his see he was in good favour with all the land folk; he was a very doughty man and of good kin. The Tronds greeted him well, for most of the great men in Trondlaw were bound by ties of kinship or marriage to the archbishop and all were his true friends. The archbishop then brought up a matter before the bonders; he spoke first about the wants of the archbishops and then of what great support the see needed if it were to be upheld more fittingly than before, as it was more distinguished now than it had been before, since it was an archbishop's see. He demanded of the bonders that they should grant him in payment of his fees a pure silver öre whereas formerly he had had a fee öre, such as passed for payment of the king's fees; and the difference between the öres was that the öre he wished to have, that is, the pure silver one, was double the value of the other.[1] But with the help of the archbishop's kinsmen and friends and by his own thrusting this was brought about and it was

[1] Since the days of Harald Hardrade the money had decreased by half its previous value.

deemed as law all through Trondlaw and throughout all the folk districts which were within his archbishopric.

17. When Sigurd and Markus had lost their ships in the Elv, they saw that they could do nothing against Erling. They then turned to the Uplands and so went north by the land-ways to Trondheim. There they were well received and Sigurd was taken as king at the Örething. The sons of many good men betook themselves to this troop; there they got themselves ships, quickly fitted themselves out, and, when summer came, went south to Möre and took all the king's dues, wherever they went. In Bergen were set—in order to ward the land—the landed men, Nicholas Sigurdson and Nökkvi[1] Paulson, and still more troop leaders—Torolv Dryll, Torbjörn Gjaldkeri and many others. Markus and his men sailed southwards and learned that Erling's men had a big army in Bergen; they then sailed outside the skerries past there to the south. Men had it in their talk that this summer Markus' men had a fair wind, wherever they wanted to go.

18. As soon as Erling Skakki learned that Markus' men had turned southwards, he sailed to the Vik; he drew folk to him and soon had a big strength of men; he also had many big ships. But when he was coming outside the Vik he got contrary wind and he lay here and there in harbours a long time during the whole summer. When Markus' men came east to Lister, they learned that Erling had a mighty army in the Vik and then they turned back to the north. And when they came to Hordaland they wished to go into Bergen, but when they came outside the town, Nicholas and the others rowed against them, and they had a much greater army and bigger ships. Markus' men then saw no other way out for themselves than to row southwards in order to escape; some sailed out to sea, some south into the sounds, and some into the fjords. But Markus and some men with him leaped up on to the island which is called Skarpa.[2] Nicholas and his men took their ships, gave quarter to John Halkelson and some others, but they slew most of those they got near. Some days later Eindridi Heidafyla found Sigurd and Markus, who were then brought to Bergen. Sigurd was beheaded outside Gravdale[3] and Markus was hanged with another man at Kvarfnes;[4] that was at Michaelmas.[5] The troop which had followed them then split up.

---

1 *Nökkvi* is considered to be the same as Nicholas.    2 *Skarpa* is now Skorpa, on the south side of the Korsfjord by the entrance to Bergen.    3 A wick or bay inside Kvarven (south-west of Bergen).    4 Kvarven.    5 29th of September, 1163.

19. Fridrek Köni and Biarne the Evil, Anund Simonson and Arnolf Skorpa had rowed out to sea with some ships and sailed outside the skerries along the coast. Wherever they came to land they robbed and slew Erling's friends. And when Erling heard of the deaths of Markus and Sigurd he gave the landed men and the levy men leave to go home and he himself went east with his men across the Fold,[1] for he learned that Markus' men were there. Erling sailed to Konungahella and stayed there during the autumn. In the first week of winter[2] Erling went out to the island of Hising with a great army and there he demanded a thing. The Hising-dwellers came down and held a thing. Erling charged them with having joined the troop of Markus' men and with having drawn up their army against him. Assur was the name of the man who was the mightiest of the bonders; he spoke on their behalf. The thing lasted a long while but at length the bonders agreed that Erling should judge; he called them to a meeting in the town within a week and he named fifteen men from the bonders to come there. And when they came Erling condemned them to pay three hundred head of cattle. The bonders went home and were ill pleased. A little later ice covered the river and Erling's ships were frozen in. The bonders then kept their fines back and lay for a time gathered together. Erling there made ready for a Yule feast, but the Hising-dwellers drank their ale by themselves and kept their men together during Yule. The night after the fifth day of Yule[3] Erling went out on the island, surrounded Assur's house and burned him inside it; in all he slew a hundred men, burned three garths and went back to Konungahella. The bonders then came to him and paid their fines.

20. Erling Skakki made himself ready in the spring, as soon as he could get his ships free from the ice, and he went from Konungahella. He learned that they who had formerly been Markus' men were harrying in the north in the Vik. Erling had their farings spied on and went after them; he found them where they lay in a harbour. Anund Simonson and Arnolf Skorpa got away, but Fridrek Köni and Biarne the Evil were taken prisoner and many of their men were slain. Erling had Fridrek bound to an anchor and cast overboard; for that deed Erling was much hated in Trondlaw, for Fridrek was of the best stock there. Erling had Biarne hanged; and before he was

---

1 The Oslofjord.    2 I.e. the week after the 14th of October, which was the first winter day.    3 I.e. the night between the 29th and 30th of December, 1163.

hanged, Biarne quoth, as was his wont, the worst of words. Thus sayeth Torbjörn Skakkascald:

In the east of the fjord Erling
Brought the Vikings ill-luck,
When he sailed there; many
A man got harm from Köni.

The anchor was tied between
Fridrek's shoulders; up was
The ill-minded Biarne
Borne to the gallow-tree.

Arnolf and Anund and the troops which had escaped fled to Denmark, but they were sometimes in Gautland or in the Vik.

21. Erling Skakki afterwards sailed to Tunsberg, and he stayed there a long time in the spring. And when summer came he sailed north to Bergen, where a crowd of people were then gathered. The legate Stefanus from Rome and Archbishop Eystein and other bishops were there; there too was Bishop Brand,[1] who was then consecrated as Bishop of Iceland, and also John Loftson,[2] King Magnus Barefoot's daughter's son; King Magnus and John's other kinsmen had acknowledged their kinship with him. Archbishop Eystein and Erling Skakki were often at meetings and private talks. And once it happened in their talk that Erling asked: "Is it true, my lord, as folks say, that you have increased the öre fee in the north of the land?" The archbishop answered: "It is certainly true that the bonders have allowed me to increase the öre in my fees. It has been done after their own counsel and without constraint; they have thereby increased God's honour and the income of our see". Erling answered: "Is this the law, my lord, of St Olav, or have you taken this matter farther than is written in the law-book?" The archbishop answered: "St Olav made a good law and obtained the ayes and assent thereto of the common people; but it is not found in his law that it is forbidden to increase God's right". Erling said: "If you will increase your right, will you then strengthen us in increasing the king's right just as much". The archbishop answered: "Thou hast already increased enough thy son's name and realm. But if I have taken the öre of the Tronds over and above the law, I think that the law-breaking is the more serious when he is king of the land who is not a king's son, for thereto is there neither law nor precedent in this land".[3] Erling said: "When Magnus was taken as king over Norway's realm, it was done with your know-

1 *Brand* Sæmundson was consecrated Bishop of Skalholt (Iceland) on the 8th of September, 1163.    2 *John Loftson* was Snorre Sturlason's foster-father. Cf. further 'History of Magnus the Blind', chapter 9.    3 King Magnus Erlingson had royal descent only through his mother, who was a daughter of Sigurd the Crusader. According to the Norse law he was not eligible for the throne.

ledge and counsel, as with that of the other bishops in this land". The archbishop answered: "Thou didst promise, Erling, that if we agreed with thee that Magnus be taken as king, thou shouldest strengthen God's right everywhere, with all thy might". "I keep to it", said Erling, "that I have promised to keep God's law and land right with all the might of myself and the king. Now I see here a better counsel for it than that each of us should charge the other with being a traitor; let us rather keep all our agreements. Strengthen King Magnus in the realm, as you have vowed, and I shall strengthen your rule with all gainful things." Thereafter all the talk between them was friendly. Then said Erling: "If Magnus has not been taken as king in such a way as the old custom is in this land, you can by your might give him the crown just as the law of God says about the anointing of a king to his realm. And even if I am not king or come of the stock of kings, most kings who have been kings in our time have not known as well as I the law or the land rights; but King Magnus' mother is the daughter born in wedlock of a king and queen; therefore King Magnus is the son of a queen and a lawful wife. But if you will crown him king, then no one will be able with right to take the kingship from him. William the Bastard was not a king's son, but he was hallowed and crowned King of England, and since then the kingship of England has been kept in his family and all the kings have been crowned. Swein Ulfson in Denmark was not a king's son but he was crowned a king, and since then his sons and one after the other of his family have been crowned kings. Now here in the land is an archbishopric and it is a great honour and dignity for our land. Let us now increase its power still more and have a crowned king, no less than the Englishmen or the Danes". After this the archbishop and Erling often talked about this matter and everything went smoothly. The archbishop then put the matter before the legate and easily got the legate to agree with him. Thereafter the archbishop held meetings with the folk bishops and other churchmen and put the matter before them. And all answered in one and the same way, saying that it was their counsel even as the archbishop would have it, and all wished the crowning to take place as soon as they found that the archbishop would decide. This then was the judgment of all.

22. Erling Skakki had a great banquet made ready in the king's residence and the great hall was covered with pall cloths and tapestries and decked out at the greatest cost. There was held a feast for the bodyguard and all the landed men; there was a great crowd

of guests and many chiefs. Magnus was then crowned by Archbishop Eystein and there at the coronation were five other bishops
and the legate and a crowd of priests. Erling Skakki and twelve
landed men with him swore oaths before the king according to the
law. And on the day of the crowning the king and Erling gave a
banquet to the archbishop and the legate and all the bishops. That
feast was of the noblest. Erling and Magnus gave many great gifts.
King Magnus was then eight years old and he had been king for
three years.

The landed men swear allegiance to the crowned king

23. The Danish king Valdemar had then learned tidings that
Magnus was sole king of Norway and that all other troops in the
land had been destroyed. The king then sent his men with a letter to
King Magnus and Erling reminding them of the terms to which
Erling had bound himself with King Valdemar, even as is written
above, namely, that King Valdemar was to have the Vik west to
Rygjarbit, if Magnus became sole king of Norway. But when the
messengers came forth and showed Erling the Danish king's letter
and he understood the claim which the Danish king had on Norway,

Erling put it before the other men, from whom he craved counsel. But they all said the same thing, that they should never give the Danes a share in Norway, for, they said, "The worst time the land has had was when the Danes had power over Norway". The messengers of the Danish king told their case to Erling and bade him settle it. Erling bade them go east with him to the Vik in the autumn and said that he would settle it then when he had met the men who were the wisest in the Vik.

24. In the autumn Erling Skakki went east to the Vik and he stayed in Tunsberg; he sent men over to Borg¹ and had a thing of four folk districts called in Borg. Erling then went thither with his men. And when the thing was sitting Erling spoke and told of the agreement that had been made between himself and the Danish king, when Erling and Magnus first took command of the army; "I also wish", he said, "to keep all the agreements we made then, if, bonders, it is your wish and desire to serve the Danish king rather than this king who has been consecrated and crowned to the realm". The bonders answered Erling and spoke thus: "On no condition do we wish to be the Danish king's men, so long as one of us Vik-men is still alive". Then the whole folk raised a great shout and cried out, bidding Erling keep the oaths which he had one time sworn to all the land folk, to protect his son's land, "and we shall all follow thee". Thus ended the thing. Afterwards the Danish king's messengers went home south to Denmark and told the outcome of their business, such as it was. The Danes spoke many hard words against Erling and all the Norsemen, and said that they never learned aught but evil of them. The word went about that in the following spring the Danish king would lead out his army and harry in Norway. In the autumn Erling went north to Bergen, where he sat during the winter and gave the guard their pay.

25. That winter certain Danish men went by the upper way through the land and said, as was their wont, that they would go to St Olav to pray. And when they came to Trondheim, they sought out many great men. They told them their business, that the Danish king had sent them to try to win their friendship and welcome if he came into the land, and he promised to give them both power and wealth. With this message there went the Danish king's letters and seal and bidding that, in return, the Tronds should send their own letters and seal. They did so, and most of them welcomed the Danish king's message. The messengers went back to the south when Lent

1 I.e. Sarpsborg.

was passing. Erling sat in Bergen; but when spring came, Erling's friends told him of the report they had heard from merchants who had come from the north from Trondheim, that the Tronds were openly hostile to him and that they had made it clear at their things that if Erling came to Trondheim he would never get away past Agdenes with his life. Erling said that such things were invented and untrue. He made it known that he would go south to Unarheim[1] to the Rogation Day thing and he had a twenty-benched craft and a fifteen-benched cutter made ready, besides a ship of burden for the food. And when the ships were ready, a keen south wind came upon them. On the Tuesday in Rogation Days[2] Erling had his men summoned to the ships, but the men were slow in coming out of the town, for they thought it ill to row against the wind. Erling brought his ships north into Bishopshaven.[3] Then said Erling: "Ye grumble at rowing against the wind; take now the masts and raise them; hoist the sails and let the ships go north". They did so and they sailed north during the day and the night. Towards Wednesday evening they sailed in past Agdenes;[4] there they came into a great fleet of merchant ships and other ferry-boats and cutters; they were folk who were going into the town for the feast day, some in front of them, some after them; for that reason the townsmen did not notice that the longships were sailing there.

26. Erling Skakki came to the town about the time when Matins was being sung in Christ Church. Erling's men ran up into the town and it was told them that the landed man Alf Red, Ottar Birting's son, was still drinking with his men. Erling went against them and Alf was slain with most of his troop. Few other men fell, for most of them had gone to church. That was the night before Ascension Day.[5] Straightway in the morning Erling had all the folk summoned to a thing at Öre. And at that thing Erling brought charges against the Tronds and blamed them for treason both to himself and the king; in that he named Bard Standali and Paul Andreasson and Rassa-Bard (who was sheriff of the town) and many others. They answered and said they were free from guilt. Then Erling's chaplain stood up, holding up many letters and seals, and he asked if they recognised the seals on them, which they had sent in the spring to the Danish king; the letters were also then read out. There with Erling were also the Danish men who had been with

---

1 *Unarheim*, now Onarheim on Tysnes (South Hordaland).   2 11th of May, 1165.
3 *Bishopshaven*, i.e. Biskopshavn in the Byfjord north of Bergen.   4 In the Trondheims-fjord.   5 13th of May.

the letters in the winter. Erling had got them to do it. They then said before all the folk the words of each one as he had spoken. "Thus spokest thou, Rassa-Bard!" they said, "and thou didst strike thyself on the breast, saying, 'From the first all these counsels came from this breast'." Bard answered: "Mad I was then, my lord, when I said such things". There was no other way out but to leave the whole matter to Erling's judgment. He forthwith took much wealth from many men, and for all who were slain no fines were to be paid. Erling afterwards went back south to Bergen.

27. King Valdemar had that spring a big army out in Denmark and with it he sailed north to the Vik. As soon as he came into the dominion of the King of Norway, the bonders had out big gatherings of men. The king went peacefully and quietly, but wherever they went past the mainland folk shot at them even if there were only one or two; the Danes deemed that the landsmen showed them much ill-will. And when they came to Tunsberg, King Valdemar called a thing at Haugar[1] but no man came to it from the lordships. Then King Valdemar spoke and said: "It is easy to see that the land folk here all oppose us. We have now two choices in our hands: one is to go through the land with the shield of war and spare neither folk nor goods; the other is to go south, things being as they are. It is more my mind to go on the easterway[2] to heathen lands, of which there are enough, rather than slay Christian folk here, even though they have well enough deserved it". All the others wished to harry, but the king decided to go back to the south. There was nevertheless much robbery in the outer isles and whenever the king was not near. They then went south to Denmark.

28. Erling Skakki learned that the Danish army had come to the Vik. He called a levy of men and ships throughout the whole land and it was the greatest gathering of men. With that army he sailed east along the coast. And when he came to Lidandisnes[3] he learned that the Danish army had gone back to the south to Denmark and that they had robbed far and wide in the Vik. He then gave the whole army leave to go home, but he himself and certain landed men sailed south with some ships after the Danes to Jutland. And when they came to where it is called Dyrsa,[4] the Danes who had come from their expedition lay there with many ships. Erling came up to them and fought with them. The Danes quickly fled and they lost many men; Erling's men robbed the ships and then the market

1 *Haugar* is now Möllebakken at Tönsberg.   2 *Easterway* was the Baltic and Baltic Provinces.   3 The Naze.   4 The most easterly point in Jutland.

town;[1] there they got many goods and then went back to Norway. There was now trouble for a time between Norway and Denmark.

29. In the autumn Kristin King's Daughter went south to Denmark; she went to her kinsman King Valdemar. They were the children of two sisters, and the king greeted her extremely well and gave her land rents there for herself, so that she could keep her men well. She was often in talk with the king, who was very blithe towards her. And the spring after, Kristin sent men to Erling and bade him go to the Danish king and make peace with him. The following summer Erling was in the Vik. He there got a longship ready and set on it his best men; he then sailed over to Jutland. He learned that King Valdemar was in Randaros.[2] Erling sailed thither and came to the town at the time the king sat at meat,[3] and most folk had their meals. And when they had covered and fastened the ship, Erling went up with eleven men; he was the twelfth; they were all in brynies and had hats over their helmets and swords under their capes; they went to the king's room. The dishes were then coming in and the door was open; Erling and his men went farther in before the high-seat. Erling said: "We will have a truce, O king, both here and for our journey home". The king looked at him and said: "Art thou there, Erling?" He answered: "Erling is here, and say now at once whether we shall have a truce". There were inside eighty men of the king's, all unarmed. The king said: "Truce thou shalt have, Erling, as thou demandest; I do no dastard's[4] deed to any man who comes to me". Erling then kissed the king on the hand and went out to his ship. He stayed there for a time with the king; they spoke of peace between themselves and their lands, and they agreed that Erling should give himself as a hostage to the Danish king, and Asbiorn Snari, Archbishop Absalon's[5] brother, was to go to Norway as a hostage in return.

30. One time when King Valdemar and Erling were talking together, Erling said: "My lord, it seems likeliest for peace that you have all that part of Norway which was promised you in our agreements. But if it be so, which chief will you set over it? Must it be a Dane?" "No", said the king. "No Danish chief will be

---

1 I.e. Grindhög, now Grenaa.    2 I.e. Randers.    3 The O.N. text reads: *Konungr sat yfir matbordum*, lit. "the king sat over the food boards or tables", *mat* meaning 'food' in O.S. as well as in M.S.    4 In O.N. *niðingr*. Dastard's deed = *niðings-verk*. 5 *Archbishop Absalon* died in 1201. Snorre naturally calls him "Archbishop", by which title he was known when Snorre wrote his history, although he did not become archbishop till 1178, or several years after the event above related. *Asbiorn* Snari was called by the Danes *Esbern* Snare. Esbern is still more like the English Osborn than the Norse Asbiorn. Cf. p. 348, n. 2. In Normandy the name became Osbern.

pleased to go to Norway and there have to do with a hard and un-
loyal folk, whilst they are well pleased to stay with me." Then said
Erling, "I came here in order not to lose your friendship at any price.
Here to Denmark have men come before from Norway—Hacon
Ivorson and Finn Arneson—and your kinsman, King Swein, made
them both his jarls. I have no less power in Norway now than they had
at that time, and the king gave them the rule of Halland, the realm he
had formerly owned. Now, my lord, it seems to me that you can well
grant me the land, if I become your liegeman, to hold the kingdom
under you, in such a way that my son, King Magnus, will not deny
it me, and I will be pledged to you and bound to all the service that
goes with the title". Such words and other like things Erling spoke
and at length it came about that Erling submitted to King Valdemar; the king led Erling to the seat and gave him the name of 'jarl'
and the fief and rule of the Vik. After that Erling went home to
Norway and was afterwards jarl as long as he lived; ever afterwards
he kept peace with the Danish king.

Erling had four illegitimate children; one was called Reidar and
the second Agmund, and these two had different mothers; the third
was called Finn and the fourth Sigurd, and their mother was Asa the
Fair and they were the youngest. Kristin King's Daughter and
Erling had a daughter called Ragnhild who married John Torbergson
of Randaberg.[1] Kristin went away from the land with a man called
Grim Rusli; they went out to Miklegarth and were there for a
time; they had several children.

31. Olav, the son of Gudbrand Skavhoggson and Maria, King
Eystein Magnusson's daughter, was fostered by Sigurd Agnhatt
in the Uplands. And whilst Erling was in Denmark Sigurd and his
foster-son Olav raised a troop and to it came many Uplanders. Olav
was there taken as king. They went with this troop through the
Uplands and sometimes to the Vik, sometimes east to Marker.
They were not on ships. And when Erling the Jarl heard of this
troop he went with his men to the Vik and was there during the
summer on his ships, but in the autumn he was in Oslo, and there he
held a feast through Yule. He kept spies about in the land to watch
this troop and he himself went up into the country to look for them;
with him went Orm King's Brother. And when they came to a lake
they took all the ships that were on the water.

32. The priest who sang at Rydjakull—which is by the water—

---

1 *Randaberg* is close to Stavanger, on the west side of the town.

asked the jarl and his men to a feast and that they should come to Candlemas.[1] The jarl promised to go; he deemed it well to hear Mass there. They rowed thither over the water on the eve of the feast day. But the priest had another plan on his hands; he sent men to bear word to Olav about Erling's journey. He gave Erling's men strong drink in the evening and let them drink a long time. And when the jarl retired to sleep, their beds were made ready in the feast chamber. And when they had slept a short while the jarl woke and asked if it were time for Matins. The priest said that but a short part of the night had passed, and bade them sleep in peace. The jarl answered: "I dream much in the night and sleep badly". He then slept. A second time he woke up and bade the priest stand up and sing Mass. The priest bade the jarl sleep and said that it was now midnight. The jarl laid himself down and slept a short while; he then leaped up and bade his men clothe themselves. They did so; they took their weapons, went to church and laid down their weapons whilst the priest sang Matins.

33. Word came to Olav in the evening, and that night his men went six miles[2] by road, and folk thought this was a remarkable feat. They came to Rydjakull during Matins and it was pitch dark. Olav's men went to the room and called out their war cry; inside they slew several men who had not gone to Matins. But when Erling and his men heard the shout they seized their weapons and then made for their ships. Olav's men met them near a wall and they went to battle. Erling's men turned away down by the wall and it covered them. They had much fewer folk and many of them fell and many were wounded. Their greatest help was that Olav's men could not see them, so dark was it; Erling's men could only make for their ships. There fell Ari Torgeirson, father of Bishop Gudmund,[3] and many others of Erling's bodyguard. Erling was wounded in the left side and some men say that he caught his own sword against himself when he was drawing it out. Orm also was badly wounded. They barely managed to reach the ships and straightway thrust off from land. It was said that Olav and his men had the greatest ill-luck at that meeting, and Erling and his men would not have escaped, if Olav had gone forth with more cunning. Olav was afterwards called the "Unlucky", and some men called the troop the "Hood-swains". With this troop they went up through the land once more. But the jarl

1 2nd of February, 1167. According to Sturlunga Saga the event happened on the 1st of November, 1166 (All Saints' Day). 2 Six Norse miles are equal to forty-two English miles. 3 The famous St Gudmund, Bishop of Holar (Iceland), died 1237.

went to the Vik to his ships and he was there the next summer; Olav and his men were in the Uplands, but sometimes in the east in Marker. They thus kept the troop together until next winter.

34. The following spring Olav and his men went to the Vik, and there took the king's dues; they stayed there a long time during the summer. Erling the Jarl learned that, and brought his army eastwards against them, and their meeting was east of the fjord at a place called Stangir.[1] There was a great battle and Erling got the victory. There fell Sigurd Agnhatt and many of Olav's men, but Olav got away by flight and then went to Denmark; he was the next winter at Alborg in Jutland. But the spring after, Olav got a sickness which brought him to his death; he is buried there in St Mary's Church, and the Danes call him 'holy'.

35. Nicholas Kuvung, son of Paul Skoftason, was a landed man of King Magnus; he seized Harald who was said to be the son of King Sigurd Haraldson and Kristin King's Daughter, and brother, through his mother, to King Magnus. Nicholas moved Harald to Bergen and handed him over to Erling the Jarl. It was Erling's way when his enemies came before him to say little or nothing to them, and what he said he said calmly when he had decided to slay them, but to those whose lives he spared he used the strongest words. Erling spoke little to Harald and they misdoubted what he had in his mind. Then folk bade King Magnus beg peace of the jarl for Harald. The king did so. The jarl answered: "Thus do thy friends counsel thee. But thou wilt rule thy kingdom freely only for a short while if thou wilt go forth with too much mercy". Afterwards Erling had Harald moved over to Nordnes and there he was beheaded.

36. Eystein was the name of a man who was called the son of King Eystein Haraldson. He was a young man, not quite full grown. It is said that he appeared one summer in the east in Sweden and went to Birger Brosa who was then married to Birgitte, the daughter of Harald Gilli, and Eystein's father's sister. Eystein brought forward his business and bade them help him. She and the jarl took his cause well and promised him their help; he stayed there a while. Birger the Jarl gave Eystein some men and much money for their upkeep; he sent him away well set up and both promised him their friendship. Eystein then went north to Norway and came down into the Vik; folk drew to him at once and his troop grew. They took Eystein as their king and went with the troop during the winter in the Vik. And because they had little money they robbed

---

1 *Stangir*, now Stange in Valer district (Östfold).

widely, and the landed men and bonders sent their army against them. And when they were beaten, they fled away to the woods and for a long time they lay in the wastes; they wore out their clothes so that they wrapped birch bark round their legs. The bonders then called them the "Birchlegs". They often rushed down into the settlements and appeared here and there, and at once fell on folk when there were not many present. They held several battles with the bonders with varying success, and held three battles in regular lines and won the victory in all. In Krokaskog[1] they were nearly defeated; the bonders came upon them with a great army. The Birchlegs felled trees in front of them and then ran into the wood. The Birchlegs were two years in the Vik, so that during that time they did not go north in the land.

37. Magnus had been king thirteen years when the Birchlegs first appeared. The third year they got themselves ships and went with them along the coast and gathered men and goods. They were at first in the Vik, but when summer was passing, they sailed north in the land and went so speedily that no news went before them until they came to Trondheim. The Birchlegs had in their troop mostly Markamen[2] and Elvgrims,[3] but they had also a great number from Telemark;[4] they were all well armed. Eystein, their king, was good-looking and fair; he had a small face and he was not big. By many he was called Eystein Meyla.[5] King Magnus and Erling the Jarl sat in Bergen when the Birchlegs sailed northwards outside the skerries and they were not aware of it. Erling was a mighty and wise man, a great warrior when there was unrest, and a good and active land ruler. He was said to be somewhat grim and hard in his rule, but that was mostly because he would only allow very few of his foes to live in the land, even though they begged it; for that reason many threw in their lot with the troops which were raised against him. Erling was a tall and strongly built man and rather high-shouldered, and he had a long sharp face; he was fair of complexion and became very grey-haired. He carried his head somewhat askew; he was merry but dignified, he had old-fashioned clothes and he wore long jerkins and long sleeves to his kirtles and shirts; he had French capes and high-laced shoes. Such dress he let the king wear whilst he was young, but when he settled things for

---

1 *Krokaskog* in Saurbö district, now Sörbygden in Bohuslän (Sweden).   2 *Markamen* were men from Marker, i.e. the wood districts, Aremark and Ömark.   3 The inhabitants round the Elv (Göta River).   4 The country district above the towns of Porsgrund and Skien.   5 The O.N. *Meyla* means 'the little maiden'.

himself, the king clothed himself grandly. King Magnus was light-hearted, and keen on games, merry, and fond of women.

38. Nicholas, son of Sigurd Ranason, was the son of Skjaldvor, who was the daughter of Brynjulv Ulvaldi and sister of Haldor Brynjulvson and had the same mother as King Magnus Barefoot. Nicholas was a great chief; he had his garth in Angel[1] in Halogaland at a place called Steig. He owned a garth in Nidaros below St John's Church, a garth which Torgeir the Chaplain afterwards owned. Nicholas was often in Kaupang and he had much say with the townsmen. Skjaldvor, Nicholas' daughter, was married to Eric Arneson; he, too, was a landed man.

39. It was on the later Feast of St Mary[2] when folk were coming to Matins in the town, that Eric went up to Nicholas and said: "Kinsman, some fishermen who are come without, say that longships have sailed in along the fjord and folk guess that it may be the Birchlegs. It would be best, kinsman, to have all the townsmen with weapons summoned out to Öre".[3] Nicholas answered: "I go not, my kinsman, according to the gabble of fishermen; I will send spies out into the fjord—but let us hold a thing to-day". Eric went home, and when they were ringing for High Mass, Nicholas went to church. Eric then came to him and said: "I believe, kinsman, that the report is true; here now are the men who say that they have seen the sails. It seems advisable to me that we ride out of the town and gather men". Nicholas answered: "Uneasy thou art, kinsman. Let us first hear Mass, and then afterwards we can make our plan". Nicholas went to church. When Mass was sung, Eric went to Nicholas and said: "Kinsman, my horses now stand ready. I will go away". Nicholas answered: "Fare thee well, then! We will hold a thing at Öre and see what strength of men there is in the town". Eric then rode away, but Nicholas went to his garth and afterwards to his table.

40. And at the time when the food was set forth a man came in and told Nicholas that the Birchlegs were now rowing up the river. Nicholas shouted that his men should arm themselves. And when they were armed, Nicholas bade them go into the loft. That was the unwisest counsel, for if they had warded the garth the townsmen would have come to help them. But the Birchlegs surrounded the garth, and then they went towards the loft from all sides. They shouted to each other and the Birchlegs offered Nicholas quarter,

1 *Angel* is now Engelöy in Steigen district (North Norway).   2 8th of September, 1176.   3 Where the Örething was held.

but he rejected it. They then fought with each other; Nicholas'
men fought with bowshots
and handshots and oven-
stones. But the Birchlegs
struck the houses down and
shot fiercely at them. Nicholas had a red shield with
golden studs thereon and a
starred St Williamband. The
Birchlegs shot so hard that
the arrows penetrated right
to the bands.[1] Nicholas said:
"Now the shield belies me".
There Nicholas fell and so
did the greatest part of his
men; folk sorrowed much
over his death. The Birch-

The Birchlegs filled the whole garth
and went towards the loft

legs gave all the townsmen quarter.

41. Eystein was then taken as king there and all the folk submitted to him. He stayed for a time in the town and then went into
Trondheim;[2] there many men came to him. Torfinn the Black of
Snaus[3] came to him and he had a troop of men. In the beginning of
the winter they went out to the town. Then there came to them the
sons of Gudrun of Saltnes,[4] John Ketling and Sigurd and William.
They went up from Nidaros to Orkedale; they then numbered
nearly twenty hundred (twenty-four hundred) men. They went to the
Uplands, thereafter out through Tote and Hadeland, and thence
to Ringerik.

42. In the autumn King Magnus went east to the Vik with some
of his army, and with him went Orm King's Brother. Erling the Jarl
was left at Bergen; he had a great army and was to meet the Birchlegs there if they passed outside. King Magnus settled in Tunsberg
with Orm and held a feast there during Yule. He learned that the
Birchlegs were up at Re.[5] Afterwards the king and Orm went from
the town with their army and came to Re. There was deep snow and
the weather was very cold. And when they came to the garth[6] they
went out of the enclosure on to the highway, and on the outside of the

---

1 *Bands* that were tied round the arrow, to fasten the point to the shaft.  2 I.e. the
country round the town.  3 In North Trondheim folk district.  4 *Saltnes* is a
farm in Buvik near Gulosen, South Trondheim folk district.  5 Cf. p. 718,
n. 2.  6 I.e. Ramnes. Cf. p. 718.

wall they drew up their line and trampled the snow hard. They had not quite fifteen hundred (eighteen hundred) men. The Birchlegs were in the other garth and some of them were here and there in the houses. And when they were aware of King Magnus' army they gathered themselves together and drew up a line. When they saw King Magnus' army, they thought (as was right) that their own

The battle of Re

army was the bigger and they went straightway into battle. But when they came forth on the highway they could only go forward in single file, and they who ran from the highway went into deep snow so that they could scarcely get forward; they thus lost their formation and those who were leading on the road were killed. The standard was then struck down, and they who were nearest to it fell back, and some went off in flight. King Magnus' men followed them and slew one after the other. The Birchlegs could not then draw up their line and they stood unprotected against the weapons; many fell and many fled. It happened then as it often does even if the men are brave and bold with weapons, that when they once have been defeated and have fled it is not easy to make them turn back. The main strength of the Birchlegs began to flee and a great number fell, for King Magnus' men slew all they could and they gave quarter to no man they got near; and the fleeing men scattered out on the highways. King Eystein fled; he ran into a house and begged quarter and implored the bonder to hide him. But the bonder slew him and then went off to King Magnus and found him at Ramnes. The king was in a room warming himself at the fire, and there were many men. Afterwards men came and moved the body there; they bore it into the room and the king bade the men go in and see if they knew it. A man was sitting on a bench in a corner and he was a Birchleg, but no man had given heed to him. But when he saw his chief's body and recognised it, he stood up quickly. He had an axe in his hand and he rushed swiftly along the floor and struck at King Magnus; the blow fell on his neck near the shoulder. A man saw him swinging the axe and thrust him aside; and thereat the axe turned down to the shoulder and there was a great wound. He then swung the axe a second time and struck at Orm King's Brother who was lying on the bench, and the blow pointed at both his legs. But when Orm saw that the man would slay him, he quickly drew his feet over his head and the axe fell on the bench and stuck there. And then the weapons were so thick round the Birchleg that he could hardly fall down. They then saw that he dragged his guts after him over the floor and the man's hardiness was much praised. King Magnus' men followed the fleeing men for a long time and slew all they could. There fell Torfinn of Snaus, and many other Tronds too.

43. This troop, which was called the Birchlegs, had gathered a great crowd; they were hard and very bold with weapons, but rather unruly, and they went forth fiercely and madly when they thought they had a great strength of men. They had few such men as understood the making of plans or were acquainted with the law and could rule the land or lead an army; and even though some had knowledge of it, the whole troop, however, would have it as they themselves thought fit. They relied more upon their numbers and courage. But of those men who escaped many were wounded and lost their weapons and clothes, and all were penniless. Some went east to Marker, and many went to Telemark (most of those who had kindred there) and some went right east to Sweden. All tried to escape, for they deemed they had little hope of quarter from King Magnus or Erling the Jarl.

44. King Magnus then went back to Tunsberg and he now became famous from that victory, for it was formerly the talk of all men that Erling the Jarl was the shield and help for his son and himself. But after King Magnus had got the victory over so strong and large a troop, though he had a smaller army, everybody deemed he would overcome all, and would become a greater warrior than the jarl his father, as he was so much younger.

# INDEX

A CATALOG OF SELECTED
# DOVER BOOKS
IN ALL FIELDS OF INTEREST

# A CATALOG OF SELECTED DOVER
# BOOKS IN ALL FIELDS OF INTEREST

CONCERNING THE SPIRITUAL IN ART, Wassily Kandinsky. Pioneering work by father of abstract art. Thoughts on color theory, nature of art. Analysis of earlier masters. 12 illustrations. 80pp. of text. 5⅜ x 8½. 23411-8 Pa. $4.95

ANIMALS: 1,419 Copyright-Free Illustrations of Mammals, Birds, Fish, Insects, etc., Jim Harter (ed.). Clear wood engravings present, in extremely lifelike poses, over 1,000 species of animals. One of the most extensive pictorial sourcebooks of its kind. Captions. Index. 284pp. 9 x 12. 23766-4 Pa. $14.95

CELTIC ART: The Methods of Construction, George Bain. Simple geometric techniques for making Celtic interlacements, spirals, Kells-type initials, animals, humans, etc. Over 500 illustrations. 160pp. 9 x 12. (USO) 22923-8 Pa. $9.95

AN ATLAS OF ANATOMY FOR ARTISTS, Fritz Schider. Most thorough reference work on art anatomy in the world. Hundreds of illustrations, including selections from works by Vesalius, Leonardo, Goya, Ingres, Michelangelo, others. 593 illustrations. 192pp. 7⅛ x 10¼. 20241-0 Pa. $9.95

CELTIC HAND STROKE-BY-STROKE (Irish Half-Uncial from "The Book of Kells"): An Arthur Baker Calligraphy Manual, Arthur Baker. Complete guide to creating each letter of the alphabet in distinctive Celtic manner. Covers hand position, strokes, pens, inks, paper, more. Illustrated. 48pp. 8¼ x 11. 24336-2 Pa. $3.95

EASY ORIGAMI, John Montroll. Charming collection of 32 projects (hat, cup, pelican, piano, swan, many more) specially designed for the novice origami hobbyist. Clearly illustrated easy-to-follow instructions insure that even beginning papercrafters will achieve successful results. 48pp. 8¼ x 11. 27298-2 Pa. $3.50

THE COMPLETE BOOK OF BIRDHOUSE CONSTRUCTION FOR WOOD-WORKERS, Scott D. Campbell. Detailed instructions, illustrations, tables. Also data on bird habitat and instinct patterns. Bibliography. 3 tables. 63 illustrations in 15 figures. 48pp. 5¼ x 8½. 24407-5 Pa. $2.50

BLOOMINGDALE'S ILLUSTRATED 1886 CATALOG: Fashions, Dry Goods and Housewares, Bloomingdale Brothers. Famed merchants' extremely rare catalog depicting about 1,700 products: clothing, housewares, firearms, dry goods, jewelry, more. Invaluable for dating, identifying vintage items. Also, copyright-free graphics for artists, designers. Co-published with Henry Ford Museum & Greenfield Village. 160pp. 8¼ x 11. 25780-0 Pa. $10.95

HISTORIC COSTUME IN PICTURES, Braun & Schneider. Over 1,450 costumed figures in clearly detailed engravings–from dawn of civilization to end of 19th century. Captions. Many folk costumes. 256pp. 8⅜ x 11¾. 23150-X Pa. $12.95

STICKLEY CRAFTSMAN FURNITURE CATALOGS, Gustav Stickley and L. & J. G. Stickley. Beautiful, functional furniture in two authentic catalogs from 1910. 594 illustrations, including 277 photos, show settles, rockers, armchairs, reclining chairs, bookcases, desks, tables. 183pp. 6½ x 9¼. 23838-5 Pa. $11.95

AMERICAN LOCOMOTIVES IN HISTORIC PHOTOGRAPHS: 1858 to 1949, Ron Ziel (ed.). A rare collection of 126 meticulously detailed official photographs, called "builder portraits," of American locomotives that majestically chronicle the rise of steam locomotive power in America. Introduction. Detailed captions. xi + 129pp. 9 x 12. 27393-8 Pa. $13.95

AMERICA'S LIGHTHOUSES: An Illustrated History, Francis Ross Holland, Jr. Delightfully written, profusely illustrated fact-filled survey of over 200 American lighthouses since 1716. History, anecdotes, technological advances, more. 240pp. 8 x 10¾. 25576-X Pa. $12.95

TOWARDS A NEW ARCHITECTURE, Le Corbusier. Pioneering manifesto by founder of "International School." Technical and aesthetic theories, views of industry, economics, relation of form to function, "mass-production split" and much more. Profusely illustrated. 320pp. 6⅛ x 9¼. (USO) 25023-7 Pa. $9.95

HOW THE OTHER HALF LIVES, Jacob Riis. Famous journalistic record, exposing poverty and degradation of New York slums around 1900, by major social reformer. 100 striking and influential photographs. 233pp. 10 x 7⅞. 22012-5 Pa. $11.95

FRUIT KEY AND TWIG KEY TO TREES AND SHRUBS, William M. Harlow. One of the handiest and most widely used identification aids. Fruit key covers 120 deciduous and evergreen species; twig key 160 deciduous species. Easily used. Over 300 photographs. 126pp. 5⅜ x 8½. 20511-8 Pa. $3.95

COMMON BIRD SONGS, Dr. Donald J. Borror. Songs of 60 most common U.S. birds: robins, sparrows, cardinals, bluejays, finches, more—arranged in order of increasing complexity. Up to 9 variations of songs of each species.
Cassette and manual 99911-4 $8.95

ORCHIDS AS HOUSE PLANTS, Rebecca Tyson Northen. Grow cattleyas and many other kinds of orchids—in a window, in a case, or under artificial light. 63 illustrations. 148pp. 5⅜ x 8½. 23261-1 Pa. $5.95

MONSTER MAZES, Dave Phillips. Masterful mazes at four levels of difficulty. Avoid deadly perils and evil creatures to find magical treasures. Solutions for all 32 exciting illustrated puzzles. 48pp. 8¼ x 11. 26005-4 Pa. $2.95

MOZART'S DON GIOVANNI (DOVER OPERA LIBRETTO SERIES), Wolfgang Amadeus Mozart. Introduced and translated by Ellen H. Bleiler. Standard Italian libretto, with complete English translation. Convenient and thoroughly portable—an ideal companion for reading along with a recording or the performance itself. Introduction. List of characters. Plot summary. 121pp. 5¼ x 8½. 24944-1 Pa. $3.95

TECHNICAL MANUAL AND DICTIONARY OF CLASSICAL BALLET, Gail Grant. Defines, explains, comments on steps, movements, poses and concepts. 15-page pictorial section. Basic book for student, viewer. 127pp. 5⅜ x 8½. 21843-0 Pa. $4.95

THE CLARINET AND CLARINET PLAYING, David Pino. Lively, comprehensive work features suggestions about technique, musicianship, and musical interpretation, as well as guidelines for teaching, making your own reeds, and preparing for public performance. Includes an intriguing look at clarinet history. "A godsend," The Clarinet, Journal of the International Clarinet Society. Appendixes. 7 illus. 320pp. $5\frac{3}{8} \times 8\frac{1}{2}$. 40270-3 Pa. $9.95

HOLLYWOOD GLAMOR PORTRAITS, John Kobal (ed.). 145 photos from 1926-49. Harlow, Gable, Bogart, Bacall; 94 stars in all. Full background on photographers, technical aspects. 160pp. $8\frac{3}{8} \times 11\frac{1}{4}$. 23352-9 Pa. $12.95

THE ANNOTATED CASEY AT THE BAT: A Collection of Ballads about the Mighty Casey/Third, Revised Edition, Martin Gardner (ed.). Amusing sequels and parodies of one of America's best-loved poems: Casey's Revenge, Why Casey Whiffed, Casey's Sister at the Bat, others. 256pp. $5\frac{3}{8} \times 8\frac{1}{2}$. 28598-7 Pa. $8.95

THE RAVEN AND OTHER FAVORITE POEMS, Edgar Allan Poe. Over 40 of the author's most memorable poems: "The Bells," "Ulalume," "Israfel," "To Helen," "The Conqueror Worm," "Eldorado," "Annabel Lee," many more. Alphabetic lists of titles and first lines. 64pp. $5\frac{3}{16} \times 8\frac{1}{4}$. 26685-0 Pa. $1.00

PERSONAL MEMOIRS OF U. S. GRANT, Ulysses Simpson Grant. Intelligent, deeply moving firsthand account of Civil War campaigns, considered by many the finest military memoirs ever written. Includes letters, historic photographs, maps and more. 528pp. $6\frac{1}{8} \times 9\frac{1}{4}$. 28587-1 Pa. $12.95

ANCIENT EGYPTIAN MATERIALS AND INDUSTRIES, A. Lucas and J. Harris. Fascinating, comprehensive, thoroughly documented text describes this ancient civilization's vast resources and the processes that incorporated them in daily life, including the use of animal products, building materials, cosmetics, perfumes and incense, fibers, glazed ware, glass and its manufacture, materials used in the mummification process, and much more. 544pp. $6\frac{1}{8} \times 9\frac{1}{4}$. (USO) 40446-3 Pa. $16.95

RUSSIAN STORIES/PYCCKNE PACCKA3bl: A Dual-Language Book, edited by Gleb Struve. Twelve tales by such masters as Chekhov, Tolstoy, Dostoevsky, Pushkin, others. Excellent word-for-word English translations on facing pages, plus teaching and study aids, Russian/English vocabulary, biographical/critical introductions, more. 416pp. $5\frac{3}{8} \times 8\frac{1}{2}$. 26244-8 Pa. $9.95

PHILADELPHIA THEN AND NOW: 60 Sites Photographed in the Past and Present, Kenneth Finkel and Susan Oyama. Rare photographs of City Hall, Logan Square, Independence Hall, Betsy Ross House, other landmarks juxtaposed with contemporary views. Captures changing face of historic city. Introduction. Captions. 128pp. $8\frac{1}{4} \times 11$. 25790-8 Pa. $9.95

AIA ARCHITECTURAL GUIDE TO NASSAU AND SUFFOLK COUNTIES, LONG ISLAND, The American Institute of Architects, Long Island Chapter, and the Society for the Preservation of Long Island Antiquities. Comprehensive, well-researched and generously illustrated volume brings to life over three centuries of Long Island's great architectural heritage. More than 240 photographs with authoritative, extensively detailed captions. 176pp. $8\frac{1}{4} \times 11$. 26946-9 Pa. $14.95

NORTH AMERICAN INDIAN LIFE: Customs and Traditions of 23 Tribes, Elsie Clews Parsons (ed.). 27 fictionalized essays by noted anthropologists examine religion, customs, government, additional facets of life among the Winnebago, Crow, Zuni, Eskimo, other tribes. 480pp. $6\frac{1}{8} \times 9\frac{1}{4}$. 27377-6 Pa. $10.95

FRANK LLOYD WRIGHT'S DANA HOUSE, Donald Hoffmann. Pictorial essay of residential masterpiece with over 160 interior and exterior photos, plans, elevations, sketches and studies. 128pp. 9¼ x 10¾. 29120-0 Pa. $12.95

THE MALE AND FEMALE FIGURE IN MOTION: 60 Classic Photographic Sequences, Eadweard Muybridge. 60 true-action photographs of men and women walking, running, climbing, bending, turning, etc., reproduced from rare 19th-century masterpiece. vi + 121pp. 9 x 12. 24745-7 Pa. $10.95

1001 QUESTIONS ANSWERED ABOUT THE SEASHORE, N. J. Berrill and Jacquelyn Berrill. Queries answered about dolphins, sea snails, sponges, starfish, fishes, shore birds, many others. Covers appearance, breeding, growth, feeding, much more. 305pp. 5¼ x 8¼. 23366-9 Pa. $9.95

ATTRACTING BIRDS TO YOUR YARD, William J. Weber. Easy-to-follow guide offers advice on how to attract the greatest diversity of birds: birdhouses, feeders, water and waterers, much more. 96pp. 5³⁄₁₆ x 8¼. 28927-3 Pa. $2.50

MEDICINAL AND OTHER USES OF NORTH AMERICAN PLANTS: A Historical Survey with Special Reference to the Eastern Indian Tribes, Charlotte Erichsen-Brown. Chronological historical citations document 500 years of usage of plants, trees, shrubs native to eastern Canada, northeastern U.S. Also complete identifying information. 343 illustrations. 544pp. 6½ x 9¼. 25951-X Pa. $12.95

STORYBOOK MAZES, Dave Phillips. 23 stories and mazes on two-page spreads: Wizard of Oz, Treasure Island, Robin Hood, etc. Solutions. 64pp. 8¼ x 11. 23628-5 Pa. $2.95

AMERICAN NEGRO SONGS: 230 Folk Songs and Spirituals, Religious and Secular, John W. Work. This authoritative study traces the African influences of songs sung and played by black Americans at work, in church, and as entertainment. The author discusses the lyric significance of such songs as "Swing Low, Sweet Chariot," "John Henry," and others and offers the words and music for 230 songs. Bibliography. Index of Song Titles. 272pp. 6½ x 9¼. 40271-1 Pa. $9.95

MOVIE-STAR PORTRAITS OF THE FORTIES, John Kobal (ed.). 163 glamor, studio photos of 106 stars of the 1940s: Rita Hayworth, Ava Gardner, Marlon Brando, Clark Gable, many more. 176pp. 8⅜ x 11¼. 23546-7 Pa. $14.95

BENCHLEY LOST AND FOUND, Robert Benchley. Finest humor from early 30s, about pet peeves, child psychologists, post office and others. Mostly unavailable elsewhere. 73 illustrations by Peter Arno and others. 183pp. 5⅜ x 8½. 22410-4 Pa. $6.95

YEKL and THE IMPORTED BRIDEGROOM AND OTHER STORIES OF YIDDISH NEW YORK, Abraham Cahan. Film Hester Street based on Yekl (1896). Novel, other stories among first about Jewish immigrants on N.Y.'s East Side. 240pp. 5⅜ x 8½. 22427-9 Pa. $6.95

SELECTED POEMS, Walt Whitman. Generous sampling from *Leaves of Grass*. Twenty-four poems include "I Hear America Singing," "Song of the Open Road," "I Sing the Body Electric," "When Lilacs Last in the Dooryard Bloom'd," "O Captain! My Captain!"–all reprinted from an authoritative edition. Lists of titles and first lines. 128pp. 5³⁄₁₆ x 8¼. 26878-0 Pa. $1.00

THE BEST TALES OF HOFFMANN, E. T. A. Hoffmann. 10 of Hoffmann's most important stories: "Nutcracker and the King of Mice," "The Golden Flowerpot," etc. 458pp. 5⅜ x 8½. 21793-0 Pa. $9.95

FROM FETISH TO GOD IN ANCIENT EGYPT, E. A. Wallis Budge. Rich detailed survey of Egyptian conception of "God" and gods, magic, cult of animals, Osiris, more. Also, superb English translations of hymns and legends. 240 illustrations. 545pp. 5⅜ x 8½. 25803-3 Pa. $13.95

FRENCH STORIES/CONTES FRANÇAIS: A Dual-Language Book, Wallace Fowlie. Ten stories by French masters, Voltaire to Camus: "Micromegas" by Voltaire; "The Atheist's Mass" by Balzac; "Minuet" by de Maupassant; "The Guest" by Camus, six more. Excellent English translations on facing pages. Also French-English vocabulary list, exercises, more. 352pp. 5⅜ x 8½. 26443-2 Pa. $9.95

CHICAGO AT THE TURN OF THE CENTURY IN PHOTOGRAPHS: 122 Historic Views from the Collections of the Chicago Historical Society, Larry A. Viskochil. Rare large-format prints offer detailed views of City Hall, State Street, the Loop, Hull House, Union Station, many other landmarks, circa 1904-1913. Introduction. Captions. Maps. 144pp. 9⅜ x 12¼. 24656-6 Pa. $12.95

OLD BROOKLYN IN EARLY PHOTOGRAPHS, 1865-1929, William Lee Younger. Luna Park, Gravesend race track, construction of Grand Army Plaza, moving of Hotel Brighton, etc. 157 previously unpublished photographs. 165pp. 8⅞ x 11¾. 23587-4 Pa. $13.95

THE MYTHS OF THE NORTH AMERICAN INDIANS, Lewis Spence. Rich anthology of the myths and legends of the Algonquins, Iroquois, Pawnees and Sioux, prefaced by an extensive historical and ethnological commentary. 36 illustrations. 480pp. 5⅜ x 8½. 25967-6 Pa. $10.95

AN ENCYCLOPEDIA OF BATTLES: Accounts of Over 1,560 Battles from 1479 B.C. to the Present, David Eggenberger. Essential details of every major battle in recorded history from the first battle of Megiddo in 1479 B.C. to Grenada in 1984. List of Battle Maps. New Appendix covering the years 1967-1984. Index. 99 illustrations. 544pp. 6½ x 9¼. 24913-1 Pa. $16.95

SAILING ALONE AROUND THE WORLD, Captain Joshua Slocum. First man to sail around the world, alone, in small boat. One of great feats of seamanship told in delightful manner. 67 illustrations. 294pp. 5⅜ x 8½. 20326-3 Pa. $6.95

ANARCHISM AND OTHER ESSAYS, Emma Goldman. Powerful, penetrating, prophetic essays on direct action, role of minorities, prison reform, puritan hypocrisy, violence, etc. 271pp. 5⅜ x 8½. 22484-8 Pa. $7.95

MYTHS OF THE HINDUS AND BUDDHISTS, Ananda K. Coomaraswamy and Sister Nivedita. Great stories of the epics; deeds of Krishna, Shiva, taken from puranas, Vedas, folk tales; etc. 32 illustrations. 400pp. 5⅜ x 8½. 21759-0 Pa. $12.95

THE TRAUMA OF BIRTH, Otto Rank. Rank's controversial thesis that anxiety neurosis is caused by profound psychological trauma which occurs at birth. 256pp. 5⅜ x 8½. 27974-X Pa. $7.95

A THEOLOGICO-POLITICAL TREATISE, Benedict Spinoza. Also contains unfinished Political Treatise. Great classic on religious liberty, theory of government on common consent. R. Elwes translation. Total of 421pp. 5⅜ x 8½. 20249-6 Pa. $9.95

MY BONDAGE AND MY FREEDOM, Frederick Douglass. Born a slave, Douglass became outspoken force in antislavery movement. The best of Douglass' autobiographies. Graphic description of slave life. 464pp. 5⅜ x 8½. 22457-0 Pa. $8.95

FOLLOWING THE EQUATOR: A Journey Around the World, Mark Twain. Fascinating humorous account of 1897 voyage to Hawaii, Australia, India, New Zealand, etc. Ironic, bemused reports on peoples, customs, climate, flora and fauna, politics, much more. 197 illustrations. 720pp. 5⅜ x 8½. 26113-1 Pa. $15.95

THE PEOPLE CALLED SHAKERS, Edward D. Andrews. Definitive study of Shakers: origins, beliefs, practices, dances, social organization, furniture and crafts, etc. 33 illustrations. 351pp. 5⅜ x 8½. 21081-2 Pa. $8.95

THE MYTHS OF GREECE AND ROME, H. A. Guerber. A classic of mythology, generously illustrated, long prized for its simple, graphic, accurate retelling of the principal myths of Greece and Rome, and for its commentary on their origins and significance. With 64 illustrations by Michelangelo, Raphael, Titian, Rubens, Canova, Bernini and others. 480pp. 5⅜ x 8½. 27584-1 Pa. $9.95

PSYCHOLOGY OF MUSIC, Carl E. Seashore. Classic work discusses music as a medium from psychological viewpoint. Clear treatment of physical acoustics, auditory apparatus, sound perception, development of musical skills, nature of musical feeling, host of other topics. 88 figures. 408pp. 5⅜ x 8½. 21851-1 Pa. $11.95

THE PHILOSOPHY OF HISTORY, Georg W. Hegel. Great classic of Western thought develops concept that history is not chance but rational process, the evolution of freedom. 457pp. 5⅜ x 8½. 20112-0 Pa. $9.95

THE BOOK OF TEA, Kakuzo Okakura. Minor classic of the Orient: entertaining, charming explanation, interpretation of traditional Japanese culture in terms of tea ceremony. 94pp. 5⅜ x 8½. 20070-1 Pa. $3.95

LIFE IN ANCIENT EGYPT, Adolf Erman. Fullest, most thorough, detailed older account with much not in more recent books, domestic life, religion, magic, medicine, commerce, much more. Many illustrations reproduce tomb paintings, carvings, hieroglyphs, etc. 597pp. 5⅜ x 8½. 22632-8 Pa. $12.95

SUNDIALS, Their Theory and Construction, Albert Waugh. Far and away the best, most thorough coverage of ideas, mathematics concerned, types, construction, adjusting anywhere. Simple, nontechnical treatment allows even children to build several of these dials. Over 100 illustrations. 230pp. 5⅜ x 8½. 22947-5 Pa. $8.95

THEORETICAL HYDRODYNAMICS, L. M. Milne-Thomson. Classic exposition of the mathematical theory of fluid motion, applicable to both hydrodynamics and aerodynamics. Over 600 exercises. 768pp. 6⅛ x 9¼. 68970-0 Pa. $20.95

SONGS OF EXPERIENCE: Facsimile Reproduction with 26 Plates in Full Color, William Blake. 26 full-color plates from a rare 1826 edition. Includes "The Tyger," "London," "Holy Thursday," and other poems. Printed text of poems. 48pp. 5¼ x 7. 24636-1 Pa. $4.95

OLD-TIME VIGNETTES IN FULL COLOR, Carol Belanger Grafton (ed.). Over 390 charming, often sentimental illustrations, selected from archives of Victorian graphics—pretty women posing, children playing, food, flowers, kittens and puppies, smiling cherubs, birds and butterflies, much more. All copyright-free. 48pp. 9¼ x 12¼. 27269-9 Pa. $7.95

PERSPECTIVE FOR ARTISTS, Rex Vicat Cole. Depth, perspective of sky and sea, shadows, much more, not usually covered. 391 diagrams, 81 reproductions of drawings and paintings. 279pp. 5⅜ x 8½. 22487-2 Pa. $7.95

DRAWING THE LIVING FIGURE, Joseph Sheppard. Innovative approach to artistic anatomy focuses on specifics of surface anatomy, rather than muscles and bones. Over 170 drawings of live models in front, back and side views, and in widely varying poses. Accompanying diagrams. 177 illustrations. Introduction. Index. 144pp. 8⅜ x11¼. 26723-7 Pa. $8.95

GOTHIC AND OLD ENGLISH ALPHABETS: 100 Complete Fonts, Dan X. Solo. Add power, elegance to posters, signs, other graphics with 100 stunning copyright-free alphabets: Blackstone, Dolbey, Germania, 97 more–including many lower-case, numerals, punctuation marks. 104pp. 8⅛ x 11. 24695-7 Pa. $8.95

HOW TO DO BEADWORK, Mary White. Fundamental book on craft from simple projects to five-bead chains and woven works. 106 illustrations. 142pp. 5⅜ x 8. 20697-1 Pa. $5.95

THE BOOK OF WOOD CARVING, Charles Marshall Sayers. Finest book for beginners discusses fundamentals and offers 34 designs. "Absolutely first rate . . . well thought out and well executed."–E. J. Tangerman. 118pp. 7¾ x 10⅝. 23654-4 Pa. $7.95

ILLUSTRATED CATALOG OF CIVIL WAR MILITARY GOODS: Union Army Weapons, Insignia, Uniform Accessories, and Other Equipment, Schuyler, Hartley, and Graham. Rare, profusely illustrated 1846 catalog includes Union Army uniform and dress regulations, arms and ammunition, coats, insignia, flags, swords, rifles, etc. 226 illustrations. 160pp. 9 x 12. 24939-5 Pa. $10.95

WOMEN'S FASHIONS OF THE EARLY 1900s: An Unabridged Republication of "New York Fashions, 1909," National Cloak & Suit Co. Rare catalog of mail-order fashions documents women's and children's clothing styles shortly after the turn of the century. Captions offer full descriptions, prices. Invaluable resource for fashion, costume historians. Approximately 725 illustrations. 128pp. 8⅜ x 11¼. 27276-1 Pa. $11.95

THE 1912 AND 1915 GUSTAV STICKLEY FURNITURE CATALOGS, Gustav Stickley. With over 200 detailed illustrations and descriptions, these two catalogs are essential reading and reference materials and identification guides for Stickley furniture. Captions cite materials, dimensions and prices. 112pp. 6½ x 9¼. 26676-1 Pa. $9.95

EARLY AMERICAN LOCOMOTIVES, John H. White, Jr. Finest locomotive engravings from early 19th century: historical (1804–74), main-line (after 1870), special, foreign, etc. 147 plates. 142pp. 11⅜ x 8¼. 22772-3 Pa. $10.95

THE TALL SHIPS OF TODAY IN PHOTOGRAPHS, Frank O. Braynard. Lavishly illustrated tribute to nearly 100 majestic contemporary sailing vessels: Amerigo Vespucci, Clearwater, Constitution, Eagle, Mayflower, Sea Cloud, Victory, many more. Authoritative captions provide statistics, background on each ship. 190 black-and-white photographs and illustrations. Introduction. 128pp. 8⅞ x 11¾. 27163-3 Pa. $14.95

LITTLE BOOK OF EARLY AMERICAN CRAFTS AND TRADES, Peter Stockham (ed.). 1807 children's book explains crafts and trades: baker, hatter, cooper, potter, and many others. 23 copperplate illustrations. 140pp. 4⅝ x 6.
23336-7 Pa. $4.95

VICTORIAN FASHIONS AND COSTUMES FROM HARPER'S BAZAR, 1867–1898, Stella Blum (ed.). Day costumes, evening wear, sports clothes, shoes, hats, other accessories in over 1,000 detailed engravings. 320pp. 9⅜ x 12¼.
22990-4 Pa. $15.95

GUSTAV STICKLEY, THE CRAFTSMAN, Mary Ann Smith. Superb study surveys broad scope of Stickley's achievement, especially in architecture. Design philosophy, rise and fall of the Craftsman empire, descriptions and floor plans for many Craftsman houses, more. 86 black-and-white halftones. 31 line illustrations. Introduction 208pp. 6½ x 9¼. 27210-9 Pa. $9.95

THE LONG ISLAND RAIL ROAD IN EARLY PHOTOGRAPHS, Ron Ziel. Over 220 rare photos, informative text document origin ( 1844) and development of rail service on Long Island. Vintage views of early trains, locomotives, stations, passengers, crews, much more. Captions. 8⅞ x 11¾. 26301-0 Pa. $13.95

VOYAGE OF THE LIBERDADE, Joshua Slocum. Great 19th-century mariner's thrilling, first-hand account of the wreck of his ship off South America, the 35-foot boat he built from the wreckage, and its remarkable voyage home. 128pp. 5⅜ x 8½.
40022-0 Pa. $4.95

TEN BOOKS ON ARCHITECTURE, Vitruvius. The most important book ever written on architecture. Early Roman aesthetics, technology, classical orders, site selection, all other aspects. Morgan translation. 331pp. 5⅜ x 8½. 20645-9 Pa. $8.95

THE HUMAN FIGURE IN MOTION, Eadweard Muybridge. More than 4,500 stopped-action photos, in action series, showing undraped men, women, children jumping, lying down, throwing, sitting, wrestling, carrying, etc. 390pp. 7⅞ x 10⅝.
20204-6 Clothbd. $27.95

TREES OF THE EASTERN AND CENTRAL UNITED STATES AND CANADA, William M. Harlow. Best one-volume guide to 140 trees. Full descriptions, woodlore, range, etc. Over 600 illustrations. Handy size. 288pp. 4½ x 6⅜.
20395-6 Pa. $6.95

SONGS OF WESTERN BIRDS, Dr. Donald J. Borror. Complete song and call repertoire of 60 western species, including flycatchers, juncoes, cactus wrens, many more–includes fully illustrated booklet. Cassette and manual 99913-0 $8.95

GROWING AND USING HERBS AND SPICES, Milo Miloradovich. Versatile handbook provides all the information needed for cultivation and use of all the herbs and spices available in North America. 4 illustrations. Index. Glossary. 236pp. 5⅜ x 8½.
25058-X Pa. $7.95

BIG BOOK OF MAZES AND LABYRINTHS, Walter Shepherd. 50 mazes and labyrinths in all–classical, solid, ripple, and more–in one great volume. Perfect inexpensive puzzler for clever youngsters. Full solutions. 112pp. 8⅛ x 11.
22951-3 Pa. $5.95

PIANO TUNING, J. Cree Fischer. Clearest, best book for beginner, amateur. Simple repairs, raising dropped notes, tuning by easy method of flattened fifths. No previous skills needed. 4 illustrations. 201pp. 5⅜ x 8½. 23267-0 Pa. $6.95

HINTS TO SINGERS, Lillian Nordica. Selecting the right teacher, developing confidence, overcoming stage fright, and many other important skills receive thoughtful discussion in this indispensible guide, written by a world-famous diva of four decades' experience. 96pp. 5⅜ x 8½. 40094-8 Pa. $4.95

THE COMPLETE NONSENSE OF EDWARD LEAR, Edward Lear. All nonsense limericks, zany alphabets, Owl and Pussycat, songs, nonsense botany, etc., illustrated by Lear. Total of 320pp. 5⅜ x 8½. (USO) 20167-8 Pa. $7.95

VICTORIAN PARLOUR POETRY: An Annotated Anthology, Michael R. Turner. 117 gems by Longfellow, Tennyson, Browning, many lesser-known poets. "The Village Blacksmith," "Curfew Must Not Ring Tonight," "Only a Baby Small," dozens more, often difficult to find elsewhere. Index of poets, titles, first lines. xxiii + 325pp. 5⅝ x 8¼. 27044-0 Pa. $8.95

DUBLINERS, James Joyce. Fifteen stories offer vivid, tightly focused observations of the lives of Dublin's poorer classes. At least one, "The Dead," is considered a masterpiece. Reprinted complete and unabridged from standard edition. 160pp. 5$\frac{3}{16}$ x 8¼. 26870-5 Pa. $1.00

GREAT WEIRD TALES: 14 Stories by Lovecraft, Blackwood, Machen and Others, S. T. Joshi (ed.). 14 spellbinding tales, including "The Sin Eater," by Fiona McLeod, "The Eye Above the Mantel," by Frank Belknap Long, as well as renowned works by R. H. Barlow, Lord Dunsany, Arthur Machen, W. C. Morrow and eight other masters of the genre. 256pp. 5⅜ x 8½. (USO) 40436-6 Pa. $8.95

THE BOOK OF THE SACRED MAGIC OF ABRAMELIN THE MAGE, translated by S. MacGregor Mathers. Medieval manuscript of ceremonial magic. Basic document in Aleister Crowley, Golden Dawn groups. 268pp. 5⅜ x 8½. 23211-5 Pa. $9.95

NEW RUSSIAN-ENGLISH AND ENGLISH-RUSSIAN DICTIONARY, M. A. O'Brien. This is a remarkably handy Russian dictionary, containing a surprising amount of information, including over 70,000 entries. 366pp. 4½ x 6⅛. 20208-9 Pa. $10.95

HISTORIC HOMES OF THE AMERICAN PRESIDENTS, Second, Revised Edition, Irvin Haas. A traveler's guide to American Presidential homes, most open to the public, depicting and describing homes occupied by every American President from George Washington to George Bush. With visiting hours, admission charges, travel routes. 175 photographs. Index. 160pp. 8¼ x 11. 26751-2 Pa. $11.95

NEW YORK IN THE FORTIES, Andreas Feininger. 162 brilliant photographs by the well-known photographer, formerly with *Life* magazine. Commuters, shoppers, Times Square at night, much else from city at its peak. Captions by John von Hartz. 181pp. 9¼ x 10¾. 23585-8 Pa. $13.95

INDIAN SIGN LANGUAGE, William Tomkins. Over 525 signs developed by Sioux and other tribes. Written instructions and diagrams. Also 290 pictographs. 111pp. 6⅛ x 9¼. 22029-X Pa. $3.95

ANATOMY: A Complete Guide for Artists, Joseph Sheppard. A master of figure drawing shows artists how to render human anatomy convincingly. Over 460 illustrations. 224pp. 8⅜ x 11¼. 27279-6 Pa. $11.95

MEDIEVAL CALLIGRAPHY: Its History and Technique, Marc Drogin. Spirited history, comprehensive instruction manual covers 13 styles (ca. 4th century thru 15th). Excellent photographs; directions for duplicating medieval techniques with modern tools. 224pp. 8⅜ x 11¼. 26142-5 Pa. $12.95

DRIED FLOWERS: How to Prepare Them, Sarah Whitlock and Martha Rankin. Complete instructions on how to use silica gel, meal and borax, perlite aggregate, sand and borax, glycerine and water to create attractive permanent flower arrangements. 12 illustrations. 32pp. 5⅜ x 8½. 21802-3 Pa. $1.00

EASY-TO-MAKE BIRD FEEDERS FOR WOODWORKERS, Scott D. Campbell. Detailed, simple-to-use guide for designing, constructing, caring for and using feeders. Text, illustrations for 12 classic and contemporary designs. 96pp. 5⅜ x 8½. 25847-5 Pa. $3.95

SCOTTISH WONDER TALES FROM MYTH AND LEGEND, Donald A. Mackenzie. 16 lively tales tell of giants rumbling down mountainsides, of a magic wand that turns stone pillars into warriors, of gods and goddesses, evil hags, powerful forces and more. 240pp. 5⅜ x 8½. 29677-6 Pa. $6.95

THE HISTORY OF UNDERCLOTHES, C. Willett Cunnington and Phyllis Cunnington. Fascinating, well-documented survey covering six centuries of English undergarments, enhanced with over 100 illustrations: 12th-century laced-up bodice, footed long drawers (1795), 19th-century bustles, 19th-century corsets for men, Victorian "bust improvers," much more. 272pp. 5⅜ x 8¼. 27124-2 Pa. $9.95

ARTS AND CRAFTS FURNITURE: The Complete Brooks Catalog of 1912, Brooks Manufacturing Co. Photos and detailed descriptions of more than 150 now very collectible furniture designs from the Arts and Crafts movement depict davenports, settees, buffets, desks, tables, chairs, bedsteads, dressers and more, all built of solid, quarter-sawed oak. Invaluable for students and enthusiasts of antiques, Americana and the decorative arts. 80pp. 6½ x 9¼. 27471-3 Pa. $8.95

WILBUR AND ORVILLE: A Biography of the Wright Brothers, Fred Howard. Definitive, crisply written study tells the full story of the brothers' lives and work. A vividly written biography, unparalleled in scope and color, that also captures the spirit of an extraordinary era. 560pp. 6⅛ x 9¼. 40297-5 Pa. $17.95

THE ARTS OF THE SAILOR: Knotting, Splicing and Ropework, Hervey Garrett Smith. Indispensable shipboard reference covers tools, basic knots and useful hitches; handsewing and canvas work, more. Over 100 illustrations. Delightful reading for sea lovers. 256pp. 5⅜ x 8½. 26440-8 Pa. $8.95

FRANK LLOYD WRIGHT'S FALLINGWATER: The House and Its History, Second, Revised Edition, Donald Hoffmann. A total revision—both in text and illustrations—of the standard document on Fallingwater, the boldest, most personal architectural statement of Wright's mature years, updated with valuable new material from the recently opened Frank Lloyd Wright Archives. "Fascinating"–*The New York Times.* 116 illustrations. 128pp. 9¼ x 10¾. 27430-6 Pa. $12.95

PHOTOGRAPHIC SKETCHBOOK OF THE CIVIL WAR, Alexander Gardner. 100 photos taken on field during the Civil War. Famous shots of Manassas Harper's Ferry, Lincoln, Richmond, slave pens, etc. 244pp. 10⅝ x 8¼. 22731-6 Pa. $10.95

FIVE ACRES AND INDEPENDENCE, Maurice G. Kains. Great back-to-the-land classic explains basics of self-sufficient farming. The one book to get. 95 illustrations. 397pp. 5⅜ x 8½. 20974-1 Pa. $7.95

SONGS OF EASTERN BIRDS, Dr. Donald J. Borror. Songs and calls of 60 species most common to eastern U.S.: warblers, woodpeckers, flycatchers, thrushes, larks, many more in high-quality recording. Cassette and manual 99912-2 $9.95

A MODERN HERBAL, Margaret Grieve. Much the fullest, most exact, most useful compilation of herbal material. Gigantic alphabetical encyclopedia, from aconite to zedoary, gives botanical information, medical properties, folklore, economic uses, much else. Indispensable to serious reader. 161 illustrations. 888pp. 6½ x 9¼. 2-vol. set. (USO)
Vol. I: 22798-7 Pa. $9.95
Vol. II: 22799-5 Pa. $9.95

HIDDEN TREASURE MAZE BOOK, Dave Phillips. Solve 34 challenging mazes accompanied by heroic tales of adventure. Evil dragons, people-eating plants, bloodthirsty giants, many more dangerous adversaries lurk at every twist and turn. 34 mazes, stories, solutions. 48pp. 8¼ x 11. 24566-7 Pa. $2.95

LETTERS OF W. A. MOZART, Wolfgang A. Mozart. Remarkable letters show bawdy wit, humor, imagination, musical insights, contemporary musical world; includes some letters from Leopold Mozart. 276pp. 5⅜ x 8½. 22859-2 Pa. $7.95

BASIC PRINCIPLES OF CLASSICAL BALLET, Agrippina Vaganova. Great Russian theoretician, teacher explains methods for teaching classical ballet. 118 illustrations. 175pp. 5⅜ x 8½. 22036-2 Pa. $5.95

THE JUMPING FROG, Mark Twain. Revenge edition. The original story of The Celebrated Jumping Frog of Calaveras County, a hapless French translation, and Twain's hilarious "retranslation" from the French. 12 illustrations. 66pp. 5⅜ x 8½.
22686-7 Pa. $3.95

BEST REMEMBERED POEMS, Martin Gardner (ed.). The 126 poems in this superb collection of 19th- and 20th-century British and American verse range from Shelley's "To a Skylark" to the impassioned "Renascence" of Edna St. Vincent Millay and to Edward Lear's whimsical "The Owl and the Pussycat." 224pp. 5⅜ x 8½.
27165-X Pa. $5.95

COMPLETE SONNETS, William Shakespeare. Over 150 exquisite poems deal with love, friendship, the tyranny of time, beauty's evanescence, death and other themes in language of remarkable power, precision and beauty. Glossary of archaic terms. 80pp. 5 3/16 x 8¼. 26686-9 Pa. $1.00

BODIES IN A BOOKSHOP, R. T. Campbell. Challenging mystery of blackmail and murder with ingenious plot and superbly drawn characters. In the best tradition of British suspense fiction. 192pp. 5⅜ x 8½. 24720-1 Pa. $6.95

THE WIT AND HUMOR OF OSCAR WILDE, Alvin Redman (ed.). More than 1,000 ripostes, paradoxes, wisecracks: Work is the curse of the drinking classes; I can resist everything except temptation; etc. 258pp. 5⅜ x 8½. 20602-5 Pa. $6.95

SHAKESPEARE LEXICON AND QUOTATION DICTIONARY, Alexander Schmidt. Full definitions, locations, shades of meaning in every word in plays and poems. More than 50,000 exact quotations. 1,485pp. 6½ x 9¼. 2-vol. set.
Vol. 1: 22726-X Pa. $17.95
Vol. 2: 22727-8 Pa. $17.95

SELECTED POEMS, Emily Dickinson. Over 100 best-known, best-loved poems by one of America's foremost poets, reprinted from authoritative early editions. No comparable edition at this price. Index of first lines. 64pp. 5³⁄₁₆ x 8¼.
26466-1 Pa. $1.00

THE INSIDIOUS DR. FU-MANCHU, Sax Rohmer. The first of the popular mystery series introduces a pair of English detectives to their archnemesis, the diabolical Dr. Fu-Manchu. Flavorful atmosphere, fast-paced action, and colorful characters enliven this classic of the genre. 208pp. 5³⁄₁₆ x 8¼. 29898-1 Pa. $2.00

THE MALLEUS MALEFICARUM OF KRAMER AND SPRENGER, translated by Montague Summers. Full text of most important witchhunter's "bible," used by both Catholics and Protestants. 278pp. 6⅝ x 10. 22802-9 Pa. $12.95

SPANISH STORIES/CUENTOS ESPAÑOLES: A Dual-Language Book, Angel Flores (ed.). Unique format offers 13 great stories in Spanish by Cervantes, Borges, others. Faithful English translations on facing pages. 352pp. 5⅜ x 8½.
25399-6 Pa. $8.95

GARDEN CITY, LONG ISLAND, IN EARLY PHOTOGRAPHS, 1869–1919, Mildred H. Smith. Handsome treasury of 118 vintage pictures, accompanied by carefully researched captions, document the Garden City Hotel fire (1899), the Vanderbilt Cup Race (1908), the first airmail flight departing from the Nassau Boulevard Aerodrome (1911), and much more. 96pp. 8⅞ x 11³⁄₄. 40669-5 Pa. $12.95

OLD QUEENS, N.Y., IN EARLY PHOTOGRAPHS, Vincent F. Seyfried and William Asadorian. Over 160 rare photographs of Maspeth, Jamaica, Jackson Heights, and other areas. Vintage views of DeWitt Clinton mansion, 1939 World's Fair and more. Captions. 192pp. 8⅞ x 11. 26358-4 Pa. $12.95

CAPTURED BY THE INDIANS: 15 Firsthand Accounts, 1750-1870, Frederick Drimmer. Astounding true historical accounts of grisly torture, bloody conflicts, relentless pursuits, miraculous escapes and more, by people who lived to tell the tale. 384pp. 5⅜ x 8½. 24901-8 Pa. $8.95

THE WORLD'S GREAT SPEECHES (Fourth Enlarged Edition), Lewis Copeland, Lawrence W. Lamm, and Stephen J. McKenna. Nearly 300 speeches provide public speakers with a wealth of updated quotes and inspiration—from Pericles' funeral oration and William Jennings Bryan's "Cross of Gold Speech" to Malcolm X's powerful words on the Black Revolution and Earl of Spenser's tribute to his sister, Diana, Princess of Wales. 944pp. 5⅜ x 8⅜. 40903-1 Pa. $15.95

THE BOOK OF THE SWORD, Sir Richard F. Burton. Great Victorian scholar/adventurer's eloquent, erudite history of the "queen of weapons"—from prehistory to early Roman Empire. Evolution and development of early swords, variations (sabre, broadsword, cutlass, scimitar, etc.), much more. 336pp. 6⅛ x 9¼.
25434-8 Pa. $9.95

AUTOBIOGRAPHY: The Story of My Experiments with Truth, Mohandas K. Gandhi. Boyhood, legal studies, purification, the growth of the Satyagraha (nonviolent protest) movement. Critical, inspiring work of the man responsible for the freedom of India. 480pp. 5⅜ x 8½. (USO) 24593-4 Pa. $8.95

CELTIC MYTHS AND LEGENDS, T. W. Rolleston. Masterful retelling of Irish and Welsh stories and tales. Cuchulain, King Arthur, Deirdre, the Grail, many more. First paperback edition. 58 full-page illustrations. 512pp. 5⅜ x 8½. 26507-2 Pa. $9.95

THE PRINCIPLES OF PSYCHOLOGY, William James. Famous long course complete, unabridged. Stream of thought, time perception, memory, experimental methods; great work decades ahead of its time. 94 figures. 1,391pp. 5⅜ x 8½. 2-vol. set.
Vol. I: 20381-6 Pa. $13.95
Vol. II: 20382-4 Pa. $14.95

THE WORLD AS WILL AND REPRESENTATION, Arthur Schopenhauer. Definitive English translation of Schopenhauer's life work, correcting more than 1,000 errors, omissions in earlier translations. Translated by E. F. J. Payne. Total of 1,269pp. 5⅜ x 8½. 2-vol. set.
Vol. 1: 21761-2 Pa. $12.95
Vol. 2: 21762-0 Pa. $12.95

MAGIC AND MYSTERY IN TIBET, Madame Alexandra David-Neel. Experiences among lamas, magicians, sages, sorcerers, Bonpa wizards. A true psychic discovery. 32 illustrations. 321pp. 5⅜ x 8½. (USO) 22682-4 Pa. $9.95

THE EGYPTIAN BOOK OF THE DEAD, E. A. Wallis Budge. Complete reproduction of Ani's papyrus, finest ever found. Full hieroglyphic text, interlinear transliteration, word-for-word translation, smooth translation. 533pp. 6½ x 9¼.
21866-X Pa. $11.95

MATHEMATICS FOR THE NONMATHEMATICIAN, Morris Kline. Detailed, college-level treatment of mathematics in cultural and historical context, with numerous exercises. Recommended Reading Lists. Tables. Numerous figures. 641pp. 5⅜ x 8½.
24823-2 Pa. $11.95

PROBABILISTIC METHODS IN THE THEORY OF STRUCTURES, Isaac Elishakoff. Well-written introduction covers the elements of the theory of probability from two or more random variables, the reliability of such multivariable structures, the theory of random function, Monte Carlo methods of treating problems incapable of exact solution, and more. Examples. 502pp. $5^3/_8$ x $8^1/_2$. 40691-1 Pa. $16.95

THE RIME OF THE ANCIENT MARINER, Gustave Doré, S. T. Coleridge. Doré's finest work; 34 plates capture moods, subtleties of poem. Flawless full-size reproductions printed on facing pages with authoritative text of poem. "Beautiful. Simply beautiful."–*Publisher's Weekly.* 77pp. 9¼ x 12. 22305-1 Pa. $7.95

NORTH AMERICAN INDIAN DESIGNS FOR ARTISTS AND CRAFTSPEOPLE, Eva Wilson. Over 360 authentic copyright-free designs adapted from Navajo blankets, Hopi pottery, Sioux buffalo hides, more. Geometrics, symbolic figures, plant and animal motifs, etc. 128pp. 8⅜ x 11. (EUK) 25341-4 Pa. $8.95

SCULPTURE: Principles and Practice, Louis Slobodkin. Step-by-step approach to clay, plaster, metals, stone; classical and modern. 253 drawings, photos. 255pp. 8⅛ x 11.
22960-2 Pa. $11.95

THE INFLUENCE OF SEA POWER UPON HISTORY, 1660–1783, A. T. Mahan. Influential classic of naval history and tactics still used as text in war colleges. First paperback edition. 4 maps. 24 battle plans. 640pp. 5⅜ x 8½. 25509-3 Pa. $14.95

THE STORY OF THE TITANIC AS TOLD BY ITS SURVIVORS, Jack Winocour (ed.). What it was really like. Panic, despair, shocking inefficiency, and a little heroism. More thrilling than any fictional account. 26 illustrations. 320pp. 5⅜ x 8½. 20610-6 Pa. $8.95

FAIRY AND FOLK TALES OF THE IRISH PEASANTRY, William Butler Yeats (ed.). Treasury of 64 tales from the twilight world of Celtic myth and legend: "The Soul Cages," "The Kildare Pooka," "King O'Toole and his Goose," many more. Introduction and Notes by W. B. Yeats. 352pp. 5⅜ x 8½. 26941-8 Pa. $8.95

BUDDHIST MAHAYANA TEXTS, E. B. Cowell and Others (eds.). Superb, accurate translations of basic documents in Mahayana Buddhism, highly important in history of religions. The Buddha-karita of Asvaghosha, Larger Sukhavativyuha, more. 448pp. 5⅜ x 8½. 25552-2 Pa. $12.95

ONE TWO THREE . . . INFINITY: Facts and Speculations of Science, George Gamow. Great physicist's fascinating, readable overview of contemporary science: number theory, relativity, fourth dimension, entropy, genes, atomic structure, much more. 128 illustrations. Index. 352pp. 5⅜ x 8½. 25664-2 Pa. $8.95

EXPERIMENTATION AND MEASUREMENT, W. J. Youden. Introductory manual explains laws of measurement in simple terms and offers tips for achieving accuracy and minimizing errors. Mathematics of measurement, use of instruments, experimenting with machines. 1994 edition. Foreword. Preface. Introduction. Epilogue. Selected Readings. Glossary. Index. Tables and figures. 128pp. 5³/₈ x 8½. 40451-X Pa. $6.95

DALÍ ON MODERN ART: The Cuckolds of Antiquated Modern Art, Salvador Dalí. Influential painter skewers modern art and its practitioners. Outrageous evaluations of Picasso, Cézanne, Turner, more. 15 renderings of paintings discussed. 44 calligraphic decorations by Dalí. 96pp. 5⅜ x 8½. (USO) 29220-7 Pa. $5.95

ANTIQUE PLAYING CARDS: A Pictorial History, Henry René D'Allemagne. Over 900 elaborate, decorative images from rare playing cards (14th–20th centuries): Bacchus, death, dancing dogs, hunting scenes, royal coats of arms, players cheating, much more. 96pp. 9¼ x 12¼. 29265-7 Pa. $12.95

MAKING FURNITURE MASTERPIECES: 30 Projects with Measured Drawings, Franklin H. Gottshall. Step-by-step instructions, illustrations for constructing handsome, useful pieces, among them a Sheraton desk, Chippendale chair, Spanish desk, Queen Anne table and a William and Mary dressing mirror. 224pp. 8⅛ x 11¼. 29338-6 Pa. $13.95

THE FOSSIL BOOK: A Record of Prehistoric Life, Patricia V. Rich et al. Profusely illustrated definitive guide covers everything from single-celled organisms and dinosaurs to birds and mammals and the interplay between climate and man. Over 1,500 illustrations. 760pp. 7½ x 10⅛. 29371-8 Pa. $29.95

*Prices subject to change without notice.*